International Adoption

International Adoption

Ruth Cabeza

Ayeesha Bhutta

Jason Braier

/f **Family Law**

Published by Family Law
a publishing imprint of
Jordan Publishing Limited
21 St Thomas Street
Bristol BS1 6JS

Whilst the publishers and the author have taken every care in preparing the material included in this work, any statements made as to the legal or other implications of particular transactions are made in good faith purely for general guidance and cannot be regarded as a substitute for professional advice. Consequently, no liability can be accepted for loss or expense incurred as a result of relying in particular circumstances on statements made in this work.

British Library Cataloguing-in-Publication Data

A catalogue record for this book is available from the British Library.

ISBN 978 1 84661 318 0

Typeset by Letterpart Ltd, Reigate, Surrey
Printed and bound by CPI Group (UK) Ltd, Croydon, CR0 4YY

FOREWORD

It is a great honour for me to be asked to write the foreword for *International Adoption*. Its publication could not be more welcome, at a time when the international movement of children and their families have become the norm.

The authors, who are all practising barristers in this field, have produced an invaluable guide in this difficult area of the law. They are to be congratulated on producing a truly comprehensive work on the law and practice relating to this complex subject.

The book is extremely well laid out; it takes the reader logically through the law and practice arising on both Hague Convention and Non-Hague Convention adoption and is helpfully divided into two parts, depending on whether the United Kingdom is the receiving state or the state of origin. In addition it brings together, in a comprehensive form, the relevant statutory provisions and rules which are set out in the Appendix.

I have no doubt all lawyers (both practising and academic) who have an interest in this area will find it immensely valuable.

Lucy Theis
The Hon Mrs Justice Theis
October 2012

CONTENTS

TABLE OF CASES

References are to paragraph numbers.

TABLE OF STATUTES

References are to paragraph numbers.

TABLE OF STATUTORY INSTRUMENTS

References are to paragraph numbers.

TABLE OF INTERNATIONAL MATERIALS

References are to paragraph numbers.

Part 1
GENERAL

Chapter 1

INTRODUCTION

1.1   The instinct to parent a child is a fundamental characteristic of human nature. The concept of adoption of children is probably as old as humanity itself. At its best it is an act of entirely selfless love. But any relationship in which there is an imbalance of power is open to abuse, and the relationship between parent and child must be one of the most extreme imbalances of power in modern society, for a child is completely dependent upon his or her parents. It is therefore imperative that children are only placed with adopters who are suitable to adopt them, are motivated to prioritise the child's needs and who have the means to provide adequately for their new child.

1.2   In the UK, as in many countries across the world, for an adoption to be recognised as establishing the legal relationship of parent and child between a child and adult who are not biologically related there must be a formal legal process. In England and Wales the adoption process is primarily governed by the Adoption and Children Act 2002 (ACA 2002) and the regulations which support it. There are two routes to adoption, private adoptions and agency adoptions.

1.3   Private adoptions are those in which the prospective adopters have not been chosen by an adoption agency. For example, a private adoption might arise when a mother wishes her new partner to adopt her child and share full parental status with her. In order to safeguard the welfare of children it is unlawful to make arrangements for the adoption of a child, except in very limited circumstances, and unless an exception applies it is a criminal offence[1] to make such arrangements. The criminal offence operates extra-territorially which means that it applies whether or not the arrangements are made in this country or another one.

1.4   In England and Wales an agency adoption occurs when an approved adoption agency finds adopters for a child who does not have parents who are able to care for it. That might be because the parents have relinquished their parental role to the local authority or have abandoned their child, or it might be because the courts have determined that the child's welfare required that alternative parents be found for the child. In such cases the adoption agency will search for and hopefully identify suitable prospective adopters with whom they can place the child. After the child has been placed for adoption with suitable prospective adopters and has lived with them for not less than 10

---

[1]   ACA 2002, s 92.

weeks, the prospective adopters can apply to adopt the child. If a child is being adopted from overseas the relevant foreign authority will need to have been involved in assessing the child's suitability to be adopted. The way in which this takes place will depend on the relevant procedures in the child's country of origin.

1.5 In England and Wales, adoption can only take place by way of a court order, and a judge who makes an adoption order must be satisfied that the adoption is in the best interests of the child throughout their whole life. A judge in such a case will take account of independent assessments of the prospective adopters and of the child, carried out by the adoption agency that placed the child with the prospective adopters, or if it is a private adoptive placement, by the local authority in whose area the child lives.

1.6 The effect of an adoption order made in England and Wales is to vest the adoptive parent with all rights and responsibilities that a natural parent would have in relation to the child and to extinguish such rights in every other person. In addition, it will vest the child with all the rights and entitlements that a natural child of the adoptive parents would have: the child becomes legally part of the adopters' family. These rights include rights to nationality, citizenship, financial support and inheritance provision. An amended birth certificate is issued for the child following adoption which reflects the new status of the child. A foreign adoption order may be similar in effect to a UK one, but that is not automatically the case. In some countries adoption does not sever the link between the birth parents and the child, although it does create a new link between the child and the adopters. When adoption does not sever the legal connection between a parent and child it is often called a 'simple' adoption. Adoptions, such those made in England and Wales, which will sever the legal connection between birth parents and child and transfer parenthood completely to the adoptive parents are known as 'full' adoptions. The effect of such orders made in foreign jurisdictions is considered later in the book.

1.7 In the context of the far-reaching legal, psychological and practical effects of adoption, it is unsurprising that great caution is exercised by the state when inter-country adoption is contemplated. In order to protect children from slavery and child trafficking and to promote their welfare, UK law does not permit the casual movement of children who are habitually resident within the British Isles out of this country for the purpose of adoption overseas. Equally it does not permit the unregulated movement into this country of children who are habitually resident outside of the British Isles for the purpose of adoption within the British Isles, and there are restrictions on the circumstances in which a foreign adoption will be recognised. A person who does not comply with the statutory and regulatory requirements which govern inter-country adoption and the movement of children may be guilty of a criminal offence which is punishable by way of a fine and/or a custodial sentence.[2]

---

[2]   ACA 2002, ss 83 and 85.

1.8 International adoption in the UK is a very complex area governed by a myriad of interacting provisions contained in primary legislation, secondary legislation (Regulations), treaty provisions, as well as case-law. Instead of having one legislative scheme for domestic adoption and a separate one for international adoption, there is a single scheme for domestic adoption law, which is augmented and modified by regulations to be fit for use in an international context. This is not intended to be a handbook for domestic adoptions, and it does not provide detailed guidance on adoption panels or their function. Instead this book aims to explain how the domestic adoption procedures are adapted by way of regulation for use in the context of a foreign adoption.

1.9 To understand foreign adoptions it is important to have some knowledge of the common law concepts of habitual residence and domicile as well as an understanding of the *Convention of 29 May 1993 on Protection of Children and Co-operation in Respect of Intercountry Adoption* ('the Convention'). Since this information is important to both incoming and outgoing adoptions we have put these chapters in Part 1 of this book. These chapters are designed to equip the reader with the skills and understanding to identify whether or not a particular adoption would be a foreign or domestic adoption, and if a foreign one whether it falls within or outside of the Convention. Armed with this information it will be possible to identify the correct legal procedures which will be involved in arranging and finalising the adoption.

1.10 Part 2 deals with incoming adoptions. These occur when an adopter is domiciled or habitually resident in the British Isles and the child is habitually resident outside of the British Isles. This is a very complex area and accounts for the majority of foreign adoptions which take place in this country. The focus in these cases is to work out which framework will apply for adoptions from the child's country of habitual residence. The adoption will fall into one of these categories:

(a) **A Convention adoption**: when the child's country of origin is in a state which is contracted into the Convention. These adoptions can take place in the child's country of origin or in this jurisdiction;

(b) **An overseas adoption**: when the child has been adopted in the country of origin and that country is designated on the Designated List;[3]

(c) **An adoption which is not recognised as an overseas or Convention adoption order**: when the adoption has taken place in the child's country of origin and that country is not a country designated on the Designated List. In these cases the child will need to be adopted in this country or an order obtained which gives recognition to the foreign adoption order;

---

[3]   Adoption (Designation of Overseas Adoptions) Order 1973, SI 1973/19, reg 3(3).

(d)   An adoption in this country of a child who has been brought to this country from their country of origin for the purpose of an adoption.

1.11   In addition to understanding the legal procedures associated with the adoption itself it is also important to understand the immigration issues which come into play when it is planned that a child without immigration status should be adopted by a family living in the UK. This is an area which is not always well understood and Chapter 9 sets out the relevant immigration law and practice which will apply in the various sorts of adoptions, and the process when at least one adoptive parent is a British Citizen, as well as situations when neither adoptive parent is a British Citizen.

1.12   Part 3 of the book is concerned with outgoing adoptions. There are two ways that a child who is habitually resident in the British Isles can be adopted by a person who is neither domiciled or habitually resident here. Either they can be adopted in this country under the Convention, or they can be removed from this country for the purpose of adoption overseas. If the latter, the prospective adopters must obtain an order under ACA 2002, s 84, commonly called 'section 84 orders'. If a child is removed from this country for the purpose of adoption overseas by a person who does not have a section 84 order, the person who removes the child, and any other person involved in making arrangements for the removal of the child, commits a criminal offence.[4]

1.13   The court process by which the adopters can apply for and obtain a section 84 order or a Convention adoption order will be the same, whether the child was placed for adoption with the adopters by an adoption agency, or whether it is a private adoption. However, the pre-issue process is very different indeed. To reflect this, Part 3 is divided into four chapters. The first (Chapter 10) provides an overview of the legal procedures which govern outgoing adoptions. Chapter 11 deals with Convention adoptions when the child is placed with the adopters by an adoption agency. Chapter 12 deals with non-Convention adoptions when the child is placed with the adopters by an adoption agency. Chapter 13 deals with private adoptions and covers both Convention and non-Convention cases.

1.14   Although we do explain the meaning of key concepts throughout the book, we have also included a glossary at the end of the book which explains some of the legal terms found within it. We have also included a table of offences to forewarn the unwary of proscribed behaviour and the consequences of pressing ahead without carefully following the statutory and regulatory framework.

1.15   International adoption is still fairly rare in the UK. Only a handful of children are adopted by foreign adopters each year, although since 2009 when *Re A (Adoption: Removal)*[5] was decided, local authorities have had more

---

4   ACA 2002, s 85.
5   [2009] EWCA Civ 41, [2010] Fam 9.

flexibility to place children with relatives who live overseas. It is hoped that in this book the reader will gain an insight into both the law governing international adoption, and the practical steps which will need to be taken in order to bring plans for international adoption to fruition.

Chapter 2

THE ROLE OF THE HAGUE CONVENTION FOR THE PROTECTION OF CHILDREN AND CO-OPERATION IN RESPECT OF INTERCOUNTRY ADOPTION

INTRODUCTION

2.1 The Hague Conference on Private International Law (HccH) is a global inter-governmental organisation. On its website it describes itself as 'a melting pot of different legal traditions, it develops and services multilateral legal instruments, which respond to global needs'. With 72 Members (71 States and the European Union) representing all continents and an increasing number of non-Member States becoming Parties to the Hague Conventions, the work of the HccH encompasses 130 countries around the world.

2.2 Although The Hague had been a centre for international conventions since 1893, in 1955 it was considered desirable for the work of the HccH to be put on a statutory basis and the UK was among the founding members who signed up to *Statute of the Hague Conference on Private International Law* which entered into force on 15 July 1955. As long ago as 1965 the HccH created a convention for the recognition of adoptions where the adopters were habitually resident in a Contracting State different to their national state and/or the child being adopted was habitually resident in a different Contracting State.[1] However, by 1988 it was apparent that this convention did not adequately regulate cross border adoptions and it was agreed by the HccH that consideration would be given to the creation of a new inter-county adoption convention. Once the HccH decided that it was appropriate to prepare a new convention it soon became clear that to be as effective as possible it would be important that the applicability of the convention was not limited to members of the HccH, and therefore from the outset non-member states and other relevant organisations were invited to participate in the discussions which in time led to the final draft of the convention. The result of all this work was the *Convention of 29 May 1993 on Protection of Children and Co-operation in Respect of Intercountry Adoption*. This convention will be the focus of this chapter and, notwithstanding the existence of the other 38 conventions which, at the date of writing, have been generated by the HccH since 1955, each of

---

[1] Convention on Jurisdiction, Applicable Law and Recognition of Decrees Relating to Adoptions (Concluded 15 November 1965). In accordance with its Article 23, this Convention ceased to have effect on 23 October 2008.

which might be known as the Hague Convention, throughout this book references to 'the Convention' will refer to this one on intercountry adoption, unless otherwise specified.

The UK and the Convention

2.3   The UK ratified the Convention on 27 February 2003, and it entered into force in the UK on 1 June 2003. The effect of the Convention is that if a child enters into this country for the purpose of adoption or leaves this country for the purpose of adoption overseas, and the other country involved has also contracted into the Convention, both countries must comply with the Articles of the Convention. Although many countries in the world have contracted into the Convention, not all have done so, and therefore two parallel legal processes exist for the purpose of intercountry adoption. One system governs the movement of children in and out of the UK where either the child or the adopters are habitually resident in a Convention country, and another governs non-Convention countries. As such, it becomes immediately apparent that the first question to be considered in any proposed intercountry adoption must be: is the other country a Convention country? Only by asking this question at the beginning of a case can the correct legal process be identified. The HccH have a very helpful website which can be found at http://www.hcch.net. In particular the HccH website maintains a status table which identifies which countries have contracted into the Convention. The status table can be found on their website using this address: http://www.hcch.net/index_en.php?act=conventions. status&cid=69.

2.4   Later chapters in this book will address the detail of the procedures to bring a child into this country or take a child out of the country for the purpose of an overseas adoption which involves another Convention state. However, it is useful at this stage to consider the legislative framework that incorporates the Convention into our domestic law. The first building block was put into place with the enactment of the Adoption (Intercountry Aspects) Act 1999 which came into force in January 2003, just before the UK ratified the Convention. Much of that Act has now been repealed but it remains the primary legislative source of authority for the Secretary of State to make regulations. This power is given by s 1, the relevant parts of which read:

'1 Regulations giving effect to Convention

(1) Subject to the provisions of this Act, regulations made by the Secretary of State may make provision for giving effect to the Convention on Protection of Children and Co-operation in respect of Intercountry Adoption, concluded at the Hague on 29th May 1993 ("the Convention").

(2) The text of the Convention (so far as material) is set out in Schedule 1 to this Act.

(3) Regulations under this section may –

(a) apply, with or without modifications, any provision of the enactments relating to adoption;

(b) provide that any person who contravenes or fails to comply with any provision of the regulations is to be guilty of an offence and liable on summary conviction to imprisonment for a term not exceeding three months, or a fine not exceeding level 5 on the standard scale, or both;

(c) make different provision for different purposes or areas; and

(d) make such incidental, supplementary, consequential or transitional provision as appears to the Secretary of State to be expedient ...

(5) Subject to subsection (6), any power to make subordinate legislation under or for the purposes of the enactments relating to adoption includes power to do so with a view to giving effect to the provisions of the Convention ...

2.5 The main regulations which have been made under this Act are the Adoptions with a Foreign Element Regulations 2005[2] ('AFER'). Later in this book we will examine the provisions of these regulations in detail, but it is important to note here that AFER regulates both Convention and Non-Convention adoptions. The regulations themselves provide direct regulation and also operate to modify various sections of other Acts and Statutory Instruments. In particular AFER imports and modifies certain provisions of the Adoption Agencies Regulations 2005[3] and the Adoption and Children Act 2002.

A DETAILED EXAMINATION OF THE KEY ARTICLES OF THE CONVENTION

2.6 The body of the Convention is divided into a preamble followed by seven chapters. The reader can find the full text in the statutory materials at the end of this book. What is intended in this section is to provide a guide to the interpretation of the Convention itself, and it draws heavily on the information provided in the Explanatory Note[4] which accompanies the Convention. As set out above, the Convention is not directly incorporated into English law, rather the obligations set out within it are given effect in the domestic legislation. However, where the domestic legislation is unclear an understanding of the Convention is likely to be a useful guide for the interpretation of those provisions. Equally, when considering the obligations of a different Contracting State it may be useful for the reader to understand the Convention when considering whether, and to what extent, the other Contracting State is failing to comply with its obligations under the Convention. This section is divided into sub-headings which mirror the chapter headings in the Convention.

---

[2] SI 2005/392 (made under sub-ss (1), (3), (5)).
[3] SI 2005/389.
[4] Ibid.

The Preamble

2.7   The first thing to note about the Convention is that it has an unusually long preamble. It is clear from the very helpful Explanatory Note[5] that this preamble was the subject of a great deal of thought and discussion, and its purpose is to guide the reader in the interpretation of the various Articles within the Convention. It reads:

'The States signatory to the present Convention,

Recognising that the child, for the full and harmonious development of his or her personality, should grow up in a family environment, in an atmosphere of happiness, love and understanding,

Recalling that each State should take, as a matter of priority, appropriate measures to enable the child to remain in the care of his or her family of origin,

Recognising that intercountry adoption may offer the advantage of a permanent family to a child for whom a suitable family cannot be found in his or her State of origin,

Convinced of the necessity to take measures to ensure that intercountry adoptions are made in the best interests of the child and with respect for his or her fundamental rights, and to prevent the abduction, the sale of, or traffic in children,

Desiring to establish common provisions to this effect, taking into account the principles set forth in international instruments, in particular the United Nations Convention on the Rights of the Child, of 20 November 1989, and the United Nations Declaration on Social and Legal Principles relating to the Protection and Welfare of Children, with Special Reference to Foster Placement and Adoption Nationally and Internationally (General Assembly Resolution 41/85, of 3 December 1986),

Have agreed upon the following provisions –'

Chapter 1 – The Objective and Scope of the Convention

2.8   The objective of the Convention is set out in its first Article which states:

'Article 1

The objects of the present Convention are –

a)   to establish safeguards to ensure that intercountry adoptions take place in the best interests of the child and with respect for his or her fundamental rights as recognised in international law;

---

[5]   The report was drawn up by G Parra-Aranguren who was the Reporter and member ex officio of the drafting committee; the Explanatory note can be viewed in full and downloaded free of charge at http://www.hcch.net/upload/expl33e.pdf.

b)   to establish a system of co-operation amongst Contracting States to ensure that those safeguards are respected and thereby prevent the abduction, the sale of, or traffic in children;

c)   to secure the recognition in Contracting States of adoptions made in accordance with the Convention.'

2.9   The means by which these objectives are achieved is by regulating the adoption processes in both the child's state of origin and the state where the adopters live and into which the child will be received if the adoption proceeds. Each Contracting State must designate a central authority which is responsible for overseeing and ensuring the correct administration of the state's domestic measures to implement the Convention and to act as the conduit of information to other states. Crucially, the Convention requires the central authorities in both states to be actively involved in the assessment and decision making process. Another key aspect of the Convention is that both states are equally bound by the adoption order, giving the child certainty of status in the receiving state. Furthermore the Convention requires all member states to recognise the adoption and accord the child and the parents the status of an adopted child in their own jurisdiction. The Convention requires Contracting States to put in place domestic legislation which gives effect to the Articles contained within it. Thus, by working together, the child's state of origin and the receiving state in which the adopters live are able to ensure, that amongst other things:

- no child is removed from their state of origin for the purpose of adoption unless they are suitable to be adopted;

- no adopter may remove a child from his or her country of origin for the purpose of adoption elsewhere unless they are suitable to adopt that child;

- no person or organisation will make a financial gain from intercountry adoption;

- no child may be placed for adoption with prospective adopters unless both states agree that the adoption of this child by these particular adopters is in the child's best interest;

- a child who is placed for adoption with the agreement of both states must be allowed to enter and permanently reside with their adoptive family in the receiving state;

- measures are available in the receiving state to monitor the child's placement and to take protective measures if that placement breaks down before the child is adopted within its jurisdiction.

2.10   The scope of the Convention is defined in Arts 2 and 3 which read:

'Article 2

(1) The Convention shall apply where a child habitually resident in one Contracting State ("the State of origin") has been, is being, or is to be moved to another Contracting State ("the receiving State") either after his or her adoption in the State of origin by spouses or a person habitually resident in the receiving State, or for the purposes of such an adoption in the receiving State or in the State of origin.

(2) The Convention covers only adoptions which create a permanent parent-child relationship.

Article 3

The Convention ceases to apply if the agreements mentioned in Article 17, sub-paragraph c, have not been given before the child attains the age of eighteen years.'

It is interesting to note that the scope of the Convention is determined by habitual residence and not by other legal concepts such as nationality or domicile. However, although it will apply to all cases where the habitual residence test is met, there is no requirement for a Contracting State to facilitate intercountry adoption under the Convention if, for example adoption is contrary to their domestic law or the child would not be eligible for a visa to enter and permanently remain in the country. In such a case the adoption would simply be unable to proceed.

2.11 Under domestic law in England it is possible for unmarried partners and civil partners jointly to adopt a child. However Art 2(1) limits the application of the Convention to adoptions by spouses or by one person. This is not an accident of drafting. The question of whether or not a couple who are unmarried heterosexuals; or homosexuals or lesbians, irrespective of whether or not they are civil partners of each other, should be allowed to adopt under the Convention, was discussed at great length in the preparatory stages of the Convention. Although some countries had very strong views that the adoption of a child by persons who were not husband and wife was likely to be contrary to the child's best interests, the term husband and wife instead of spouses was not adopted, and 'a person' is allowed to adopt under the Convention. It was accepted that each Contracting State had the power to find a person unsuitable to adopt if the adoption by him or her by reason of his or her relationship status or otherwise would be contrary to their domestic laws. Therefore if in country A, persons who are openly homosexual are prohibited by law from adopting a child, and the adopter in country B is a homosexual man X who lives with his partner Y, and country B has assessed X to be suitable to adopt a child, it would remain open to country A to refuse to consent to the adoption and the adoption would not proceed. Equally if both country A and B allow homosexual partners to adopt children, the adoption by X alone could proceed, even though the adoption by X and Y as a couple could not.

2.12 Notwithstanding that the adoption by X and Y as a couple could not proceed under the Convention, there does not appear to be any provision within the Convention that could act to prohibit the subsequent adoption of the child by both X and Y, if in country B, under its internal adoption laws, this would be lawful once the child had established its place of habitual residence within country B's borders. However, the first paragraph of Art 2 should be read in conjunction with Art 26, paras 2 and 3, because the Convention is to be applied not only for the granting of the adoption, when the child is transferred the receiving State from another Contracting State, but also to determine his or her rights as an adopted child. Likewise with Art 27, since the scope of the Convention covers the possible conversion of the adoption too. If in the scenario considered above X and Y did subsequently adopt the child, that adoption would not have the benefit of being recognised internationally pursuant to the Convention: its recognition in other countries would depend on the domestic law of those particular countries.

2.13 Consideration was given to defining the term 'adoption' but in the end the idea of incorporating a single definition of adoption was rejected and instead the only pre-requisite to an adoption being treated as such under the Convention is that it must create a permanent parent and child relationship. It would appear from the wording of Art 2(2) that the Convention does not apply to arrangements such as Kafala agreements or fostering or guardianship as these do not create a permanent parent and child relationship. Note that, provided that a permanent parent-child relationship is formed with the adopter, there is no requirement that the child's legal relationship to its birth parents is terminated. This allows for the inclusion of limited adoptions or 'simple adoptions', such as exist for example within the French legal system, to be covered by the Convention. This inclusive approach is reflected in both Arts 26 and 27 which are considered later in this chapter.

2.14 Article 3 defines the scope of the Convention in terms of the age of the child. It limits the applicability of the Convention to children about whom the agreement to the adoption is given under Art 17. In this country a child can be adopted at any stage before his or her nineteenth birthday provided the application has been issued before the child attains the age of 18 years. Thus, a Convention Adoption order could be made in this country in relation to a child of 18 years, provided that both central authorities had agreed to the adoption and the application had been issued before the child's eighteenth birthday. However, if a country prohibited a child's adoption after a certain age which was younger than 18, for example 16 years old, the provisions of Art 3 would not act to extend or take precedence over that domestic provision as, pursuant to that country's internal laws, a child over 16 years old would not be suitable for adoption.

Chapter 2 – Requirements for Intercountry Adoptions

2.15 Having considered the scope of the Convention, the next issue that is addressed is the minimum requirements that need to be met before an intercountry adoption between Contracting States can take place. There are only two Articles in this Chapter of the Convention: Art 4, which sets out the duties of the state of origin and Art 5, which sets out the duties of the receiving state. Notwithstanding the apparent delineation of responsibility between the two Contracting States, at the heart of the Convention is the need to make intercountry adoption a collaborative process. For this reason, the agreement of each Contracting State to the adoption is required by Art 17(c) before the child can be placed for adoption with the adopters. Accordingly, each state can exert influence over the other to ensure that the provisions of Arts 4 and 5 are fully met. In this way both states can be confident that the adoption is in the best interests of the child concerned, whose welfare is always the paramount consideration. Within that context it is worth taking a closer look at each of these two provisions, turning first to Art 4 which reads:

'Article 4

An adoption within the scope of the Convention shall take place only if the competent authorities of the State of origin –

a)   have established that the child is adoptable;
b)   have determined, after possibilities for placement of the child within the State of origin have been given due consideration, that an intercountry adoption is in the child's best interests;
c)   have ensured that
    (1)   the persons, institutions and authorities whose consent is necessary for adoption, have been counselled as may be necessary and duly informed of the effects of their consent, in particular whether or not an adoption will result in the termination of the legal relationship between the child and his or her family of origin,
    (2)   such persons, institutions and authorities have given their consent freely, in the required legal form, and expressed or evidenced in writing,
    (3)   the consents have not been induced by payment or compensation of any kind and have not been withdrawn, and
    (4)   the consent of the mother, where required, has been given only after the birth of the child; and
d)   have ensured, having regard to the age and degree of maturity of the child, that
    (1)   he or she has been counselled and duly informed of the effects of the adoption and of his or her consent to the adoption, where such consent is required,
    (2)   consideration has been given to the child's wishes and opinions,
    (3)   the child's consent to the adoption, where such consent is required, has been given freely, in the required legal form, and expressed or evidenced in writing, and
    (4)   such consent has not been induced by payment or compensation of any kind.'

2.16   One of the first things to note about Art 4 is that it places responsibility for compliance on the competent authorities of the state of origin. It does not specify what those authorities should be or how their respective responsibilities should be devolved between them. The competent authorities may be a mixture of privately run – albeit government accredited – bodies, government bodies, the judiciary or the central authority itself. The child must be adoptable, which is to say that there should be no impediment, legal or otherwise to the child being adopted. The options available to place the child in the country of origin must have been explored and discounted by reason of their being contrary to the child's best interests before intercountry adoption can be considered. This means that if there are placements in the state of origin and abroad which offer the same benefits to the child, the placement in the child's state should always be preferred. Finally, all necessary consents, including where appropriate that of the child, must be given freely, on a fully informed basis and without the promise of remuneration. In respect of the consent of a mother, where it is necessary it must be given following the birth of the child. Subject to compliance with the minimum requirements set out in Art 4, the specific provisions as to who must consent and the conditions under which their consent is given are matters to be determined by the internal law of the state of origin. So, for example, under the Adoption and Children Act 2002, the mother's consent must be provided not less than 6 weeks following the birth of the child.[6] This is more onerous than the requirement in Art 4(4), and it still must be complied with. Article 4 therefore includes all the factors which need to be taken into account pursuant to Art 21(a) of the United Nations Convention on the Rights of the Child[7] which states that:

'States Parties that recognize and/or permit the system of adoption shall ensure that the best interests of the child shall be the paramount consideration and they shall:

(a)   Ensure that the adoption of a child is authorized only by competent authorities who determine, in accordance with applicable law and procedures and on the basis of all pertinent and reliable information, that the adoption is permissible in view of the child's status concerning parents, relatives and legal guardians and that, if required, the persons concerned have given their informed consent to the adoption on the basis of such counselling as may be necessary;'

2.17   Article 5, set out below, is more concise in its wording, although the responsibilities contained within it are certainly no less onerous. Note in particular the use again of the term 'competent authorities' as in Art 4. Finally, and from the point of view of the security of the child, the receiving state must certify that it has determined that the child is or will be allowed to enter and permanently reside in that jurisdiction. This confirmation must be received by the state of origin before the child is placed for adoption with the adopters, and is specifically required pursuant to Art 17(d).

---

6   Adoption and Children Act 2002, s 52(3).
7   The United Nations Convention. Adopted and opened for signature, ratification and accession by General Assembly Resolution 44/25 of 20 November 1989, entry into force 2 September 1990, in accordance with Art 49 and ratified by the UK on 16 December 1991.

'Article 5

An adoption within the scope of the Convention shall take place only if the competent authorities of the receiving State –

a)   have determined that the prospective adoptive parents are eligible and suited to adopt;

b)   have ensured that the prospective adoptive parents have been counselled as may be necessary; and

c)   have determined that the child is or will be authorised to enter and reside permanently in that State.'

Chapter 3 – Central Authorities and Accredited Bodies

2.18   Chapter 3 of the Convention, which contains Arts 6–13, governs the designation and function of central authorities, and also sets out which of those functions must be carried out by the central authority and which can be delegated. Each Contracting State must create or designate a central authority, the primary function of which is to act as the interface through which the state communicates with other Contracting States and the HccH. Its role as a conduit of information and communication at an inter-state level must be carried out directly by the central authority, and it cannot delegate its ultimate responsibility to eliminate any obstacle to the application of the Convention. Additionally, Art 8 only allows the central authority to delegate to 'public authorities' the task of taking 'all appropriate measures to prevent improper financial or other gain in connection with an adoption and to deter all practices contrary to the objects of the Convention', although it does not specify what sort of public body and leaves it open to the individual state to determine whether they are judicial or administrative bodies. In particular this provision needs to be read alongside Arts 32 and 33, which together prohibit the obtaining of improper financial or other gain from intercountry adoption and prevent violation of the Convention. In relation to the other functions of the central authority, pursuant to Art 9, it is a matter for each state to determine the extent to which they are carried out by its central authority, by public authorities, or by other bodies duly accredited in that state. This is not an unfettered freedom though, since Art 10 restricts the accreditation of non-public bodies to 'bodies demonstrating their competence to carry out properly the tasks with which they may be entrusted' and Art 11 sets out that accredited bodies must be non-profit making, staffed by suitably qualified personnel, and subject to supervision by the competent authorities in that state. By Art 12, accredited bodies are allowed to operate in more than one Contracting State provided that the competent authorities in both states have authorised it to do so. Article 13 completes this Chapter and states:

'Article 13

The designation of the Central Authorities and, where appropriate, the extent of their functions, as well as the names and addresses of the accredited bodies shall be communicated by each Contracting State to the Permanent Bureau of the Hague Conference on Private International Law.'

The HccH therefore acts as the depository for retaining records of the details of each Contracting State's central authority and accredited bodies, enabling it to communicate with the relevant bodies in each Contracting State in order to carry out its function in monitoring the effectiveness of the Convention and providing guidelines to Contracting States.

2.19 Article 22 is not in fact in Chapter 3 of the Convention but merits consideration at this stage. It reads:

'**Article 22**

(1) The functions of a Central Authority under this Chapter may be performed by public authorities or by bodies accredited under Chapter III, to the extent permitted by the law of its State.

(2) Any Contracting State may declare to the depositary of the Convention that the functions of the Central Authority under Articles 15 to 21 may be performed in that State, to the extent permitted by the law and subject to the supervision of the competent authorities of that State, also by bodies or persons who –

a)   meet the requirements of integrity, professional competence, experience and accountability of that State; and
b)   are qualified by their ethical standards and by training or experience to work in the field of intercountry adoption.

(3) A Contracting State which makes the declaration provided for in paragraph 2 shall keep the Permanent Bureau of the Hague Conference on Private International Law informed of the names and addresses of these bodies and persons.

(4) Any Contracting State may declare to the depositary of the Convention that adoptions of children habitually resident in its territory may only take place if the functions of the Central Authorities are performed in accordance with paragraph 1.

(5) Notwithstanding any declaration made under paragraph 2, the reports provided for in Articles 15 and 16 shall, in every case, be prepared under the responsibility of the Central Authority or other authorities or bodies in accordance with paragraph 1.'

So, if any person is authorised under Art 22(2) to carry out any of the functions of the central authority, under Art 22(3) their details must also be sent to the HccH. The HccH provides unrestricted access to the contact details of the relevant bodies in each Contracting State, and this information is available free of charge on the HccH website.[8] While it is the right of one state

---

8   http://www.hcch.net/index_en.php?act=conventions.authorities&cid=69.

to declare that an unaccredited person or body can carry out some of the functions of the central authority pursuant to subpara (2), it is also the right of any other Contracting State to declare under subpara (4), that they will only allow the adoption of children resident in their territory if the other Contracting State ensures that the functions of the central authority are carried out only by those bodies specified in subpara (1). So, country B can stipulate that it will only allow children from country A to be adopted under the Convention in country B if the obligations of the central authority in country A are carried out by public authorities or accredited bodies. In the absence of a declaration under sub-para (4) a state will be assumed to have agreed that some of the functions of the central authority in a different state can be carried out by an unaccredited person or body pursuant to subpara (2).

2.20 It is of note that while a person or body authorised under Art 22(2) to carry out some of the functions of the central authority is bound by the Convention, and in particular by Art 32, they are not required to operate within the boundaries imposed by Art 11. This means that a person or organisation may undertake profit-related business as part of their general enterprise, although may not do so insofar as any part of their business relates to the carrying out of the functions of the central authority. Finally, while a non-accredited person or body may be authorised to undertake some of the functions of the central authority set out in Arts 15–21, the final responsibility for the reports required by Arts 15 and 16 lies with the central authority or other public authorities or accredited bodies in accordance with subpara (1) in every case.

Chapter 4 – Procedural Requirements in Intercountry Adoption

2.21 The provisions of Chapter 4 of the Convention regulate the adoption process itself, from the application, through the assessment process, specifying the minimum conditions to be met before the child is placed for adoption with the adopters, regulating the transfer of the child across state borders and the monitoring and protection of the child in the receiving state until the adoption in that state is finalised if it has not taken place in the state of origin. The purpose of this Chapter of the Convention is neatly summarised in the Explanatory Report[9] which accompanies it, which states:

> 'Chapter IV aims at designing a procedure that will protect the fundamental interests of all the parties involved in intercountry adoptions, in particular the child, the biological parents and the prospective adoptive parents. Consequently, it establishes important safeguards for the protection of those interests, but, at the same time, an effort was made to simplify the existing procedures and to maximize the chances of homeless children being integrated into adequate homes in other Contracting States.'

---

[9]   The report was drawn up by G Parra-Aranguren who was the Reporter and member ex officio of the drafting committee; the Explanatory Note can be viewed in full and downloaded free of charge at http://www.hcch.net/upload/expl33e.pdf – see para 282.

2.22 This Chapter is comprised of Arts 14–22. During the drafting phase of the Convention there was some discussion as to the order in which the various provisions should sit in the Convention as the order in which the provisions are set out could be interpreted as signifying their relative importance. However, the framework eventually agreed upon approaches the order of this Chapter from a chronological perspective and within that context it makes sense that the first provision deals with the application, which in line with the scope of the Convention expressed in Art 2, directs itself to persons habitually resident in a Contracting State who wish to adopt a child habitually resident in another one. Article 14 reads:

'Article 14

Persons habitually resident in a Contracting State, who wish to adopt a child habitually resident in another Contracting State, shall apply to the Central Authority in the State of their habitual residence.'

2.23 The key point about this Article is that it requires the adopters to apply to their own central authority, and not to the child's central authority. At first glance it might appear that the Convention requires the Convention adoption order itself to be made in the receiving state (ie the state in which the applicants are based), but it is doubtful that this is the intention. It is more likely that what is being referred to here by the use of the word 'apply' is the sort of application that a person makes to a local authority when they wish to adopt a child and need to be assessed. As will become clear in Art 15 the assessment of the adopters is carried out by the central authority in the receiving state and it is only after the full rigour of the assessments of both the adopters and the child, and after careful consideration by both central authorities of the match has taken place and agreement reached, that an adopter can find themselves in a position to make an application to a court for an adoption order pursuant to the Convention in relation to a child.

2.24 Once an application by a person or a married couple who are habitually resident in a Contracting State and who wish to adopt a child who is habitually resident in another Contracting State is received, it is the duty of the central authority in the receiving state (the country in which the applicants are habitually resident) to assess that person or married couple. This duty is imposed by Art 9, which states:

'Article 9

Central Authorities shall take, directly or through public authorities or other bodies duly accredited in their State, all appropriate measures, in particular to –

a)   collect, preserve and exchange information about the situation of the child and the prospective adoptive parents, so far as is necessary to complete the adoption;

b)   facilitate, follow and expedite proceedings with a view to obtaining the adoption;

c)   promote the development of adoption counselling and post-adoption services in their States;

d)   provide each other with general evaluation reports about experience with intercountry adoption;

e)   reply, in so far as is permitted by the law of their State, to justified requests from other Central Authorities or public authorities for information about a particular adoption situation.'

In particular it is a requirement of Art 9(b) that they need to do so expeditiously. The matters which must be taken into account are specified in the terms of Art 15 which reads:

'Article 15

If the Central Authority of the receiving State is satisfied that the applicants are eligible and suited to adopt, it shall prepare a report including information about their identity, eligibility and suitability to adopt, background, family and medical history, social environment, reasons for adoption, ability to undertake an intercountry adoption, as well as the characteristics of the children for whom they would be qualified to care.

(2) It shall transmit the report to the Central Authority of the State of origin.'

2.25   However, it must always be understood that the list of factors enumerated in this Article is not supposed to represent the limit of the assessment of the adopters. Rather it is the absolute minimum extent of the considerations which must be taken into account before the receiving state can be satisfied that the applicants are eligible and suited to adopt. Although it does not specifically require the receiving state to ensure that all necessary consents are obtained, it is implicit that if the application is by a single person who is party to a marriage, the other spouse's consent will need to be obtained where such an adoption is possible under the internal law of the receiving state. When assessing their suitability to adopt a child, the receiving state must also consider the characteristics of the children that they would be able to care for. This does not necessarily mean specific characteristics of a particular child, but rather it directs the central authority to consider what sort of child or children the adopters could offer a home to. This may, for example, refer to the adopters' own parenting capacity, experience, economic circumstances, religious beliefs and preferences. This does not mean that if the report is being prepared with a view to the adoption of a particular child, for example a relative of the applicants, the report could not take into account their suitability to adopt that particular child. If the identity of the child is known when the assessment is being carried out, as it would be in an adoption by a relative, there are obvious advantages for the decision-making process if the assessment of the adopters is conducted in the light of that child's particular needs. In this way there can be a much more reliable determination of the adopters' suitability to adopt that particular child. These reports have come to be referred to as 'Article 15 reports'.

2.26 Pursuant to Art 4 it is the responsibility of the central authority in the state of origin (the country in which the child is habitually resident) to assess whether or not intercountry adoption is in the best interests of a particular child. The central authority can delegate this task pursuant to Art 9, and the assessment must be carried out expeditiously. The content of the assessment and the report is regulated by Art 16 which reads:

'Article 16

(1) If the Central Authority of the State of origin is satisfied that the child is adoptable, it shall –

a) prepare a report including information about his or her identity, adoptability, background, social environment, family history, medical history including that of the child's family, and any special needs of the child;
b) give due consideration to the child's upbringing and to his or her ethnic, religious and cultural background;
c) ensure that consents have been obtained in accordance with Article 4; and
d) determine, on the basis in particular of the reports relating to the child and the prospective adoptive parents, whether the envisaged placement is in the best interests of the child.

(2) It shall transmit to the Central Authority of the receiving State its report on the child, proof that the necessary consents have been obtained and the reasons for its determination on the placement, taking care not to reveal the identity of the mother and the father if, in the State of origin, these identities may not be disclosed.'

2.27 The report specified at Art 16(1)(a) should be prepared by the state of origin once it is satisfied that the child's best interests would be served by an intercountry adoption. It is not necessary for the state of origin to wait until it receives an Article 15 report to start this work. Indeed it is the duty of the state of origin to keep a list of children who have been assessed as suitable to be adopted overseas so that, if an enquiry is received from a foreign central authority with approved adopters who are looking to adopt a child from another Convention country, consideration of matching any available child can be carried out expeditiously to avoid delay for that child.

2.28 Once an Article 15 report has been received, the actual matching process is carried out under Art 16(1)(d). Although this sub-clause is quite clearly about matching the child to the adopters, apparently there was no equivalent word in French, hence the way it is set out in the Convention. When giving consideration to the match between the child and the adopter, it is necessary for the state of origin to consider the report specified in subpara (1)(a), and taking into account the information in that report, turn its attention specifically to the matters specified at subparas (1)(b) and (c). If, having carried out all of the tasks specified in Art 16(1), the state of origin approves the match, it must transmit to the central authority in the receiving state all the information contained in Art 16(2). The totality of the information sent pursuant to

Art 16(2) is generally referred to as the 'Article 16 report'. It is important not to confuse the *report on the child* specified at Art 16(1)(a) with the Article 16 Report, which must include the totality of the information required by Art 16(2). The Article 16 Report confirms the suitability of the child for an overseas adoption per se; provides proof of all necessary consents; takes into account the specific features of the child and those of the adopters; and in the light of that information the agreement of the child's state of origin to the adoption. Once the receiving state has all the information in the Article 16 Report it must consider the matching process, and form its own independent view as to whether or not the adoption is in the best interests of the child concerned.

'Article 17

Any decision in the State of origin that a child should be entrusted to prospective adoptive parents may only be made if –

a)   the Central Authority of that State has ensured that the prospective adoptive parents agree;
b)   the Central Authority of the receiving State has approved such decision, where such approval is required by the law of that State or by the Central Authority of the State of origin;
c)   the Central Authorities of both States have agreed that the adoption may proceed; and
d)   it has been determined, in accordance with Article 5, that the prospective adoptive parents are eligible and suited to adopt and that the child is or will be authorised to enter and reside permanently in the receiving State.'

2.29   The key to understanding Art 17 is to understand what is meant by the word 'entrusted' within the context of 'entrusted to prospective adoptive parents'. The Explanatory Note[10] confirms that this Article is intended to regulate the *placement* of the child with the prospective adopters. It is therefore curious that the Article uses the term 'entrusted' rather than 'placement'. It would appear from the Explanatory Note that the use of 'entrusted' would ensure that confusion over the term 'placement' was avoided, as it explains:

'Notwithstanding the persistence of some delegations all along the Conference to insert the word "placement" in Article 17, as in other articles of the Convention, the term "entrust-ment" was maintained for the sake of clarity and because it offers the advantage that whoever does not understand its exact meaning will try to find it out and therefore obtain a satisfactory explanation.'[11]

Clearly, being entrusted with the child means more in this context than simply being given the day-to-day care of the child. The meaning of 'entrusted' within the context of Art 17 was considered at first instance in the case of *Haringey London Borough Council v MA, JN, IA*.[12] In that case Charles J said this:

---

[10]   Ibid, para 324.
[11]   Ibid, para 328.
[12]   [2008] EWHC 1722 (Fam), [2008] 2 FLR 1857.

'[95] To my mind "entrusted to prospective adopters":

(i)   has a meaning that relates the placement much more closely to the proposed adoption than giving or entrusting day-to-day care to potential adopters for the purpose of an assessment; and thus

(ii)   in English terms the concept equates to the making of a parental responsibility order under s 84 of the ACA 2002,[13] or a placement for adoption, with their respective consequences.

In both cases those consequences involve changes in status and the relationship between the child and the prospective adopters which can be assessed without reference to the detailed conditions precedent required by English law (or the laws of other Hague Convention States) before such a step can be taken or order made.'

Although this case went on to be considered by the Court of Appeal and is reported as *Re A (Adoption: Removal)*,[14] this aspect of Charles J's judgment was not challenged and therefore remains the only case-law on this issue.

2.30   Paragraph 17 (b) is a form of double check and will not always apply. However, subpara 17(c) is a keystone of the Convention. The agreement given in Art 17(c) does not pre-judge the adoption process. That must still be carried out in accordance with the law of the state in which it takes place. Rather the agreement in Art 17(c) is a prerequisite of the relevant adoption proceedings even being able to be considered. Unless both central authorities agree to the adoption proceeding, the child cannot be entrusted to the prospective adopters. Each state therefore has a right of veto in relation to the adoption if, in the view of its own central authority, the adoption of the child by the proposed adopters is not in the child's best interests. This short provision is how the Convention ensures that children do not fall unseen through the child protection net. The left hand always knows and agrees with what the right hand is doing and vice versa. The importance of this agreement is reflected in the requirement in Art 23 that the certificate issued for recognition purposes, by the state in which the adoption order is made, must specify on that certificate 'when and by whom the agreements under Article 17, sub-paragraph c), were given'.

2.31   Subparagraph 17(d) cross-references with the obligation in Art 5 to ensure that the child is able to enter and permanently remain within the jurisdiction of the receiving state following the making of the relevant adoption order, which in the UK would be a Convention Adoption Order or a Section 84 Order.[15] It ensures that children are not entrusted to prospective adopters until all relevant immigration issues have been resolved in the favour of the child.

---

[13]   This provision allows a person to lawfully remove a child from the jurisdiction of the court for the purpose of adoption overseas. Please see Chapter 12 for full details.

[14]   [2009] EWCA Civ 41.

[15]   For a full explanation of what these orders are and when and how to apply for them, please refer to Chapter 11.

'**Article 18**

The Central Authorities of both States shall take all necessary steps to obtain permission for the child to leave the State of origin and to enter and reside permanently in the receiving State.'

2.32 Article 18 adds very little to what is specified in Arts 5 and 17(d), but does add the requirement that both states have to take all steps necessary to obtain permission for the child to leave its country of origin as well as to enter and permanently reside in the receiving state. Certainly within Europe where there is free movement of persons this provision is not likely to have much impact.

'**Article 19**

(1) The transfer of the child to the receiving State may only be carried out if the requirements of Article 17 have been satisfied.

(2) The Central Authorities of both States shall ensure that this transfer takes place in secure and appropriate circumstances and, if possible, in the company of the adoptive or prospective adoptive parents.

(3) If the transfer of the child does not take place, the reports referred to in Articles 15 and 16 are to be sent back to the authorities who forwarded them.'

2.33 Article 19 concerns the physical transfer of the child. It is clear from the Explanatory Note that when formulating this provision of the Convention it was envisaged that the transfer of the child in this context might take place before or after the entrustment to the prospective adopters and indeed before or after the making of the adoption order itself.[16] The Explanatory Note does not define what is meant by the term transfer. The question therefore arises: does the term transfer mean 'enter within the jurisdiction of the receiving state for any purpose' or does it mean 'enter for the purpose of permanently residing within that jurisdiction'? If the answer is the latter, then a visit by the child to stay with family members in the receiving state while assessments are being carried out by the state of origin would be permitted. If the answer is the former then such a visit would be in contravention of Art 19.

2.34 The English courts in two cases have implicitly favoured the latter approach, allowing the child to move internationally on a temporary basis before the making of an adoption order. The meaning of the word 'transfer' within this context was not expressly considered by either the High Court or the Court of Appeal in the case of *Re A (Adoption: Removal)*.[17] In that case the plan which was endorsed by both courts involved the child (IA) being taken to the United States of America for a temporary visit with her relatives who lived there while assessments were being carried out to see if this placement had

---

[16]   Explanatory Note, para 347.
[17]   [2009] EWCA Civ 41.

the potential to become an adoptive placement. The proposed visit was intended to occur after receipt of the Article 15 Report but prior to the completion of the Article 16 Report, and the information obtained during the proposed visit was intended to inform the local authority's decision-making process when it considered the relevant factors pursuant to Art 16. The child was subject to a care order and parental responsibility for (and rights of custody over – within the meaning of the Hague Convention on International Child Abduction) the child remained always with the parents and the local authority. Furthermore, since the child was a looked-after child the proposed placement would therefore be categorised as a foster placement, and accordingly the child's place of ordinary residence remained throughout the visit within the local authority in England.[18] Although not expressly stated, it might be thought that it is implicit within this context, that when the court accepted that para 19 of Sch 2 to the Children Act 1989 could be used to authorise a visit of this sort, the court did not consider the proposed visit to constitute a transfer within the terms of Art 19.

2.35 The case of *ECC (The Local Authority) v SM*[19] considered a similar set of facts to those in *Re A*,[20] in that the local authority wished to place a looked-after child with relatives overseas in the context of a possible Convention adoption. However, in that case at the time when it was proposed that the placement overseas would be effected, the child would already be the subject of a placement order. Therefore it was not possible for the court to authorise the proposed temporary visit with the family members overseas under para 19 of Sch 2 to the Children Act 1989. This is because once a placement order has been made, any placement overseas of a looked-after child, for a period of more than 28 days, can only take place with the agreement of all persons with parental responsibility or with the permission of the court. Such permission must be obtained from the court under s 28 of the Adoption and Children Act 2002 once a child is the subject of a placement order. The situation in ECC differed from *Re A* in that the local authority had put together almost all the information required for the Article 16 report and had sent most of this to the central authority for England and Wales (the only outstanding information from the Article 16 report was the placement order itself which was granted at the same time as the s 28 order). The central authority of the receiving state (the USA) had not at that time provided the Art 17(c) agreement or the certificate required under Art 5. It was therefore not permissible to place the child for adoption with the family at the time the permission under s 28 was obtained but it was envisaged that the child would be so placed in the near future. However, it was the local authority case that permission could be given pursuant to s 28 in circumstances where it was planned that the child would remain in the USA until shortly before the final hearing in the proposed Convention Adoption application. Hedley J was not specifically addressed in relation to Art 19 of the Convention, but he was satisfied that the proposed trip was not for the purpose of an adoption

---

[18] Children Act 1989, s 105(6).
[19] [2010] EWHC 1694 (Fam), [2011] 1 FLR 234.
[20] [2009] EWCA Civ 41.

overseas, and therefore was not prohibited by ACA 2002, s 85.[21] Further, he was satisfied that ACA 2002, s 1 applied to the making of orders under s 28. Additionally, the prospective adopters had offered to give the court an undertaking to return the child to the jurisdiction of the court at the request of the local authority or the court and to do so in any event by a specified date. Accordingly, Hedley J was satisfied that the order under s 28 allowing the child to travel to the USA was both lawful and in the best interests of the child, and he gave permission for a visit on the basis that the child was returned to this jurisdiction before the final hearing. In giving his permission Hedley J directed that the order had to contain a number of recitals, and suggested that these should be included in any similar order. In particular an order under s 28 should set out that:

(a)   the child's place of habitual residence will remain in England and Wales and it is not intended that this status will change by virtue of the proposed temporary visit;

(b)   the local authority and the parents will retain parental responsibility for and rights of custody over the child throughout the visit;

(c)   the prospective adopters (who should be named in the order) have undertaken to the court to return the child to the jurisdiction at the request of the local authority or the court and in event by no later than a specified date.

In that case the receiving state (the USA) was also a party to the Hague Convention on International Child Abduction[22] and if necessary an application in the US Court under that Convention would have been available to secure the child's return to the UK if the prospective adopters breached their undertakings. It is therefore clear that in this context, as in the *Re A* case, the child remained subject to the protection of the English Court and for that reason the child had not 'transferred' to the receiving state within the meaning of Art 19 of the Convention.

2.36   The Explanatory Note states that the transfer can take place before or after the entrustment and/or before or after the adoption itself.[23] It would seem unlikely that a child could be entrusted to prospective adopters without being in their physical control. If that is correct, the logical corollary would be that Art 19 was not intended to prevent a child from travelling to the receiving state for the purpose of a temporary visit prior to the formal transfer of the child to that jurisdiction. Within that context, it would appear that the English court has interpreted ACA 2002 to treat the transfer referred to in Art 19 as the permanent movement of the child into the receiving state, whereupon the child's habitual residence would change and the child would be subject to the

---

[21]   For further details of s 85 please see **12.6**.
[22]   Convention of 25 October 1980 on the Civil Aspects of International Child Abduction, Entry into force: 1 December 1983.
[23]   See footnote 6 for details of the report; para 347 of the report.

jurisdiction of the court in that country. If that is correct, the effect of the provisions of ACA 2002 limit the transfer of the child to a time after the making of a Convention Adoption Order or a s 84 order.

2.37   Article 20 imposes a duty on the central authorities to keep each other informed. This duty is already imposed under Art 9(b) and is implicit in many of the other provisions, and one might wonder why it is duplicated in Art 20 which reads:

> **'Article 20**
>
> The Central Authorities shall keep each other informed about the adoption process and the measures taken to complete it, as well as about the progress of the placement if a probationary period is required.'

Perhaps the reason is that by giving this duty its own separate place in one simple Article it casts a focused spotlight which emphasises the importance of communication at the state level and ensures that the state of origin does not hold on to any illusion that once the child has transferred to the receiving state its obligations to the child are severed. Sandwiched as it is, between Art 19 (which deals with the transfer) and Art 21 (defining the duties of the central authorities when an adoptive placement breaks down in the receiving state prior to finalisation of the adoption) it reminds both states, that until the adoption has been finalised, they share an ongoing responsibility for welfare of the child.

2.38   Between them, Arts 20 and 21 of the Convention implicitly impose a duty on the receiving state to monitor the child's placement with the prospective adopters once the transfer has taken place and pending any final adoption order made in that country. Although it does not state expressly that the receiving state must monitor the placement during any probationary period, it does state what should happen in the event that it appears to the receiving state that the continued placement of the child with the prospective adopters is not in the child's best interests. Article 21 states:

> **'Article 21**
>
> (1) Where the adoption is to take place after the transfer of the child to the receiving State and it appears to the Central Authority of that State that the continued placement of the child with the prospective adoptive parents is not in the child's best interests, such Central Authority shall take the measures necessary to protect the child, in particular –
>
> a)   to cause the child to be withdrawn from the prospective adoptive parents and to arrange temporary care;
> b)   in consultation with the Central Authority of the State of origin, to arrange without delay a new placement of the child with a view to adoption or, if this is not appropriate, to arrange alternative long-term care; an adoption

shall not take place until the Central Authority of the State of origin has been duly informed concerning the new prospective adoptive parents;

c)   as a last resort, to arrange the return of the child, if his or her interests so require.

(2) Having regard in particular to the age and degree of maturity of the child, he or she shall be consulted and, where appropriate, his or her consent obtained in relation to measures to be taken under this Article.'

2.39   Clearly if the adoption has taken place in the state of origin, before the transfer of the child, Art 21 will not apply, as it only covers the situation when the child is entrusted to the adopters and transferred to the receiving state prior to the adoption order being made. Notwithstanding the joint responsibility towards the child indicated by Art 20, it is clear from Art 21, that following transfer of the child, and pending the adoption being finalised, the receiving state has primary and ultimate responsibility for the child. This is apparent from the approach taken in sub-paragraph (b) which, while obliging the receiving state to consult with the state of origin as to the new placement for the child, adoptive or otherwise, does not require the consent of both Contracting States to any new adoptive placement in the same way as Art 17 does. The rationale for this approach would appear to be the need to ensure that decisions are made expeditiously for the child to avoid the child being left in a state of limbo for any significant period. Thus, there is a duty to consult with the child's state of origin, and in particular to inform them about any new prospective adopters prior to the child being placed for adoption with them (which in this context should be taken to have the same meaning as entrustment), but there is no power of veto on the part of the state of origin if it disagrees with the decisions of the receiving state. It is also clear that the expectation will be that the receiving state is expected to exhaust the options for the long term care of the child within its jurisdiction before returning the child to its country of origin, as pursuant to subpara (c) return of the child is the option of last resort.

2.40   Article 22, as we have seen, already serves to regulate the circumstances within which people or organisations can perform the various functions of the central authorities defined within this chapter of the Convention and requires each state to keep the depositary (the HccH) up to date with information as to the persons or bodies carrying out these functions within their state. As a consequence it should always be possible for a central authority in one state to identify the relevant person or body responsible for carrying out the functions of the central authority in any other Contracting State. It would appear that among other things, the purpose of this Article is to allow for 'private' or 'independent' adoptions. An adoption is a private adoption when the child is not placed for adoption by the state. In this country private adoptions can only be lawfully arranged in very limited circumstances.[24]

---

[24]   ACA 2002, s 92 which is considered in **13.1**.

Chapter 5 – Recognition and Effects of the Adoption

2.41 In order to ensure that an adoption which has been granted in compliance with the provisions of the Convention is recognised in all Contracting States, the competent authority in the state in which the adoption was carried out must prepare a certificate stating that the adoption has been made in accordance with the Convention, and that certificate must specify when and by whom the agreements under Art 17(c), were given. An adoption certified in this way is recognised by operation of law in all other Contracting States pursuant to Art 23 of the Convention which reads:

> **'Article 23**
>
> (1) An adoption certified by the competent authority of the State of the adoption as having been made in accordance with the Convention shall be recognised by operation of law in the other Contracting States. The certificate shall specify when and by whom the agreements under Article 17, sub-paragraph c), were given.
>
> (2) Each Contracting State shall, at the time of signature, ratification, acceptance, approval or accession, notify the depositary of the Convention of the identity and the functions of the authority or the authorities which, in that State, are competent to make the certification. It shall also notify the depositary of any modification in the designation of these authorities.'

2.42 It appears from the Explanatory Note that during the drafting phase of the Convention there was a great deal of thought given to what should be stipulated on the certificate and the extent to which a breach of one of more of the Articles of the Convention would be a bar to the recognition of the adoption. Ultimately it was agreed that all of the Articles are important and none should be seen as optional. To stipulate one or two might suggest that these were of a fundamental nature and others were of secondary importance. Furthermore, an unwillingness to recognise the legal and family relationship between a child and their adoptive parents, in consequence of a failure by a Contracting State to carry out its obligations by the letter of the Convention, would not be likely to further the welfare of the child in question. The balance was struck by the requirement that the certificate must certify when and by whom the agreements under Art 17(c) were given, emphasising the critical importance of this agreement being reached before the child is entrusted, or placed for adoption, with the adopters. It is of note that Art 23 binds all Contracting States, not just the two which were involved in the adoption.

2.43 The only basis for a Contracting State to refuse to recognise a Convention adoption, certified according to Art 23, is if the terms of Art 24 are met, these being:

'**Article 24**

The recognition of an adoption may be refused in a Contracting State only if the adoption is manifestly contrary to its public policy, taking into account the best interests of the child.'

2.44   Where it says 'manifestly contrary to public policy' this should be read restrictively in that it would have to go against the fundamental principles of the objecting state, but even if this criteria is met, the state would still need to consider the impact on the refusal on the child and must take that child's best interests into account.

2.45   However, although Art 24 is the only basis for refusal of recognition of a standard Convention Adoption order, Art 39(2) allows states to agree with other states ways of improving the operation of the Convention as between themselves, by allowing a bilateral agreement that enables modifications to some, but not all, of the Articles of the Convention. It reads:

'**Article 39(2)**

Any Contracting State may enter into agreements with one or more other Contracting States, with a view to improving the application of the Convention in their mutual relations. These agreements may derogate only from the provisions of Articles 14 to 16 and 18 to 21. The States which have concluded such an agreement shall transmit a copy to the depositary of the Convention.'

If two Contracting States should come to such an arrangement and register it with the depositary in accordance with Art 39(2), every Contracting State will be bound to recognise an adoption granted in compliance with that agreement, unless a Contracting State has made a declaration that they will not be bound to recognise such adoptions in which case that particular Contracting State will not be obliged to recognise them. Art 25 reads:

'**Article 25**

Any Contracting State may declare to the depositary of the Convention that it will not be bound under this Convention to recognise adoptions made in accordance with an agreement concluded by application of Article 39, paragraph 2.'

2.46   Article 26 clarifies what is meant by recognition of an adoption. To understand this provision it must be remembered that there is more than one kind of adoption outside of the UK. In the British Isles, adoption is pretty straightforward. When a child is adopted the adoptive parents become the legal parents and the child's former parents (whether by birth or earlier adoption) cease to the child's legal parents. A child who is adopted in the UK can only have a maximum of two legal parents at any one time. However, some countries have a different approach to adoption and while an adoption will create a permanent parent-child relationship, it does not always terminate the former parent-child relationship. It was therefore necessary to clarify the status of birth parents in a Contracting State that does not terminate the parental relationship between the child and its birth parents upon adoption. The result is set out in Art 26, which reads:

'Article 26

(1) The recognition of an adoption includes recognition of

a) the legal parent-child relationship between the child and his or her adoptive parents;
b) parental responsibility of the adoptive parents for the child;
c) the termination of a pre-existing legal relationship between the child and his or her mother and father, if the adoption has this effect in the Contracting State where it was made.

(2) In the case of an adoption having the effect of terminating a pre-existing legal parent-child relationship, the child shall enjoy in the receiving State, and in any other Contracting State where the adoption is recognised, rights equivalent to those resulting from adoptions having this effect in each such State.

(3) The preceding paragraphs shall not prejudice the application of any provision more favourable for the child, in force in the Contracting State which recognises the adoption.'

2.47 The effect of this provision is that if, in the country in which the adoption takes place, the adoption entails the termination of legal parenthood in the former parents, that status will be recognised in all other Contracting States, including Contracting States in which such termination would not be a consequence of adoption. On the other hand, if the adoption takes place in a country that does not terminate the legal relationship between the child and his or her mother then that relationship will have to be respected in other states, even if an adoption would terminate that relationship under their laws. However, in this case, there is provision under Art 27 for the receiving state to convert the adoption if their domestic law allows this, and provided that the conversion is registered in accordance with Art 23, it shall be recognised by all other Contracting States. However, it is important to remember that in order to convert the adoption to a full adoption, all consents required under Art 4(c) and (d) must have been obtained.

Chapter 6 – General Provisions and Chapter 7 – Final Clauses

2.48 It is not proposed to go through Arts 28–48 individually although they are set out in full in the statutory materials at the end of the book and are fairly self-explanatory. However, it is worth noting that it is not the role of the HccH to enforce the terms of the Convention. Pursuant to Art 33 which states:

'Article 33

A competent authority which finds that any provision of the Convention has not been respected or that there is a serious risk that it may not be respected, shall immediately inform the Central Authority of its State. This Central Authority shall be responsible for ensuring that appropriate measures are taken.'

it is clear that if a breach of the Convention is identified by a competent authority, that person or body must immediately notify their own central authority which then becomes responsible for addressing and resolving the problem. However, the HccH does have an ongoing duty to review the effectiveness of the Convention, set down in Art 42, which reads:

'Article 42

The Secretary General of the Hague Conference on Private International Law shall at regular intervals convene a Special Commission in order to review the practical operation of the Convention.'

and has distributed questionnaires to the Contracting States for the purpose of reviewing the effectiveness of the Hague Convention and to analyse the different ways that the Contracting States have incorporated within their domestic legislative framework the provisions of the Convention.[25] These responses offer a useful starting place for developing an understanding of the way in which another Contracting State applies the Convention within its jurisdiction. Such an understanding is likely to be very helpful when advising clients on what to expect in terms of procedures in the Contracting State, irrespective of whether the UK is the state of origin or the receiving state.

---

[25]   They can be found on the HccH website currently to be found at: http://www.hcch.net/index_ en.php?act=text.display&tid=45.

Chapter 3

DOMICILE, HABITUAL RESIDENCE AND ADOPTION

INTRODUCTION

3.1   An understanding of what is meant by the terms domicile and habitual residence is essential when considering any adoption application. The domicile/habitual residence of the adopters will determine the basis of the court's jurisdiction to make an adoption order in their favour, and a child's place of habitual residence will determine the court's jurisdiction to make an order in respect of that child. Unlike those countries which operate on Roman Law principles, in common law countries these terms have very different meanings. A person's place of habitual residence will be the place where they are in the habit of living. A person is domiciled in their homeland. At first glance it may seem that these two concepts are just different ways of saying the same thing, but as will be made clear in this chapter, they are not necessarily the same thing at all, and it is possible for some purposes, that a person may have two places of habitual residence and a third and different country of domicile.

HABITUAL RESIDENCE – GENERAL PRINCIPLES

3.2   Unless a particular statute requires otherwise, in English law habitual residence is a common law concept and its meaning must therefore be gleaned from examination of case-law. In order to establish that a person has a habitual residence in a particular place the court must be satisfied that as a matter of fact a person:

(a)   has a voluntary residence in a particular place;

(b)   has been residing in that place for an appreciable amount of time; and

(c)   has an intention to remain there for a settled purpose as part of the regular order of their life.

3.3   The first ingredient is relatively easy to establish. Is a person voluntarily living in a particular place? The second ingredient is less straightforward because it appears that what constitutes an appreciable amount of time has to be determined within the context of the third ingredient. The third ingredient is a state of mind. It is not simply an intention to remain in a place, but a settled intention to live there. This must be determined with reference to the stated intentions of the person, their conduct and other relevant factors. The existence of a habitual residence will be a question of fact in every case, to be determined taking into account all the relevant evidence. Perhaps for this reason the case-law does not provide a strict formulaic approach to determine the issue. However, there are a number of useful principles which can be extracted:

(a)   It is not necessary to establish that a person intends to remain in a place indefinitely, only that they intend to remain there for settled purposes as part of the regular order of their life for the time being, whether of short or long duration.[1]

(b)   It has been held that a person's presence in a country as an illegal immigrant may not be relied upon to establish habitual residence (*Shah v Barnet London Borough Council*[2] – in the context of 'ordinary residence'); however, a person who has overstayed her leave to remain in the United Kingdom and remains in the United Kingdom unlawfully may assert habitual residence in the jurisdiction for the purposes of a divorce (*Mark v Mark*[3]).

(c)   A person will need to have lived in a place for an appreciable period of time; however, what constitutes an appreciable period of time will be linked to the strength of their settled intention. 'Appreciable' appears to be a contextual matter.[4]

(d)   A person can lose a place of habitual residence in a day.[5]

(e)   A person can be without a period of habitual residence if they have lost their former place of habitual residence and not formed a settled intention to live in another place.[6]

(f)   A person can acquire a new place of habitual residence in a day.[7]

(g)   A person can acquire a new place of habitual residence in a month.[8]

(h)   A person can acquire a new place of habitual residence in 7 weeks.[9]

---

[1]   *Shah v Barnet London Borough Council* [1983] 1 All ER 226 at 235, [1983] 2 AC 309 at 343.
[2]   [1983] 2 AC 309, [1983] 1 All ER 226, HL.
[3]   [2005] UKHL 42, [2006] 1 AC 98, [2005] 3 All ER 912.
[4]   *L-K v K (No 2)* [2006] EWHC 3280 (Fam), [2007] 2 FLR 729.
[5]   *C v S (A Minor) (Abduction)* [1990] 2 FLR 442.
[6]   *Re J (Abduction: Custody Rights)* [1990] 2 AC 562 at 578–579.
[7]   *Marinos v Marinos* [2007] EWHC 2047 (Fam), [2007] 2 FLR 1018 at [89].
[8]   *Re F (A Minor) (Child Abduction)* [1992] 1 FLR 548.
[9]   *Re S (Habitual Residence)* [2009] EWCA Civ 1021, [2010] 1 FLR 1146.

(i)   A person might need to live in a place for longer than 3 months if there is other evidence which suggests that their continued presence in an area is uncertain.[10]

(j)   A person does not lose a habitual residence by virtue of a temporary visit to another place if that visit would not form part of the fabric of their day-to-day life, for example the essence of a holiday is that it is a break from the fabric of one's normal routine.

(k)   A person can have more than one place of habitual residence if they maintain two homes in different places.[11]

(l)   For the purpose of establishing jurisdiction under some EU conventions, for example, a person can only have one place of habitual residence.[12]

(m) For the purposes of the Hague Convention on the Civil Aspects of International Child Abduction 1980 a child can only have one place of habitual residence at any one time, although they may have two alternating places of habitual residence which apply when the child is in the home of parents who live in different countries for the purpose of agreed shared residence arrangements.[13]

(n)   The habitual residence of a child who is provided with accommodation by or on behalf of a local authority will not change during the period they are so accommodated, even if that accommodation is provided overseas.[14]

(o)   A settled purpose is not something to be searched for under a microscope. If it is there at all it will stand out clearly as a matter of general impression.[15]

Perhaps the only consistent feature of habitual residence is that it is a question of fact to be determined in every case according to the factual and legal context within which it is being applied.

DOMICILE – GENERAL PRINCIPLES

3.4   Domicile is in many ways a lot more straightforward than habitual residence. It is the means by which a person's personal law is identified. Domicile is required to establish the relevant law where matters such as

---

[10]   *London Borough of Redbridge v Newport City Council* [2003] EWHC 2967 (Fam), [2004] 2 FLR 226.
[11]   *Ikimi v Ikimi* [2001] EWCA Civ 873, [2001] 2 FLR 1288; also *V v V (Divorce: Jurisdiction)* [2011] EWHC 1190 (Fam), [2011] 2 FLR 778.
[12]   *Marinos v Marinos* [2007] EWHC 2047 (Fam), [2007] 2 FLR 1018.
[13]   *Re V (Abduction: Habitual Residence)* [1995] 2 FLR 992.
[14]   Children Act 1989, s 105(6)(c) and also *Greenwich London Borough Council v S* [2007] EWHC 820 (Fam), [2007] 2 FLR 154.
[15]   *Re B (Minors) (Abduction) (No 2)* [1993] 1 FLR 993, at 998E–G.

inheritance, tax, marriage, divorce, parental orders and of course adoption are involved. In the case of *Z v C (Parental Order: Domicile)*[16] Mrs Justice Theis DBE had to determine whether at least one of the two applicants for a parental order had acquired a domicile of choice in England. The following extract from her judgment provides a thorough and very useful exposition of the law governing domicile:

> '13 The general principles of domiciliary law (described in the Dicey text as "rules") are set down in Dicey, Morris and Collins, on The Conflict of Laws 14th edition 2006 ("Dicey"). In the bankruptcy case *Barlow Clowes International Ltd (In Liquidation) & Ors v Henwood* [2008] EWCA Civ 577, the Court summarised a number of the Dicey principles of law on domicile as uncontentious (paragraph [8] per Arden LJ). Relevant to the domicile of choice issues raised in this case the uncontentious principles include:
>
> (1) A person is, in general, domiciled in the country in which he is considered by English law to have his permanent home. A person may sometimes be domiciled in a country although he does not have his permanent home in it.
> (2) No person can be without a domicile.
> (3) No person can at the same time for the same purpose have more than one domicile.
> (4) An existing domicile is presumed to continue until it is proved that a new domicile has been acquired.
> (5) Every person receives at birth a domicile of origin.
> (6) Every independent person can acquire a domicile of choice by the combination of residence and an intention of permanent or indefinite residence, but not otherwise.
> (7) Any circumstance that is evidence of a person's residence, or of his intention to reside permanently or indefinitely in a country, must be considered in determining whether he has acquired a domicile of choice.
> (8) In determining whether a person intends to reside permanently or indefinitely, the court may have regard to the motive for which residence was taken up, the fact that residence was not freely chosen, and the fact that residence was precarious.
> (9) A person abandons a domicile of choice in a country by ceasing to reside there and by ceasing to intend to reside there permanently, or indefinitely, and not otherwise. A person who has formed the intention of leaving a country does not cease to have his home in it until he acts according to that intention.
> (10) When a domicile of choice is abandoned, a new domicile of choice may be acquired, but if it is not acquired, the domicile of origin revives.

14 In *Mark v Mark* [2005] UKHL 42 Baroness Hale referred to a further principle concerning the ascertainment of domicile at paragraph 47 – namely that:

> "English law requires only that the intention [of the person claiming to be domiciled by reason of their intention to reside permanently in the UK] be bona fide, in the sense of being genuine and not pretended for some other purpose, such as getting a divorce to which one would not be entitled by the law of the true domicile."

---

[16] [2011] EWHC 3181 (Fam) at [13]–[18].

She noted at paragraph 44:

> "The object of the rules determining domicile is to discover the system of law with which the propositus is most closely connected for the range of [family and other status] purposes .... Sometimes that connection will be an advantage to him. Sometimes it will not. As Hughes J put it, at para 73:

> 'the concept of domicile is not that of a benefit to the propositus. Rather, it is a neutral rule of law for determining that system of personal law with which the individual has the appropriate connection, so that it shall govern his personal status and questions relating to him and his affairs ...'

15 The burden of proving the abandonment of a domicile of origin and the acquisition of a domicile of choice is upon the person asserting the change. The standard of proof is the balance of probability (see *Barlow Clowes International Ltd (In Liquidation) & Ors v Henwood* [2008] EWCA Civ 577 per Arden LJ at paragraphs 85–88).

16 Dicey notes that the intention required for the acquisition of a domicile is the intention to reside permanently or for an unlimited time in a country (Dicey paragraph 6-039). The authors note that it is rare for the animus manendi to exist in this explicit, positive form, more frequently a person simply resides in a country without any intention of leaving it and such a state of mind may suffice for the acquisition of a domicile of choice. If the person has in mind the vague possibility of a return to his domicile of origin, this might not negate the acquisition of a domicile of choice where there has been a long residence in the country of chosen domicile, but if there is a "clearly foreseen and reasonably anticipated contingency" upon which it is intended to return to the home domicile, this may prevent the acquisition of a domicile of choice. (Dicey paragraph 6-040)

17 In this case, Z must satisfy the court not only that he resides in the UK as his permanent home, but also that he has a fixed intention to remain here indefinitely.

> "Residence [is] fixed not for a limited period or particular purpose, but general and indefinite in its future contemplation" (*Udny v Udny* (1869) LR 1 Sc & D 441, page 458).

18 In *IRC v Bullock* (1976) All ER 353 at p 357, Buckley LJ (with whom Roskill LJ and Scarman LJ agreed) said at p 359:

> "... I do not think that it is necessary to show that the intention to make a home in the new country is irrevocable [in order to show the person has a new domicile of choice]. In my judgment, the true test is whether he intends to make his home in the new country until the end of his days unless and until something happens to make him change his mind."

3.5　Domicile is what ties you to a particular legal system. It is your homeland. Every person is born with a domicile of origin which they will take from their parents. A child's habitual residence will be dependent on that of their parents while they are a minor. They will be domiciled in that country unless and until they adopt a different domicile of choice. If they abandon their domicile of choice their domicile of origin will revive unless and until they adopt a new domicile of choice.

3.6   Habitual residence is where you make your home from time to time. It does not need to be forever, but there must be an attachment of sorts, whether it is a 3-month contract of employment, a year-long course of education or a second home where you always spend your summer. It is a place where you put down roots, but they do not need to be permanent ones. Each status is a matter of fact. Often they will coincide but they do not need to.

DOMICILE AND HABITUAL RESIDENCE IN THE CONTEXT OF ADOPTION

3.7   Probably the most important issues to establish when first considering an adoption case are: where are the adopters habitually resident and where is the child habitually resident? It is therefore important to know, within the context of adoption, the principles which enable those questions to be answered.

How long will it take to establish a habitual residence?

3.8   Section 49 of the Adoption and Children Act 2002 (ACA 2002), provides the basis for eligibility to apply for an adoption order in the UK. There are two alternate bases: either the applicant, or one them is domiciled in a part of the British Islands, or both of them have been habitually resident in a part of the British Islands for a year on the date of the application. For this purpose the length of time it takes to establish a habitual residence will be capable of determination with the benefit of hindsight. It is likely, for example, that after a year of residence in England a person who moved to England a year earlier will be able to say with a large amount of credibility that they intended from their arrival to remain for a settled purpose, since they will have remained here for a year by the time they need to establish that fact.

3.9   However, even then just their presence is unlikely to be enough; the stopwatch will run from the point in time when they had the state of mind that this move was to be part of the regular order of their life.

Example 3.1

Xavier is domiciled and habitually resident in France when he accepts a 3-year employment contract which requires him to move to England and work in the London office on 1 January 2010. Xavier has a girlfriend called Yvette who is also domiciled and habitually resident in France when Xavier gets his job. Between January 2010 and March 2010 Yvette visits Xavier a few times for long weekends. On 1 March 2010 Yvette travels to England from France for the purpose of a 3-week holiday staying with Xavier in his London flat. By 21 March 2010 Yvette decides she would like to extend her holiday for a further 3 weeks. On 14 April 2010 Yvette decides that she loves London and Xavier too much to go back to France until he does and she makes arrangements to live with Xavier in his flat in London and arranges for a significant part of her belongings to be shipped to London for that purpose. In December 2010 Xavier and Yvette decide that they would like to adopt a child.

In these circumstances it is likely that:

(i)   Both Xavier and Yvette remain domiciled in France throughout their visit since neither of them have formed an intention to remain in England permanently or for an indefinite period. The length of their stay is linked to the duration of Xavier's employment contract. Therefore they would not be eligible to apply on the domicile basis.

(ii)   Xavier will have been habitually resident in England for a year on 1 January 2011. It is likely that the court would accept that the stopwatch should run from the date of his arrival since he arrived with a settled intention to remain for 3 years as part of his day-to-day life, and a year later this plan is clearly evidenced. If he wished to adopt as a single person this would be the date he would become eligible to make the application.

(iii)   Yvette will have been habitually resident in England for a year on 14 April 2011. Although she arrived in London on 1 March 2010, she did not have the requisite intention to remain until she decided to stay here for the length of Xavier's contract. However, having made that decision and evidenced it by moving her belongings over to London and a year later still being here the court is likely to accept that the period of habitual residence began when she changed her mind. On 14 April 2011 Yvette would meet the habitual residence test to apply to adopt a child.

(iv)   If Yvette and Xavier wished to apply to adopt a child as a couple they will have both been habitually resident in England for a year on 14 April 2011. Although Xavier has been habitually resident since 1 January 2010, the stopwatch would not run until the date that both of them were habitually resident, which is the date that Yvette also became habitually resident in England.

3.10 By contrast, there is no statutory period of time that a child must be habitually resident within the British Islands to make them suitable for adoption by applicants who meet the criteria of ACA 2002, s 49, or to restrict their removal for the purpose of overseas adoption under ACA 2002, s 85. Equally there is no statutory period of time during which a child must be habitually resident outside of the British Islands for the provisions of ACA 2002, s 83(1) to apply. It would appear that the existence of a habitual residence, however short, is what is required to establish their status under each of these provisions.

Can an applicant adopter have more than one place of habitual residence?

3.11 The Adoption Statutory Guidance issued by the Department for Education in February 2011 considers the issue of domicile and habitual residence in Chapter 3,[17] and it says at paragraph 9:

> '9. It is also possible to be habitually resident in two countries at the same time. Factors such as possession of a property, type of employment contract, financial arrangements and location of bank accounts, and local connections are just some of the many factors that may be relevant to any question relating to habitual residence.'

This would suggest that in principle it is accepted that, for the purposes of a domestic adoption, joint habitual residence would suffice to establish eligibility but it does not distinguish between a situation where the other country of habitual residence is a Convention or a non-Convention country. Neither does it appear that this issue has been explored in case-law.

3.12 Since there is no direct case-law on this issue the court is likely to look at the way in which this issue has been approached in other reported cases which have had to grapple with dual habitual residence. Matrimonial cases provide a useful source of guidance in this area since habitual residence provides one of the grounds upon which a petitioner can establish that the court has jurisdiction to hear their divorce petition. In such cases the court has taken a different approach towards matrimonial cases which are governed by EU Conventions and those which are not. The two cases which most clearly highlight these different approaches are *Ikimi v Ikimi* – a case which did not involve an international treaty and could therefore be considered on English legal principles alone, and *Marinos v Marinos* – a case which had to be determined in the context of Brussels II Revised, and which therefore involved consideration of that treaty as well as domestic case-law. Since these two cases are very fact specific it is helpful to look at the headnotes of each case to illustrate these differing approaches.

'Ikimi v Ikimi

> The husband and wife, both Nigerian, married in 1977. Throughout the marriage they retained a residence in Nigeria, but from 1978 onwards they also had a home in England. At first they rented, then, in 1982, they purchased a substantial home in London which was at all times available for their exclusive occupation. The four children were all born in England, the three elder children held British as well as Nigerian citizenship, and all four were educated almost entirely in England. Between November 1995 and July 1998, EU sanctions imposed on Nigeria made it impossible for the husband and wife to travel to England, but the children remained in London. When restrictions on her entry were lifted in 1998, the wife immediately took steps to return to England, arriving on 5 August 1998. The husband issued divorce proceedings in Nigeria on 18 November 1998. In Spring

---

[17]   See pp 60–61 of first revision February 2011.

1999, the wife filed an answer and cross-petition in the Nigerian proceedings, pleading permanent residence and domicile in Nigeria. The wife issued divorce proceedings in England on 14 September 1999, on the basis that she had, by then, been habitually resident in England for one year. The preliminary issue arose whether the wife had in fact been habitually resident in England for one year, given that she had spent only 161 days of that year in England.

The wife argued that her habitual residence was based on her very strong ties with England, which had endured for over 20 years, and her regular periods of residence in England, which had been interrupted only by the sanctions. The husband argued that the wife was habitually resident in Nigeria rather than England at all times, and alternatively, if the wife were to be held resident in England for any period, that in computing residence for jurisdictional purposes no account should be taken of any period spent by her in her Nigerian residence. The judge concluded that the court had jurisdiction to hear the wife's petition, based on the wife's habitual residence in England for the relevant year. He held that a person with two habitual residences occupied them concurrently, providing she spent some time in each, but otherwise regardless of the precise time she spent in each during the relevant period, rejecting the argument that in dual residence cases occupation of each residence should be considered consecutively.

Held – dismissing the appeal – a person could be 'habitually resident in England and Wales' for the whole one-year period required to found jurisdiction in matrimonial proceedings, under Domicile and Matrimonial Proceedings Act 1973, s 5(2), even though they were also habitually resident in another country. A person may be ordinarily resident in two countries at the same time. In the context of the court's divorce jurisdiction, 'ordinarily' and 'habitually' must be regarded as synonymous, and the same meaning should be given to 'habitually' wherever it appeared in a family law statute. The test proposed by the judge for habitual residence was too relaxed, and a petitioner would have to have spent an appreciable part of the relevant year within the jurisdiction to establish habitual residence. However, even on this stricter formulation, there was just sufficient foundation for jurisdiction on the facts of this case.'[18]

'Marinos v Marinos

The Greek husband and the English wife had been married for 15 years, and had two children. The family had moved to Greece when the youngest child was about 2 years old. The move was initially on a trial basis, but the family remained in Greece for a number of years, and the children attended Greek schools. The family lived with the husband's family; they did not buy property in Greece, but retained their two English properties, both of which were let. Some months after moving to Greece, the wife resumed part-time work as a flight attendant with a British airline, working 3 weeks out of 9; her home base for employment was in the UK. Just over a year later the wife also enrolled on a part-time LPC in the UK, requiring her attendance 13 times a year. During her many visits to the UK for work and study, the wife stayed with her parents, or at a hotel close to the airport. In addition, the family spent holidays in the UK, usually at the home of the wife's parents. The wife spent roughly equal amounts of time in the UK and Greece, although she acknowledged a slight emphasis on Greece. Having successfully

---

[18] (2001) EWCA Civ 873 [2001] 2 FLR 1288 (extract from the headnote in that case).

completed her LPC, the wife temporarily increased her workload with the airline to 4 weeks out of 8. She also began preparations to return to the UK, in particular organising schools for the children. Five months later, when school places became available, the wife gave the letting agents instructions to serve notice to quit on the tenants of the London property, and returned to the UK with the children. The husband remained in Greece. The day after her return, the wife issued a petition for divorce in the UK, stating that she was domiciled and habitually resident in the UK, having resided there for at least 6 months immediately prior to the presentation of the petition; she gave her parents' address as her place of residence during this period. The husband filed an acknowledgement of service, disputing the jurisdiction of the English court; he sought a stay of the wife's petition. Although the husband also brought Hague Convention proceedings, seeking the summary return of the children to Greece, an English court found that he had consented to his wife and children moving to the UK without him. The husband's Greek petition for divorce, and Greek proceedings concerning the children were still ongoing. At the stay hearing the husband accepted that the wife was domiciled in the UK, but disputed that she had been habitually resident in the UK when the divorce petition was issued, arguing that she did not satisfy the Brussels II (Revised), Art 3(1)(a) jurisdictional requirement of habitual residence based on domicile with at least 6 months' residence immediately before the application was made.

Held – that the English court had jurisdiction, and, being the jurisdiction first seised, was entitled to exercise that jurisdiction in priority to the Greek court – (1) For the purposes of Brussels II (Revised), 'habitually resident' meant 'the place where the person had established, on a fixed basis, his permanent or habitual centre of interests, with all the relevant facts being taken into account for the purpose of determining such residence'. In deciding where the person had established his or her habitual centre of interests, the court had to have regard to the context: in a case concerning a worker's rights, the place of work was obviously key; when identifying the court with jurisdiction in family matters, the place where the matrimonial home was to be found, the place where the family lived, was an important factor. The presumption that a worker resided in the Member State where he had stable employment, qua worker, even if his family resided in a different Member State, carried less weight and was more easily rebutted when considering him qua spouse (see paras [34], [36]).

(2) For the purposes of Brussels II (Revised) a person could have only one habitual residence at any given time, and could not therefore be habitually resident in more than one country at the same time. The entire ECJ case-law was framed in terms of the place or state in which someone had the centre of interests. In English domestic law a party could have two habitual residences, because a different definition of habitual residence was used (see paras [38], [40]–[43]).

(3) Brussels II (Revised) clearly distinguished between two concepts: habitual residence and residence. Mere residence connoted something less than habitual residence; a pattern of occupation of a base in a country was sufficient. To establish jurisdiction two separate things were required: (i) habitual residence on a particular day; and (ii) residence, though not necessarily habitual residence, during the relevant immediately preceding period. This was not surprising, given that the ECJ case-law recognised that it was possible to be resident in more than one

country at a time, although it was not possible to be habitually resident in more than one country at a time (see paras [45], [46], [48]).

(4) The wife had been entitled to petition for divorce in the UK on the basis of habitual residence over the previous 6 months. Throughout the period of 28 months before the wife brought the children to the UK it could sensibly and appropriately be said that the wife was resident in both Greece and the UK. It was more difficult to determine the question of habitual residence, but in a finely balanced case, over the same period the wife's habitual centre of interest, and thus her place of habitual residence for the purposes of Brussels II (Revised), had been England. In the particular circumstances of the case there were three factors of preponderant importance: the fact that the matrimonial home was in Greece; the fact that the wife worked in and from the UK; and the fact that the wife was educating herself in the UK, with a view to obtaining a qualification for future employment in the UK. The factors were finely balanced, but the overall balance pointed to the wife's centre of gravity as being in the UK (see paras [75], [78]–[84]).

(5) When someone was undertaking a planned, purposeful and permanent relocation from one country to another, there was nothing in Community law to prevent the acquisition of a new habitual residence contemporaneously or virtually contemporaneously with the loss of the previous habitual residence. Therefore, even if the wife had been habitually resident in Greece before the final move to the UK, she would have been able to acquire habitual residence in the UK for the purposes of Brussels II (Revised) in the very short period between returning to the UK and issuing her petition for divorce. She would thus have been entitled to petition on the basis of habitual residence on the day of the petition, plus residence for at least 6 months previously (see paras [89]–[90]).'[19]

3.13 These two cases highlight the fact that habitual residence must be viewed through the lens of the statutory instruments it is being applied within. However, unlike Brussels II Revised, the Convention itself does not govern the jurisdiction of the court. It is a matter for the domestic law of the countries concerned to grant the adoption orders made after both contracting states have agreed that the adoption should proceed. The purpose of the Convention[20] is to determine which of two contracting states should assess the child and the adopters and to ensure that when a child crosses state borders in connection with an international adoption both states are aware of the child's situation and responsible for ensuring the arrangements are in the child's best interest and to ensure that adoptions made in compliance with the Convention are given full recognition in all Convention countries. Quite how the court will approach the issue of dual habitual residence in an international adoption is uncertain. What these cases suggest is that if a person asserts that they meet the eligibility criteria in ACA 2002, s 49 to adopt a child on that basis that they have a dual habitual residence in the British Isles and somewhere else, the court will take into account the fact that the other country is, or is not, a Convention country.

---

[19]   [2007] EWHC 2047 (Fam) [2007] 2 FLR 1018 (extract taken from the headnote).
[20]   See Chapter 2 and in particular **2.7–2.9** for full details of the purpose of the Convention.

Domicile, habitual residence, dual habitual residence and s 49 in the context of non-Convention countries

3.14   If the other country is a non-Convention country the court cannot make an adoption order unless the applicant meets the criteria in either ACA 2002, s 49(2) or (3). If a person is domiciled in the British Islands, the court cannot grant an order under ACA 2002, s 84 unless s 84(2) is met. Therefore, if a person who is domiciled in the British Islands, but habitually resident in a non-Convention country, wishes to adopt a child who meets the criteria in ACA 2002, s 85(1), he must apply to adopt the child in England and Wales under the domestic provisions irrespective of his place of habitual residence.

3.15   If a person is not domiciled in the British Islands but has a dual habitual residence within the British Isles and in a non-Convention country the court will have to consider whether or not for the purpose of ACA 2002 s 49(3) a person can have dual habitual residence. In a non-Convention case there will be no international treaty to consider and accordingly it is likely that the approach in *Ikimi v Ikimi* would be followed and he would be treated as meeting the habitual residence requirement in s 49(3) with the result that the eligibility requirement in that section would be met and he would as a consequence fail to meet the provisions of s 84(2).

Example 3.2

Jenny and her husband Simon are both domiciled in England and Jenny works for a multi-national media company based in London. She is offered the chance to head up a new department in Russia and she and Simon agree that this is a great career move. They rent out their house in London, and on 1 January 2011 move out to live in Russia having decided that they will give themselves a maximum of 5 years there during which time Simon will do a post graduate degree in archaeology. In any event, they intend to return to live in London by no later than 1 January 2016. In January 2012, they hear that a child in their family needs to be placed outside of the parents' care and they agree to be assessed to adopt the child. What would be the appropriate legal framework under which they would need to adopt the child?

The first point to note in this example is that Jenny and Simon have not abandoned their English domicile. The second point to note is that Russia is not for the time being a Convention country. Because they retain their English domicile they are eligible to adopt under s 49(2) and not eligible to apply for an order under s 84. Jenny and Simon must therefore adopt the child according to the same statutory and regulatory provisions which would have applied if they were still living in London.

Example 3.3

Peter and his wife Felicity are both domiciled in England. Peter works for a multi-national mining company based in Sheffield and has always harboured dreams of living and working in Russia. When he is offered the chance to work on a mine in Russia he persuades Felicity that this would be a wonderful opportunity to make a fresh start and they agree to make a go of it. They sell their house in Sheffield, and on 1 January 2011 move out to live in Russia having decided that they will make Russia their new home. Although they continue to visit their family and friends in England, they do not have any plans to return to live in England in the future. In January 2012, they hear that a child in their family needs to be placed outside of the parents' care and they agree to be assessed to adopt the child. What would be the appropriate legal framework under which they would need to adopt the child?

Unlike Simon and Jenny, in this example Peter and Felicity appear to have abandoned their domicile in England and taken up a domicile of choice in Russia where they have been habitually resident for a year. They would not be eligible to adopt the child under s 49(2) or (3). They would need to apply to adopt the child in Russia, and in order to take the child out of England and Wales they would need to apply for an order under s 84. They do meet the criteria under s 84(2) and so this is not a problem.

Example 3.4

Angelina is a Jamaican national whose domicile of origin is Jamaica. She has lived in Jamaica all her life, but in 2006 she bought a home in London as well as keeping a home in Jamaica. She has a business which has developed operations in both London and Jamaica. She has friends and family on both sides of the Atlantic and moves seamlessly between her two homes, although in some years she is more often in Jamaica and in some years she spends a larger part of the year in London, depending on where she is needed. In January 2012 Angelina is informed that her niece has been made subject of care proceedings and there are no family members based in the British Isles that can offer her a home. Angelina agrees to be assessed to adopt the child, but which is the correct legal framework for the assessments and the adoption?

In this case s 49(2) does not apply because Angelina appears to remain domiciled in Jamaica. Her habitual residence is less clear though as she has two homes in which she resides. It would be possible to argue that by applying the principles in *Ikimi v Ikimi* Angelina is habitually resident in both Jamaica and England and therefore meets the criteria of ACA 2002, s 49(3) and is eligible to apply to adopt the child under the domestic provisions.

3.16 While Angelina's scenario presents an interesting conundrum from an academic perspective, if the issue of dual habitual residence arises within the context of a proposed non-Convention adoption, it is likely to be prudent to seek a declaration on the applicant's habitual residence status before the child is placed with the adopter in order to ensure that the correct legal processes and applications are applied.

Domicile, habitual residence, dual habitual residence and s 49 in the context of Convention countries

3.17 In Convention cases a person may apply to remove a child under ACA 2002, s 84 or apply for a Convention adoption order. If a person remains domiciled in the British Islands but is habitually resident in another Convention country he will not be eligible to apply for a s 84 order because he will not meet the criteria at ACA 2002, s 84(2). However, he will be eligible to apply for a Convention adoption order under ACA 2002, s 49 as amended by the Adoptions with a Foreign Element Regulations 2005 (AFER 2005),[21] reg 58, and there is nothing in AFER 2005, reg 50 which would prevent the Convention adoption order being made provided that he was habitually resident in a Convention country outside the British Islands for a period of not less than one year at the date of the application. For the purpose of a Convention adoption order the eligibility criteria rests on a person's habitual residence not on their domicile.

3.18 This raises two interesting questions:

(a) In a case where a person remains domiciled in the UK but is habitually resident in a Convention country, may they rely on s 49(2) and apply to adopt a child habitually resident in the British Isles under the domestic provisions?

(b) For the purpose of s 49(3) is it possible for a person to assert a dual habitual residence status in a case where on the facts it would be said that he has homes in two Convention countries in which he spends significant albeit unequal amounts of time?

3.19 Let us look again at the three examples in **3.15**, but switch countries.

Example 3.5

Jenny and her husband Simon are both domiciled in England and Jenny works for a multi-national media company based in London. She is offered the chance to head up a new department in Madrid and she and Simon agree that this is a great career move. They rent out their house in London, and on 1 January 2011 move out to live in Madrid having decided that they will give themselves a maximum of 5 years there during which time Simon will do a post graduate degree in archaeology. In any event, they intend to return to live in London by no later than 1 January 2016. In January 2012, they hear that a child in their family needs to be placed outside of the parents' care and they agree to be assessed to adopt the child. What would be the appropriate legal framework under which they would need to adopt the child?

---

[21] SI 2005/392.

(1) Jenny and Simon's case illustrates the question at **3.15**. They retain their English domicile so they cannot apply for a s 84 order because they do not meet the eligibility criteria under ACA 2002 s 84(2). They have been habitually resident in Madrid for one year and therefore meet the criteria for a Convention adoption order.[22] They also meet the criteria in s 49(2) and are therefore eligible to adopt under the domestic provisions. Under the provisions of Article 2 of the Convention the adoption must proceed in accordance with that instrument because the adopters are habitually resident in one contracting state and the child is habitually resident in another. This would suggest that Jenny and Simon would need to apply to the English courts for a Convention adoption order. However, as discussed in Chapter 2 of this book[23] the Convention itself is not directly incorporated into English law, rather its provisions are given effect through the AFER 2005 regulations. In order to know if the provisions of AFER 2005, Part 3, Ch 2 apply to a particular case it is necessary to look at reg 35 which reads:

'35 Application of Chapter 2

The provisions in this Chapter shall apply where a couple or a person habitually resident in a Convention country outside the British Islands, wishes to adopt a child who is habitually resident in the British Islands in accordance with the Convention.'

(2) This regulation makes it clear that if a person wishes to adopt a child in accordance with the Convention the provisions of AFER 2005, Part 3, Ch 2 apply. However, if a person does not need to apply under the Convention because he is eligible to apply pursuant to ACA 2002, s 49(2), and he wishes to adopt in accordance with the standard domestic process, does this regulation operate to prohibit him from doing so? It does not appear that there is anything in the plain ordinary meaning of the words used in reg 35 to prohibit the use of s 49 where an applicant meets the criteria at s 49(2) or (3). In addition, although the AFER 2005, reg 58 does operate to modify ACA 2002 s 49, it does so by removing subs (2) and (3). At no point before or after the coming into force of the ACA 2002 has provision been made to alter the wording of s 49(2), by regulations or direct amendment to add to the statute itself wording such as 'unless the applicant is habitually resident in a state which is a party to the Convention on Intercountry adoption'. It might therefore be said that Simon and Jenny have a choice as to which adoption route they would like to take. If they wish to adopt in accordance with the Convention then as a result of AFER 2005, reg 35 that chapter will apply. However, if they do not wish to adopt in accordance with the Convention, and prefer instead to adopt in accordance with the domestic provisions, relying as they are entitled to on their domicile in England then the provisions of AFER 2005, Part 3, Ch 2 will not apply.

---

[22] The combined effect of s 49 as amended by AFER 2005, reg 58 and the conditions for making a Convention adoption order at AFER 2005, reg 50.

[23] See **2.3–2.5** and also **2.10**.

(3) The difficulty with this interpretation of AFER 2005, reg 35 is that it involves a construction of that provision which implicitly accepts that the UK intended to allow adoptions to take place in breach of its obligations under the Convention.[24] This potential conflict between the UK's treaty obligations under Article 2 and the law which gives effect to those obligations does not appear to have been explored in any reported case and it is unhelpful that our statutory and regulatory framework is so unclear in this regard.

Example 3.6

Peter and his wife Felicity are both domiciled in England. Peter works for a multi-national mining company based in Sheffield and has always harboured dreams of living and working in Spain. When he is offered the chance to work on a mine near Madrid he persuades Felicity that this would be a wonderful opportunity to make a fresh start and they agree to make a go of it. They sell their house in Sheffield, and on 1 January 2011 move out to live in Spain having decided that they will make Spain their new home. Although they continue to visit their family and friends in England, they do not have any plans to return to live in England in the future. In January 2012, they hear that a child in their family needs to be placed outside of the parents' care and they agree to be assessed to adopt the child. What would be the appropriate legal framework under which they would need to adopt the child?

This is a little bit more straightforward. Peter and Felicity have abandoned their domicile in England and taken up a domicile of choice in Spain where they have been habitually resident for a year. They are therefore not eligible to apply for a domestic adoption order under s 49(2) or (3). They are eligible to apply for a s 84 order or a Convention adoption order.

Example 3.7

Angelina is a German national whose domicile of origin is Germany. She has lived in Germany all her life, but in 2006 she bought a home in London as well as keeping a home in Germany. She has a business which has developed operations in both London and Germany. She has friends and family on both sides of the Channel and moves seamlessly between her two homes, although in some years she is more often in Germany and in some years she spends a larger part of the year in London, depending on where she is needed. In January 2012 Angelina is informed that her niece has been made the subject of care proceedings and there are no family members based in the British Isles that can offer her a home. Angelina agrees to be assessed to adopt the child, but which is the correct legal framework for the assessments and the adoption?

(1) In this scenario Angelina is domiciled in Germany and cannot apply to adopt under s 49(2). However she appears to have a dual habitual residence in both England and Germany. Can she assert that she is habitually resident in

---

[24]   Specifically Article 2(1) of the Convention.

England for the purpose of s 49(3)? This question raises a very interesting question of law. Would the court take the same approach to the Convention that it took in relation to Brussels II revised in *Marinos v Marinos*?

(2) The answer is not straightforward. Brussels II revised is an instrument used to establish the jurisdiction of the court. The Convention is an instrument governing the assessment of children and adopters and protecting children from child slavery and trafficking. The purpose of the Convention is not to avoid forum shopping, it is to ensure that children do not fall between the two stools of different child protection regimes when adopted children cross state borders. For those reasons it might be possible to argue that the approach in *Marinos v Marinos* can be distinguished from a dual habitual residence in a Convention case.

(3) On the other hand, while not a mechanism for identifying the relevant court with jurisdiction to make decisions about children, the Convention is a mechanism for establishing which country's adoption agency should be responsible for making decisions which are of enormous importance to the welfare of the child concerned. It might be argued that assessments of a person wishing to adopt a child should be undertaken by the state in which they have their 'centre of interests' so that the most reliable information can be obtained in the state which will become the child's centre of interests following the adoption.

(4) Until a case comes before the court and the arguments are fully rehearsed and the issues determined it is not possible to predict with certainty whether the court will adopt a similar approach to that taken in Hague Abduction and Brussels II revised cases, such as is seen in *Marinos v Marinos*, or adopt the approach in *Ikimi v Ikimi* in relation to the concept of the dual habitual residence and its availability as a means of establishing the criteria in s 49(3).

3.20 According to the Department for Education which is the central authority for England, there have only been about five Convention adoptions involving children habitually resident in England and Wales each year since the Convention came into force in 2003. This probably explains why many of the issues identified in **3.17–3.18** remain unresolved. However, the Department for Education is only aware of cases where Convention adoptions are applied for as they are not involved in domestic adoptions. It is impossible to know the extent to which adopters falling into the categories discussed in examples 3.5 and 3.7 pass through the court as domestic adoptions, which for reasons explored above may well be the most appropriate route in any event.

Part 2

INTERNATIONAL ADOPTION WHEN THE UNITED KINGDOM IS THE RECEIVING STATE

Chapter 4

OVERVIEW OF INTERNATIONAL ADOPTIONS WHERE THE UNITED KINGDOM IS THE RECEIVING STATE

4.1 Chapters 5–9 examine the process that needs to be undertaken by prospective adopters who are habitually resident in the UK seeking to adopt a child habitually resident in another country. The social work, immigration and legal procedure for such adoptions is complicated. Prospective adopters run the risk of committing criminal offences if a child is brought into the UK without the correct process being undertaken.

4.2 The first question to ask is: where is the child habitually resident? This will determine whether the adoption falls within the Convention or not.

CONVENTION ADOPTIONS

4.3 As detailed in Chapter 2 the Convention provides a framework to regulate the movement of children across borders for adoption. It constructs a system of assessments in the child's state of origin and the receiving state (where the adopters are habitually resident).

4.4 The practical application of the Convention in England and Wales is achieved through the Adoptions with a Foreign Element Regulations 2005 (AFER 2005).[1] These set out a scheme for assessment of prospective adopters. The assessment process is broadly similar to that imposed on adopters seeking to adopt a child resident in the UK. The assessment process is followed by liaison between the Department for Education (the central authority for England) and the Central Authority in the child's state and matching of the child to the adoptive parents. This process culminates with the child being 'entrusted' to the adoptive parents. The assessment and liaison process is set out in detail in Chapter 5.

4.5 Following this process the prospective adopters can either seek an adoption order in the child's state of origin or seek an order within the UK courts. The process for the latter option is detailed in Chapter 5.

---

[1] SI 2005/392.

4.6   AFER 2005 impose certain duties upon local authorities when a child is brought into the UK and no adoption order has been made in the child's home country. These duties are also examined within Chapter 5.

NON-CONVENTION ADOPTIONS

4.7   The process of adopting a child who is not habitually resident in a Convention country is more complicated. Section 83(1) of the Adoption and Children Act 2002 (ACA 2002) creates a criminal offence of bringing a child into the UK for the purposes of adoption, or within 12 months of an adoption abroad, without complying with the regulations in AFER 2005. Convention countries are exempt from this section.

4.8   Chapter 6 examines the regulations that apply for non-Convention adoptions and the assessment process imposed on prospective adopters. Whilst in some respects this process mirrors that for Convention adoptions, it is not identical. In addition, there are criminal penalties for non-compliance with the process.

4.9   The AFER 2005 regulations set down the assessment and social work process for prospective adopters. They do not deal with the legal status of the child once the process is complete. Chapter 7 examines the various routes open to prospective adopters to legal recognition of their adoption.

4.10   The majority of the case-law in this field arises from situations where children have been brought into the United Kingdom in breach of the AFER 2005 regulations. The court's approach to children 'adopted' in such circumstances is also considered in Chapter 7.

IMMIGRATION ASPECTS

4.11   The process of adopting a child who is not present in the UK does not just require an eye on adoption law, but also on immigration law. For unless an adopted (or prospective adopted) child has a right to enter the UK or is given leave to enter the UK, the adoptive parents cannot achieve their intended purpose of bringing the child to the UK to be part of their family.

4.12   Immigration law provides for specific – and sometimes onerous – requirements that have to be satisfied before a right or leave to enter the UK will be granted. Chapter 9 examines these immigration requirements and provides guidance as to which requirements need to be met in a given situation.

Chapter 5

HAGUE CONVENTION ADOPTIONS

INTRODUCTION

5.1   This chapter will explore adoptions made in accordance with the provisions of the *Convention on Protection of Children and Co-operation in Respect of Intercountry Adoption 1993* (the Convention). The Convention was concluded on 23 May 1993. Its aim is to facilitate and regulate intercountry adoptions in the best interests of the children concerned and to prevent the abduction, sale and trafficking of children. The Convention has its foundations in the United Nations Convention on the Rights of the Child (UNCRC) (20 November 1989) and is underpinned by the UNCRC principles. The full background to the Convention can be found in Chapter 1.

5.2   The importance of the Convention for adopters from England and Wales is twofold: first that a 'Convention adoption' is regarded as an adoption under Adoption and Children Act 2002 (ACA 2002), s 66. Secondly that ACA 2002 s 83 does not apply to Convention adoptions. Therefore, whilst the procedural requirements of a Convention adoption may seem both numerous and onerous, the process is simpler than for a non-Convention adoption and, importantly, criminal sanctions attach to fewer provisions of the Convention adoption process than non-Convention adoptions.

Statutes, regulations and guidance

5.3   The Convention was signed by the United Kingdom in 1994 and incorporated into law by the Adoption (Intercountry Aspects) Act 1999. It came into force on 1 June 2003.

5.4   ACA 2002 provides the overall statutory scheme for adoptions. Parts of ACA 2002 are applicable to Convention adoptions as modified by regulations.

5.5   The most recent legislation in this area is the Children and Adoption Act 2006 (CAA 2006), in particular Part 2 (ss 9–13) (in force variously from 7 July and 1 August 2008). This Act is significant in that it allows the Secretary of State to declare restrictions on adoptions from countries where the practices mean that to allow children to be brought into the UK would contravene public policy. This applies equally to Convention countries as well as other countries.[1]

---

[1]   CAA 2006, s 9(1).

5.6   Two sets of dense and interconnected regulations provide much of the detailed working of Convention adoptions. First, the Adoptions with a Foreign Element Regulations 2005 (AFER 2005)[2] and second, the Adoption Agency Regulations 2005 (AAR 2005)[3] both of which came into force on 30 December 2005. AAR 2005 apply to all domestic adoptions and parts of the regulations apply also to Convention adoptions.

5.7   Furthermore, non-statutory guidance on the practical working of the Convention can be found on the HccH website: www.hcch.net. This includes a 2005 Guide to Good Practice[4] (currently being reviewed) and an up-to-date list of states.

5.8   The central authority for England was previously the Department of Health. The duties have now moved to the Department for Education who carry easy to understand fact-sheets and other information on their website: www.education.gov.uk in the 'international adoption' section.[5] This contains helpful information sheets about the requirements each country may place on adopters, up-to-date information on restricted countries and guidance notes to the relevant sections of ACA 2002. At the time of writing, the latter is in the process of being re-written and updated.

Countries and applicability

5.9   The Convention applies when the child is habitually resident in one state which has contracted to the convention and the adopter or adopters are habitually resident is a second Contracting State. The child's state of residence is known within the Convention as the 'state of origin'; the adopter or adopters' state is the 'receiving state'.[6]

5.10   The Convention only covers adoptions 'which create a permanent parent-child relationship'.[7] Therefore private fostering arrangements, temporary family or other arrangements are not covered by the Convention. Significantly the Islamic concept of *Kafala* (long-term care in countries where adoption is excluded or simply not a culturally and religiously recognised concept) is outwith the parameters of the Convention.

5.11   The working of the Convention depends on co-operation between the central authorities of the two states regarding information about the child, assessment of adopters and 'matching' of a child to his placement. The Guide to Good Practice specifically excludes from the workings of the Convention

---

2   SI 2005/392.
3   SI 2005/389.
4   The Implementation and Operation of the 1993 Hague Intercountry Adoption Convention, Guide to Good Practice, no 1.
5   The Department for Education uses the nomenclature of 'international adoption' and not 'intercountry adoption'.
6   Hague Convention 1993, Article 2(1).
7   Ibid, Article 2(2).

independent adoptions and private adoptions. In the former, adopters approved by the receiving state travel independently to find a child to adopt in the state of origin.[8] In the latter private arrangements between the birth parents and adoptive parents are made.[9] UK adopters should be aware that such arrangements may fall foul of ACA 2002, s 83 and place them at risk of committing various criminal offences.[10]

5.12 The UK can place further restrictions on adoptions from specified countries even though they apply the provisions of the Convention.[11] There are currently restrictions on adoptions from Cambodia, Guatemala, Nepal and Haiti[12] and the procedures outlined in this chapter do not apply to these countries. In addition at the time of writing the Department for Education has expressed concern about certain adoption agencies in India and placed restrictions upon their use. Such restrictions are reviewed regularly. Further details on these restrictions and the regulations and statutes governing them can be found in Chapter 8.

5.13 As well as restrictions imposed by the UK, many countries make further requirements on those planning to adopt their children. For example China requires that prospective adopters are married, between 30 and 50 (55 if the child has special needs), have no history of drug use, and priority will be given to childless couples.[13]

Full and simple adoption

5.14 There is more than one form of 'adoption' recognised by some Convention countries. Adoption in the British Isles has the effect of severing all legal ties between the child and his birth parents. However, many Convention countries recognise more than one form of adoption. The UK system extinguishes the birth parent's parental responsibility and transfers parenthood to the adoptive parents and no other.[14] This is known as a 'full adoption'. In some countries adoption establishes a legal relationship between the child and his adopters but does not terminate the child's legal connection to his birth parents. Where a legal connection remains between the child and his birth parents this is known as a 'simple adoption'. Some Convention States (notably France) have a dual system whereby a child can be adopted under either a full or a simple adoption.

5.15 Articles 26 and 27 of the Convention provide a system whereby these different ideas of adoption can co-exist. ACA 2002, s 88 provides a mechanism for incorporating different concepts of adoption in Convention cases.

---

[8]   Hague Convention 1993, Guide to Good Practice, no 1, p 16.
[9]   Ibid.
[10] See Chapter 7.
[11] CAA 2006, s 9.
[12] See Chapter 7.
[13] Department for Children, Schools and Families, June 2008, Adoption from China.
[14] ACA 2002, s 67(2) and (3).

5.16   Article 26(1) of the Convention states:

'The recognition of an adoption includes recognition of

a.   the legal parent-child relationship between the child and his or her adoption parents;
b.   parental responsibility of the adoptive parents for the child;
c.   the termination of a pre-existing legal relationship between the child and her or her mother and father, if the adoption has this effect in the Contracting State where it was made.'

5.17   Article 27(1) adds:

'Where an adoption granted in the state of origin does not have the effect of terminating a pre-existing legal relationship, it may, in the receiving State which recognises the adoption under the Convention, be converted into an adoption having such an effect –

a.   if the law of the receiving state so permits; and
b.   if the consents [of the parents, institutions and agencies as required and, if appropriate the child] have been or are given for a full adoption.'

5.18   The decision, therefore, as to whether an adoption is a full or simple one is taken by the child's state of origin and not the receiving state. As simple adoption is not a concept normally recognised by the UK courts, ACA 2002, s 88 provides that the court can make directions to disapply or limit the application of ACA 2002, s 67(3).[15] To exercise this discretion, certain conditions must be met:

(a)   there was a Convention adoption in the child's state of origin;[16]

(b)   under the law of the Convention State where the adoption has effect the adoption was not a full adoption;

(c)   the birth parents, and agencies or institutions, and, if appropriate, the child have not consented to a full adoption; and

(d)   it would be more favourable to the adopted child for a direction limiting or disapplying s 67(3) to be made.

OVERVIEW OF CONVENTION ADOPTION PROCEDURE

5.19   The Convention sets out a process of assessment and agreement between the two Contracting States. In summary:

---

[15]   Which states the child is the child of the adoptive parents and no other person.
[16]   ACA 2002, s 88(1).

(1)   the child is determined to be 'adoptable' within the terms of the Convention;

(2)   adoptive parents are considered to be eligible to adopt under the Convention;

(3)   adoptive parents are assessed by the receiving state (their home state);

(4)   the child's state of origin matches the child to the adoptive parents;

(5)   there is liaison between the receiving state and the proposed state of origin resulting in an agreement that the adoptive parents can adopt the child;

(6)· either the child is adopted by the adoptive parents within the state of origin and enters England and Wales with his new adoptive parents or the child enters England and Wales with his adoptive parents and a Convention adoption order is applied for in the English courts.

THE CHILD

5.20 Article 4 of the Convention requires the child's state of origin to establish that:

(1)   the child is 'adoptable';

(2)   possibilities for placement within the state of origin have been given due consideration;

(3)   intercountry adoption is in the child's best interests;

(4)   consent has been obtained freely and expressed or evidenced in writing from all persons, agencies and institutions;

(5)   consents were not induced by payments;

(6)   the mother's consent was not given before the child's birth.

5.21 If appropriate the child's views must be taken into account. If the child's consent is required it, as with all others, should be given freely and without inducement.

5.22 Whilst the burden of establishing the above is placed on the state of origin, the issue of consent is relevant if a Convention adoption order is sought in the UK. This is because Form A59, used to apply for a Convention adoption order, requires the adopters to give the details of the birth parents and declare that they consent to the adoption. However, as an Article 17 agreement cannot be made without the central authority being assured of the birth parent's consent it is arguable that the existence of the Article 17 agreement alone is sufficient.

THE PROSPECTIVE ADOPTER OR ADOPTERS

5.23   The process of assessment for adoptive parents follows that for domestic adoptions. Where requirements are altered it is usually to add additional requirements to the domestic adoption framework. Even prior to the current statutory and regulatory structure the family courts expressed disquiet about the prospect of parents who were not (or would never be) approved to adopt a British child being subsequently becoming the adopters of foreign children. For a high profile example of this see *Flintshire County Council v K*.[17]

5.24   As a result the approval process for prospective adopters can be a lengthy one taking at least 6 months and up to 2 years. The process is also costly. The Department for Education has used powers granted under CAA 2006, s 13 to insert s 91A into ACA 2002 and thus has the power to apply fees in an international adoption case. Currently the Department for Education charges a fee of £1,775 for all international adoptions. The fee is not charged where the prospective adopters are relatives of the child. For other adopters it is means tested: those with a household income of between £25,000 and £45,000 per annum pay 50% (£885) and those with a household income of less than £25,000 pay nothing.

5.25   In addition, specific countries may have additional fees. For example those adopting Chinese children are expected to make a contribution to the child's orphanage. Travel costs and local court and other bureaucratic fees can be added to this. If the adopters later need to apply for a Convention adoption order in the UK courts further fees are incurred. Due to the complexity of this area of law, applicants would be strongly advised to seek legal advice prior to any proceedings.

Eligibility and initial requirements

5.26   A couple or individual wishing to adopt a child from a Convention State will only be considered by an adoption agency if they are over 21 and have been habitually resident in Britain for a period of not less than one year before the date of the application to adopt.[18] In the case of a couple wishing to adopt, both prospective adopters must meet these initial requirements.[19] See Chapter 3 for details of the court's approach to determining habitual residence and domicile.

---

[17]   [2001] 2 FLR 476.
[18]   AFER 2005, reg 13(2).
[19]   AFER 2005, reg 13(2)(a).

5.27 The first stage for the couple or individual wishing to adopt a child from a Convention State is to apply in writing to an adoption agency for a determination of their eligibility and suitability to adopt.[20] The prospective adopters are required to give the adoption agency any information it may need for this purpose.[21] This notice triggers certain duties of the adoption agency. They are obliged to 'consider' the prospective adopter or adopters' application and set up a case record which will contain the application and all further records and reports made during the adoption process, including information regarding the specific country the adopters propose to adopt from.[22]

5.28 The prospective adopters must be counseled and prepared for adoption by the adoption agency in the initial stages. Further work around adoption takes place during the in-depth assessment process. The adoption agency must provide counseling and information on adoption.[23] This includes information on the legal implications of a placement for adoption and information given in writing.[24] In a Convention adoption the agency has additional requirements to explain the implication of adopting a child from the proposed state of origin.[25]

5.29 It should be noted that prospective adopters are expected from a very early stage to decide from which country they wish to adopt a child. The adoption agency's provision of information, assessment and approval is country specific and not general to any child from any Convention State. If the adopters are unsure and change the proposed country the processes described in this chapter will need to be repeated for the new proposed country.

5.30 Prior to commencing the in depth assessment the adoption agency will carry out police checks (often known as an 'enhanced criminal records bureau' checks).[26] As with domestic adoptions certain convictions or cautions for 'specified offences' by the adopter or a member of his household who is over the age of 18 will preclude the prospective adopter from adopting.[27] The adoption agency 'may not' consider the prospective adopter suitable and the assessment process ceases. The specified offences are detailed in AAR 2005 and include:

- an offence against a child as defined by the Criminal Justice Act 2000, s 26(1);

- offences relating to the import of child pornography;[28]

---

[20] AFER 2005, reg 13(1)(a).
[21] AFER 2005, reg 13(1)(b).
[22] AFER 2005, reg 15(1) and AAR 2005, reg 22.
[23] AFER 2005, reg 14(1) and AAR 2005, reg 21.
[24] AAR 2005, reg 21(1).
[25] AFER 2005, reg 14(1)(a).
[26] AFER 2005, reg 15(2)(b) and AAR 2005, reg 23.
[27] AAR 2005, reg 23 and AFER 2005, reg 15(2)(b).
[28] AAR 2005, reg 23(3)(c).

- serious sexual offences against an adult contrary to the Sexual Offences Act 2003, such as rape, sexual activity without consent and sexual activity with those suffering a mental impairment;[29]

- serious sexual offences under repealed legislation.[30]

5.31 Certain limited offences are excluded such as battery or common assault against a child.[31] The 'young man's' defence is also relevant and the offence of sexual activity with a child over 13 will not preclude a person adopting if at the time of the offence the victim was over 13 and the perpetrator under 20.[32] Clearly, convictions for other offences may not automatically bar a person from being considered as an adopter but will be highly relevant during the assessment and recommendation process.

Assessment of the prospective adopters

5.32 Following the criminal convictions checks and the initial counseling the adoption agency must prepare the couple for adoption.[33] In many areas local authorities and adoption agencies run courses for prospective adopters to fulfil this requirement in the regulations. Whether they are domestic or intercountry, the prospective adopters are obliged to learn about adoption and its implications, post-adoption contact, the range of likely children and the skills necessary for an adoptive parent.[34] AFER 2005 do not alter the domestic regulation in this regard and it may be that some of the contents of training, aimed at domestic adopters, is irrelevant to those seeking a child from overseas.

5.33 Once the preparatory work has been undertaken the adoption agency prepares an in-depth report on the adopters.[35] This report must contain the following:

- a medical report following a full examination of the prospective adopters to include matters such as family medical history, alcohol and drug use;[36]

- information from the local authority where the prospective adopters reside;[37]

- interviews with referees;[38]

---

[29]   AAR 2005, reg 23(3)(b) and Sch 3, para (1).
[30]   Ibid, reg 23(3)(c) and Sch 3, para (2).
[31]   Ibid, reg 23(3)(d).
[32]   Ibid, reg 23.
[33]   AFER 2005, reg 15(2)(b) and AAR 2005, reg 22(2).
[34]   AAR 2005, reg 22(2)(a)–(f).
[35]   AFER 2005, reg 15(2).
[36]   AAR 2005, reg 25(1) and Sch 2, Part 4.
[37]   Ibid, reg 25(4).
[38]   Ibid, reg 25(3).

- detailed information on the prospective adopters and their family;[39]

- the state of origin that the prospective adopter wishes to adopt a child from and confirmation that they are eligible to adopt a child from that state;[40]

- assessment of the prospective adopters' suitability to adopt a child from the proposed state.[41]

5.34 The report and assessment process is detailed and lengthy. If at an early stage the adoption agency's enquiries suggest that the prospective adopters are unlikely to be considered suitable to adopt a child they can finish the report without the very detailed information required and take the matter to an adoption recommendations panel.[42] This may happen, for example, if local authority checks showed matters of concern. The prospective adopters have means of redress in this situation by their right to comment on the report and to challenge the panel's recommendation (see below).

5.35 The report is sent to the prospective adopters who have 10 working days to provide their comments on it.[43] These comments should be retained by the adoption agency.[44] The prospective adopters' suitability to adopt is then considered by the adoption agency's panel. The panel is sent the reports and other information obtained (save for the medical report which is not sent unless the medical examiner advises this to be done).[45] Information obtained about the proposed country is included within the documents sent.[46] The panel may request further documents which the adoption agency must send if reasonably practicable.[47] Prior to making their recommendation (in reality usually on the same day) the panel must invite the prospective adopters to attend a meeting.[48]

5.36 Following consideration of the relevant information, their own enquiries and meeting with the adopters the panel make a recommendation as to whether or not the prospective adopters are suitable to adopt a child.[49] Certain limitations or requirements can be placed on the recommendations such as the number, age and gender of children the adopters are recommended as being suitable to care for.[50]

---

[39] AAR 2005, Sch 4, Part 1.
[40] AFER 2005, reg 15(4)(a), (b).
[41] Ibid, reg 15(4)(d).
[42] AAR 2005, reg 25(7).
[43] Ibid, reg 25(8).
[44] Ibid, reg 22(3)(c).
[45] Ibid, reg 25(7).
[46] AFER 2005, reg 15(5).
[47] AAR 2005, reg 25(10).
[48] Ibid, reg 26(4).
[49] Ibid, reg 26(1).
[50] Ibid, reg 26(3).

5.37 The outcome of the panel is only a recommendation and not a final decision on the issue. The responsibility for the final decision on whether or not the prospective adopters are suitable rests with the adoption agency.[51] The final decision should be taken by a person or persons who are not on the panel that made the recommendation.[52] The prospective adopters are notified of the decision in writing.

5.38 If the prospective adopters are considered suitable to adopt a child from their chosen Convention country the focus then shifts to the 'matching' process and liaison between the Department for Education and central authority of the state of origin.

5.39 A positive decision by the adoption panel is not everlasting and must be reviewed within one year of approval and thereafter every year.[53] These reviews must take into account any updating information and the adopters' own views.[54] In Convention adoption cases the clock stops ticking on these reviews once agreement has been reached between the two states pursuant to Article 17(c) of the Convention that the adoption should proceed.[55] If prospective adopters are not considered suitable they must be sent the reasons for the decision, and, if different from the adoption agency's final decision, the record of the panel's recommendation.[56]

Appealing a decision not to approve prospective adopters

5.40 If the prospective adopters are not considered suitable they have two possible forms of redress. These also apply to prospective adopters who are ruled out at an early stage. Either they can make further representations to the adoption agency which may then refer the matter back to a panel for a fresh recommendation.[57] Any further representations must be made within 40 working days. The adoption agency must advise the unsuccessful adopters of these options and the time limits.[58] There is no obligation on the agency to refer the matter back to panel and the final decision still rests with the agency, although they must take into account the views of the second panel.[59] Alternatively, the prospective adopters may make representations to the Secretary of State for a review by an independent panel. Again such representations must be made within 40 days. The final decision still comes back to the adoption agency who should take into account the decision of the independent panel and inform the Secretary of State of their final decision.[60]

---

[51] AAR 2005. reg 27(1); AFER 2005, reg 16.
[52] AAR 2005, reg 27(2).
[53] Ibid, reg 29(2); AFER 2005, reg 17.
[54] AAR 2005, reg 29(3)(a), (b).
[55] AFER 2005, reg 17.
[56] AAR 2005, reg 27(4).
[57] Ibid, reg 27(6) and (7).
[58] Ibid, reg 27(4)(c).
[59] Ibid, reg 27(8)(a).
[60] Ibid, regs 27(8)(b) and 27(10).

5.41 The above two routes are given in the alternative in AAR 2005. There is no indication that they need to be completed sequentially. After completing one or both routes of appeal a still unsatisfied potential adopter may be able to judicially review the relevant body. Such proceedings are outside the scope of this work.

Liaison between states and Article 17(c) agreement

5.42 Following a decision that prospective adopters are suitable to adopt a child from their chosen country the focus shifts to liaison between the adoption agency and Department for Education (the central authority for England) and later to communications between the Department for Education and the central authority in the relevant Convention country. First the adoption agency sends to the Department for Education:[61]

- written confirmation of the prospective adopters' suitability to adopt;

- any recommendation the agency make about the number and type of children that should be matched with the adopter;

- the enhanced criminal records bureau check;

- all the documents given to the adoption panel (this will include the full report on the adopter and information about how they meet the specific country's requirements);

- a record of the panel meeting; and

- any other relevant information, in particular information required by the central authority in the state of origin.

5.43 If the Department for Education is satisfied that the duties laid down in AFER 2005 and AAR 2005 have been complied with and all relevant information has been supplied it will send to the central authority in the proposed state of origin the report on the adopters (this is the Article 15 report[62]), the decision and panel recommendations, and other required information.[63] Together with these documents is sent a certificate of eligibility confirming that the prospective adopter is eligible to adopt and that the regulations have been complied with. The certificate should also confirm that:

> 'the child will be authorized to enter and reside permanently in the United Kingdom if entry clearance, and leave to enter or remain as may be necessary, is granted and not revoked or curtailed and a Convention adoption order or Convention adoption is made.'[64]

---

[61] AFER 2005, reg 18(1).
[62] See **2.24–2.25** for full discussion of Article 15.
[63] AFER 2005, reg 18(2)(a)–(d).
[64] Ibid, reg 18(2)(e).

5.44 It should be noted that the above does not give a guarantee to the state of origin that the child will be allowed to enter and/or reside permanently in the UK; it merely states that if they pass the relevant immigration tests they will be allowed to do so. The immigration requirements are considered in detail in Chapter 9.

5.45 AFER 2005, Sch 1 contains the required form of the certificate. The Department for Education then notifies the adoption agency and the prospective adopter that they have sent the relevant documents and certificate.[65]

5.46 Following receipt and consideration of the information sent the state of origin sends the Article 16 information to the Department for Education.[66] This information includes:[67]

- a report on the children's identity, adoptability, background, social environment, family history, medical history and any special needs;

- proof of confirmation that consent has been obtained as necessary; and

- the reasons for the determination on the placement.

5.47 This information is sent to the Department for Education to give to the adoption agency which must consider the information, send it to the adopters and meet with the adopters to discuss the information, the proposed placement and any support services.[68] The Department for Education cautions in their guidance that this process of transmission of the Article 16 information must be followed strictly:

> 'occasionally prospective adopters or their adoption agency have received information directly from the State of origin of the child. If that were to happen and the prospective adopters were to act on the information received there is a risk that the adoption may then no longer meet the requirements of the Hague Convention. If prospective adopters receive information direction they should immediately notify their adoption agency and the DfE. It will be necessary for them to wait for information about the child to be sent to them by their UK adoption agency once the agency has received the information from the DfE. In cases where the information is initially misrouted the DfE contacts the Central Authority in the State of origin to request that they provide the information directly to the DfE, thus ensuring that the requirements of the Convention may be met; the information will then be passed on as required.'[69]

---

[65] AFER 2005, reg 18(3).
[66] Ibid, reg 19.
[67] Hague Convention 1993, Article 16(2) and AFER 2005, reg 19(6).
[68] AFER 2005, reg 19(2).
[69] Department for Education, Hague Convention Adoption Procedures, Annex A: http://media.education.gov.uk/assets/files/pdf/a/an/annex%20%20a%20-%20hague%20convention%20adoption%20procedures.pdf.

5.48 After their meeting with the adoption agency and consideration of the information received from the state of origin the prospective adopters need to confirm in writing to the adoption agency that they are willing to proceed with the adoption of the child proposed.[70] The adoption agency then notifies the Department for Education of this and at the same time confirms it is satisfied that the adoption should proceed.[71]

5.49 Although not a requirement of the regulations, the Department for Education guidance suggests that following the discussion of the Article 16 information the prospective adoptions may travel to the state of origin to meet the child. Previous versions of the regulations required this to happen before the Article 17(c) agreement was reached.[72] However, some countries may require that the adopters meet the child before giving their consent for the adoption to proceed.

5.50 Once the adopters have confirmed their intention to proceed with the adoption, the two central authorities work towards agreement that the adoption can proceed. The Department for Education notifies the child's state of origin that the prospective adopter wishes to proceed and that it is prepared to agree the same.[73] The Department for Education also confirms either if the child meets the requirements of the British Nationality Act 1981 or that if entry clearance is granted and not revoked the child will be allowed to enter and reside in the UK.[74] As stated above this is not a guarantee that entry clearance will be granted. The criteria for entry clearance and of the British Nationality Act 1981 are considered in Chapter 9.

5.51 At this stage the requirements of Article 17 of the Convention are met:

'Any decision in the State of origin that a child should be entrusted to prospective adoptive parents many only be made if –

a.   the Central Authority of that State has ensured that the prospective adoptive parents agree;

b.   the Central Authority of the receiving State has approved such decision, where such approval is required by the law of that State or by the Central Authority of the State of origin;

c.   the Central Authorities of both States have agreed the adoption may proceed; and

d.   it has been determined, in accordance with Article 5, that the prospective adoptive parents are eligible and suited to adopt and that the child is or will be authorised to enter and reside permanently in the receiving state.'

---

[70]   AFER 2005, reg 19(3)(b).
[71]   Ibid, reg 19(3).
[72]   Adoptions with a Foreign Element (Amendment) Regulations 2009, SI 2009/2563, reg 2(1) and (2).
[73]   AFER 2005, reg 19(4)(a).
[74]   Ibid, reg 19(4)(b).

5.52 Once the Article 17(c) agreement is reached the Department for Education notifies the adoption agency and the prospective adopter. The child can only be 'entrusted' to the care of the adopters following this agreement.[75] The Department for Education notes in its guidance on ACA 2002 that adopters should not try and leap ahead of the process (even if pushed by the institution or authority caring for the child in the state of origin) and take over care of the child for an overnight stay or longer period prior to the completion of the Article 17(c) agreement being reached. As discussed in Chapter 1, the meaning of the term 'entrusted' has been taken to mean more than day-to-day care of a child when the child is subject to a care order. However, what is meant by the 'decision to entrust' and when that decision will be given effect may vary from country to country. In some countries it may be that the child is not 'entrusted' until after the making of a Convention adoption order; in other countries the child may be entrusted to the adopters for a probationary period prior to the Convention adoption order being made in the child's state of origin. In some countries the child may be placed in the care of the adopters under an order made by a competent authority which allows the adopters to exercise parental responsibility for the child and transfer the child to the UK for the purpose of a Convention adoption order being made in this jurisdiction.

5.53 The making of the Article 17(c) agreement triggers a requirement for the adoption agency to:[76]

- inform the adopters' GP in writing of the proposed placement and send to the doctor a written report detailing the child's health history and current state of health (insofar as it is known to them);

- notify the local authority where the child will reside on the proposed arrival of the child (this does not apply if the adoption agency is the local authority);

- inform the primary care trust of the child's proposed arrival;

- if the child is of school age, send written notification to the local education authority of the child's educational history and whether he is likely to have special education needs.

Decision not to proceed with adoption

5.54 The adoption agency and/or state of origin may decide prior to the Article 17 agreement being reached that the adoption should not proceed.

5.55 If the state of origin decides, prior to the Article 17(c) agreement, that the placement should not proceed it will notify the Department for Education who in turn inform the adoption agency. It falls to the adoption agency to tell

---

[75]   Pursuant to Article 5 of the Convention.
[76]   AFER 2005, reg 22.

the prospective adopter. The Article 16 documents are returned by the agency to the state of origin via the Department for Education.[77] If the adoption agency decides, prior to the Article 17(c) agreement, following a review of the prospective adopters approval to adopt[78] that the adopter is no longer considered suitable the Department for Education must be informed and the Article 16 documents similarly returned.[79]

5.56 If the prospective adopters decide before a Convention adoption order is made and before the child's entry into the UK, that they do not wish to proceed they need to notify their adoption agency. This agency will notify the Department for Education who in turn notify the state of origin. This decision by the adopters can come after the Article 17(c) agreement but not after a Convention adoption in the state of origin or the child's entry into the UK. If the adopters no longer wish to care for the child or the placement breaks down once the adopters are in the UK different procedures apply. These are considered below at **5.83**.

CONVENTION ADOPTION AND CONVENTION ADOPTION ORDER

5.57 Prior to this stage the procedure and requirements for all prospective adopters is the same and deviation from them can lead to invalidating the process. Following the Article 17(c) agreement the prospective adopters have two options: to apply for a Convention adoption in the state of origin or return to the UK with the child with the intention of applying for a Convention adoption order in the English or Welsh courts.

5.58 In all cases the prospective adopters must, following the Article 17(c) agreement, notify their adoption agency of:[80]

- the date of their expected entry into the UK with the child;

- when the child is placed with them by the authorities in the state of origin.

5.59 The prospective adopters must accompany the child to the UK. In the case of a couple both must travel with the child unless the adoption agency and the central authority of the state of origin have agreed that it is necessary for only one of them to.[81]

---

[77]   AFER 2005, reg 20(1).
[78]   AAR 2005, reg 29.
[79]   AFER 2005, reg 20(2).
[80]   AFER 2005, reg 21(a), (b).
[81]   Ibid, reg 21(c).

Convention adoption

5.60 In some cases the adopters may complete all the necessary legal requirements in the child's state of origin and a final adoption order will be made. In these circumstances the state of origin issues a certificate under Article 23 of the Convention certifying that the adoption was made in accordance with the Convention. Article 23 states:

> 'an adoption certified by the competent authority of State of the adoption as having been made in accordance with the Convention shall be recognised by operation of law in the other Contracting States. The certificate shall specify when and by whom the agreement under Article 17 sub-paragraph (c) were given.'

5.61 In accordance with the requirement of Article 23 that Convention adoptions are recognised by operation of law in contracting states, ACA 2002, s 66(1)(c) provides that an adoption effected under the law of a Convention Country outside of the British Isles and certified under Article 23 is an adoption. Therefore following the Article 23 certificate the prospective adopters are recognised as the child's parents and can apply for and obtain a British passport for the child and enter the UK with the child. Upon entry to the UK there are no further requirements placed upon the adoptive parents.

5.62 However, it is a requirement in some states of origin that before a Convention adoption can be granted, the child must have been entrusted to the prospective adopter and lived with them in the receiving state for a probationary period. In such a case, before returning to the UK the prospective adopter must have applied for a Convention adoption in the state of origin. The prospective adopters should notify the local authority of any private fostering arrangements when they enter the UK with the child. The local authority may be required to complete a report for the state of origin prior to a Convention adoption being finalised in that state.[82]

Procedure on an application for a 'simple' adoption

5.63 Whilst there is no need for a further adoption order from the English and Welsh courts,[83] in cases where the adoption in the state of origin was a simple adoption (see above), there may need to be an application to the High Court for a direction under ACA 2002, s 88 to modify the effects of s 67(3) of the same Act.

5.64 Such an application is made to the High Court and can be made by the child, adoptive parents, birth parents or any other person (such as the local authority).[84] The application is made on Form 62 which can be found on the Courts and Tribunals Service website.[85] The respondents to the application are

---

[82]   AFER 2005, reg 29.
[83]   ACA 2002, s 66(1)(c).
[84]   FPR 2010, SI 2010/2955, r 14.3.
[85]   www.justice.gov.uk/courts.

(if not the applicants) the adoptive parents, birth parents, local authority and the adoption agency.[86] ACA 2002 provides that the Attorney-General may, if directed by the court, be sent the papers and may intervene in the proceedings.[87] The Family Procedure Rules 2010 (FPR 2010) state that he should be a party from the outset and a respondent to the application for a s 88 direction.[88]

Registration of Convention adoptions

5.65 If a Convention adoption is effected in the child's state of origin the adopters may register the adoption in the UK. However, this is not required of them. Convention adoptions are registered with the Registrar General if he is satisfied he has sufficient particulars of the adoption.[89]

5.66 The application to register is made by the adoptive parents, any other person with parental responsibility or, if over 18, the child.[90] The application must be in writing and signed.[91] At the time of the application the adoptive parents (both if a couple) must be habitually resident in England and Wales.[92] The applicant must provide details regarding the child, his birth parents and the adoptive parents. If not all details are known (for example an abandoned child's birth parents) those that are known should be stated.[93] In the case of a Convention adoption a copy of the Article 23 certificate should be sent to the adoptive parents by the central authority of the child's state of origin.[94] Any documents not in English should be translated to include the name and address of the person translating and a statement of truth.[95]

CONVENTION ADOPTION ORDER

Notification of the local authority

5.67 The procedure is more complex in cases were no order was obtained or applied for in the child's state of origin and further responsibility is placed upon the prospective adopters and the local authority in whose area they reside. If an order was applied for in the state of origin but subject to a probationary period the requirements below do not apply.[96]

---

[86] FPR 2010, r 14.3.
[87] ACA 2002, s 88(4) and Family Law Act 1986, s 59.
[88] FPR 2010, r 14.3.
[89] ACA 2002, Sch 1, para (3)(1) and (5).
[90] Adopted Children and Adoption Contact Registers Regulations, SI 2005/924, reg 4.
[91] Ibid, reg 5.
[92] Ibid, reg 3.
[93] Ibid, reg 5(3).
[94] Ibid, reg 5(2)(a).
[95] Ibid, reg 5(4).
[96] AFER 2005, reg 24(1).

5.68   The first and most significant requirement on the prospective adopters is to inform the local authority in whose area they reside within 14 days of the child's entry into the UK of the child's arrival in the UK and the prospective adopter's intention to apply for an adoption order.[97] If the placement has broken down the prospective adopter must inform the local authority of his intention not to give the child a home.[98] If the adopter moves into the area of another local authority he must notify his new local authority that notice of his intention to adopt the child has been given or tell the authority that he does not intend to give the child a home.[99] Failure to give the requisite notice to the local authority is a criminal offence and if found guilty on summary conviction the prospective adopter can be sentenced to imprisonment for 6 months and/or a fine of up to £5,000.[100] This applies both when the adopter enters the UK with the child and if the adopter moves to an area covered by a different local authority.

5.69   Receipt of notification under AFER 2005, reg 24(1) or (2) imposes certain duties upon the local authority in respect of the child who has arrived in the UK.[101] The local authority must:

- set up a case record containing information received from the central authority of the child's state of origin, the adoption agency (if not the local authority) the adopter and records of visits and reviews;

- visit the child and prospective adopter within one week of receipt of the notice of intention;

- visit the prospective adopter and child once each week until a review to be held within 4 weeks;

- review the case within 4 weeks, then 3 months and thereafter at least every 6 months until an adoption order is made. These reviews are to consider the child's needs, welfare and development, the support services available and the need for further visits;

- ensure that the prospective adopters are advised about the child's needs and availability of support services.

5.70   If the prospective adopters fail to make an application to adopt within 2 years of giving notice of their intention so to do the local authority must further review the case considering the child's needs, the arrangements for the exercise of parental responsibility for the child, the terms of any immigration status and the arrangement for support.[102]

---

[97]   AFER 2005, reg 24(1)(a), (b)(i).
[98]   Ibid, reg 24(1)(b)(ii).
[99]   Ibid, reg 24(2).
[100] Ibid, reg 59(a).
[101] Ibid, reg 5 applied to Hague Convention 1993 cases by ibid, reg 25.
[102] Ibid, reg 24(4).

Limits on rights of prospective adopters prior to Convention adoption order

5.71 Before any Convention adoption order is made there are limits on the changes that the prospective adopters can effect. In particular they cannot change the child's surname unless the state of origin consents to this.[103] Further, they cannot remove the child from the UK for a period of more than one month.[104]

Application for a Convention adoption order

5.72 The adopters need to make an application for a Convention adoption order. To do so they must meet the initial requirements that:[105]

- they have been habitually resident in the British Isles for a period of at least one year. In the case of a couple wishing to adopt, both must meet this criteria;

- at the date on which the Article 17(c) agreement was reached the child was habitually resident in a Convention State;

- if one member of a couple or, in the case of a sole application, the applicant, is not a British citizen the Home Office has confirmed that the child is authorised to enter and reside permanently in the UK.

5.73 As the above requirements need to be met in order to allow the prospective adopters to complete the assessment process and for the Article 17(c) agreement to be reached, it is unlikely that many will fall at this hurdle. The final initial requirement is that the child must be under 18 on the date the application is made.[106]

Forms and court procedure

5.74 The procedure for Convention adoption application is governed by FPR 2010, Part 14. The application is made on form A59 which can be found on the Courts and Tribunal Service website together with guidance notes on its completion.[107] The form requires detailed information about both adopters (in the case of a couple). If an individual wishes to adopt but is married, he or she will need to satisfy the court that they are permanently separated from their spouse; that their spouse cannot be located or that the spouse in incapable of making the application due to ill health.

---

[103] ACA 2002, s 28(2), (3) as modified by AFER 2005, reg 53(c).
[104] Ibid.
[105] AFER 2005, reg 31.
[106] ACA 2002, s 55(4). However, an order may be made after the child's eighteenth birthday but before their nineteenth birthday,
[107] www.justice.gov.uk/courts.

5.75 Form A59 also requires the adopters to declare that the birth parents of the child consent to the adoption. Details of the birth parents are required.

5.76 Once completed the form should normally be taken to a county court that is an intercountry adoption centre to be issued.[108] There are currently only 13 (including the Principal Registry of the Family Division) such courts in England and Wales. At the time of writing they are:[109]

Birmingham County Court	Chester County Court	Manchester County Court
Bournemouth County Court	Exeter County Court	Nottingham County Court
Bristol County Court	Leeds County Court	Portsmouth County Court
Cardiff County Court	Liverpool County Court	Wrexham County Court

5.77 Proceedings for Convention adoption orders should only be started in the High Court if they are exceptionally complex, the outcome is of general public importance or for another substantial reason.[110]

5.78 Following completion of the form it is issued by the court and notice of the proceedings is given by the court to the relevant parties. The respondents to the application will be the birth parents and the child.[111] The application form is not sent to the child's parents, but is sent (without supporting documents) to the adoption agency and the child's guardian.[112]

5.79 In applications for a Convention adoption order, the court will list a first directions hearing and not proceed directly to a final hearing. The first directions hearing will:[113]

- fix a timetable for the filing of any reports (eg from the local authority or child's guardian);

- consider whether any other person should be a party to the proceedings (eg the local authority);

- consider whether the requirements in AFER 2005 have been complied with;

---

[108] Allocation and Transfer of Proceedings Order 2008, SI 2008/2836, arts 6(c) and 11(2)(a).
[109] Ibid, Sch (1).
[110] Ibid, art 7.
[111] FPR 2010, r 14.3.
[112] Ibid, r 14.6(1)(b) and Practice Direction 14A.
[113] Ibid, r 14.8 and Practice Direction 14B.

- consider whether all relevant documents have been translated into English;

- decide whether the applicants need to file any affidavit evidence regarding the circumstances in which the child was brought into the UK;

- give directions for the production of the child's passport;

- consider whether Cafcass should be involved;

- consider whether a representative from the Home Office should attend court;

- give directions regarding service upon birth parents, via the central authority of the state of origin including information about the role of Cafcass and the availability of legal aid.

5.80 At the first directions hearing the appropriate forum for the final hearing may also be reconsidered. The county court may transfer to the High Court if the requirements of AFER 2005 have not been complied with or if it considers the proceedings to be:

- exceptionally complex; or

- the outcome is of general public importance; or

- for another substantial reason.

If Cafcass is involved the court may fix a further directions hearing within 6 weeks and Cafcass should file an interim report for this hearing.[114]

5.81 Following the making of a Convention adoption order at a final hearing the court will within 7 days send the order to the central authority in the state of origin.[115]

5.82 It is the practice of some courts following the making of final adoption orders to have a short ceremony or celebratory event with the adopters to acknowledge the importance of the order for the child and new parents. Children are often permitted to attend court for these events which are separate from any contested hearings regarding the making of the order.[116] Ordinarily photography is prohibited within the court building, but it is recognised that these are joyful and momentous occasions in a child's life and it is not unusual for judges to agree to the use of a camera so that photographs can be taken. If

---

[114] FPR 2010, Practice Direction 14B.
[115] FPR 2010, r 14.26.
[116] *Re F (Adoption: Natural Parents)* [2007] 1 FLR 363.

a prospective adopter would like to take photographs they must obtain permission from the court to do so before the hearing so that liaison with security can be organised.

PLACEMENT BREAKDOWN AND ANNULMENT OF CONVENTION ADOPTION ORDERS

Return of child prior to a Convention adoption order

5.83 AFER 2005 makes provision for the child in the event of the breakdown of a placement prior to the making of a Convention adoption or Convention adoption order or its annulment. Before the making of an order the prospective adopters can notify the local authority that they no longer wish to provide a home for the child. The prospective adopters have the option to do this when notifying the local authority of the child's arrival in the UK.[117] The prospective adopters have 7 days from their notification to return the child to the relevant local authority.[118] Failure to do so is an offence punishable by 3 months in prison or a fine at level 5 on the standard scale (£5,000).[119]

5.84 The alternative situation is where the local authority decides that the continued placement of the child with the prospective adopters is not in the child's best interests. If no application for a Convention adoption order has been issued, the local authority must give notice of its opinion to the prospective adopters and request the return of the child.[120] The prospective adopter must hand the child over to the local authority within 7 days. Again, a failure to hand the child over is an offence punishable by 3 months in prison or a fine at level 5 on the standard scale (£5,000).[121] If proceedings are ongoing for a Convention adoption order the adopters do not have to hand the child over to the local authority unless ordered to do so by the court.[122] In addition to the powers given to the local authority by AFER 2005, reg 27, they retain their powers under other legislation to protect children.[123]

5.85 Other circumstances in which a placement is terminated are when:

- a child is placed under probationary arrangements by the state of origin after which a Convention adoption is not made;

- the court declines to make a Convention adoption order;

- a Convention adoption or Convention adoption order is annulled.

---

[117] AFER 2005, reg 24(1)(b)(ii).
[118] AFER 2005, reg 26(1).
[119] AFER 2005, reg 59.
[120] AFER 2005, reg 27(1).
[121] AFER 2005, reg 59.
[122] AFER 2005, reg 27(3).
[123] AFER 2005, reg 27(4).

5.86 In all the above circumstances the local authority must decide whether it is in the child's best interests to be placed with another prospective adopter who is habitually resident in the UK. Such an adopter must be as fully assessed as the original adopter and undergo the necessary preparatory work. If an adopter is identified the local authority informs the Department for Education and confirmed that AFER 2005, regs 14–16 (assessment, preparation and panel) have been complied with. The Department for Education informs the central authority in the child's state of origin and liaises with that central authority to agree the placement.[124]

5.87 If the local authority decide it is not in the child's interests to remain with another adopter in England and Wales it must inform the Department for Education and arrange for the return of the child to his or her state of origin.[125]

5.88 Any decision regarding the future of the child should have regard to the child's wishes and feelings in light of his or her age and understanding. If appropriate the child should consent to any steps taken.[126]

Annulment of a Convention adoption or Convention adoption order

5.89 A Convention adoption or Convention adoption order can only be annulled by the High Court on the basis that the order is contrary to public policy.[127] However the state of origin may also retain powers to give decision annulling a Convention adoption.[128] Such a decision can only be challenged in the High Court on the grounds that it is contrary to public policy or the body making the decision was not competent to make the decision.[129]

5.90 An application for annulment is made on Form 62 to the High Court. It can be made by the adopter, child, birth parents, local authority, adoption agency, Home Secretary or any other person. The respondents are the birth parent, adopters, adoption agency and local authority.[130]

---

[124] AFER 2005, reg 28(2), (3).
[125] AFER 2005, reg 28(5).
[126] AFER 2005, reg 28(6).
[127] ACA 2002, s 89(1).
[128] ACA 2002, s 91(1)(b).
[129] ACA 2002, s 88(2), (4).
[130] FPR 2010, r 14.3.

Chapter 6

NON-CONVENTION ADOPTIONS: ASSESSMENT PROCESS

INTRODUCTION

6.1   This chapter will consider the position where prospective adopters wish to adopt children outwith the parameters of the Convention. This would be either where the country is not signed up to the Convention or where the circumstances of the adoption do not fall within the terms of the Convention (such as a private or independent adoption).

6.2   The adoption of foreign children is highly regulated and breach of the regulations can give rise to a number of criminal offences. The Adoption and Children Act 2002 (ACA 2002) and associated regulations bring into force a stringent scheme of preparation and assessment that must be complied with before a child enters the jurisdiction. There are public policy reasons for the safeguards in place and the courts have reinforced these reasons. Munby J, as he then was, powerfully states in *Re M (International Adoption Trade)*:[1]

> 'It is high time that this evil and exploitative trade was stamped out. It is a trade because, however it is dressed up, it involved the buying and selling of babies by intermediaries who pocket most of the large sums of money which change hands during the course of the transaction. It is evil and exploitative because in battens on would-be adopters who, unable to adopt through more conventional channels, are induced in their desperation to part with large sums of money to intermediaries whose motives are purely mercenary; because it battens on the emotional turmoil of disadvantaged and desperately vulnerable birth mothers who are induced to part with their babies within days of birth, who see little for the large sums of money paid to the intermediaries by the adopters and who too often, as in the present case, soon come to regret their hasty and ill-considered decision; and because it can cause untold harm to children, untold misery to their birth mothers and untold heartache to adopters.'[2]

Outline of process

6.3   In summary there are two stages to the process of adopting a child outside the Convention.

---

[1]   [2003] 1 FLR 1111, sub nom *A LA v M* [2003] EHWC 219.
[2]   Ibid, at [4].

(1) First, there are the requirements adopters must comply with prior to the child entering the country and, in some cases, after the child enters.

(2) Second, there is legal process of the child being adopted by the proposed adopters. There are a number of routes to this:

    (a) the adoption may be made in the child's home state and recognised in England and Wales;

    (b) If there is no, or no recognised, adoption in the child's home state, the adopters will have to apply to the UK courts for an adoption order.

6.4 The legal process is considered in Chapter 7.

6.5 As well as the above the prospective adopters will need to consider immigration issues. These are detailed in Chapter 9.

Statutes, Regulations and Guidance

6.6 The governing statutes are the ACA 2002 which has been in force since 30 December 2005. In relation to international adoption, ACA 2002 builds on restrictions developed in earlier statutes, in particular the Adoption and Children Act 1976. However, in many respects the ACA 2002 and regulations impose additional and more stringent requirements and with more serious criminal sanctions for breach than their predecessors.

6.7 Much of the detail of the requirements is found in the Adoptions with a Foreign Element Regulations 2005[3] (AFER 2005), which incorporate significant parts of the Adoption Agency Regulations 2005 (AAR 2005).[4] In some circumstances, where the child enters the UK without a recognised external adoption order, parts of the Children (Private Arrangements for Fostering) Regulations 2005[5] are also applicable.

6.8 As in Convention cases the Department for Education offers guidance on international adoption on its website (www.education.gov.uk). The Department for Education has guidance to ACA 2002 requirements including helpful flowcharts; up-to-date information on the requirements of specific countries and the latest ministerial statements on restricted countries.

---

[3] SI 2005/392.
[4] SI 2005/389.
[5] SI 2005/1533.

REQUIREMENTS BEFORE THE CHILD ENTERS THE JURISDICTION

6.9 ACA 2002, s 83 applies where a person or couple habitually resident in the British Isles bring a child habitually resident in another country into the UK either:

- for the purpose of adopting that child; or

- within 12 months of the child being adopted by them under an external adoption.[6]

6.10 An external adoption is any adoption, save for a Convention adoption, effected under the law of a country outside the British Isles. It is immaterial whether the adoption confers the full status of a UK adoption. In addition s 83(1) applies even if the adoption is an 'overseas' adoption or is otherwise automatically recognised in the UK.[7] The period of time that needs to lapse between an external order and the child being brought into the UK was initially 6 months. This was increased to 12 months and applies to children adopted and brought into the UK after 1 October 2007.[8]

6.11 In either case the prospective adopter must comply with the conditions and regulations of AFER 2005, Chapter 1.[9] Failure to do so is a criminal offence punishable on summary conviction with 6 months' imprisonment and/or a fine not exceeding the statutory maximum. On indictment breach of s 83 can result in a sentence of up to 12 months and/or an unlimited fine.[10]

6.12 It is important to note that the only exceptions to s 83 are Convention adopters. Adopters adopting children from countries whose adoption orders are 'Overseas adoptions orders' must still comply with the regulations before the child is brought into the country. Once the child is in the country an overseas adoption order does simplify the remaining stages of the process.

6.13 ACA 2002 does make provision for the requirements of s 83 to be modified in the case of step-parents and relatives applying to adopt a child.[11] However, at the time of writing, no regulations in this regard have been made and thus all prospective adopters must go through the same, lengthy, process.

6.14 Whilst s 83 applies only to children brought into the UK, ACA 2002 also prohibits any person who is neither an adoption agency or acting pursuant to a High Court order arranging adoptions; restricts who can prepare reports on prospective adopters; and, prohibits certain payments in connection with an

---

6   ACA 2002, s 83(1).
7   Ibid, s 83(3)(a) and (b).
8   Children and Adoption Act 2006.
9   ACA 2002, s 83(7).
10 ACA 2002, s 83(8).
11 Ibid, s 86(1).

adoption.[12] Breach of these restrictions can also constitute a criminal offence. These restrictions are considered further below.

6.15   The process prescribed by AFER 2005 pursuant to ACA 2002, s 83 is shown at **Figure 6.1** below.

Notification, preparation and assessment process

6.16   AFER 2005 sets out in detail the process for prospective adopters. The first requirement placed on prospective adopters is to apply in writing to an adoption agency for an assessment of their suitability to adopt and give the agency any necessary information.[13]

6.17   The requirements pursuant to ACA 2002, s 83(4) are laid out in AFER 2005, reg 4. In order to comply with these regulations and, in particular, to obtain a certificate from the Department for Education the adopters must undergo an assessment that complies with AAR 2005, Part 4.[14] The process of assessment is country specific and if the adopters are assessed for one country and later change their minds as to their proposed country a new assessment must be completed. Following the notification from the prospective adopters, the adoption agency should provide a counseling service to the prospective adopters. In addition they should explain to the prospective adopter the proceedings relating to adopting a child from the proposed country and provide written information regarding this.[15]

6.18   Following the above proceedings, the prospective adopters must apply on the form provided by the adoption agency for their suitability to adopt a child to be assessed.[16] The adoption agency then sets up a case record containing information already received and that obtained in the course of their later enquiries.[17] The adoption agency can seek any reasonably required further information from the prospective adopters prior to or as part of the assessment process.[18]

6.19   Prior to embarking on a full report the adoption agency will undertake enhanced police checks on the prospective adopter and members of his household over the age of 18. As with domestic adoptions, certain convictions or cautions for 'specified offences' by the adopter or a member of his household who is over the age of 18 will preclude the prospective adopter from

---

[12]   ACA 2002, s 92, 94 and 96.
[13]   AFER 2005, reg 3; ACA 2002, s 83(4).
[14]   AFER 2005, reg 4(2)(a)(i).
[15]   AAR 2005, reg 21(1)(a), (b) and (d).
[16]   Ibid, reg 22(1).
[17]   Ibid, reg 22(3).
[18]   Ibid, reg 22(2).

Figure 6.1

Prospective adopter gives notice to the adoption agency of his intention to adopt

The prospective adopter undergoes the preparation and assessment process. A report is prepared and a recommendation made by panel. The agency approves (or not) him as an appropriate person to adopt a child

The adoption agency sends the relevant information to the secretary of state (Department of Education) who issue a certificate confirming that the prospective adopter is suitable to adopt and that if entry clearance granted the child will be allowed to remain in the UK.

The adopters tell the adoption agency details of the child they wish to adopt

The adopters visit the child in his or her home country and confirm to the adoption agency that they wish to proceed to adopt the child.

The adopters accompany the child to the UK

[The adopters may obtain an order in the child's home state]

If no order is obtained in the child's home state, or, if the order is not recognised by the UK, the adopters must inform the LA of the child's arrival. The prospective adopters apply for an adoption order once the child has remained with them for a period of 6 months.

adopting.[19] The adoption agency 'may not' consider the prospective adopter suitable and the assessment process ceases. The specified offences are detailed in the AAR 2005 and include:

---

[19]   AAR 2005, reg 23 and AFER 2005, reg 15(2)(b).

- an offence against a child as defined by Criminal Justice Act 2000, s 26(1);

- offences relating to the import of child pornography;[20]

- serious sexual offences against an adult contrary to the Sexual Offences Act 2003, such as rape, sexual activity without consent and sexual activity with those suffering a mental impairment;[21]

- serious sexual offences under repealed legislation.[22]

6.20 Certain limited offences are excluded such as battery or common assault against a child.[23] The 'young man's' defence is also relevant and the offence of sexual activity with a child over 13 will not preclude a person adopting if at the time of the offence the victim was over 13 and the perpetrator under 20.[24] If a specified offence is uncovered during the police checks that is the end of the adoption process. Clearly, convictions for other offences may not automatically bar a person from being considered as an adopter but will be highly relevant during the assessment and recommendation process.

6.21 The adoption agency must then commence preparation work with the prospective adopters.[25] This work builds on the initial preparation undertaken prior to the application to adopt, and includes the provision of information about the age, sex and needs of any children; the significance of adoption to the child and their birth family; issues of contact with the birth family; the skills an adopter needs[26] as well as such other preparation the adoption agency considers appropriate.[27] The same list of information is given to all prospective adopters irrespective of whether they are adopting: domestically, from Convention countries or from non-Convention countries. Additional matters, such as difficulties that may arise in transracial adoptions, that are more relevant to international adoption, are not specifically covered by the preparation required by the regulations.

Adoption Report – contents

6.22 If the above phases are completed and the adoption agency considers the prospective adopters suitable to adopt a child, they then prepare a full adoption report.[28] This report must contain significant and detailed information about the adopters and their family. It includes a full written report on the health and medical history of the adopter and information from the local authority where

---

[20] AAR 2005, reg 23(3)(c).
[21] Ibid, reg 23(3)(b) and Sch 3, para (1).
[22] Ibid, reg 23(3)(c) and Sch 3, para (2).
[23] Ibid, reg 23(3)(d).
[24] Ibid, reg 23.
[25] Ibid, reg 24.
[26] Ibid, reg 24(2).
[27] Ibid, reg 24(1).
[28] Ibid, reg 25(1).

the adopter resides.[29] As well as matters common to all those who wish to adopt, where s 83(1) applies the report must also include the name of the country proposed, confirmation that the prospective adopter meets the requirements to adopt from that country, and additional information obtained as a result of any additional requirements of the proposed country. The adoption agency must also assess the suitability of the prospective adopter to adopt a child from their proposed country.[30]

6.23 The report can be completed without all the required information and submitted to the adoption panel for reference if it seems to the agency that the prospective adopter is unlikely to be considered suitable to adopt a child.[31]

Who can prepare the report

6.24 ACA 2002, s 94 allows only 'prescribed' persons to prepare reports on prospective adopters. Such persons are defined in the Restriction on the Preparation of Adoption Reports Regulations 2005.[32] The report must be prepared by either:

- a social worker of more than 3 years post-qualification experience who is employed by a local authority or adoption agency;

- a training social worker (on an approved course) employed by or placed with an agency who is supervised by a social worker employed by the adoption agency who is more than 3 years qualified; or

- a social worker of more than 3 years post-qualification experience who is acting on behalf of the adoption agency or local authority and is supervised by a social worker within the agency or local authority with at least 3 years post-qualification experience.[33]

6.25 A social worker is someone who is registered on the register for social workers.[34]

6.26 It is a criminal offence for someone other than the above categories of people to prepare a report on prospective adopters and is punishable on conviction by up to 6 months' imprisonment and/or a fine not exceeding level 5 on the standard scale (£5,000).[35] Adopters who pay for a report to be prepared

---

[29] AAR 2005, reg 25(3).
[30] Ibid, reg 25(6).
[31] Ibid, reg 24(7).
[32] SI 2005/1711.
[33] Restrictions on the Preparation of Adoption Reports Regulations 2005, reg (3).
[34] Care Standards Act 2000, s 56.
[35] ACA 2002, s 94(5).

or cause a report to be prepared by someone other than a prescribed person also commit an offence and can be sentenced to 6 months' imprisonment and a fine not exceeding £10,000 or both.[36]

6.27 Serious judicial concern has been expressed about privately commissioned 'home study' reports.

> 'I doubt whether any privately commissioned home study report has ever reached a conclusion unfavourable to the application. However I cannot be sure about this because it is obvious that any report that proved to be unfavourable would not be used in the overseas adoption nor placed before the court in the proceedings here. The reality is that these privately commissioned home study reports are simply sought to support, the statutory word is facilitate, the adoption application overseas. Lacking the facilities and opportunities for investigation which are available to a social worker employed by an adoption agency or local authority, the independent social worker does not have access to a whole range of information that would be relevant, and, as this case shows, important.'[37]

Procedure after report – panel recommendation and decision

6.28 Once the report is completed it is sent to the prospective adopter who has 10 working days to consider and comment on it.[38] The report and adopter's observations are then sent to the adoption agency panel. The panel may request any reasonably practical further information.[39] The panel must consider the report and other relevant information and meet with the prospective adopters.[40] The panel then makes a recommendation as to whether or not the prospective adopters are suitable to adopt a child. The recommendation may specify the number, ages and characteristics of the child(ren) the prospective adopter may be suitable to adopt.[41]

6.29 The final decision on the adopter's suitability to adopt remains with the adoption agency. It is taken independently of the panel in that no panel member may take part in the decision. If the prospective adopter is not suitable to adopt, the agency must the send the reasons for the decision, and, if different from the adoption panel's recommendation, the record of the panel's recommendation, to the prospective adopter.[42] If the potential adopters are not considered suitable they have two possible forms of redress. These also apply to prospective adopters who are ruled out at an early stage. The adoption agency must advise the unsuccessful adopters of these options and the time limits.[43]

---

[36]   ACA 2002, s 94(1)(e) and (4).
[37]   *Re C (A Minor) (Adoption: Legality)* [1999] 1 FLR 370 per Johnson J at 379–380. See also *Flintshire County Council v K* [2001] 2 FLR 476 at 487; *Re JS (Private International Adoption)* [2000] 2 FLR 638; *Re M (International Adoption Trade)* [2003] 1 FLR 1111 at [38].
[38]   AAR 2005, reg 25(8).
[39]   Ibid, reg 25(10).
[40]   Ibid, reg 26(2) and (4).
[41]   Ibid, reg 26(3).
[42]   Ibid, reg 27(4).
[43]   Ibid, reg 27(4)(c).

6.30 First, the adopters can make further representations to the adoption agency which may then refer the matter back to a panel for a fresh recommendation.[44] Any further representations must be made within 40 working days. There is no obligation on the agency to refer the matter back to the panel and the final decision still rests with the agency, although they must take into account the views of the second panel.[45]

6.31 Secondly, the prospective adopters may make representations to the Secretary of State for a review by an independent panel. Again such representations must be made within 40 days. The final decision still comes back to the adoption agency which should take into account the decision of the independent panel and inform the Secretary of State of their final decision.[46]

6.32 The above two routes are given in the alternative in the AAR 2005. There is no indication that they need to be completed sequentially. After completing one or both routes of appeal a still unsatisfied potential adopter may be able to judicially review the relevant body. Such proceedings are outside the scope of this work.

6.33 If the prospective adopter is suitable to adopt a child where s 83 applies the agency must send to the Department for Education:

- written confirmation of the decision made and any recommendation by the agency as to the number and characteristics of any adopted children;

- the report and any other documents placed before the adoption panel;

- the record of panel proceedings; and

- other relevant information that may be required by the Department for Education or relevant foreign authority.[47]

6.34 The adoption agency approval must be reviewed within a year of being granted and thereafter at yearly intervals until the adopter has visited the proposed child in the child's country of origin and confirmed that he wishes to proceed with the adoption.[48] These reviews should seek updating information and the adopter's views.[49] If the adopter is no longer considered suitable to adopt a child a report is prepared and the matter referred to the panel.[50]

---

[44]   AAR 2005, reg 27(6) and (7).
[45]   Ibid, reg 27(8)(a).
[46]   Ibid, reg 27(8)(b) and 27(10).
[47]   Ibid, reg 30.
[48]   Ibid, reg 29(1), (2).
[49]   Ibid, reg 29(3).
[50]   Ibid, reg 29(4)–(8).

Visiting child in state of origin and bringing to UK

6.35 After receiving the adoption panel recommendation but *before* visiting the child the prospective adopter must tell the adoption agency details of the child to be adopted together with any relevant information or reports. The adopter must meet with the adoption agency to discuss the adoption and the information received from the relevant foreign authority.[51]

6.36 Prior to the child's entry into the UK the prospective adopter must receive notification from the Department for Education that a certificate has been issued to the relevant foreign authority. This certificate confirms that the prospective adopter has been properly assessed and approved and that, if entry clearance is granted, the child will be allowed to remain in the UK.[52] Although the regulations state this must be received before entry into the UK, in reality the adoptive parents may be wise to wait until such certificate has been issued before visiting the child.

6.37 The prospective adopters, after their discussions with the adoption agency about the child, must visit the child in their home country. If the adoption is by a couple both must visit the child. After the visit the adopters must confirm to the adoption agency that they have met the child and wish to proceed with the adoption. They must also provide the agency with any additional reports and information received. The child's expected date of entry into the UK should also be given to the adoption agency.[53] The prospective adopter must accompany the child to the UK. If the adoption is by a couple both must accompany the child unless the adoption agency and relevant foreign authority have agreed that only one person may do so.[54]

REQUIREMENTS ONCE CHILD IS IN THE UK

6.38 Once the child is in the UK the adopter must, within 14 days, inform his local authority of the child's arrival and his intention to apply for an adoption order. If the adopter does not intend to give the child a home he must tell the local authority (for details on the procedure if this happens, see **6.46**).[55] If the adopter moves prior to the adoption order being made then the adopter must inform the local authority of his new home that he has given notification of his intention to adopt the child.[56]

6.39 The adopters are not required to give the above notification if an overseas adoption has been obtained or is to be effected.[57]

---

[51] AFER 2005, reg 4(2)(b).
[52] Ibid, reg 4(2)(a).
[53] Ibid, reg 4(2)(c) and (d).
[54] Ibid, reg 4(3).
[55] Ibid, reg 4(4).
[56] Ibid, reg 4(5).
[57] Ibid, reg 4(4).

6.40 Upon receipt of the notification from the prospective adopters the local authority has certain duties. In particular they must:

- set up a case record containing information received from the relevant foreign agency, the adoption agency (if not the local authority), the prospective adopter, entry clearance and information from the Department for Education;

- notify the adopter's GP in writing of the child's arrival into England and Wales and send a report as to the child's health;

- send notification to the local Primary Care Trust.

6.41 The child should be visited within one week of the notification and thereafter on a weekly basis until a review. The review should be held within 4 weeks and should consider the child's needs, arrangements for support services and the need for further visits. The child should be visited further within 3 months and 6-monthly thereafter. The local authority should give the adopters advice as to the child's needs, welfare and development and adoption support services.[58]

6.42 If no application for an adoption order has been made within 2 years of the adopters giving notice, the local authority must further review the case and consider the child's needs, the arrangements for the exercise of parental responsibility for the child, any immigration issues and the arrangements for meeting the child's needs.[59]

Restrictions on adoptive parents

6.43 If the child has entered the country with the intention to apply for an adoption order the adoptive parents may not change the child's surname or remove the child from the UK for more than one month.[60]

Private fostering arrangements

6.44 If the child enters the country and an overseas adoption is in the process of being made, the adopters should notify the local authority of a private fostering arrangement.[61] The local authority has a duty to 'satisfy themselves that the welfare of children who are or are proposed to be privately fostered within their area is being or will be satisfactorily safeguarded and promoted ...'.[62]

---

[58] AFER 2005, reg 5(1).
[59] AFER 2005, reg 5(3) and (4).
[60] ACA 2002, s 28(2) as amended by AFER 2005, reg 7.
[61] Private fostering as defined by the Children Act 1989, s 66.
[62] Children Act 1989, s 67(1).

6.45 The associated regulations[63] provide, amongst other things, that:

- the local authority should be notified 6 weeks prior to the start of a private fostering arrangement, or, if the arrangement has already begun, immediately;

- the local authority should visit the child's home within 7 working days and prepare a written report;

- the local authority should visit every 6 weeks for the first year of the arrangement;

- the private foster carer should inform the local authority of any change of circumstances.[64]

PLACEMENT BREAKDOWN

6.46 In non-Convention adoption cases, where ACA 2002, s 83(1) applies, placement breakdown is covered by ACA 2002, s 35 as amended by AFER 2005, reg 8.

6.47 If, after the child enters the UK, the adopters notify the local authority that they do not wish to provide the child with a home, the local authority must receive the child into their care within 7 days. The local authority must also notify the Department for Education of the prospective adopters' decision.[65]

6.48 If the adopters wish to apply to adopt the child but the local authority is of the opinion that the child should not remain with the prospective adopters, the local authority should give the prospective adopters notice of this opinion. Upon being given such notice, the prospective adopters must return the child within 7 days.[66] Failure to do so is an offence punishable on summary conviction with 3 months' imprisonment and/or a level five fine.[67] However, the requirement to return the child within 7 days does not apply if the prospective adopters have commenced court proceedings. In these circumstances, they do not have to return the child to the local authority unless the court so orders. The court proceedings need not be for an adoption order but can be for residence or special guardianship or leave to apply for such orders.[68]

---

[63] Children (Private Arrangements for Fostering) Regulations 2005, SI 2005/1533.
[64] Ibid, regs 3, 5, 7, 8 and 9.
[65] ACA 2002, s 35(1).
[66] Ibid, s 35(2).
[67] Ibid, s 35(4).
[68] Ibid, s 35(5).

Chapter 7

ADOPTIONS FROM NON-HAGUE CONVENTION COUNTRIES: LEGAL RECOGNITION

INTRODUCTION

7.1   This chapter will consider the legal and court processes involved when a child is adopted from a non-Convention Country. As stated in Chapter 6 there are two stages to adopting a child who is habitually resident in a state that is not a party to the Convention:

- first, there are the requirements adopters must comply with prior to the child entering the country and, in some cases, after the child enters; and

- second, there is the legal process of the child being adopted by the proposed adopters.

7.2   This chapter considers in detail the second stage of the process.

7.3   Under UK law, the status of an adoption order made overseas will vary according to the country in which it was made. It is therefore important to identify at the outset of any proposed adoption, the correct legal process to ensure that a valid and recognised adoption order is secured in relation to a child to whom s 83 of the Adoption and Children Act 2002 (ACA 2002) applies. There are three routes to this:

(1)   An adoption order is made in the child's home state and is recognised by virtue of being an 'overseas' adoption (also known as a designated list adoption).

(2)   An adoption order is made in the child's home state but is not recognised under UK law, in which case the prospective adopter can either apply for:

   (a)   an adoption order;
   (b)   a declaration that the foreign adoption order be recognised.

(3)   No adoption is made in the child's home state and an adoption order must be obtained through the UK courts.

7.4 The legal process above does not operate independently of the restrictions in ACA 2002, s 83(1). These restrictions state that where a person (or couple) habitually resident in the British Isles brings a child habitually resident in another country into the UK either:

- for the purpose of adopting that child; or

- within 12 months of the child being adopted by them under an external adoption;[1]

they must comply with the Adoptions with a Foreign Element Regulations 2005 (AFER 2005)[2] as detailed in Chapter 6.

7.5 It is important to note that the restrictions in this chapter and in Chapter 6 do not apply where the child is adopted outside the UK and then the adopters wait 12 months before the child is brought into the UK.

7.6 This chapter will consider the various routes through the legal process as follows:

- Overseas or Designation List adoptions
  This section will:

  - define and detail the requirements for an overseas adoption;
  - consider the impact of a breach of AFER 2005 on an overseas adoption; and
  - explain the process of registration of an overseas adoption.

- Application for an adoption order: court process
  Such an application will be needed when there is no recognised adoption in the child's home country or no order made at all in the child's home country. This section will:

  - consider when an application for an adoption order is needed;
  - detail the court process for applying for such an order; and
  - examine the issue relating to consent of birth parents and guardians when such orders are applied for.

- Applications for an adoption order: breaches of AFER 2005
  The majority of the case-law is focused on cases where adoptions have 'gone wrong' and the child is brought into the country without proper safeguards. This section will consider the implications for adopters of breaching the rules on their application for an adoption order.

- Common law declarations

---

[1]   ACA 2002, s 83(1).
[2]   SI 2005/392.

This final section will:

- consider what such declarations are and when they can be used; and
- examine the criteria applied by the courts when deciding whether or not to grant such a declaration.

OVERSEAS (ALSO KNOWN AS DESIGNATED LIST) ADOPTIONS

Definition and requirements

7.7   ACA 2002, Chapter 2 governs the status and effect of adoption orders. Under ACA 2002, s 66, for the purposes of English law, an 'overseas' adoption has the same status as an adoption order made in this jurisdiction. However, what constitutes an 'overseas adoption' for the purpose of that section is limited to adoptions which:[3]

(a)   take place in specific countries outside the British Isles in accordance with regulations;

(b)   are effected under the law of that country. Adoptions that take place under 'customary law' are excluded;[4]

(c)   are not Convention adoptions; and

(d)   at the time of the adoption the child was under 18 and unmarried.[5]

7.8   The specified countries are detailed in the Adoption (Designation of Overseas Adoptions) Order 1973.[6] In essence these are some, but not all, commonwealth countries and British Overseas Territories and other countries. These countries are:[7]

Australia	Fiji	Lesotho	Seychelles
Austria	Finland	Luxembourg	Singapore
Bahamas	France (including Reunion, Guadeloupe and French Guyana)	Malawi	South Africa

---

[3]   ACA 2002, s 87.
[4]   Adoption (Designation of Overseas Adoptions) Order 1973, SI 1973/19, reg 3(3).
[5]   Adoption (Designation of Overseas Adoptions) Order 1973, SI 1973/19, reg 3(3).
[6]   SI 1973/19.
[7]   NB: parts of the Adoption (Designation of Overseas Adoptions) Order 1973 are outdated: for example in relation to Germany only 'West Germany and Land Berlin' are included; 'Southern 'Rhodesia (now Zimbabwe)' is stated as a country and 'Yugoslavia' is listed as one country.

Barbados	Germany	Malaysia	Spain (including Balearics and Canary Isles)
Belgium	Ghana	Malta	Swaziland
Bermuda	Gibraltar	Mauritius	Sweden
Botswana	Greece	Montserrat	Switzerland
British Honduras	Guyana	Netherlands	Tanzania
British Virgin Islands	Hong Kong	New Zealand	Tango
Canada	Iceland	Nigeria	Trinidad and Tobago
Cayman Islands	Ireland	Norway	Turkey
China	Israel	Pitcairn	USA
Cyprus (the Republic of)	Italy	Portugal (including the Azores and Madeira)	Zambia
Denmark (including Greenland and the Faros)	Jamaica	St Christopher, Nevis and Anguilla	Yugoslavia
Dominica	Kenya	St Vincent	

7.9   The adopters may prove the fact that an overseas adoption has taken place by producing a certified copy of an entry made in any public register of adoptions of the overseas country or a certificate signed by an authorised person.[8] Whilst these are the two specific forms of proof specifically detailed in the regulations, this does not prevent the adopters proving the adoption in any other way.[9]

Breaches of AFER 2005 and overseas adoption

7.10   ACA 2002, s 83(1) applies to overseas adoptions and therefore prospective adopters who bring a child into the country within 12 months of the child being adopted under an overseas order must comply with the requirements of AFER 2005.

7.11   When the adoptive parents apply at the relevant diplomatic post for entry clearance in order to bring the child into the UK, the Entry Clearance

---

[8]   Adoption (Designation of Overseas Adoptions) Order 1973, reg 4(1).
[9]   Ibid, reg 4(3).

Officer will liaise with the Department for Education or other relevant authority to ascertain that the adoption processes have been adhered to prior to issuing entry clearance.[10]

Registration

7.12 If such an adoption is effected overseas the adopters may wish to register the adoption in the UK. However, this is not required of them. Overseas adoptions are registered with the Registrar General if he is satisfied he has sufficient particulars of the adoption.[11]

7.13 The Adoption Register has existed since 1927 and is not a publicly searchable record. Adopted children and their families can obtain a certificate of adoption following registration and, once over 18, adoptive children can use the register to obtain details of their birth parents.

7.14 The application to register is made by the adoptive parents, any other person with parental responsibility or, if over 18, the child.[12] The application must be in writing and signed.[13] At the time of the application the adoptive parents (both if a couple) must be habitually resident in England and Wales.[14] The applicant must provide details regarding the child, his birth parents and the adoptive parents. If not all details are known (for example an abandoned child's birth parents) those that are known should be stated.[15] In the case of an overseas adoption the date of the overseas adoption and evidence of the adoption should also be provided. The evidence is the same as required by the Adoption (Designation of Overseas Adoptions) Order 1973.[16] Any documents not in English should be translated to include the name and address of the person translating and a statement of truth.[17]

Invalidation of overseas adoptions

7.15 The High Court can determine that an overseas adoption is invalid on the basis that the order is contrary to public policy or that the authority overseas making the order was not competent so to do.[18] However, the overseas state may also retain powers to make a decision revoking or annulling an overseas adoption.[19] Such a decision can only be challenged in the High Court

---

[10] UK Border Agency, *Intercountry Adoption and the Immigration Rules, 1 No 2008*. For further details on the immigration rules see Chapter 9.
[11] ACA 2002, Sch 1, para (3).
[12] Adopted Children and Adoption Contact Registers Regulations 2005, SI 2005/924, reg 4.
[13] Ibid, reg 5.
[14] Ibid, reg 3.
[15] Ibid, reg 5(3).
[16] Ibid, reg 5(2)(b).
[17] Ibid, reg 5(4).
[18] ACA 2002, s 89(2) and (3).
[19] Ibid, s 91(1)(b).

on the grounds that it is contrary to public policy or the body making the decision was not competent to make the decision.[20]

7.16 An application for annulment is made on Form A63 to the High Court. It can be made by the adopter, child, birth parent, local authority, an adoption agency, the Home Secretary or any other person. The respondents are the birth parent, adopter, adoption agency and local authority.[21]

APPLICATION FOR ADOPTION ORDER: COURT PROCESS

When an adoption order is needed

7.17 The adoptive parents will need to make an application for an adoption order under ACA 2002, s 44 in the following circumstances:

- no adoption order has been made in the child's home country;

- an order has been made in the child's home country but it is not recognised by the English courts as the country is not in the list of 'overseas countries';

- an order has been made in an overseas country but it is not recognised as it is not effected under the law of that country (for example under customary law).

7.18 In some cases the adopters may be able to apply for a declaration of adoptive status. The circumstances in which this is appropriate are considered at **7.74** ff.

Court process

Preconditions

7.19 There are certain preconditions to any applications.

(1) Placement of child:

    (a) if all the requirements of AFER 2005 are met, the child must have lived with the prospective adopters for a period of 6 months prior to the application;[22]

---

[20] ACA 2002, s 88(2), (4).
[21] FPR 2010, SI 2010/2955, r 14.3.
[22] ACA 2002, s 42(5) as amended by AFER 2005, reg 9(1).

(b)   if the requirements of AFER 2005 have not been met, the child must have lived with the prospective adopters for a period of 12 months prior to the application.[23]

(2)   Residence/domicile:

(a)   at least one of the adoptive parents must be domiciled in the United Kingdom; or

(b)   the adopters (both if a couple) must have been habitually resident in the United Kingdom for a year prior to the application.

Application

7.20   The procedure for applications is governed by the Family Procedure Rules 2010 (FPR 2010), Part 14. The application is made on Form A60 which is available, along with explanatory notes, on the HM Court and Tribunal service website.[24] The adopters may need to attach birth, death and marriage certificates to the form. These must be certified copies and not simply photocopies.

7.21   Single adopters who are married/civil partners but not divorced from their spouse/civil partner will need to satisfy the court that they have either: separated permanently from their spouse/civil partner, or that the spouse/civil partner cannot be found or is incapable of making an application to adopt.

7.22   Details regarding the child's parents and guardian(s) and their attitude to the adoption are required. Issues around the consent of the child's birth parents and any guardian can cause difficulties within proceedings. These are considered at **7.32** ff.

7.23   Attached to the form should be various documents including:

- certified copies of the child's birth certificate, any abandonment certificate and any documents proving an adoption in the child's home state;

- a medical report on the health of the child and applicants;

- notification from the Department for Education that the 'certificate of eligibility' was issued;

- photo page and entry stamp page from the child's passport (photocopy permissible); and

- photo page and any visa/entry stamp from the adopter's passport (photocopy permissible).

---

[23]   ACA 2002, s 42(5) as amended by AFER 2005, reg 9(2).
[24]   http://hmctscourtfinder.justice.gov.uk/HMCTS/FormFinder.do.

7.24   The respondents to the proceedings are:[25]

- each parent with parental responsibility;

- any guardian of a child;

- person in whose favour there is provision for contact;

- the adoption agency;

- the child.

7.25   In intercountry adoptions the issue of who has parental responsibility and who can be considered to be a guardian of the child can be contentious and may require expert evidence on foreign law. This is considered at **7.32 ff.**

Where to issue?

7.26   If s 83(1) does not apply then the application should be issued in a county court that is an adoption centre.[26]

7.27   If ACA 2002, s 83(1) applies and all the requirements of AFER 2005 have been met then the application should be issued in a county court that is an intercountry adoption centre.[27] There are 13 such courts:[28]

Birmingham County Court	Exeter County Court	Nottingham County Court
Bournemouth County Court	Leeds County Court	Portsmouth County Court
Bristol County Court	Liverpool County Court	Wrexham County Court
Cardiff County Court	Manchester County Court	
Chester County Court	Newcastle-upon-Tyne County Court	

7.28   If ACA 2002, s 83(1) applies but there have been breaches of the regulations the application should be issued in the High Court.[29] If the case has other complicating features it should also be started in the High Court.

7.29   In all cases the application should be listed before a District Judge of the Principal Registry of the Family Division, a Circuit Judge or a High Court

---

[25]   FPR 2010, r 14.3.
[26]   President's Guidance, 24 November 2008, para 6.
[27]   Ibid, para 4.
[28]   Allocation and Transfer of Proceedings Order 2008, SI 2008/2836, Sch (1).
[29]   Practice Direction 3 November 2008 [2009] 1 FLR 365, para 5.1(4).

Judge. Recorders may hear intercountry adoption cases if they are authorised to do so by the Family Division Liaison Judge. Some local arrangements may allow District Judges to hear directions.[30]

First directions hearing and reports

7.30 In cases were s 83(1) applies the court will list a first directions appointment. This hearing will consider:[31]

(1)   the timetable for reports and evidence;

(2)   who is a party to the proceedings, including whether the Official Solicitor and Home Office should be involved;

(3)   directions regarding service on parents;

(4)   whether AFER 2005 has been complied with and, if not, whether the case should be transferred to the High Court;

(5)   translation of documents;

(6)   whether the prospective adopters need to file affidavit evidence concerning the child's entry into the UK.

7.31 The local authority will be directed to file a report in the proceedings.[32] This report must include detailed information about the child and the adoptive parents. In addition, the report must also consider specific issues that arise in intercountry cases. These include: the child's knowledge of their racial and cultural origins; confirmation that the requirements of AFER 2005 have been complied with; and information regarding the child from their home country.

Consent of birth parents and guardians

7.32 In cases where s 83 applies, particular difficulties can arise with the issues of consent and service. These stem from questions of whose consent is required and how it was obtained in the child's home country. Due to the circumstances and, often, the distances involved in intercountry cases, these issues can make adoption applications lengthy and complicated. While each case will be decided according to its own facts, the issue of consent has been the subject of a substantial body of case-law which is explored in the following paragraphs.

---

[30]   President's Guidance, 3 November 2008, para (8).
[31]   FPR 2010, r 14.8(1) and PD 14B.
[32]   Pursuant to ACA 2002, s 43. This report must comply with FPR 2010, PD 14C.

Who should consent to the adoption?

7.33   ACA 2002, s 47 ('conditions for making adoption orders') states:

> '(1)   An adoption order may not be made if the child has a parent or guardian
>   unless one of the following three conditions is met; but this section is subject
>   to section 52 (parental etc consent);
> (2)   The first condition is that, in the case of each parent or guardian of the
>   child, the court is satisfied:
>   (a)   that the parent or guardian consents to the making of the adoption
>   order;
>   (b)   ...
>   (c)   that the parent's or guardian's consent should be dispensed with.'

7.34   ACA 2002, s 52(5) states that 'consent' means: 'consent given
unconditionally and with full understanding of what is involved ...'.

7.35   For the purpose of ss 52 and 47 a 'parent' is someone with parental
responsibility for the child.[33]

7.36   The court will need to ascertain whether the consent of the child's birth
parents is required: ie do they have parental responsibility for the child.

7.37   In *Re AMR (Adoption: Procedure)*[34] a Polish great grandmother had
obtained orders in Poland depriving the parents of responsibility for the child
and appointing her as a guardian for the child. Expert evidence was obtained
on Polish law as to the effect of these orders. Johnson J stated:[35]

> 'Here we have orders made by a competent court in respect of parties and a child
> domiciled and resident within its jurisdiction. It should be noted that Poland is a
> Hague Convention Country and, indeed, has both signed and ratified the Hague
> Convention in respect of intercountry adoption. Both judicial comity, judicial
> authority and, it seems to me, common sense, points to the fact that this court
> should recognise the Polish orders for the purposes of these proceedings ...
>
> It seems to me that I have to look closely at the effect of the orders depriving the
> parents of parental responsibility and decide whether that also had the effect of
> depriving them of what, under English law, would have been their parental
> responsibility.'

7.38   Johnson J considered the expert evidence to show the Polish concept of
parental responsibility to be similar to the English concept. He therefore
concluded that the birth parents did not have parental responsibility and thus
their consent was not required.

---

[33]   ACA 2002, s 52(6).
[34]   [1999] 2 FLR 807.
[35]   [1999] 2 FLR 807 at 813E–F.

7.39 In intercountry cases the child may have been abandoned and parental rights given by an institution. A declaration of abandonment may, after relevant expert evidence is considered, be enough to deprive a birth parent of parental responsibility.[36] In these circumstances their consent is also not required.

Guardians

7.40 ACA 2002, s 144 defines guardians as having the same meaning as the Children Act 1989 (CA 1989) and including special guardians. CA 1989, s 5 makes specific provision for the appointment of guardians (distinct from 'guardians ad litem' in Children Act proceedings) and for guardians so appointed to have parental responsibility for the child.[37]

7.41 In intercountry adoption cases it is not uncommon for an official, institution or authority to be called the child's 'guardian'. In some cases the consent of this 'guardian' will be required to adoption. Failure to properly inform the 'guardian' of the proceedings may result in the adoption being set aside. In a case involving a Bosnian child adopted by an English couple who were aware of the existence of a 'guardian' in Bosnia, it was stated:

> 'The guardian was appointed by the Bosnian government to protect the interests of a Bosnian child in England and the English system of justice has failed to give him the notice he was entitled to about the intention of the [adopters to] make the child a member of their family and cut the link with her natural family ... The welfare of the child herself dictated that proper steps should be taken to balance the natural family with the prospective adoptive family.'[38]

7.42 In *Re K* the definition of 'guardian' was not further considered. *Re AGN*[39] endorsed a general, wide definition of guardian in the earlier decision of *Re AMR*. In *Re AGN* Cazelet J stated that:

> 'My conclusion is that a foreign guardian, invested with rights under a foreign order recognised under English law, is capable of being a guardian whose agreement to an adoption order needs either to be given or dispensed with.'[40]

7.43 In *Re J (Adoption: Consent of Foreign Public Authority)*,[41] Charles J echoed the above and made clear the purpose of the court's considerations of whether or not a person is guardian:

---

[36] *Re AGN (A Child) (Adoption: Foreign Guardianship)* [2000] 2 FLR 431. This case was decided prior to the Convention coming into effect in the United Kingdom and therefore it was not automatically recognised as it would have been had the order been made after June 2003.
[37] CA 1989, s 5(6).
[38] *Re K (Adoption and Wardship)* [1997] 2 FLR 221.
[39] [2000] 2 FLR 431.
[40] [2000] 2 FLR 431 at 442C.
[41] [2002] EWHC 766 (Fam), [2002] 2 FLR 618.

'In my view that purpose is to ensure that the consent of the appropriate persons is either given to the adoption order, or is dispensed with, and those persons are identified as the persons with parental responsibility (but excluding a local authority who is named in a care order).'[42]

7.44 Charles J developed the court's approach to whether or not a body or person was a foreign 'guardian' further. First, the court should consider the extent to which the 'guardian's' duties, rights and responsibilities equate to a person who has parental responsibility and whose consent is required for an adoption order. Second, whether, having regard to the purpose of the relevant parts of the legislation, whether in all the circumstances the 'guardian's' consent should be given or dispensed with, before an adoption order is made.[43]

7.45 *Re J* concerned the question of whether the Jordanian Minster of Social Development or a public authority in Jordan was a child's guardian. Charles J decided in the context of the case neither should be treated as guardians as their position and responsibilities were analogous to a local authority in care proceedings and not a guardian.[44]

7.46 However, it should be noted that the above case-law was decided under the now repealed Adoption and Children Act 1976. The 'definitions' section of that Act (s 72) was prefaced by the caveat 'In this Act, *unless the context otherwise requires*, [guardian] shall mean ...' (emphasis supplied). The definition section of the ACA 2002 has no such 'disclaimer'. Whether the courts will continue to apply such a wide definition of 'guardian' has not yet been tested.

Consent obtained – nature of consent

7.47 In many intercountry cases the birth parents and in particular the birth mother may have consented to the adoption of their child. If there is an order in the child's home state (even if such order is not recognised by English law) the birth parent's consent may well have been required.

7.48 However, consent to an unrecognised adoption or advance consent to an intended adoption in this jurisdiction, given otherwise than in accordance with the relevant provisions of the ACA 2002, is not necessarily sufficient for the purpose of any adoption proceedings brought under ACA 2002. Following the decision in *Re G (Foreign Adoption: Consent)*,[45] precisely what was consented to needs to be examined. In *Re G* a Paraguayan mother consented to an adoption order being made in Paraguay. She was aware that the prospective adopters were an English couple. However, adoptions in Paraguay had different legal consequences from those in England, in particular, the mother's legal relationship to the child was not extinguished and the adoption was revocable.

---

[42]   [2002] EWHC 766 (Fam), [2002] 2 FLR 618 at [30].
[43]   [2002] EWHC 766 (Fam), [2002] 2 FLR 618 at [31].
[44]   [2002] EWHC 766 (Fam), [2002] 2 FLR 618 at [38].
[45]   [1995] 2 FLR 534.

In these circumstances the court declined to hold that the mother had consented to an English adoption and ordered that she be served and her consent sought via the British Embassy in Paraguay.

7.49 A number of subsequent cases have sought to distinguish themselves from *Re G* and the conclusion that valid parental agreement must include specific consent to an English adoption has been doubted, albeit obiter.[46]

- In *Re WM (Adoption: Non-patrial)*[47] an El Salvadorian mother consented to an adoption in El Salvador. However, she was aware that there may be a further adoption in England and the consequences of such an adoption were explained to her. The consent included provision for this. It was held that the mother's further consent was not required.

- *Re C (A Child) (Foreign Adoption: Natural Mother's Consent: Service)*.[48] In *Re C* the child was 12 and had lived with the prospective adopters for over 10 years. The birth mother had consented unconditionally to an adoption order being made in Papua New Guinea and to her parental rights being extinguished. She was aware that the adopters were English and had met the adoptive mother. Again it was held that her further consent was not required as the consent already given was 'sufficient to embrace [the UK] adoption application'.

7.50 How and when consent was obtained may also be relevant. ACA 2002 states that a birth mother cannot give her consent to adoption within 6 weeks of giving birth. *Re A (Adoption of a Russian Child)*[49] concerned a birth mother whose consent to adoption was obtained only 2 days after birth. Expert evidence on Russian law stated it would be illegal to contact the birth mother and to do so would place the person doing so at risk of proceedings for damages. The court decided to dispense with the birth mother's consent rather than seek to confirm her consent.

Service

7.51 The question of how and when birth parents should be served with proceedings may arise regardless of the issue of consent. The general rule is that where a parent is believed to hold parental responsibility under the law of another state, they should be given notice of the proceedings.[50] The court has the power to dispense with service upon the parents even if parental responsibility is held. In *Re A* service was dispensed with as it was not possible, legally, under the law of her native country (Russia) to contact the mother.[51] In *Re C*, despite the fact a (possibly out-of-date) telephone number existed for the

---

[46]   *Re A (Adoption of a Russian Child)* [2000] 1 FLR 539.
[47]   [1997] 1 FLR 132.
[48]   [2006] 1 FLR 318.
[49]   [2000] 1 FLR 539.
[50]   FPR 2010, r 14.4.
[51]   [2000] 1 FLR 539.

mother, service was dispensed with due to the length of time since her original consent to the adoption and the concern that service of the proceedings might cause difficulties for the mother within her home community.[52]

APPLICATION FOR AN ADOPTION ORDER – BREACHES OF AFER

7.52   The most difficult and complex issues arise in cases where a child has entered the country illegally (ie in breach of ACA 2002, ss 83(1), (4) and (5) and the associated regulations) and is living with his prospective adopters. In these circumstances the court has to balance the often competing considerations of the public policy of discouraging unregulated international movement of children and the welfare of the child concerned. The courts will not sacrifice the best interests of an individual child upon the altar of public policy.

7.53   The public policy case was clearly enunciated by Parliamentary Assembly of the Council of Europe on 26 January 2000 in Recommendation 1443 (2000) – *International Adoption: Respecting Children's Rights*:[53]

> 'The purpose of international adoption must be to provide children with a mother and father in a way that respects their rights, and not to enable foreign parents to satisfy their wish for a child at any price ...
>
> the current transformation of international adoption into nothing short of a market regulated by the capitalist laws of supply and demand, and characterised by a one-way flow of children from poor states or states in transition to developed countries.'

Welfare v public policy

7.54   One consequence of the detailed system laid down in AFER 2005 is that those wishing to adopt a foreign child are subjected to the same scrutiny and assessment as those wishing to adopt domestically. In many cases where the regulations are breached the prospective adopters have been rejected by adoption agencies as adopters for British children or would not have been approved, had such an application been made. For example the prospective adoptive mother in *Re C (Adoption: Legality)*[54] was rejected by two different local authorities and an adoption agency before (successfully) adopting a Guatemalan child.[55]

> 'the Applicant has sought to achieve her objective [of adoption] in disregard of the legal processes laid down by Parliament for the protection of child ... There are

---

[52]   [2006] 1 FLR 318.
[53]   Quoted in *Singh v Entry Clearance Officer (New Delhi)* [2004] EWCA Civ 1075, [2005] 1 FLR 308.
[54]   [1999] 1 FLR 370.
[55]   See also *Flintshire County Council v K* [2001] 2 FLR 476.

some 300 overseas adoptions every year conducted in accordance with the proper procedures. There are between 75 and 100 which are made after disregard of those procedures. Most of those will be by applicants who have been previously rejected as suitable for the adoption of a British child, yet ask the court for an adoption order in respect of an overseas child in disregard of the safeguard laid down to protect a British child.'[56]

7.55 The reason that prospective adopters must undergo a rigorous assessment process before they are allowed to adopt a child is to ensure that children who have already suffered the misfortune of not being raised by their birth parents are only placed with new parents who are suitable to care for them. It is plainly undesirable to have in place a system which condones the adoption of a foreign child by a person who has been, or would have been, deemed unsuitable to adopt a child under the Adoption Agency Regulations 2005 (AAR 2005).[57] This desire to avoid a 'two tier' system in which lower standards are applied in relation to the adoption of foreign children than would apply to a child habitually resident in the British Isles is a strong one. It is not unusual for children who are the subject of overseas adoptions to have particular care needs arising out of their early childhood experiences, for example children who have become institutionalised or who have lost parents in traumatic circumstances. In addition such children may need help acclimatising to British culture and there may be transracial issues to consider.

7.56   However, once the fact of such breaches is established how is the court to approach them?

'If such breaches are to count for nothing, at least nothing of any practical consequence, what one might ask is the point of maintaining the authorised procedures.'[58]

7.57   In *Re X (A Child)*[59] Munby J (as he then was) gave detailed consideration to the welfare of the child versus the public policy regarding international adoption.[60] He extracted the following principles from previous case-law:

'(i)   public policy is relevant to welfare and that policy includes the attitude of the country of origin to adoption; ...
(ii)   dishonesty/subterfuge are relevant to welfare; ...
(iii)   where, after analysis, welfare and public policy point towards differing outcomes for the child, then welfare will prevail; put bluntly ... welfare trumps public policy ...

---

[56]   *Re C (Adoption: Legality)* [1999] 1 FLR 370 at 376G per Johnson J.
[57]   SI 2005/389.
[58]   *Re C (Adoption: Legality)* [1999] 1 FLR 370 at 318.
[59]   [2009] EWHC 498 (Fam).
[60]   [2009] EWHC 498 (Fam) at [112]–[122].

the court must not refuse to make any order which is otherwise required by the dictates of X's welfare so as in any way to punish or to penalise the "parents". Nor must it be used here to deter others from acting in a similar vein whilst of course offering such people no possible encouragement'.[61]

Case-law

7.58 A discussion of cases where a child has entered the country in breach of the regulations and the final outcome follows. The factual backgrounds of the cases are diverse and the results turn on the facts. However, some factors emerge as relevant when the court is deciding how to approach the application of adopters when a child is placed illegally. These are:

(1)   the nature and extent of the breaches of AFER 2005;

(2)   the length of time the child has been with the adopters;

(3)   the alternatives available for care of the child;

(4)   the local authorities' involvement and position;

(5)   other concerns about the adopters' parenting.

The nature and extent of the breaches of the regulations

7.59 AFER 2005 are very detailed regulations and it is possible for otherwise conscientious adopters to inadvertently breach aspects of them. In these cases the court may look leniently on such breaches. In *Re N (Children) (Recognition of Foreign Adoption Orders)*[62] the court excused unintentional breaches of the regulations and found a way for the adoption to proceed by making a declaration of status for an otherwise unrecognised Indian adoption.

7.60 At the other end of the spectrum are adopters who deliberately breach the regulations in order to frustrate the intentions of Parliament so that, at final hearing, the court will be presented with a *fait accompli* and be unable to remove the child. In *Re R (No 1) (Intercountry Adoption)*[63] the prospective adopters deliberately sought to delay the adoption proceedings. They prevaricated before informing the local authority of the presence of the child; delayed in giving information to help the local authority and the court; and failed to provide translations of some highly relevant documents. The court dismissed their application for an adoption order and instead made the child a ward of court. More recently in *Re X (A Child) Northumberland CC v Z*,[64] the prospective adopters sought to exploit a perceived 'loophole' in the law and bring a Kenyan child to the UK as 'privately fostered', deceiving both the

---

[61]   [2009] EWHC 498 (Fam) at [119] and [120].
[62]   [2008] EWHC 403, sub nom *D v D* [2008] 1 FLR 1475.
[63]   [1999] 1 FLR 1014.
[64]   [2009] EWHC 498 (Fam).

Kenyan and British authorities. The child was concealed from the local authority and other agencies (including not being registered with a doctor).

7.61 Both *Re R* and *Re X* involved serious and prolonged deceit which continued into the court proceedings. In neither case was the adoption order made.

7.62 The importance of breaches of the regulations is twofold:

(1) public policy: the importance of encouraging compliance and not 'rewarding' breaches of the regulations;

(2) welfare: the effect of the adopter's deceit on the child and their ability to meet the child's needs in the future. The process of deceiving the authorities may place the child's welfare at risk.[65] In addition the prospective adopters' lying and disregard for the truth may have implications for their ability to meet the child's needs in future. How will they tell the child about his or her origins? How can the court be confident that relevant facts are not being withheld from the local authority and other professionals?

Length of time child has lived with proposed adopters

7.63 A further concern of the court is the issue of delay. The length of time taken to investigate such cases can mean that it is impossible to then remove a settled and attached child from the prospective adopters. In *Re R (No 1) (Intercountry Adoption)*[66] it took 4½ years for the case to come to a final hearing. Following this case Bracewell J set out detailed guidance for public bodies, including the court, to minimise such delay.[67] In *Re K (Adoption: Wardship)*[68] the court noted many missed chances to return a child to her birth family. By the time the case got to a full hearing it was simply too damaging to the child to do so.

7.64 By contrast in *Flintshire County Council v K*[69] the children (twins) were with their prospective adopters for a period of only 16 days before the local authority sought an emergency protection order.[70] In *Re X (A Child)*, the child was with the proposed adopters for 9 months before the local authority, alerted by an anonymous referral to a 'trafficked child' removed her under an emergency protection order. In neither case were the child(ren) ultimately returned to their adopters.

---

[65]   *Flintshire County Council v K* [2001] 2 FLR 476 at 496.
[66]   [1999] 1 FLR 1014.
[67]   See also *Re R (Intercountry Adoptions: Practice)* [1999] 1 FLR 1042. Much of the guidance regarding the court's role is incorporated in FPR 2010, PD 14B.
[68]   [1997] 2 FLR 221.
[69]   [2001] 2 FLR 476.
[70]   This case received widespread publicity as the prospective adopters gave interviews to various media regarding their 'internet twins'.

Available alternatives to adoption

7.65 Upon being given notice of the proceedings the child's birth parents, guardian, state of origin or adoption agency may seek his return.

7.66 In circumstances where the child is placed provisionally the adoption agency may retain rights in relation to the child and seek the return of the child if presented with, previously unrevealed, negative information regarding the proposed adopters.[71]

7.67 Even if a birth family is not 'successful' in having the child returned their involvement may prevent the court making an adoption order. Instead the child may be made a ward of court with care and control to the proposed adopters and contact to the extended family. The court may keep control of the proceedings to allow the situation to be monitored further.[72]

7.68 The court, where no birth parents can be located, may invite the child's state of origin to intervene in the proceedings. The court will attach importance to the child's welfare being decided in his home state. This must be balanced against the realities of the child's situation:

> 'On the one hand M has powerful interests in being brought up by her birth parents and, let me make this clear, in being brought up as an American in the country of her birth and nationality. On the other hand, the fact is that she has spent all but the first ten days of her short life not in the United States of America but in the UK.'[73]

7.69 When assessing the claim of the child's state of origin to have the child returned, the court should not assess the child's welfare purely through 'Western' eyes:

> 'When considering welfare in an international case such as this, the children's circumstances and welfare should not be viewed from an entirely domestic perspective. X is a Kenyan child and ... Kenyan concepts of welfare are relevant ...
>
> the court cannot automatically apply Western standards and concepts of welfare given the international nature of this case and Kenyan concepts of welfare. The views and principles of the [General Republic of Kenya] as to what constitute or at least influence the best interests of the child are part of X's welfare. Although it must apply English law, the court ... should take an international perspective when considering X's background and future.'[74]

---

[71] *Re JS (Private International Adoption)* [2000] 2 FLR 638.
[72] *Re R (Intercountry Adoptions: Practice) (No 1)* [1999] 1 FLR 1014; *Re K (Adoption and Wardship)* [1997] 2 FLR 221.
[73] *Re M (Adoption: International Adoption Trade)* [2003] EWHC 219, [2003] 1 FLR 1111 at [94].
[74] *Re X (A Child)* [2008] EWHC 1324 at [105] and [108].

7.70   However, in some cases the only options before the court may be a known placement with the (perhaps inadequate) adopters; or the removal of the child into foster care to be placed again for adoption.

Local authority involvement and position

7.71   Local authorities are sometimes criticised for not carrying out their duties to investigate and report in these cases fully and swiftly.[75] In *Re R (Inter-Country Adoptions: Practice)*,[76] local authorities were given the following guidance in international adoption cases:[77]

'(1)   Upon being notified of the child's presence, the local authority should strictly comply with their duties under s 67 Children Act 1967.

(2)   The matter should be considered at director level and allocated to a member of staff with particular experience. Progress reports should be submitted to the director.

(3)   Legal advice should be sought within the legal department.

(4)   The local authority should immediately attempt to contact the natural parents of the child and ascertain their views ... If the local authority is unable to do so, they should ask the British Embassy in the parents' country of origin ...

(5)   In the event that the local authority is not satisfied in respect of the welfare issues and adoption proceedings have not been started, then proceedings under Parts IV and V Children Act 1989 should be considered and, if appropriate, instituted forthwith in order to bring the case urgently before the court.

(6)   If it appears to the local authority that the natural parents do not consent to the child remaining in the UK then the local authority should immediately inform the Department of [Education] and the Home Office of that fact.'[78]

7.72   If the local authority acts swiftly to remove the child it can prevent a *'fait accompli'* adoption order being made.

Other concerns re prospective adoptions

7.73   There may be other concerns regarding the prospective adopters which the court will need to take into account when carrying out the welfare test in ACA 2002, s 1. These are over and above the issues that arise from any deception in bringing the child into the jurisdiction. These concerns will clearly vary between cases.

---

[75]   *Re R (No 1) (Intercountry Adoption)* [1999] 1 FLR 1014; *Re K (Adoption and Wardship)* [1997] 2 FLR 221.

[76]   [1999] 1 FLR 1042.

[77]   NB: *Re R (Inter-Country Adoptions: Practice)* was decided prior to AFER 2005 and the Children (Private Arrangements for Fostering) Regulations 1991, SI 1991/2050 coming into force and the guidance should be read in light of the more recent regulations.

[78]   [1999] 1 FLR 1042, per Bracewell J at 1049–1050.

RECOGNITION AT COMMON LAW AND DECLARATIONS

7.74 Historically, recognition at common law was one of the few routes available to adoptive parents who effected an adoption outside England and Wales. This route is preserved by ACA 2002, s 66(1)(e) which states that 'adoption' includes an adoption 'recognised by the law of England and Wales and effected under the law of any other country'. Section 66(1)(e) therefore provides a statutory basis for the recognition of foreign adoptions at common law. Adoptees who wish for their adoption to be so recognised can apply for a declaration under Family Law Act 1986, s 57 that they are or are not the adopted child of their adopters.[79] The procedure for doing this is detailed below.

7.75 Given the comprehensive statutory schemes now in place, the need for common law recognition will be limited. Situations where it may be used include:

(1)   an adoptee over the age of 18 seeking to affirm his status where the adoption order is not otherwise recognised;

(2)   an overseas adoption made under 'customary law';

(3)   an adoption order made in a country that is not an 'overseas' country.

7.76 The cases where it may be theoretically possible to apply for a declaration are therefore quite wide. In most cases it would also be open to the adoptive parents to apply for an adoption order. There is little guidance on which process, if both are available to choose. Nonetheless, it is suggested that, as there is a detailed statutory scheme in place, the application of the common law jurisdiction is limited. In particular it would run counter to the strong public policy motivations for the statutory scheme (AFER 2005 and ACA 2002) if it were possible to avoid the stringent statutory requirements by seeking common law recognition.

7.77 In at least one case the courts have used common law recognition and declarations where the requirements of AFER 2005 have not been met.[80] However, in *Re N*,[81] the breaches were minor and entirely innocent. It is doubtful that the courts would allow prospective adopters to use common law recognition to subvert the strict requirements of AFER 2005 and ACA 2002 s 83. Such a 'loophole' would run counter to the public policy reasons for having such a stringent scheme.

---

[79]   Family Law Act 1986, s 57(1)(a) and 57(2).
[80]   *Re N (Recognition of Foreign Adoption Order)* [2010] 1 FLR 1102.
[81]   [2008] EWHC 403, sub nom *D v D* [2008] 1 FLR 1475.

7.78   It is therefore suggested that in the majority of cases an application for an adoption order will be the most appropriate course of adoptive parents to take.

Criteria for common law recognition

7.79   The starting point for the court's recognition of foreign adopters at common law is found in the dicta of James LJ in *Re Goodman's Trusts*:[82]

> '... the family relation is at the foundation of all society, and it would appear almost an axiom that the family relation, once duly constituted by the law of any civilised country, should be respected and acknowledged by every other member of the great community nations ...'

7.80   The matter was given its fullest consideration in *Re Valentine's Settlement*.[83] *Re Valentine's* concerned the status in English law of two adopted children in the context of a dispute regarding whether they were the proper beneficiaries of a family trust. Their adoption order was effected in South African but the adopter domiciled in Southern Rhodesia (as it then was).

7.81   Giving the lead judgment, Denning MR stated:

> 'But when is the status of adoption duly constituted. Clearly it is so when it is constituted in another country in similar circumstances as we claim for ourselves. Our courts should recognise a jurisdiction which mutatis mutandis they claim for themselves ... We claim jurisdiction when the adopting parents are domiciled in this country and the child is resident here. So also, out of the comity of nations, we should recognise an adoption order made by another country when the adopting parents are domiciled there and the child is resident there ...

> Apart from international comity we reach the same result on principle. When a court of any country makes an adoption order for an infant child, it does two things: (1) it destroys the legal relationship theretofore existing between the child and its natural parents, be it legitimate or illegitimate; (2) it creates the legal relationship of parent and child between the child and its adopting parents, making it their legitimate child. It creates a new status in both, namely, the status of parent and child. Now it has long been settled that questions affecting status are determined by the law of the domicile. The new status of parent and child, in order to be recognised everywhere, must be validly created by the law of the domicile of the adopting parent. You do not look to the domicile of the child: for that has no separate domicile of its own. It takes its parents' domicile. You look to the parents' domicile only. If you find that a legitimate relationship of parent and child has been validly created, then the status so created should be universally recognised throughout the civilised world provided always that there is nothing contrary to public policy in recognising it.'[84]

---

[82]   [1881] 17 ChD 266 at 296.
[83]   [1965] Ch 831.
[84]   [1965] Ch 831 at 842B–G.

7.82 Dankwerts LJ, somewhat reluctantly, followed Denning MR that for an foreign adoption order to be valid at common law 'if the adoptive parents are regarded by the law of this country as domiciled there' but doubted whether there was any requirement that the child be 'ordinarily resident' in the same country.[85] This requirement was based on the conditions precedent for an adoption in England at the time of the decision in *Re Valentine's*. ACA 2002 no longer attaches any condition to the child's residence or domicile; it is doubtful that there is any need for a child to be ordinarily resident in the jurisdiction where the order is made.[86]

7.83 In a dissenting opinion whose force was acknowledged,[87] Salmon LJ dissented from the requirement of domicile. He struggled with the issue of the conflict between the domicile of the adoptive parents and adoptive child:

> 'Whilst it is of course a principle of English law that it will not recognise the right of a foreign court to impose a change of status upon anyone domiciled within its jurisdiction, it is equally a principle of English law generally to recognise the right of a foreign court to make an order changing the status of anyone over whom it has jurisdiction. What happens, as here, when these two principles conflict? When the adopted child and its natural parents are domiciled within the jurisdiction of the foreign court and the adoptive father is not domiciled within its jurisdiction? There is no escape from choosing between the two principles, no escape is possible.'[88]

7.84 Salmon LJ concluded that:

> 'Adoption – providing there are proper safeguards – is greatly for the benefit of the adopted child and of the adoptive parents, and also, I think, of civilised society, since this is founded on the family relationship. It seems to me that we should be slow to refuse recognition to an adoption order made by a foreign court which applies the same safeguard as we do and which undoubtedly has jurisdiction over the adopted child and its natural parents.'[89]

7.85 Due to the conflicting decision in *Re Valentine's* what, if any, requirements of domicile exist for common law adoption is the subject of debate.[90] However, the focus of the court in recent decisions regarding common law recognition has shifted from domicile to the requirements in the foreign jurisdiction pending the making of an adoption order.[91] In *Re N* an Armenian adoption order in favour of a British stepfather was recognised. The court

---

[85]   Ibid, at 846F.
[86]   ACA 2002, s 49.
[87]   By Denning MR, [1965] 1 Ch 831 at 843F.
[88]   Ibid, at 852B, followed in *Re G (Foreign Adoption: Consent)* [1995] 2 FLR 534.
[89]   *Re Valentine's Settlement* [1965] 1 Ch 831 at 852F.
[90]   For full discussion see Dicey, Morris and Collins, *The Conflict of Laws*, (Sweet and Maxwell, 2006), 20-126–20-131.
[91]   *D v D (Foreign Adoption)* [2008] EWHC 203 (Fam), [2008] 1 FLR 1475; *Re N (Recognition of a Foreign Adoption Order)* [2010] 1 FLR 1102; *Re T and M (Adoption)* [2010] EHWC 964, [2011] 1 FLR 1487.

noted that the order was made after very thorough investigation in Armenia.[92] In *D v D* an order was made under the Hindu Adoption and Maintenance Act 1956, the court observing that the procedures followed in India were largely similar to those in Hague Convention cases (at the time India was not a party to the Hague Convention 1993).[93]

7.86 In *Re T and M (Adoption)*[94] Hedley J succinctly summarised the three questions before the court:

(1) Was the adoption order obtained wholly lawfully in the foreign jurisdiction?

(2) Does the concept of adoption in the foreign jurisdiction substantially conform to that in England?

(3) Is there any public policy consideration that should mitigate against recognition?[95]

Public policy

7.87 The courts may refuse common law recognition on grounds of public policy. This relates to matters that are 'repugnant' such as the buying and selling of children disregarding their needs.[96]

> 'If the foreign adoption was designed to provide some immoral or mercenary object, like prostitution or financial gain, it is improbable that it would be recognised in England. But, apart from exceptional cases like these, it is submitted that the courts should be slow to refuse recognition to a foreign adoption on the grounds of public policy merely because the requirements for adoption in the foreign law differ from those of the English Law.'[97]

Declarations

7.88 The Family Law Act 1986 (FLA 1986), s 57 allows any person whose status as an adopted child of a person depends on whether he has been adopted by a Convention Adoption, an overseas adoption or a foreign adoption recognised at common law to apply for declarations as to his status.[98] The declarations that can be sought are that:[99]

• the applicant is for the purposes of ACA 2002, s 67 (or Adoption Act 1976, s 39) the adopted child of the adopter;

---

[92] *Re N (Recognition of a Foreign Adoption Order)* [2010] 1 FLR 1102 at [4].
[93] *D v D (Foreign Adoption)* [2008] EWHC 203 (Fam), [2008] 1 FLR 1475 at [9].
[94] [2010] EHWC 964, [2011] 1 FLR 1487.
[95] Ibid, at [12].
[96] Ibid, at [13].
[97] Dicey, Morris and Collins, 20-133, cited with approval in *Re N* at [28] and *D v D* at [15].
[98] FLA 1986, s 57(1).
[99] Ibid, s 57(2).

- the applicant is not the adopted child of the adopter.

7.89 The effect of these declarations is that the child is the child of the adopters and no other person.[100] However, in the case of a step-parent adopting, the declaration does not operate so as to extinguish his partner's (the child's biological parent) parental responsibility.[101]

Court process

7.90 An application for a declaration is made to the High Court or the county court. The application is made on Form C65[102] and the procedure is governed by FPR 2010, Parts 8 and 19. The applicant is the adopted child (acting if necessary through his litigation friend). The respondents are the adoptive parents. However, the applicant should include on the form details of each person who may be affected by the proceedings and their relation to the applicant.[103] This suggests details of the birth parent should be included.

7.91 Form C65 is a relatively simple form with one section for 'brief details' of the applications. The accompanying guidance notes state that this should include the question for the court to decide or the order sought and legal basis and, if relevant, the rule or practice direction. However, FPR 2010, Part 19, which governs the application, requires more detailed information to be filed with the application, including written evidence relied upon.[104]

7.92 One month prior to the applicant issuing proceedings the application form and accompanying documents should be sent to the Attorney General. The Attorney General may intervene in the proceedings and notify the court.[105] Following issue, the court may give directions as to who should be joined as respondents or given notice of the proceedings.[106]

7.93 Prior to making a decision, the court may require expert evidence regarding the foreign adoption order. This is in relation to the process for obtaining the order and the effect of the order.

---

[100] ACA 2002, s 67.
[101] *Re N (Recognition of Foreign Adoption Order)* [2010] 1 FLR 1102.
[102] www.justice.gov.uk/courts.
[103] FPR 2010, r 8.20(2).
[104] Ibid, r 19.3.
[105] Ibid, r 8.21. This requirement is over and above those stated in FLA 1986, s 59.
[106] FPR 2010, r 8.20(4).

CASE-LAW

7.94

Name of Case	Child's Country of Origin	Age of child when placed with adopters	Age of child at final hearing	Breaches of regulations and/or concerns re prospective adopters	Outcome (including costs)
Re A (Adoption: Placement) [1988] 2 FLR 133	El Salvador	4½ years	6½ years	All requirements in El Salvador met but child not placed for adoption by adoption agency.	Court exercised its dispensing power to allow the adoption application to proceeding despite the breach.
Re An Adoption Application [1992] 1 FLR 341	El Salvador	1 month	2½ years	Child not placed by an adoption agency and payments made. Adoptive father imprisoned for fraud. Pending proceedings not disclosed to El Salvador assessors or the UK local authority. Concerns re honesty, emotional insight and ability to promote child's cultural needs.	Adoption order made.

Name of Case	Child's Country of Origin	Age of child when placed with adopters	Age of child at final hearing	Breaches of regulations and/or concerns re prospective adopters	Outcome (including costs)
Re AW (Adoption Application) [1993] 1 FLR 62	England	c. 1 month	4½ years	Child's existence concealed from the local authority; failure to co-operate with local authority enquiries. Adoptive father had difficulties with alcohol; concerns regarding adoptive parents' marriage and health.	Interim adoption order made under ACA 1976, s 25 with terms. Adopters ordered to pay half the Official Solicitor's costs.
Re Adoption Application (Non-patrial Breach of Procedures) [1993] 1 FLR 947	El Salvador	1 month	3 years	Child not placed for adoption by an agency but this found to be due to ignorance. Prospective adopters made full disclosure to the local authority and no concerns about their care.	Adoption order made.

Name of Case	Child's Country of Origin	Age of child when placed with adopters	Age of child at final hearing	Breaches of regulations and/or concerns re prospective adopters	Outcome (including costs)
Re WM (Adoption: Non-patrial) [1997] 1 FLR 132	El Salvador	Just under 1 year	3½ years	Child not placed by an adoption agency and illegal payments made. Some 'reservations' about prospective adopters (not detailed in the judgment).	Adoption order made.
Re K (Adoption and Wardship) [1997] 2 FLR 221	Bosnia	2½ months	5 years	Adopters misled court regarding the child's origins and avoided enquiries from her formal guardian in the state of origin. Birth family wanted child returned to them. Concerns regarding adopters' ability to promote child's religious and cultural heritage.	Initial adoption order set aside by Court of Appeal. Final outcome: adoption application dismissed. Wardship with care and control to proposed adopters and extensive contact to birth family.

Name of Case	Child's Country of Origin	Age of child when placed with adopters	Age of child at final hearing	Breaches of regulations and/or concerns re prospective adopters	Outcome (including costs)
Re C (Adoption: Legality) [1999] 1 FLR 370	Guatemala	8 months	2 years	Adopter turned down for adoption by three agencies in England. Private 'home study' report superficial and prepared and paid for illegally. Lack of insight into racial and cultural issues.	Adoption order made.
Re R (No 1) (Inter-country Adoption) [1999] 1 FLR 1014	Romania	5 years	10 years	Birth parents allowed child to come to UK for three months for medical treatment. Proposed adopters did not return child and parents did not pursue return. Birth parents opposed adoption and sought child's return. Concerns regarding the standard of care birth family could offer.	Adoption application dismissed. Child made ward with care and control granted to proposed adopters and contact to birth family.

Name of Case	Child's Country of Origin	Age of child when placed with adopters	Age of child at final hearing	Breaches of regulations and/or concerns re prospective adopters	Outcome (including costs)
Re JS (Private International Adoption) [2000] 2 FLR 638	USA	2 days (removed by local authority at 6 months)	7 months	Child placed with adopters who paid $19,000. Inadequate assessment undertaken by US agency. Local authority concerns regarding safety of child. US adoption agency sought return of child.	Child removed by local authority. Child returned to USA.
Flintshire County Council v K [2001] 2 FLR 476	USA	6 months (removed by local authority 16 days after placed)	1 year	Children (twins) placed illegally and payments made for adoption. Home study report inadequate. Adoptive parents sold story to a tabloid newspaper and embarked on media campaign. Concerns regarding parents' ability to meet children's emotional needs, put children's needs first and understanding of racial issues.	Final care order and return to USA. Children in UK foster care until US court reached decisions about their future.

Name of Case	Child's Country of Origin	Age of child when placed with adopters	Age of child at final hearing	Breaches of regulations and/or concerns re prospective adopters	Outcome (including costs)
Re M (International Adoption Trade) [2003] 1 FLR 1111	USA	11 days (accommodated by local authority at 18 months)	3 years	Child placed illegally; inadequate home study report. Adoptive parents separated after child placed. Adoptive mother committed suicide and adoptive father did not seek to care for the child. US did not seek return of the child.	'Freeing order' child to be placed to adoption in UK.
Re A [2005] 2 FLR 727	England	5 days	5 years	Child placed illegally (domestic adoption) but in good faith. No deception by adopters. No concerns regarding care of child.	Adoption order made.

Name of Case	Child's Country of Origin	Age of child when placed with adopters	Age of child at final hearing	Breaches of regulations and/or concerns re prospective adopters	Outcome (including costs)
X (A Child), *Re*, *Northumberland CC v Z* [2008] EWHC 1342	Kenya	1½ years (removed by local authority after 9 months)	3½ years	Child brought to UK illegally. Deliberate deception of Kenyan and UK authorities. Kenyan Government sought return of the child. Concerns regarding impact of deception on child, emotional insight and cultural issues.	Interim care order, care plan for child to return to Kenya.
ASB v MQS [2010] 1 FLR 748	Pakistan	15 years (but adopted when 10)	17 years	Family adoption. No breaches of Adoption Act. Birth parents deceived immigration authorities – unknown to adoptive parents. No concerns regarding child's welfare.	Adoption order made.

Name of Case	Child's Country of Origin	Age of child when placed with adopters	Age of child at final hearing	Breaches of regulations and/or concerns re prospective adopters	Outcome (including costs)
Re N (Recognition of Foreign Adoption Order) [2010] 1 FLR 1102	Armenia	Not stated	17 years	Application to adopt by stepfather. Adoption order made in Armenia. Breaches of AFER, regs 3 and 4; no intention to deceive.	Declaration that Armenian adoption order recognised.

Chapter 8

RESTRICTIONS ON ADOPTIONS FROM SPECIFIED COUNTRIES

RESTRICTED COUNTRIES

8.1   Despite the international conventions, agreements and pronouncements, abuses of intercountry adoption remain. Although the statutory scheme laid down by the Adoption and Children Act 2002 (ACA 2002) and the Adoptions with a Foreign Element Regulations 2005 (AFER 2005)[1] largely regulates intercountry adoption, there is little that the United Kingdom can do to regulate practices in other jurisdictions. Due to concerns regarding the practices of intercountry adoption in some (particularly South American) countries, a mechanism exists whereby movement of children from specified countries can be restricted.

8.2   The Secretary of State for Education has the power to restrict adoptions from a country if he believes that it would be contrary to public policy to allow children to be brought into the United Kingdom from that country. The Secretary of State's reasons must be based on the practices occurring in that country in relation to adoption.[2] The restriction applies both to children brought to the United Kingdom for the purpose of adoption and those brought to the United Kingdom within 12 months of an adoption abroad.[3] A country being a signatory to the Convention does not prevent it being designated a restricted country.[4]

8.3   The Secretary of State may declare (by order) that 'special restrictions' apply to the country in question. The special restrictions are that the Department for Education may not take any steps to further adoption from that country.[5] For example, in a Convention adoption the Department for Education could not undertake the process of securing Article 17(c) agreement. In a non-Hague Convention 1993 case the Department for Education could not issue a certificate of eligibility. Countries subject to special restrictions are known as 'restricted countries'.[6] The decision to order a country to be a restricted country must be kept under review.[7]

---

[1]   SI 2005/392.
[2]   Children and Adoption Act 2006 (CAA 2006), s 9(1).
[3]   Ibid, s 9(2).
[4]   Ibid, s 9(3).
[5]   Ibid, s 9(4) and 11.
[6]   Ibid, s 9(6).
[7]   Ibid, s 10.

8.4   The effect of the Children and Adoption Act 2006 (CAA 2006) is that the proposed adopters would not be able to bring the child into the UK without breaching ACA 2002, s 83(1). CAA 2006 makes provision for extra restrictions to be imposed on restricted countries backed up by criminal penalties.[8] At the time of writing, no such extra restrictions are in force.

COUNTRIES CURRENTLY DESIGNATED AS 'RESTRICTED'

8.5   There are currently four 'restricted' countries.

Cambodia

8.6   Adoptions from Cambodia have been suspended since June 2004,[9] prior to the CAA 2006 coming into force. Following a review in April 2008 the suspension remained. A wide ranging judicial review against the Secretary of State's decision to suspend adoptions from Cambodia was unsuccessful.[10]

Guatemala

8.7   Adoptions from Guatemala have been suspended since December 2007.[11] This was due to:

'New evidence which demonstrates that: there are insufficient safeguards in the Guatemalan system to prevent a child being adopted without proper consents being given and improper financial gain being made by individuals in the adoption process. In particular that: there is a trade in babies being sold; and mothers being paid, or otherwise encouraged, to give up children for adoption.'[12]

Nepal

8.8   Special restrictions have applied to adoptions from Nepal since 3 May 2010.[13]

Haiti

8.9   Special restrictions have been in place since 15 October 2010.[14] This follows issues after the earthquake in that country.

---

[8]   CAA 2006, s 12.
[9]   Special Restrictions on Adoptions from Abroad (Cambodia) Order 2008, SI 2008/1808.
[10]   *R (Charlton Thomas) v Secretary of State of Education and Skills* [2005] EWHC 1378, [2005] All ER (D) 25 (Jul).
[11]   Special Restrictions on Adoptions from Abroad (Guatemala) Order 2008, SI 2008/1809.
[12]   Suspension of Adoptions from Guatemala, Ministerial Statement, 6 December 2007.
[13]   Special Restrictions on Adoptions from Abroad (Nepal) Order 2010, SI 2010/951.
[14]   Special Restrictions on Adoptions from Abroad (Haiti) Order 2010, SI 2010/2265.

EXCEPTIONAL CIRCUMSTANCES

8.10 The Secretary of State can lift the special restrictions to allow an adoption to proceed in exceptional circumstances. The prospective adopter must apply in writing to the Secretary of State which must be acknowledged and investigated by the Department for Education.[15] If a child has been identified by the prospective adopter, the Department for Education will take into account the following matters when deciding whether to allow a specific adoption.[16]

- The circumstances leading to the child's availability for adoption, including whether a competent authority in the child's home state has made a decision regarding adoption. A competent authority is a court or person who performs functions analogous to those of the Secretary of State or an adoption agency.

- If the child has formed a relationship with the prospective adopters and how and when that relationship was formed.

- The child's particular needs and the capacity of the adopters to meet those needs.

- The reasons why the child's home country was placed on the restricted list.

8.11 If a child has not been identified the only matter that must be considered is the reason(s) the country has been placed on the restricted list.[17]

8.12 The prospective adopters should be notified of the decision in writing including the reasons for the conclusions reached. Whilst it is open to adopters to make further requests to the Department for Education, these will only be considered if there is new information. Even if there is new information it must be sufficient to lead the Department for Education to consider that the case is exceptional.[18]

---

[15] Adoptions with a Foreign Element (Special Restrictions on Adoptions from Abroad) Regulations 2008, SI 2008/1807, regs 2 and 3.
[16] Ibid, reg 6.
[17] Ibid, reg 6(3).
[18] Ibid, reg 4(2).

Chapter 9

IMMIGRATION CONSEQUENCES OF INTERCOUNTRY ADOPTION INTO THE UNITED KINGDOM

INTRODUCTION

9.1   This chapter concentrates on the immigration status of those adopted through intercountry adoptions where the receiving state is the UK. The chapter concentrates on those children who either require leave to enter the UK or who undergo a change of nationality as part of the adoption process (ie who become a British citizen as part of the adoption process) in order to enter the UK. The chapter is not concerned with the intercountry adoption of British citizens abroad or children who are citizens of the European Economic Area (EEA).[1] British citizens have a right of abode in the UK as an integral part of their British citizenship, and thus do not have to satisfy any immigration requirements to enter the UK (other than to produce their passport). EEA citizens have a right of admission on producing on arrival a valid national identity card or a passport issued by an EEA state.[2]

9.2   In respect of adopted (or prospective adopted) children who are neither British citizens nor EEA citizens, as will be seen below, only in certain circumstances does the fact a lawful intercountry adoption has taken place confer automatic lawful immigration status on the adopted child in the UK. In many cases, there are a number of substantive requirements to be fulfilled before a status (temporary or permanent) can be acquired and before the child can lawfully enter the UK. As can be seen from Chapters 5 to 7, there are a number of routes through which an intercountry adoption can take place between a state of origin and the UK, or through which an adoption overseas can be recognised in the UK. The immigration requirements that have to be fulfilled by an adoptive child without British or EEA citizenship before entering the UK depend upon which route is taken. The various routes and the means of lawfully entering or remaining in the UK under each route are considered in this chapter. Save in respect of adoptive parents who are EEA citizens (as to which see below), there are two possible routes for entering the

---

[1]   Ie a national of an EEA state as defined under the Immigration (European Economic Area) Regulations 2006, SI 2006/1003 (the EEA Regs) – namely, the UK, Austria, Belgium, Bulgaria, Cyprus, Czech Republic, Denmark, Estonia, Finland, France, Germany, Greece, Hungary, Iceland, Ireland, Italy, Latvia, Liechtenstein, Lithuania, Luxembourg, Malta, Netherlands, Norway, Poland, Portugal, Romania, Slovakia, Slovenia, Spain, Sweden and Switzerland.
[2]   EEA Regs, reg 11(1).

UK where British citizenship is not automatically acquired: through an application for registration of the child as a British citizen, or through an application for leave to enter. Both types of application are considered in this chapter in respect of each basis of intercountry adoption. The first type of application relies upon the unfettered discretion of the Home Secretary pursuant to the British Nationality Act 1981 (BNA 1981), s 3(1). This chapter considers the guidance provided by the UK Border Agency on how the discretion will be exercised. The second type of application is governed, in most circumstances, by substantive requirements set out in paras 309A to 316F of the Immigration Rules.[3] Those rules are set out in Part 5 of this book. This chapter provides guidance as to which rule is relevant for each adoption situation, and will explain how particular elements of the rules are interpreted, but will not set out the full wording of the relevant rules. Cross-reference should be made to the full wording in Part 5. This chapter explains in detail the terms of the rules in the section on 'Provisions of the Immigration Rules'. Where the adoptive parents are citizens of the EEA exercising Treaty rights in the UK, the entry requirements for immigration purposes are, to an extent, distinct from in other situations, and this issue is also explored below. Even where the requirements for entry clearance are not satisfied, it may be that refusal of leave to an adoptive child to enter or remain in the UK will be in breach of the right to respect for family and private life under Article 8 of the European Convention for the Protection of Human Rights and Fundamental Freedoms (ECHR). The tests applied in those circumstances are considered. Finally, guidance is given on the right of appeal in circumstances where a negative immigration decision is made.

9.3   This chapter is divided into the following sections:

- Convention Adoptions where there is a full order

- Convention Adoptions where there is not a full order before entry into the UK

- Adoptions from a country on the Designated List

- Adoptions from a country not on the Designated List

- De facto adoptions

- Adoptions by relatives

- Definitions within paragraphs 309A to 316 of the Immigration Rules

- Adoption by EEA nationals

---

[3]   HC 395, originally laid before Parliament on 23 May 1994 by the Secretary of State for the Home Department, pursuant to s 3(2) of the Immigration Act 1971 (IA 1971) and amended on numerous occasions since.

- Article 8 and decisions on the grant of leave to enter or remain

- Rights of appeal

CONVENTION ADOPTIONS WHERE THERE IS A FULL ORDER

9.4 Where a Convention adoption of a child[4] who is not a British citizen takes place overseas and a certificate under Article 23 of the Convention is issued, British citizenship is automatically acquired on the date of issue, so long as at that date:

- the adoptive parent (or, if a joint adoption, at least one of them) is a British citizen; and

- the adoptive parent is (or, if a joint adoption, both are) habitually resident in the UK.[5]

9.5 Where a child automatically acquires British citizenship in this way, the adoptive parents can apply for the child to be issued with a British passport[6] or a certificate of entitlement to the right of abode.[7]

9.6 If the adoption order under a Convention adoption is subsequently annulled or ceases to have effect, the British citizenship automatically acquired by the adopted child is not revoked.[8]

9.7 Where, however, the above requirements for the conferring of automatic British citizenship are not met, there are two available possibilities. An application can be made for the Secretary of State for the Home Department to exercise her discretion to register the child as a British citizen, or an application for leave to enter the UK will need to be made. Each is dealt with in turn below.

---

4   The term used in the BNA 1981 is 'minor', but the term 'child' will be used throughout the course of this chapter. A minor is defined at BNA 1981, s 50(1) as a person who has not reached the age of 18.

5   BNA 1981, s 1(5) and (5A). For guidance on the definition of 'habitual residence', see Chapter 2.

6   Applications for British passports from outside the UK are to be made at the regional passport processing centre relevant to the country the applicant is in. Advice on the application process relevant to each country can be found at http://www.fco.gov.uk/en/travel-and-living-abroad/passports1/how-to-apply/.

7   An application for a certificate of entitlement can be made either online through the Visa4UK website at www.visa4uk.fco.gov.uk or through use of form VAF7. In all countries, the online application process should be used, save for Afghanistan, Cuba, Kiribati, Malawi, Mozambique, Namibia, North Korea, Pakistan, Turkmenistan and Zimbabwe (in which form VAF7 must be used) and Bangladesh, Maldives, Mongolia, Nepal, Nigeria, Sri Lanka and Uganda (in which either process can be used). The cost of application is currently £265.

8   BNA 1981, s 1(6).

Application for registration as a British citizen on discretionary grounds

9.8   An application for registration on discretionary grounds is made pursuant to BNA 1981, s 3(1). Registration under this subsection is entirely at the discretion of the Home Secretary.[9] There is no authoritative case-law on the application of the discretion under s 3(1), but the UK Border Agency does provide extensive guidance about the manner in which the discretion will be exercised. That guidance is, however, by no means entirely prescriptive and is not much more than indicative of the process and requirements for the Home Secretary's exercise of the discretion. The guidance leaves a lot of room for the exercise of discretion. As explained by the UK Border Agency at para 9.1.5 of *Nationality Instructions*, Chapter 9: Registration of minors at discretion:

> 'IT IS IMPORTANT TO REMEMBER that the guidance in this Chapter does not amount to hard and fast rules. It will enable the majority of cases to be dealt with, but because the law gives complete discretion each case must be considered on its merits. All the relevant factors must be taken into account, together with any representations made to us. If we do not, we are open to criticism for not exercising our discretion differently.'

9.9   The application is made on Form MN1 and will, according to the guidance, normally be approved when each of the following criteria are satisfied:[10]

- one of the adoptive parents or the sole adopter is a British citizen otherwise than by descent; and

- the adoptive parent(s) have signified their consent to the registration; and

- the Home Secretary is satisfied that the adoption is not one of convenience arranged to facilitate the child's admission to or stay in the UK; and

- the adoption is recognised in the UK; and

- the Home Secretary is satisfied that all relevant laws have been complied with (ie the laws of the country in which the adoption has taken place, any applicable laws in the child's country of origin and any applicable laws in the country where the adopters are habitually resident); and

---

9   Where the application is refused, there would be a right to bring a claim in judicial review, though not a right to bring an appeal before the First-Tier Tribunal of the Immigration and Asylum Chamber.

10   UK Border Agency guidance *Inter-Country Adoption and the Immigration Rules* at para 46. Also see UK Border Agency document *Guide MN1 – Registration as a British citizen – A guide about the registration of children under 18* at p 13, and UK Border Agency *Nationality Instructions,* Chapter 9: Registration of minors at discretion at para 9.8.3.

- there is no reason to refuse registration on grounds of the child's character.

9.10 It can be seen from the first criterion that it will be rare for a child subject to a Convention adoption where the UK is the receiving state to fall short of the requirements for automatic British citizenship but to satisfy those for registration as a British citizen under BNA 1981, s 3(1). The guidance to immigration officers indicates that it will rarely be right to register a child as a British citizen if neither of his parents is or is about to become a British citizen.[11] However, even if the criteria are not all satisfied, the application will be considered on its merits, and the child will be registered as a British citizen if British citizenship is demonstrably in the child's best interests.[12]

9.11 If the child is 10 or older, checks will be carried out to ascertain that the child is of good character. The checks will consider, for example, whether the child satisfies any obligations to pay income tax, whether there are any civil judgments against the child, and whether the child has any outstanding convictions which are not considered spent under the Rehabilitation of Offenders Act 1974.[13] Any offences for which the child has been arrested albeit not formally charged or convicted should also be disclosed.[14]

9.12 The evidence that is required to be provided with the application form is:[15]

- the child's birth certificate or (if abandoned) a certificate of abandonment from the authorities previously responsible for the child;

- evidence of the relevant adoptive parent's claim to British citizenship otherwise than by descent;

- the consent of the adoptive parent(s) to the registration;

- the adoption order;

- a contemporary report from the overseas equivalent of the social services department, detailing:

    - the child's parentage and history;

---

[11] UK Border Agency *Nationality Instructions,* Chapter 9: Registration of minors at discretion at para 9.17.11.

[12] *Guide MN1 – Registration as a British citizen – A guide about the registration of children under 18* at p 13. UK Border Agency *Nationality Instructions,* Chapter 9: Registration of minors at discretion at para 9.8.3.

[13] *Guide MN1 – Registration as a British citizen – A guide about the registration of children under 18* at pp 22–23.

[14] Ibid, at p 24.

[15] *Guide MN1 – Registration as a British citizen – A guide about the registration of children under 18* at pp 29–30. UK Border Agency *Nationality Instructions,* Chapter 9: Registration of minors at discretion at para 9.8.6.

- the degree of contact with the original parents;
- the reasons for adoption;
- the date, reasons and arrangements for the child's entry into an institution or foster placement;
- when, how and why the child came to be offered to the adoptive parent(s);
- evidence of the parents' country of habitual residence; and
- if the parents are habitually resident in the UK, confirmation from the Department for Education or relevant devolved authority that they have been assessed and approved as eligible to become an adoptive parent, or if not habitually resident in the UK, confirmation from the equivalent of the social services department in their country of residence that all relevant adoption laws have been complied with.

9.13 The application must be supported by two referees who know the child personally. One referee should be a professional who has engaged with the child in a professional capacity (eg as a teacher or social worker). The other should be either a professional or over the age of 25. Ideally the second referee should be a British citizen, but if the child knows no British citizen qualified to act as a referee, a Commonwealth citizen or citizen of the country in which the child resides will suffice. The referee cannot have been convicted of an imprisonable offence in the last 10 years unless the conviction has become spent under the Rehabilitation of Offenders Act 1974.[16]

9.14 If an application is successful and British citizenship is conferred, the adoptive child will become a British citizen otherwise than by descent and will have the right of abode, and an application for a passport or certificate of entitlement to the right of abode can be made, as detailed above.[17] In those circumstances no application would need to be made for leave to enter the UK where registration occurs before the adoptive child has entered the UK.

Application for indefinite leave to enter the UK

9.15 In most countries, applications are required to be made online at www.visa4uk.fco.gov.uk.[18] Where that facility is not available, the application is made by filling in Form VAF 4A Settlement, including Appendix 1 and Appendix 2 and sending it to the relevant visa application centre for the child's state of origin.[19] Either way, an appointment will need to be made to visit the

---

[16] *Guide MN1 – Registration as a British citizen – A guide about the registration of children under 18* at p 26; UK Border Agency *Nationality Instructions*, Chapter 9, Registration of minors at discretion, at para 9.1.3.

[17] See **9.5**.

[18] See note 7 for the list of countries that require a paper application or where the applicant can choose between applying online or on paper.

[19] Forms and details of visa application centres can be found on the UK Border Agency website: www.ukba.homeoffice.gov.uk.

visa application centre. The application will be considered by an entry clearance officer working for the UK Border Agency at the relevant visa application centre.

9.16   Guidance from the UK Border Agency provides that the following evidence should be provided with the application:[20]

'a)   settlement application form VAF2 (available from U.K. Visas, address above), the child's passport, 2 recent passport sized photographs and the appropriate fee;

b)   the child's original birth certificate showing his name at birth;

c)   a contemporary report from the overseas equivalent of the social services department, which details: the child's parentage and history; the degree of contact with the original parent(s); the reasons for the adoption; the date, reasons and arrangements for the child's entry into an institution or foster placement and when, how and why the child came to be offered to the adoptive parent(s). Where no legal adoption has taken place, a full written account covering the background should be provided;

d)   where the child has been abandoned, a certificate of abandonment from the authorities previously responsible for the child's care;

e)   the adoption/guardianship order (where applicable);

f)   passport(s) of the adoptive parent(s) or other evidence to show that they have settled status in the United Kingdom, such as a birth certificate, registration or naturalisation certificate;

g)   evidence that the DCSF or Devolved Authority have issued a Certificate of Eligibility attesting to the suitability of the adopters & allowing them to approach the adoption authorities of the country in question;

h)   bank statements and an accountant's letter or pay slips which show the monthly incomings and outgoings of the adoptive parent(s) and details of their accommodation in the United Kingdom;

i)   For Scotland, where a child is of sufficient age and understanding to be able to make a decision in relation to the adoption, (normally from 7 years on), a report of an interview with the child confirming that the child has been informed and understands the circumstances of the adoption is required;

j)   In England, Wales and Northern Ireland the child's views must be taken into account where they are of sufficient age and understanding to be able to make a decision in relation to their adoption. The court in England, Wales and Northern Ireland will wish to see a report about the child, prepared by the, (court appointed), Children's Guardian.'

In addition to subpara (g) of the guidance, a new para 309B of the Immigration Rules was inserted in September 2012 to make expressly clear that a Certificate of Eligibility **must** be presented with all entry clearance adoption applications under paras 310 to 316F, save for where there is a de facto adoption.

---

[20]   *Inter-country adoption and the Immigration Rules* at para 34.

9.17 For the application for indefinite leave to enter to succeed, the child will need to satisfy the requirements of para 310 of the Immigration Rules,[21] which is set out in full in Part 5 of this book. Paragraph 310 sets out the requirements to be fulfilled by a person seeking indefinite leave[22] to enter the UK as the adopted child of a parent or parents present and settled[23] or being admitted for settlement in the UK.[24] One element of the requirements under para 310 requires express mention at this point, in order to explain why para 310 applies to a Convention adoption where British citizenship is not automatically conferred. Paragraph 310(vi)(a) requires, for para 310 to apply, that the child:

> 'was adopted in accordance with a decision taken by the competent administrative authority or court in his country of origin or the country in which he is resident, being a country whose adoption orders are recognised by the United Kingdom ...'

9.18 That requirement covers completed Convention adoptions, adoptions made through a lawful court process in countries designated for the purposes of the Adoption (Designation of Overseas Adoptions) Order 1973 ('Designated List Adoption'),[25] and adoptions through neither means but declared as lawful by the UK courts following application under the Family Law Act 1986, s 57.[26] Whichever process is used, before issuing entry clearance the entry clearance officer will seek confirmation from the Department for Education or relevant devolved authority that the adoption processes have been properly adhered to.[27]

9.19 A cursory examination of para 310 of the Immigration Rules in Part 5 of this book will highlight that the paragraph contains a number of onerous requirements as to the reasons for the adoption and the relationship of the adopted child with his family of origin. Those requirements, insofar as they require explanation, are explored in detail in **9.48** ff.[28] It is by no means inevitable that when persons adopt via a Convention adoption but do not satisfy the requirements for British citizenship to be conferred automatically on the adopted child, that child will be granted leave to enter the UK under the Immigration Rules.

---

[21] Save where leave is given outside the Immigration Rules, usually where Article 8 of the ECHR applies, as to which see below.

[22] Ie leave for an unrestricted period of time.

[23] The definition of 'present and settled' is explained below.

[24] An adoption under the Convention satisfies the requirement under HC395, para 310(vi).

[25] SI 1973/19.

[26] The latter two methods of lawful adoption are dealt with in detail in Chapter 7. The immigration consequences of an overseas adoption under the Adoption (Designation of Overseas Adoptions) Order 1973 are set out at **9.28–9.30**. The immigration consequences of adoptions subject to a s 57 declaration are dealt with at **9.36**.

[27] UK Border Agency guide *Inter-country adoption and the Immigration Rules* (1 November 2008), at para 25. See also the requirement under HC395, para 309B, to provide a Certificate of Eligibility with the entry clearance application.

[28] See **9.49** ff.

CONVENTION ADOPTIONS WHERE THERE IS NOT A FULL ORDER BEFORE ENTRY INTO THE UK

9.20 Where a Convention adoption is not subject to a full order overseas, but the child is either subject to an interim order or is to be brought to the UK for the adoption to progress through the UK courts, British citizenship is not conferred automatically. In these circumstances, an application needs to be made for limited leave to enter, so that the adopted child can enter the UK and undertake the requirements necessary for the adoption to be finalised. The application is made through the same process as in the section above.

9.21 If the child is to be brought to the UK for the Convention adoption to progress through the UK courts, the application for limited leave to enter is considered under para 316D of the Immigration Rules. On satisfaction of the requirements set out under that paragraph, the child will be granted leave to enter for a period of up to 24 months so that the Convention Adoption can be effected.[29]

9.22 If, on the other hand, the prospective parents are waiting for the interim adoption order to be made final in the Convention country rather than through the UK courts, the situation does not fall directly under any paragraph of the Immigration Rules, and the entry clearance officer is required to consider the case exceptionally outside the rules.[30] The UK Border Agency provides no specific guidance on the matters to be considered in such circumstances, but the situation is clearly analogous with one to which para 316D applies, and the authors take the view that the entry clearance officer's decision ought to follow the lines of para 316D. The UKBA Guidance[31] provides that entry clearance in these circumstances should be granted for 12 months and marked 'Adoption CYR'.[32]

9.23 When the Convention adoption is finalised (either in the UK courts or in the courts of the state of origin), British citizenship will be acquired automatically by the adopted child as at the date the adoption order takes effect, so long as at that date:

- the adoptive parent (or, if a joint adoption, at least one of them) is a British citizen; and

- the adoptive parent is (or, if a joint adoption, both are) habitually resident in the UK.[33]

---

[29]   HC395, para 316E.
[30]   UK Border Agency Guidance – *Adopted children* – version 3.0 (11 July 2012), p 23. Once the adoption procedure is completed, an application can then be made for the time limit on the child's leave to be removed.
[31]   Ibid.
[32]   Which stands for Child Probationary Year.
[33]   BNA 1981, s 1(5) and (5A).

9.24 Where British citizenship is not acquired automatically after an adoption is finalised, an application will either need to be made for registration of the child as a British citizen on discretionary grounds, or for indefinite leave to remain as the adopted child of a parent or parents present and settled in the UK.

9.25 For guidance on an application for registration as a British citizen on discretionary grounds, see **9.4** ff.[34]

9.26 An application for indefinite leave to remain is made on Form SET(F). Paragraph 311 of the Immigration Rules sets out the requirements to be fulfilled by a person seeking indefinite leave to remain in the UK as the adopted child of a parent or parents present and settled in the UK.

ADOPTIONS FROM A COUNTRY ON THE DESIGNATED LIST

9.27 Where an adoption is not a Convention Adoption but takes place in a country designated for the purposes of the Adoption (Designation of Overseas Adoptions) Order 1973, the adoption is recognised by the UK as a legal overseas adoption[35] ('a Designated List adoption'). Such an adoption does not automatically confer any lawful British immigration status on the child,[36] and either an application for registration as a British citizen on discretionary grounds[37] or an application for indefinite leave to enter the UK[38] must be made in the same manner as explained above in respect of Convention adoptions where British citizenship is not automatically acquired. Any application for indefinite leave to enter will be determined against the requirements of para 310 of the Immigration Rules.

9.28 If, for some reason, the child is already in the UK, then the application will be for indefinite leave to remain and will be determined against the requirements of para 311 of the Immigration Rules. That application is to be made on Form SET(F),[39] which can either be sent by post or can be taken in person to a public enquiry office.[40]

---

[34] At **9.8–9.15**.

[35] See Chapter 7. Where in the present chapter reference is made to a country on the Designated List, it refers to a country designated for the purposes of the Adoption (Designation of Overseas Adoptions) Order 1973, described in this chapter as a Designated List adoption. The phrase 'Designated List' is used consistently throughout UK Border Agency guidance on intercountry adoption, and accordingly this chapter uses that phrase to fall in line with the guidance. The Immigration Rules do not contemplate a refusal to accept the validity of a valid order of a competent court in a country on the Designated List: *Buama (Inter-country Adoption – Competent Court)* [2012] UKUT 00146 (IAC) at [17].

[36] ACA 2002, s 74(2) read together with ss 66(1)(d) and 67.

[37] On Form MN1.

[38] Ie online at www.visa4uk.fco.gov.uk or by filling in a VAF 4A Settlement form along with Appendices 1 and 2.

[39] The form can be downloaded from the UKBA website at www.ukba.gov.uk.

[40] The fee for a postal application is £991. For an application taken in person to a public enquiry

9.29 If one of the adoptive parents is not present and settled in the UK or being admitted for settlement,[41] but has limited leave or is being given limited leave to enter or remain, then the child's application will need to be for limited leave to enter or remain with a view to settlement. Such an application is determined against the requirements of para 314 of the Immigration Rules. Paragraph 314 mirrors the requirements set out under paras 310 (for leave to enter) and 311 (for leave to remain), save for the parental situations in which it applies. The application for limited leave to enter is made on the same form as an application for indefinite leave to enter. Where the application is for limited leave to remain, it is made on form FLR(O).[42]

9.30 Where there has been a Designated List adoption, an application can be made for registration of the child as a British citizen on discretionary grounds under BNA 1981, s 3(1). These applications are dealt with in detail at **9.8–9.15**.

ADOPTIONS FROM A COUNTRY NOT ON THE DESIGNATED LIST WHERE THE CHILD IS TO BE BROUGHT INTO THE UK TO BE ADOPTED IN THE UK

9.31 Where an adoption takes place outside the UK and it is neither a Convention adoption nor a Designated List adoption, the adoption is not recognised for the purpose of domestic law.[43] This is so even though the adoption was lawfully entered into under the law of the country in which it took place. In those circumstances, the child will not be recognised in the UK as an adopted child of the persons who adopted him in the state of origin.

9.32 As explained in Chapter 7, there are two options open to the adoptive parents in these circumstances in order to effect an adoption recognised as lawful in the UK. They can (i) seek to bring the child to apply for an adoption order in the UK; or (ii) apply for a declaration pursuant to Family Law Act 1986, s 57 that the adoption is recognised at common law.

9.33 The immigration rules applicable to an application for entry clearance from such a child are dependent upon which path is taken.

9.34 If the first route is taken, para 316A of the Immigration Rules applies. That paragraph provides the requirements to be satisfied by a child seeking limited leave to enter the UK for the purpose of being adopted. The application is made by the same procedure as already described above in respect of

---

office, the fee is £1,377. The higher fee is justified on the basis that applications delivered in person will be subject to a premium service whereby decisions are made the same day.
[41] See **9.50–9.55**.
[42] Available to be downloaded from the UKBA website at www.ukba.gov.uk.
[43] ACA 2002, s 66(1).

Convention adoptions.[44] If leave to enter is granted, it will be for a period not exceeding 24 months,[45] to enable the adoption to take place.

9.35 If, however, a declaration is sought as to the validity of the adoption, then once the declaration is made an application can be made for indefinite leave to remain pursuant to para 310 of the Immigration Rules.[46] Until the declaration is granted, the Immigration Rules provide no adoption-related basis upon which the child can lawfully enter the UK pursuant to a grant of leave to enter.

9.36 Whilst it is open to a person subject to an adoption that is neither a Convention adoption nor a Designated List adoption to apply for registration of the child as a British citizen by exercise of the Home Secretary's discretion pursuant to BNA 1981, s 3(1), the guidance provides that such applications should normally be refused, although the child should be registered if it is demonstrably in the child's best interests.[47]

DE FACTO ADOPTIONS

9.37 Paragraph 309A of the Immigration Rules provides for the category of 'de facto adoption'. A de facto adoption is not recognised formally as an adoption in the UK. Unlike the other adoptions set out above, the existence of a de facto adoption is not reliant on there having been an adoption lawfully carried out in either the state of origin or in the UK. The category of de facto adoption provides a mechanism enabling the lawful entry to the UK of a child who has not been formally adopted, but whose care by the de facto adoptive parents meets specified criteria. It is a mechanism that is most useful where the child is from a country in which children cannot be formally adopted. It can also, however, be relied upon in circumstances where adoption orders in the country in which the child was adopted are not recognised in the UK, or where the child lives in a country that is a signatory of the Convention or is on the Designated List but where the adoptive parents are unable to satisfy that country's particular requirements.[48]

9.38 A de facto adoption is held under para 309A of the Immigration Rules to exist where:

---

[44] Ie online at www.visa4uk.fco.gov.uk or by filling in a VAF 4A Settlement form along with Appendices 1 and 2.

[45] HC395, para 316B.

[46] See *N (Children) (Recognition of Foreign Adoption Orders), Re*, [2008] EWHC 403 (Fam); sub nom *D v D (Foreign Adoption)* [2008] 1 FLR 1475 at [19].

[47] *Guide MN1 – Registration as a British citizen – a guide about the registration of children under 18'* at p 14; *Nationality Instructions*, Chapter 9: Registration of minors at discretion at para 9.8.4.

[48] See UK Border Agency document *Guidance – Adopted children – version 4.0* (valid from 22 August 2012), p 24.

'(a) at the time immediately preceding the making of the application for entry clearance under these Rules the adoptive parent or parents have been living abroad (in applications involving two parents both must have lived abroad together) for at least a period of time equal to the first period mentioned in sub-paragraph (b)(i) and must have cared for the child for at least a period of time equal to the second period material in that sub-paragraph; and

(b) during their time abroad, the adoptive parent or parents have:

   (i) lived together for a minimum period of 18 months, of which the 12 months immediately preceding the application for entry clearance must have been spent living together with the child; and

   (ii) have assumed the role of the child's parents, since the beginning of the 18 month period, so that there has been a genuine transfer of parental responsibility.'

9.39 The requirements are self-explanatory. The term 'genuine transfer of parental responsibility' is explained at **9.78**.

9.40 Where the requirements are satisfied, the child is considered to be subject to a de facto adoption for the purpose of paras 310 to 316C of the Immigration Rules.

9.41 So long as one of the de facto adoptive parents (i) has either a right of abode in the UK or indefinite leave to enter or remain in the UK and (ii) is seeking admission to the UK on the same occasion as the de facto adoptive child for the purposes of settlement, then the de facto adoptive child can apply for the following bases of leave (presuming, of course, the other requirements of the relevant rule are satisfied):

- indefinite leave to enter the UK as the adopted child of a parent or parents present and settled or being admitted for settlement in the UK;[49]

- indefinite leave to remain in the UK as the adopted child of a parent or parents present and settled in the UK;[50] or

- limited leave to enter or remain in the UK with a view to settlement as the adopted child of a parent or parents given limited leave to enter or remain in the UK with a view to settlement.[51]

9.42 Where there is a de facto adoption and one or both of the adopters are British, application can be made for the child's registration as a British citizen under the discretionary arrangements of BNA 1981, s 3(1).[52]

---

[49] HC395, para 310(i)(g).
[50] HC395, para 311(i)(e).
[51] HC395, para 314(i)(d).
[52] Applications are made using Form MN1, as explained above. It is advisable to apply for a residence order first, to clarify the adoptive parents' responsibility for the child and the status of the child vis-à-vis the adoptive parents.

ADOPTION BY RELATIVES

9.43   Where a child is adopted by close relatives, the case may be considered not only under the relevant rules under paras 309A to 316F of the Immigration Rules, but also under para 297, which is the rule under which an application for indefinite leave to enter the UK can be made as the child of a parent, parents or a relative present and settled or being admitted for settlement in the UK. Paragraph 297 cannot be relied upon ordinarily in an adoption case because reliance upon it is expressly prohibited by the definition of 'parent' under paragraph 6 of the Immigration Rules, which provides that:

> '... an adopted child or child who is the subject of a de facto adoption may not make an application for leave to enter or remain in order to accompany, join or remain with an adoptive parent under paragraphs 297 to 303 ...'

9.44   That rule does not preclude a person who claims to be an adoptive child (whether by way of an adoption lawfully recognised or otherwise) from relying on para 297 as the child of a *relative* (as opposed to parent) present and settled in the UK or being admitted for settlement in the UK.[53]

9.45   The only basis upon which para 297 of the Immigration Rules can be relied upon as the child of a relative is set out in para 297(i)(f), which provides as a requirement for the rule to apply that:

> '... a relative is present and settled in the United Kingdom or being admitted on the same occasion for settlement and there are serious and compelling family or other considerations which make exclusion of the child undesirable and suitable arrangements have been made for the child's care.'

9.46   The other requirements are that the child:

- is under the age of 18;

- is not leading an independent life, is unmarried and is not a civil partner, and has not formed an independent family unit;

- will be accommodated adequately by the relative without recourse to public funds in accommodation the relative owns or occupies exclusively;

- will be maintained adequately by the relative without recourse to public funds;

- holds valid entry clearance; and

- does not have one or more unspent convictions under the Rehabilitation of Offenders Act 1974.

---

[53]   See *SZ (Applicable Immigration Rules) Bangladesh* [2007] UKAIT 00037.

9.47   Each of these terms are mirrored within parts of the paragraphs of the Immigration Rules dealing specifically with adoption, and the reader should refer to the definitions section at **9.48** ff.

DEFINITIONS WITHIN PARAGRAPHS 309A TO 316 OF THE IMMIGRATION RULES

9.48   In the sections above, the reader is directed to the relevant paragraphs of the Immigration Rules whose requirements have to be satisfied for an entry clearance officer[54] or an immigration officer on behalf of the Home Secretary[55] to grant leave to enter or remain respectively. In this section, explanation is provided as to the meaning behind those requirements where those meanings may not be self-evident. The terms requiring clarification are dealt with below in the order in which they appear in the paragraphs of the Immigration Rules.

Present and settled

9.49   'Present and settled' is defined in para 6 of the Immigration Rules to mean that:

> 'the person concerned is settled in the United Kingdom, and, at the time that an application under these Rules is made, is physically present here or is coming here with or to join the applicant and intends to make the United Kingdom their home with the applicant if their application is successful'

9.50   There is also a definition under para 6 of 'settled in the United Kingdom' which provides that a person is settled if free from any restriction on the period for which he may remain (save for an exception in respect of aircrew, sea crew, members of diplomatic missions and members of armed forces posted in the UK), and is either:

> '(i) ordinarily resident in the United Kingdom without having entered or remained in breach of the immigration laws; or (ii) despite having entered or remained in breach of the immigration laws, has subsequently entered lawfully or has been granted leave to remain and is ordinarily resident'

9.51   The definition of 'settlement' is inferred from the above definitions.

9.52   'Ordinary residence' was defined by Lord Scarman in *R v Barnet London Borough Council, ex parte Shah*[56] as referring:

> '... to a man's abode in a particular place or country which he has adopted voluntarily and for settled purposes as part of the regular order of his life for the time being, whether of short or of long duration.'

---

[54]   For applications for leave to enter.
[55]   For applications for leave to remain.
[56]   [1983] 2 AC 309 at 343G.

9.53   A person cannot be ordinarily resident for immigration purposes during a period in which they are in the UK in breach of immigration laws.[57] This is not the same in the family law sphere.[58] A person can be ordinarily resident in two places at the same time.[59] For there to be ordinary residence in the UK, the person must be habitually and normally resident in the UK, apart from temporary or occasional absences of either long or short duration.[60]

9.54   In *Ikimi v Ikimi*,[61] the Court of Appeal held within the divorce jurisdiction that the terms 'ordinary residence' and 'habitual residence' were interchangeable. However, some care should be taken in relying on family case-law when determining the meaning of ordinary residence for immigration law purposes. As explained in *Mark v Mark*,[62] the policy reasons for requiring ordinary or habitual residence differ in different contexts. It should be borne in mind that under the Immigration Rules, the reference to ordinary residence within the definition of 'settled in the United Kingdom' is made in a context where an applicant seeks to rely on their sponsor's present and settled status in order to gain an immigration status for themselves. It is unlikely that case-law in which very short periods of stay in the UK have sufficed to show habitual residence (for example in child abduction cases) will be of assistance in showing ordinary residence for the purpose of the definition of 'settled in the United Kingdom' under the Immigration Rules.[63]

Sole responsibility

9.55   The definition of *'sole responsibility'* is relevant where there are two parents alive but only one is present and settled in the UK or being admitted for settlement on the same occasion as the child. Although included under the provisions of the Immigration Rules, it is unusual for this requirement to be relevant to an intercountry adoption case.

9.56   In essence, the phrase 'sole responsibility' seeks to reflect a situation where the sponsor parent is primarily responsible for the child's upbringing,

---

[57]   IA 1971, s 33(2) and (2A); *R v Barnet London Borough Council, ex parte Shah* [1983] 2 AC 309 at 343H–344B; *R v Secretary of State for the Home Department, ex parte Margueritte* [1983] QB 180.

[58]   For example, in *Mark v Mark* [2005] UKHL 42, [2006] 1 AC 98, Baroness Hale held, at [34]–[36], that lawfulness of residence was not a prerequisite for habitual residence under s 5(2) of the Domicile and Matrimonial Proceedings Act 1973.

[59]   *R v Barnet London Borough Council, ex parte Shah* [1983] 2 AC 309 at 342F.

[60]   Ibid, at 342D. See also *Ikimi v Ikimi* [2001] EWCA Civ 873, [2001] 2 FLR 1288, in which, in considering whether a wife was habitually resident in the UK for the purposes of s 5(2) of the Domicile and Matrimonial Proceedings Act 1973, when she spent 44% of her time in the UK and 56% in Nigeria and had five periods outside the UK within the relevant 12 months, the Court of Appeal held there was just sufficient foundation for a finding of jurisdiction.

[61]   *Ikimi v Ikimi* [2001] EWCA Civ 873, [2001] 2 FLR 1288 at [31]. Also see *Mark v Mark* [2005] UKHL 42, [2006] 1 AC 98 at [33].

[62]   [2005] UKHL 42, [2006] 1 AC 98.

[63]   Accordingly the principles on habitual residence outlined in Chapter 2 should be treated with care when considering whether there is ordinary residence for the purpose of the Immigration Rules.

including ultimate responsibility for making the major decisions about the child's life[64] (such as where the child lives, educational, medical, legal and religious decisions) and providing the majority of the financial and emotional support that the child requires.[65] Where – as would often be the case where sole responsibility needs to be shown in an adoption case – the parent claiming sole responsibility is separated from the child, clearly the parent cannot have physical day-to-day care of the child. It is accepted in such circumstances that this will be entrusted to others.[66] However, the parent claiming sole responsibility must still be able to show he has retained ultimate responsibility for the child's upbringing, and that what is done in respect of the child's upbringing is done under that parent's direction,[67] and that he provides the majority of emotional and financial support.[68] Whilst the provision of financial support is a relevant factor, it is not conclusive but merely one factor to be taken into account.[69] It is arguable that there can be sole responsibility where the financial support provided by the sponsor comes from other members of his family.[70] The period of sole responsibility does not necessarily have to be a long period (in one case it was just 2½ months[71]), but the burden is more difficult to discharge when the period relied upon is short.[72]

Serious and compelling family or other considerations which make exclusion of the child undesirable

9.57 The *'serious and compelling'* test is not an easy one to satisfy.[73] The test is a question of fact that can involve consideration of a myriad of circumstances and issues, and it is not possible to give a definitive list of what constitutes serious and compelling circumstances. The guidance to immigration officers[74] explains two routes for determining whether there are serious and compelling family or other considerations, depending on whether the sponsor is or is not a parent. If the sponsor is not a parent, the only circumstances to be taken into account are those relating to the child and not the UK-based sponsor. If the sponsor is a parent settled in the UK, then the circumstances of the parent in the UK (of an emotional or a physical nature) may be taken into account. In both cases, the guidance specifies that the circumstances surrounding the child must be exceptional in relation to those of other children living in the country

---

[64] *TD (Para 297(i)(e): 'sole responsibility')* [2006] UKAIT 00049 at [13].

[65] See *Immigration Directorate Instructions*, Chapter 8, Annex FM3.2 at 4.1.

[66] See, e g *Ramos v Immigration Appeal Tribunal* [1989] Imm AR 148, per Dillon LJ at 151.

[67] *Cenir v Entry Clearance Officer* [2003] EWCA Civ 572, [2003] All ER (D) 286 (Mar), per Buxton LJ at [6].

[68] *Immigration Directorate Instructions*, Chapter 8, Annex FM3.2 at 4.2.

[69] *TD (Para 297(i)(e): 'sole responsibility')* [2006] UKAIT 00049 at [16].

[70] *NA (Bangladesh) v Secretary of State for the Home Department* [2007] EWCA Civ 128, per Pill LJ at [24].

[71] *Nmaju v Secretary of State for the Home Department* [2001] INLR 26.

[72] *TD (Para 297(i)(e): 'sole responsibility')* [2006] UKAIT 00049 at [28]. The *Immigration Directorate Instructions*, Chapter 8, Annex FM3.2 notes (at 4.1) that sole responsibility is usually demonstrated for a substantial period of time.

[73] See *Tiwana v Entry Clearance Officer – Islamabad* [2002] UKIAT 04889 at [8]; *SK ('Adoption' not recognised in UK)* [2006] UKAIT 00068 at [39].

[74] *Immigration Directorate Instructions*, Chapter 8, Annex FM3.2, Part 1.

in which the child lives. It is not sufficient to show that the applicant would be better off with the sponsor.[75] When considering this comparative test, the decision-maker should consider as relevant the applicant's age, growing maturity and independence.[76] Where the child regards the sponsors as her natural parents as well as her adoptive parents, that may also tend towards a finding of serious and compelling family considerations.[77]

Under the age of 18

9.58   Where in the Immigration Rules there is reference to a person being under the age of 18, the person must be under that age at the date of the application, not the date of decision.[78]

Independent life

9.59   The requirement not to be leading an independent life was not defined in any way in the Immigration Rules until an amendment was made to the Rules on 9 July 2012. Under the interpretive provision of para 6 of the Immigration Rules, the term 'must not be leading an independent life' is defined as meaning that:

> '... the applicant does not have a partner as defined in Appendix FM, is living with their parents (except where they are at boarding school, college or university as part of their full-time education), is not employed full-time (unless aged 18 years or over), is wholly or mainly dependent upon their parents for financial support (unless aged 18 years or over) and is wholly or mainly dependent on their parents for emotional support ...'

9.60   The precise term 'must not be leading an independent life' is used solely within Appendix FM, which is not directly concerned with applications in respect of adopted children or children it is intended to adopt. It will be self-evident that some elements of the above definition are wholly inappropriate to many adoption situations.

9.61   There is no case-law on the meaning of the term 'independent life' within the provisions of the Immigration Rules focusing on adoption. It is likely that some elements of the definition set out above will be instructive. For example, emotional and financial independence from carers and adopters/prospective adopters and full-time or significant employment are likely to be considered factors tending towards a finding of an independent life.

---

[75]   *Tiwana v Entry Clearance Officer – Islamabad* [2002] UKIAT 04889 at [8].
[76]   *SO (Nigeria) v Secretary of State for the Home Department* [2007] EWCA Civ 76, per Hallett LJ at [15].
[77]   *Buama (Inter-country Adoption – Competent Court)* [2012] UKUT 00146 (IAC) at [25].
[78]   Paragraph 27 of the Immigration Rules.

9.62 Before the new definition set out above, authoritative case-law on the meaning of 'independent life' had been sparse. In *MI (paragraph 298(iii) 'independent life') Pakistan*,[79] the Tribunal reached the (acknowledged) unhelpful conclusion that:[80]

> 'As with the proverbial elephant, it may be harder to explain what an "independent life" is, than to recognise it when one sees it. It has to be looked at (in that much-abused phrase) "in the round".'

9.63 The Tribunal further explained that dependency need not be borne out of necessity but can be a matter of choice.[81]

9.64 In *NM ('leading an independent life') Zimbabwe*,[82] the Tribunal held[83] that to fail under the requirement not to be leading an independent life one has to have formed a separate social unit, whether alone or with others (such as a boyfriend or a girlfriend). The Tribunal then clarified this further by explaining that:[84]

> 'The crucial issue is always to ask whether the child has, through choice, separated from his parents' family to form his own social unit, whether alone, by marrying or as part of his own independent social unit.'

9.65 The Tribunal also held[85] that financial self-sufficiency does not in itself lead to the conclusion that a person is leading an independent life. This conclusion may not withstand the element of the new definition under para 6 of the Immigration Rules which requires that – in order not to be leading an independent life – a child must be wholly or mainly financially dependent on his parents. It remains to be seen whether the courts will allow the new definition set out under para 6 in respect of the wording under Appendix FM to influence the definition of the similarly worded tests in other parts of the Immigration Rules.

Adequacy of maintenance

9.66 There are two different tests for the adequacy of maintenance, depending on whether the case falls within or outside of Appendix FM of the Immigration Rules. In respect of the adoption rules at paras 309A to 316F of the Immigration Rules, Appendix FM only applies in respect of applications made after 9 July 2012 and only in the following circumstances:[86]

---

[79]   [2007] UKAIT 00052.
[80]   Ibid, at [4].
[81]   Ibid, at [3].
[82]   [2007] UKAIT 00051.
[83]   Ibid, at [13].
[84]   Ibid, at [14].
[85]   Ibid, at [21].
[86]   Set out under the Transitional Provisions at HC395, para A280.

- where the application is for limited leave to enter or remain in the UK with a view to settlement as the adopted child of a parent or parents given limited leave to enter or remain in the UK with a view to settlement, in circumstances where one parent is present and settled in the UK or being admitted on the same occasion for settlement and the other parent is being or has been given limited leave to enter or remain in the UK with a view to settlement;[87]

- where the application is the same as above, but the circumstances are that there is a de facto adoption where one parent has a right of abode in the UK or indefinite leave to enter or remain in the UK and is seeking admission on the same occasion for the purpose of settlement and the other parent is not present and settled or being admitted for settlement on the same occasion as the applicant;[88]

- where the application is for limited leave to enter the UK with a view to settlement as a child for adoption, and one prospective parent is present and settled in the UK and the other is being given limited leave to enter or remain with a view to settlement on the same occasion that the child is seeking admission, or has previously been given such leave;[89]

- where the application is on the same basis as that above, and one prospective parent is being admitted for settlement on the same occasion that the other is being granted limited leave to enter with a view to settlement, which is also on the same occasion that the child is seeking admission.[90]

9.67 Where Appendix FM applies, the application must meet the financial requirements set out under Appendix FM.[91] In short, those requirements provide that the applicant's parent and parent's partner must provide evidence of a specified gross annual income of at least £18,600 plus £3,800 for the first child included in the application and £2,400 for each additional child included in the application. Savings over and above £16,000 can be counted towards the requisite gross annual income figure, though at 40% of their total amount. For example, if a person has £26,000 of savings, then £4,000 (40% of the £10,000 savings over and above the £16,000 figure) can be counted towards the gross annual income figure. Third party support cannot be relied upon to prove the requisite figure.

9.68 Where the applicant's parent's partner receives disability living allowance, severe disablement allowance, industrial injury disablement benefit, attendance allowance or carer's allowance, the financial requirements of

---

[87] HC395, para 314(i)(a).
[88] HC395, para 314(i)(d).
[89] HC395, para 316(i)(d).
[90] HC395, para 316(i)(e).
[91] HC395, Appendix FM paras E-ECC 2.1–2.3 for entry clearance applications and E-LTRC 2.1-2.3 for leave to remain applications.

Appendix FM do not apply so long as the applicant's parent's partner is able to maintain and accommodate themselves, the applicant's parent, the applicant and any dependants adequately without recourse to public funds.[92]

9.69 There is very detailed and clear prescriptive guidance as to when income and savings can be counted, and what evidence needs to be provided to prove the level of income and savings to the immigration officer. The guidance can be found in Appendix FM-SE and is also helpfully explained in the *Immigration Directorate Instructions, Family Members under Appendix FM of the Immigration Rules, Annex FM Section FM 1.7 Financial Requirements*.[93] A full explanation of this guidance is outside the remit of this book, but reference should be made to the terms of Appendix FM-SE and to the Immigration Directorate Instruction if an application is being made in one of the rare adoption situations in which Appendix FM applies to intercountry adoption.

9.70 Where Appendix FM does not apply, the level of maintenance is deemed adequate where the level of income available to the family after deduction of income tax, national insurance contributions and housing costs equates to or exceeds the level of income the family would receive were they in receipt of income support.[94] Where the sponsor is in receipt of public funds, those can be relied upon in calculating the adequacy of maintenance.[95] Where a sponsor is in receipt of disability living allowance, that amount can be considered as part of the sponsor's income to show adequacy of maintenance to the extent the sponsor can establish that it will be used to maintain the applicant rather than to be spent on assistance for the sponsor's disability.[96] The Supreme Court held in *Mahad v Entry Clearance Officer* that maintenance can be provided by way of third party support,[97] albeit the case did not refer specifically to the paragraphs of the Immigration Rules concerned with adoption. Whilst the financial requirements under Appendix FM preclude reliance on third party support, it does not appear that that guidance will impact on circumstances in which Appendix FM does not impact on the terms of the Immigration Rules.

---

[92]   HC395, paras E-ECC 2.3 and E-LTRC 2.3 of Appendix FM.
[93]   Which can be found at http://www.ukba.homeoffice.gov.uk/sitecontent/documents/policyandlaw/IDIs/chp8-annex/section-FM-1.7.pdf?view=Binary.
[94]   HC395, para 6, definitions of 'adequate' and 'adequately'. This effectively places on a more formal footing the test set out in *KA (Adequacy of Maintenance) Pakistan* [2006] UKAIT 00065, [2007] Imm AR 155, as approved by the Court of Appeal in *French v Entry Clearance Officer, Kingston* [2011] EWCA Civ 35, [2011] Imm AR 387.
[95]   *Mahad v Entry Clearance Officer* [2009] UKSC 16, [2010] 1 WLR 48 at [14]. This is also implicit from para 6A of the Immigration Rules. However, see **9.72** as to the definition of 'without recourse to public funds'.
[96]   *MK (Somalia)* [2007] EWCA Civ 1521, [2008] Imm AR 412 (Pill LJ dissenting).
[97]   [2009] UKSC 16, [2010] 1 WLR 48. Although that case specifically concerned the maintenance provisions under para 281, 297 and 317 of the Immigration Rules, the Supreme Court notes that all maintenance requirements under Part 8 are similarly drafted, and no distinction can sensibly be drawn between the provisions considered in that case and those in the paragraphs of the Immigration Rules relating to adoption. The application of *Mahad* to the adoption paragraphs has not yet been tested in case-law.

Accommodation

9.71 Accommodation must be owned or occupied exclusively by the adoptive parent(s). The requirement for accommodation to be occupied exclusively[98] by the adoptive parent(s) merely requires that they have exclusive use of part of the accommodation.[99] Thus exclusive use of a bedroom in a home owned and otherwise occupied by a third party would, for example, suffice (so long as the overcrowding provisions set out below were not breached). To be adequate, accommodation must also not breach public health requirements and must not be overcrowded. For England and Wales, overcrowding is defined by Part X of the Housing Act 1985.[100] There is overcrowding in any of the following circumstances:

- When the number of persons sleeping in a dwelling and the number of rooms available as sleeping accommodation[101] is such that two persons of opposite sex, aged ten or over, who are not living together as husband and wife, must sleep in the same room.[102]

- The number of persons sleeping in a dwelling is in excess of the lowest number permitted in line with the two tables below (with a child under the age of one not counting, and a child over one but under ten counting as half of a unit):[103]

Number of rooms available as sleeping accommodation	Number of persons
1	2
2	3
3	5
4	7 $\frac{1}{2}$
5 or more	2 for each room

Floor area of each room available as sleeping accommodation	Number of persons
110 sq ft or more	2
90 sq ft or more but less than 110 sq ft	1$\frac{1}{2}$
70 sq ft or more but less than 90 sq ft	1
50 sq ft or more but less than 70 sq ft	$\frac{1}{2}$

---

[98] As the alternative to ownership.
[99] HC395, para 6, definition of 'occupy exclusively'.
[100] For Scotland see the Housing (Scotland) Act 1987, and for Northern Ireland see the Housing (Northern Ireland) Order 1988.
[101] Defined by Housing Act 1985 (HA 1985), s 325(2)(b) as bedrooms and living rooms.
[102] HA 1985, s 325.
[103] HA 1985, s 326.

Without recourse to public funds

9.72 The rules on recourse to public funds are set out in paras 6 and 6A–6C of the Immigration Rules, which can be found in the statutory material in Part 5 of this book.

9.73 'Public funds' are defined under para 6 as:

'(a) housing under Part VI or VII of the Housing Act 1996 and under Part II of the Housing Act 1985, Part I or II of the Housing (Scotland) Act 1987, Part II of the Housing (Northern Ireland) Order 1981 or Part II of the Housing (Northern Ireland) Order 1988;

(b) attendance allowance, severe disablement allowance, carer's allowance and disability living allowance under Part III of the Social Security Contribution and Benefits Act 1992;, income support, council tax benefit and housing benefit under Part VII of that Act; a social fund payment under Part VIII of that Act; child benefit under Part IX of that Act; income based jobseeker's allowance under the Jobseekers Act 1995, income related allowance under Part 1 of the Welfare Reform Act 2007 (employment and support allowance) state pension credit under the State Pension Credit Act 2002; or child tax credit and working tax credit under Part 1 of the Tax Credits Act 2002;

(c) attendance allowance, severe disablement allowance, carer's allowance and disability living allowance under Part III of the Social Security Contribution and Benefits (Northern Ireland) Act 1992; income support, council tax benefit and, housing benefit under Part VII of that Act; a social fund payment under Part VIII of that Act; child benefit under Part IX of that Act; income based jobseeker's allowance under the Jobseekers (Northern Ireland) Order 1995 or income related allowance under Part 1 of the Welfare Reform Act (Northern Ireland) 2007.'

9.74 An applicant is not treated as having had recourse to public funds if reliant on public funds provided to his sponsor, so long as the sponsor has not/will not become entitled to increased or additional public funds as a result of the applicant's presence in the UK.[104]

9.75 An applicant is also not treated as having recourse to public funds if allowed to have those benefits under exceptions set out in regulations made under the Immigration and Asylum Act 1999, s 115 or the Tax Credits Act 2002, s 42.[105] Those regulations provide for various specific circumstances where a person subject to immigration control is expressly excluded from the restrictions on entitlement to specific benefits.

---

[104] HC395, para 6A. If the entitlement is a joint entitlement of the sponsor and the applicant due to regulations made under s 115 of the Immigration and Asylum Act 1999 or s 42 of the Tax Credits Act 2002 (which provide for exceptions when a person subject to immigration control may receive some of those benefits defined as 'public funds' in HC395, para 6) then the applicant will not be regarded as having recourse to public funds even though the sponsor is entitled to increased or additional public funds as a result of the applicant's presence in the UK.

[105] HC395, para 6B.

9.76 However, where an application for entry clearance is made from outside the UK, the applicant will be regarded as having recourse to public funds where the applicant relies on future entitlement to any public funds that would be payable to himself or his sponsor as a result of his presence in the UK, notwithstanding that the entitlement is as a result of the exclusions under the statutory provisions referred to in the above paragraph.[106]

Inability of the original parent(s) or current carer(s) to care for him

9.77 The inability requirement covers children whose natural parents are *unable* to care for them, as opposed to those with the ability but who *choose* not to care for them.[107] For example, parents who gave birth to a daughter and rejected her because they had wanted a son, may have been unwilling to care for her but were not unable to do so, and accordingly the requirement under the rules was held not to be satisfied.[108]

Genuine transfer of parental responsibility

9.78 This sits in the Immigration Rules as a corollary to the requirement that the original parents or current carers are unable to care for the adopted child. There is scant authority on what constitutes a genuine transfer of parental responsibility. In *MF (Immigration – Adoption – Genuine Transfer of Parental Responsibility) (Philippines)*,[109] an adoption had taken place in The Phillippines, which was accepted as a lawful adoption in the UK. However, in considering whether the terms of para 310(ix) of the Immigration Rules were satisfied, the Immigration Appeal Tribunal held that sending money, making telephone calls and writing letters did not constitute sufficient evidence of a transfer of parental responsibility. The Tribunal stated that there was no evidence of the adoptive parents making the sort of decisions that would be part of the transfer of parental responsibility, but unhelpfully the Tribunal did not go on to explain the decisions it expected adoptive parents to make as part of that transfer. The Tribunal in *Aman Gill v Secretary of State for the Home Department*[110] also held that the taking of financial responsibility did not in itself equate to a transfer of parental responsibility, but once more gave no guidance on what would constitute such a transfer. In *Buama (Inter-country*

---

[106] HC395, para 6C. This paragraph prevents, for example, a couple from seeking to show adequacy of maintenance by relying on tax credits to which they would be entitled under regulations made under s 42 of the Tax Credits Act 2002.

[107] *Sharma v Entry Clearance Officer, New Delhi* [2005] EWCA Civ 89, [2005] 2 FLR 219.

[108] *Sharma v Entry Clearance Officer, New Delhi* [2005] EWCA Civ 89, [2005] 2 FLR 219.

[109] [2004] UKIAT 00094 at [19].

[110] TH/8624/97 (24 March 2000) (Unreported). It is also notable that *Pawandeep Singh v Entry Clearance Officer, New Delhi* [2004] EWCA Civ 1075, [2005] QB 608 at [9], the adjudicator had found that there had been a genuine transfer of parental responsibility by supporting the adoptive child financially and making all major decisions about his care and future, notwithstanding that the adoptive child's family in India retained day-to-day responsibility for him when he was not at school. This point was not subject to appeal in that case.

Adoption – Competent Court),[111] the Upper Tribunal held that there had plainly been a genuine transfer of parental responsibility in circumstances where the child considered her adoptive parents to be her natural parents, her real mother was dead, her father had abandoned her, the adoptive parties underwent a formal adoption through the Ghanaian courts and her adoptive parents had appointed the adoptive mother's sister as the child's guardian in Ghana and had been solely responsible for the child's upkeep for 8½ years.

9.79 It is worth bearing in mind that these cases were cases of adoptions by relatives, where the adoption processes were conducted entirely within the state of origin. Although there is no case-law on point, it is less likely that an entry clearance officer would take issue on the genuine transfer of parental responsibility where the relevant UK authorities had been involved in the adoption process, whether the adoption is pursuant to the Convention or otherwise.

Lost or broken his ties with his family of origin

9.80 There are three points to note in respect of the requirement to have broken ties with the family of origin.

9.81 First, 'family of origin' is not limited to the natural parents, but includes the family with whom a child was living and by whom the child was being brought up and cared for before the adoption took place.[112]

9.82 Secondly, the break in ties need not be a break of all emotional ties, but of the ties of responsibility.[113] The purpose of the requirement is to ensure the adoption is not temporary (with the family of origin intending to take back responsibility once the child gains entry clearance to the UK). There is no need for all contact with the family of origin to be lost. In *Boadi v Entry Clearance Officer, Ghana*,[114] Collins J gave the example of a child whose single parent was smitten with a terminal illness and was wholly unable to care for the child. That child would not fall foul of the 'broken ties' requirement because of a retention of affection for his dying parent, or because he visited the parent. In the later case of *MF (Immigration – Adoption – Genuine Transfer of Parental Responsibility) (Philippines)*,[115] the IAT held a child could not be said to have broken ties with her biological father when she saw him once a week and was accompanied by him to the immigration interview. This does not appear to stand on all fours with the earlier decision in *Boadi*. The *Boadi* judgment is not referred to in *MF*. In *MF*, the child was living with her siblings and her maternal uncle and his family, she saw her father weekly when he visited her

---

[111] *Buama (Inter-country Adoption – Competent Court)* [2012] UKUT 00146 (IAC).
[112] *Boadi v Entry Clearance Officer, Ghana* [2002] UKIAT 01323, [2003] INLR 54 at [13]. *MF (Immigration – Adoption – Genuine Transfer of Parental Responsibility) (Philippines)* [2004] UKIAT 00094 at [17].
[113] *Boadi* at [14]–[15].
[114] *Boadi* at [15].
[115] [2004] UKIAT 00094.

siblings, and there were questions raised as to whether there was sufficient evidence of a genuine transfer of parental responsibility. In *Boadi*, the child's mother had died, her father had left her to the care of his mother, and her grandmother had left her in the care of a reverend. The remaining tie between the child and her family of origin was that she visited her grandmother once a month. It may be that the difference between the two judgments can be explained as a question of fact and degree, albeit it is difficult to see precisely where the courts will draw the line.

9.83 Thirdly, where the application is being made under para 316A (ie an application for limited leave to enter the UK with a view to settlement as a child for adoption), the ties need not already be broken at the time of the application for entry clearance. A mere intention to break the ties with the family of origin suffices.[116]

Adoption of convenience

9.84 The relevant paragraphs of the Immigration Rules require that the adoption is not one of convenience arranged to facilitate the child's admission to, or his remaining in, the UK.[117] The distinction to be drawn in this requirement is between adoption where admission to, or remaining in, the UK is a by-product of the adoption on the one hand, and adoption where admission to, or remaining in, the UK is its sole purpose, on the other.[118] The distinction was explained in powerful terms by Thorpe LJ in *In re J (Adoption: Non-patrial)*[119] where he spoke of applications for sham adoptions as being:

> 'solely designed to achieve a legal status unsupported by the fundamental foundations: ... the creation of the psychological relationship of parent and child with all its far-reaching manifestations and consequences.'

9.85 It is instructive in the context of this requirement to note the approach taken by the courts when an application is made to the family court by a British citizen habitually resident in the UK to adopt a foreign child who is already in the UK but without permanency of status (either because they have limited leave to enter or remain, or are an overstayer or an illegal entrant). As we have seen above, the effect of the court making an adoption order in those circumstances will be to confer British citizenship on the child.[120] In *Re B (A Minor) (Adoption Order: Nationality)*,[121] B and her mother were given 6

---

[116] HC395, para 316A(vii).
[117] HC395, paras 310(xi), 311(xi), 314(x) and 316A(viii).
[118] See, e g *Boadi v Entry Clearance Officer, Ghana* [2002] UKIAT 01323, [2003] INLR 54 at [8]–[9]. In *Re A (A Minor) (Adoption: Non-patrial)* [1996] 3 FCR 1, Thorpe LJ focuses on whether the adoption is a device to circumvent immigration regulations and controls. In *VB v Entry Clearance Officer, Ghana* [2002] UKIAT 01323, the IAT pointed out that most overseas adoptions take place in order to facilitate entry into the UK, and this factor by itself does not render the adoption one of convenience.
[119] [1998] 1 FLR 225.
[120] BNA 1981, s 1(5) and (5A).
[121] [1999] 2 AC 136.

months' leave to enter the UK to visit B's mother's parents. She was enrolled at school for that period. B's mother returned to Jamaica but B remained in the UK with her grandparents. They applied for an adoption order, having been advised that that was the only basis on which B could acquire the right of abode in the UK. The House of Lords held that case-law supported two modest exclusionary principles in respect of the making of an adoption order in favour of a foreign child already in the UK without permanent status:[122]

- First, the court would not make an adoption order when the adopters did not intend to exercise any parental responsibility but merely wished to assist the child to acquire a right of abode.

- Secondly, the court would rarely make an adoption order when it would confer no benefits on the child during its childhood but give it the right of abode for the rest of its life.

THE POSITION OF EEA NATIONALS AS ADOPTIVE PARENTS

9.86 EEA nationals[123] residing in the UK and exercising Treaty rights in the UK[124] only fall within the definition of 'settled' under the relevant paragraphs of the Immigration Rules if they have the status of permanent residency in the UK.[125] Except for under para 316D,[126] it is a prerequisite of the relevant paragraphs of the Immigration Rules that an adoptive parent is either settled or being admitted for settlement, and therefore the adoptive child of an EEA national will not satisfy the requirements for leave to enter or remain unless the EEA national parent has permanent residency status. This will not, of course, affect those adoptions to which the Immigration Rules are not relevant. Thus, for example, where there is a Hague Convention adoption with one adoptive parent a British citizen and the other an EEA national without permanent residency status, then so long as the adoptive parents are habitually resident in the UK the child will have British citizenship conferred automatically on him.[127]

---

[122] [1999] 2 AC 136 at 141G–H.
[123] Ie a national of an EEA State as defined under the Immigration (European Economic Area) Regulations 2006, SI 2006/1003 (the EEA Regs) – namely, the UK, Austria, Belgium, Bulgaria, Cyprus, Czech Republic, Denmark, Estonia, Finland, France, Germany, Greece, Hungary, Iceland, Ireland, Italy, Latvia, Liechtenstein, Lithuania, Luxembourg, Malta, Netherlands, Norway, Poland, Portugal, Romania, Slovakia, Slovenia, Spain, Sweden and Switzerland.
[124] Ie is residing in the UK in accordance with the EEA Regs.
[125] In accordance with the EEA Regs, reg 15 and Sch 2, para 2. The EEA Regs are complex and an explanation of the EEA Regs and how a person acquires a permanent right of residence fall outside the scope of this chapter. It should be noted, however, that reg 15(2) and (3) provides that once acquired, the right of permanent residence shall be lost only through absence from the UK for a period exceeding two consecutive years, or where removal is justified on grounds of public policy, public security or public health.
[126] Setting out requirements for limited leave to enter the UK with a view to settlement as a child for adoption under the Convention.
[127] BNA 1981, s 1(5) and (5A).

9.87   EEA nationals, including those who are not settled in the UK[128] but are exercising Treaty rights in the UK, can also rely on the EEA Family Permit scheme to bring a child adopted through a Designated List Adoption into the UK.

9.88   The EEA Family Permit scheme is set out under reg 12 of the EEA Regs. It provides for a number of circumstances in which an entry clearance officer must issue an EEA family permit to a person who applies for one. A person who, on arrival in the UK, produces a valid passport and an EEA Family Permit must be admitted to the UK.[129] The relevant circumstance for present purposes is that provided under reg 12(1), which provides that:

> 'An entry clearance officer must issue an EEA family permit to a person who applies for one if the person is the family member of an EEA national and –
>
> (a)   the EEA national –
>   (i)   is residing in the UK in accordance with these Regulations; or
>   (ii)   will be travelling to the United Kingdom within six months of the date of the application and will be an EEA national residing in the United Kingdom in accordance with these Regulations on arrival in the United Kingdom; and
> (b)   the family member will be accompanying the EEA national to the United Kingdom or joining the EEA national there.'

9.89   'Family member' is defined as including:[130]

> '(b)   direct descendants of his, his spouse or his civil partner who are –
>   (i)   under 21; and
>   (ii)   dependants of his, his spouse or his civil partner.'

9.90   'Direct descendants' is not defined in the EEA Regs and there has been no case-law expressing conclusions as to how far the term extends in respect of children who are not the natural descendants of the EEA national. In *FK and MK (EEA Regulations: 'Descendants': meaning) Sierra Leone*,[131] the AIT accepted by implication that a child of a formal adoption fell within the definition of 'direct descendants'. In respect of the question whether de facto adoptions come within the EEA Regs, the AIT accepted that de facto adoptions may be recognised in English law where the applicable law prevents a formal legally-effective adoption from taking place. The AIT held that the definition of 'de facto adoption' under para 309A of the Immigration Rules should not be held as a formal definition outside the ambit of those rules. Unfortunately, the AIT neither reached a conclusion on whether de facto adoptions could fall within the definition of 'direct descendants' nor did the AIT explain what constitutes a de facto adoption outside of the purposes of the definition in para 309A of the Immigration Rules (save to assert that there

---

[128]   Ie do not have permanent residency status.
[129]   EEA Regs, reg 11(2).
[130]   EEA Regs, reg 7(1)(b).
[131]   [2007] UKAIT 00038.

needs, as a prerequisite, to be an intention to adopt). It is notable, however, that the current guidance given to immigration officers, updated most recently on 22 August 2012, contradicts this decision. The guidance acknowledges that children adopted lawfully in a country on the Designated List are direct descendants, as are those subject to a de facto adoption as defined under para 309A of the Immigration Rules.[132]

9.91   An EEA national cannot rely upon the EEA Family Permit scheme to bring in to the UK a child adopted in a country not on the Designated List, save where it meets the requirements of a de facto adoption, as explained above. Where there is not a de facto adoption, the requirements of the relevant paragraphs of the Immigration Rules[133] have to be satisfied in order to obtain leave to enter so that adoption proceedings can be carried out in the UK, or a declaration has to be sought for the recognition of the adoption. This is because the child will not otherwise be recognised in the UK as the adoptive child of the EEA national parent(s), and accordingly will not fall within the remit of the EEA Family Permit scheme by reason of that relationship.

ARTICLE 8 AND DECISIONS ON THE GRANT OF LEAVE TO ENTER OR REMAIN

9.92   Even where an applicant does not satisfy the requirements of the relevant Immigration Rules, the decision-maker should give consideration to whether leave to enter or remain should be granted to avoid a breach of the right to family life under Article 8 of the ECHR.[134] Article 8 of the ECHR reads as follows:

> '(1)   Everyone has the right to respect for his private and family life, his home and his correspondence.
>
> (2)   There shall be no interference by a public authority with the exercise of this right except such as is in accordance with the law and is necessary in a democratic society in the interests of national security, public safety or the economic well-being of the country, for the prevention of disorder or crime, for the protection of health or morals, or for the protection of the rights and freedoms of others.'

9.93   The general test for determining whether there has been a breach of Article 8 is provided by the House of Lords decision in *R (Razgar) v Secretary of State for the Home Department*,[135] where Lord Bingham set out the following five questions:[136]

---

[132]   See *Guidance – Adopted Children – version 4.0* (valid from 22 August 2012) at pp 27–28.

[133]   Ie HC395, para 316A or 316D.

[134]   Incorporated into UK law on 2 October 2000 pursuant to the Human Rights Act 1998 (HRA 1998). HC395, para 2 requires all entry clearance officers, immigration officers and Home Office staff in the Immigration and Nationality Directorate to carry out their duties in compliance with HRA 1998. This accords with the requirements of HRA 1998, s 6.

[135]   [2004] UKHL 27, [2004] 2 AC 368, per Lord Bingham at [17].

[136]   Albeit a removal case, this test is also relied upon in respect of applications to enter the UK.

'(1) Will the proposed removal be an interference by a public authority with the exercise of the applicant's right to respect for his private or (as the case may be) family life?

(2) If so, will such interference have consequences of such gravity as potentially to engage the operation of article 8?

(3) If so, is such interference in accordance with the law?

(4) If so, is such interference necessary in a democratic society in the interests of national security, public safety or the economic well-being of the country, for the prevention of disorder or crime, for the protection of health or morals, or for the protection of the rights and freedoms of others?

(5) If so, is such interference proportionate to the legitimate public end sought to be achieved?'

9.94 Looking at Lord Bingham's first question in *Razgar*, the European Court of Human Rights has consistently held that the relationship between an adoptive parent and adopted child can constitute family life within the meaning of Article 8.[137] Domestic courts have held likewise, even in cases in which the adoption is not recognised as an adoption in the UK courts.[138] The question of whether the relationship between child and adoptive parent suffices to constitute family life is one of fact and degree.[139] An adoptive relationship which arises from a lawful adoption that is not a sham can be considered sufficient to fall within the protection of Article 8.[140] Although the question of whether there is family life in an adoption case must be considered in light of international instruments, including the Convention, the fact that an adoption does not meet the requirements of those international instruments does not necessarily mean that little weight should be accorded to the adoption in considering whether family life exists. The relevant question is whether the departure from the requirements is substantive or procedural.[141] It is highly relevant to the existence of family life under Article 8(1) whether the adoption can be seen as being in the best interests of the adopted child, even if consideration of the child's best interests was not part of the process for

---

See, eg *R (Aguilar Quila) v Secretary of State for the Home Department (AIRE Centre and Others intervening), R (Bibi) v Same (Same intervening)* [2011] UKSC 45, [2012] 1 AC 621, in which Lord Wilson JSC relied upon para [17] of *Razgar* in respect of appeals concerning leave to enter *and* leave to remain. In jurisprudence of the European Court of Human Rights, it has been made clear that the principles applicable to positive obligations of the state (to allow somebody to enter) and negative obligations (not to remove somebody) are similar: see *Tuquabo-Tekle v The Netherlands* [2006] 1 FLR 798, and the discussion of positive and negative obligations in the *Aguilar Quila* case at [38]–[43].

[137] See, eg *X v France* (App No 9993/82) 31 DR 241 (5 October 1982); *Aminoff v Sweden* (App No 10554/83); 43 DR 120 (15 May 1985); *Pini v Romania* (2005) 40 EHRR 13.

[138] *Pawandeep Singh v Entry Clearance Officer, New Delhi* [2004] EWCA Civ 1075, [2005] QB 608. In *FK and MK (EEA Regulations: 'Descendants': Meaning) Sierra Leone* [2007] UKAIT 00038, the AIT accepted that de facto adoptions could constitute family life for the purposes of Article 8.

[139] *Pawandeep Singh v Entry Clearance Officer, New Delhi* [2004] EWCA Civ 1075; [2005] QB 608, per Dyson LJ at [25].

[140] *Pini v Romania* (2005) 40 EHRR 13 at [148].

[141] *Pawandeep Singh v Entry Clearance Officer, New Delhi* [2004] EWCA Civ 1075, [2005] QB 608, per Dyson LJ at [33].

granting the adoption order.[142] In determining whether family life exists, regard should be had not merely to the fact of the adoption, but also to all of the personal, emotional, psychological, social, cultural and religious consequences that flow from it.[143]

9.95   In a controversial decision, the Asylum and Immigration Tribunal in *SK* *('Adoption' not recognised in UK) India*[144] held that:[145]

'There can be no "human right" to enjoy in any particular state the consequences of an adoption, unless the adoption is one recognised as such in that state.'

9.96   This statement seems to contradict the Court of Appeal's decision in *Pawandeep Singh v Entry Clearance Officer, New Delhi*[146] that one looks to the substance of the adoptive relationship rather than merely the legalities of the adoption. The decision in *SK* has been heavily criticised by leading commentators.[147]

9.97   Moving on to the question of the proportionality of any decision to refuse leave to enter or to remain, in the case of *Huang v Secretary of State for the Home Department*[148] the House of Lords set out the balancing test to be carried out at Lord Bingham's question (5) in the following manner:

'In an article 8 case where this question is reached, the ultimate question for the appellate immigration authority is whether the refusal of leave to enter or remain, in circumstances where the life of the family cannot reasonably be expected to be enjoyed elsewhere, taking full account of all considerations weighing in favour of the refusal, prejudices the family life of the applicant in a manner sufficiently serious to amount to a breach of the fundamental right protected by article 8.'

9.98   The function of a court or tribunal presented with a claim that an immigration decision breaches Article 8 of the ECHR is to decide whether the decision is compatible or incompatible with Article 8, rather than merely a secondary, reviewing function of determining whether the decision-maker misdirected himself, made an irrational decision or acted with procedural impropriety.[149]

---

[142]   Ibid, per Dyson LJ at [34].

[143]   Ibid, per Munby LJ at [86].

[144]   [2006] UKAIT 00068.

[145]   Ibid, at [22].

[146]   [2004] EWCA Civ 1075, [2005] QB 608.

[147]   See Ian Macdonald QC and Ronan Toal, *'Macdonald's Immigration Law and Practice'* (8th edn, LexisNexis, 2010) at [11.116].

[148]   [2007] UKHL 11, [2007] 2 AC 167 at [20].

[149]   Ibid, at [11]. Where HC395, Appendix FM applies, para GEN 1.1 of the Appendix explains that the requirements in the Appendix reflect the balance to be struck between the right to respect for private and family life on the one hand, and the legitimate aims set out under Article 8(2) ECHR on the other. It is intended that where Appendix FM applies, failure to comply with the requirements of the rules will generally mean failure to establish an Article 8 claim to enter or remain in the UK: see the Home Office document *Statement of Intent: Family Migration* (June 2012) at paras 7 and 31–43. The Home Office also expects the role of the

9.99   A court or tribunal will not just look at whether a decision to refuse leave to enter or remain breaches the Article 8 rights of the individual applicant, but also whether or not it breaches the Article 8 rights of that applicant's family members.[150]

9.100   Where the applicant's adoption is not one recognised by the UK courts, the availability to the applicant and adoptive parents of the avenue provided by para 316A of the Immigration Rules is a relevant consideration of substantial weight when considering the proportionality of a decision whether or not to grant leave to enter.[151]

9.101   Where the child is in the UK, and accordingly a decision on whether or not to grant leave to remain as an adoptive child is made, s 55 of the Borders, Citizenship and Immigration Act 2009 (BCIA 2009) needs to be taken into account. That section requires the Secretary of State for the Home Department to ensure that immigration decisions are discharged having regard to the need to safeguard and promote the welfare of children who are in the UK. In *ZH (Tanzania) v Secretary of State for the Home Department*,[152] the Supreme Court explained[153] that the impact of s 55 is that the best interests of the child must be a primary consideration (ie must be considered first). Being a primary consideration should not be confused with a paramount consideration, and the best interests of a child can be outweighed by the cumulative effect of other considerations. If an immigration decision is made about an adoptive child and s 55 is not complied with, the decision will not be in accordance with the law and accordingly will be in breach of Article 8(2) ECHR.[154] Where the child is outside the UK, BCIA 2009, s 55 does not apply.[155] However an Entry Clearance Officer should apply the spirit of s 55 if there is reason to suspect the child is in need of protection.[156] Where there is reason to believe that the welfare of a child may be compromised by refusing his application, it is incumbent on the decision-maker to sufficiently explore disputed material in

---

courts and tribunals to shift from reviewing the proportionality of individual administrative decisions to the proportionality of the Immigration Rules: *Immigration Rules on Family and Private Life* (HC 194). *Grounds of Compatibility with Article of the European Convention on Human Rights, Statement by the Home Office* (13 June 2012) at para 22. It remains to be seen whether the Home Office will attempt to extend this intention to other parts of the Immigration Rules (including those regarding adoption) to which Appendix FM does not apply, and also the approach that courts and tribunals will actually take to the manner in which the Home Office seek to restrict their role in considering interferences with a person's Article 8 rights.

[150]   *Beoku-Betts v Secretary of State for the Home Department* [2008] UKHL 39, [2009] AC 115.

[151]   *MN (India) v Entry Clearance Officer (New Delhi) and the Secretary of State for the Home Department* [2008] EWCA Civ 38, [2008] 2 FLR 87, per Wilson LJ at [32]–[33].

[152]   [2011] UKSC 4, [2011] 2 AC 166.

[153]   Ibid, per Baroness Hale JSC at [33].

[154]   Ibid, per Baroness Hale JSC at [24].

[155]   See *T (s 55 BCIA 2009 – entry clearance) Jamaica* [2011] UKUT 00483 at [21].

[156]   Ibid, at [23].

reaching a conclusion. That requirement includes taking account of the child's views if the child is capable of forming them.[157]

9.102 The European Court of Human Rights has held the following to be the basic applicable principles that provide the context to the scope of a state's obligations to admit children for the purpose of family reunion:[158]

- The extent of a state's obligation to admit to its territory relatives of settled immigrants will vary according to the particular circumstances of the persons involved and the general interest.

- As a matter of well-established international law and subject to its treaty obligations, a state has the right to control the entry of non-nationals to its territory.

- Where immigration is concerned, Article 8 cannot be considered to impose on a state a general obligation to respect the choice by married couples of the country of their matrimonial residence and to authorise family reunion in its territory.

9.103 Factors held to be relevant to whether or not there is a positive obligation on a state to admit a child for the purpose of family reunion include:[159]

- the age of the child concerned;

- their situation in their country of origin, including the presence of relatives there and the linguistic and cultural links with that country;

- their degree of dependence on their parents;

- the immigration status of the parents in the receiving country;

- the reasonableness of the applicant's family reuniting in the state of origin.

9.104 Where considering the removal of a person from the contracting state (ie the state that is a signatory to the ECHR), the European Court of Human Rights has consistently held the following to be relevant factors:[160]

---

[157] See *T (s 55 BCIA 2009 – entry clearance) Jamaica* [2011] UKUT 00483 at [36-37]; *ZH (Tanzania) v Secretary of State for the Home Department* [2011] UKSC 4, [2011] 2 AC 166 at [34]–[37].

[158] *Gul v Switzerland* (1996) 22 EHRR 93 at [38]; *Ahmut v The Netherlands* (1997) 24 EHRR 62 at [67]; *Sen v The Netherlands* (2003) 36 EHRR 7 at [36]; *Tuquabo-Tekle v The Netherlands* [2006] 1 FLR 798 at [43].

[159] *Sen v The Netherlands* (2003) 36 EHRR 7 at [37]–[40]; *Tuquabo-Tekle v The Netherlands* [2006] 1 FLR 798 at [44]–[52].

[160] See, e g *Rodrigues da Silva, Hoogkamer v The Netherlands* (2006) 44 EHRR 729; *Haghighi v The Netherlands* (2009) 49 EHRR SE8.

'Factors to be taken into account in this context are the extent to which family life is effectively ruptured, the extent of the ties in the Contracting State, whether there are insurmountable obstacles in the way of the family living in the country of origin of one or more of them, whether there are factors of immigration control (eg a history of breaches of immigration law) or considerations of public order weighing in favour of exclusion. Another important consideration will also be whether family life was created at a time when the persons involved were aware that the immigration status of one of them was such that the persistence of that family life within the host state would from the outset be precarious. The Court has previously held that where this is the case it is likely only to be in the most exceptional circumstances that the removal of the non-national family member will constitute a violation of Article 8.'

9.105 In *ZH (Tanzania)*[161] the Supreme Court quoted the above with approval and also held the following factors[162] set out by the European Court of Human Rights in *Boultif v Switzerland*[163] and *Üner v The Netherlands*[164] relevant to consideration of proportionality under Article 8 where a person is to be removed because he has no right to remain in the country (the factors are phrased in respect of the expulsion of a married person, but are analogously relevant where the person without leave is the child of the family):[165]

- the length of the applicant's stay in the country from which he or she is to be expelled;

- the nationalities of the various persons concerned;

- the applicant's family situation, such as the length of the marriage, and other factors expressing the effectiveness of a couple's family life;

- whether there are any children of the marriage, and is so, their age;

- the seriousness of the difficulties which the spouse is likely to encounter in the country to which the appellant is to be expelled;

- the best interests and well-being of the children, in particular the seriousness of the difficulties which any children of the applicant are likely to encounter in the country of removal;

- the solidity of social, cultural and family ties with the host country and with the country of destination.

---

[161] [2011] UKSC 4, [2011] 2 AC 166, per Baroness Hale JSC at [19].
[162] Ibid, at [17]–[18].
[163] (2001) 33 EHRR 1179.
[164] (2006) 45 EHRR 421.
[165] *Üner* and *Boultif* were both cases where deportation orders had been made following the commission by the applicant of criminal offences. Additional factors are set out in both cases to be considered where there has been a deportation order made, though those factors are not relevant in the situation of an ordinary removal.

RIGHTS OF APPEAL

9.106 There are two potentially relevant statutory schemes for appeals in intercountry adoption cases – the general scheme and that specific to appeals under the EEA Regs. This section deals first, with the general right of appeal, and second, with that under the EEA Regs. The purpose of this section is not to be a comprehensive guide to immigration appeals, but to raise those elements of the immigration appeal structure of central relevance to first appeals against immigration decisions in intercountry adoption cases.[166] Accordingly, matters such as deportation orders, exclusion orders and national security are not dealt with below.

The general scheme

9.107 Where an application for entry clearance or leave to enter the UK is refused, the applicant is entitled to appeal against that decision.[167] Likewise where an application for leave to remain is refused in circumstances where this constitutes a refusal to vary a person's leave to enter or remain in the UK and the consequence of the refusal is that the person has no such extant leave.[168] The application has to have been made during an extant period of leave. If leave had already expired before the application was made, the person is an overstayer and there is no right of appeal against the refusal.[169]

9.108 The appeal is made to the First-tier Tribunal of the Immigration and Asylum Chamber.[170]

9.109 The grounds on which an appeal can be brought are set out under NIAA 2002 s 84(1), as follows:

'(a) that the decision is not in accordance with immigration rules;
(b) that the decision is unlawful by virtue of ... [Article 20A of the Race Relations (Northern Ireland) Order 1997] (discrimination by public authorities);
(c) that the decision is unlawful under section 6 of the Human Rights Act 1998 (c 42) (public authority not to act contrary to Human Rights Convention) as being incompatible with the appellant's Convention rights;

---

[166] This section does not deal with onward appeals to the Upper Tribunal, Court of Appeal or Supreme Court.
[167] Nationality Immigration and Asylum Act 2002 (NIAA 2002), s 82(1) together with s 82(2)(a) or (b).
[168] NIAA 2002, s 82(1) together with s 82(2)(d). Where at the date of refusal of extension of leave the person has extant leave, the refusal is not an 'immigration decision' for the purpose of NIAA 2002, s 82(1) and (2): *SA (s 82(2)(d): interpretation and effect) (Pakistan)* [2007] UKAIT 00083. There are also rights of appeal in various other circumstances, including upon a decision to remove a person unlawfully in the UK (s 82(2)(g)) or illegal entrant (under s 82(2)(h)), or a family member of such a person (s 82(2)(i)).
[169] In those circumstances reliance would have to be placed on an application for judicial review. As explained in the footnote above, an overstayer or illegal entrant does, however, have a right of appeal against removal directions.
[170] NIAA 2002, s 82(1).

(d)   that the appellant is an EEA national or a member of the family of an EEA national and the decision breaches the appellant's rights under the [EU] Treaties in respect of entry to or residence in the United Kingdom;

(e)   that the decision is otherwise not in accordance with the law;

(f)   that the person taking the decision should have exercised differently a discretion conferred by immigration rules;

(g)   that removal of the appellant from the United Kingdom in consequence of the immigration decision would breach the United Kingdom's obligations under the Refugee Convention or would be unlawful under section 6 of the Human Rights Act 1998 as being incompatible with the appellant's Convention rights.'

9.110 In certain circumstances, the right of appeal is restricted to an appeal solely on the grounds set out at NIAA 2002, s 84(1)(b), (c) and (g). Those include where an immigration decision is taken on grounds that the applicant or a person of whom he is a dependant:

- does not satisfy a requirement as to age;[171]

- does not have an entry clearance or a passport;[172] or

- is seeking to be in the UK for a period greater than that permitted in his case by immigration rules.[173]

9.111 A person may also not appeal against refusal of leave to enter the UK, save on the grounds set out in NIAA 2002, s 84(1)(b), (c) or (g), unless on arrival in the UK he had entry clearance, and the purpose of entry specified in the entry clearance is the same as that specified in the application for leave to enter.[174] Where, before arrival in the UK, a person already has entry clearance operating as leave to enter,[175] this exclusion from a right of appeal will not apply.[176]

9.112 A person in the UK can only bring their appeal whilst in the UK[177] in circumstances specified in NIAA 2002, s 92. Circumstances in which there is an in-country right of appeal include:

---

[171]   Ibid, s 88(2)(a).

[172]   Ibid, s 88(2)(b) and (3)(a) and (b).

[173]   Ibid, s 88(2)(c).

[174]   Ibid, s 89.

[175]   Ie in accordance with the Immigration (Leave to Enter and Remain) Order 2000, SI 2000/1161, art 3, the entry clearance specifies the purpose for which the holder wishes to enter the UK, is endorsed with the conditions to which entry is subject or has a statement on it that it is to have effect as indefinite leave to enter the UK, and it is not endorsed on a travel document issued outside of the UK under Article 28 of the 1951 Convention relating to the Status of Refugees (unless issued before 27 February 2004).

[176]   *GO (Right of appeal: ss 89 and 92) (Nigeria)* [2008] UKAIT 00025.

[177]   When relying on the right of appeal under NIAA 2002, s 82(1).

- an appeal against refusal to vary a person's leave to enter or remain where the result of that refusal is the person has no leave to enter or remain;[178]

- an appeal against refusal of leave to enter if at the time of refusal the appellant is in the UK, and on arrival the appellant had entry clearance;[179]

- an appeal on asylum or human rights grounds, made whilst in the UK;[180]

- an appeal by an EEA national on grounds that the decision breaches the appellant's rights under the Community Treaties in respect of entry to or residence in the UK.[181]

9.113 Refusals of leave in intercountry adoption cases will most often occur when the applicant is outside the UK and entry clearance is refused. In those circumstances, the applicant has to put in a notice of appeal within 28 days of service of notice of the immigration decision.[182] Where the appeal is in-country, the time limit is 10 days from service of the notice of decision,[183] unless the appellant is in detention in which case it is 5 days.[184] Where notice of appeal is given out of time, an application may be made for an extension of time.[185] The First-tier Tribunal may extend time for appealing if satisfied that by reason of special circumstances it would be unjust not to do so.[186]

9.114 Appeals from within the UK are on Form IAFT-1. Appeals against decisions of entry clearance officers are on Form IAFT-2. Where the appeal can only be made after leaving the UK or an appellant chooses to leave the UK before exercising the right of appeal, notice of appeal must be on Form IAFT-3.[187]

9.115 Where a person is in the UK with limited leave to enter or remain and applies for a variation of leave before the leave expires, the leave is deemed extended whilst the application remains undecided and has not been

---

[178] Ibid, s 92(2).
[179] Ibid, s 92(3). There is, however, not an in-country right of appeal in a situation covered by s 92(3) where an immigration officer cancels leave on grounds that the person's purpose in arriving in the UK is different to that specified in the entry clearance: ibid, s 92(3A) to (3C).
[180] Ibid, s 92(4)(a).
[181] Ibid, s 92(4)(b).
[182] Asylum and Immigration Tribunal (Procedure) Rules 2005, SI 2005/230, r 7(2)(b). Where the appellant is in the UK at the date on which the decision is made but may not appeal in-country, the time limit is 28 days after his departure: r 7(2)(a).
[183] Ibid, r 7(1)(b).
[184] Ibid, r 7(1)(a).
[185] Under ibid, r 10(1), or, if a notice of appeal is given out of time and there is no application for extension, the Tribunal will notify in writing if it proposes to treat the appeal as being out of time, and the appellant can then file written evidence to contend the notice was given in time or there were special circumstances for failing to give notice in time which could not reasonably have been stated in the notice of appeal: ibid, r 10(2) to (4).
[186] Ibid, r 10(5).
[187] All forms are available at http://www.justice.gov.uk/forms/hmcts/immigration-and-asylum.

withdrawn,[188] an appeal under NIAA 2002, s 82(1) could be brought,[189] or an appeal under s 82(1) against the decision on the application for variation of leave is pending.[190] A person can also not be removed from the UK or required to leave the UK whilst an in-country appeal is pending,[191] although removal directions may be given, a deportation order may be made and other interim or preparatory action may be taken.[192]

The EEA Regulations

9.116   For the purpose of intercountry adoption, the appeal mechanism under the EEA Regs is of relevance insofar as it allows appeals against refusal of an entry clearance officer to issue an EEA Family Permit.[193]

9.117   A person claiming to be the family member of an EEA national can only rely on the appeal rights under the EEA Regs if he produces either a family permit or other proof that he is related as claimed to an EEA national.[194]

9.118   Where there is a right of appeal under the EEA Regs, it lies to the First-tier Tribunal of the Immigration and Asylum Chamber,[195] and the 2005 Procedure Rules have effect in relation to the appeal.[196]

9.119   A person may not appeal under the EEA Regs whilst in the UK against an EEA decision to refuse to issue him with an EEA family permit.[197] An appeal in those circumstances will need to be made out of country. Where the decision is a refusal to admit the person to the UK, then the appeal cannot be made in-country unless:

---

[188]   IA 1971, s 3C(1) and (2)(a).
[189]   IA 1971, s 3C(2)(b).
[190]   IA 1971, s 3C(2)(c). For this purpose, time begins when the appeal is instituted and ends when finally determined, withdrawn or abandoned: NIAA 2002, s 104(1). It is not finally determined while an application for permission to appeal could be made or is awaiting determination, permission to appeal has been granted and the appeal awaits determination, or the appeal has been remitted: NIAA 2002, s 104(2). Circumstances in which an appeal is treated as abandoned include if the appellant leaves the UK (ibid, s 104(4)), or is granted leave to enter or remain in the UK (save for an exception in respect of an appeal on asylum grounds): ibid, s 104(4A)–(4C).
[191]   Ibid, s 78(1) and (4).
[192]   Ibid, s 78(3).
[193]   Under the EEA Regs, reg 12(1).
[194]   Ibid, reg 26(3).
[195]   Ibid, reg 26(6).
[196]   Ibid, Sch 1, para 2. Accordingly the time limits under the Asylum and Immigration Tribunal (Procedure) Rules 2005 also apply.
[197]   EEA Regs, reg 27(1)(c).

- he held a valid EEA family permit, registration certificate, residence card, derivative residence card, document certifying permanent residence or permanent residence card on arrival in the UK, or can otherwise prove he is resident in the UK;[198]

- he has been in the UK for at least 3 months on the date of the refusal decision, but is deemed not to have been admitted to the UK by reason of detention, temporary admission or temporary release pursuant to IA 1971, Sch 2;[199] or

- he has made an asylum or human rights claim, not certified as clearly unfounded.[200]

9.120 A pending in-country appeal has a suspensory effect on any removal directions not yet carried out.[201] The definition of a pending appeal mirrors that under the NIAA 2002, save that a pending appeal is not to be treated as abandoned solely because the appellant leaves the UK.[202]

9.121 The grounds of appeal which can be relied upon in an appeal under the EEA Regs are those set out under NIAA 2002, s 84(1)[203] save for those relating specifically to the Immigration Rules.[204]

9.122 The forms to be used are the same as for appeals under the NIAA 2002.[205]

---

[198] Ibid, reg 27(2)(a).
[199] Ibid, reg 27(2)(b).
[200] Ibid, reg 27(2)(c).
[201] Ibid, reg 29(2) and (3).
[202] Ibid, reg 25(4).
[203] See **9.110**.
[204] Those under NIAA 2002, s 84(1)(a) and (f). Specified in the EEA Regs, Sch 1, para 1.
[205] See **9.114**.

Part 3

INTERNATIONAL ADOPTION WHEN THE UNITED KINGDOM IS THE STATE OF ORIGIN

Chapter 10

OVERVIEW OF INTERNATIONAL ADOPTION WHEN THE UNITED KINGDOM IS THE STATE OF ORIGIN

10.1 If a child is habitually resident in the British Islands then for the purpose of any international adoption, the UK will be the state of origin and the country into which the child is being removed for the purpose of adoption is the receiving state. There are two categories of receiving states, those which have contracted to the Convention[1] (Convention countries) and those which have not (non-Convention countries).

NON-CONVENTION COUNTRIES

10.2 If the receiving state is a non-Convention country then the prospective adopters must adopt the child in that country pursuant to the internal domestic law of that jurisdiction. Before the child can be lawfully removed from the British Islands for the purpose of such an adoption the court must grant the prospective adopters parental responsibility pursuant to the Adoption and Children Act 2002 (ACA 2002), s 84. These orders are commonly referred to as section 84 orders. The effect of a section 84 order is to give the prospective adopters parental responsibility and to extinguish parental responsibility in every other person or body. Only after the making of a section 84 order can a child be lawfully removed from the jurisdiction for the purpose of adoption.[2] Part 2 Chapter 2 of the Adoptions with a Foreign Element Regulations 2005 (AFER 2005)[3] governs the process for applying for a section 84 order in a non-Convention international adoption.

CONVENTION COUNTRIES

10.3 If the receiving state is a Convention country then the Convention will apply and Part 3, Chapter 2 of AFER 2005 provides the legal framework for these adoptions. If the receiving state is a Convention country, the prospective adopters can choose whether to apply for the child's adoption in their own

---

[1]   See Chapter 1.
[2]   Pursuant to ACA 2002, s 86.
[3]   SI 2005/392.

country after obtaining a section 84 order in this jurisdiction, or whether in the alternative, they wish to finalise the adoption in the UK by way of a Convention adoption order.

PRIVATE ADOPTIONS AND AGENCY ADOPTIONS

10.4 If a child is placed for adoption by an adoption agency then the adoption is known as an agency adoption. An adoption agency can place a child for adoption with prospective adopters if the parents have consented to this or if the court has made a placement order. Because of the involvement of the state, and the fact that the adopters may be unrelated to the child, agency adoptions are carefully regulated by both primary legislation in the ACA 2002 and also secondary legislation in the Adoption Agency Regulations 2005 (AAR 2005).[4] When an adoption agency is considering placing a child with foreign adopters the process is even more carefully regulated and changes are made to both the primary and secondary legislation by AFER 2005. Due to the complexity involved in agency adoptions, Chapter 11 will address the legal framework in a Convention adoption, and Chapter 12 will deal with the legal framework in a non-Convention adoption.

10.5 If the application to adopt is being made by a person in circumstances where they assumed the care of the child other than by the child being placed with them for adoption by an adoption agency it is a private adoption. As with domestic private adoptions which take place in England and Wales, the local authority in the area in which the child lives must prepare a report for the court in relation to the adoption application. AFER 2005 applies to private adoptions and in Chapter 13 the reader will find information on the process for both Convention and non-Convention private adoptions.

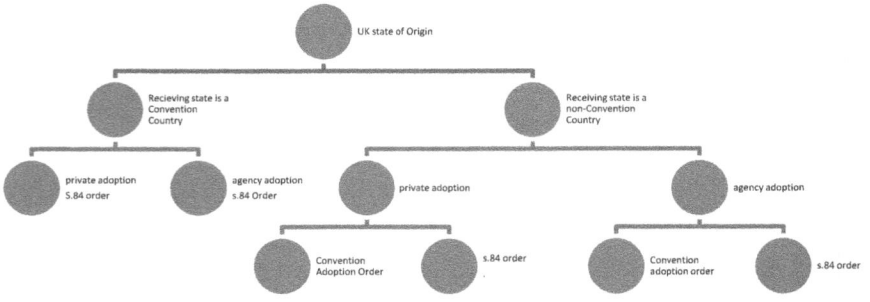

---

4   SI 2005/389.

Chapter 11

AGENCY ADOPTIONS IN A CONVENTION COUNTRY

INTRODUCTION

11.1 Part 3, Chapter 2 of the Adoptions with a Foreign Element Regulations 2005 (AFER 2005)[1] provides the regulatory framework which governs the adoption of a child habitually resident in the British Islands by a person who is habitually resident in a Convention country. This chapter will provide a step-by-step guide to the placement and adoption of children when there is a plan, or contemplation of a plan, in which it is envisaged that a child who is habitually resident in England or Wales will be placed for adoption by an adoption agency with foreign adopters who live in a Convention country. It will cover:

- assessment of both adopters and child;

- matching;

- placement for adoption;

- section 84 orders/Convention adoption orders;

- transfer to the receiving state post adoptive order; and

- tips to bear in mind if the receiving state is the USA.

11.2 As set out in Chapter 2, all Convention countries must hold a register of children who have been assessed to be suitable for adoption overseas. In England and Wales the requirement to have a Convention List is met by AFER 2005, reg 41. The information contained on the register is confidential and can only be accessed by other central authorities within the British Islands.[2] The extent to which the Convention List contains details of children who are not already provisionally matched to connected persons habitually resident outside the British Islands is therefore outside of the public domain; however, the Department for Education has confirmed that at the date of this publication no children's names have been held on the Convention List for England and Wales.

---

[1]   SI 2005/392.
[2]   AFER 2005, reg 41(1).

11.3   What is known is that sometimes, when a child cannot be looked after by their parents or by family members living in this country, there are relatives or other connected persons who live outside of the British Islands who would be able to offer the child a good long term home, and in those circumstances sometimes the best legal framework for that child will be an international adoption within their extended family network. This is particularly so where family members live in countries such as the USA, which have strict immigration policies that restrict the permanent movement of children into their country to live with people who are not their natural parents.

11.4   It is unlikely that a child in the care of a local authority will be placed for adoption with foreign adopters unless those adopters are connected to the child in some way, most likely by family relationships. Often, although not always, the overseas family member will be identified during care proceedings relating to the child. When that happens it is important that careful consideration is given to the assessment process within the context of the care and placement order proceedings in order to avoid unnecessary delay to those proceedings.

STEP 1 – VIABILITY ASSESSMENT OF PROSPECTIVE ADOPTERS

11.5   Upon being notified that there is an extended family member who would like to be assessed as a long term carer for a child, the local authority should carry out a viability assessment. This duty arises out of s 22C of the Children Act 1989, which states that the local authority should place children in their care with suitable family members before placing them with unconnected persons and s 1(4)(f) of the Adoption and Children Act 2002 (ACA 2002) which specifically requires the court to take into account:

> '(f)   the relationship which the child has with relatives, and with any other person in relation to whom the court or agency considers the relationship to be relevant, including –
>   (i)   the likelihood of any such relationship continuing and the value to the child of its doing so,
>   (ii)   the ability and willingness of any of the child's relatives, or of any such person, to provide the child with a secure environment in which the child can develop, and otherwise to meet the child's needs,
>   (iii)   the wishes and feelings of any of the child's relatives, or of any such person, regarding the child.'

11.6   The initial viability assessment can be done by phone or Skype in order to ascertain preliminary information and to ensure that the proposed carer is fully aware of the child's physical and emotional needs and of the concerns which led to the issue of care proceedings or the making of a final care order if proceedings are completed. It should include discussions in general terms as to the prospective adopters' expectations in relation to the child's needs in terms of post adoptive contact with birth parents, and the sort of financial and other support that the adopters might be entitled to. It would be appropriate to discuss their:

- primary family unit and the ages of all their children and their hopes for any future children;

- financial circumstances;

- child care arrangements and how these might change if they adopted the child in question;

- housing;

- local support network;

- connections with the parents;

- current relationship if any with the child in question;

- knowledge of adoption;

- current relationships with the child's parents, and in the light of those relationships their attitudes towards direct/indirect contact with the birth parents; and

- how they would feel about being subjected to a thorough assessment process which would involve examination by local agencies of their parenting capacity, including investigations into their financial and criminal background.

11.7 Armed with this information the local authority should be in a position to determine whether or not it proposes to move forward with a full assessment of the family. This is an important decision which will have significant financial implications for the local authority and will inevitably involve delay within the permanency decision-making process for the child.

11.8 Unlike in a domestic case, with Convention adoptions the assessment of the adopters must be carried out by the receiving state's central authority or such organisation as is authorised by it to conduct that assessment. In many countries the state does not provide Article 15 reports (see **11.16**) free of charge, and therefore when the adopters apply to be assessed there will be a cost involved. Consideration must therefore be given to the funding of the assessment.

11.9 When considering whether or not to proceed with the Article 15 report the local authority may wish to take into account not just the cost of that assessment but also the costs of the whole adoptive process if that assessment is positive. If the Convention adoption is successful then in financial terms those costs will involve:

- direct legal costs;

- assessment costs;

- indirect legal costs if they would be responsible for meeting the legal costs of the adopters;

- the transition costs in terms of travel arrangements (for some or all of the prospective adopters, the child, the social worker and the foster carer); and

- the post adoption support plan (which may need to include provision for private health and educational costs if these are not provided free of charge by the state in the receiving state).

11.10 Additionally there is the non-financial, but also important, cost of delay to the child in his or her permanency planning. To be balanced against these costs are the benefits to the child of being raised within his or her family, where his or her sense of identity and cultural and familial heritage can be promoted.

11.11 Upon receipt of a positive viability assessment it might be prudent therefore for a local authority to convene a meeting with members of the Adoption Panel and the Resource Panel to carefully consider whether or not it is appropriate to pursue a plan for overseas adoption. If such a meeting is considered likely to be necessary for the internal decision-making process within the local authority, in the event that the outcome of the viability assessment is positive, this meeting should be fixed when the decision is made to undertake the viability assessment. If thought is not given to this part of the planning process until after a positive viability assessment is complete it is likely to add unnecessary delay to the planning for the child.

11.12 If the decision is made not to proceed to the next step, notwithstanding the positive viability assessment, the local authority should notify the parents and the prospective adopters as soon as possible. Although there does not appear to be a rule within the adoption regulations which requires the reasons for refusing to progress to a full assessment of the foreign family member be given in writing, it is suggested that it would be good practice to do so, and for the reasons to be set out clearly and fully, in order to ensure that there is complete transparency in the decision-making process. If the child's case is in court proceedings at the time this decision is made, it would be appropriate to seek a direction that the social worker files a statement dealing with the reasons for not proceeding beyond the viability assessment.

11.13 If a sufficiently closely connected person (a parent, an Independent Reviewing Officer, a children's guardian or the prospective adopter, for example) took the view that the decision not to proceed was so unreasonable as to be reviewable, the only remedy would be to seek a judicial review of that decision in the Administrative Court. If the child's case is in care or placement order proceedings at that time, then, subject to there being a sufficient basis to justify an application to the Administrative Court, the respondents could ask the court to adjourn final decisions until the outcome of the judicial review proceedings is known. In such circumstances it is likely to be appropriate to seek transfer of the case to a High Court Judge and request that the case is heard by a High Court Judge who can sit in both the family and the Administrative Court.

11.14 If the child's case is in care or placement order proceedings when the local authority decision not to pursue overseas adoption is made, then subject to the prospective adopters and or the parties to the proceedings being able to obtain funding or the prospective adopters being in a position to fund the Home study report themselves (by way of legal aid funding or otherwise), the court could timetable the case taking that assessment into account and direct that the Home study report is filed by the party or parties who are responsible for that instruction.

11.15 If the decision is made that it is appropriate to undertake a full assessment of the prospective adopters, the planning will move to the next step.

STEP 2 – FULL ASSESSMENT OF THE ADOPTERS – ARTICLE 15 REPORT

11.16 The preparation of the Article 15 report is usually done in two stages. The first stage is a social work assessment of the suitability of the adopters which is carried out by (i) a public body; (ii) an accredited private body; or (iii) a private person or body qualifying under Article 22. That assessment is referred to as the Home study report. The Home study report is then sent to the receiving state's central authority which, having satisfied itself of the suitability of the prospective adopters in the light of the Home study report, prepares the Article 15 report for onward transmission by the receiving state's central authority to the relevant central authority in the state of origin (ie the Department for Education which is the central authority for England in the UK).

11.17 The prospective adopters must apply to their central authority to assess their suitability to adopt a child from overseas. The assessment must cover the information specified in Article 15 of the Convention, but as we have seen in Chapter 2, it is not limited to that information. Ultimately the Home study report must satisfy both the receiving state and the state of origin that the prospective adopters are suitable to adopt the child in question. Therefore, the local authority, in consultation with the prospective adopters (and the other parties if they are in court proceedings) may wish to prepare a letter of instruction setting out detailed requirements in terms of the aspects of the prospective adopters' history, lifestyle, insight, protective abilities, etc which will need to be addressed in the assessment process and report.

11.18 It is likely to be helpful to the assessing organisation to have sight of information about the child's history, and it is likely to be appropriate for the assessors to see some of the papers in the care proceedings. If the assessment is directed within the course of care or placement order proceedings the assessors will be allowed to see the court papers automatically,[3] although it is likely to be sensible to limit the bundle of documents sent to the assessor to that which is strictly relevant to the assessment process. If the case is no longer in proceedings then an application to disclose particular key documents to the assessor can be made to the court which dealt with those proceedings. In any event, a separate direction that the prospective adopters be allowed to see relevant papers will be necessary if the parties agree that such disclosure would be appropriate. For example, it is likely that the prospective adopters would need to see any psychiatric, psychological, or paediatric assessment of the child which sheds light on the child's particular care needs. It is also likely to be useful for the prospective adopters to see the threshold document and the parent's response to it so that they can have an understanding of the risks that the parents might pose to the child. There may be other documents such as the parties' statements which will enable the prospective adopters properly to understand and discuss issues relating to contact between the child and his or her parents, and if appropriate, the reasons such contact must be limited/promoted in order to meet the child's needs. Every case will be different and the issue of disclosure should be looked at carefully, always keeping in mind the purpose of that disclosure, and balancing the privacy of the parents and the child against the need to ensure that decisions are made on a fully informed, and therefore more reliable, basis.

11.19 The Home study report is likely to be sent to the adopters by the assessor once it is complete and may also be sent directly to the local authority. It will also be sent to the receiving state's central authority. Once it is received, the local authority will be able to see if the family has been approved in principle as suitable to adopt a child from overseas. If there are outstanding questions that it would like clarified it can seek that clarification. If it is of the view that it would like to carry out a supplementary assessment of its own it can make arrangements to do so by phone, email or Skype, or by sending a social worker to carry out that piece of work with the prospective adopters. There is no prohibition on the state of origin (ie the UK) carrying out any independent assessment it considers necessary in order to inform its own decision making in relation to the child.

11.20 In itself though, this report is not the Article 15 report. The Article 15 report will be sent by the receiving state's central authority to the relevant UK

---

[3]   FPR 2010, r 12.73(vii).

central authority (currently the Department for Education for cases involving children living in England) and from there to the local authority.[4] The local authority cannot proceed to matching the child to the adopters until it receives the official Article 15 report.[5]

STEP 3 – ASSESSMENT OF THE CHILD AS SUITABLE TO BE ADOPTED UNDER THE CONVENTION

11.21   The next step is the preparation and dispatch of the Article 16 report to the receiving state. However, as will become clear below, there are three stages involved in the preparation of the information required for completion of the Article 16 report:

- the assessment of the child as being suitable for adoption overseas;

- obtaining of consents/placement orders; and

- the matching of the child to the adoptive parents who are specified in the Article 15 report.

While the third task must follow the receipt of the Article 15 report, the first and second task can be pursued in parallel to the assessment of the adopters, and if the case is in proceedings then it will be in the interest of the child in avoiding delay if that approach is taken.

11.22   The point at which the prospect of a Convention adoption arises in relation to a child who is looked after by a local authority will vary from case to case. In some cases it may be a live issue from the start of the adoption agency's involvement, in most cases it will arise during the course of care proceedings, but it may not arise until after care and placement orders have been made, or when a child has already been relinquished for adoption by the parents. The regulations which govern the decision as to the child's suitability to be adopted under the Convention and matching process with the adopters approved under Article 15 will apply equally in all of these situations, but the dynamic of complying with these regulations in parallel with the court process for care and placement order proceedings adds a layer of complexity, which if not managed carefully can lead to unnecessary delay for the child. For that reason it may be easier to consider first the process as it would be if consideration of an overseas placement arises for the first time after the adoption agency is authorised to place the child for adoption. In any event, the final stage in this step is the preparation of the Article 16 report and that cannot be completed unless there is a placement order or parental consent to the Convention adoption.

---

[4]   AFER 2005, reg 40.
[5]   Ibid, reg 43.

Approval of a child as suitable for a Convention adoption when that issue arises for the first time when the child is available for adoption

11.23   AFER 2005 do not affect the care planning and decision making for a child until the stage where it is clear that not only is the child suitable for adoption per se, but there is an issue as to whether or not he or she is suitable to be adopted overseas. For the purposes of this section it is assumed that the possibility of a family adoption overseas is being considered at a time when the child is available for adoption by virtue of parental agreement or a placement order.

11.24   Before a child can be placed for adoption an adoption agency must consider whether or not that option is in the child's best interest. This decision is governed by Part 3 of the Adoption Agencies Regulations 2005 (AAR 2005),[6] which have recently been amended.[7] If the adoption agency is considering adoption for a child it must open a case record for the child and, among other things, place on it the child's permanence report.[8] The content of the child's permanence report is dictated by AAR 2005, reg 17(1) which states:

> **'17 Requirement to prepare child's permanence report**
>
> (1) The adoption agency must prepare a written report ("the child's permanence report") which shall include –
>
> (a)   the information about the child and his family as specified in Parts 1 and 3 of Schedule 1;
>
> (b)   a summary, written by the agency's medical adviser, of the state of the child's health, his health history and any need for health care which might arise in the future;
>
> (c)   the wishes and feelings of the child regarding the matters set out in regulation 13(1)(c);
>
> (d)   the wishes and feelings of the child's parent or guardian, and where regulation 14(4)(a) applies, his father, and any other person the agency considers relevant, regarding the matters set out in regulation 14(1)(c);
>
> (e)   the views of the agency about the child's need for contact with his parent or guardian or other relative or with any other person the agency considers relevant and the arrangements the agency proposes to make for allowing any person contact with the child;
>
> (f)   an assessment of the child's emotional and behavioural development and any related needs;
>
> (g)   an assessment of the parenting capacity of the child's parent or guardian and, where regulation 14(4)(a) applies, his father;
>
> (h)   a chronology of the decisions and actions taken by the agency with respect to the child;

---

[6]   SI 2005/389.
[7]   Adoption Agencies (Panel and Consequential Amendments) Regulations, SI 2012/1410.
[8]   AAR 2005, reg 12(1)(b).

(i) an analysis of the options for the future care of the child which have been considered by the agency and why placement for adoption is considered the preferred option; and

(j) any other information which the agency considers relevant.'

11.25 At such time as the adoption agency forms the view that particular adopters who live in a Convention country should be considered for matching with a child, the child's permanence report will need to be updated to include a summary of the possibilities for placement of the child within the United Kingdom; and an assessment of whether an adoption by a person in a particular receiving state is in the child's best interests.[9] In this scenario the decision that the child should be placed for adoption has already been made by the adoption agency and consent has been given by the parents and/or a placement order has already been granted by the court. It does not appear that the decision that the child is suitable for adoption needs to be revisited simply because the question of an overseas placement has arisen.

11.26 However, even if a decision has been made by the adoption agency in accordance with AAR 2005, reg 19 that the child is suitable for adoption, and even if a court has made a placement order in relation to the child in question, it would appear that if the local authority subsequently wishes to expand the remit of that decision to include a decision that the child is suitable for a Convention adoption, the provisions of AFER 2005, regs 38 and 40 will require the local authority to update the child's permanence report and revisit that specific issue, and it may do so even before the Article 15 report has been recieved.

Approval of a child as suitable for a Convention adoption when that issue arises for the first time during care proceedings

11.27 For the purposes of this section it is assumed that the local authority has issued an application for a care order and when the family have been asked to provide details of potential alternative carers for the child, in the event that a care order is made, they have put forward a foreign family member who lives in a Convention country. At that stage the viability assessment of the foreign family member would be undertaken along with any other family members or connected persons in this jurisdiction, and that process is already explained in steps 1 and 2 above.

11.28 As soon as the local authority considers adoption as a potential outcome for the child within proceedings it must open the child's case record[10] and prepare the child's permanence report.[11] While the assessment of the foreign family member is rolling forward, there may be assessment of the parents and/or the child directed within the care proceedings. Once all the assessments of the parents and/or the child and/or other family members in the

---

9   AFER 2005, reg 38(1).
10 AAR 2005, reg 12.
11 Ibid, reg 17.

UK or abroad are completed the local authority will be directed to file and serve its final evidence which will include its care plan for the child. In preparing the care plan for the child the local authority will have given consideration as to whether or not the child is suitable for adoption.

11.29 Prior to the coming into force of the Adoption Agencies (Panel and Consequential Amendments) Regulations 2012[12] on 1 September 2012, if the view of the local authority was that adoption might be the best long term option for a child, it was obliged to send the child's case to the adoption panel who would need to consider the case and make a recommendation, before the agency decision maker could make a decision pursuant to AAR 2005, reg 19(1) that the child should be placed for adoption. As amended, AAR 2005, reg 17(2)–(2D) reads:

'(2) In a case where –

(a)   the adoption agency is a local authority and is considering whether the child ought to be placed for adoption, and
(b)   either paragraph (2A) or paragraph (2B) applies,

the adoption agency may not refer the case to the adoption panel.

(2A) This paragraph applies where –

(a)   the child is placed for adoption by the adoption agency or is being provided with accommodation by them,
(b)   no adoption agency is authorised to place the child for adoption, and
(c)   the child has no parent or guardian, or the agency consider that the conditions in section 31(2) of the 1989 Act are met in relation to the child.

(2B) This paragraph applies where –

(a)   an application has been made, and has not been disposed of, on which a care order might be made in respect of the child, or
(b)   the child is subject to a care order and the adoption agency are not authorised to place the child for adoption.

(2C) In a case not falling within paragraph (2), the adoption agency must send the information and reports referred to in paragraph (2D) to the adoption panel.

(2D) For the purposes of paragraph (2C) and regulation 19(1A) the information and reports are –

(i)   the child's permanence report,
(ii)   the child's health report and any other reports referred to in regulation 15, and
(iii) the information relating to the health of each of the child's natural parents,

---

[12]   SI 2012/1410.

except that, in a case falling within paragraph (2C), the adoption agency may only send to the adoption panel the documents referred to in subparagraphs (ii) and (iii) if the agency's medical adviser advises it to do so.'

11.30 This significant amendment to AAR 2005 means that if a case meets the criteria in reg 17(2A) or (2B), local authorities must now decide whether or not adoption is in the best interest of a child without referring the case to the adoption panel. The decision-making process by the local authority is governed by AAR 2005, reg 19, which in its amended form reads:

'19 Adoption agency decision and notification

(1) In any case falling within regulation 17(2C) the adoption agency must take into account the recommendation of the adoption panel in coming to a decision about whether the child should be placed for adoption.

(1A) In any case falling within regulation 17(2) the adoption agency must take into account the information and reports referred to in regulation 17(2D), and any other relevant information, in coming to a decision about whether the child ought to be placed for adoption.

(2) No member of the adoption panel or person on the central list shall take part in any decision made by the adoption agency under paragraph (1).

(3) The adoption agency must, if their whereabouts are known to the agency, notify in writing the parent or guardian and, where regulation 14(3) applies and the agency considers it is appropriate, the father of the child of its decision.'

11.31 In a case such as this therefore, the local authority will need to have (i) completed the child's permanence report before it makes a decision as to whether or not the child should be adopted, and (ii) taken that into account when reaching its decision. Since this is a case where consideration is being given to an overseas adoption, reg 38 of AFER 2005 also applies, which now[13] reads:

'38 Requirements in respect of the child's permanence report and information for the adoption panel

(1) The child's permanence report which the adoption agency is required to prepare in accordance with regulation 17 of the Agencies Regulations or corresponding Welsh provision must include –

(a)   a summary of the possibilities for placement of the child within the United Kingdom; and
(b)   an assessment of whether an adoption by a person in a particular receiving State is in the child's best interests.

---

[13]   As amended by the Adoption Agencies (Panel and Consequential Amendments) Regulations, SI 2012/1410, reg 10.

(2) In a case falling within regulation 17(2C) of the Agencies Regulations or the corresponding Welsh provision, the adoption agency must send –

(a)   if received, the Article 15 Report; and
(b)   their observations on that Report,

together with the reports and information referred to in regulation 17(2D) of the Agencies Regulations or corresponding Welsh provision to the adoption panel.

(3) In a case falling within regulation 17(2) of the Agencies Regulations or the corresponding Welsh provision, the adoption agency must consider –

(a)   if received, the Article 15 Report; and
(b)   their observations on that Report together with the reports and information referred to in regulation 17(2D) of the Agencies Regulations or the corresponding Welsh provision

in deciding whether the child should be placed for adoption in accordance with the Convention.'

11.32   Accordingly, the child's permanence report will need to include the information specified in reg 38(1) and the local authority will need to take into account the Article 15 report '*if received*' and their observations on that report.

11.33   The issue will then arise – should the local authority wait until it has received the Article 15 report before making its decision pursuant to AAR 2005, reg 19? It is suggested that the answer to this question should be 'no'. An argument in favour of waiting is that there would be no point in considering the suitability of the child for a Convention adoption before the receipt of the Home study report. As we saw in step 2 above, there may be a delay of a month or more between the receipt of the Home study report from the assessing agency and receipt of the Article 15 report from the English central authority. To wait for the Article 15 report in order to make a decision under reg 19 may cause a disproportionate delay to the child of up to 3 months while the central authority in the receiving state processes the Article 15 report and forwards it to the UK central authority to forward to the local authority. In countries such as the USA part of the reason for that delay is that criminal history and immigration checks need to be carried out at federal level.

11.34   The effect of the reg 19 decision is that it puts the local authority in a position to apply to the court for a placement order. The child cannot be matched for adoption until the full Article 15 report has been obtained, and cannot be placed for adoption until after a placement order has been obtained. For those reasons it is likely that the most child-focused approach will be for the local authority to consider whether or not the child should be placed for adoption overseas under AAR 2005, reg 19 and AFER 2005, reg 38 once the Home study report is available, but without having to wait for the full official Article 15 report.

11.35 The decision of the local authority may be to agree that adoption overseas is appropriate in the light of the Home study report, or that adoption in the UK is appropriate, or that adoption is not appropriate at all. If it decides that the foreign adoption is not in the child's best interests, then subject to any successful review of that decision in the Administrative Court, that would appear to be the end of the subject. There does not appear to be any mechanism for a looked-after child to be placed for adoption with foreign adopters unless the placement is made with the approval of the adoption agency, which must then match the child for adoption and prepare the reports which form the Article 16 report.

11.36 If the local authority determines that the child is suitable to be adopted under the Convention it must notify the English central authority and provide the information specified in AFER 2005, reg 40. In terms of the ongoing court proceedings it can prepare its final evidence and issue its application for a placement order, and the case can be listed for final hearing of both applications.

STEP 4 – MATCHING THE CHILD WITH THE CONVENTION ADOPTERS AND THE PREPARATION OF THE ARTICLE 16 REPORT

11.37 The next step in the Convention adoption process is the matching of the child with the adopters. This can be carried out before or after the child is available for adoption. Before moving on to consider the mechanism of the matching process in detail it is worth considering how the matching process fits into the court process if there are ongoing care and/or placement order proceedings.

11.38 As we will see below, the child cannot be matched with the adopters until the formal Article 15 report has been received by the adoption agency. The timing of this event is not within the control of the parties to the care proceedings or the court. The question may therefore arise: if the Article 15 report is not available prior to the final hearing of the care and placement order proceedings, should either or both sets of proceedings be adjourned? In answering this question it is suggested that the court should be invited to consider the relevance of the Article 15 report to the two separate enquiries before it. The Article 15 report will not shed light on either threshold or the parents' ability to care for the child. Nor will it shed light on whether or not a care order is necessary for the child. Unless it can be shown that there is a real forensic reason why the evidence contained within the Article 15 report would assist the court in relation to the care proceedings, there would be no reason to delay the resolution of that case, particularly if the parents seek the return of the child to the care of one or both parents, or seek placement with a family in the UK which is not supported by the local authority.

11.39 The issues before the court in a placement order application are different. The availability of the Article 15 report and the local authority's decision in relation to matching are likely to be very relevant considerations when the court considers whether or not the local authority should be allowed to place the child with any adopters of their choosing. From a practical perspective, there are other advantages to adjourning the placement order proceedings to await the Article 15 report, in that the child's solicitor and the children's guardian will remain appointed, and the court can diarise hearings to consider the case further once the matching process is finalised.

11.40 It is therefore suggested that if the Article 15 report and/or the decision as to matching are not available before the final hearing in the care and placement order proceedings, the court should proceed to hear the care proceedings but adjourn the placement order proceedings, with directions being made for the filing of final evidence in the placement order proceedings shortly after the local authority expects to have made its decision on matching.

The procedure for matching a child with a Convention adopter

11.41 Part 5 of the AAR 2005 governs the matching and placement of a child with prospective adopters. Regulation 31 specifically requires the adoption agency to give a recommendation as to the suitability of particular adopters to adopt a particular child.[14] This requirement is not changed by the Adoption Agencies (Panel and Consequential Amendments) Regulations 2012. Regulation 43 of AFER 2005 confirms that the procedure dictated by AAR 2005, reg 31 must still be followed in a Convention adoption. However, in addition to the material stipulated in reg 31, the adoption panel must also be sent a copy of the Article 15 report. It is clear therefore that matching cannot take place until this formal document, which includes but is not limited to, the Home study report, has been received by the adoption agency from the relevant central authority in the UK (currently the Department for Education in England).

11.42 By virtue of AAR 2005, reg 31(2) the relevant local authority must prepare a support plan for the adoption, which must include consideration of financial support if this would be payable under the relevant Adoption Support Services Regulations 2005.[15] The fact that the placement is overseas does not appear to alter the obligation to support the placement.

11.43 The adoption panel must make a recommendation as to whether the child should be placed with the prospective adopters, and it must take into account the Article 15 report, in addition to the other documents specified in AAR 2005, reg 32(2).[16] Pursuant to AAR 2005, reg 33 as amended by AFER 2005, reg 45 the adoption agency must then decide whether or not to place the child with the prospective adopters. In doing so, it must take into account the

---

[14]   AAR 2005, reg 31.
[15]   Adoption Support Services Regulations 2005, SI 2005/691 or Adoption Support Services (Local Authorities) (Wales) Regulations 2005, SI 2005/1512.
[16]   Pursuant to AFER 2005, reg 44.

recommendation of the adoption panel. Since sub-paragraph (3) of reg 33 is omitted, there is no obligation on the adoption agency to tell the adopters or the parents of its decision. However, they must notify the relevant central authority (for England that is currently the Department for Education) of its decision. If the decision is that the child should not be placed with the foreign prospective adopters, the adoption agency must return the Article 15 report and any other documents received from the UK central authority. It is the responsibility of the relevant central authority in the UK to send these papers back to the central authority in the receiving state.[17]

11.44 There is no regulatory requirement that the child must be available for adoption in order to be matched with a particular prospective adopter. Indeed the regulations provide that the panel can both recommend the child as suitable for adoption and match them with the adopter in the same panel meeting.[18] If the panel is in a position to make its recommendation before the court is in a position to make a final placement order, there is no reason why this should not happen. Unlike a domestic adoption, in a Convention case the recommendation of the panel and the decision of the agency decision maker[19] are not the final word on the match. The ultimate approval must come from the two central authorities, pursuant to Article 17(c) of the Convention, before the child may be lawfully placed for adoption, and this determination at an inter-country level can only take place once the child's Article 16 report has been prepared. The child's Article 16 report requires evidence of all consents necessary for the adoption. If the parents do not consent to the adoption, a placement order will be necessary.

Information required in the Article 16 report

11.45 If the child is matched with the foreign adopters the next stage is to prepare the Article 16 report. The preparation of this report is governed by AFER 2005, reg 46 which states:

'**46 Preparation of the Article 16 Information**

(1) If the adoption agency decides that the proposed placement should proceed, it must prepare a report for the purposes of Article 16(1) of the Convention which must include –

(a)   the information about the child which is specified in Schedule 1 to the Agencies Regulations or corresponding Welsh provision; and
(b)   the reasons for their decision.

(2) The adoption agency must send the following to the relevant Central Authority –

---

[17]   Pursuant to ibid, reg 45.
[18]   Ibid, reg 32(5)(a).
[19]   AFER 2005, reg 33.

    (a)   the report referred to in paragraph (1);

    (b)   details of any placement order or other orders, if any, made by the courts; and

    (c)   confirmation that the parent or guardian consents to the proposed adoption.

(3) The relevant Central Authority must then send the documents referred to in paragraph (2) to the CA of the receiving State.'

11.46   It is of note that reg 46(2) appears to require both a placement order and the parents' consent to the adoption. This would be a rather strange situation since if the parents gave their consent to the adoption a placement order would not be required. Additionally, within this jurisdiction at least, if a child is placed with prospective adopters by an adoption agency while the child is subject to a placement order, a parent's consent to adoption is not required,[20] and a parent may not oppose the making of an adoption order without the court's leave.[21] Since parental consent is therefore unnecessary for the making of an adoption order if there is a placement order in force, and there is no statutory provision which requires parental consent for the making of an order under ACA 2002, s 84 or for a Convention adoption order, it is incongruous that such consent is required for the preparation of the Article 16 report. Furthermore, Article 16 of the Convention requires the central authority in the state of origin to ensure that the consents required by Article 4 are obtained. In turn Article 4(c) only requires the consent of 'the persons, institutions and authorities whose consent is necessary for adoption'. Since the Convention does not require the consent of the parents if that consent is not necessary for the adoption, it is suggested that the reg 46(2)(c) only applies if the child is not subject to a placement order. Certainly this approach has been adopted in a number of unreported Convention adoption cases in which final Convention adoption orders were granted by the High Court during 2011 and 2012.

STEP 5 – PLACEMENT OF THE CHILD FOR ADOPTION

11.47   AFER 2005, reg 47(2) sets out the requirements which have to be complied with before the UK central authority is permitted to agree with the receiving state's central authority that the adoption should proceed pursuant to Article 17(c). It then goes on to specify that an adoption agency may not place a child for adoption with the adopters unless the Article 17 agreement has been reached. It is the duty of the UK central authority to let the adoption agency know when this has happened.[22] These requirements are mandatory and apply whether or not the adopters are related to the child. It is also clear within reg 47 that the receiving state must confirm all the matters specified in reg 47(1) to the UK central authority before the UK central authority can confirm that it is willing to agree to the adoption. However, before the UK central authority can

---

[20]   ACA 2002, s 47(4).
[21]   ACA 2002, s 47(5).
[22]   AFER 2005, reg 47(3).

actually enter into the agreement under Article 17(c), the adoption agency must double check three matters independently, these being:

'(i)   it has met the prospective adopter and explained the requirement to make an application for an order under section 84 of the Act before the child can be removed from the United Kingdom;
(ii)   the prospective adopter has visited the child; and
(iii)   the prospective adopter is content for the adoption to proceed.'[23]

11.48   AFER 2005, reg 47(2)(ii) therefore imposes a requirement that the adopters must meet the child before the agreement under Article 17(c) is entered into, whether or not they are related. However, although it is not specifically mentioned in the regulations, it is suggested that if the placement is outside the family network, for example a placement with a family friend, the prospective adopters should not meet the child until the requirements in Article 29 of the Convention have been met.[24]

11.49   As soon as the adoption agency is notified that the Article 17(c) agreement has been reached it is free to place the child with the adopters for adoption.

Timing of the child's placement with their foreign family members

11.50   It is important to bear in mind that the requirements of AFER 2005, reg 47 do not prevent a local authority placing a child with family members who are being assessed as suitable adopters or who have been approved by a local authority as suitable adopters, if that placement is a placement under s 22C of the Children Act 1989, and not a placement for adoption pursuant to ACA 2002, s 18.[25] Equally, there is no prohibition in Article 29 of the Convention of contact taking place between prospective Convention adopters and the child, if it is an adoption within a family. Accordingly, a local authority has the flexibility to place a child with family members at any time before or after the child has been matched with the adopters for adoption by the adoption agency. In the case of *Re A*[26] the child was placed with her family members pursuant to para 19 of Sch 2 to the Children Act 1989 before a placement order was made. However, Sch 2 cannot be used if a placement order is in force, and the correct provision to facilitate the placement of a child overseas when a placement order is in force is s 28 of ACA 2002. The court has approved the use of ACA 2002, s 28 for placement of a child overseas with

---

[23]   AFER 2005, reg 47(2).
[24]   Article 29 of the Convention reads: 'There shall be no contact between the prospective adoptive parents and the child's parents or any other person who has care of the child until the requirements of Article 4, sub-paragraphs a) to c), and Article 5, sub-paragraph a), have been met, unless the adoption takes place within a family or unless the contact is in compliance with the conditions established by the competent authority of the State of origin.'
[25]   *A LBC v Department for Children, Schools and Families* [2009] EWCA Civ 41, [2009] 2 FLR 597.
[26]   *A LBC v Department for Children, Schools and Families* [2009] EWCA Civ 41, [2009] 2 FLR 597.

relatives who it is contemplated will be approved as adopters pursuant to Article 17(c) in the case of *ECC (The Local Authority) v SM*.[27] In either case it is clear that the child remains in the care of the local authority, and that his or her country of habitual residence remains England and Wales. In addition, in the case of *ECC*, the carers were required to undertake to return the child on or before a date specified in the order or earlier if so required by the placing local authority or the court. These matters should be included in the order which permits the temporary removal.

11.51   It is important to note that in *ECC* the adopters intended to apply for a Convention adoption order, and therefore the proposed adoption would not take place overseas, but in the High Court in England. On that basis the court was satisfied that the permission given under s 28 did not give rise to any criminal liability under ACA 2002, s 85. The *ECC* case did not look at removal when an application under s 84 was contemplated. It is suggested that similar arguments can be advanced, but at the time of writing the court has not specifically contemplated that scenario in any reported case.

11.52   It is clear therefore that the court may give permission for a proposed placement with family members overseas who are being assessed as prospective adopters or who have been successfully matched for adoption with the child, and may do so before the child is formally placed for adoption with them, provided that it is intended that any adoption application will be made in a court within this jurisdiction. It will be a matter for the local authority in each case to determine at what point it is in the child's best interests to place him or her with his or her family members and to make the appropriate application at that time.

11.53   From a practical perspective a local authority may wish to take into account the following matters:

- the emotional harm to the child of multiple placements and the corresponding need to be confident that the placement has the potential to meet the child's needs in the long term before moving the child;

- the benefits to the child of moving to long term carers as early as practicable;

- the additional information as to the family's ability to meet the child's needs if assessments are carried out in part while the child is living with the carers in their natural home environment;

- immigration issues which may limit the time a child may lawfully visit family members overseas; and

---

[27]   [2011] 1 FLR 234.

- the requirement that the child must have had his or her home with the adopters for not less than 10 weeks prior to the date that they issue an application to adopt the child under the Convention or an application for a section 84 order.

11.54 One particular consideration to bear in mind when determining this question is the length of time that a child can stay in the receiving state on a temporary basis. If a child is being placed with adopters in an EU country, there is no time limit placed on the child's visit by immigration, since there is free movement of citizens within the EU. It may be that once a local authority has made its decision on placement, it is best for the child to move to live with their family members, particularly if the local authority would consider an alternative option such as a special guardianship order[28] if the central authorities did not ultimately approve the adoption.

11.55 There are different considerations if the child is being placed in a country where there are strict time limits on temporary visits of minors to that country. For example, it is possible for a child to visit family members in the USA for a period of up to 3 months on the visa waiver transfer scheme. In summary this scheme allows UK citizens to visit the US for up to 3 months without needing to apply for a formal visa. Advance notification of the intention to travel to the US is required, but the visa is granted upon entry to the US. Once the 3-month period is up, the child will need to return to the UK since a failure to do so would make the child an overstayer in that country. While it is correct that if a child is taken out of the USA within the 3-month period they can apply to re-enter shortly afterwards under the same scheme, there is no guarantee that the child will be allowed to re-enter, and in some cases the approach of both the UK and the USA immigration services has been very unsettling to the families when they have tried to re-enter the USA for a second 3-month period when only a few days had elapsed after they had left the USA. The alternative method of entering the USA on a temporary basis is with a 6-month visiting visa. This brings with it the advantage of a 6-month visit which can be extended. However, if the application for a 6-month visitor visa is unsuccessful, the 3-month visa waiver scheme cannot be used. It is therefore a risky strategy to apply for a 6-month visa for the child, because a refusal of that visa will mean that the child cannot enter that country at all until after the Convention adoption order is made and he or she has been granted a visa which allows him or her to enter and permanently reside in that country. For these reasons it might be more prudent to delay the visit of the child to stay with their relatives until such time as the local authority is allowed to place the child for adoption with their US family members, unless these potential adopters are able to spend significant periods of time in the UK if the child is refused entry to the USA before the final Convention adoption order is granted.

---

[28]   Children Act 1989, s 14A.

STEP 6 – APPLICATION FOR CONVENTION ADOPTION/SECTION 84 ORDER

11.56 When a child is to be adopted under the Convention the adopters may choose whether they wish to conclude the adoption proceedings in the UK or in the receiving state. If they wish to adopt the child in the receiving state, they must obtain a section 84 order in this country before they can lawfully remove the child from the UK for the purpose of the adoption overseas. However, unlike non-Convention adoptions, the adopters may, if they wish, adopt the child in the UK, even though they are neither habitually resident nor domiciled in the British Islands. A Convention adoption order is a final adoption order and will be recognised as such by all Convention countries. The clear advantage to this option is that it negates the need for further legal proceedings in the receiving state.

11.57 If a child is being adopted under the Convention in the UK there is no need to obtain a section 84 order as a preliminary step to a Convention adoption order. If a child is removed from this country with a section 84 order the adopters will need to apply to adopt the child in the receiving state. In either situation there is only one set of proceedings in this country and the options of a section 84 order and a Convention adoption order are clearly alternatives. For both types of order the assessment, matching and placement processes are identical, as is the requirement that the child must have his or her home with the adopters for not less than 10 weeks before the relevant application is issued. The differences between the two final orders come into play at the time of issue. Accordingly at this point it is necessary to look at the two applications separately.

APPLICATION FOR A SECTION 84 ORDER

The court's power to make the order

11.58 An application for a section 84 order is made under ACA 2002, s 84. The effect of the order is to give the applicants parental responsibility and to extinguish it in every other person or body.[29] Once a person has been granted a section 84 order they may lawfully remove the subject child for the purpose of adopting that child under the law of a country or territory outside of the British Islands.[30] A section 84 order is not an adoption order and does not transfer parenthood from the parents of the child to the prospective adopters.

11.59 A section 84 order may not be made in favour of any person who meets the requirements as to habitual residence or domicile which would have to be met if an adoption order was to be made in their favour.[31]

---

[29] ACA 2005, s 84(5).
[30] ACA 2005, s 85.
[31] ACA 2005, s 84(2).

11.60 Before a court can make a section 84 order it must satisfy itself that the regulatory requirements imposed by s 84(3) are met. These requirements are enumerated in AFER 2005, reg 48. In effect, this regulation requires the court to double check that the matters which needed to be in place before a local authority was allowed to place the child for adoption have been met. It also confirms that the report required by ACA 2002, s 43(a) or (b), as modified by AFER 2005, reg 11, details any placement reviews or visits.

11.61 In addition the provisions of the ACA 2002 which are amended pursuant to AFER 2005, reg 11 will also apply in section 84 applications governed by the Convention.[32]

11.62 Before a person may apply to the court for a section 84 order the child must have had his or her home with the adopters for a period of not less than 10 weeks.[33] The court has found that in an agency adoption the home referred to in this section can be the home of the applicant wherever in the world that home may be.[34] Part of the reasoning for this conclusion was that in an agency placement there is no requirement in ACA 2002, s 42(7)(a) that the child has a home in the area of a local authority. In addition the time can be time spent before and/or after the child was placed for adoption, provided that it is more than 10 weeks in total before the date of the application.

11.63 Provided that the requirements of s 84 are met, the court may go on to consider whether or not the order would be in the interest of the child pursuant to ACA 2002, s 1.

The procedure for making the application

11.64 The procedure for making an application under s 84 is governed by Part 14 of the FPR 2010 and the associated Practice Directions. Pursuant to FPR 2010, r 14.3 the parties to a section 84 order are the same as for an adoption order. The application is made using Form A61.[35]

11.65 In some courts there can be a significant delay between the date that a posted application is received by the court and the date when the court issues that application. If the circumstances of the case require that the matter is dealt with quickly it may therefore be advisable to issue the application at the court counter. In addition, when the court makes a placement order in circumstances where it is envisaged that a section 84 application will be issued in due course, the court can be invited to make contingent directions which would come into effect at issue of the section 84 application. Those contingent directions can provide for preliminary matters that will enable the matter to be heard swiftly

---

[32] AFER 2005, reg 55 (see also Chapter 12 for more details).
[33] ACA 2002, s 84(4).
[34] *Re A (Adoption: Removal)* [2009] EWCA Civ 41, [2009] 2 FLR 597.
[35] This form can be downloaded for free at http://hmctscourtfinder.justice.gov.uk/courtfinder/forms/a061-bil.pdf.

and effectively upon issue, and avoiding unnecessary delay. Contingent directions may, for example, provide that:

'upon issue of an application for a s 84 order in relation to the child

- the child is joined as party to the proceedings and CAFCASS is invited to appoint the children's guardian [name] who has acted for the child in the placement order proceedings;
- [name of solicitor in placement order proceedings] shall be appointed to act for the child;
- provided that the application is issued in person the court list office shall issue the matter forthwith and allocate a case number and list the matter for a first directions appointment not more than 7 days thereafter to be heard by [name of judge who determines placement order proceedings] if possible.'

11.66 At the first hearing the court will need to consider the position of the parents. If the parents have not given their consent to the section 84 order and a placement order is in force, the parents will need to be served with the application, and may apply for leave to oppose the making of the section 84 order. Accordingly the court needs to take this into account at the first directions hearing. If the parents are not in attendance at the first directions hearing, an effective approach which has been taken in some cases such as this has been to direct the applicants or the local authority personally to serve the parents with a copy of the application, and to provide that if the parents wish to apply to oppose the making of the section 84 order they must do so within a specified number of days of being served with the application. If there is no urgency in terms of disposal then this period can be more generous. In a case where there is a real need for an expedited final hearing owing to visa time limits expiring, the court might be willing to reduce the time allowed for a parent to apply for permission to oppose the application.

APPLICATION FOR A CONVENTION ADOPTION ORDER

The court's power to make the order

11.67 It is important to note that AFER 2005, reg 52 provides that, subject to the modifications made within Chapter 3 of Part 3 of AFER 2005, 'the provisions of the Act shall apply to adoptions within the scope of the Convention so far as the nature of the provision permits and unless the contrary intention is shown'. This means that a Convention adoption order will confer the same rights on the child and the adopters as an ordinary domestic adoption would.

11.68 The eligibility criteria for a Convention adoption order is set out in ACA 2002, s 49 which, as amended by AFER 2005, reg 58 reads:

'49 Applications for Convention adoption order

(1) An application for an adoption order may be made by –

(a)   a couple, or
(b)   one person ...

(4) An application for an adoption order may only be made if the person to be adopted has not attained the age of 18 years on the date of the application.

(5) References in this Act to a child, in connection with any proceedings (whether or not concluded) for adoption, (such as "child to be adopted" or "adopted child") include a person who has attained the age of 18 years before the proceedings are concluded.'

11.69   Unlike the s 84 provisions, a person who is domiciled in the UK may apply for a Convention adoption order. As with domestic adoptions, it is a requirement that the child must live with the adopters before the application for a Convention adoption order is made. This requirement is derived from ACA 2002, s 42, as amended by AFER 2005, reg 56. Section 42 in its amended form reads:

'42 Child to live with adopters before application

(1) An application for an adoption order may not be made unless –

(a)   if subsection (2) applies, the condition in that subsection is met ...

(2) In the case of an adoption under the Convention the condition is that the child must have had his home with the applicant or, in the case of an application by a couple, with one or both of them at all times during the period of ten weeks preceding the application.

...

(7) An adoption order may not be made unless the court is satisfied that sufficient opportunities to see the child with the applicant or, in the case of an application by a couple, both of them together in the home environment have been given –

(a)   where the child was placed for adoption with the applicant or applicants by an adoption agency, to that agency,
(b)   in any other case, to the local authority within whose area the home is.

(8) In this section and sections 43 and 44(1) –

(a)   references to an adoption agency include a Scottish or Northern Irish adoption agency,
(b)   references to a child placed for adoption by an adoption agency are to be read accordingly.'

11.70 It is of note that ACA 2002, s 42(7) continues to have effect in a Convention adoption application. The Court of Appeal has confirmed that the home in s 42(a) can be anywhere in the world, so for the purposes of a Convention adoption arranged by an adoption agency, the home environment referred to in s 42(7) can be the adopters' ordinary home in the receiving state. The effect of s 42(7)(b) is that, in a private adoption under the Convention, it is a requirement that the adopters set up a temporary home in England and Wales, so that the local authority in that area can carry out the assessments required pursuant to s 42(7).

11.71 As with an ordinary agency adoption, the local authority will need to prepare a report pursuant to ACA 2002, s 43(a). In addition to the matters which would otherwise need to be addressed the report must also include a copy of:

(a)   the Article 15 Report;

(b)   the report prepared for the purposes of Article 16(1); and

(c)   written confirmation of the agreement under Article 17(c) of the Convention.[36]

11.72 At the final hearing the court will need to be satisfied that all matters set out in AFER 2005, reg 50 have been complied with. This provision reads:

'50 Convention adoption order

An adoption order shall not be made as a Convention adoption order unless –

(a)   in the case of –
  (i)   an application by a couple, both members of the couple have been habitually resident in a Convention country outside the British Islands for a period of not less than one year ending with the date of the application; or
  (ii)   an application by one person, the applicant has been habitually resident in a Convention country outside the British Islands for a period of not less than one year ending with the date of the application;
(b)   the child to be adopted was, on the date on which the agreement under Article 17(c) of the Convention was made, habitually resident in any part of the British Islands; and
(c)   the competent authority has confirmed that the child is authorised to enter and remain permanently in the Convention country in which the applicant is habitually resident.'

---

[36]   AFER 2005, reg 49.

11.73   Again we see that there is a requirement that the applicants are not habitually resident in the British Isles, but there is nothing to prevent the court from making a Convention adoption order in favour of a person domiciled in England and Wales.

11.74   In addition, it is interesting to note that there is no prohibition anywhere in AFER 2005 limiting the eligibility criteria either to apply for, or be granted, a Convention adoption order, to a married couple. As seen in Chapter 2 of this book the Convention itself does limit the making of a Convention adoption order to either a person or a married couple. There do not appear to be any reported cases of a Convention adoption order being granted to an unmarried couple. By the application of the rules of normal statutory construction, it is likely that the court will construe the regulations which amend the primary legislation in such a way as to make them compliant with the Convention that they seek to implement. However, since the regulations themselves are not clear on this point it is likely to be appropriate for any application by an unmarried couple for a Convention adoption order to be listed before a High Court judge so that the these provisions can be considered and the decision reported in due course.

The procedure for making the application

11.75   As with section 84 applications the procedure is governed by FPR 2010, Part 14. The application must be made on Form A59.[37] In the past there has been some confusion as to whether or not an application for a Convention adoption order must be accompanied by an application for a section 84 order. This has led in a couple of cases to members of the court staff responsible for issuing court proceedings refusing to issue an application for a Convention order unless the applicants also complete a section 84 application. The confusion has arisen due to some rather convoluted guidance on the form itself which reads:

> 'You shall need to complete Form A61 (Application for parental responsibility prior to adoption abroad) if you intend to adopt a child who is habitually resident in the United Kingdom (or who is a Commonwealth citizen) *in a place outside of the British Islands* (and provided you do not already have an order to remove the child under the Adoption (Scotland) Act 1978 or the Adoption (Northern Ireland) Order 1987), *even if you will be applying for a Convention adoption order in a place outside the British Islands.*' (emphasis added)

11.76   For the avoidance of doubt, a section 84 order is not required as a preliminary step to the making of a Convention adoption order, if the Convention adoption order is being made in England and Wales. A section 84 order is to be used if the application for a Convention adoption will be made in a court outside the British Isles. If the application for the Convention adoption order is going to be heard by a court in England and Wales, the correct form is A59 and it is the only application which needs to be issued.

---

[37]   http://hmctscourtfinder.justice.gov.uk/courtfinder/forms/a059-eng.pdf.

11.77 Apart from the use of the different application form, the considerations for timetabling the case to a final hearing will be the same as set out in **11.64–11.66**. The key difference is that upon the making of a Convention adoption order the child becomes the legal child of the adopters and the parent-child relationship between the child and its former parents is extinguished.

11.78 Following the making of the Convention adoption order the applicants should send a copy of the Convention adoption order to the UK central authority which must then prepare a certificate pursuant to Sch 2 to AFER 2005, which meets the requirements of Article 23(1) of the Convention.[38] The Schedule 2 certificate is then sent to the central authority in the receiving state and also to the relevant local authority. It is likely to be useful for the applicants to have their own copy of this certificate, and it would seem reasonable to expect a local authority to provide a copy if requested to do so by the applicants. It certifies that the adoption was made in compliance with the Convention and must therefore be recognised by all Convention states. The only justification for refusing to recognise the adoption would be if the very limited circumstances in Article 24 of the Convention are found to apply in a particular contracting state in which case that state may refuse to recognise the adoption (see **2.43–2.44** for more details).

TRANSFER TO THE RECEIVING STATE POST ADOPTION ORDER

11.79 Once the adoption has been finalised the child can be transferred to the receiving state. By contrast with temporary visits made while the child was looked after by the local authority, this visit is permanent and the child's place of habitual residence will become that of his or her new parents. Accordingly when the child leaves English soil he or she will lose his or her place of habitual residence here, and on arrival in the receiving state he or she will become habitually resident there. The child should enter the receiving state with his or her adoptive parent, and if adopted by a couple with both of them if possible.

11.80 If the child is travelling outside the EU, it may be necessary for the applicants to obtain a visa facilitating the child's entry to the receiving state and allowing the child permission to permanently remain there. Since that state will have already granted such permission in principle pursuant to Article 5, this process should be reasonably quick and straightforward, but it is worth bearing in mind that appointments with the relevant Embassy or Consulate may be needed to finalise his or her visa before the child can travel with his or her new parents to the receiving state.

---

[38] Pursuant to AFER 2005, reg 51(1).

TIPS TO BEAR IN MIND IF THE RECEIVING STATE IS THE USA

11.81 It is beyond the remit of this book to give advice as to USA immigration law and practice. It is strongly suggested that when planning a move to the USA, very careful advice on the likely approach of the US consulate towards an application for a 6-month visa is obtained before any such application is made. It may be that the approach of the US consulate to such applications becomes more liberal as this sort of application becomes more familiar. However, for the time being, if the adopters live in the US the least risky strategy in terms of placing the child would appear to be:

- **Do not place the child with the adopters until after Article 17 agreement is reached**. Placement before this agreement is reached leaves open the possibility that the administrative matters which must be complete before the child can be placed for adoption will not be completed in time for the child to be adopted within the 3-month window given by the visa waiver transit scheme. Once the Article 17 agreement is reached the only variable is the court timetable, and the courts have been very accommodating in finding court time in these cases, as they are aware of the difficulties imposed by immigration matters.

- **Issue an application for a Convention adoption order as soon as 10 weeks have elapsed**. To do this the application forms should be prepared in advance and the applications should be issued in person at the court counter. There is no reason why the application should not be issued 10 weeks and 1 day after the child moved to live with the adopters.

- **Seek an expedited final hearing**. If the court has made contingent directions as set out above it should be possible for the matter to be listed for a directions appointment within days of the case being issued. There should be close liaison between the child's solicitor and Cafcass before the issue date so that they are aware of the intended application and they can attend the first directions appointment. The local authority section 43(a) report should be ready by the date of issue so that it can be filed and served within days of the matter being issued. In one case, where there was parental agreement, the time between the date of issue and the final order was less than one week. This case was exceptional, but does show what can be achieved if parties work together and engage in careful pre-issue planning.

- **Fix Consulate appointments to fit with the final hearing**. Book appointments with the US Consulate in London to complete the child's long term visa application so that they take place about 4 days after the final hearing. These appointments usually need to be made at least 2 weeks in advance, and so as soon as the date of the final hearing is known it would be sensible to make the Consulate appointments. It is suggested that a window of at least 4 days is allowed because the court staff will need to prepare the Convention adoption order, following which the UK central authority will need to prepare the Schedule 2 certificate. Both of these documents will be required by the Consulate when processing the child's long term visa.

Chapter 12

NON-CONVENTION AGENCY ADOPTIONS

INTRODUCTION

12.1 This chapter will look at the law and procedures which govern international adoption of a child habitually resident in the British Isles who is placed for adoption by an adoption agency with adopters who are habitually resident in a non-Convention country and are not domiciled in the British Isles. Unlike Convention cases which are addressed in Chapter 11, adopters who are not habitually resident in a Convention country cannot apply for a Convention adoption order. Therefore, section 84 orders provide the only means of facilitating adoption when a child is to be placed with prospective adopters who are habitually resident in a non-Convention country. In this chapter, the term 'receiving state' will be used to denote the foreign country to which the child is to be removed pursuant to the section 84 order. The Adoptions with a Foreign Element Regulations 2005 (AFER 2005),[1] Part 2 Chapter 2 provides the regulatory framework which governs these applications. In particular this chapter will look at:

(1)   assessment of both adopters and child;

(2)   matching;

(3)   placement for adoption;

(4)   applying for section 84 orders.

WHAT IS A SECTION 84 ORDER?

12.2   The Adoption and Children Act 2002 (ACA 2002), s 84 gives the court a power to make an order which invests the applicants with parental responsibility for a child. However, unlike an order under the Children Act 1989 (CA 1989), s 4 or s 12, this parental responsibility is not only conferred on the applicants, but stripped from every other person or body that

---

[1]   SI 2005/392.

had parental responsibility for the child before the order was made.[2] It does this by importing ACA 2002, s 46(2)–(4) to have effect when a section 84 order is made. Those provisions read:

'(2) The making of an adoption order operates to extinguish –

(a)   the parental responsibility which any person other than the adopters or adopter has for the adopted child immediately before the making of the order,

(b)   any order under the 1989 Act or the Children (Northern Ireland) Order 1995 (SI 1995/755 (NI 2)),

(c)   any order under the Children (Scotland) Act 1995 (c 36) other than an excepted order, and

(d)   any duty arising by virtue of an agreement or an order of a court to make payments, so far as the payments are in respect of the adopted child's maintenance or upbringing for any period after the making of the adoption order.

"Excepted order" means an order under section 9, 11(1)(d) or 13 of the Children (Scotland) Act 1995 or an exclusion order within the meaning of section 76(1) of that Act.

(3) An adoption order –

(a)   does not affect parental responsibility so far as it relates to any period before the making of the order, and

(b)   in the case of an order made on an application under section 51(2) by the partner of a parent of the adopted child, does not affect the parental responsibility of that parent or any duties of that parent within subsection (2)(d).

(4) Subsection (2)(d) does not apply to a duty arising by virtue of an agreement –

(a)   which constitutes a trust, or

(b)   which expressly provides that the duty is not to be extinguished by the making of an adoption order.'

12.3   Following the making of a section 84 order the prospective adopters are at liberty to remove the child from this jurisdiction and travel with the child to their own country, where they may lawfully commence adoption proceedings.

WHEN AND WHY IS A SECTION 84 ORDER NECESSARY?

12.4   ACA 2002, s 49 sets out the eligibility criteria which applicants must meet if they wish to apply for an adoption order in any court within England and Wales. It reads:

---

[2]   ACA 2002, s 84(5).

'49 Applications for adoption

(1) An application for an adoption order may be made by –

(a)   a couple, or
(b)   one person,

but only if it is made under section 50 or 51 and one of the following conditions is met.

(2) The first condition is that at least one of the couple (in the case of an application under section 50) or the applicant (in the case of an application under section 51) is domiciled in a part of the British Islands.

(3) The second condition is that both of the couple (in the case of an application under section 50) or the applicant (in the case of an application under section 51) have been habitually resident in a part of the British Islands for a period of not less than one year ending with the date of the application.

(4) An application for an adoption order may only be made if the person to be adopted has not attained the age of 18 years on the date of the application.

(5) References in this Act to a child, in connection with any proceedings (whether or not concluded) for adoption, (such as "child to be adopted" or "adopted child") include a person who has attained the age of 18 years before the proceedings are concluded.'

12.5   Accordingly, any person who is unable to satisfy the court that these criteria are met will be unable to adopt a child in a court within England and Wales. The only exception to this rule is the making of a Convention adoption order if the applicants live in a Convention country. A person who is habitually resident in a non-Convention country and who is neither domiciled nor habitually resident here and thus unable to adopt a child in this country, must therefore remove the child from this country and adopt the child in their own country, according to the relevant law of that country.

12.6   A person cannot remove a child from the British Islands for the purpose of adoption overseas without the permission of the court. ACA 2002, s 85 limits the circumstances in which a child can be removed from the British Isles for the purpose of adoption overseas. Section 85 reads:

'85 Restriction on taking children out

(1) A child who –

(a)   is a Commonwealth citizen, or
(b)   is habitually resident in the United Kingdom,

must not be removed from the United Kingdom to a place outside the British Islands for the purpose of adoption unless the condition in subsection (2) is met.

(2) The condition is that –

(a) the prospective adopters have parental responsibility for the child by virtue of an order under section 84, or
(b) the child is removed under the authority of an order under [section 59 of the Adoption and Children (Scotland) Act 2007 (asp 4)] or Article 57 of the Adoption (Northern Ireland) Order 1987 (SI 1987/2203 (NI 22)).

(3) Removing a child from the United Kingdom includes arranging to do so; and the circumstances in which a person arranges to remove a child from the United Kingdom include those where he –

(a) enters into an arrangement for the purpose of facilitating such a removal of the child,
(b) initiates or takes part in any negotiations of which the purpose is the conclusion of an arrangement within paragraph (a).

An arrangement includes an agreement (whether or not enforceable).

(4) A person who removes a child from the United Kingdom in contravention of subsection (1) is guilty of an offence.

(5) A person is not guilty of an offence under subsection (4) of causing a person to take any step mentioned in paragraph (a) or (b) of subsection (3) unless it is proved that he knew or had reason to suspect that the step taken would contravene subsection (1). But this subsection only applies if sufficient evidence is adduced to raise an issue as to whether the person had the knowledge or reason mentioned.

(6) A person guilty of an offence under this section is liable –

(a) on summary conviction to imprisonment for a term not exceeding six months, or a fine not exceeding the statutory maximum, or both,
(b) on conviction on indictment, to imprisonment for a term not exceeding twelve months, or a fine, or both.

(7) In any proceedings under this section –

(a) a report by a British consular officer or a deposition made before a British consular officer and authenticated under the signature of that officer is admissible, upon proof that the officer or the deponent cannot be found in the United Kingdom, as evidence of the matters stated in it, and
(b) it is not necessary to prove the signature or official character of the person who appears to have signed any such report or deposition.'

12.7 The combined effect of s 49 and s 85 is to require a person who does not fulfill the s 49 criteria, but who wishes to adopt a child to whom s 85(1) applies, to obtain a s 84 order before he or she may lawfully remove the child from this jurisdiction for the purpose of adoption overseas.

ASSESSING THE ADOPTERS

12.8   If the parents of a child request that a local authority looking after their child consider a connected person as a potential long term carer for their child, the local authority will have to consider that person's ability to meet the child's needs. The first step in that assessment process will be for the local authority to carry out a viability assessment. If the potential carer lives abroad, it may be appropriate that in the first instance that assessment is carried out by way of phone, Skype or video-conferencing, and the considerations which are set out in **11.5–11.15** apply equally to assessments for the purpose of non-Convention section 84 placements as they do to potential Convention adoption placements.

12.9   As with Convention adoptions, the relevant foreign authority in the receiving state[3] must assess the suitability of the prospective adopter to be an adoptive parent, to counsel them on the implications of the adoption and to confirm their eligibility to adopt the child. It must also confirm that the child will be allowed to enter and permanently reside in that foreign country or territory. Additionally the relevant foreign authority must have confirmed that the prospective adopters will accompany the child into the receiving country. These obligations arise out of AFER 2005, reg 10(b) and (c) which read:

'(b)   in the case of a child placed by an adoption agency the relevant foreign authority has –

(i)   confirmed in writing to that agency that the prospective adopter has been counselled and the legal implications of adoption have been explained to him;

(ii)   prepared a report on the suitability of the prospective adopter to be an adoptive parent;

(iii)   determined and confirmed in writing to that agency that he is eligible and suitable to adopt in the country or territory in which the adoption is to be effected; and

(iv)   confirmed in writing to that agency that the child is or will be authorised to enter and reside permanently in that foreign country or territory; and

(c)   in the case of a child placed by an adoption agency the prospective adopter has confirmed in writing to the adoption agency that he will accompany the child on taking him out of the United Kingdom and entering the country or territory where the adoption is to be effected, or in the case of a couple, the agency and relevant foreign authority have confirmed that it is necessary for only one of them to do so.'

12.10   The local authority will have to ascertain the identity of the relevant foreign authority for these purposes. It may be that the information required by AFER 2005, reg 10(b) and (c) is supplied by one public body, or it may be that the information needs to be obtained from more than one public or private body.

---

[3]   As explained at the beginning of this Chapter, this term is used in this chapter to mean the overseas country to which the child is to be removed pursuant to the section 84 order, whether or not the country is a party to the Convention.

12.11 Although it is not a requirement of the regulations, an adoption agency is likely to find it helpful to seek the advice of a suitably qualified legal expert in the receiving state. Such advice would help to ensure that the correct authorities are contacted for the purpose of providing the necessary information, and to assist in the planning for the child. It is suggested that the adoption agency should seek advice in relation to both the adoption and immigration laws of that country. Such advice should seek clarification in relation to:

(a) the identity and contact details of the agencies responsible for assessing the suitability of the adopters to adopt the child;

(b) the form of the assessment undertaken (including the extent to which criminal history checks are undertaken);

(c) the likely timescales and costs (if any) of the assessment;

(d) the adoption law and procedure in that state and in particular the role (if any) that the birth parents would be expected to play in the adoption proceedings;

(e) confirmation as to whether or not parental consent is required for the adoption to proceed in the receiving state, and the extent to which that country would have regard to the effect of the section 84 order (this is not a requirement of the regulations but it is suggested that it is an important consideration);

(f) the immigration issues, and in particular how the relevant foreign authority responsible for providing the information required by AFER 2005, reg 10(b)(iv) can be contacted, along with the evidential requirements and application procedure for obtaining the required authorisation and confirmation thereof.

12.12 At first glance it may seem strange that the foreign authority is responsible for assessing the suitability of the adopters to adopt the child, even in a non-Convention case. The reason for this is that following the making of the section 84 order, the child's parents will lose parental responsibility. Before the order is made in this country, there needs to be a degree of confidence that once in the receiving state, the child can be adopted by the adopters and achieve the sense of permanence and security, both emotionally and legally, that flows from adoption. The final decision on the adoption will be made by the relevant authority in the receiving state. Therefore, in order to ascertain the likelihood that any adoption application made by the prospective adopters will succeed in that country, it is necessary to confirm that they are deemed to be both suitable and eligible to adopt the child according to the law of that country. It would also be important to know what, if any, role the birth parents would have in the adoption proceedings, and whether or not the receiving state would recognize the effect of the section 84 order. Certainly the courts of this country do not always recognise similar orders which are made in other countries, eg orders made in a foreign country which transfer parenthood from a surrogate mother and her husband to the intended parents, following a lawful commercial surrogacy in that country, are not recognised in England and Wales.[4]

12.13 The requirement that the foreign authority assess the adopters does not appear to relieve the adoption agency of its duty to assess the adopters as being suitable to adopt. There does not appear to be any reason why the adoption panel and the decision maker cannot rely on the report provided by the foreign authority for the purpose of approving the adopters. However, if the agency/panel consider that additional information is necessary in order for the adoption panel to make a recommendation and/or for the agency to make a decision, either for approval or for matching purposes, that additional information should be obtained.

12.14 To all intents and purposes, the report required by AFER 2005, reg 10(b)(ii) is the same as the Home study report considered in Chapter 11. Therefore, in terms of:

(a)   disclosure to the assessing organisation of evidence in the care or placement order proceedings relating to the child; and

(b)   timetabling of court proceedings if the decisions of the panel/agency are being made during the course of care proceedings,

the considerations are the same as with a Convention application.[5]

12.15 AFER 2005, reg 10(a) specifies that before the court can make a section 84 order the adoption agency must confirm that it has complied with Part 3 of the Adoption Agency Regulations 2005 (AAR 2005),[6] which relate to the assessment of the child. By contrast, in relation to the information which must be provided to the court in respect of the adopters, there is no requirement for the adoption agency to confirm that it has complied with AAR 2005, Part 4, which is the part covering the assessment of the adopter. Furthermore, certain tasks in the assessment process under Part 4, such as obtaining of police reports etc, could not be relied upon as being proof of a clean criminal history if the adopter is habitually resident out of the jurisdiction and has been so for at least a year. However, ACA 2002, s 43 requires the local authority to prepare a report for the court, and the contents of that report must confirm, among other things,[7] that the adopters are still approved as adopters.[8] It does appear therefore that the provisions of AAR 2005, Part 4 do apply, or at least apply insofar as they can reasonably be carried

---

4   *Re X & Y (Foreign Surrogacy)* [2008] EWHC 3030 (Fam), [2009] 1 FLR 733.
5   See **11.16–11.20**.
6   SI 2005/389.
7   FPR 2010, r 14.11(3), as supplemented by PD 14C.
8   FPR 2010, PD 14C Annexe A, section C(r).

out. Indeed, part of the ratio in *Re A (Adoption: Removal)*[9] was that it was a matter for the local authority to carry out its assessment either in this country, or in the receiving country in the most effective way. The local authority will therefore need to prepare a report as to the suitability of the adopter pursuant to AAR 2005, reg 25. Within that report it is necessary to obtain a health report from a registered medical practitioner. The term 'registered medical practitioner' is not defined in AAR 2005, reg 2, and it is therefore suggested that provided the health report is obtained from a suitably qualified medical practitioner recognised by the receiving state as authorised to provide this information within their own adoption procedures, the requirement in reg 25(3)(a) should be met. If this report is not provided within the body of the AFER 2005, reg 10(b)(ii) report, the local authority should commission the report independently.

ASSESSING THE CHILD

12.16   The local authority will need to assess the child as being suitable to be adopted. This decision needs to be made according to the normal regulatory framework which applies in terms of determining that the child is suitable for adoption. AFER 2005, Part 2, Chapter 2 does not alter the regulations which govern this process. However, if any information is available as a result of the investigations into the possibility of the adoption with foreign adopters, this will need to be taken into account as it will fall into the 'any other relevant information' category when this is called for in the applicable regulations.

MATCHING THE CHILD AND PLACING THE CHILD FOR ADOPTION

12.17   AFER 2005 does not amend the normal regulatory process for the matching of a child with the adopters for the purpose of a non-Convention section 84 application. However, those regulations require the local authority to include in the child's placement report 'any other relevant information'.[10] It is very likely that the adoption panel would find all the information which is required for the court by virtue of AFER 2005, reg 10(b) and (c) relevant information with regard to their matching decision; indeed it is hard to see how they could recommend the match without it. Therefore, although the regulations do not impose a requirement that matching is delayed until all that information is available, it would be sensible to timetable the matching panel to take place once it has become available. Equally, although the child's permanence report does not need to set out the options for adoption in the UK, this information is likely to be very relevant and it would be prudent to include it in the child's permanence report, as well as the full reasons why the match with foreign adopters is proposed.

---

[9]   [2009] EWCA Civ 41, [2009] 2 FLR 597, [2010] Fam 9.
[10]   AFER 2005, reg 31(2)(c)(v).

12.18 In terms of the child's support plan, the considerations set out in **11.42** have equal applicability in non-Convention applications for section 84 orders.

12.19 Once the local authority has successfully matched the child with the adopters in accordance with the standard regulations, it can proceed to place the child for adoption with them pursuant to ACA 2002, s 18.

12.20 Once the child has been placed for adoption the effect of AFER 2005, reg 11 is to import, in a modified form, statutory provisions from ACA 2002 to govern that placement, so that the prospective adopters in this situation have the same rights and duties as prospective adopters who would be eligible to apply for an adoption order in this jurisdiction.[11]

LEGAL PROCEDURE TO BE FOLLOWED IN APPLICATIONS FOR SECTION 84 ORDERS

12.21 As with Convention applications, non-Convention section 84 applications are governed by FPR 2010, Part 14. The application form is A61.[12] Pursuant to ACA 2002, s 84(4) the child must have had his or her home with the adopters for not less than 10 weeks at the date of application, but that 10 weeks can take place before or after the child is placed for adoption. Furthermore, the home can be anywhere in the world.[13]

12.22 In addition to the eligibility requirement set out in s 84 itself, the provisions of ACA 2002, ss 50 and 51, as modified by AFER 2005, reg 11, specify the same minimum age for applicants for section 84 orders as for domestic adoptions.

12.23 Pursuant to FPR 2010, r 14.3 the respondents to the application will be:

(a) each parent who has parental responsibility for the child unless that parent has given notice under ACA 2002, s 20(4)(a) (statement of wish not to be informed of any application for an adoption order);

(b) any guardian of the child unless that guardian has given notice under ACA 2002, s 20(4)(a) (statement of wish not to be informed of any application for an adoption order);

(c) any person in whose favour there is provision for contact;

(d) any adoption agency having parental responsibility for the child under ACA 2002, s 25;

---

[11] See the appendix at the end of this chapter which sets out the provisions of ACA 2002 amended by AFER 2005, reg 11 in their modified form.

[12] Available to download for free at http://hmctsformfinder.justice.gov.uk/courtfinder/forms/a061-eng.pdf.

[13] *Re A (Adoption: Removal)* [2009] EWCA Civ 41, [2009] 2 FLR 597, [2010] Fam 9.

(e) any adoption agency which has taken part at any stage in the arrangements for adoption of the child;

(f) any local authority to whom notice under ACA 2002, s 44 (notice of intention to adopt or apply for a section 84 order) has been given;

(g) any local authority or voluntary organisation which has parental responsibility for, is looking after or is caring for, the child;

(h) the child (since the application is for a section 84 order).

12.24 Pursuant to FPR 2010, r 14.5, the court is ordinarily responsible for the service of proceedings on the respondents. However, this may not be the most expeditious way of effecting service. For the reasons set out in **11.65–11.66**, it may be advisable if contingent directions are sought at the conclusion of the placement order proceedings to seek a direction that the applicants will be responsible for effecting service of the application on the respondents. Also, because this is a foreign adoption case and the child will be made a party, Cafcass will need to appoint a children's guardian who will have to prepare a report for the court. If possible this should be the same person as the children's guardian in the placement order proceedings and again that is something that can be included in any contingent directions.

12.25 At the first directions appointment, the court will need to check that the information required for the final hearing will be available. FPR 2010, PD 14B, para 2.1(a)–(b) require the court in particular to:

'(a) consider whether the requirements of the Act and the Adoptions with a Foreign Element Regulations 2005 (SI 2005/392) appear to have been complied with and, if not, consider whether or not it is appropriate to transfer the case to the High Court;

(b) consider whether all relevant documents are translated into English and, if not, fix a timetable for translating any outstanding documents;'

The remaining provisions of this Practice Direction are relevant to applications when a child is brought into the British Islands from overseas and so do not apply to section 84 cases. As well as considering these particular matters the court will need to consider all the other matters which need to be addressed at a first directions appointment under FPR 2010, r 14.8(1).

12.26 The local authority will need to prepare a report pursuant to s 43, and will need to set out in that report the information obtained from their visits to the family pursuant to s 42(7). In addition the adoption agency will need to place before the court all the information required by AFER 2005, reg 10. The report will need to take the form required by FPR 2010, r 14.11(3), as supplemented by PD 14C. In relation to that report, the requirements of Section C, Part 1 still requires the following information:

'(r) Confirmation that the applicants have not been convicted of, or cautioned for, a specified offence within the meaning of regulation 23(3) of the Adoption Agencies Regulations 2005 (SI 2005/389).

(s) Confirmation that the prospective adopter is still approved.

(t) Confirmation that any referees have been interviewed, with a report of their views and opinion of the weight to be placed thereon and whether they are still valid.'

If the adopters have never lived in the UK, there is not likely to be a record of their having any convictions under (r), but this can be checked. Of more importance will be their criminal history in their own country. It is suggested that in this section the information obtained from the foreign authority is provided along with confirmation that criminal checks have been undertaken in the UK. In relation to the prospective adopter being approved, it is suggested that in answering this question the report should confirm that the adopter is still approved by their own adoption agency as suitable to adopt in that country as well as being approved by the adoption agency. In relation to (t), provided that the referees have been interviewed by the foreign authority and the local authority is satisfied that the referees have been properly interviewed and their views reported within the assessment carried out by the relevant authority, and that their view are still valid, it does not appear that there is a need for the local authority to re-interview the referees. If there is any doubt as to the way in which the references have been taken, while the local authority is carrying out its visits under ACA 2002, s 42(7) it would be appropriate for the visiting social worker to carry out their own interviews of the referees, with the assistance of an interpreter if necessary.

PHYSICAL PLACEMENT OF THE CHILD WITH THE FOREIGN FAMILY MEMBERS AND COURT TIMETABLING CONSIDERATIONS

12.27 With respect to the physical placement of the child with the adopters the situation may be different to that which pertained in the case of *ECC (The Local Authority) v SM*.[14] In the case of *ECC*, the court was able to justify the removal of the child from the jurisdiction of the court for the purpose of a temporary overseas visit with relatives pursuant to ACA 2002, s 28, because it could not be said to be for the purpose of an adoption overseas. Insofar as anyone might say the removal was for the purpose of an adoption at all, it was for the purpose of a Convention adoption which would in due course be made within the British Islands. Accordingly there was no conflict with the use of this section for this purpose and ACA 2002, s 85. However, since a Convention adoption is not available to adopters living in a non-Convention country, any adoption would need to be obtained overseas. Section 84 orders are obtained for the purpose of facilitating an adoption overseas. The question therefore arises: can ACA 2002, s 28 be used to authorise a temporary removal of a child placed for adoption with foreign adopters in circumstances where the removal

---

[14] [2011] 1 FLR 234.

is intended to facilitate their application for a section 84 order? This question has not yet been addressed in a reported case. It is difficult to predict at this stage what the answer would be to that question should it arise in the future, since there are valid points to be advanced for both sides of the argument.

12.28   However, the case of *Re A*,[15] would appear to support the contention that such an application could be allowed. In the case of *Re A* at first instance, it was argued that s 85 did not apply to the intended removal because the trip to the USA was not for the purpose of adoption but was for the purpose of assessment. Charles J did not accept that proposition and determined that but for para 19(6) of Sch 2 to CA 1989, the removal would be unlawful under the terms of ACA 2002, s 85. Although the appellant did not seek to overturn that finding as to the law, the issue was addressed in the judgment of Moore-Bick LJ in the Court of Appeal who stated:

> '[98] The plan in the present case contemplates that IA will travel to the USA in order to assess one possible option for her future care, namely, adoption by Mr and Mrs N. It also contemplates that she will return to this country in any event, whatever the outcome of the visit and whether the assessment is in favour of or against adoption. That means that the court will retain control over the process and even if the assessment favours adoption, no adoption is contemplated otherwise than in accordance with the relevant statutory provisions. I do not think, therefore, that the removal of IA from this country to live for a period with Mr and Mrs N and their family as envisaged by Step 1 can be said to be removal for the purposes of adoption in anything but the loosest sense. *In reality it is no more than temporary removal for purposes connected with a care plan in which adoption is the preferred but not the only possible outcome, so I doubt whether it falls within s 85 of the Act at all.* Even if it does, however, it does not amount to placing a child for adoption with prospective adopters within the meaning of para 19(9). Accordingly, the court can, in my view, lawfully give its approval to Step 1. The problem, as the judge recognised, lies with Step 4.' (emphasis added)

12.29   While it is correct to say that in the case of *Re A* that the child had not been matched with the adopters or placed for adoption with them, it does seem clear that the court has given the word 'purpose' within ACA 2002, s 85 a fairly narrow meaning. If the court is satisfied that the trip abroad under s 28 is for the purposes of obtaining a s 84 order and not for the purpose of obtaining a foreign adoption, the court would be in a position to authorise the visit. It was accepted in *Re A* at both first instance and in the Court of Appeal that the adopters would return to this jurisdiction before the placement order was granted and that they would spend such time as necessary between the placement order and the final order in this jurisdiction, and that was something which the adopters were able to do for a short time at least. So it is unclear whether or not the court would be willing to authorise a visit under s 28 in a section 84 case. However, if permission was granted under s 28 in these circumstances, it is likely that the requirements set out in *ECC* for declarations as to the child's habitual residence, etc would still need to appear on the face of the drawn order granting permission under ACA 2002, s 28 (see **11.50**).

---

[15]   [2009] EWCA Civ 41, [2009] 2 FLR 597, [2010] Fam 9.

12.30 Given the uncertainty of the law in this regard, it would be prudent to ensure that before a child is placed with a family under CA 1989, Sch 2, para 19 in these circumstances, they must have confirmed that they (or in the case of a couple at least one of them[16]) would be in a position to spend a period of time in the UK should that become necessary. *Re A* established that a child can be placed with their family members under para 19 before a placement order has been granted by the court, that the assessments required by s 42(7) can be undertaken during that period, and that the time spent with the family in these circumstances can count towards the 10-week time limit in s 84(4). Furthermore, upon the making of a placement order a local authority can place the child for adoption in a non-Convention case without waiting for authorisation from any third party. Taking all of these factors into account, and allowing for the possibility that the child might not be permitted to leave the jurisdiction following the making of the placement order, careful planning will be required in order to minimise the time which the prospective adopters will need to spend in England or Wales. Accordingly it is recommended that order of the key events leading up to a final section 84 order ought to be planned to take place as follows:

(a) determine the child's suitability to be adopted pursuant to AAR 2005, reg 19;

(b) obtain an expert legal opinion on the law in relation to adoption and immigration in the receiving state;

(c) support the adopters to commission such reports as required in order for the information required by AAR 2005, reg 10(b) and (c);

(d) subject to the adoption agency remaining of the view that adoption with the prospective adopters is still in the child's best interests, apply for a placement order;

(e) apply for an order under CA 1989, Sch 2, para 19 to place the child overseas with the family members acting as foster carers to be heard at the first appointment in the placement order proceedings (which may or may not be within the context of ongoing care proceedings);

(f) subject to permission being granted, place the child with the family under para 19 for the purpose of visits with the family;[17]

(g) carry out visits to the family pursuant to ACA 2002, s 42(7), and complete the adopters report pursuant to AAR 2005, reg 25;

---

[16] *Re G (Adoption: Placement Outside Jurisdiction)* [2008] EWCA Civ 105, [2008] 1 FLR 1484.
[17] The order should recite that the local authority have parental responsibility for the child and that the child remains habitually resident in England or Wales and that the carers have provided the court with solemn undertakings to return to the jurisdiction of the court if required to do so by the court or the local authority and in any event by no later than [insert date as applicable].

(h)   approve the adopters pursuant to AAR 2005, reg 27;

(i)   match the child with the adopters pursuant to AAR 2005, reg 33;

(j)   list the matter for a final hearing of the placement order proceedings not less than 10 weeks after the child has had a home with the potential adopters in the receiving state, and in any event not before all the information required for the purposes of the section 43 report is available and that report is capable of being filed with the court within a very short timescale;

(k)   arrange for the adopter (or if a couple at least one of them) to bring the child back to the jurisdiction on a date which precedes the final hearing of the placement order proceedings;

(l)   issue an application for leave to remove the child from the jurisdiction pursuant to ACA 2002, s 28 to be heard at the same time as the placement order proceedings are finally determined;

(m)   at the final hearing of the placement order proceedings obtain contingent directions for the section 84 application, on the basis that application will issued shortly thereafter;

(n)   place the child for adoption with the adopters soon after the placement order is granted;

(o)   the adopters should issue their section 84 application as soon as the child is placed for adoption with them;

(p)   if the section 28 order is granted the child can return to the receiving state pending the final hearing of the section 84 order; *or*

(q)   if the section 28 order is refused, the child will need to remain with the prospective adopters within the jurisdiction of the court pending the grant of the section 84 order;

(r)   list the matter for first directions in a section 84 application if necessary (the contingent directions may be capable of dealing with all directions matters since the factual matrix will be clear at the time of the placement order final hearing);

(s)   list the final hearing of the section 84 order (subject to any directions to serve the parents with a copy of the application and allow them time to apply for leave to oppose the making of the order, this may be capable of being listed between 2–4 weeks following the date of issue of the application);

(t)   once they have been granted the section 84 order, the adopters may lawfully remove the child for the purpose of adoption overseas.

12.31   Until there is clarity on the law with regard to section 28 orders sought in the context of section 84 orders, it cannot be guaranteed that the adopters will not be required to spend some time post-placement order in this country. That fact will need to be taken into account in the assessment stage before matching the child and placing them with the family overseas. The advantage of this approach is that it enables the preparation of the evidence for the section 84 proceedings to take place prior to the granting of the placement order. This has the effect of reducing the time that the adopters will need to spend in the UK to the absolute minimum if section 28 permission is refused.

APPENDIX

Provisions of the Act modified by AFER 2005, reg 11

1 Considerations applying to the exercise of powers

(1) This section applies whenever a court or adoption agency is coming to a decision relating to the adoption of a child.

(2) The paramount consideration of the court or adoption agency must be the child's welfare, throughout his life.

(3) The court or adoption agency must at all times bear in mind that, in general, any delay in coming to the decision is likely to prejudice the child's welfare.

(4) The court or adoption agency must have regard to the following matters (among others) —

(a)   the child's ascertainable wishes and feelings regarding the decision (considered in the light of the child's age and understanding),
(b)   the child's particular needs,
(c)   the likely effect on the child (throughout his life) of having ceased to be a member of the original family and become an adopted person,
(d)   the child's age, sex, background and any of the child's characteristics which the court or agency considers relevant,
(e)   any harm (within the meaning of the Children Act 1989 (c 41)) which the child has suffered or is at risk of suffering,
(f)   the relationship which the child has with relatives, and with any other person in relation to whom the court or agency considers the relationship to be relevant, including —
      (i)   the likelihood of any such relationship continuing and the value to the child of its doing so,
      (ii)   the ability and willingness of any of the child's relatives, or of any such person, to provide the child with a secure environment in which the child can develop, and otherwise to meet the child's needs,
      (iii) the wishes and feelings of any of the child's relatives, or of any such person, regarding the child.

(5) In placing the child for adoption, the adoption agency must give due consideration to the child's religious persuasion, racial origin and cultural and linguistic background.

(6) The court or adoption agency must always consider the whole range of powers available to it in the child's case (whether under this Act or the Children Act 1989); and the court must not make any order under this Act unless it considers that making the order would be better for the child than not doing so.

(7) In this section, 'coming to a decision relating to the adoption of a child', in relation to a court, includes —

(a) coming to a decision in any proceedings where the orders that might be made by the court include a section 84 order (or the revocation of such an order), a placement order (or the revocation of such an order) or an order under section 26 (or the revocation or variation of such an order),

(b) coming to a decision about granting leave in respect of any action (other than the initiation of proceedings in any court) which may be taken by an adoption agency or individual under this Act, but does not include coming to a decision about granting leave in any other circumstances.

(8) For the purposes of this section —

(a) references to relationships are not confined to legal relationships,
(b) references to a relative, in relation to a child, include the child's.

18 Placement for adoption by agencies

...

(4) If an application for a section 84 order has been made by any persons in respect of a child and has not been disposed of —

(a) an adoption agency which placed the child with those persons may leave the child with them until the application is disposed of, but
(b) apart from that, the child may not be placed for adoption with any prospective adopters.

'Adoption order' includes a Scottish or Northern Irish adoption order.

21 Placement orders

(4) A placement order continues in force until —

...

(b) A section 84 order is made in respect of the child, or ...

22 Applications for placement orders

...

(5) Subsections (1) to (3) do not apply in respect of a child —

(a) if any persons have given notice of intention to adopt, unless the period of four months beginning with the giving of the notice has expired without them applying for a section 84 order or their application for such an order has been withdrawn or refused, or
(b) if an application for a section 84 order has been made and has not been disposed of.

24 Revoking placement orders

...

(4) If the court determines, on an application for a section 84 order, not to make the order, it may revoke any placement order in respect of the child.

28 Further consequences of placement

(1) Where a child is placed for adoption under section 19 or an adoption agency is authorised to place a child for adoption under that section —

(a)   a parent or guardian of the child may not apply for a residence order unless an application for a section 84 order has been made and the parent or guardian has obtained the court's leave under subsection (3) or (5) of section 47,

(b)   if an application has been made for a section 84 order, a guardian of the child may not apply for a special guardianship order unless he has obtained the court's leave under subsection (3) or (5) of that section.

29 Further consequences of placement orders

...

(3) Where a placement order is in force —

(a)   no prohibited steps order, residence order or specific issue order, and
(b)   no supervision order or child assessment order,

may be made in respect of the child.

(4) Subsection (3)(a) does not apply in respect of a residence order if —

(a)   an application for a section 84 has been made in respect of the child, and
(b)   the residence order is applied for by a parent or guardian who has obtained the court's leave under subsection (3) or (5) of section 47 or by any other person who has obtained the court's leave under this subsection.

32 Recovery by parent etc where child placed and consent withdrawn

(1) This section applies where —

(a)   a child is placed for adoption by an adoption agency under section 19, and
(b)   consent to placement under that section has been withdrawn,

unless an application is, or has been, made for a placement order and the application has not been disposed of.

(2) If a parent or guardian of the child informs the agency that he wishes the child to be returned to him —

(a)   the agency must give notice of the parent's or guardian's wish to the prospective adopters, and

(b)   the prospective adopters must return the child to the agency within the period of 14 days beginning with the day on which the notice is given.

(3) A prospective adopter who fails to comply with subsection (2)(b) is guilty of an offence and liable on summary conviction to imprisonment for a term not exceeding three months, or a fine not exceeding level 5 on the standard scale, or both.

(4) As soon as a child is returned to an adoption agency under this section, the agency must return the child to the parent or guardian in question.

(5) Where a notice under subsection (2) is given, but —

(a)   before the notice was given, an application for a section 84 order (including a Scottish or Northern Irish section 84 order), special guardianship order or residence order, or for leave to apply for a special guardianship order or residence order, was made in respect of the child, and

(b)   the application (and, in a case where leave is given on an application to apply for a special guardianship order or residence order, the application for the order) has not been disposed of, the prospective adopters are not required by virtue of the notice to return the child to the agency unless the court so orders.

35 Return of child in other cases

(1) Where a child is placed for adoption by an adoption agency and the prospective adopters give notice to the agency of their wish to return the child, the agency must —

(a)   receive the child from the prospective adopters before the end of the period of seven days beginning with the giving of the notice, and

(b)   give notice to any parent or guardian of the child of the prospective adopters' wish to return the child.

(2) Where a child is placed for adoption by an adoption agency, and the agency —

(a)   is of the opinion that the child should not remain with the prospective adopters, and

(b)   gives notice to them of its opinion,

the prospective adopters must, not later than the end of the period of seven days beginning with the giving of the notice, return the child to the agency.

(3) If the agency gives notice under subsection (2)(b), it must give notice to any parent or guardian of the child of the obligation to return the child to the agency.

(4) A prospective adopter who fails to comply with subsection (2) is guilty of an offence and liable on summary conviction to imprisonment for a term not exceeding three months, or a fine not exceeding level 5 on the standard scale, or both.

(5) Where —

(a) an adoption agency gives notice under subsection (2) in respect of a child,
(b) before the notice was given, an application for a section 84 order, special guardianship order or residence order, or for leave to apply for a special guardianship order or residence order, was made in respect of the child, and
(c) the application (and, in a case where leave is given on an application to apply for a special guardianship order or residence order, the application for the order) has not been disposed of, prospective adopters are not required by virtue of the notice to return the child to the agency unless the court so orders.

(6) This section applies whether or not the child in question is in England and Wales.

42 Child to live with adopters before application

...

(7) A section 84 order may not be made unless the court is satisfied that sufficient opportunities to see the child with the applicant or, in the case of an application by a couple, both of them together in the home environment have been given —

(a) where the child was placed for adoption with the applicant or applicants by an adoption agency, to that agency,
(b) in any other case, to the local authority within whose area the home is.

43 Reports where child placed by agency

Where an application for a section 84 order relates to a child placed for adoption by an adoption agency, the agency must —

(a) submit to the court a report on the suitability of the applicants and on any other matters relevant to the operation of section 1, and
(b) assist the court in any manner the court directs.

44 Notice of intention to adopt

(1) This section applies where persons (referred to in this section as 'proposed adopters') wish to adopt a child who is not placed for adoption with them by an adoption agency.

(2) A section 84 order may not be made in respect of the child unless the proposed adopters have given notice to the appropriate local authority of their intention to apply for the adoption order (referred to in this Act as a 'notice of intention to adopt').

(3) The notice must be given not more than two years, or less than three months, before the date on which the application for the adoption order is made.

(5) On receipt of a notice of intention to adopt, the local authority must arrange for the investigation of the matter and submit to the court a report of the investigation.

(6) In particular, the investigation must, so far as practicable, include the suitability of the proposed adopters and any other matters relevant to the operation of section 1 in relation to the application.

(7) If a local authority receive a notice of intention to adopt in respect of a child whom they know was (immediately before the notice was given) looked after by another local authority, they must, not more than seven days after the receipt of the notice, inform the other local authority in writing that they have received the notice.

(8) Where —

(a)   a local authority have placed a child with any persons otherwise than as prospective adopters, and
(b)   the persons give notice of intention to adopt, the authority are not to be treated as leaving the child with them as prospective adopters for the purposes of section 18(1)(b).

(9) In this section, references to the appropriate local authority, in relation to any proposed adopters, are —

(a)   in prescribed cases, references to the prescribed local authority,
(b)   in any other case, references to the local authority for the area in which, at the time of giving the notice of intention to adopt, they have their home, and 'prescribed' means prescribed by regulations.

47 Conditions for making adoption orders

(1) A section 84 order may not be made if the child has a parent or guardian unless one of the following three conditions is met; but this section is subject to section 52 (parental etc consent).

(2) The first condition is that, in the case of each parent or guardian of the child, the court is satisfied —

(a)   that the parent or guardian consents to the making of the section 84 order,
(b)   that the parent or guardian has consented under section 20 (and has not withdrawn the consent) and does not oppose the making of the section 84 order, or
(c)   that the parent's or guardian's consent should be dispensed with.

(3) A parent or guardian may not oppose the making of a section 84 order under subsection (2)(b) without the court's leave.

(4) The second condition is that —

(a)   the child has been placed for adoption by an adoption agency with the prospective adopters in whose favour the order is proposed to be made,

(b)   either —

    (i)   the child was placed for adoption with the consent of each parent or guardian and the consent of the mother was given when the child was at least six weeks old, or

    (ii)   the child was placed for adoption under a placement order, and

(c)   no parent or guardian opposes the making of the adoption order.

(5) A parent or guardian may not oppose the making of a section 84 order under the second condition without the court's leave.

...

(8) a section 84 order may not be made in relation to a person who is or has been married.

[(8A) a section 84 order may not be made in relation to a person who is or has been a civil partner.]

(9) a section 84 order may not be made in relation to a person who has attained the age of 19 years.

48 Restrictions on making Section 84 orders

(1) The court may not hear an application for a section 84 order in relation to a child, where a previous application to which subsection (2) applies made in relation to the child by the same persons was refused by any court, unless it appears to the court that, because of a change in circumstances or for any other reason, it is proper to hear the application.

...

50 Adoption by couple

(1) A section 84 order may be made on the application of a couple where both of them have attained the age of 21 years.

(2) A section 84 order may be made on the application of a couple where —

(a)   one of the couple is the mother or the father of the person to be adopted and has attained the age of 18 years, and

(b)   the other has attained the age of 21 years.

51 Adoption by one person

(1) A section 84 order may be made on the application of one person who has attained the age of 21 years and is not married [or a civil partner].

(2) A section 84 order may be made on the application of one person who has attained the age of 21 years if the court is satisfied that the person is the partner of a parent of the person to be adopted.

(3) A section 84 order may be made on the application of one person who has attained the age of 21 years and is married if the court is satisfied that —

(a)   the person's spouse cannot be found,
(b)   the spouses have separated and are living apart, and the separation is likely to be permanent,
(c)   the person's spouse is by reason of ill-health, whether physical or mental, incapable of making an application for an adoption order.

[(3A) A section 84 order may be made on the application of one person who has attained the age of 21 years and is a civil partner if the court is satisfied that —

(a)   the person's civil partner cannot be found,
(b)   the civil partners have separated and are living apart, and the separation is likely to be permanent, or
(c)   the person's civil partner is by reason of ill-health, whether physical or mental, incapable of making an application for an adoption order.]

(4) A section 84 order may not be made on an application under this section by the mother or the father of the person to be adopted unless the court is satisfied that —

(a)   the other natural parent is dead or cannot be found,
[(b)   by virtue of the provisions specified in subsection (5), there is no other parent, or]
(c)   there is some other reason justifying the child's being adopted by the applicant alone, and, where the court makes an adoption order on such an application, the court must record that it is satisfied as to the fact mentioned in paragraph (a) or (b) or, in the case of paragraph (c), record the reason.

[(5) The provisions referred to in subsection (4)(b) are —

(a)   section 28 of the Human Fertilisation and Embryology Act 1990 (disregarding subsections (5A) to (5I) of that section), or
(b)   sections 34 to 47 of the Human Fertilisation and Embryology Act 2008 (disregarding sections 39, 40 and 46 of that Act).]

52 Parental etc consent

(1) The court cannot dispense with the consent of any parent or guardian of a child to the child being placed for adoption or to the making of a section 84 order in respect of the child unless the court is satisfied that —

(a)   the parent or guardian cannot be found or [lacks capacity (within the meaning of the Mental Capacity Act 2005) to give consent], or
(b)   the welfare of the child requires the consent to be dispensed with.

(2) The following provisions apply to references in this Chapter to any parent or guardian of a child giving or withdrawing —

(a)   consent to the placement of a child for adoption, or
(b)   consent to the making of a section 84 order (including a future section 84 order).

(3) Any consent given by the mother to the making of a section 84 order is ineffective if it is given less than six weeks after the child's birth.

(4) The withdrawal of any consent to the placement of a child for adoption, or of any consent given under section 20, is ineffective if it is given after an application for a section 84 order is made.

(5) 'Consent' means consent given unconditionally and with full understanding of what is involved; but a person may consent to adoption without knowing the identity of the persons in whose favour the order will be made.

(6) 'Parent' (except in subsections (9) and (10) below) means a parent having parental responsibility.

(7) Consent under section 19 or 20 must be given in the form prescribed by rules, and the rules may prescribe forms in which a person giving consent under any other provision of this Part may do so (if he wishes).

(8) Consent given under section 19 or 20 must be withdrawn —

(a)   in the form prescribed by rules, or
(b)   by notice given to the agency.

(9) Subsection (10) applies if —

(a)   an agency has placed a child for adoption under section 19 in pursuance of consent given by a parent of the child, and
(b)   at a later time, the other parent of the child acquires parental responsibility for the child.

(10) The other parent is to be treated as having at that time given consent in accordance with this section in the same terms as those in which the first parent gave consent.

53 Modification of 1989 Act in relation to adoption

(1) Where —
(a)   a local authority are authorised to place a child for adoption, or
(b)   a child who has been placed for adoption by a local authority is less than six weeks old,

regulations may provide for the following provisions of the 1989 Act to apply with modifications, or not to apply, in relation to the child.

(2) The provisions are —

(a) section 22(4)(b), (c) and (d) and (5)(b) (duty to ascertain wishes and feelings of certain persons),

(b) paragraphs 15 and 21 of Schedule 2 (promoting contact with parents and parents' obligation to contribute towards maintenance).

(3) Where a registered adoption society is authorised to place a child for adoption or a child who has been placed for adoption by a registered adoption society is less than six weeks old, regulations may provide —

(a) for section 61 of that Act to have effect in relation to the child whether or not he is accommodated by or on behalf of the society,

(b) for subsections (2)(b) to (d) and (3)(b) of that section (duty to ascertain wishes and feelings of certain persons) to apply with modifications, or not to apply, in relation to the child.

(4) Where a child's home is with persons who have given notice of intention to adopt, no contribution is payable (whether under a contribution order or otherwise) under Part 3 of Schedule 2 to that Act (contributions towards maintenance of children looked after by local authorities) in respect of the period referred to in subsection (5).

(5) That period begins when the notice of intention to adopt is given and ends if —

(a) the period of four months beginning with the giving of the notice expires without the prospective adopters applying for a section 84 order, or

(b) an application for such an order is withdrawn or refused.

(6) In this section, 'notice of intention to adopt' includes notice of intention to apply for a Scottish or Northern Irish adoption order.

141 Rules of procedure

(1) [Family Procedure Rules may make provision] in respect of any matter to be prescribed by rules made by virtue of this Act and dealing generally with all matters of procedure.

(2) ...

(3) In the case of an application for a placement order, for the variation or revocation of such an order, or for a section 84 order, the rules must require any person mentioned in subsection (4) to be notified —

(a) of the date and place where the application will be heard, and

(b) of the fact that, unless the person wishes or the court requires, the person need not attend.

(4) The persons referred to in subsection (3) are —

(a) in the case of a placement order, every person who can be found whose consent to the making of the order is required under subsection (3)(a) of section 21 (or would be required but for subsection (3)(b) of that section) or, if no such person can be found, any relative prescribed by rules who can be found,

(b)   in the case of a variation or revocation of a placement order, every person who can be found whose consent to the making of the placement order was required under subsection (3)(a) of section 21 (or would have been required but for subsection (3)(b) of that section),

(c)   in the case of a section 84 order —

   (i)   every person who can be found whose consent to the making of the order is required under subsection (2)(a) of section 47 (or would be required but for subsection (2)(c) of that section) or, if no such person can be found, any relative prescribed by rules who can be found,

   (ii)   every person who has consented to the making of the order under section 20 (and has not withdrawn the consent) unless he has given a notice under subsection (4)(a) of that section which has effect,

   (iii) every person who, if leave were given under section 47(5), would be entitled to oppose the making of the order.

(5) Rules made in respect of magistrates' courts may provide —

(a)   for enabling any fact tending to establish the identity of a child with a child to whom a document relates to be proved by affidavit, and

(b)   for excluding or restricting in relation to any facts that may be so proved the power of a justice of the peace to compel the attendance of witnesses.

[(6) Rules may, for the purposes of the law relating to contempt of court, authorise the publication in such circumstances as may be specified of information relating to proceedings held in private involving children.]

[(7) In subsection (6) 'proceedings held in private' means proceedings at which the public have no right to be present.]

Chapter 13

PRIVATE ADOPTIONS WHEN THE UK IS THE STATE OF ORIGIN

INTRODUCTION

13.1   Chapters 11 and 12 examine the adoption process when a child is placed for adoption by a local authority. This chapter will look at the adoption process if the adoption is arranged privately. Private adoptions can only be arranged in circumstances which are permitted by the Adoption and Children Act 2002 (ACA 2002), s 92. This section effectively prohibits private arrangements for the adoption of children being made unless the adopters fall into one of the following categories:

(a)   parents;

(b)   relatives or guardians of the child; or

(c)   a person who is the partner of a parent of the child.

Arranging adoptions in breach of this provision is a criminal offence, and the maximum penalty for a person convicted is 6 months' imprisonment and or a fine of up to £10,000.[1]

13.2   In a private adoption the child is placed into the care of the applicant adopters by either:

•   the people who have parental responsibility for the child, which will be the child's mother if she is alive and any other person who shares parental responsibility with her; or

•   the court under a residence order or special guardianship order; or

•   a local authority who place the adopters in their capacity as foster carers.

When an adoption agency places a child for adoption with prospective adopters those adopters acquire parental responsibility for the child. By contrast, in a non-agency case, a person will not acquire parental responsibility for a child when that child is placed into his or her day-to-day care by the parents/guardian/local authority. The parents or guardian or local authority

---

[1]   ACA 2002, s 93.

who placed the child into the care of the adopters will continue to hold parental responsibility for the child, but they are permitted to make arrangements for some or all of it to be met by one or more persons acting on their behalf.[2] If the prospective adopters are relatives who do not have parental responsibility for the child, and it is considered important for them to share it with the parents and/or guardians of the child, they could apply for a residence order, which would grant them parental responsibility, which they would then share with the parents, but this is not a legal requirement.[3] Although for the sake of completeness reference is made to the fact that foster carers who have looked after a child for over a year can apply to adopt that child, nothwithstanding that the child has not been placed for adoption with them, the reality is that local authority foster parents are likely to be eligible to adopt under the domestic provisions and so the remainder of this chapter will assume that the private adoption is not made by a local authority foster parent but rather by a person who has assumed the care of the child by agreement with the child's parent(s).

13.3   Only persons who qualify as eligible to adopt a child pursuant to ACA 2002, ss 50 and 51 can adopt a child in this country, whether it is a domestic adoption or a foreign adoption. This means that a single adopter must be at least 21 years old, and an application by a couple can only be made if both applicants have attained the age of 21. The one exception to the requirement that an applicant must be at least 21 years old is if he or she is the parent of the child and he or she jointly applies to adopt with another person who is at least 21 years old.

13.4   As with agency adoptions, the rules which govern Convention cases and non-convention cases are different, and so when considering how best to prepare for the issue of adoption proceedings, the first question to ask is: is the receiving state[4] a Convention country or not? This chapter is divided into two sections; the first will examine the adoption process if the receiving state is a Convention country, the second when the receiving state is a non-Convention country.

PRIVATE CONVENTION ADOPTIONS

13.5   Before a court can consider making any Convention adoption/section 84 order, the relevant central authority in the UK will need to prepare an Article 16[5] report confirming that the child is suitable to be adopted and the relevant central authority in the receiving state will need to prepare the

---

2   Children Act 1989, s 2(9).
3   Ibid, s 8.
4   Again, in this chapter, as in Chapter 12, the term 'receiving state' is used to denote the foreign country to which the child will be removed to live with the adopters, whether or not that country is a party to the Convention.
5   See **11.45**.

Article 15[6] report confirming that the adopters are suitable to adopt a child from overseas. Both central authorities will need to agree the match and the receiving state will need to provide the Article 5 confirmation that the child will be allowed to enter and permanently reside within its jurisdiction. These mandatory conditions apply to private adoptions just as they do to agency adoptions.

13.6 It will be the responsibility of the adopters and their legal representatives to ensure that all necessary evidence is obtained and placed before the court in the adoption proceedings. Accordingly they will need to:

(a) commission and obtain an Article 15 report from the relevant central authority in their country;

(b) set up a temporary home in England and Wales so that the local authority can see them with the child for the purposes of preparing the necessary court report;

(c) give notice of their intention to adopt to the local authority in the area of their temporary home in England or Wales, which will trigger the assessment process by the local authority;

(d) when the child has been in their care for not less than 10 weeks, issue their application for Convention adoption order/section 84 order.

Physical placement of the child with the adopters

13.7 There is no provision which regulates the placement of the child by the parents into the physical care of the prospective adopter, who will in any event either be a relative, a partner of a parent, or a guardian of the child. Furthermore, if it is intended that the proposed Convention adoption order will be sought in a court within England and Wales, it does not appear that the parents, guardian or prospective adopters would commit any offence under ACA 2002, s 85 if they took the child overseas with them for a temporary visit while assessments were being carried out.[7]

The Article 15 report

13.8 As set out in Chapter 2, it is the responsibility of the receiving state to determine whether or not a person habitually resident in their country is suitable to adopt a child habitually resident in a different contracting state. Accordingly, the prospective adopters will need to apply to their own central authority for an assessment of their suitability to adopt and it will be their responsibility to fund the assessment if necessary. The adopters will need to identify the appropriate agency to carry out this assessment, and when it is

---

[6] See **11.16**.
[7] *ECC (The Local Authority) v SM* [2011] 1 FLR 234.

complete request that their central authority forward the report to the relevant UK central authority. It is likely that they will need to be in their own country for a large part of the time that it takes for this report to be carried out. The adopters may wish to consider instructing qualified lawyers in their own country who have expertise in this area of law to assist them to obtain the Home study report and resolve any immigration issues, and to assist in liaising with their central authority.

Notice to the local authority

13.9 If a person wishes to adopt a child who has not been placed for adoption with them by an adoption agency, they must give notice to the local authority in the area in which they are living with the child. Since there is no agency involved in the placement of the child for adoption, the effect of ACA 2002, s 42(7)(b) is to require the adopters to set up a temporary home in the UK, so that the local authority can assess their suitability to adopt the child.

13.10 The conditions for this notice are defined in ACA 2002, s 44. This provision is amended by the Adoptions with a Foreign Element Regulations 2005 (AFER 2005),[8] reg 57 which has the effect of removing subsection (3). Subsection (3) makes provision for the minimum and maximum amount of notice that must be given to the adoption agency. Accordingly, in a Convention adoption or Convention section 84 application, there is no minimum amount of notice that needs to be given to the prescribed local authority. In addition, in subsection (2) the words 'adoption order' are amended to read 'section 84 order' if the application is being made for a section 84 order instead of an adoption order.[9] In its amended form therefore s 44 will read:

'44 Notice of intention to adopt

(1) This section applies where persons (referred to in this section as "proposed adopters") wish to adopt a child who is not placed for adoption with them by an adoption agency.

(2) An adoption order/section 84 Order may not be made in respect of the child unless the proposed adopters have given notice to the appropriate local authority of their intention to apply for the adoption order/section 84 Order (referred to in this Act as a "notice of intention to adopt").

(3) [deleted]

(4) Where –

(a)   if a person were seeking to apply for an adoption order, subsection (4) or (5) of section 42 would apply, but

---

8   SI 2005/392.
9   By virtue of AFER 2005, reg 55 which imports the amendments in reg 11 for the purposes of section 84 orders under the Convention.

(b)   the condition in the subsection in question is not met, the person may not give notice of intention to adopt unless he has the court's leave to apply for an adoption order.

(5) On receipt of a notice of intention to adopt, the local authority must arrange for the investigation of the matter and submit to the court a report of the investigation.

(6) In particular, the investigation must, so far as practicable, include the suitability of the proposed adopters and any other matters relevant to the operation of section 1 in relation to the application.

(7) If a local authority receive a notice of intention to adopt in respect of a child whom they know was (immediately before the notice was given) looked after by another local authority, they must, not more than seven days after the receipt of the notice, inform the other local authority in writing that they have received the notice.

(8) Where –

(a)   a local authority have placed a child with any persons otherwise than as prospective adopters, and
(b)   the persons give notice of intention to adopt,

the authority are not to be treated as leaving the child with them as prospective adopters for the purposes of section 18(1)(b).

(9) In this section, references to the appropriate local authority, in relation to any proposed adopters, are—in prescribed cases, references to the prescribed local authority, in any other case, references to the local authority for the area in which, at the time of giving the notice of intention to adopt, they have their home, and "prescribed" means prescribed by regulations.'

13.11   Once notice has been given the local authority are obliged, pursuant to subsection (5), to investigate the matter and prepare a report for the court. As part of the local authority's investigations, it will need to have sight of the Article 15 report from the receiving state's central authority. There does not appear to be any requirement that the notice of intention to adopt required by s 44 should be given before or after the Home study report is complete. However, it may be helpful for the appropriate local authority to be given as much notice as possible and there may be advantages to making contact with the appropriate local authority at or around the time that the Home study report is being commissioned. Once the Home study report is finished the prospective adopters will need to make such arrangements as necessary to ensure that the Article 15 report prepared by their central authority is sent to the relevant central authority in England or Wales.

13.12   It would appear that if in the course of their investigations the local authority comes to the view that the adoption should proceed, the provisions of AFER 2005, reg 46 will apply. This provision requires the local authority in its capacity as an adoption agency to prepare the Article 16 report. However, the applicability of this provision in the context of a private adoption is not entirely clear cut. The wording used in reg 46 says 'if the adoption agency decides that the placement should proceed', and of course in a private adoption, the local authority is not responsible for making the decision to place the child for adoption. However, there is a clear obligation on the local authority to prepare a report.[10] That report must include the Article 16 report. The Article 16 report is prepared by the local authority and sent to the relevant central authority pursuant to reg 46. Therefore, it is suggested that the only sensible interpretation of regs 46 and 49, within the context of a private adoption, is that reg 46 will have effect when the local authority reaches the conclusion that adoption with the applicants is in the best interests of the child, taking into account the welfare checklist contained in ACA 2002, s 1.

13.13 In preparing the Article 16 report, the local authority will need to carry out an assessment of the child, which must include the information specified in AAR 2005, Sch 1. Since the child in this situation will not be the subject of a placement order, there is a requirement of parental consent to the adoption, which must also be included in the Article 16 report. Once the report is ready, it must be sent to the appropriate UK central authority who will then liaise with the foreign central authority.

13.14 The adopters will then need to keep in close liaison with both the local authority and the relevant UK central authority, as well as their own central authority, to track the progress of the decision making at a central authority level.

13.15 AFER 2005, reg 49 places a requirement on the local authority to include within the report which is prepared pursuant to ACA 2002, s 44(5) the following information:

(a)   Article 15 report;

(b)   report prepared for the purposes of Article 16(1); and

(c)   written confirmation of the agreement under Article 17(c) of the Convention.

Issuing the application for a Convention Adoption/section 84 order

13.16 Provided that the applicants fulfil the criteria as set out in:

(a)   AFER 2005, reg 50; and

(b)   ACA 2002, s 50 or 51;[11] and

---

[10]   AFER 2005, reg 49.
[11]   As to which, see **13.3**.

(c)   ACA 2002, s 49 as amended by AFER 2005, reg 58,[12] ie the child has had his or her home with them for a period of not less than 10 weeks,

they may apply for a Convention adoption order. Since there is no clear regulatory framework to govern the interaction between the local authority and the relevant central authority in the UK, it is likely to be beneficial if the court is involved at an early stage to make such directions as necessary to ensure that the relevant local and/or central government departments act with reasonable expedition. Save in relation to the advantage that springs from an early application, the law and procedure relating to Convention adoption applications is the same as in agency adoptions, as set out in full in Chapter 11.[13]

13.17   The court's powers in relation to a section 84 order are also dealt with in Chapter 11. However, for reasons set out in both Chapters 11 and 12, removing a child from the jurisdiction of the court when there is a clear intention to apply for a section 84 order may constitute an offence under ACA 2002, s 85. Until there is case-law which confirms that making arrangements to take a child overseas on a temporary basis, with the intention that no application to adopt the child will be issued in a overseas country unless and until the applicants have obtained a section 84 order, does not contravene s 85, it is likely to be safer and more straightforward if section 84 applications are avoided when Convention adoption orders are available.

NON-CONVENTION APPLICATIONS FOR A SECTION 84 ORDER

13.18   A person who does not meet the eligibility criteria to adopt a child to whom ACA 2002, s 85 applies must obtain a section 84 order before they can remove the child from this jurisdiction for the purpose of adoption in their own country.[14] In a private adoption AFER 2005, reg 10 does not apply. Therefore the only applicable regulation is AFER 2005, reg 11. This is an important provision because it alters the provisions of ACA 2002 to provide a legal framework for these orders. The sections of the ACA 2002 which are modified are set out in the modified form in the Appendix at the end of Chapter 12. Only ss 42–52 and s 141 apply to private adoptions.

Notice to the local authority

13.19   The prospective adopters will need to set up a home in England and Wales, and the child will need to live with them in that home. For the reasons set out in **13.16** it is likely that the child will need to live with the adopters in this jurisdiction until they have obtained a section 84 order. AFER 2005, reg 11 provides that ACA 2002, s 44 applies to section 84 orders. It does not delete

---

[12]   See **11.68** which sets out this provision in its amended form.
[13]   See **11.67–11.80**.
[14]   Please refer to **11.2–11.7** for full discussion of the details of the relevant statutory provision.

subsection (3), and that provision therefore remains relevant for non-Convention cases. The adopters will therefore need to give the local authority in the area in which they live not less than 3 months' notice of their intention to adopt the child before they issue their application. The effect of this provision is that the adopters will need to be in a position to set up a home in the UK for at least 6 months, taking into account the 3 months required by s 44(3) and the time it will take proceedings to conclude once issued. That home can obviously be a temporary base with family, and does not need to be a separate home, which may save on living expenses while the adopters are living in this jurisdiction. In the case of a couple there does not seem to be any reason why they would both need to remain full time in this jurisdiction, and the case of *Re G (Adoption: Placement Outside Jurisdiction)*[15] is clear authority that, provided that both potential adopters are sufficiently available for the local authority to carry out its investigations, the requirement of s 84(4) will be met, even if one of them returns to the receiving state for part of the 10 weeks. By logical extension, these principles should also apply to the requirement of s 44(3). However, the overall time constraints do appear to be fixed. Therefore, the adopter, or in the case of a couple the adopters between them, must ensure that they can satisfy the requirements of both s 44 and s 84, and can stay here with the child throughout this period.

13.20   Once notified, the local authority will need to carry out an investigation of their suitability to adopt the child and prepare a report pursuant to ACA 2002, s 44(5). The report must address all the relevant factors set out in ACA 2002, s 1, and include the information specified in FPR 2010, PD 14C. There is no specific requirement in the regulations or PD 14C that this report should inform the court as to the eligibility of the adopters to adopt the child in the receiving state, or that the child has been given permission to enter and permanently reside in that country. However, these issues are clearly relevant to the welfare decisions and it is suggested that they should be included in the local authority investigations and report in any event.

13.21   There is no reason why the prospective adopters should not issue their application for a section 84 order as soon as the 3-months' notice period has expired. The law and procedure relating to section 84 applications in private cases is the same as in agency adoptions, and is set out in full in Chapter 12.[16]

---

[15]   [2008] EWCA Civ 105, [2008] 1 FLR 1484.
[16]   See **12.21–12.26** for full details.

Part 4

GLOSSARY AND OFFENCES

GLOSSARY

adoption agency	Within England and Wales an adoption agency is defined as either a local authority's adoption service or a local authority or registered adoption society, (ACA 2002, s 2(1)).
adoption panel	An independent panel constituted in accordance with AAR 2005, reg 3 for the purpose of making recommendations to an adoption agency in relation to approval of adopters, matching of adopters to children and (in limited circumstances) to the suitability of children to be adopted.
adoption order	An order made under ACA 2002, s 46(1) which confers the status of legal parent and gives parental responsibility to the adopter(s) and extinguishes parenthood and the parental responsibility of the child's biological (or former adoptive) parents and others.
Convention	Within the confines of this book, and unless otherwise specified, the term 'Convention' will always refer to the Convention on Protection of Children and Co-operation in respect of Inter-country Adoption, 1993.
Convention adoption	In an adoption under the Convention, an adoption order made outside of England and Wales.
Convention adoption order	In an adoption under the Convention, an adoption order made in England and Wales.
Designated List adoption	An adoption carried out in a country which is included in the Adoption (Designated of Overseas Adoptions) Order 1973.
domicile	A legal concept by which a person's system of personal law is identified. See Chapter 2 for a full discussion of this concept.
ECHR	The European Convention for the Protection of Human Rights and Fundamental Freedoms, incorporating in part into UK statute law under the Human Rights Act 1998.
entry clearance	A sticker or vignette attached to a passport or travel document, providing permission to enter the UK for a prescribed purpose for either a limited or indefinite period, and containing any conditions of entry.

full adoption	An adoption which operates to transfer parenthood from the parents to the adopters and extinguish the child's parents' legal parenthood.
habitual residence	The place where a person is living for an appreciable amount of time, for a settled purpose within the fabric of their day-to-day life. See Chapter 2 for full discussion of this concept.
Home study report	The assessment of the prospective adopters carried out by the relevant authority in the receiving state.
indefinite leave to enter or remain	Leave to enter or remain in the UK without restriction of time.
leave to enter	Leave given to an applicant outside the UK by an entry clearance officer to lawfully enter the UK (ordinarily for a prescribed purpose).
leave to remain	Leave given by the Home Secretary (via an immigration officer) for a person in the UK to lawfully remain in the UK.
overseas adoption	An adoption made under the law of a country listed in the Adoption (Designated of Overseas Adoptions) Order 1973.
simple adoption	An adoption in which the child's birth parents retain the status of legal parents for some or all legal purposes.
receiving state	In a Convention adoption, the state where the prospective adopters are habitually resident. For convenience this term has also been used in this book to denote the state to which a child will removed following the making of a section 84 order in a non-Convention adoption.
restricted country	A country where additional restrictions on inward intercountry adoption have been imposed.
right of abode	The right to live in and to enter and exit the UK without let or hindrance except as may be required to enable the right of abode to be established (e g by a requirement to produce a passport).
state of origin	In a Convention adoption, the state where the child to be adopted is habitually resident.

TABLE OF OFFENCES

ALL INTERNATIONAL ADOPTION CASES[1]

Statute	Offence	Defence/Exceptions	Sentence
ACA 2002, s 92	Taking steps to arrange an adoption if not an adoption agency or acting pursuant to a High Court Order.	**EXCEPTION** No offence is committed under (d), (e) or (g) (h) or (i) if:	Summary conviction: 6 months' imprisonment and/or a fine not exceeding £10,000 (ACA 2002, s 93(5))
	(a) asking a person other than an adoption agency to provide a child for adoption	(a) the prospective adopters are parents, relatives or guardians of the child (or one of them is), or	
	(b) asking a person other than an adoption agency to provide prospective adopters for a child	(b) the prospective adopter is the partner of a parent of the child (ACA 2002, s 92(3)–(4))	

---

1   ACA 2002, ss 92–96 have international effect and include the adoption of persons habitually residence outside the British Isles effected under the law of a country outside the British Isles (ACA 2002, s 97(c) and s 123(9)).

Statute	Offence	Defence/Exceptions	Sentence
	(c) offering to find a child for adoption	**DEFENCE**	
	(d) offering a child for adoption to a person other than an adoption agency	If sufficient evidence is adduced to raise an issue of whether the person had knowledge or reasons to suspect an offence was committed, a person is not guilty unless it is proved they knew or had sufficient knowledge to suspect that the step would contravene s 92(1) (ACA 2002, s 93(2)–(4))	
	(e) handing a child to any person other than an adoption agency with a view to the child's adoption by that or another person		
	(f) receiving a child as (e)		
	(g) entering into an agreement for adoption or to facilitate adoption where no adoption agency is acting on behalf of the child		
	(h) taking part in negotiations with the purpose of reaching an agreement for adoption		
	(i) causing another person to take any of the above steps.		

Statute	Offence	Defence/Exceptions	Sentence
ACA 2002, s 94	If not a 'prescribed person', preparing a report on suitability of prospective adopters or commissioning or distributing a report.	Prescribed persons are social workers working for or training within an adoption agency with three years' experience in adoption work, or supervised by someone so qualified. (Restrictions on the Preparation of Adoption Reports Regulations 2005)	Summary conviction: 6 months' imprisonment and/or a level five fine (ACA 2002, s 94(5))
ACA 2002, s 95	Offering, agreeing, making or receiving payment in consideration of (a) the adoption of a child (b) giving any consent connected to the adoption of a child (c) taking any step to arrange an adoption (d) preparing a report in contravention of s 94(1)	Payment of reasonable expenses to an adoption agency by parent or guardian or prospective adopter (ACA 2002 s 96(2)) Payment of legal or medical expenses incurred in connection with an adoption application (ACA 2002, s 96(3))	Summary conviction: 6 months' imprisonment and/or a fine not exceeding £10,000 (ACA 2002, s 95(5))

Statute	Offence	Defence/Exceptions	Sentence
ACA 2002, s 123	Publishing or distributing an advert (including electronically) indicating that a parent wants a child adopted; a person wants to adopt a child; a person other than an adoption agency is prepared to take steps to arrange an adoption; a person other than an adoption agency is prepared to receive a for the purpose of adoption.	If sufficient evidence is adduced to raise an issue of whether the person had knowledge or reasons to suspect an offence was committed, a person is not guilty unless it is proved they knew or had sufficient knowledge to suspect that the advert would contravene s 123(1) (ACA 2002, s 124(3)).	Summary conviction: 3 months' imprisonment and/or level 5 fine (ACA 2002, s 124(3))

HAGUE CONVENTION 1993 ADOPTIONS

Regulation	Offence	Defence/Exceptions	Sentence
AFER 24(1)	Where no Convention adoption in state of origin, failure to notify the local authority within 14 days of child's arrival into the UK that: (a) child has arrived in UK (b) prospective adopter's intention to apply for a Convention adoption order or not to give the child a home	Reg 27(1): where proceedings for a Convention adoption order are before the court the child does not have to be returned unless the court so orders.	Summary Conviction: 3 months imprisonment and/or a level five fine.
AFER 26(1), 27(1)(b) and 33	Failure to return the child to the local authority either: • Reg 26(1): 7 days after proposed adopter has notified local authority that he does not intend to give the child a home • Reg 27(1)(b): 7 days after local authority has notified proposed adopters that the child should be returned • Reg 33: following refusal of a convention adoption order by the court, within period specified by the court		Summary Conviction: 3 months imprisonment and/or a level five fine.

NON-HAGUE CONVENTION ADOPTION

Statute	Offence	Defence/Exceptions	Sentence
ACA 2002, s 83(1)(a)	Bring or cause to bring a child into the UK for the purpose of adoption without complying with AFER 2005 Regs 3 and 4		Summary conviction: 6 months imprisonment and/or fine not exceeding statutory maximum. Indictment: 12 months imprisonment and unlimited fine
ACA 2002, s 83(1)(b)	Bring or cause to bring a child into the UK who has been adopted under an external adoption effected within the previous 12 months without complying with AFER 2005 Regs 3 and 4		Summary conviction: 6 months imprisonment and/or fine not exceeding statutory maximum. Indictment: 12 months imprisonment and/or unlimited fine
ACA 2002, s 35(2) and AFER 2005, reg 8	Failure to return the child to the local authority within seven days if local authority gives notice that child should be returned	If an application for an adoption order, residence order or special guardianship order or leave to apply for a special guardianship or residence order is before the court, child does not have to be returned unless ordered by the court (ACA 2002 s 35(5))	Summary conviction: 3 months imprisonment and/or level 5 fine.

Statute	Offence	Defence/Exceptions	Sentence
ACA 2002, s 85	Removing a child from the United Kingdom to a place outside the British Islands for the purpose of adoption when that child is: (a) a Commonwealth citizen, or (b) habitually resident in the United Kingdom UNLESS (a) the prospective adopters have parental responsibility for the child by virtue of an order under s 84, or	A person is not guilty of an offence under subsection (4) of causing a person to take any step mentioned in paragraph (a) or (b) of subsection (3) unless it is proved that he knew or had reason to suspect that the step taken would contravene subsection (1). But this subsection only applies if sufficient evidence is adduced to raise an issue as to whether the person had the knowledge or reason mentioned.	(a) on summary conviction to imprisonment for a term not exceeding six months, or a fine not exceeding the statutory maximum, or both, (b) on conviction on indictment, to imprisonment for a term not exceeding twelve months, or a fine, or both.

Statute	Offence	Defence/Exceptions	Sentence
	(b) the child is removed under the authority of an order under (s 59 of the Adoption and Children (Scotland) Act 2007 (asp 4)] or art 57 of the Adoption (Northern Ireland) Order 1987 (SI 1987/2203 (NI 22)).		
	Removing a child from the United Kingdom includes arranging to do so; and the circumstances in which a person arranges to remove a child from the United Kingdom include those where he:		
	(a) enters into an arrangement for the purpose of facilitating such a removal of the child,		
	(b) initiates or takes part in any negotiations of which the purpose is the conclusion of an arrangement within paragraph (a), or		
	an arrangement includes an agreement (whether or not enforceable).		

Appendix 1

ADOPTION AND CHILDREN ACT 2002

PART I
ADOPTION

Chapter 1
Introductory

1 Considerations applying to the exercise of powers

(1) This section applies whenever a court or adoption agency is coming to a decision relating to the adoption of a child.

(2) The paramount consideration of the court or adoption agency must be the child's welfare, throughout his life.

(3) The court or adoption agency must at all times bear in mind that, in general, any delay in coming to the decision is likely to prejudice the child's welfare.

(4) The court or adoption agency must have regard to the following matters (among others) –

- (a) the child's ascertainable wishes and feelings regarding the decision (considered in the light of the child's age and understanding),
- (b) the child's particular needs,
- (c) the likely effect on the child (throughout his life) of having ceased to be a member of the original family and become an adopted person,
- (d) the child's age, sex, background and any of the child's characteristics which the court or agency considers relevant,
- (e) any harm (within the meaning of the Children Act 1989) which the child has suffered or is at risk of suffering,
- (f) the relationship which the child has with relatives, and with any other person in relation to whom the court or agency considers the relationship to be relevant, including –
  - (i) the likelihood of any such relationship continuing and the value to the child of its doing so,
  - (ii) the ability and willingness of any of the child's relatives, or of any such person, to provide the child with a secure environment in which the child can develop, and otherwise to meet the child's needs,
  - (iii) the wishes and feelings of any of the child's relatives, or of any such person, regarding the child.

(5) In placing the child for adoption, the adoption agency must give due consideration to the child's religious persuasion, racial origin and cultural and linguistic background.

(6) The court or adoption agency must always consider the whole range of powers available to it in the child's case (whether under this Act or the Children Act 1989); and the court must not make any order under this Act unless it considers that making the order would be better for the child than not doing so.

(7) In this section, 'coming to a decision relating to the adoption of a child', in relation to a court, includes –

    (a)   coming to a decision in any proceedings where the orders that might be made by the court include an adoption order (or the revocation of such an order), a placement order (or the revocation of such an order) or an order under section 26 (or the revocation or variation of such an order),

    (b)   coming to a decision about granting leave in respect of any action (other than the initiation of proceedings in any court) which may be taken by an adoption agency or individual under this Act,

but does not include coming to a decision about granting leave in any other circumstances.

(8) For the purposes of this section –

    (a)   references to relationships are not confined to legal relationships,
    (b)   references to a relative, in relation to a child, include the child's mother and father.

Chapter 2
The Adoption Service

2 Basic definitions

(1) The services maintained by local authorities under section 3(1) may be collectively referred to as 'the Adoption Service', and a local authority or registered adoption society may be referred to as an adoption agency.

(2) In this Act, 'registered adoption society' means a voluntary organisation which is an adoption society registered under Part 2 of the Care Standards Act 2000; but in relation to the provision of any facility of the Adoption Service, references to a registered adoption society or to an adoption agency do not include an adoption society which is not registered in respect of that facility.

(3) A registered adoption society is to be treated as registered in respect of any facility of the Adoption Service unless it is a condition of its registration that it does not provide that facility.

(4) No application for registration under Part 2 of the Care Standards Act 2000 may be made in respect of an adoption society which is an unincorporated body.

(5) In this Act –

'the 1989 Act' means the Children Act 1989,

'adoption society' means a body whose functions consist of or include making arrangements for the adoption of children,

'voluntary organisation' means a body other than a public or local authority the activities of which are not carried on for profit.

(6) In this Act, 'adoption support services' means –

(a)   counselling, advice and information, and

(b)   any other services prescribed by regulations,

in relation to adoption.

(7) The power to make regulations under subsection (6)(*b*) is to be exercised so as to secure that local authorities provide financial support.

(8) In this Chapter, references to adoption are to the adoption of persons, wherever they may be habitually resident, effected under the law of any country or territory, whether within or outside the British Islands.

3 Maintenance of Adoption Service

(1) Each local authority must continue to maintain within their area a service designed to meet the needs, in relation to adoption, of –

(a)   children who may be adopted, their parents and guardians,

(b)   persons wishing to adopt a child, and

(c)   adopted persons, their parents, natural parents and former guardians;

and for that purpose must provide the requisite facilities.

(2) Those facilities must include making, and participating in, arrangements –

(a)   for the adoption of children, and

(b)   for the provision of adoption support services.

(3) As part of the service, the arrangements made for the purposes of subsection (2)(b) –

(a)   must extend to the provision of adoption support services to persons who are within a description prescribed by regulations,

(b)   may extend to the provision of those services to other persons.

(4) A local authority may provide any of the requisite facilities by securing their provision by –

(a)   registered adoption societies, or

(b)   other persons who are within a description prescribed by regulations of persons who may provide the facilities in question.

(5) The facilities of the service must be provided in conjunction with the local authority's other social services and with registered adoption societies in their area, so that help may be given in a co-ordinated manner without duplication, omission or avoidable delay.

(6) The social services referred to in subsection (5) are the functions of a local authority which are social services functions within the meaning of the Local Authority Social Services Act 1970 (which include, in particular, those functions in so far as they relate to children).

4 Assessments etc for adoption support services

(1) A local authority must at the request of –

  (a) any of the persons mentioned in paragraphs (a) to (c) of section 3(1), or

  (b) any other person who falls within a description prescribed by regulations (subject to subsection (7)(a)),

carry out an assessment of that person's needs for adoption support services.

(2) A local authority may, at the request of any person, carry out an assessment of that person's needs for adoption support services.

(3) A local authority may request the help of the persons mentioned in paragraph (a) or (b) of section 3(4) in carrying out an assessment.

(4) Where, as a result of an assessment, a local authority decide that a person has needs for adoption support services, they must then decide whether to provide any such services to that person.

(5) If –

  (a) a local authority decide to provide any adoption support services to a person, and

  (b) the circumstances fall within a description prescribed by regulations,

the local authority must prepare a plan in accordance with which adoption support services are to be provided to the person and keep the plan under review.

(6) Regulations may make provision about assessments, preparing and reviewing plans, the provision of adoption support services in accordance with plans and reviewing the provision of adoption support services.

(7) The regulations may in particular make provision –

  (a) as to the circumstances in which a person mentioned in paragraph (b) of subsection (1) is to have a right to request an assessment of his needs in accordance with that subsection,

  (b) about the type of assessment which, or the way in which an assessment, is to be carried out,

  (c) about the way in which a plan is to be prepared,

  (d) about the way in which, and time at which, a plan or the provision of adoption support services is to be reviewed,

  (e) about the considerations to which a local authority are to have regard in carrying out an assessment or review or preparing a plan,

  (f) as to the circumstances in which a local authority may provide adoption support services subject to conditions,

(g)   as to the consequences of conditions imposed by virtue of paragraph
       (f) not being met (including the recovery of any financial support
       provided by a local authority),
(h)   as to the circumstances in which this section may apply to a local
       authority in respect of persons who are outside that local authority's
       area,
(i)   as to the circumstances in which a local authority may recover from
       another local authority the expenses of providing adoption support
       services to any person.

(8) A local authority may carry out an assessment of the needs of any person
under this section at the same time as an assessment of his needs is made under
any other enactment.

(9) If at any time during the assessment of the needs of any person under this
section, it appears to a local authority that –

(a)   there may be a need for the provision of services to that person by a
       Primary Care Trust (in Wales, a Health Authority or Local Health
       Board), or
(b)   there may be a need for the provision to him of any services which fall
       within the education functions (as defined in section 579(1) of the
       Education Act 1996) of another local authority (as defined in
       section 579(1) of that Act),

the local authority must notify that Primary Care Trust, Health Authority,
Local Health Board or other local authority.

(10) Where it appears to a local authority that another local authority could,
by taking any specified action, help in the exercise of any of their functions
under this section, they may request the help of that other local authority,
specifying the action in question.

(11) A local authority whose help is so requested must comply with the request
if it is consistent with the exercise of their functions.

Amendments: SI 2010/1158; SI 2005/691; SI 2005/1512.

5   (*repealed*)

Amendments: Section repealed: Children Act 2004, s 64, Sch 5, Pt 1; SI 2005/394; SI 2006/885.

6 Arrangements on cancellation of registration

Where, by virtue of the cancellation of its registration under Part 2 of the Care
Standards Act 2000, a body has ceased to be a registered adoption society, the
appropriate Minister may direct the body to make such arrangements as to the
transfer of its functions relating to children and other transitional matters as
seem to him expedient.

7 Inactive or defunct adoption societies etc

(1) This section applies where it appears to the appropriate Minister that –

    (a)   a body which is or has been a registered adoption society is inactive or defunct, or

    (b)   a body which has ceased to be a registered adoption society by virtue of the cancellation of its registration under Part 2 of the Care Standards Act 2000 has not made such arrangements for the transfer of its functions relating to children as are specified in a direction given by him.

(2) The appropriate Minister may, in relation to such functions of the society as relate to children, direct what appears to him to be the appropriate local authority to take any such action as might have been taken by the society or by the society jointly with the authority.

(3) A local authority are entitled to take any action which –

    (a)   apart from this subsection the authority would not be entitled to take, or would not be entitled to take without joining the society in the action, but

    (b)   they are directed to take under subsection (2).

(4) The appropriate Minister may charge the society for expenses necessarily incurred by him or on his behalf in securing the transfer of its functions relating to children.

(5) Before giving a direction under subsection (2) the appropriate Minister must, if practicable, consult both the society and the authority.

8 Adoption support agencies

(1) In this Act, 'adoption support agency' means an undertaking the purpose of which, or one of the purposes of which, is the provision of adoption support services; but an undertaking is not an adoption support agency –

    (a)   merely because it provides information in connection with adoption other than for the purpose mentioned in section 98(1), or

    (b)   if it is excepted by virtue of subsection (2).

'Undertaking' has the same meaning as in the Care Standards Act 2000.

(2) The following are excepted –

    (a)   a registered adoption society, whether or not the society is registered in respect of the provision of adoption support services,

    (b)   a local authority,

    (c)   (*repealed*)

    (d)   a Special Health Authority, Primary Care Trust (in Wales, a Health Authority or Local Health Board), NHS trust or NHS foundation trust,

    (e)   the Registrar General,

    (f)   any person, or description of persons, excepted by regulations.

(3) (*repealed*)

(4) In this section 'local authority' includes any body that is a local authority as defined in section 579(1) of the Education Act 1996 (in addition to the bodies mentioned in the definition in section 144(1)).

Amendments: Health and Social Care (Community Health and Standards) Act 2003, s 34, Sch 4, paras 125, 126; SI 2010/1158.

Regulations

9 General power to regulate adoption etc agencies

(1) Regulations may make provision for any purpose relating to –

   (a)   the exercise by local authorities or voluntary adoption agencies of their functions in relation to adoption, or

   (b)   the exercise by adoption support agencies of their functions in relation to adoption.

(2) The extent of the power to make regulations under this section is not limited by sections 10 to 12, 45, 54, 56 to 65 and 98 or by any other powers exercisable in respect of local authorities, voluntary adoption agencies or adoption support agencies.

(3) Regulations may provide that a person who contravenes or fails to comply with any provision of regulations under this section is to be guilty of an offence and liable on summary conviction to a fine not exceeding level 5 on the standard scale.

(4) In this section and section 10, 'voluntary adoption agency' means a voluntary organisation which is an adoption society.

10 Management etc of agencies

(1) In relation to local authorities, voluntary adoption agencies and adoption support agencies, regulations under section 9 may make provision as to –

   (a)   the persons who are fit to work for them for the purposes of the functions mentioned in section 9(1),

   (b)   the fitness of premises,

   (c)   the management and control of their operations,

   (d)   the number of persons, or persons of any particular type, working for the purposes of those functions,

   (e)   the management and training of persons working for the purposes of those functions,

   (f)   the keeping of information.

(2) Regulations made by virtue of subsection (1)(a) may, in particular, make provision for prohibiting persons from working in prescribed positions unless they are registered in, or in a particular part of, one of the registers maintained under section 56(1) of the Care Standards Act 2000 (registration of social care workers).

(3) In relation to voluntary adoption agencies and adoption support agencies, regulations under section 9 may –

- (a)   make provision as to the persons who are fit to manage an agency, including provision prohibiting persons from doing so unless they are registered in, or in a particular part of, one of the registers referred to in subsection (2),
- (b)   impose requirements as to the financial position of an agency,
- (c)   make provision requiring the appointment of a manager,
- (d)   in the case of a voluntary adoption agency, make provision for securing the welfare of children placed by the agency, including provision as to the promotion and protection of their health,
- (e)   in the case of an adoption support agency, make provision as to the persons who are fit to carry on the agency.

(4) Regulations under section 9 may make provision as to the conduct of voluntary adoption agencies and adoption support agencies, and may in particular make provision –

- (a)   as to the facilities and services to be provided by an agency,
- (b)   as to the keeping of accounts,
- (c)   as to the notification to the registration authority of events occurring in premises used for the purposes of an agency,
- (d)   as to the giving of notice to the registration authority of periods during which the manager of an agency proposes to be absent, and specifying the information to be given in such a notice,
- (e)   as to the making of adequate arrangements for the running of an agency during a period when its manager is absent,
- (f)   as to the giving of notice to the registration authority of any intended change in the identity of the manager,
- (g)   as to the giving of notice to the registration authority of changes in the ownership of an agency or the identity of its officers,
- (h)   requiring the payment of a prescribed fee to the registration authority in respect of any notification required to be made by virtue of paragraph (g),
- (i)   requiring arrangements to be made for dealing with complaints made by or on behalf of those seeking, or receiving, any of the services provided by an agency and requiring the agency or manager to take steps for publicising the arrangements.

11 Fees

(1) Regulations under section 9 may prescribe –

- (a)   the fees which may be charged by adoption agencies in respect of the provision of services to persons providing facilities as part of the Adoption Service (including the Adoption Services in Scotland and Northern Ireland),
- (b)   the fees which may be paid by adoption agencies to persons providing or assisting in providing such facilities.

(2) Regulations under section 9 may prescribe the fees which may be charged by local authorities in respect of the provision of prescribed facilities of the Adoption Service where the following conditions are met.

(3) The conditions are that the facilities are provided in connection with –

(a)   the adoption of a child brought into the United Kingdom for the purpose of adoption, or

(b)   a Convention adoption, an overseas adoption or an adoption effected under the law of a country or territory outside the British Islands.

(4) Regulations under section 9 may prescribe the fees which may be charged by adoption agencies in respect of the provision of counselling, where the counselling is provided in connection with the disclosure of information in relation to a person's adoption.

12 Independent review of determinations

(1) Regulations under section 9 may establish a procedure under which any person in respect of whom a qualifying determination has been made by an adoption agency may apply to the appropriate Minister for a review of that determination by a panel constituted by that Minister.

(2) The regulations must make provision as to the description of determinations which are qualifying determinations for the purposes of subsection (1).

(3) The regulations may include provision as to –

(a)   the duties and powers of a panel,

(b)   the administration and procedures of a panel,

(c)   the appointment of members of a panel (including the number, or any limit on the number, of members who may be appointed and any conditions for appointment),

(d)   the payment of fees to members of a panel,

(e)   the duties of adoption agencies in connection with reviews conducted under the regulations,

(f)   the monitoring of any such reviews.

(3A) Regulations made by virtue of subsection (3)(e) may impose a duty to pay to the appropriate Minister such sum as that Minister may determine.

(3B) The appropriate Minister must secure that, taking one financial year with another, the aggregate of the sums which become payable to him under regulations made by virtue of subsection (3A) does not exceed the cost to him of performing his independent review functions.

(4) The appropriate Minister may make an arrangement with an organisation under which independent review functions are performed by the organisation on his behalf.

(5) If the appropriate Minister makes such an arrangement with an organisation, the organisation is to perform its functions under the arrangement in accordance with any general or special directions given by the appropriate Minister.

(6) The arrangement may include provision for payments to be made to the organisation by the appropriate Minister.

(6A) Payments made by the appropriate Minister in accordance with such provision shall be taken into account in determining (for the purpose of subsection (3B)) the cost to that Minister of performing his independent review functions.

(7) Where the appropriate Minister is the Assembly, subsections (4) and (6) also apply as if references to an organisation included references to the Secretary of State.

(8) In this section –

'financial year' means a period of twelve months ending with 31st March,
'independent review function' means a function conferred or imposed on an appropriate Minister by regulations made by virtue of this section,
'organisation' includes a public body and a private or voluntary organisation.

Amendments: Children Act 2004, s 57; Children and Young Persons Act 2008, ss 34(1)–(7), 42, Sch 4.

Supplemental

13 Information concerning adoption

(1) Each adoption agency must give to the appropriate Minister any statistical or other general information he requires about –

(a)   its performance of all or any of its functions relating to adoption,
(b)   the children and other persons in relation to whom it has exercised those functions.

(2) The following persons –

(a)   the designated officer for each magistrates' court,
(b)   the relevant officer of each county court,
(c)   the relevant officer of the High Court,

must give to the appropriate Minister any statistical or other general information he requires about the proceedings under this Act of the court in question.

(3) In subsection (2), 'relevant officer', in relation to a county court or the High Court, means the officer of that court who is designated to act for the purposes of that subsection by a direction given by the Lord Chancellor.

(4) The information required to be given to the appropriate Minister under this section must be given at the times, and in the form, directed by him.

(5) The appropriate Minister may publish from time to time abstracts of the information given to him under this section.

Amendments: Courts Act 2003, s 109(1), Sch 8, para 411.

14 Default power of appropriate Minister

(1) If the appropriate Minister is satisfied that any local authority have failed, without reasonable excuse, to comply with any of the duties imposed on them by virtue of this Act or of section 1 or 2(4) of the Adoption (Intercountry Aspects) Act 1999, he may make an order declaring that authority to be in default in respect of that duty.

(2) An order under subsection (1) must give the appropriate Minister's reasons for making it.

(3) An order under subsection (1) may contain such directions as appear to the appropriate Minister to be necessary for the purpose of ensuring that, within the period specified in the order, the duty is complied with.

(4) Any such directions are enforceable, on the appropriate Minister's application, by a mandatory order.

15 Inspection of premises etc

(1) The appropriate Minister may arrange for any premises in which –

    (a)   a child is living with a person with whom the child has been placed by an adoption agency, or

    (b)   a child in respect of whom a notice of intention to adopt has been given under section 44 is, or will be, living,

to be inspected from time to time.

(2) The appropriate Minister may require an adoption agency –

    (a)   to give him any information, or

    (b)   to allow him to inspect any records (in whatever form they are held),

relating to the discharge of any of its functions in relation to adoption which the appropriate Minister specifies.

(3) An inspection under this section must be conducted by a person authorised by the appropriate Minister.

(4) An officer of a local authority may only be so authorised with the consent of the authority.

(5) A person inspecting any premises under subsection (1) may –

    (a)   visit the child there,

    (b)   make any examination into the state of the premises and the treatment of the child there which he thinks fit.

(6) A person authorised to inspect any records under this section may at any reasonable time have access to, and inspect and check the operation of, any computer (and associated apparatus) which is being or has been used in connection with the records in question.

(7) A person authorised to inspect any premises or records under this section may –

(a)   enter the premises for that purpose at any reasonable time,

(b)   require any person to give him any reasonable assistance he may require.

(8) A person exercising a power under this section must, if required to do so, produce a duly authenticated document showing his authority.

(9) Any person who intentionally obstructs another in the exercise of a power under this section is guilty of an offence and liable on summary conviction to a fine not exceeding level 3 on the standard scale.

****

17   (*repealed*)

Amendments: Section repealed; Inquiries Act 2005, s 48(1), 49(2), Sch 2, Pt 1, para 23, Sch 3.

Chapter 3
Placement for Adoption and Adoption Orders

Placement of children by adoption agency for adoption

18 Placement for adoption by agencies

(1) An adoption agency may –

(a)   place a child for adoption with prospective adopters, or

(b)   where it has placed a child with any persons (whether under this Part or not), leave the child with them as prospective adopters,

but, except in the case of a child who is less than six weeks old, may only do so under section 19 or a placement order.

(2) An adoption agency may only place a child for adoption with prospective adopters if the agency is satisfied that the child ought to be placed for adoption.

(3) A child who is placed or authorised to be placed for adoption with prospective adopters by a local authority is looked after by the authority.

(4) If an application for an adoption order has been made by any persons in respect of a child and has not been disposed of –

(a)   an adoption agency which placed the child with those persons may leave the child with them until the application is disposed of, but

(b)   apart from that, the child may not be placed for adoption with any prospective adopters.

'Adoption order' includes a Scottish or Northern Irish adoption order.

(5) References in this Act (apart from this section) to an adoption agency placing a child for adoption –

(a)   are to its placing a child for adoption with prospective adopters, and

(b)   include, where it has placed a child with any persons (whether under this Act or not), leaving the child with them as prospective adopters;

and references in this Act (apart from this section) to a child who is placed for adoption by an adoption agency are to be interpreted accordingly.

(6) References in this Chapter to an adoption agency being, or not being, authorised to place a child for adoption are to the agency being or (as the case may be) not being authorised to do so under section 19 or a placement order.

(7) This section is subject to sections 30 to 35 (removal of children placed by adoption agencies).

19 Placing children with parental consent

(1) Where an adoption agency is satisfied that each parent or guardian of a child has consented to the child –

(a)   being placed for adoption with prospective adopters identified in the consent, or
(b)   being placed for adoption with any prospective adopters who may be chosen by the agency,

and has not withdrawn the consent, the agency is authorised to place the child for adoption accordingly.

(2) Consent to a child being placed for adoption with prospective adopters identified in the consent may be combined with consent to the child subsequently being placed for adoption with any prospective adopters who may be chosen by the agency in circumstances where the child is removed from or returned by the identified prospective adopters.

(3) Subsection (1) does not apply where –

(a)   an application has been made on which a care order might be made and the application has not been disposed of, or
(b)   a care order or placement order has been made after the consent was given.

(4) References in this Act to a child placed for adoption under this section include a child who was placed under this section with prospective adopters and continues to be placed with them, whether or not consent to the placement has been withdrawn.

(5) This section is subject to section 52 (parental etc consent).

20 Advance consent to adoption

(1) A parent or guardian of a child who consents to the child being placed for adoption by an adoption agency under section 19 may, at the same or any subsequent time, consent to the making of a future adoption order.

(2) Consent under this section –

(a)   where the parent or guardian has consented to the child being placed for adoption with prospective adopters identified in the consent, may be consent to adoption by them, or

(b)   may be consent to adoption by any prospective adopters who may be chosen by the agency.

(3) A person may withdraw any consent given under this section.

(4) A person who gives consent under this section may, at the same or any subsequent time, by notice given to the adoption agency –

(a)   state that he does not wish to be informed of any application for an adoption order, or

(b)   withdraw such a statement.

(5) A notice under subsection (4) has effect from the time when it is received by the adoption agency but has no effect if the person concerned has withdrawn his consent.

(6) This section is subject to section 52 (parental etc consent).

21 Placement orders

(1) A placement order is an order made by the court authorising a local authority to place a child for adoption with any prospective adopters who may be chosen by the authority.

(2) The court may not make a placement order in respect of a child unless –

(a)   the child is subject to a care order,

(b)   the court is satisfied that the conditions in section 31(2) of the 1989 Act (conditions for making a care order) are met, or

(c)   the child has no parent or guardian.

(3) The court may only make a placement order if, in the case of each parent or guardian of the child, the court is satisfied –

(a)   that the parent or guardian has consented to the child being placed for adoption with any prospective adopters who may be chosen by the local authority and has not withdrawn the consent, or

(b)   that the parent's or guardian's consent should be dispensed with.

This subsection is subject to section 52 (parental etc consent).

(4) A placement order continues in force until –

(a)   it is revoked under section 24,

(b)   an adoption order is made in respect of the child, or

(c)   the child marries, forms a civil partnership or attains the age of 18 years.

'Adoption order' includes a Scottish or Northern Irish adoption order.

Amendments: Civil Partnership Act 2004, s 79(1), (2).

22 Applications for placement orders

(1) A local authority must apply to the court for a placement order in respect of a child if –

  (a) the child is placed for adoption by them or is being provided with accommodation by them,
  (b) no adoption agency is authorised to place the child for adoption,
  (c) the child has no parent or guardian or the authority consider that the conditions in section 31(2) of the 1989 Act are met, and
  (d) the authority are satisfied that the child ought to be placed for adoption.

(2) If –

  (a) an application has been made (and has not been disposed of) on which a care order might be made in respect of a child, or
  (b) a child is subject to a care order and the appropriate local authority are not authorised to place the child for adoption,

the appropriate local authority must apply to the court for a placement order if they are satisfied that the child ought to be placed for adoption.

(3) If –

  (a) a child is subject to a care order, and
  (b) the appropriate local authority are authorised to place the child for adoption under section 19,

the authority may apply to the court for a placement order.

(4) If a local authority –

  (a) are under a duty to apply to the court for a placement order in respect of a child, or
  (b) have applied for a placement order in respect of a child and the application has not been disposed of,

the child is looked after by the authority.

(5) Subsections (1) to (3) do not apply in respect of a child –

  (a) if any persons have given notice of intention to adopt, unless the period of four months beginning with the giving of the notice has expired without them applying for an adoption order or their application for such an order has been withdrawn or refused, or
  (b) if an application for an adoption order has been made and has not been disposed of.

'Adoption order' includes a Scottish or Northern Irish adoption order.

(6) Where –

  (a) an application for a placement order in respect of a child has been made and has not been disposed of, and
  (b) no interim care order is in force,

the court may give any directions it considers appropriate for the medical or psychiatric examination or other assessment of the child; but a child who is of sufficient understanding to make an informed decision may refuse to submit to the examination or other assessment.

(7) The appropriate local authority –

    (a)   in relation to a care order, is the local authority in whose care the child is placed by the order, and

    (b)   in relation to an application on which a care order might be made, is the local authority which makes the application.

23 Varying placement orders

(1) The court may vary a placement order so as to substitute another local authority for the local authority authorised by the order to place the child for adoption.

(2) The variation may only be made on the joint application of both authorities.

24 Revoking placement orders

(1) The court may revoke a placement order on the application of any person.

(2) But an application may not be made by a person other than the child or the local authority authorised by the order to place the child for adoption unless –

    (a)   the court has given leave to apply, and

    (b)   the child is not placed for adoption by the authority.

(3) The court cannot give leave under subsection (2)(a) unless satisfied that there has been a change in circumstances since the order was made.

(4) If the court determines, on an application for an adoption order, not to make the order, it may revoke any placement order in respect of the child.

(5) Where –

    (a)   an application for the revocation of a placement order has been made and has not been disposed of, and

    (b)   the child is not placed for adoption by the authority,

the child may not without the court's leave be placed for adoption under the order.

25 Parental responsibility

(1) This section applies while –

    (a)   a child is placed for adoption under section 19 or an adoption agency is authorised to place a child for adoption under that section, or

    (b)   a placement order is in force in respect of a child.

(2) Parental responsibility for the child is given to the agency concerned.

(3) While the child is placed with prospective adopters, parental responsibility is given to them.

(4) The agency may determine that the parental responsibility of any parent or guardian, or of prospective adopters, is to be restricted to the extent specified in the determination.

26 Contact

(1) On an adoption agency being authorised to place a child for adoption, or placing a child for adoption who is less than six weeks old, any provision for contact under the 1989 Act ceases to have effect and any contact activity direction relating to contact with the child is discharged.

(2) While an adoption agency is so authorised or a child is placed for adoption –

   (a)   no application may be made for any provision for contact under that Act, but
   (b)   the court may make an order under this section requiring the person with whom the child lives, or is to live, to allow the child to visit or stay with the person named in the order, or for the person named in the order and the child otherwise to have contact with each other.

(3) An application for an order under this section may be made by –

   (a)   the child or the agency,
   (b)   any parent, guardian or relative,
   (c)   any person in whose favour there was provision for contact under the 1989 Act which ceased to have effect by virtue of subsection (1),
   (d)   if a residence order was in force immediately before the adoption agency was authorised to place the child for adoption or (as the case may be) placed the child for adoption at a time when he was less than six weeks old, the person in whose favour the order was made,
   (e)   if a person had care of the child immediately before that time by virtue of an order made in the exercise of the High Court's inherent jurisdiction with respect to children, that person,
   (f)   any person who has obtained the court's leave to make the application.

(4) When making a placement order, the court may on its own initiative make an order under this section.

(5) This section does not prevent an application for a contact order under section 8 of the 1989 Act being made where the application is to be heard together with an application for an adoption order in respect of the child.

(6) In this section, 'contact activity direction' has the meaning given by section 11A of the 1989 Act and 'provision for contact under the 1989 Act' means a contact order under section 8 of that Act or an order under section 34 of that Act (parental contact with children in care).

Amendments: Children and Adoption Act 2006, s 15(1), Sch 2, paras 13, 14(1)–(3); SI 2008/2870.

27 Contact: supplementary

(1) An order under section 26 –

    (a)   has effect while the adoption agency is authorised to place the child for adoption or the child is placed for adoption, but

    (b)   may be varied or revoked by the court on an application by the child, the agency or a person named in the order.

(2) The agency may refuse to allow the contact that would otherwise be required by virtue of an order under that section if –

    (a)   it is satisfied that it is necessary to do so in order to safeguard or promote the child's welfare, and

    (b)   the refusal is decided upon as a matter of urgency and does not last for more than seven days.

(3) Regulations may make provision as to –

    (a)   the steps to be taken by an agency which has exercised its power under subsection (2),

    (b)   the circumstances in which, and conditions subject to which, the terms of any order under section 26 may be departed from by agreement between the agency and any person for whose contact with the child the order provides,

    (c)   notification by an agency of any variation or suspension of arrangements made (otherwise than under an order under that section) with a view to allowing any person contact with the child.

(4) Before making a placement order the court must –

    (a)   consider the arrangements which the adoption agency has made, or proposes to make, for allowing any person contact with the child, and

    (b)   invite the parties to the proceedings to comment on those arrangements.

(5) An order under section 26 may provide for contact on any conditions the court considers appropriate.

28 Further consequences of placement

(1) Where a child is placed for adoption under section 19 or an adoption agency is authorised to place a child for adoption under that section –

    (a)   a parent or guardian of the child may not apply for a residence order unless an application for an adoption order has been made and the parent or guardian has obtained the court's leave under subsection (3) or (5) of section 47,

    (b)   if an application has been made for an adoption order, a guardian of the child may not apply for a special guardianship order unless he has obtained the court's leave under subsection (3) or (5) of that section.

(2) Where –

(a) a child is placed for adoption under section 19 or an adoption agency is authorised to place a child for adoption under that section, or

(b) a placement order is in force in respect of a child,

then (whether or not the child is in England and Wales) a person may not do either of the following things, unless the court gives leave or each parent or guardian of the child gives written consent.

(3) Those things are –

(a) causing the child to be known by a new surname, or

(b) removing the child from the United Kingdom.

(4) Subsection (3) does not prevent the removal of a child from the United Kingdom for a period of less than one month by a person who provides the child's home.

29 Further consequences of placement orders

(1) Where a placement order is made in respect of a child and either –

(a) the child is subject to a care order, or

(b) the court at the same time makes a care order in respect of the child,

the care order does not have effect at any time when the placement order is in force.

(2) On the making of a placement order in respect of a child, any order mentioned in section 8(1) of the 1989 Act, and any supervision order in respect of the child, ceases to have effect.

(3) Where a placement order is in force –

(a) no prohibited steps order, residence order or specific issue order, and

(b) no supervision order or child assessment order,

may be made in respect of the child.

(4) Subsection (3)(a) does not apply in respect of a residence order if –

(a) an application for an adoption order has been made in respect of the child, and

(b) the residence order is applied for by a parent or guardian who has obtained the court's leave under subsection (3) or (5) of section 47 or by any other person who has obtained the court's leave under this subsection.

(5) Where a placement order is in force, no special guardianship order may be made in respect of the child unless –

(a) an application has been made for an adoption order, and

(b) the person applying for the special guardianship order has obtained the court's leave under this subsection or, if he is a guardian of the child, has obtained the court's leave under section 47(5).

(6) Section 14A(7) of the 1989 Act applies in respect of an application for a special guardianship order for which leave has been given as mentioned in subsection (5)(b) with the omission of the words 'the beginning of the period of three months ending with'.

(7) Where a placement order is in force –

    (a)   section 14C(1)(b) of the 1989 Act (special guardianship: parental responsibility) has effect subject to any determination under section 25(4) of this Act,

    (b)   section 14C(3) and (4) of the 1989 Act (special guardianship: removal of child from UK etc) does not apply.

Removal of children who are or may be placed by adoption agencies

30 General prohibitions on removal

(1) Where –

    (a)   a child is placed for adoption by an adoption agency under section 19, or

    (b)   a child is placed for adoption by an adoption agency and either the child is less than six weeks old or the agency has at no time been authorised to place the child for adoption,

a person (other than the agency) must not remove the child from the prospective adopters.

(2) Where –

    (a)   a child who is not for the time being placed for adoption is being provided with accommodation by a local authority, and

    (b)   the authority have applied to the court for a placement order and the application has not been disposed of,

only a person who has the court's leave (or the authority) may remove the child from the accommodation.

(3) Where subsection (2) does not apply, but –

    (a)   a child who is not for the time being placed for adoption is being provided with accommodation by an adoption agency, and

    (b)   the agency is authorised to place the child for adoption under section 19 or would be so authorised if any consent to placement under that section had not been withdrawn,

a person (other than the agency) must not remove the child from the accommodation.

(4) This section is subject to sections 31 to 33 but those sections do not apply if the child is subject to a care order.

(5) This group of sections (that is, this section and those sections) apply whether or not the child in question is in England and Wales.

(6) This group of sections does not affect the exercise by any local authority or other person of any power conferred by any enactment, other than section 20(8) of the 1989 Act (removal of children from local authority accommodation).

(7) This group of sections does not prevent the removal of a child who is arrested.

(8) A person who removes a child in contravention of this section is guilty of an offence and liable on summary conviction to imprisonment for a term not exceeding three months, or a fine not exceeding level 5 on the standard scale, or both.

31 Recovery by parent etc where child not placed or is a baby

(1) Subsection (2) applies where –

   (a)   a child who is not for the time being placed for adoption is being provided with accommodation by an adoption agency, and
   (b)   the agency would be authorised to place the child for adoption under section 19 if consent to placement under that section had not been withdrawn.

(2) If any parent or guardian of the child informs the agency that he wishes the child to be returned to him, the agency must return the child to him within the period of seven days beginning with the request unless an application is, or has been, made for a placement order and the application has not been disposed of.

(3) Subsection (4) applies where –

   (a)   a child is placed for adoption by an adoption agency and either the child is less than six weeks old or the agency has at no time been authorised to place the child for adoption, and
   (b)   any parent or guardian of the child informs the agency that he wishes the child to be returned to him,

unless an application is, or has been, made for a placement order and the application has not been disposed of.

(4) The agency must give notice of the parent's or guardian's wish to the prospective adopters who must return the child to the agency within the period of seven days beginning with the day on which the notice is given.

(5) A prospective adopter who fails to comply with subsection (4) is guilty of an offence and liable on summary conviction to imprisonment for a term not exceeding three months, or a fine not exceeding level 5 on the standard scale, or both.

(6) As soon as a child is returned to an adoption agency under subsection (4), the agency must return the child to the parent or guardian in question.

32 Recovery by parent etc where child placed and consent withdrawn

(1) This section applies where –

(a)   a child is placed for adoption by an adoption agency under section 19, and

(b)   consent to placement under that section has been withdrawn,

unless an application is, or has been, made for a placement order and the application has not been disposed of.

(2) If a parent or guardian of the child informs the agency that he wishes the child to be returned to him –

(a)   the agency must give notice of the parent's or guardian's wish to the prospective adopters, and

(b)   the prospective adopters must return the child to the agency within the period of 14 days beginning with the day on which the notice is given.

(3) A prospective adopter who fails to comply with subsection (2)(b) is guilty of an offence and liable on summary conviction to imprisonment for a term not exceeding three months, or a fine not exceeding level 5 on the standard scale, or both.

(4) As soon as a child is returned to an adoption agency under this section, the agency must return the child to the parent or guardian in question.

(5) Where a notice under subsection (2) is given, but –

(a)   before the notice was given, an application for an adoption order (including a Scottish or Northern Irish adoption order), special guardianship order or residence order, or for leave to apply for a special guardianship order or residence order, was made in respect of the child, and

(b)   the application (and, in a case where leave is given on an application to apply for a special guardianship order or residence order, the application for the order) has not been disposed of,

the prospective adopters are not required by virtue of the notice to return the child to the agency unless the court so orders.

33 Recovery by parent etc where child placed and placement order refused

(1) This section applies where –

(a)   a child is placed for adoption by a local authority under section 19,

(b)   the authority have applied for a placement order and the application has been refused, and

(c)   any parent or guardian of the child informs the authority that he wishes the child to be returned to him.

(2) The prospective adopters must return the child to the authority on a date determined by the court.

(3) A prospective adopter who fails to comply with subsection (2) is guilty of an offence and liable on summary conviction to imprisonment for a term not exceeding three months, or a fine not exceeding level 5 on the standard scale, or both.

(4) As soon as a child is returned to the authority, they must return the child to the parent or guardian in question.

34 Placement orders: prohibition on removal

(1) Where a placement order in respect of a child –

(a)   is in force, or
(b)   has been revoked, but the child has not been returned by the prospective adopters or remains in any accommodation provided by the local authority,

a person (other than the local authority) may not remove the child from the prospective adopters or from accommodation provided by the authority.

(2) A person who removes a child in contravention of subsection (1) is guilty of an offence.

(3) Where a court revoking a placement order in respect of a child determines that the child is not to remain with any former prospective adopters with whom the child is placed, they must return the child to the local authority within the period determined by the court for the purpose; and a person who fails to do so is guilty of an offence.

(4) Where a court revoking a placement order in respect of a child determines that the child is to be returned to a parent or guardian, the local authority must return the child to the parent or guardian as soon as the child is returned to the authority or, where the child is in accommodation provided by the authority, at once.

(5) A person guilty of an offence under this section is liable on summary conviction to imprisonment for a term not exceeding three months, or a fine not exceeding level 5 on the standard scale, or both.

(6) This section does not affect the exercise by any local authority or other person of a power conferred by any enactment, other than section 20(8) of the 1989 Act.

(7) This section does not prevent the removal of a child who is arrested.

(8) This section applies whether or not the child in question is in England and Wales.

35 Return of child in other cases

(1) Where a child is placed for adoption by an adoption agency and the prospective adopters give notice to the agency of their wish to return the child, the agency must –

(a)   receive the child from the prospective adopters before the end of the period of seven days beginning with the giving of the notice, and
(b)   give notice to any parent or guardian of the child of the prospective adopters' wish to return the child.

(2) Where a child is placed for adoption by an adoption agency, and the agency –

  (a)   is of the opinion that the child should not remain with the prospective adopters, and
  (b)   gives notice to them of its opinion,

the prospective adopters must, not later than the end of the period of seven days beginning with the giving of the notice, return the child to the agency.

(3) If the agency gives notice under subsection (2)(*b*), it must give notice to any parent or guardian of the child of the obligation to return the child to the agency.

(4) A prospective adopter who fails to comply with subsection (2) is guilty of an offence and liable on summary conviction to imprisonment for a term not exceeding three months, or a fine not exceeding level 5 on the standard scale, or both.

(5) Where –

  (a)   an adoption agency gives notice under subsection (2) in respect of a child,
  (b)   before the notice was given, an application for an adoption order (including a Scottish or Northern Irish adoption order), special guardianship order or residence order, or for leave to apply for a special guardianship order or residence order, was made in respect of the child, and
  (c)   the application (and, in a case where leave is given on an application to apply for a special guardianship order or residence order, the application for the order) has not been disposed of,

prospective adopters are not required by virtue of the notice to return the child to the agency unless the court so orders.

(6) This section applies whether or not the child in question is in England and Wales.

Removal of children in non-agency cases

36 Restrictions on removal

(1) At any time when a child's home is with any persons ('the people concerned') with whom the child is not placed by an adoption agency, but the people concerned –

  (a)   have applied for an adoption order in respect of the child and the application has not been disposed of,
  (b)   have given notice of intention to adopt, or
  (c)   have applied for leave to apply for an adoption order under section 42(6) and the application has not been disposed of,

a person may remove the child only in accordance with the provisions of this group of sections (that is, this section and sections 37 to 40).

The reference to a child placed by an adoption agency includes a child placed by a Scottish or Northern Irish adoption agency.

(2) For the purposes of this group of sections, a notice of intention to adopt is to be disregarded if –

    (a)   the period of four months beginning with the giving of the notice has expired without the people concerned applying for an adoption order, or

    (b)   the notice is a second or subsequent notice of intention to adopt and was given during the period of five months beginning with the giving of the preceding notice.

(3) For the purposes of this group of sections, if the people concerned apply for leave to apply for an adoption order under section 42(6) and the leave is granted, the application for leave is not to be treated as disposed of until the period of three days beginning with the granting of the leave has expired.

(4) This section does not prevent the removal of a child who is arrested.

(5) Where a parent or guardian may remove a child from the people concerned in accordance with the provisions of this group of sections, the people concerned must at the request of the parent or guardian return the child to the parent or guardian at once.

(6) A person who –

    (a)   fails to comply with subsection (5), or

    (b)   removes a child in contravention of this section,

is guilty of an offence and liable on summary conviction to imprisonment for a term not exceeding three months, or a fine not exceeding level 5 on the standard scale, or both.

(7) This group of sections applies whether or not the child in question is in England and Wales.

37 Applicants for adoption

If section 36(1)(a) applies, the following persons may remove the child –

    (a)   a person who has the court's leave,

    (b)   a local authority or other person in the exercise of a power conferred by any enactment, other than section 20(8) of the 1989 Act.

38 Local authority foster parents

(1) This section applies if the child's home is with local authority foster parents.

(2) If –

    (a)   the child has had his home with the foster parents at all times during the period of five years ending with the removal and the foster parents have given notice of intention to adopt, or

(b)   an application has been made for leave under section 42(6) and has not been disposed of,

the following persons may remove the child.

(3) They are –

(a)   a person who has the court's leave,
(b)   a local authority or other person in the exercise of a power conferred by any enactment, other than section 20(8) of the 1989 Act.

(4) If subsection (2) does not apply but –

(a)   the child has had his home with the foster parents at all times during the period of one year ending with the removal, and
(b)   the foster parents have given notice of intention to adopt,

the following persons may remove the child.

(5) They are –

(a)   a person with parental responsibility for the child who is exercising the power in section 20(8) of the 1989 Act,
(b)   a person who has the court's leave,
(c)   a local authority or other person in the exercise of a power conferred by any enactment, other than section 20(8) of the 1989 Act.

39 Partners of parents

(1) This section applies if a child's home is with a partner of a parent and the partner has given notice of intention to adopt.

(2) If the child's home has been with the partner for not less than three years (whether continuous or not) during the period of five years ending with the removal, the following persons may remove the child –

(a)   a person who has the court's leave,
(b)   a local authority or other person in the exercise of a power conferred by any enactment, other than section 20(8) of the 1989 Act.

(3) If subsection (2) does not apply, the following persons may remove the child –

(a)   a parent or guardian,
(b)   a person who has the court's leave,
(c)   a local authority or other person in the exercise of a power conferred by any enactment, other than section 20(8) of the 1989 Act.

40 Other non-agency cases

(1) In any case where sections 37 to 39 do not apply but –

(a)   the people concerned have given notice of intention to adopt, or
(b)   the people concerned have applied for leave under section 42(6) and the application has not been disposed of,

the following persons may remove the child.

(2) They are –

- (a) a person who has the court's leave,
- (b) a local authority or other person in the exercise of a power conferred by any enactment, other than section 20(8) of the 1989 Act.

Breach of restrictions on removal

41 Recovery orders

(1) This section applies where it appears to the court –

- (a) that a child has been removed in contravention of any of the preceding provisions of this Chapter or that there are reasonable grounds for believing that a person intends to remove a child in contravention of those provisions, or
- (b) that a person has failed to comply with section 31(4), 32(2), 33(2), 34(3) or 35(2).

(2) The court may, on the application of any person, by an order –

- (a) direct any person who is in a position to do so to produce the child on request to any person mentioned in subsection (4),
- (b) authorise the removal of the child by any person mentioned in that subsection,
- (c) require any person who has information as to the child's whereabouts to disclose that information on request to any constable or officer of the court,
- (d) authorise a constable to enter any premises specified in the order and search for the child, using reasonable force if necessary.

(3) Premises may only be specified under subsection (2)(d) if it appears to the court that there are reasonable grounds for believing the child to be on them.

(4) The persons referred to in subsection (2) are –

- (a) any person named by the court,
- (b) any constable,
- (c) any person who, after the order is made under that subsection, is authorised to exercise any power under the order by an adoption agency which is authorised to place the child for adoption.

(5) A person who intentionally obstructs a person exercising a power of removal conferred by the order is guilty of an offence and liable on summary conviction to a fine not exceeding level 3 on the standard scale.

(6) A person must comply with a request to disclose information as required by the order even if the information sought might constitute evidence that he had committed an offence.

(7) But in criminal proceedings in which the person is charged with an offence (other than one mentioned in subsection (8)) –

(a)   no evidence relating to the information provided may be adduced, and

(b)   no question relating to the information may be asked,

by or on behalf of the prosecution, unless evidence relating to it is adduced, or a question relating to it is asked, in the proceedings by or on behalf of the person.

(8) The offences excluded from subsection (7) are –

(a)   an offence under section 2 or 5 of the Perjury Act 1911 (false statements made on oath otherwise than in judicial proceedings or made otherwise than on oath),

(b)   an offence under section 44(1) or (2) of the Criminal Law (Consolidation) (Scotland) Act 1995 (false statements made on oath or otherwise than on oath).

(9) An order under this section has effect in relation to Scotland as if it were an order made by the Court of Session which that court had jurisdiction to make.

Preliminaries to adoption

42 Child to live with adopters before application

(1) An application for an adoption order may not be made unless –

(a)   if subsection (2) applies, the condition in that subsection is met,

(b)   if that subsection does not apply, the condition in whichever is applicable of subsections (3) to (5) applies.

(2) If –

(a)   the child was placed for adoption with the applicant or applicants by an adoption agency or in pursuance of an order of the High Court, or

(b)   the applicant is a parent of the child,

the condition is that the child must have had his home with the applicant or, in the case of an application by a couple, with one or both of them at all times during the period of ten weeks preceding the application.

(3) If the applicant or one of the applicants is the partner of a parent of the child, the condition is that the child must have had his home with the applicant or, as the case may be, applicants at all times during the period of six months preceding the application.

(4) If the applicants are local authority foster parents, the condition is that the child must have had his home with the applicants at all times during the period of one year preceding the application.

(5) In any other case, the condition is that the child must have had his home with the applicant or, in the case of an application by a couple, with one or both of them for not less than three years (whether continuous or not) during the period of five years preceding the application.

(6) But subsections (4) and (5) do not prevent an application being made if the court gives leave to make it.

(7) An adoption order may not be made unless the court is satisfied that sufficient opportunities to see the child with the applicant or, in the case of an application by a couple, both of them together in the home environment have been given –

(a) where the child was placed for adoption with the applicant or applicants by an adoption agency, to that agency,
(b) in any other case, to the local authority within whose area the home is.

(8) In this section and sections 43 and 44(1) –

(a) references to an adoption agency include a Scottish or Northern Irish adoption agency,
(b) references to a child placed for adoption by an adoption agency are to be read accordingly.

43 Reports where child placed by agency

Where an application for an adoption order relates to a child placed for adoption by an adoption agency, the agency must –

(a) submit to the court a report on the suitability of the applicants and on any other matters relevant to the operation of section 1, and
(b) assist the court in any manner the court directs.

44 Notice of intention to adopt

(1) This section applies where persons (referred to in this section as 'proposed adopters') wish to adopt a child who is not placed for adoption with them by an adoption agency.

(2) An adoption order may not be made in respect of the child unless the proposed adopters have given notice to the appropriate local authority of their intention to apply for the adoption order (referred to in this Act as a 'notice of intention to adopt').

(3) The notice must be given not more than two years, or less than three months, before the date on which the application for the adoption order is made.

(4) Where –

(a) if a person were seeking to apply for an adoption order, subsection (4) or (5) of section 42 would apply, but
(b) the condition in the subsection in question is not met,

the person may not give notice of intention to adopt unless he has the court's leave to apply for an adoption order.

(5) On receipt of a notice of intention to adopt, the local authority must arrange for the investigation of the matter and submit to the court a report of the investigation.

(6) In particular, the investigation must, so far as practicable, include the suitability of the proposed adopters and any other matters relevant to the operation of section 1 in relation to the application.

(7) If a local authority receive a notice of intention to adopt in respect of a child whom they know was (immediately before the notice was given) looked after by another local authority, they must, not more than seven days after the receipt of the notice, inform the other local authority in writing that they have received the notice.

(8) Where –

(a)   a local authority have placed a child with any persons otherwise than as prospective adopters, and
(b)   the persons give notice of intention to adopt,

the authority are not to be treated as leaving the child with them as prospective adopters for the purposes of section 18(1)(b).

(9) In this section, references to the appropriate local authority, in relation to any proposed adopters, are –

(a)   in prescribed cases, references to the prescribed local authority,
(b)   in any other case, references to the local authority for the area in which, at the time of giving the notice of intention to adopt, they have their home,

and 'prescribed' means prescribed by regulations.

45 Suitability of adopters

(1) Regulations under section 9 may make provision as to the matters to be taken into account by an adoption agency in determining, or making any report in respect of, the suitability of any persons to adopt a child.

(2) In particular, the regulations may make provision for the purpose of securing that, in determining the suitability of a couple to adopt a child, proper regard is had to the need for stability and permanence in their relationship.

The making of adoption orders

46 Adoption orders

(1) An adoption order is an order made by the court on an application under section 50 or 51 giving parental responsibility for a child to the adopters or adopter.

(2) The making of an adoption order operates to extinguish –

(a)   the parental responsibility which any person other than the adopters or adopter has for the adopted child immediately before the making of the order,
(b)   any order under the 1989 Act or the Children (Northern Ireland) Order 1995 (SI 1995/755 (NI 2)),

(c)   any order under the Children (Scotland) Act 1995 other than an excepted order, and

(d)   any duty arising by virtue of an agreement or an order of a court to make payments, so far as the payments are in respect of the adopted child's maintenance or upbringing for any period after the making of the adoption order.

'Excepted order' means an order under section 9, 11(1)(d) or 13 of the Children (Scotland) Act 1995 or an exclusion order within the meaning of section 76(1) of that Act.

(3) An adoption order –

(a)   does not affect parental responsibility so far as it relates to any period before the making of the order, and

(b)   in the case of an order made on an application under section 51(2) by the partner of a parent of the adopted child, does not affect the parental responsibility of that parent or any duties of that parent within subsection (2)(d).

(4) Subsection (2)(d) does not apply to a duty arising by virtue of an agreement –

(a)   which constitutes a trust, or

(b)   which expressly provides that the duty is not to be extinguished by the making of an adoption order.

(5) An adoption order may be made even if the child to be adopted is already an adopted child.

(6) Before making an adoption order, the court must consider whether there should be arrangements for allowing any person contact with the child; and for that purpose the court must consider any existing or proposed arrangements and obtain any views of the parties to the proceedings.

47 Conditions for making adoption orders

(1) An adoption order may not be made if the child has a parent or guardian unless one of the following three conditions is met; but this section is subject to section 52 (parental etc consent).

(2) The first condition is that, in the case of each parent or guardian of the child, the court is satisfied –

(a)   that the parent or guardian consents to the making of the adoption order,

(b)   that the parent or guardian has consented under section 20 (and has not withdrawn the consent) and does not oppose the making of the adoption order, or

(c)   that the parent's or guardian's consent should be dispensed with.

(3) A parent or guardian may not oppose the making of an adoption order under subsection (2)(b) without the court's leave.

(4) The second condition is that –

  (a)   the child has been placed for adoption by an adoption agency with the prospective adopters in whose favour the order is proposed to be made,
  (b)   either –
        (i)   the child was placed for adoption with the consent of each parent or guardian and the consent of the mother was given when the child was at least six weeks old, or
        (ii) the child was placed for adoption under a placement order, and
  (c)   no parent or guardian opposes the making of the adoption order.

(5) A parent or guardian may not oppose the making of an adoption order under the second condition without the court's leave.

(6) The third condition is that the child –

  (a)   is the subject of a Scottish permanence order which includes provision granting authority for the child to be adopted, or
  (b)   is free for adoption by virtue of an order made, under Article 17(1) or 18(1) of the Adoption (Northern Ireland) Order 1987 (SI 1987/2203 (NI 22)).

(7) The court cannot give leave under subsection (3) or (5) unless satisfied that there has been a change in circumstances since the consent of the parent or guardian was given or, as the case may be, the placement order was made.

(8) An adoption order may not be made in relation to a person who is or has been married.

(8A) An adoption order may not be made in relation to a person who is or has been a civil partner.

(9) An adoption order may not be made in relation to a person who has attained the age of 19 years.

Amendments: Civil Partnership Act 2004, s 79(1), (3); SI 2011/1740.

48 Restrictions on making adoption orders

(1) The court may not hear an application for an adoption order in relation to a child, where a previous application to which subsection (2) applies made in relation to the child by the same persons was refused by any court, unless it appears to the court that, because of a change in circumstances or for any other reason, it is proper to hear the application.

(2) This subsection applies to any application –

  (a)   for an adoption order or a Scottish or Northern Irish adoption order, or
  (b)   for an order for adoption made in the Isle of Man or any of the Channel Islands.

49 Applications for adoption

(1) An application for an adoption order may be made by –

(a)   a couple, or

(b)   one person,

but only if it is made under section 50 or 51 and one of the following conditions is met.

(2) The first condition is that at least one of the couple (in the case of an application under section 50) or the applicant (in the case of an application under section 51) is domiciled in a part of the British Islands.

(3) The second condition is that both of the couple (in the case of an application under section 50) or the applicant (in the case of an application under section 51) have been habitually resident in a part of the British Islands for a period of not less than one year ending with the date of the application.

(4) An application for an adoption order may only be made if the person to be adopted has not attained the age of 18 years on the date of the application.

(5) References in this Act to a child, in connection with any proceedings (whether or not concluded) for adoption, (such as 'child to be adopted' or 'adopted child') include a person who has attained the age of 18 years before the proceedings are concluded.

50 Adoption by couple

(1) An adoption order may be made on the application of a couple where both of them have attained the age of 21 years.

(2) An adoption order may be made on the application of a couple where –

(a)   one of the couple is the mother or the father of the person to be adopted and has attained the age of 18 years, and

(b)   the other has attained the age of 21 years.

51 Adoption by one person

(1) An adoption order may be made on the application of one person who has attained the age of 21 years and is not married or a civil partner.

(2) An adoption order may be made on the application of one person who has attained the age of 21 years if the court is satisfied that the person is the partner of a parent of the person to be adopted.

(3) An adoption order may be made on the application of one person who has attained the age of 21 years and is married if the court is satisfied that –

(a)   the person's spouse cannot be found,

(b)   the spouses have separated and are living apart, and the separation is likely to be permanent, or

(c)   the person's spouse is by reason of ill-health, whether physical or mental, incapable of making an application for an adoption order.

(3A) An adoption order may be made on the application of one person who has attained the age of 21 years and is a civil partner if the court is satisfied that –

(a) the person's civil partner cannot be found,

(b) the civil partners have separated and are living apart, and the separation is likely to be permanent, or

(c) the person's civil partner is by reason of ill-health, whether physical or mental, incapable of making an application for an adoption order.

(4) An adoption order may not be made on an application under this section by the mother or the father of the person to be adopted unless the court is satisfied that –

(a) the other natural parent is dead or cannot be found,

(b) by virtue of the provisions specified in subsection (5), there is no other parent, or

(c) there is some other reason justifying the child's being adopted by the applicant alone,

and, where the court makes an adoption order on such an application, the court must record that it is satisfied as to the fact mentioned in paragraph (a) or (b) or, in the case of paragraph (c), record the reason.

(5) The provisions referred to in subsection (4)(b) are –

(a) section 28 of the Human Fertilisation and Embryology Act 1990 (disregarding subsections (5A) to (5I) of that section), or

(b) sections 34 to 47 of the Human Fertilisation and Embryology Act 2008 (disregarding sections 39, 40 and 46 of that Act).

Amendments: Civil Partnership Act 2004, s 79(1), (4), (5); Human Fertilisation and Embryology (Deceased Fathers) Act 2003, s 2(1), Schedule, para 18; Human Fertilisation and Embryology Act 2008, s 56, Sch 6, Pt 1, para 39; SI 2009/479.

Placement and adoption: general

52 Parental etc consent

(1) The court cannot dispense with the consent of any parent or guardian of a child to the child being placed for adoption or to the making of an adoption order in respect of the child unless the court is satisfied that –

(a) the parent or guardian cannot be found or lacks capacity (within the meaning of the Mental Capacity Act 2005) to give consent, or

(b) the welfare of the child requires the consent to be dispensed with.

(2) The following provisions apply to references in this Chapter to any parent or guardian of a child giving or withdrawing –

(a) consent to the placement of a child for adoption, or

(b) consent to the making of an adoption order (including a future adoption order).

(3) Any consent given by the mother to the making of an adoption order is ineffective if it is given less than six weeks after the child's birth.

(4) The withdrawal of any consent to the placement of a child for adoption, or of any consent given under section 20, is ineffective if it is given after an application for an adoption order is made.

(5) 'Consent' means consent given unconditionally and with full understanding of what is involved; but a person may consent to adoption without knowing the identity of the persons in whose favour the order will be made.

(6) 'Parent' (except in subsections (9) and (10) below) means a parent having parental responsibility.

(7) Consent under section 19 or 20 must be given in the form prescribed by rules, and the rules may prescribe forms in which a person giving consent under any other provision of this Part may do so (if he wishes).

(8) Consent given under section 19 or 20 must be withdrawn –

(a)   in the form prescribed by rules, or
(b)   by notice given to the agency.

(9) Subsection (10) applies if –

(a)   an agency has placed a child for adoption under section 19 in pursuance of consent given by a parent of the child, and
(b)   at a later time, the other parent of the child acquires parental responsibility for the child.

(10) The other parent is to be treated as having at that time given consent in accordance with this section in the same terms as those in which the first parent gave consent.

Amendments: Mental Capacity Act 2005, s 67(1), Sch 6, para 45.

53 Modification of 1989 Act in relation to adoption

(1) Where –

(a)   a local authority are authorised to place a child for adoption, or
(b)   a child who has been placed for adoption by a local authority is less than six weeks old,

regulations may provide for the following provisions of the 1989 Act to apply with modifications, or not to apply, in relation to the child.

(2) The provisions are –

(a)   section 22(4)(b), (c) and (d) and (5)(b) (duty to ascertain wishes and feelings of certain persons),
(b)   paragraphs 15 and 21 of Schedule 2 (promoting contact with parents and parents' obligation to contribute towards maintenance).

(3) Where a registered adoption society is authorised to place a child for adoption or a child who has been placed for adoption by a registered adoption society is less than six weeks old, regulations may provide –

(a) for section 61 of that Act to have effect in relation to the child whether or not he is accommodated by or on behalf of the society,

(b) for subsections (2)(b) to (d) and (3)(b) of that section (duty to ascertain wishes and feelings of certain persons) to apply with modifications, or not to apply, in relation to the child.

(4) Where a child's home is with persons who have given notice of intention to adopt, no contribution is payable (whether under a contribution order or otherwise) under Part 3 of Schedule 2 to that Act (contributions towards maintenance of children looked after by local authorities) in respect of the period referred to in subsection (5).

(5) That period begins when the notice of intention to adopt is given and ends if –

(a) the period of four months beginning with the giving of the notice expires without the prospective adopters applying for an adoption order, or

(b) an application for such an order is withdrawn or refused.

(6) In this section, 'notice of intention to adopt' includes notice of intention to apply for a Scottish or Northern Irish adoption order.

54 Disclosing information during adoption process

Regulations under section 9 may require adoption agencies in prescribed circumstances to disclose in accordance with the regulations prescribed information to prospective adopters.

55 Revocation of adoptions on legitimation

(1) Where any child adopted by one natural parent as sole adoptive parent subsequently becomes a legitimated person on the marriage of the natural parents, the court by which the adoption order was made may, on the application of any of the parties concerned, revoke the order.

(2) In relation to an adoption order made by a magistrates' court, the reference in subsection (1) to the court by which the order was made includes a court acting for the same local justice area.

Amendment: Courts Act 2003, s 109(1), Sch 8, para 412.

Disclosure of information in relation to a person's adoption

56 Information to be kept about a person's adoption

(1) In relation to an adopted person, regulations may prescribe –

(a) the information which an adoption agency must keep in relation to his adoption,

(b) the form and manner in which it must keep that information.

(2) Below in this group of sections (that is, this section and sections 57 to 65), any information kept by an adoption agency by virtue of subsection (1)(a) is referred to as section 56 information.

(3) Regulations may provide for the transfer in prescribed circumstances of information held, or previously held, by an adoption agency to another adoption agency.

57 Restrictions on disclosure of protected etc information

(1) Any section 56 information kept by an adoption agency which –

(a) is about an adopted person or any other person, and
(b) is or includes identifying information about the person in question,

may only be disclosed by the agency to a person (other than the person the information is about) in pursuance of this group of sections.

(2) Any information kept by an adoption agency –

(a) which the agency has obtained from the Registrar General on an application under section 79(5) and any other information which would enable the adopted person to obtain a certified copy of the record of his birth, or
(b) which is information about an entry relating to the adopted person in the Adoption Contact Register,

may only be disclosed to a person by the agency in pursuance of this group of sections.

(3) In this group of sections, information the disclosure of which to a person is restricted by virtue of subsection (1) or (2) is referred to (in relation to him) as protected information.

(4) Identifying information about a person means information which, whether taken on its own or together with other information disclosed by an adoption agency, identifies the person or enables the person to be identified.

(5) This section does not prevent the disclosure of protected information in pursuance of a prescribed agreement to which the adoption agency is a party.

(6) Regulations may authorise or require an adoption agency to disclose protected information to a person who is not an adopted person.

58 Disclosure of other information

(1) This section applies to any section 56 information other than protected information.

(2) An adoption agency may for the purposes of its functions disclose to any person in accordance with prescribed arrangements any information to which this section applies.

(3) An adoption agency must, in prescribed circumstances, disclose prescribed information to a prescribed person.

59 Offence

Regulations may provide that a registered adoption society which discloses any information in contravention of section 57 is to be guilty of an offence and liable on summary conviction to a fine not exceeding level 5 on the standard scale.

60 Disclosing information to adopted adult

(1) This section applies to an adopted person who has attained the age of 18 years.

(2) The adopted person has the right, at his request, to receive from the appropriate adoption agency –

  (a)   any information which would enable him to obtain a certified copy of the record of his birth, unless the High Court orders otherwise,

  (b)   any prescribed information disclosed to the adopters by the agency by virtue of section 54.

(3) The High Court may make an order under subsection (2)(a), on an application by the appropriate adoption agency, if satisfied that the circumstances are exceptional.

(4) The adopted person also has the right, at his request, to receive from the court which made the adoption order a copy of any prescribed document or prescribed order relating to the adoption.

(5) Subsection (4) does not apply to a document or order so far as it contains information which is protected information.

61 Disclosing protected information about adults

(1) This section applies where –

  (a)   a person applies to the appropriate adoption agency for protected information to be disclosed to him, and

  (b)   none of the information is about a person who is a child at the time of the application.

(2) The agency is not required to proceed with the application unless it considers it appropriate to do so.

(3) If the agency does proceed with the application it must take all reasonable steps to obtain the views of any person the information is about as to the disclosure of the information about him.

(4) The agency may then disclose the information if it considers it appropriate to do so.

(5) In deciding whether it is appropriate to proceed with the application or disclose the information, the agency must consider –

  (a)   the welfare of the adopted person,

  (b)   any views obtained under subsection (3),

(c)   any prescribed matters,

and all the other circumstances of the case.

(6) This section does not apply to a request for information under section 60(2) or to a request for information which the agency is authorised or required to disclose in pursuance of regulations made by virtue of section 57(6).

62 Disclosing protected information about children

(1) This section applies where –

(a)   a person applies to the appropriate adoption agency for protected information to be disclosed to him, and

(b)   any of the information is about a person who is a child at the time of the application.

(2) The agency is not required to proceed with the application unless it considers it appropriate to do so.

(3) If the agency does proceed with the application, then, so far as the information is about a person who is at the time a child, the agency must take all reasonable steps to obtain –

(a)   the views of any parent or guardian of the child, and

(b)   the views of the child, if the agency considers it appropriate to do so having regard to his age and understanding and to all the other circumstances of the case,

as to the disclosure of the information.

(4) And, so far as the information is about a person who has at the time attained the age of 18 years, the agency must take all reasonable steps to obtain his views as to the disclosure of the information.

(5) The agency may then disclose the information if it considers it appropriate to do so.

(6) In deciding whether it is appropriate to proceed with the application, or disclose the information, where any of the information is about a person who is at the time a child –

(a)   if the child is an adopted child, the child's welfare must be the paramount consideration,

(b)   in the case of any other child, the agency must have particular regard to the child's welfare.

(7) And, in deciding whether it is appropriate to proceed with the application or disclose the information, the agency must consider –

(a)   the welfare of the adopted person (where subsection (6)(a) does not apply),

(b)   any views obtained under subsection (3) or (4),

(c)   any prescribed matters,

and all the other circumstances of the case.

(8) This section does not apply to a request for information under section 60(2) or to a request for information which the agency is authorised or required to disclose in pursuance of regulations made by virtue of section 57(6).

63 Counselling

(1) Regulations may require adoption agencies to give information about the availability of counselling to persons –

    (a)   seeking information from them in pursuance of this group of sections,

    (b)   considering objecting or consenting to the disclosure of information by the agency in pursuance of this group of sections, or

    (c)   considering entering with the agency into an agreement prescribed for the purposes of section 57(5).

(2) Regulations may require adoption agencies to make arrangements to secure the provision of counselling for persons seeking information from them in prescribed circumstances in pursuance of this group of sections.

(3) The regulations may authorise adoption agencies –

    (a)   to disclose information which is required for the purposes of such counselling to the persons providing the counselling,

    (b)   where the person providing the counselling is outside the United Kingdom, to require a prescribed fee to be paid.

(4) The regulations may require any of the following persons to provide counselling for the purposes of arrangements under subsection (2) –

    (a)   a local authority, a council constituted under section 2 of the Local Government etc (Scotland) Act 1994 or a Health and Social Services Board established under Article 16 of the Health and Personal Social Services (Northern Ireland) Order 1972 (SI 1972/1265 (NI 14)),

    (b)   a registered adoption society, an organisation within section 144(3)(b) or an adoption society which is registered under Article 4 of the Adoption (Northern Ireland) Order 1987 (SI 1987/2203 (NI 22)),

    (c)   an adoption support agency in respect of which a person is registered under Part 2 of the Care Standards Act 2000.

(5) For the purposes of subsection (4), where the functions of a Health and Social Services Board are exercisable by a Health and Social Services Trust, the reference in sub-paragraph (a) to a Board is to be read as a reference to the Health and Social Services Trust.

64 Other provision to be made by regulations

(1) Regulations may make provision for the purposes of this group of sections, including provision as to –

    (a)   the performance by adoption agencies of their functions,

    (b)   the manner in which information may be received, and

    (c)   the matters mentioned below in this section.

(2) Regulations may prescribe –

(a) the manner in which agreements made by virtue of section 57(5) are to be recorded,

(b) the information to be provided by any person on an application for the disclosure of information under this group of sections.

(3) Regulations may require adoption agencies –

(a) to give to prescribed persons prescribed information about the rights or opportunities to obtain information, or to give their views as to its disclosure, given by this group of sections,

(b) to seek prescribed information from, or give prescribed information to, the Registrar General in prescribed circumstances.

(4) Regulations may require the Registrar General –

(a) to disclose to any person (including an adopted person) at his request any information which the person requires to assist him to make contact with the adoption agency which is the appropriate adoption agency in the case of an adopted person specified in the request (or, as the case may be, in the applicant's case),

(b) to disclose to the appropriate adoption agency any information which the agency requires about any entry relating to the adopted person on the Adoption Contact Register.

(5) Regulations may provide for the payment of a prescribed fee in respect of the disclosure in prescribed circumstances of any information in pursuance of section 60, 61 or 62; but an adopted person may not be required to pay any fee in respect of any information disclosed to him in relation to any person who (but for his adoption) would be related to him by blood (including half-blood), marriage or civil partnership.

(6) Regulations may provide for the payment of a prescribed fee by an adoption agency obtaining information under subsection (4)(b).

Amendments: Civil Partnership Act 2004, s 79(1), (6).

65 Sections 56 to 65: interpretation

(1) In this group of sections –

'appropriate adoption agency', in relation to an adopted person or to information relating to his adoption, means –
    (a) if the person was placed for adoption by an adoption agency, that agency or (if different) the agency which keeps the information in relation to his adoption,
    (b) in any other case, the local authority to which notice of intention to adopt was given,

'prescribed' means prescribed by subordinate legislation,
'regulations' means regulations under section 9,
'subordinate legislation' means regulations or, in relation to information to be given by a court, rules.

(2) But –

    (a)   regulations under section 63(2) imposing any requirement on a council constituted under section 2 of the Local Government etc (Scotland) Act 1994, or an organisation within section 144(3)(b), are to be made by the Scottish Ministers,

    (b)   regulations under section 63(2) imposing any requirement on a Health and Social Services Board established under Article 16 of the Health and Personal Social Services (Northern Ireland) Order 1972 (SI 1972/1265 (NI 14)), or an adoption society which is registered under Article 4 of the Adoption (Northern Ireland) Order 1987 (SI 1987/2203 (NI 22)), are to be made by the Department of Health, Social Services and Public Safety.

(3) The power of the Scottish Ministers or of the Department of Health, Social Services and Public Safety to make regulations under section 63(2) includes power to make –

    (a)   any supplementary, incidental or consequential provision,
    (b)   any transitory, transitional or saving provision,

which the person making the regulations considers necessary or expedient.

(4) Regulations prescribing any fee by virtue of section 64(6) require the approval of the Chancellor of the Exchequer.

(5) Regulations making any provision as to the manner in which any application is to be made for the disclosure of information by the Registrar General require his approval.

Chapter 4
Status of Adopted Children

66 Meaning of adoption in Chapter 4

(1) In this Chapter 'adoption' means –

    (a)   adoption by an adoption order or a Scottish or Northern Irish adoption order,
    (b)   adoption by an order made in the Isle of Man or any of the Channel Islands,
    (c)   an adoption effected under the law of a Convention country outside the British Islands, and certified in pursuance of Article 23(1) of the Convention (referred to in this Act as a 'Convention adoption'),
    (d)   an overseas adoption, or
    (e)   an adoption recognised by the law of England and Wales and effected under the law of any other country;

and related expressions are to be interpreted accordingly.

(2) But references in this Chapter to adoption do not include an adoption effected before the day on which this Chapter comes into force (referred to in this Chapter as 'the appointed day').

(3) Any reference in an enactment to an adopted person within the meaning of this Chapter includes a reference to an adopted child within the meaning of Part 4 of the Adoption Act 1976.

67 Status conferred by adoption

(1) An adopted person is to be treated in law as if born as the child of the adopters or adopter.

(2) An adopted person is the legitimate child of the adopters or adopter and, if adopted by –

(a)   a couple, or
(b)   one of a couple under section 51(2),

is to be treated as the child of the relationship of the couple in question.

(3) An adopted person –

(a)   if adopted by one of a couple under section 51(2), is to be treated in law as not being the child of any person other than the adopter and the other one of the couple, and
(b)   in any other case, is to be treated in law, subject to subsection (4), as not being the child of any person other than the adopters or adopter;

but this subsection does not affect any reference in this Act to a person's natural parent or to any other natural relationship.

(4) In the case of a person adopted by one of the person's natural parents as sole adoptive parent, subsection (3)(b) has no effect as respects entitlement to property depending on relationship to that parent, or as respects anything else depending on that relationship.

(5) This section has effect from the date of the adoption.

(6) Subject to the provisions of this Chapter and Schedule 4, this section –

(a)   applies for the interpretation of enactments or instruments passed or made before as well as after the adoption, and so applies subject to any contrary indication, and
(b)   has effect as respects things done, or events occurring, on or after the adoption.

68 Adoptive relatives

(1) A relationship existing by virtue of section 67 may be referred to as an adoptive relationship, and –

(a)   an adopter may be referred to as an adoptive parent or (as the case may be) as an adoptive father or adoptive mother,
(b)   any other relative of any degree under an adoptive relationship may be referred to as an adoptive relative of that degree.

(2) Subsection (1) does not affect the interpretation of any reference, not qualified by the word 'adoptive', to a relationship.

(3) A reference (however expressed) to the adoptive mother and father of a child adopted by –

(a)   a couple of the same sex, or
(b)   a partner of the child's parent, where the couple are of the same sex,

is to be read as a reference to the child's adoptive parents.

69 Rules of interpretation for instruments concerning property

(1) The rules of interpretation contained in this section apply (subject to any contrary indication and to Schedule 4) to any instrument so far as it contains a disposition of property.

(2) In applying section 67(1) and (2) to a disposition which depends on the date of birth of a child or children of the adoptive parent or parents, the disposition is to be interpreted as if –

(a)   the adopted person had been born on the date of adoption,
(b)   two or more people adopted on the same date had been born on that date in the order of their actual births;

but this does not affect any reference to a person's age.

(3) Examples of phrases in wills on which subsection (2) can operate are –

1   Children of A 'living at my death or born afterwards'.
2   Children of A 'living at my death or born afterwards before any one of such children for the time being in existence attains a vested interest and who attain the age of 21 years'.
3   As in example 1 or 2, but referring to grandchildren of A instead of children of A.
4   A for life 'until he has a child', and then to his child or children.

Note. Subsection (2) will not affect the reference to the age of 21 years in example 2.

(4) Section 67(3) does not prejudice –
(a)   any qualifying interest, or
(b)   any interest expectant (whether immediately or not) upon a qualifying interest.

'Qualifying interest' means an interest vested in possession in the adopted person before the adoption.

(5) Where it is necessary to determine for the purposes of a disposition of property effected by an instrument whether a woman can have a child –

(a)   it must be presumed that once a woman has attained the age of 55 years she will not adopt a person after execution of the instrument, and
(b)   if she does so, then (in spite of section 67) that person is not to be treated as her child or (if she does so as one of a couple) as the child of the other one of the couple for the purposes of the instrument.

(6) In this section, 'instrument' includes a private Act settling property, but not any other enactment.

70 Dispositions depending on date of birth

(1) Where a disposition depends on the date of birth of a person who was born illegitimate and who is adopted by one of the natural parents as sole adoptive parent, section 69(2) does not affect entitlement by virtue of Part 3 of the Family Law Reform Act 1987 (dispositions of property).

(2) Subsection (1) applies for example where –

(a) a testator dies in 2001 bequeathing a legacy to his eldest grandchild living at a specified time,
(b) his unmarried daughter has a child in 2002 who is the first grandchild,
(c) his married son has a child in 2003,
(d) subsequently his unmarried daughter adopts her child as sole adoptive parent.

In that example the status of the daughter's child as the eldest grandchild of the testator is not affected by the events described in paragraphs (c) and (d).

71 Property devolving with peerages etc

(1) An adoption does not affect the descent of any peerage or dignity or title of honour.

(2) An adoption does not affect the devolution of any property limited (expressly or not) to devolve (as nearly as the law permits) along with any peerage or dignity or title of honour.

(3) Subsection (2) applies only if and so far as a contrary intention is not expressed in the instrument, and has effect subject to the terms of the instrument.

72 Protection of trustees and personal representatives

(1) A trustee or personal representative is not under a duty, by virtue of the law relating to trusts or the administration of estates, to enquire, before conveying or distributing any property, whether any adoption has been effected or revoked if that fact could affect entitlement to the property.

(2) A trustee or personal representative is not liable to any person by reason of a conveyance or distribution of the property made without regard to any such fact if he has not received notice of the fact before the conveyance or distribution.

(3) This section does not prejudice the right of a person to follow the property, or any property representing it, into the hands of another person, other than a purchaser, who has received it.

73 Meaning of disposition

(1) This section applies for the purposes of this Chapter.

(2) A disposition includes the conferring of a power of appointment and any other disposition of an interest in or right over property; and in this subsection a power of appointment includes any discretionary power to transfer a beneficial interest in property without the furnishing of valuable consideration.

(3) This Chapter applies to an oral disposition as if contained in an instrument made when the disposition was made.

(4) The date of death of a testator is the date at which a will or codicil is to be regarded as made.

(5) The provisions of the law of intestate succession applicable to the estate of a deceased person are to be treated as if contained in an instrument executed by him (while of full capacity) immediately before his death.

74 Miscellaneous enactments

(1) Section 67 does not apply for the purposes of –

(a)   section 1 of and Schedule 1 to the Marriage Act 1949 or Schedule 1 to the Civil Partnership Act 2004 (prohibited degrees of kindred and affinity), or

(b)   sections 64 and 65 of the Sexual Offences Act 2003 (sex with an adult relative).

(2) Section 67 does not apply for the purposes of any provision of –

(a)   the British Nationality Act 1981,

(b)   the Immigration Act 1971,

(c)   any instrument having effect under an enactment within paragraph (a) or (b), or

(d)   any other provision of the law for the time being in force which determines British citizenship, British overseas territories citizenship, the status of a British National (Overseas) or British Overseas citizenship.

Amendments: Civil Partnership Act 2004, s 79(1), (7); Sexual Offences Act 2003, s 139, Sch 6, para 47.

75 Pensions

Section 67(3) does not affect entitlement to a pension which is payable to or for the benefit of a person and is in payment at the time of the person's adoption.

76 Insurance

(1) Where a child is adopted whose natural parent has effected an insurance with a friendly society or a collecting society or an industrial insurance company for the payment on the death of the child of money for funeral expenses, then –

(a)   the rights and liabilities under the policy are by virtue of the adoption transferred to the adoptive parents, and

(b) for the purposes of the enactments relating to such societies and companies, the adoptive parents are to be treated as the person who took out the policy.

(2) Where the adoption is effected by an order made by virtue of section 51(2), the references in subsection (1) to the adoptive parents are to be read as references to the adopter and the other one of the couple.

Chapter 5
The Registers

Adopted Children Register etc

77 Adopted Children Register

(1) The Registrar General must continue to maintain in the General Register Office a register, to be called the Adopted Children Register.

(2) The Adopted Children Register is not to be open to public inspection or search.

(3) No entries may be made in the Adopted Children Register other than entries –

(a) directed to be made in it by adoption orders, or
(b) required to be made under Schedule 1.

(4) A certified copy of an entry in the Adopted Children Register, if purporting to be sealed or stamped with the seal of the General Register Office, is to be received as evidence of the adoption to which it relates without further or other proof.

(5) Where an entry in the Adopted Children Register contains a record –

(a) of the date of birth of the adopted person, or
(b) of the country, or the district and sub-district, of the birth of the adopted person,

a certified copy of the entry is also to be received, without further or other proof, as evidence of that date, or country or district and sub-district, (as the case may be) in all respects as if the copy were a certified copy of an entry in the registers of live-births.

(6) Schedule 1 (registration of adoptions and the amendment of adoption orders) is to have effect.

78 Searches and copies

(1) The Registrar General must continue to maintain at the General Register Office an index of the Adopted Children Register.

(2) Any person may –

(a) search the index,
(b) have a certified copy of any entry in the Adopted Children Register.

(3) But a person is not entitled to have a certified copy of an entry in the Adopted Children Register relating to an adopted person who has not attained the age of 18 years unless the applicant has provided the Registrar General with the prescribed particulars.

'Prescribed' means prescribed by regulations made by the Registrar General with the approval of the Secretary of State.

(4) The terms, conditions and regulations as to payment of fees, and otherwise, applicable under the Births and Deaths Registration Act 1953, and the Registration Service Act 1953, in respect of –

(a) searches in the index kept in the General Register Office of certified copies of entries in the registers of live-births,

(b) the supply from that office of certified copies of entries in those certified copies,

also apply in respect of searches, and supplies of certified copies, under subsection (2).

Amendments: SI 2008/678.

79 Connections between the register and birth records

(1) The Registrar General must make traceable the connection between any entry in the registers of live-births or other records which has been marked 'Adopted' and any corresponding entry in the Adopted Children Register.

(2) Information kept by the Registrar General for the purposes of subsection (1) is not to be open to public inspection or search.

(3) Any such information, and any other information which would enable an adopted person to obtain a certified copy of the record of his birth, may only be disclosed by the Registrar General in accordance with this section.

(4) In relation to a person adopted before the appointed day the court may, in exceptional circumstances, order the Registrar General to give any information mentioned in subsection (3) to a person.

(5) On an application made in the prescribed manner by the appropriate adoption agency in respect of an adopted person a record of whose birth is kept by the Registrar General, the Registrar General must give the agency any information relating to the adopted person which is mentioned in subsection (3).

'Appropriate adoption agency' has the same meaning as in section 65.

(6) In relation to a person adopted before the appointed day, Schedule 2 applies instead of subsection (5).

(7) On an application made in the prescribed manner by an adopted person a record of whose birth is kept by the Registrar General and who –

(a) is under the age of 18 years, and

(b) intends to be married or form a civil partnership,

the Registrar General must inform the applicant whether or not it appears from information contained in the registers of live-births or other records that the applicant and the intended spouse or civil partner may be within the prohibited degrees of relationship for the purposes of the Marriage Act 1949 or for the purposes of the Civil Partnership Act 2004 (c.33).

(8) Before the Registrar General gives any information by virtue of this section, any prescribed fee which he has demanded must be paid.

(9) In this section –

'appointed day' means the day appointed for the commencement of sections 56 to 65,
'prescribed' means prescribed by regulations made by the Registrar General with the approval of the Secretary of State.

Amendments: Civil Partnership Act 2004, s 79(1), SI 2005/3542; SI 2008/678.

Adoption Contact Register

80 Adoption Contact Register

(1) The Registrar General must continue to maintain at the General Register Office in accordance with regulations a register in two Parts to be called the Adoption Contact Register.

(2) Part 1 of the register is to contain the prescribed information about adopted persons who have given the prescribed notice expressing their wishes as to making contact with their relatives.

(3) The Registrar General may only make an entry in Part 1 of the register for an adopted person –

(a) a record of whose birth is kept by the Registrar General,
(b) who has attained the age of 18 years, and
(c) who the Registrar General is satisfied has such information as is necessary to enable him to obtain a certified copy of the record of his birth.

(4) Part 2 of the register is to contain the prescribed information about persons who have given the prescribed notice expressing their wishes, as relatives of adopted persons, as to making contact with those persons.

(5) The Registrar General may only make an entry in Part 2 of the register for a person –

(a) who has attained the age of 18 years, and
(b) who the Registrar General is satisfied is a relative of an adopted person and has such information as is necessary to enable him to obtain a certified copy of the record of the adopted person's birth.

(6) Regulations may provide for –

(a) the disclosure of information contained in one Part of the register to persons for whom there is an entry in the other Part,

    (b)   the payment of prescribed fees in respect of the making or alteration of entries in the register and the disclosure of information contained in the register.

81 Adoption Contact Register: supplementary

(1) The Adoption Contact Register is not to be open to public inspection or search.

(2) In section 80, 'relative', in relation to an adopted person, means any person who (but for his adoption) would be related to him by blood (including half-blood), marriage or civil partnership.

(3) The Registrar General must not give any information entered in the register to any person except in accordance with subsection (6)(*a*) of that section or regulations made by virtue of section 64(4)(*b*).

(4) In section 80, 'regulations' means regulations made by the Registrar General with the approval of the Secretary of State, and 'prescribed' means prescribed by such regulations.

Amendments: Civil Partnership Act 2004, s 79(1), (9); SI 2008/678.

General

82 Interpretation

(1) In this Chapter –

    'records' includes certified copies kept by the Registrar General of entries in any register of births,
    'registers of live-births' means the registers of live-births made under the Births and Deaths Registration Act 1953.

(2) Any register, record or index maintained under this Chapter may be maintained in any form the Registrar General considers appropriate; and references (however expressed) to entries in such a register, or to their amendment, marking or cancellation, are to be read accordingly.

Chapter 6
Adoptions with a Foreign Element

Bringing children into and out of the United Kingdom

83 Restriction on bringing children in

(1) This section applies where a person who is habitually resident in the British Islands (the 'British resident') –

    (a)   brings, or causes another to bring, a child who is habitually resident outside the British Islands into the United Kingdom for the purpose of adoption by the British resident, or

(b) at any time brings, or causes another to bring, into the United Kingdom a child adopted by the British resident under an external adoption effected within the period of twelve months ending with that time.

The references to adoption, or to a child adopted, by the British resident include a reference to adoption, or to a child adopted, by the British resident and another person.

(2) But this section does not apply if the child is intended to be adopted under a Convention adoption order.

(3) An external adoption means an adoption, other than a Convention adoption, of a child effected under the law of any country or territory outside the British Islands, whether or not the adoption is –

(a) an adoption within the meaning of Chapter 4, or
(b) a full adoption (within the meaning of section 88(3)).

(4) Regulations may require a person intending to bring, or to cause another to bring, a child into the United Kingdom in circumstances where this section applies –

(a) to apply to an adoption agency (including a Scottish or Northern Irish adoption agency) in the prescribed manner for an assessment of his suitability to adopt the child, and
(b) to give the agency any information it may require for the purpose of the assessment.

(5) Regulations may require prescribed conditions to be met in respect of a child brought into the United Kingdom in circumstances where this section applies.

(6) In relation to a child brought into the United Kingdom for adoption in circumstances where this section applies, regulations may –

(a) provide for any provision of Chapter 3 to apply with modifications or not to apply,
(b) if notice of intention to adopt has been given, impose functions in respect of the child on the local authority to which the notice was given.

(7) If a person brings, or causes another to bring, a child into the United Kingdom at any time in circumstances where this section applies, he is guilty of an offence if –

(a) he has not complied with any requirement imposed by virtue of subsection (4), or
(b) any condition required to be met by virtue of subsection (5) is not met,

before that time, or before any later time which may be prescribed.

(8) A person guilty of an offence under this section is liable –

(a) on summary conviction to imprisonment for a term not exceeding six months, or a fine not exceeding the statutory maximum, or both,

(b) on conviction on indictment, to imprisonment for a term not exceeding twelve months, or a fine, or both.

(9) In this section, 'prescribed' means prescribed by regulations and 'regulations' means regulations made by the Secretary of State, after consultation with the Assembly.

Amendment: Children and Adoption Act 2006, s 14(1).

84 Giving parental responsibility prior to adoption abroad

(1) The High Court may, on an application by persons who the court is satisfied intend to adopt a child under the law of a country or territory outside the British Islands, make an order giving parental responsibility for the child to them.

(2) An order under this section may not give parental responsibility to persons who the court is satisfied meet those requirements as to domicile, or habitual residence, in England and Wales which have to be met if an adoption order is to be made in favour of those persons.

(3) An order under this section may not be made unless any requirements prescribed by regulations are satisfied.

(4) An application for an order under this section may not be made unless at all times during the preceding ten weeks the child's home was with the applicant or, in the case of an application by two people, both of them.

(5) Section 46(2) to (4) has effect in relation to an order under this section as it has effect in relation to adoption orders.

(6) Regulations may provide for any provision of this Act which refers to adoption orders to apply, with or without modifications, to orders under this section.

(7) In this section, 'regulations' means regulations made by the Secretary of State, after consultation with the Assembly.

85 Restriction on taking children out

(1) A child who –

(a) is a Commonwealth citizen, or
(b) is habitually resident in the United Kingdom,

must not be removed from the United Kingdom to a place outside the British Islands for the purpose of adoption unless the condition in subsection (2) is met.

(2) The condition is that –

(a) the prospective adopters have parental responsibility for the child by virtue of an order under section 84, or

(b) the child is removed under the authority of an order under section 59 of the Adoption and Children (Scotland) Act 2007 (asp 4) or Article 57 of the Adoption (Northern Ireland) Order 1987 (SI 1987/2203 (NI 22)).

(3) Removing a child from the United Kingdom includes arranging to do so; and the circumstances in which a person arranges to remove a child from the United Kingdom include those where he –

(a) enters into an arrangement for the purpose of facilitating such a removal of the child,

(b) initiates or takes part in any negotiations of which the purpose is the conclusion of an arrangement within paragraph (a), or

(c) causes another person to take any step mentioned in paragraph (a) or (b).

An arrangement includes an agreement (whether or not enforceable).

(4) A person who removes a child from the United Kingdom in contravention of subsection (1) is guilty of an offence.

(5) A person is not guilty of an offence under subsection (4) of causing a person to take any step mentioned in paragraph (*a*) or (*b*) of subsection (3) unless it is proved that he knew or had reason to suspect that the step taken would contravene subsection (1).

But this subsection only applies if sufficient evidence is adduced to raise an issue as to whether the person had the knowledge or reason mentioned.

(6) A person guilty of an offence under this section is liable –

(a) on summary conviction to imprisonment for a term not exceeding six months, or a fine not exceeding the statutory maximum, or both,

(b) on conviction on indictment, to imprisonment for a term not exceeding twelve months, or a fine, or both.

(7) In any proceedings under this section –

(a) a report by a British consular officer or a deposition made before a British consular officer and authenticated under the signature of that officer is admissible, upon proof that the officer or the deponent cannot be found in the United Kingdom, as evidence of the matters stated in it, and

(b) it is not necessary to prove the signature or official character of the person who appears to have signed any such report or deposition.

Amendment: SI 2011/1740.

86 Power to modify sections 83 and 85

(1) Regulations may provide for section 83 not to apply if –

(a) the adopters or (as the case may be) prospective adopters are natural parents, natural relatives or guardians of the child in question (or one of them is), or

(b)   the British resident in question is a partner of a parent of the child,

and any prescribed conditions are met.

(2) Regulations may provide for section 85(1) to apply with modifications, or not to apply, if –

(a)   the prospective adopters are parents, relatives or guardians of the child in question (or one of them is), or

(b)   the prospective adopter is a partner of a parent of the child,

and any prescribed conditions are met.

(3) On the occasion of the first exercise of the power to make regulations under this section –

(a)   the statutory instrument containing the regulations is not to be made unless a draft of the instrument has been laid before, and approved by a resolution of, each House of Parliament, and

(b)   accordingly section 140(2) does not apply to the instrument.

(4) In this section, 'prescribed' means prescribed by regulations and 'regulations' means regulations made by the Secretary of State after consultation with the Assembly.

Overseas adoptions

87 Overseas adoptions

(1) In this Act, 'overseas adoption' –

(a)   means an adoption of a description specified in an order made by the Secretary of State, being a description of adoptions effected under the law of any country or territory outside the British Islands, but

(b)   does not include a Convention adoption.

(2) Regulations may prescribe the requirements that ought to be met by an adoption of any description effected after the commencement of the regulations for it to be an overseas adoption for the purposes of this Act.

(3) At any time when such regulations have effect, the Secretary of State must exercise his powers under this section so as to secure that subsequently effected adoptions of any description are not overseas adoptions for the purposes of this Act if he considers that they are not likely within a reasonable time to meet the prescribed requirements.

(4) In this section references to this Act include the Adoption Act 1976.

(5) An order under this section may contain provision as to the manner in which evidence of any overseas adoption may be given.

(6) In this section –

'adoption' means an adoption of a child or of a person who was a child at the time the adoption was applied for, 'regulations' means regulations made by the Secretary of State after consultation with the Assembly.

Miscellaneous

88 Modification of section 67 for Hague Convention adoptions

(1) If the High Court is satisfied, on an application under this section, that each of the following conditions is met in the case of a Convention adoption, it may direct that section 67(3) does not apply, or does not apply to any extent specified in the direction.

(2) The conditions are –

(a) that under the law of the country in which the adoption was effected, the adoption is not a full adoption,

(b) that the consents referred to in Article 4(c) and (d) of the Convention have not been given for a full adoption or that the United Kingdom is not the receiving State (within the meaning of Article 2 of the Convention),

(c) that it would be more favourable to the adopted child for a direction to be given under subsection (1).

(3) A full adoption is an adoption by virtue of which the child is to be treated in law as not being the child of any person other than the adopters or adopter.

(4) In relation to a direction under this section and an application for it, sections 59 and 60 of the Family Law Act 1986 (declarations under Part 3 of that Act as to marital status) apply as they apply in relation to a direction under that Part and an application for such a direction.

89 Annulment etc of overseas or Hague Convention adoptions

(1) The High Court may, on an application under this subsection, by order annul a Convention adoption or Convention adoption order on the ground that the adoption is contrary to public policy.

(2) The High Court may, on an application under this subsection –

(a) by order provide for an overseas adoption or a determination under section 91 to cease to be valid on the ground that the adoption or determination is contrary to public policy or that the authority which purported to authorise the adoption or make the determination was not competent to entertain the case, or

(b) decide the extent, if any, to which a determination under section 91 has been affected by a subsequent determination under that section.

(3) The High Court may, in any proceedings in that court, decide that an overseas adoption or a determination under section 91 is to be treated, for the purposes of those proceedings, as invalid on either of the grounds mentioned in subsection (2)(*a*).

(4) Subject to the preceding provisions, the validity of a Convention adoption, Convention adoption order or overseas adoption or a determination under section 91 cannot be called in question in proceedings in any court in England and Wales.

90 Section 89: supplementary

(1) Any application for an order under section 89 or a decision under subsection (2)(b) or (3) of that section must be made in the prescribed manner and within any prescribed period.

'Prescribed' means prescribed by rules.

(2) No application may be made under section 89(1) in respect of an adoption unless immediately before the application is made –

(a)   the person adopted, or
(b)   the adopters or adopter,

habitually reside in England and Wales.

(3) In deciding in pursuance of section 89 whether such an authority as is mentioned in section 91 was competent to entertain a particular case, a court is bound by any finding of fact made by the authority and stated by the authority to be so made for the purpose of determining whether the authority was competent to entertain the case.

91 Overseas determinations and orders

(1) Subsection (2) applies where any authority of a Convention country (other than the United Kingdom) or of the Channel Islands, the Isle of Man or any British overseas territory has power under the law of that country or territory –

(a)   to authorise, or review the authorisation of, an adoption order made in that country or territory, or
(b)   to give or review a decision revoking or annulling such an order or a Convention adoption.

(2) If the authority makes a determination in the exercise of that power, the determination is to have effect for the purpose of effecting, confirming or terminating the adoption in question or, as the case may be, confirming its termination.

(3) Subsection (2) is subject to section 89 and to any subsequent determination having effect under that subsection.

91A Power to charge

(1) This section applies to adoptions to which –

(a)   section 83 applies, or
(b)   regulations made under section 1 of the Adoption (Intercountry Aspects) Act 1999 apply.

(2) The Secretary of State may charge a fee to adopters for services provided or to be provided by him in relation to adoptions to which this section applies.

(3) The Assembly may charge a fee to adopters for services provided or to be provided by it as the Central Authority in relation to adoptions to which this section applies by virtue of subsection (1)(b).

(4) The Secretary of State and the Assembly may determine the level of fee as he or it sees fit, and may in particular –

(a) charge a flat fee or charge different fees in different cases or descriptions of case, and
(b) in any case or description of case, waive a fee.

(5) But the Secretary of State and the Assembly must each secure that, taking one financial year with another, the income from fees under this section does not exceed the total cost to him or, as the case may be, to it of providing the services in relation to which the fees are imposed.

(6) In this section –

references to adoptions and adopters include prospective adoptions and prospective adopters,
'Central Authority' is to be construed in accordance with section 2 of the Adoption (Intercountry Aspects) Act 1999,
'financial year' means a period of twelve months ending with 31st March.

Amendment: Children and Adoption Act 2006, s 13.

Chapter 7
Miscellaneous

Restrictions

92 Restriction on arranging adoptions etc

(1) A person who is neither an adoption agency nor acting in pursuance of an order of the High Court must not take any of the steps mentioned in subsection (2).

(2) The steps are –

(a) asking a person other than an adoption agency to provide a child for adoption,
(b) asking a person other than an adoption agency to provide prospective adopters for a child,
(c) offering to find a child for adoption,
(d) offering a child for adoption to a person other than an adoption agency,
(e) handing over a child to any person other than an adoption agency with a view to the child's adoption by that or another person,
(f) receiving a child handed over to him in contravention of paragraph (e),

(g)   entering into an agreement with any person for the adoption of a child, or for the purpose of facilitating the adoption of a child, where no adoption agency is acting on behalf of the child in the adoption,

(h)   initiating or taking part in negotiations of which the purpose is the conclusion of an agreement within paragraph (g),

(i)   causing another person to take any of the steps mentioned in paragraphs (a) to (h).

(3) Subsection (1) does not apply to a person taking any of the steps mentioned in paragraphs (d), (e), (g), (h) and (i) of subsection (2) if the following condition is met.

(4) The condition is that –

(a)   the prospective adopters are parents, relatives or guardians of the child (or one of them is), or

(b)   the prospective adopter is the partner of a parent of the child.

(5) References to an adoption agency in subsection (2) include a prescribed person outside the United Kingdom exercising functions corresponding to those of an adoption agency, if the functions are being exercised in prescribed circumstances in respect of the child in question.

(6) The Secretary of State may, after consultation with the Assembly, by order make any amendments of subsections (1) to (4), and any consequential amendments of this Act, which he considers necessary or expedient.

(7) In this section –

(a)   'agreement' includes an arrangement (whether or not enforceable),

(b)   'prescribed' means prescribed by regulations made by the Secretary of State after consultation with the Assembly.

93 Offence of breaching restrictions under section 92

(1) If a person contravenes section 92(1), he is guilty of an offence; and, if that person is an adoption society, the person who manages the society is also guilty of the offence.

(2) A person is not guilty of an offence under subsection (1) of taking the step mentioned in paragraph (f) of section 92(2) unless it is proved that he knew or had reason to suspect that the child was handed over to him in contravention of paragraph (e) of that subsection.

(3) A person is not guilty of an offence under subsection (1) of causing a person to take any of the steps mentioned in paragraphs (a) to (h) of section 92(2) unless it is proved that he knew or had reason to suspect that the step taken would contravene the paragraph in question.

(4) But subsections (2) and (3) only apply if sufficient evidence is adduced to raise an issue as to whether the person had the knowledge or reason mentioned.

(5) A person guilty of an offence under this section is liable on summary conviction to imprisonment for a term not exceeding six months, or a fine not exceeding £10,000, or both.

94 Restriction on reports

(1) A person who is not within a prescribed description may not, in any prescribed circumstances, prepare a report for any person about the suitability of a child for adoption or of a person to adopt a child or about the adoption, or placement for adoption, of a child.

'Prescribed' means prescribed by regulations made by the Secretary of State after consultation with the Assembly.

(2) If a person –

(a) contravenes subsection (1), or
(b) causes a person to prepare a report, or submits to any person a report which has been prepared, in contravention of that subsection,

he is guilty of an offence.

(3) If a person who works for an adoption society –

(a) contravenes subsection (1), or
(b) causes a person to prepare a report, or submits to any person a report which has been prepared, in contravention of that subsection,

the person who manages the society is also guilty of the offence.

(4) A person is not guilty of an offence under subsection (2)(*b*) unless it is proved that he knew or had reason to suspect that the report would be, or had been, prepared in contravention of subsection (1).

But this subsection only applies if sufficient evidence is adduced to raise an issue as to whether the person had the knowledge or reason mentioned.

(5) A person guilty of an offence under this section is liable on summary conviction to imprisonment for a term not exceeding six months, or a fine not exceeding level 5 on the standard scale, or both.

95 Prohibition of certain payments

(1) This section applies to any payment (other than an excepted payment) which is made for or in consideration of –

(a) the adoption of a child,
(b) giving any consent required in connection with the adoption of a child,
(c) removing from the United Kingdom a child who is a Commonwealth citizen, or is habitually resident in the United Kingdom, to a place outside the British Islands for the purpose of adoption,
(d) a person (who is neither an adoption agency nor acting in pursuance of an order of the High Court) taking any step mentioned in section 92(2),

(e) preparing, causing to be prepared or submitting a report the preparation of which contravenes section 94(1).

(2) In this section and section 96, removing a child from the United Kingdom has the same meaning as in section 85.

(3) Any person who –

(a) makes any payment to which this section applies,
(b) agrees or offers to make any such payment, or
(c) receives or agrees to receive or attempts to obtain any such payment,

is guilty of an offence.

(4) A person guilty of an offence under this section is liable on summary conviction to imprisonment for a term not exceeding six months, or a fine not exceeding £10,000, or both.

96 Excepted payments

(1) A payment is an excepted payment if it is made by virtue of, or in accordance with provision made by or under, this Act, the Adoption (Scotland) Act 1978, the Adoption and Children (Scotland) Act 2007 (asp 4) or the Adoption (Northern Ireland) Order 1987 (SI 1987/2203 (NI 22)).

(2) A payment is an excepted payment if it is made to a registered adoption society by –

(a) a parent or guardian of a child, or
(b) a person who adopts or proposes to adopt a child,

in respect of expenses reasonably incurred by the society in connection with the adoption or proposed adoption of the child.

(3) A payment is an excepted payment if it is made in respect of any legal or medical expenses incurred or to be incurred by any person in connection with an application to a court which he has made or proposes to make for an adoption order, a placement order, or an order under section 26 or 84.

(4) A payment made as mentioned in section 95(1)(c) is an excepted payment if –

(a) the condition in section 85(2) is met, and
(b) the payment is made in respect of the travel and accommodation expenses reasonably incurred in removing the child from the United Kingdom for the purpose of adoption.

Amendment: SI 2011/1740.

97 Sections 92 to 96: interpretation

In sections 92 to 96 –

(a) 'adoption agency' includes a Scottish or Northern Irish adoption agency,
(b) 'payment' includes reward,

(c)   references to adoption are to the adoption of persons, wherever they may be habitually resident, effected under the law of any country or territory, whether within or outside the British Islands.

Information

98 Pre-commencement adoptions: information

(1) Regulations under section 9 may make provision for the purpose of –

(a)   assisting persons adopted before the appointed day who have attained the age of 18 to obtain information in relation to their adoption, and
(b)   facilitating contact between such persons and their relatives.

(2) For that purpose the regulations may confer functions on –

(a)   registered adoption support agencies,
(b)   the Registrar General,
(c)   adoption agencies.

(3) For that purpose the regulations may –

(a)   authorise or require any person mentioned in subsection (2) to disclose information,
(b)   authorise or require the disclosure of information contained in records kept under section 8 of the Public Records Act 1958 (court records),

and may impose conditions on the disclosure of information, including conditions restricting its further disclosure.

(4) The regulations may authorise the charging of prescribed fees by any person mentioned in subsection (2) or in respect of the disclosure of information under subsection (3)(b).

(5) An authorisation or requirement to disclose information by virtue of subsection (3)(a) has effect in spite of any restriction on the disclosure of information in Chapter 5.

(6) The making of regulations by virtue of subsections (2) to (4) which relate to the Registrar General requires the approval of the Secretary of State.

(7) In this section –

'appointed day' means the day appointed for the commencement of sections 56 to 65,
'registered adoption support agency' means an adoption support agency in respect of which a person is registered under Part 2 of the Care Standards Act 2000,
'relative', in relation to an adopted person, means any person who (but for his adoption) would be related to him by blood (including half-blood), marriage or civil partnership.

Amendments: Civil Partnership Act 2004, s 79(1), (10); SI 2008/678.

Proceedings

99 Proceedings for offences

Proceedings for an offence by virtue of section 9 or 59 may not, without the written consent of the Attorney General, be taken by any person other than Her Majesty's Chief Inspector of Education, Children's Services and Skills or the Assembly.

100 Appeals

In section 94 of the 1989 Act (appeals under that Act), in subsections (1)(a) and (2), after 'this Act' there is inserted 'or the Adoption and Children Act 2002'.

101 Privacy

(1) Proceedings under this Act in the High Court or a County Court may be heard and determined in private.

(2)–(3) *(amend Administration of Justice Act 1960, s 12(1) and Children Act 1989, s 97(1), (2)).*

The Children and Family Court Advisory and Support Service

102 Officers of the Service

(1) For the purposes of –

    (a)   any relevant application,
    (b)   the signification by any person of any consent to placement or adoption,

rules must provide for the appointment in prescribed cases of an officer of the Children and Family Court Advisory and Support Service ('the Service') or a Welsh family proceedings officer.

(2) The rules may provide for the appointment of such an officer in other circumstances in which it appears to the Lord Chancellor to be necessary or expedient to do so.

(3) The rules may provide for the officer –

    (a)   to act on behalf of the child upon the hearing of any relevant application, with the duty of safeguarding the interests of the child in the prescribed manner,
    (b)   where the court so requests, to prepare a report on matters relating to the welfare of the child in question,
    (c)   to witness documents which signify consent to placement or adoption,
    (d)   to perform prescribed functions.

(4) A report prepared in pursuance of the rules on matters relating to the welfare of a child must –

    (a)   deal with prescribed matters (unless the court orders otherwise), and
    (b)   be made in the manner required by the court.

(5) A person who –

(a) in the case of an application for the making, varying or revocation of a placement order, is employed by the local authority which made the application,

(b) in the case of an application for an adoption order in respect of a child who was placed for adoption, is employed by the adoption agency which placed him, or

(c) is within a prescribed description,

is not to be appointed under subsection (1) or (2).

(6) In this section, 'relevant application' means an application for –

(a) the making, varying or revocation of a placement order,

(b) the making of an order under section 26, or the varying or revocation of such an order,

(c) the making of an adoption order, or

(d) the making of an order under section 84.

(7) Rules may make provision as to the assistance which the court may require an officer of the Service or a Welsh family proceedings officer to give to it.

(8) In this section and section 103 'Welsh family proceedings officer' has the meaning given by section 35 of the Children Act 2004.

Amendments: Children Act 2004, s 40, Sch 3, paras 15, 16.

103 Right of officers of the Service to have access to adoption agency records

(1) Where an officer of the Service or a Welsh family proceedings officer has been appointed to act under section 102(1), he has the right at all reasonable times to examine and take copies of any records of, or held by, an adoption agency which were compiled in connection with the making, or proposed making, by any person of any application under this Part in respect of the child concerned.

(2) Where an officer of the Service or a Welsh family proceedings officer takes a copy of any record which he is entitled to examine under this section, that copy or any part of it is admissible as evidence of any matter referred to in any –

(a) report which he makes to the court in the proceedings in question, or

(b) evidence which he gives in those proceedings.

(3) Subsection (2) has effect regardless of any enactment or rule of law which would otherwise prevent the record in question being admissible in evidence.

Amendments: Children Act 2004, s 40, Sch 3, paras 15, 17.

Evidence

104 Evidence of consent

(1) If a document signifying any consent which is required by this Part to be given is witnessed in accordance with rules, it is to be admissible in evidence without further proof of the signature of the person by whom it was executed.

(2) A document signifying any such consent which purports to be witnessed in accordance with rules is to be presumed to be so witnessed, and to have been executed and witnessed on the date and at the place specified in the document, unless the contrary is proved.

****

General

109 Avoiding delay

(1) In proceedings in which a question may arise as to whether an adoption order or placement order should be made, or any other question with respect to such an order, the court must (in the light of any rules made by virtue of subsection (2)) –

    (a)   draw up a timetable with a view to determining such a question without delay, and

    (b)   give such directions as it considers appropriate for the purpose of ensuring that the timetable is adhered to.

(2) Rules may –

    (a)   prescribe periods within which prescribed steps must be taken in relation to such proceedings, and

    (b)   make other provision with respect to such proceedings for the purpose of ensuring that such questions are determined without delay.

110 Service of notices etc

Any notice or information required to be given by virtue of this Act may be given by post.

PART 2
AMENDMENTS OF THE CHILDREN ACT 1989

111 Parental responsibility of unmarried father

(1)–(6) *(amend Children Act 1989 (c.41), ss 2(2), 4(1), 104(2), (3), inserts s 4(1A), (1B), (2A) and substitutes s 4(3)).*

(7) Paragraph (a) of section 4(1) of the 1989 Act, as substituted by subsection (2) of this section, does not confer parental responsibility on a man who was registered under an enactment referred to in paragraph (a), (b) or (c) of section 4(1A) of that Act, as inserted by subsection (3) of this section, before the commencement of subsection (3) in relation to that paragraph.

****

121 Care plans

(1), (2) *(insert Children Act 1989 (c.41) ss 31(1A), 31A).*

(3) If –

(a) before subsection (2) comes into force, a care order has been made in respect of a child and a plan for the future care of the child has been prepared in connection with the making of the order by the local authority designated in the order, and

(b) on the day on which that subsection comes into force the order is in force, or would be in force but for section 29(1) of this Act,

the plan is to have effect as if made under section 31A of the 1989 Act.

****

PART 3
MISCELLANEOUS AND FINAL PROVISIONS

Chapter 1
Miscellaneous

Advertisements in the United Kingdom

123 Restriction on advertisements etc

(1) A person must not –

(a) publish or distribute an advertisement or information to which this section applies, or

(b) cause such an advertisement or information to be published or distributed.

(2) This section applies to an advertisement indicating that –

(a) the parent or guardian of a child wants the child to be adopted,

(b) a person wants to adopt a child,

(c) a person other than an adoption agency is willing to take any step mentioned in paragraphs (a) to (e), (g) and (h) and (so far as relating to those paragraphs) (i) of section 92(2),

(d) a person other than an adoption agency is willing to receive a child handed over to him with a view to the child's adoption by him or another, or

(e) a person is willing to remove a child from the United Kingdom for the purposes of adoption.

(3) This section applies to –

(a) information about how to do anything which, if done, would constitute an offence under section 85 or 93, Article 11 or 58 of the Adoption (Northern Ireland) Order 1987 (SI 1987/2203 (NI 22)) or section 60 or 75 of the Adoption and Children (Scotland) Act 2007 (asp 4) (whether or not the information includes a warning that doing the thing in question may constitute an offence),

(b)   information about a particular child as a child available for adoption.

(4) For the purposes of this section and section 124 –

(a)   publishing or distributing an advertisement or information means publishing it or distributing it to the public and includes doing so by electronic means (for example, by means of the internet),

(b)   the public includes selected members of the public as well as the public generally or any section of the public.

(5) Subsection (1) does not apply to publication or distribution by or on behalf of an adoption agency.

(6) The Secretary of State may by order make any amendments of this section which he considers necessary or expedient in consequence of any developments in technology relating to publishing or distributing advertisements or other information by electronic or electro-magnetic means.

(7) References to an adoption agency in this section include a prescribed person outside the United Kingdom exercising functions corresponding to those of an adoption agency, if the functions are being exercised in prescribed circumstances.

'Prescribed' means prescribed by regulations made by the Secretary of State.

(8) Before exercising the power conferred by subsection (6) or (7), the Secretary of State must consult the Scottish Ministers, the Department of Health, Social Services and Public Safety and the Assembly.

(9) In this section –

(a)   'adoption agency' includes a Scottish or Northern Irish adoption agency,

(b)   references to adoption are to the adoption of persons, wherever they may be habitually resident, effected under the law of any country or territory, whether within or outside the British Islands.

Amendments: Adoption and Children (Scotland) Act 2007, s 120(1), (2), Sch 2, para 12, Sch 3 (the repeal and insertion of words in s 123(3)(a) is extended to England, Wales and Northern Ireland by the Adoption and Children (Scotland) Act 2007 (Consequential Modifications) Order 2011, SI 2011/1740, art 3, Sch 2, Pt 1, para 5, Pt 3).

124 Offence of breaching restriction under section 123

(1) A person who contravenes section 123(1) is guilty of an offence.

(2) A person is not guilty of an offence under this section unless it is proved that he knew or had reason to suspect that section 123 applied to the advertisement or information.

But this subsection only applies if sufficient evidence is adduced to raise an issue as to whether the person had the knowledge or reason mentioned.

(3) A person guilty of an offence under this section is liable on summary conviction to imprisonment for a term not exceeding three months, or a fine not exceeding level 5 on the standard scale, or both.

Adoption and Children Act Register

125 Adoption and Children Act Register

(1) Her Majesty may by Order in Council make provision for the Secretary of State to establish and maintain a register, to be called the Adoption and Children Act Register, containing –

 (a) prescribed information about children who are suitable for adoption and prospective adopters who are suitable to adopt a child,

 (b) prescribed information about persons included in the register in pursuance of paragraph (a) in respect of things occurring after their inclusion.

(2) For the purpose of giving assistance in finding persons with whom children may be placed for purposes other than adoption, an Order under this section may –

 (a) provide for the register to contain information about such persons and the children who may be placed with them, and

 (b) apply any of the other provisions of this group of sections (that is, this section and sections 126 to 131), with or without modifications.

(3) The register is not to be open to public inspection or search.

(4) An Order under this section may make provision about the retention of information in the register.

(5) Information is to be kept in the register in any form the Secretary of State considers appropriate.

Commencement: (not yet in force).

126 Use of an organisation to establish the register

(1) The Secretary of State may make an arrangement with an organisation under which any function of his under an Order under section 125 of establishing and maintaining the register, and disclosing information entered in, or compiled from information entered in, the register to any person is performed wholly or partly by the organisation on his behalf.

(2) The arrangement may include provision for payments to be made to the organisation by the Secretary of State.

(3) If the Secretary of State makes an arrangement under this section with an organisation, the organisation is to perform the functions exercisable by virtue of this section in accordance with any directions given by the Secretary of State and the directions may be of general application (or general application in any part of Great Britain) or be special directions.

(4) An exercise of the Secretary of State's powers under subsection (1) or (3) requires the agreement of the Scottish Ministers (if the register applies to Scotland) and of the Assembly (if the register applies to Wales).

(5) References in this group of sections to the registration organisation are to any organisation for the time being performing functions in respect of the register by virtue of arrangements under this section.

Commencement: (not yet in force).

127 Use of an organisation as agency for payments

(1) An Order under section 125 may authorise an organisation with which an arrangement is made under section 126 to act as agent for the payment or receipt of sums payable by adoption agencies to other adoption agencies and may require adoption agencies to pay or receive such sums through the organisation.

(2) The organisation is to perform the functions exercisable by virtue of this section in accordance with any directions given by the Secretary of State; and the directions may be of general application (or general application in any part of Great Britain) or be special directions.

(3) An exercise of the Secretary of State's power to give directions under subsection (2) requires the agreement of the Scottish Ministers (if any payment agency provision applies to Scotland) and of the Assembly (if any payment agency provision applies to Wales).

Commencement: (not yet in force).

128 Supply of information for the register

(1) An Order under section 125 may require adoption agencies to give prescribed information to the Secretary of State or the registration organisation for entry in the register.

(2) Information is to be given to the Secretary of State or the registration organisation when required by the Order and in the prescribed form and manner.

(3) An Order under section 125 may require an agency giving information which is entered on the register to pay a prescribed fee to the Secretary of State or the registration organisation.

(4) But an adoption agency is not to disclose any information to the Secretary of State or the registration organisation –

   (a)   about prospective adopters who are suitable to adopt a child, or persons who were included in the register as such prospective adopters, without their consent,
   (b)   about children suitable for adoption, or persons who were included in the register as such children, without the consent of the prescribed person.

(5) Consent under subsection (4) is to be given in the prescribed form.

Commencement: (not yet in force).

129 Disclosure of information

(1) *Information entered in the register, or compiled from information entered in the register, may only be disclosed under subsection (2) or (3).*

(2) *Prescribed information entered in the register may be disclosed by the Secretary of State or the registration organisation –*

    (a) *where an adoption agency is acting on behalf of a child who is suitable for adoption, to the agency to assist in finding prospective adopters with whom it would be appropriate for the child to be placed,*

    (b) *where an adoption agency is acting on behalf of prospective adopters who are suitable to adopt a child, to the agency to assist in finding a child appropriate for adoption by them.*

(3) *Prescribed information entered in the register, or compiled from information entered in the register, may be disclosed by the Secretary of State or the registration organisation to any prescribed person for use for statistical or research purposes, or for other prescribed purposes.*

(4) *An Order under section 125 may prescribe the steps to be taken by adoption agencies in respect of information received by them by virtue of subsection (2).*

(5) *Subsection (1) does not apply –*

    (a) *to a disclosure of information with the authority of the Secretary of State, or*

    (b) *to a disclosure by the registration organisation of prescribed information to the Scottish Ministers (if the register applies to Scotland) or the Assembly (if the register applies to Wales).*

(6) *Information disclosed to any person under subsection (2) or (3) may be given on any prescribed terms or conditions.*

(7) *An Order under section 125 may, in prescribed circumstances, require a prescribed fee to be paid to the Secretary of State or the registration organisation –*

    (a) *by a prescribed adoption agency in respect of information disclosed under subsection (2), or*

    (b) *by a person to whom information is disclosed under subsection (3).*

(8) *If any information entered in the register is disclosed to a person in contravention of subsection (1), the person disclosing it is guilty of an offence.*

(9) *A person guilty of an offence under subsection (8) is liable on summary conviction to imprisonment for a term not exceeding three months, or a fine not exceeding level 5 on the standard scale, or both.*

Commencement: (not yet in force).

130 Territorial application

(1) *In this group of sections, 'adoption agency' means –*

    (a) *a local authority in England,*

   (b)   a registered adoption society whose principal office is in England.

(2)   An Order under section 125 may provide for any requirements imposed on adoption agencies in respect of the register to apply –

   (a)   to Scottish local authorities and to voluntary organisations providing a registered adoption service,
   (b)   to local authorities in Wales and to registered adoption societies whose principal offices are in Wales,

and, in relation to the register, references to adoption agencies in this group of sections include any authorities or societies mentioned in paragraphs (a) and (b) to which an Order under that section applies those requirements.

(3)   For the purposes of this group of sections, references to the register applying to Scotland or Wales are to those requirements applying as mentioned in paragraph (a) or, as the case may be, (b) of subsection (2).

(4)   An Order under section 125 may apply any provision made by virtue of section 127 –

   (a)   to Scottish local authorities and to voluntary organisations providing a registered adoption service,
   (b)   to local authorities in Wales and to registered adoption societies whose principal offices are in Wales.

(5)   For the purposes of this group of sections, references to any payment agency provision applying to Scotland or Wales are to provision made by virtue of section 127 applying as mentioned in paragraph (a) or, as the case may be, (b) of subsection (4).

Commencement: (not yet in force).

131 Supplementary

(1)   In this group of sections –

   (a)   'organisation' includes a public body and a private or voluntary organisation,
   (b)   'prescribed' means prescribed by an Order under section 125,
   (c)   'the register' means the Adoption and Children Act Register,
   (d)   'Scottish local authority' means a local authority within the meaning of the Public Services Reform (Scotland) Act 2010 (asp 8)[1],
   (e)   'voluntary organisation providing a registered adoption service' has the same meaning as in section 144(3).

(2)   For the purposes of this group of sections –

   (a)   a child is suitable for adoption if an adoption agency is satisfied that the child ought to be placed for adoption,
   (b)   prospective adopters are suitable to adopt a child if an adoption agency is satisfied that they are suitable to have a child placed with them for adoption.

(3) Nothing authorised or required to be done by virtue of this group of sections constitutes an offence under section 93, 94 or 95.

(4) No recommendation to make an Order under section 125 is to be made to Her Majesty in Council unless a draft has been laid before and approved by resolution of each House of Parliament.

(5) If any provision made by an Order under section 125 would, if it were included in an Act of the Scottish Parliament, be within the legislative competence of that Parliament, no recommendation to make the Order is to be made to Her Majesty in Council unless a draft has been laid before, and approved by resolution of, the Parliament.

(6) No recommendation to make an Order under section 125 containing any provision in respect of the register is to be made to Her Majesty in Council if the register applies to Wales or the Order would provide for the register to apply to Wales, unless a draft has been laid before, and approved by resolution of, the Assembly.

(7) No recommendation to make an Order under section 125 containing any provision by virtue of section 127 is to be made to Her Majesty in Council if any payment agency provision applies to Wales or the Order would provide for any payment agency provision to apply to Wales, unless a draft has been laid before, and approved by resolution of, the Assembly.

Commencement: (not yet in force).

Amendment: Words substituted: Public Services Reform (Scotland) Act 2010 (Consequential Modifications of Enactments) Order 2011, SI 2011/2581, art 2, Sch 2, Pt 1, para 4(a).

137 Extension of the Hague Convention to British overseas territories

(1) Her Majesty may by Order in Council provide for giving effect to the Convention in any British overseas territory.

(2) An Order in Council under subsection (1) in respect of any British overseas territory may, in particular, make any provision corresponding to provision which in relation to any part of Great Britain is made by the Adoption (Intercountry Aspects) Act 1999 (c. 18) or may be made by regulations under section 1 of that Act.

(3)–(7) (amend British Nationality Act 1981 (c.61)).

138 Proceedings in Great Britain

Proceedings for an offence by virtue of section 9, 59, 93, 94, 95 or 129 –

  (a) may not be brought more than six years after the commission of the offence but, subject to that,
  (b) may be brought within a period of six months from the date on which evidence sufficient in the opinion of the prosecutor to warrant the proceedings came to his knowledge.

****

Amendments etc.

139 Amendments, transitional and transitory provisions, savings and repeals

(1) Schedule 3 (minor and consequential amendments) is to have effect.

(2) Schedule 4 (transitional and transitory provisions and savings) is to have effect.

(3) The enactments set out in Schedule 5 are repealed to the extent specified.

Chapter 2
Final provisions

140 Orders, rules and regulations

(1) Any power to make subordinate legislation conferred by this Act on the Lord Chancellor, the Secretary of State, the Scottish Ministers, the Assembly or the Registrar General is exercisable by statutory instrument.

(2) A statutory instrument containing subordinate legislation made under any provision of this Act (other than section 14 or 148 or an instrument to which subsection (3) applies) is to be subject to annulment in pursuance of a resolution of either House of Parliament.

(3) A statutory instrument containing subordinate legislation –

    (a)   under section 9 which includes provision made by virtue of section 45(2),
    (b)   under section 92(6), 94 or 123(6), or
    (c)   which adds to, replaces or omits any part of the text of an Act,

is not to be made unless a draft of the instrument has been laid before, and approved by resolution of, each House of Parliament.

(4) Subsections (2) and (3) do not apply to an Order in Council or to subordinate legislation made –

    (a)   by the Scottish Ministers, or
    (b)   by the Assembly, unless made jointly by the Secretary of State and the Assembly.

(5) A statutory instrument containing regulations under section 63(2) made by the Scottish Ministers is to be subject to annulment in pursuance of a resolution of the Scottish Parliament.

(6) The power of the Department of Health, Social Services and Public Safety to make regulations under section 63(2) is to be exercisable by statutory rule for the purposes of the Statutory Rules (Northern Ireland) Order 1979 (SI 1979/ 1573 (NI 12)); and any such regulations are to be subject to negative resolution within the meaning of section 41(6) of the Interpretation Act (Northern Ireland) 1954 as if they were statutory instruments within the meaning of that Act.

(7) Subordinate legislation made under this Act may make different provision for different purposes.

(8) A power to make subordinate legislation under this Act (as well as being exercisable in relation to all cases to which it extends) may be exercised in relation to –

(a)   those cases subject to specified exceptions, or
(b)   a particular case or class of case.

(9) In this section, 'subordinate legislation' does not include a direction.

141 Rules of procedure

(1) Family Procedure Rules may make provision[1] in respect of any matter to be prescribed by rules made by virtue of this Act and dealing generally with all matters of procedure.

(2) (*repealed*)

(3) In the case of an application for a placement order, for the variation or revocation of such an order, or for an adoption order, the rules must require any person mentioned in subsection (4) to be notified –

(a)   of the date and place where the application will be heard, and
(b)   of the fact that, unless the person wishes or the court requires, the person need not attend.

(4) The persons referred to in subsection (3) are –

(a)   in the case of a placement order, every person who can be found whose consent to the making of the order is required under subsection (3)(a) of section 21 (or would be required but for subsection (3)(b) of that section) or, if no such person can be found, any relative prescribed by rules who can be found,
(b)   in the case of a variation or revocation of a placement order, every person who can be found whose consent to the making of the placement order was required under subsection (3)(a) of section 21 (or would have been required but for subsection (3)(b) of that section),
(c)   in the case of an adoption order –
      (i)   every person who can be found whose consent to the making of the order is required under subsection (2)(a) of section 47 (or would be required but for subsection (2)(c) of that section) or, if no such person can be found, any relative prescribed by rules who can be found,
      (ii)   every person who has consented to the making of the order under section 20 (and has not withdrawn the consent) unless he has given a notice under subsection (4)(a) of that section which has effect,
      (iii) every person who, if leave were given under section 47(5), would be entitled to oppose the making of the order.

(5) Rules made in respect of magistrates' courts may provide –

(a)   for enabling any fact tending to establish the identity of a child with a child to whom a document relates to be proved by affidavit, and

(b)   for excluding or restricting in relation to any facts that may be so
proved the power of a justice of the peace to compel the attendance of
witnesses.

(6) Rules may, for the purposes of the law relating to contempt of court,
authorise the publication in such circumstances as may be specified of
information relating to proceedings held in private involving children.

Amendments: Courts Act 2003, s 109(1), (3), Sch 8, para 413(1), Sch 103; Children Act 2004,
s 62(6).

142 Supplementary and consequential provision

(1) The appropriate Minister may by order make –

(a)   any supplementary, incidental or consequential provision,
(b)   any transitory, transitional or saving provision,

which he considers necessary or expedient for the purposes of, in consequence
of or for giving full effect to any provision of this Act.

(2) For the purposes of subsection (1), where any provision of an order extends
to England and Wales, and Scotland or Northern Ireland, the appropriate
Minister in relation to the order is the Secretary of State.

(3) Before making an order under subsection (1) containing provision which
would, if included in an Act of the Scottish Parliament, be within the legislative
competence of that Parliament, the appropriate Minister must consult the
Scottish Ministers.

(4) Subsection (5) applies to any power of the Lord Chancellor, the Secretary
of State or the Assembly to make regulations, rules or an order by virtue of any
other provision of this Act or of Her Majesty to make an Order in Council by
virtue of section 125.

(5) The power may be exercised so as to make –

(a)   any supplementary, incidental or consequential provision,
(b)   any transitory, transitional or saving provision,

which the person exercising the power considers necessary or expedient.

(6) The provision which may be made under subsection (1) or (5) includes
provision modifying Schedule 4 or amending or repealing any enactment or
instrument.

In relation to an Order in Council, 'enactment' in this subsection includes an
enactment comprised in, or in an instrument made under, an Act of the
Scottish Parliament.

(7) The power of the Registrar General to make regulations under Chapter 5
of Part 1 may, with the approval of the Secretary of State, be exercised so as to
make –

(a)   any supplementary, incidental or consequential provision,
(b)   any transitory, transitional or saving provision,

which the Registrar General considers necessary or expedient.

Amendments: SI 2008/678.

143 Offences by bodies corporate and unincorporated bodies

(1) Where an offence under this Act committed by a body corporate is proved to have been committed with the consent or connivance of, or to be attributable to any neglect on the part of, any director, manager, secretary or other similar officer of the body, or a person purporting to act in any such capacity, that person as well as the body is guilty of the offence and liable to be proceeded against and punished accordingly.

(2) Where the affairs of a body corporate are managed by its members, subsection (1) applies in relation to the acts and defaults of a member in connection with his functions of management as it applies to a director of a body corporate.

(3) Proceedings for an offence alleged to have been committed under this Act by an unincorporated body are to be brought in the name of that body (and not in that of any of its members) and, for the purposes of any such proceedings in England and Wales or Northern Ireland, any rules of court relating to the service of documents have effect as if that body were a corporation.

(4) A fine imposed on an unincorporated body on its conviction of an offence under this Act is to be paid out of the funds of that body.

(5) If an unincorporated body is charged with an offence under this Act –

 (a) in England and Wales, section 33 of the Criminal Justice Act 1925 and Schedule 3 to the Magistrates' Courts Act 1980 (procedure on charge of an offence against a corporation),
 (b) in Northern Ireland, section 18 of the Criminal Justice Act (Northern Ireland) 1945 and Schedule 4 to the Magistrates' Courts (Northern Ireland) Order 1981 (SI 1981/1675 (NI 26)) (procedure on charge of an offence against a corporation),

have effect in like manner as in the case of a corporation so charged.

(6) Where an offence under this Act committed by an unincorporated body (other than a partnership) is proved to have been committed with the consent or connivance of, or to be attributable to any neglect on the part of, any officer of the body or any member of its governing body, he as well as the body is guilty of the offence and liable to be proceeded against and punished accordingly.

(7) Where an offence under this Act committed by a partnership is proved to have been committed with the consent or connivance of, or to be attributable to any neglect on the part of, a partner, he as well as the partnership is guilty of the offence and liable to be proceeded against and punished accordingly.

144 General interpretation etc

(1) In this Act –

'appropriate Minister' means –
    (a)   in relation to England, Scotland or Northern Ireland, the Secretary of State,
    (b)   in relation to Wales, the Assembly,
    and in relation to England and Wales means the Secretary of State and the Assembly acting jointly,

'the Assembly' means the National Assembly for Wales,

'body' includes an unincorporated body,

'by virtue of' includes 'by' and 'under',

'child', except where used to express a relationship, means a person who has not attained the age of 18 years,

'the Convention' means the Convention on Protection of Children and Co-operation in respect of Intercountry Adoption, concluded at the Hague on 29th May 1993,

'Convention adoption order' means an adoption order which, by virtue of regulations under section 1 of the Adoption (Intercountry Aspects) Act 1999 (regulations giving effect to the Convention), is made as a Convention adoption order,

'Convention country' means a country or territory in which the Convention is in force,

'court' means, subject to any provision made by virtue of Part 1 of Schedule 11 to the 1989 Act, the High Court, a county court or a magistrates' court,

'enactment' includes an enactment comprised in subordinate legislation,

'fee' includes expenses,

'guardian' has the same meaning as in the 1989 Act and includes a special guardian within the meaning of that Act,

'information' means information recorded in any form,

'local authority' means any unitary authority, or any county council so far as they are not a unitary authority,

'Northern Irish adoption agency' means an adoption agency within the meaning of Article 3 of the Adoption (Northern Ireland) Order 1987 (SI 1987/2203 (NI 22)),

'Northern Irish adoption order' means an order made, or having effect as if made, under Article 12 of the Adoption (Northern Ireland) Order 1987,

'notice' means a notice in writing,

'registration authority' (in Part 1) has the same meaning as in the Care Standards Act 2000,

'regulations' means regulations made by the appropriate Minister, unless they are required to be made by the Lord Chancellor, the Secretary of State or the Registrar General,

'relative', in relation to a child, means a grandparent, brother, sister, uncle or aunt, whether of the full blood or half-blood or by marriage or civil partnership,

'rules' means Family Procedure Rules made by virtue of section 141(1),

'Scottish adoption order' means an order made, or having effect as if made, under section 12 of the Adoption (Scotland) Act 1978or section 28(1) of the Adoption and Children (Scotland) Act 2007 (asp 4),

'subordinate legislation' has the same meaning as in the Interpretation Act 1978,

'unitary authority' means –

    (a)   the council of any county so far as they are the council for an area for which there are no district councils,

    (b)   the council of any district comprised in an area for which there is no county council,

    (c)   the council of a county borough,

    (d)   the council of a London borough,

    (e)   the Common Council of the City of London.

(2) Any power conferred by this Act to prescribe a fee by Order in Council or regulations includes power to prescribe –

    (a)   a fee not exceeding a prescribed amount,

    (b)   a fee calculated in accordance with the Order or, as the case may be, regulations,

    (c)   a fee determined by the person to whom it is payable, being a fee of a reasonable amount.

(3) In this Act, 'Scottish adoption agency' means –

    (a)   a local authority, or

    (b)   a voluntary organisation providing a registered adoption service;

but in relation to the provision of any particular service, references to a Scottish adoption agency do not include a voluntary organisation unless it is registered in respect of that service or a service which, in Scotland, corresponds to that service.

Expressions used in this subsection have the same meaning as in the Public Services Reform (Scotland) Act 2010 (asp 8) and 'registered' means registered under Chapter 3 of Part 5 of that Act.

(4) In this Act, a couple means –

    (a)   a married couple, or

    (aa)   two people who are civil partners of each other, or

    (b)   two people (whether of different sexes or the same sex) living as partners in an enduring family relationship.

(5) Subsection (4)(b) does not include two people one of whom is the other's parent, grandparent, sister, brother, aunt or uncle.

(6) References to relationships in subsection (5) –

    (a)   are to relationships of the full blood or half blood or, in the case of an adopted person, such of those relationships as would exist but for adoption, and

    (b)   include the relationship of a child with his adoptive, or former adoptive, parents, but do not include any other adoptive relationships.

(7) For the purposes of this Act, a person is the partner of a child's parent if the person and the parent are a couple but the person is not the child's parent.

Amendments: Civil Partnership Act 2004, s 79(1), (11), (12); Courts Act 2003, s 109(1), Sch 8, para 414; Adoption and Children (Scotland) Act 2007 (Consequential Modifications) Order 2011, SI 2011/1740, art 2, Sch 1, para 6(1), (7); Public Services Reform (Scotland) Act 2010 (Consequential Modifications of Enactments) Order 2011, SI 2011/2581, art 2, Sch 2, Pt 1, para 4(b).

145 Devolution: Wales

(1) The references to the Adoption Act 1976 and to the 1989 Act in Schedule 1 to the National Assembly for Wales (Transfer of Functions) Order 1999 (SI 1999/672) are to be treated as referring to those Acts as amended by virtue of this Act.

(2) This section does not affect the power to make further Orders varying or omitting those references.

(3) In Schedule 1 to that Order, in the entry for the Adoption Act 1976, '9' is omitted.

(4) The functions exercisable by the Assembly under sections 9 and 9A of the Adoption Act 1976 (by virtue of paragraphs 4 and 5 of Schedule 4 to this Act) are to be treated for the purposes of section 44 of the Government of Wales Act 1998 (parliamentary procedures for subordinate legislation) as if made exercisable by the Assembly by an Order in Council under section 22 of that Act.

146 Expenses

There shall be paid out of money provided by Parliament –

(a)　any expenditure incurred by a Minister of the Crown by virtue of this Act,
(b)　any increase attributable to this Act in the sums payable out of money so provided under any other enactment.

147 Glossary

Schedule 6 (glossary) is to have effect.

148 Commencement

(1) This Act (except sections 116 and 136, this Chapter and the provisions mentioned in subsections (5) and (6)) is to come into force on such day as the Secretary of State may by order appoint.

(2) Before making an order under subsection (1) (other than an order bringing paragraph 53 of Schedule 3 into force) the Secretary of State must consult the Assembly.

(3) Before making an order under subsection (1) bringing sections 123 and 124 into force, the Secretary of State must also consult the Scottish Ministers and the Department of Health, Social Services and Public Safety.

(4) Before making an order under subsection (1) bringing sections 125 to 131 into force, the Secretary of State must also consult the Scottish Ministers.

(5) The following are to come into force on such day as the Scottish Ministers may by order appoint –

    (a)   section 41(5) to (9), so far as relating to Scotland,
    (b)   sections 132 to 134,
    (c)   paragraphs 21 to 35 and 82 to 84 of Schedule 3,
    (d)   paragraphs 15 and 23 of Schedule 4,
    (e)   the entries in Schedule 5, so far as relating to the provisions mentioned in paragraphs (c) and (d),
    (f)   section 139, so far as relating to the provisions mentioned in the preceding paragraphs.

(6) Sections 2(6), 3(3) and (4), 4 to 17, 27(3), 53(1) to (3), 54, 56 to 65 and 98, paragraphs 13, 65, 66 and 111 to 113 of Schedule 3 and paragraphs 3 and 5 of Schedule 4 are to come into force on such day as the appropriate Minister may by order appoint.

149 Extent

(1) The amendment or repeal of an enactment has the same extent as the enactment to which it relates.

(2) Subject to that and to the following provisions, this Act except section 137 extends to England and Wales only.

(3) The following extend also to Scotland and Northern Ireland –

    (a)   sections 63(2) to (5), 65(2)(a) and (b) and (3), 123 and 124,
    (b)   this Chapter, except sections 141 and 145.

(4) The following extend also to Scotland –

    (a)   section 41(5) to (9),
    (b)   sections 125 to 131,
    (c)   section 138,
    (d)   section 139, so far as relating to provisions extending to Scotland.

(5) In Schedule 4, paragraph 23 extends only to Scotland.

150 Short title

This Act may be cited as the Adoption and Children Act 2002.

Schedule 1
Registration of Adoptions

1 Registration of adoption orders

(1) Every adoption order must contain a direction to the Registrar General to make in the Adopted Children Register an entry in the form prescribed by regulations made by the Registrar General with the approval of the Secretary of State.

(2) Where, on an application to a court for an adoption order in respect of a child, the identity of the child with a child to whom an entry in the registers of live-births or other records relates is proved to the satisfaction of the court, any adoption order made in pursuance of the application must contain a direction to the Registrar General to secure that the entry in the register or, as the case may be, record in question is marked with the word 'Adopted'.

(3) Where an adoption order is made in respect of a child who has previously been the subject of an adoption order made by a court in England or Wales under Part 1 of this Act or any other enactment –

    (a)   sub-paragraph (2) does not apply, and

    (b)   the order must contain a direction to the Registrar General to mark the previous entry in the Adopted Children Register with the word 'Re-adopted'.

(4) Where an adoption order is made, the prescribed officer of the court which made the order must communicate the order to the Registrar General in the prescribed manner; and the Registrar General must then comply with the directions contained in the order.

'Prescribed' means prescribed by rules.

Amendments: SI 2008/678.

2 Registration of adoptions in Scotland, Northern Ireland, the Isle of Man and the Channel Islands

(1) Sub-paragraphs (2) and (3) apply where the Registrar General is notified by the authority maintaining a register of adoptions in a part of the British Islands outside England and Wales that an order has been made in that part authorising the adoption of a child.

(2) If an entry in the registers of live-births or other records (and no entry in the Adopted Children Register) relates to the child, the Registrar General must secure that the entry is marked with –

    (a)   the word 'Adopted', followed by

    (b)   the name, in brackets, of the part in which the order was made.

(3) If an entry in the Adopted Children Register relates to the child, the Registrar General must mark the entry with –

    (a)   the word 'Re-adopted', followed by

(b)   the name, in brackets, of the part in which the order was made.

(4) Where, after an entry in either of the registers or other records mentioned in sub-paragraphs (2) and (3) has been so marked, the Registrar General is notified by the authority concerned that –

(a)   the order has been quashed,
(b)   an appeal against the order has been allowed, or
(c)   the order has been revoked,

the Registrar General must secure that the marking is cancelled.

(5) A copy or extract of an entry in any register or other record, being an entry the marking of which is cancelled under sub-paragraph (4), is not to be treated as an accurate copy unless both the marking and the cancellation are omitted from it.

3 Registration of other adoptions

(1) If the Registrar General is satisfied, on an application under this paragraph, that he has sufficient particulars relating to a child adopted under a registrable foreign adoption to enable an entry to be made in the Adopted Children Register for the child he must make the entry accordingly.

(2) If he is also satisfied that an entry in the registers of live-births or other records relates to the child, he must –

(a)   secure that the entry is marked 'Adopted', followed by the name, in brackets, of the country in which the adoption was effected, or
(b)   where appropriate, secure that the overseas registers of births are so marked.

(3) An application under this paragraph must be made, in the prescribed manner, by a prescribed person and the applicant must provide the prescribed documents and other information.

(4) An entry made in the Adopted Children Register by virtue of this paragraph must be made in the prescribed form.

(5) In this Schedule 'registrable foreign adoption' means an adoption which satisfies prescribed requirements and is either –

(a)   adoption under a Convention adoption, or
(b)   adoption under an overseas adoption.

(6) In this paragraph –

(a)   'prescribed' means prescribed by regulations made by the Registrar General with the approval of the Secretary of State,
(b)   'overseas register of births' includes –
   (i)   a register made under regulations made by the Secretary of State under section 41(1)(g), (h) or (i) of the British Nationality Act 1981,

(ii) a record kept under an Order in Council made under section 1 of the Registration of Births, Deaths and Marriages (Special Provisions) Act 1957 (other than a certified copy kept by the Registrar General).

Amendments: SI 2008/678.

4 Amendment of orders and rectification of Registers and other records

(1) The court by which an adoption order has been made may, on the application of the adopter or the adopted person, amend the order by the correction of any error in the particulars contained in it.

(2) The court by which an adoption order has been made may, if satisfied on the application of the adopter or the adopted person that within the period of one year beginning with the date of the order any new name –

(a) has been given to the adopted person (whether in baptism or otherwise), or
(b) has been taken by the adopted person,

either in place of or in addition to a name specified in the particulars required to be entered in the Adopted Children Register in pursuance of the order, amend the order by substituting or, as the case may be, adding that name in those particulars.

(3) The court by which an adoption order has been made may, if satisfied on the application of any person concerned that a direction for the marking of an entry in the registers of live-births, the Adopted Children Register or other records included in the order in pursuance of paragraph 1(2) or (3) was wrongly so included, revoke that direction.

(4) Where an adoption order is amended or a direction revoked under sub-paragraphs (1) to (3), the prescribed officer of the court must communicate the amendment in the prescribed manner to the Registrar General.

'Prescribed' means prescribed by rules.

(5) The Registrar General must then –

(a) amend the entry in the Adopted Children Register accordingly, or
(b) secure that the marking of the entry in the registers of live-births, the Adopted Children Register or other records is cancelled,

as the case may be.

(6) Where an adoption order is quashed or an appeal against an adoption order allowed by any court, the court must give directions to the Registrar General to secure that –

(a) any entry in the Adopted Children Register, and
(b) any marking of an entry in that Register, the registers of live-births or other records as the case may be, which was effected in pursuance of the order,

is cancelled.

(7) Where an adoption order has been amended, any certified copy of the relevant entry in the Adopted Children Register which may be issued pursuant to section 78(2)(b) must be a copy of the entry as amended, without the reproduction of –

    (a)   any note or marking relating to the amendment, or

    (b)   any matter cancelled in pursuance of it.

(8) A copy or extract of an entry in any register or other record, being an entry the marking of which has been cancelled, is not to be treated as an accurate copy unless both the marking and the cancellation are omitted from it.

(9) If the Registrar General is satisfied –

    (a)   that a registrable foreign adoption has ceased to have effect, whether on annulment or otherwise, or

    (b)   that any entry or mark was erroneously made in pursuance of paragraph 3 in the Adopted Children Register, the registers of live-births, the overseas registers of births or other records,

he may secure that such alterations are made in those registers or other records as he considers are required in consequence of the adoption ceasing to have effect or to correct the error.

'Overseas register of births' has the same meaning as in paragraph 3.

(10) Where an entry in such a register is amended in pursuance of sub-paragraph (9), any copy or extract of the entry is not to be treated as accurate unless it shows the entry as amended but without indicating that it has been amended.

5 Marking of entries on re-registration of birth on legitimation

(1) Without prejudice to paragraphs 2(4) and 4(5), where, after an entry in the registers of live-births or other records has been marked in accordance with paragraph 1 or 2, the birth is re-registered under section 14 of the Births and Deaths Registration Act 1953 (re-registration of births of legitimated persons), the entry made on the re-registration must be marked in the like manner.

(2) Without prejudice to paragraph 4(9), where an entry in the registers of live-births or other records is marked in pursuance of paragraph 3 and the birth in question is subsequently re-registered under section 14 of that Act, the entry made on re-registration must be marked in the like manner.

6 Cancellations in registers on legitimation

(1) This paragraph applies where an adoption order is revoked under section 55(1).

(2) The prescribed officer of the court must communicate the revocation in the prescribed manner to the Registrar General who must then cancel or secure the cancellation of –

(a)   the entry in the Adopted Children Register relating to the adopted person, and

(b)   the marking with the word 'Adopted' of any entry relating to the adopted person in the registers of live-births or other records.

'Prescribed' means prescribed by rules.

(3) A copy or extract of an entry in any register or other record, being an entry the marking of which is cancelled under this paragraph, is not to be treated as an accurate copy unless both the marking and the cancellation are omitted from it.

Schedule 2
Disclosure of Birth Records by Registrar General

1 On an application made in the prescribed manner by an adopted person –

(a)   a record of whose birth is kept by the Registrar General, and

(b)   who has attained the age of 18 years,

the Registrar General must give the applicant any information necessary to enable the applicant to obtain a certified copy of the record of his birth.

'Prescribed' means prescribed by regulations made by the Registrar General with the approval of the Secretary of State.

Amendments: SI 2008/678.

2 (1) Before giving any information to an applicant under paragraph 1, the Registrar General must inform the applicant that counselling services are available to the applicant –

(a)   from a registered adoption society, an organisation within section 144(3)(b) or an adoption society which is registered under Article 4 of the Adoption (Northern Ireland) Order 1987 (SI 1987/2203 (NI 22)),

(b)   if the applicant is in England and Wales, at the General Register Office or from any local authority or registered adoption support agency,

(c)   if the applicant is in Scotland, from any council constituted under section 2 of the Local Government etc (Scotland) Act 1994,

(d)   if the applicant is in Northern Ireland, from any Board.

(2) In sub-paragraph (1)(b), 'registered adoption support agency' means an adoption support agency in respect of which a person is registered under Part 2 of the Care Standards Act 2000.

(3) In sub-paragraph (1)(d), 'Board' means a Health and Social Services Board established under Article 16 of the Health and Personal Social Services (Northern Ireland) Order 1972 (SI 1972/1265 (NI 14)); but where the functions of a Board are exercisable by a Health and Social Services Trust, references in that sub-paragraph to a Board are to be read as references to the Health and Social Services Trust.

(4) If the applicant chooses to receive counselling from a person or body within sub-paragraph (1), the Registrar General must send to the person or body the information to which the applicant is entitled under paragraph 1.

3 (1) Where an adopted person who is in England and Wales –

(a)   applies for information under paragraph 1 or Article 54 of the Adoption (Northern Ireland) Order 1987, or
(b)   is supplied with information under section 55(4)(b) of the Adoption and Children (Scotland) Act 2007 (asp 4),

the persons and bodies mentioned in sub-paragraph (2) must, if asked by the applicant to do so, provide counselling for the applicant.

(2) Those persons and bodies are –

(a)   the Registrar General,
(b)   any local authority,
(c)   a registered adoption society, an organisation within section 144(3)(b) or an adoption society which is registered under Article 4 of the Adoption (Northern Ireland) Order 1987.

Amendment: SI 2011/1740.

4 (1) Where a person –

(a)   was adopted before 12th November 1975, and
(b)   applies for information under paragraph 1,

the Registrar General must not give the information to the applicant unless the applicant has attended an interview with a counsellor arranged by a person or body from whom counselling services are available as mentioned in paragraph 2.

(2) Where the Registrar General is prevented by sub-paragraph (1) from giving information to a person who is not living in the United Kingdom, the Registrar General may give the information to any body which –

(a)   the Registrar General is satisfied is suitable to provide counselling to that person, and
(b)   has notified the Registrar General that it is prepared to provide such counselling.

Schedule 3
Minor and Consequential Amendments

****

16 The Legitimacy Act 1976

The Legitimacy Act 1976 is amended as follows.

17 In section 4 (legitimation of adopted child) –

(a)   in subsection (1), after '1976' there is inserted 'or section 67 of the Adoption and Children Act 2002',

(b)   in subsection (2) –

  (i)   in paragraph (*a*), after '39' there is inserted 'or subsection (3)(*b*) of the said section 67',

  (ii)   in paragraph (*b*), after '1976' there is inserted 'or section 67, 68 or 69 of the Adoption and Children Act 2002'.

18 In section 6 (dispositions depending on date of birth), at the end of subsection (2) there is inserted 'or section 69(2) of the Adoption and Children Act 2002'.

****

36 The Magistrates' Courts Act 1980

The Magistrates' Courts Act 1980 is amended as follows.

37 In section 65 (meaning of family proceedings), in subsection (1), for paragraph (h) there is substituted –

  '(h)   the Adoption and Children Act 2002;'.

38 In section 69 (sitting of magistrates' courts for family proceedings), in subsections (2) and (3), for 'the Adoption Act 1976' there is substituted 'the Adoption and Children Act 2002'.

39 In section 71 (newspaper reports of family proceedings) –

(a)   in subsection (1), '(other than proceedings under the Adoption Act 1976)' is omitted,

(b)   in subsection (2) –

  (i)   for 'the Adoption Act 1976' there is substituted 'the Adoption and Children Act 2002',

  (ii)   the words following '(a) and (b)' are omitted.

40 In Part 1 of Schedule 6 (fees to be taken by justices' chief executives), in the entry relating to family proceedings –

(a)   for 'the Adoption Act 1976, except under section 21 of that Act', there is substituted 'the Adoption and Children Act 2002, except under section 23 of that Act',

(b)   in paragraph (c), for 'section 21 of the Adoption Act 1976' there is substituted 'section 23 of the Adoption and Children Act 2002'.

****

44 The Matrimonial and Family Proceedings Act 1984

(*repealed*)

Amendments: Paragraph repealed: Courts Act 2003, s 109(3), Sch 10.

45 The Child Abduction and Custody Act 1985

In Schedule 3 to the Child Abduction and Custody Act 1985 (custody orders), in paragraph 1, the 'and' at the end of paragraph (*b*) is omitted and after that paragraph there is inserted –

> '(bb) a special guardianship order (within the meaning of the Act of 1989); and',

and paragraph (*c*)(v) is omitted.

46 The Family Law Act 1986

The Family Law Act 1986 is amended as follows.

47 In section 1 (orders to which Part 1 applies), in subsection (1), after paragraph (*a*) there is inserted –

> '(aa) a special guardianship order made by a court in England and Wales under the Children Act 1989;
> (ab) an order made under section 26 of the Adoption and Children Act 2002 (contact), other than an order varying or revoking such an order'.

48 In section 2 (jurisdiction: general), after subsection (2) there is inserted –

> '(2A) A court in England and Wales shall not have jurisdiction to make a special guardianship order under the Children Act 1989 unless the condition in section 3 of this Act is satisfied.
> (2B) A court in England and Wales shall not have jurisdiction to make an order under section 26 of the Adoption and Children Act 2002 unless the condition in section 3 of this Act is satisfied.'

49 In section 57 (declarations as to adoptions effected overseas) –

(a) for subsection (1)(a) there is substituted –

> '(a) a Convention adoption, or an overseas adoption, within the meaning of the Adoption and Children Act 2002, or',

(b) in subsection (2)(a), after '1976' there is inserted 'or section 67 of the Adoption and Children Act 2002'.

50 The Family Law Reform Act 1987

The Family Law Reform Act 1987 is amended as follows.

51 In section 1 (general principle), for paragraph (*c*) of subsection (3) there is substituted –

> '(c) is an adopted person within the meaning of Chapter 4 of Part 1 of the Adoption and Children Act 2002'.

52 In section 19 (dispositions of property), in subsection (5), after '1976' there is inserted 'or section 69 of the Adoption and Children Act 2002'.

****

76 The Human Fertilisation and Embryology Act 1990

The Human Fertilisation and Embryology Act 1990 is amended as follows.

77 In section 27 (meaning of mother), in subsection (2), for 'child of any person other than the adopter or adopters' there is substituted 'woman's child'.

78 In section 28 (meaning of father), in subsection (5)(*c*), for 'child of any person other than the adopter or adopters' there is substituted 'man's child'.

79 In section 30 (parental orders in favour of gamete donors), in subsection (10) for 'Adoption Act 1976' there is substituted 'Adoption and Children Act 2002'.

****

81 In section 26 of the Child Support Act 1991 (disputes about parentage), in subsection (3), after '1976' there is inserted 'or Chapter 4 of Part 1 of the Adoption and Children Act 2002'.

****

85 The Family Law Act 1996

The Family Law Act 1996 is amended as follows.

86 In section 62 (meaning of 'relevant child' etc) –

    (a)   in subsection (2), in paragraph (b), after 'the Adoption Act 1976' there is inserted ', the Adoption and Children Act 2002',

    (b)   in subsection (5), for the words from 'has been freed' to '1976' there is substituted 'falls within subsection (7)'.

87 At the end of that section there is inserted –

    '(7) A child falls within this subsection if –

        (a)   an adoption agency, within the meaning of section 2 of the Adoption and Children Act 2002, has power to place him for adoption under section 19 of that Act (placing children with parental consent) or he has become the subject of an order under section 21 of that Act (placement orders), or

        (b)   he is freed for adoption by virtue of an order made –

            (i)   in England and Wales, under section 18 of the Adoption Act 1976,

            (ii)   in Scotland, under section 18 of the Adoption (Scotland) Act 1978, or

            (iii)   in Northern Ireland, under Article 17(1) or 18(1) of the Adoption (Northern Ireland) Order 1987.'

88 In section 63 (interpretation of Part 4) –

        (a)   in subsection (1), for the definition of 'adoption order', there is substituted –

"adoption order' means an adoption order within the meaning of section 72(1) of the Adoption Act 1976 or section 46(1) of the Adoption and Children Act 2002;',

  (b)   in subsection (2), after paragraph (h) there is inserted –
        '(i)   the Adoption and Children Act 2002.'

****

118 The Criminal Justice and Court Services Act 2000

In section 12(5) of the Criminal Justice and Court Services Act 2000 (meaning of 'family proceedings' in relation to CAFCASS), paragraph (*b*) (supervision orders under the 1989 Act) and the preceding 'and' are omitted.

Schedule 4
Transitional and Transitory Provisions and Savings

1 General rules for continuity

(1) Any reference (express or implied) in Part 1 or any other enactment, instrument or document to –

  (a)   any provision of Part 1, or
  (b)   things done or falling to be done under or for the purposes of any provision of Part 1,

must, so far as the nature of the reference permits, be construed as including, in relation to the times, circumstances or purposes in relation to which the corresponding provision repealed by this Act had effect, a reference to that corresponding provision or (as the case may be) to things done or falling to be done under or for the purposes of that corresponding provision.

(2) Any reference (express or implied) in any enactment, instrument or document to –

  (a)   a provision repealed by this Act, or
  (b)   things done or falling to be done under or for the purposes of such a provision,

must, so far as the nature of the reference permits, be construed as including, in relation to the times, circumstances or purposes in relation to which the corresponding provision of Part 1 has effect, a reference to that corresponding provision or (as the case may be) to things done or falling to be done under or for the purposes of that corresponding provision.

2 General rule for old savings

(1) The repeal by this Act of an enactment previously repealed subject to savings does not affect the continued operation of those savings.

(2) The repeal by this Act of a saving made on the previous repeal of an enactment does not affect the operation of the saving in so far as it is not specifically reproduced in this Act but remains capable of having effect.

****

Amendment: Paragraphs 3–5 repealed by s 139(3), Sch 5 of this Act with effect from 30 December 2005 (SI 2005/2897).

6 Pending applications for freeing orders

Nothing in this Act affects any application for an order under section 18 of the Adoption Act 1976 (freeing for adoption) where –

(a) the application has been made and has not been disposed of immediately before the repeal of that section, and

(b) the child in relation to whom the application is made has his home immediately before that repeal with a person with whom he has been placed for adoption by an adoption agency.

7 Freeing orders

(1) Nothing in this Act affects any order made under section 18 of the Adoption Act 1976 and –

(a) sections 19 to 21 of that Act are to continue to have effect in relation to such an order, and

(b) Part 1 of Schedule 6 to the Magistrates' Courts Act 1980 is to continue to have effect for the purposes of an application under section 21 of the Adoption Act 1976 in relation to such an order.

(2) Section 20 of that Act, as it has effect by virtue of this paragraph, is to apply as if, in subsection (3)(*c*) after '1989' there were inserted –

'(iia) any care order, within the meaning of that Act'.

(3) Where a child is free for adoption by virtue of an order made under section 18 of that Act, the third condition in section 47(6) is to be treated as satisfied.

8 Pending applications for adoption orders

Nothing in this Act affects any application for an adoption order under section 12 of the Adoption Act 1976 where –

(a) the application has been made and has not been disposed of immediately before the repeal of that section, and

(b) the child in relation to whom the application is made has his home immediately before that repeal with a person with whom he has been placed for adoption by an adoption agency.

9 Notification of adoption applications

Where a notice given in respect of a child by the prospective adopters under section 22(1) of the Adoption Act 1976 is treated by virtue of paragraph 1(1) as having been given for the purposes of section 44(2) in respect of an application to adopt the child, section 42(3) has effect in relation to their application for an adoption order as if for 'six months' there were substituted 'twelve months'.

****

Amendments: Paragraphs 10–16 repealed by s 139(3), Sch 5 of this Act with effect from 30 December 2005 (SI 2005/2897).

17 Status

(1) Section 67 –

    (a)   does not apply to a pre-1976 instrument or enactment in so far as it contains a disposition of property, and

    (b)   does not apply to any public general Act in its application to any disposition of property in a pre-1976 instrument or enactment.

(2) Section 73 applies in relation to this paragraph as if this paragraph were contained in Chapter 4 of Part 1; and an instrument or enactment is a pre-1976 instrument or enactment for the purposes of this Schedule if it was passed or made at any time before 1st January 1976.

18 Section 69 does not apply to a pre-1976 instrument.

19 In section 70(1), the reference to Part 3 of the Family Law Reform Act 1987 includes Part 2 of the Family Law Reform Act 1969.

20 Registration of adoptions

(1) The power of the court under paragraph 4(1) of Schedule 1 to amend an order on the application of the adopter or adopted person includes, in relation to an order made before 1st April 1959, power to make any amendment of the particulars contained in the order which appears to be required to bring the order into the form in which it would have been made if paragraph 1 of that Schedule had applied to the order.

(2) In relation to an adoption order made before the commencement of the Adoption Act 1976, the reference in paragraph 4(3) of that Schedule to paragraph 1(2) or (3) is to be read –

    (a)   in the case of an order under the Adoption of Children Act 1926, as a reference to section 12(3) and (4) of the Adoption of Children Act 1949,

    (b)   in the case of an order under the Adoption Act 1950, as a reference to section 18(3) and (4) of that Act,

    (c)   in the case of an order under the Adoption Act 1958, as a reference to section 21(4) and (5) of that Act.

21 The Child Abduction Act 1984

Paragraph 43 of Schedule 3 does not affect the Schedule to the Child Abduction Act 1984 in its application to a child who is the subject of –

    (a)   an order under section 18 of the Adoption Act 1976 freeing the child for adoption,

    (b)   a pending application for such an order, or

(c)   a pending application for an order under section 12 of that Act.

22 The Courts and Legal Services Act 1990

Paragraph 80 of Schedule 3 does not affect section 58A(2)(*b*) of the Courts and Legal Services Act 1990 in its application to proceedings under the Adoption Act 1976.

23 The Children (Scotland) Act 1995

(*Applies to Scotland only*)

Schedule 5
Repeals

Short title and chapter	Extent of repeal
Adoption Act 1976 (c 36).	The whole Act, except Part 4 and paragraph 6 of Schedule 2.
Domestic Proceedings and Magistrates' Courts Act 1978 (c 22).	Sections 73(2), 74(2) and 74(4).
Magistrates' Courts Act 1980 (c 43).	In section 71(1) the words '(other than proceedings under the Adoption Act 1976)'. In section 71(2) the words following '(a) and (b)'. In Schedule 7, paragraphs 141 and 142.
Matrimonial and Family Proceedings Act 1984 (c 42).	In section 40(2)(a), after 'the Adoption Act 1968', the word 'or'. In Schedule 1, paragraph 20.
Child Abduction and Custody Act 1985 (c 60).	In Schedule 3, in paragraph 1, the 'and' at the end of paragraph (b). In Schedule 3, in paragraph 1(c), paragraph (v).
Family Law Reform Act 1987 (c 42).	In Schedule 3, paragraphs 2 to 5.
Children Act 1989 (c 41).	Section 9(4). Section 12(3)(a). In section 20(9), the 'or' at the end of paragraph (a).

Short title and chapter	Extent of repeal
	In section 26(2)(e) and (f), the words 'to consider'.
	Section 33(6)(b)(i).
	Section 80(1)(e) and (f).
	Section 81(1)(b).
	Section 88(1).
	Section 102(6)(c).
	In section 105(1), the definition of 'protected child'.
	In Schedule 10, Part 1.
Human Fertilisation and Embryology Act 1990 (c 37).	In Schedule 4, paragraph 4.
Adoption (Intercountry Aspects) Act 1999 (c 18).	In section 2(6), the words 'in its application to Scotland'.
	Section 7(3).
	Section 14.
	In section 16(1), the words ', or section 17 or 56A of the 1976 Act,'.
	In Schedule 2, paragraph 3.
Criminal Justice and Court Services Act 2000 (c 43).	Section 12(5)(b) and the preceding 'and'.
	In Schedule 7, paragraphs 51 to 53.

Schedule 6
Glossary

In this Act, the expressions listed in the left-hand column below have the meaning given by, or are to be interpreted in accordance with, the provisions of this Act or (where stated) of the 1989 Act listed in the right-hand column.

Expression	Provision
the 1989 Act	section 2(5)
Adopted Children Register	section 77
Adoption and Children Act Register	section 125
adoption (in relation to Chapter 4 of Part 1)	section 66

Expression	*Provision*
adoption agency	section 2(1)
adoption agency placing a child for adoption	section 18(5)
Adoption Contact Register	section 80
adoption order	section 46(1)
Adoption Service	section 2(1)
adoption society	section 2(5)
adoption support agency	section 8
adoption support services	section 2(6)
appointed day (in relation to Chapter 4 of Part 1)	section 66(2)
appropriate Minister	section 144
Assembly	section 144
body	section 144
by virtue of	section 144
care order	section 105(1) of the 1989 Act
child	sections 49(5) and 144
child assessment order	section 43(2) of the 1989 Act
child in the care of a local authority	section 105(1) of the 1989 Act
child looked after by a local authority	section 22 of the 1989 Act
child placed for adoption by an adoption agency	section 18(5)
child to be adopted, adopted child	section 49(5)
consent (in relation to making adoption orders or placing for adoption)	section 52
the Convention	section 144

Expression	Provision
Convention adoption	section 66(1)(c)
Convention adoption order	section 144
Convention country	section 144
couple	section 144(4)
court	section 144
disposition (in relation to Chapter 4 of Part 1)	section 73
enactment	section 144
fee	section 144
guardian	section 144
information	section 144
interim care order	section 38 of the 1989 Act
local authority	section 144
local authority foster parent	section *23(3)* 22C of the 1989 Act
Northern Irish adoption agency	section 144
Northern Irish adoption order	section 144
notice	section 144
notice of intention to adopt	section 44(2)
overseas adoption	section 87
parental responsibility	section 3 of the 1989 Act
partner, in relation to a parent of a child	section 144(7)
placement order	section 21
placing, or placed, for adoption	sections 18(5) and 19(4)
prohibited steps order	section 8(1) of the 1989 Act
records (in relation to Chapter 5 of Part 1)	section 82

Expression	*Provision*
registered adoption society	section 2(2)
registers of live-births (in relation to Chapter 5 of Part 1)	section 82
registration authority (in Part 1)	section 144
regulations	section 144
relative	section 144, read with section 1(8)
residence order	section 8(1) of the 1989 Act
rules	section 144
Scottish adoption agency	section 144(3)
Scottish adoption order	section 144
specific issue order	section 8(1) of the 1989 Act
subordinate legislation	section 144
supervision order	section 31(11) of the 1989 Act
unitary authority	section 144
voluntary organisation	section 2(5)

Amendment: Children and Young Persons Act 2008, s 8(2), Sch 1, para 14.

Appendix 2

ADOPTIONS WITH A FOREIGN ELEMENT REGULATIONS 2005

SI 2005/392

PART I
GENERAL

1 Citation, commencement and application

(1) These Regulations may be cited as the Adoptions with a Foreign Element Regulations 2005 and shall come into force on 30th December 2005.

(2) These Regulations apply to England and Wales.

2 Interpretation

In these Regulations –

'the Act' means the Adoption and Children Act 2002;

'adoption support services' has the meaning given in section 2(6)(a) of the Act and any regulations made under section 2(6)(b) of the Act;

'adoptive family' has the same meaning as in regulation 31(2)(a) of the Agencies Regulations or corresponding Welsh provision;

'adoption panel' means a panel established in accordance with regulation 3 of the Agencies Regulations or corresponding Welsh provision;

'the Agencies Regulations' means the Adoption Agencies Regulations 2005;

'child's case record' has the same meaning as in regulation 12 of the Agencies Regulations or corresponding Welsh provision;

'CA of the receiving State' means, in relation to a Convention country other than the United Kingdom, the Central Authority of the receiving State;

'CA of the State of origin' means, in relation to a Convention country other than the United Kingdom, the Central Authority of the State of origin;

'Convention adoption' is given a meaning by virtue of section 66(1)(c) of the Act;

'Convention country' has the same meaning as in section 144(1) of the Act;

'Convention list' means –

    (a)   in relation to a relevant Central Authority, a list of children notified to that Authority in accordance with regulation 40; or

    (b)   in relation to any other Central Authority within the British Islands, a list of children notified to that Authority in accordance with provisions, which correspond to regulation 40.

'corresponding Welsh provision' in relation to a Part or a regulation of the Agencies Regulations means the provision of regulations made by the Assembly under section 9 of the Act which corresponds to that Part or regulation;

'prospective adopter's case record' has the same meaning as in regulation 22(1) of the Agencies Regulations or corresponding Welsh provision;

'prospective adopter's report' has the same meaning as in regulation 25(5) of the Agencies Regulations or corresponding Welsh provisions;

'receiving State' has the same meaning as in Article 2 of the Convention;

'relevant Central Authority' means –

    (a)   in Chapter 1 of Part 3, in relation to a prospective adopter who is habitually resident in –
        (i)   England, the Secretary of State; and
        (ii)   Wales, the National Assembly for Wales; and

    (b)   in Chapter 2 of Part 3 in relation to a local authority in –
        (i)   England, the Secretary of State; and
        (ii)   Wales, the National Assembly for Wales;

'relevant local authority' means in relation to a prospective adopter –

    (a)   the local authority within whose area he has his home; or

    (b)   in the case where he no longer has a home in England or Wales, the local authority for the area in which he last had his home;

'relevant foreign authority' means a person, outside the British Islands performing functions in the country in which the child is, or in which the prospective adopter is, habitually resident which correspond to the functions of an adoption agency or to the functions of the Secretary of State in respect of adoptions with a foreign element;

'State of origin' has the same meaning as in Article 2 of the Convention.

PART 2
BRINGING CHILDREN INTO AND OUT OF THE UNITED KINGDOM

Chapter 1
Bringing Children into the United Kingdom

3 Requirements applicable in respect of bringing or causing a child to be brought into the United Kingdom

A person intending to bring, or to cause another to bring, a child into the United Kingdom in circumstances where section 83(1) of the Act applies must –

    (a)   apply in writing to an adoption agency for an assessment of his suitability to adopt a child; and

    (b)   give the adoption agency any information it may require for the purpose of the assessment.

4 Conditions applicable in respect of a child brought into the United Kingdom

(1) This regulation prescribes the conditions for the purposes of section 83(5) of the Act in respect of a child brought into the United Kingdom in circumstances where section 83 applies.

(2) Prior to the child's entry into the United Kingdom, the prospective adopter must –

    (a)   receive in writing, notification from the Secretary of State that she has issued a certificate confirming to the relevant foreign authority –

        (i)   that the person has been assessed and approved as eligible and suitable to be an adoptive parent in accordance with Part 4 of the Agencies Regulations or corresponding Welsh provision; and

        (ii)   that if entry clearance and leave to enter and remain, as may be necessary, is granted and not revoked or curtailed, and an adoption order is made or an overseas adoption is effected, the child will be authorised to enter and reside permanently in the United Kingdom;

    (b)   before visiting the child in the State of origin –

        (i)   notify the adoption agency of the details of the child to be adopted;

        (ii)   provide the adoption agency with any information and reports received from the relevant foreign authority; and

        (iii)   meet with the adoption agency to discuss the proposed adoption and information received from the relevant foreign authority;

    (c)   visit the child in the State of origin (and where the prospective adopters are a couple each of them); and

    (d)   after that visit –

        (i)   confirm in writing to the adoption agency that he has done so and wishes to proceed with the adoption;

        (ii)   provide the adoption agency with any additional reports and information received on or after that visit; and

        (iii)   notify the adoption agency of his expected date of entry into the United Kingdom with the child.

(3) The prospective adopter must accompany the child on entering the United Kingdom unless, in the case of a couple, the adoption agency and the relevant foreign authority have agreed that it is necessary for only one of them to do so.

(4) Except where an overseas adoption is or is to be effected, the prospective adopter must within the period of 14 days beginning with the date on which the child is brought into the United Kingdom give notice to the relevant local authority –

    (a)   of the child's arrival in the United Kingdom; and

    (b)   of his intention –

        (i)   to apply for an adoption order in accordance with section 44(2) of the Act; or

        (ii)   not to give the child a home.

(5) In a case where a prospective adopter has given notice in accordance with paragraph (4) and subsequently moves his home into the area of another local authority, he must within 14 days of that move confirm in writing to that authority, the child's entry into the United Kingdom and that notice of his intention –

    (a)   to apply for an adoption order in accordance with section 44(2) of the Act has been given to another local authority; or

    (b)   not to give the child a home,

has been given.

5 Functions imposed on the local authority

(1) Where notice of intention to adopt has been given to the local authority, that authority must –

    (a)   if it has not already done so, set up a case record in respect of the child and place on it any information received from the –
        (i)   relevant foreign authority;
        (ii)   adoption agency, if it is not the local authority;
        (iii) prospective adopter;
        (iv)   entry clearance officer; and
        (v)   Secretary of State, or as the case may be, the Assembly;

    (b)   send the prospective adopter's general practitioner written notification of the arrival in England or Wales of the child and send with that notification a written report of the child's health history and current state of health, so far as is known;

    (c)   send to the Primary Care Trust or Local Health Board (Wales), in whose area the prospective adopter has his home, written notification of the arrival in England or Wales of the child;

    (d)   (*revoked*)

    (e)   ensure that the child and the prospective adopter are visited within one week of receipt of the notice of intention to adopt and thereafter not less than once a week until the review referred to in sub-paragraph (f) and thereafter at such frequency as the authority may decide;

    (f)   carry out a review of the child's case not more than 4 weeks after receipt of the notice of intention to adopt and –
        (i)   visit and, if necessary, review not more than 3 months after that initial review; and
        (ii)   thereafter not more than 6 months after the date of the previous visit,

unless the child no longer has his home with the prospective adopter or an adoption order is made;

    (g)   when carrying out a review consider –
        (i)   the child's needs, welfare and development, and whether any changes need to be made to meet his needs or assist his development;

      (ii)   the arrangements for the provision of adoption support services and whether there should be any re-assessment of the need for those services; and

      (iii)   the need for further visits and reviews; and

(h)   ensure that –

      (i)   advice is given as to the child's needs, welfare and development;

      (ii)   written reports are made of all visits and reviews of the case and placed on the child's case record; and

      (iii)   on such visits, where appropriate, advice is given as to the availability of adoption support services.

(2) Part 7 of the Agencies Regulations or corresponding Welsh provision (case records) shall apply to the case record set up in respect of the child as a consequence of this regulation as if that record had been set up under the Agencies Regulations or corresponding Welsh provision.

(3) In a case where the prospective adopter fails to make an application under section 50 or 51 of the Act within two years of the receipt by a local authority of the notice of intention to adopt the local authority must review the case.

(4) For the purposes of the review referred to in paragraph (3), the local authority must consider –

(a)   the child's needs, welfare and development, and whether any changes need to be made to meet his needs or assist his development;

(b)   the arrangements, if any, in relation to the exercise of parental responsibility for the child;

(c)   the terms upon which leave to enter the United Kingdom is granted and the immigration status of the child;

(d)   the arrangements for the provision of adoption support services for the adoptive family and whether there should be any re-assessment of the need for those services; and

(e)   in conjunction with the appropriate agencies, the arrangements for meeting the child's health care and educational needs.

(5) In a case where the local authority to which notice of intention to adopt is given ('the original authority') is notified by the prospective adopter that he intends to move or has moved his home into the area of another local authority, the original authority must notify the local authority into whose area the prospective adopter intends to move or has moved, within 14 days of receiving information in respect of that move, of –

(a)   the name, sex, date and place of birth of child;

(b)   the prospective adopter's name, sex and date of birth;

(c)   the date on which the child entered the United Kingdom;

(d)   where the original authority received notification of intention to adopt, the date of receipt of such notification whether an application for an adoption order has been made and the stage of those proceedings; and

(e)   any other relevant information.

Amendment: SI 2010/1172.

6 Application of Chapter 3 of the Act

In the case of a child brought into the United Kingdom for adoption in circumstances where section 83 of the Act applies –

    (a)   the modifications in regulations 7 to 9 apply;

    (b)   section 36(2) and (5) (restrictions on removal) and section 39(3)(a) (partners of parents) of the Act shall not apply.

7 Change of name and removal from the United Kingdom

Section 28(2) of the Act (further consequences of placement) shall apply as if from the words 'is placed' to 'then', there is substituted 'enters the United Kingdom in the circumstances where section 83(1)(a) of this Act applies'.

8 Return of the child

(1) Section 35 of the Act (return of child) shall apply with the following modifications.

(2) Subsections (1), (2) and (3) shall apply as if in each place where –

    (a)   the words 'is placed for adoption by an adoption agency' occur there were substituted 'enters the United Kingdom in circumstances where section 83(1) applies';

    (b)   the words 'the agency' occur there were substituted the words 'the local authority'; and

    (c)   the words 'any parent or guardian of the child' occur there were substituted 'the Secretary of State or, as the case may be, the Assembly'.

(3) Subsection (5) shall apply as if for the words 'an adoption agency' or 'the agency' there were substituted the words 'the local authority'.

9 Child to live with adopters before application

(1) In a case where the requirements imposed by section 83(4) of the Act have been complied with and the conditions required by section 83(5) of the Act have been met, section 42 shall apply as if –

    (a)   subsection (3) is omitted; and

    (b)   in subsection (5) the words from 'three years' to 'preceding' there were substituted 'six months'.

(2) In a case where the requirements imposed by section 83(4) of the Act have not been complied with or the conditions required by section 83(5) have not been met, section 42 shall apply as if –

    (a)   subsection (3) is omitted; and

    (b)   in subsection (5) the words from 'three years' to 'preceding' there were substituted 'twelve months'.

Chapter 2
Taking Children out of the United Kingdom

10 Requirements applicable in respect of giving parental responsibility prior to adoption abroad

The prescribed requirements for the purposes of section 84(3) of the Act (requirements to be satisfied prior to the making of an order) are that –

(a) in the case of a child placed by an adoption agency, that agency has –
 (i) confirmed to the court that it has complied with the requirements imposed in accordance with Part 3 of the Agencies Regulations or corresponding Welsh provision;
 (ii) submitted to the court –
  (aa) the reports and information referred to in regulation 17(2D) and (3), as appropriate of the Agencies Regulations or corresponding Welsh provision;
  (bb) the recommendations made by the adoption panel in accordance with regulations 18 (placing child for adoption), where applicable, and 33 (proposed placement) of the Agencies Regulations or corresponding Welsh provision;
  (cc) the adoption placement report prepared in accordance with regulation 31(2)(d) of the Agencies Regulations or corresponding Welsh provision;
  (dd) the reports of and information obtained in respect of the visits and reviews referred to in regulation 36 of the Agencies Regulations or corresponding Welsh provision; and
  (ee) the report referred to in section 43 of the Act as modified by regulation 11;

(b) in the case of a child placed by an adoption agency the relevant foreign authority has –
 (i) confirmed in writing to that agency that the prospective adopter has been counselled and the legal implications of adoption have been explained to him;
 (ii) prepared a report on the suitability of the prospective adopter to be an adoptive parent;
 (iii) determined and confirmed in writing to that agency that he is eligible and suitable to adopt in the country or territory in which the adoption is to be effected; and
 (iv) confirmed in writing to that agency that the child is or will be authorised to enter and reside permanently in that foreign country or territory; and

(c) in the case of a child placed by an adoption agency the prospective adopter has confirmed in writing to the adoption agency that he will accompany the child on taking him out of the United Kingdom and entering the country or territory where the adoption is to be effected, or in the case of a couple, the agency and relevant foreign authority have confirmed that it is necessary for only one of them to do so.

Amendments: SI 2012/1410.

11 Application of the Act in respect of orders under section 84

(1) The following provisions of the Act which refer to adoption orders shall apply to orders under section 84 as if in each place where the words 'adoption order' appear there were substituted 'order under section 84' –

(a)   section 1(7)(a) (coming to a decision relating to adoption of a child);
(b)   section 18(4) (placement for adoption by agencies);
(c)   section 21(4)(b) (placement orders);
(d)   section 22(5)(a) and (b) (application for placement orders);
(e)   section 24(4) (revoking placement orders);
(f)   section 28(1) (further consequences of placement);
(g)   section 29(4)(a) and (5)(a) (further consequences of placement orders);
(h)   section 32(5) (recovery by parent etc where child placed and consent withdrawn);
(i)   section 42(7) (sufficient opportunity for adoption agency to see the child);
(j)   section 43 (reports where child placed by agency);
(k)   section 44(2) (notice of intention to adopt);
(l)   section 47(1) to (5), (8) and (9) (conditions for making orders);
(m)   section 48(1) (restrictions on making applications);
(n)   section 50(1) and (2) (adoption by a couple);
(o)   section 51(1) to (4) (adoption by one person);
(p)   section 52(1) to (4) (parental etc consent);
(q)   section 53(5) (contribution towards maintenance); and
(r)   section 141(3) and (4)(c) (rules of procedure).

(2) Section 35(5) of the Act (return of child in other cases) shall apply to orders under section 84 of that Act as if in paragraph (b) of that subsection –

(a)   for the first reference to 'adoption order' there were substituted 'order under section 84(1)'; and
(b)   the words in brackets were omitted.

PART 3
ADOPTIONS UNDER THE CONVENTION

Chapter 1
Requirements, Procedure, Recognition and Effect of Adoptions where the United Kingdom is the Receiving State

12 Application of Chapter 1

The provisions in this Chapter shall apply where a couple or a person, habitually resident in the British Islands, wishes to adopt a child who is habitually resident in a Convention country outside the British Islands in accordance with the Convention.

13 Requirements applicable in respect of eligibility and suitability

(1) A couple or a person who wishes to adopt a child habitually resident in a Convention country outside the British Islands shall –

(a) apply in writing to an adoption agency for a determination of eligibility, and an assessment of his suitability, to adopt; and
(b) give the agency any information it may require for the purposes of the assessment.

(2) An adoption agency may not consider an application under paragraph (1) unless at the date of that application –

(a) in the case of an application by a couple, they have both –
  (i) attained the age of 21 years; and
  (ii) been habitually resident in a part of the British Islands for a period of not less than one year ending with the date of application; and
(b) in the case of an application by one person, he has –
  (i) attained the age of 21 years; and
  (ii) been habitually resident in a part of the British Islands for a period of not less than one year ending with the date of application.

14 Counselling and information

(1) An adoption agency must provide a counselling service in accordance with regulation 21(1)(a) of the Agencies Regulations or corresponding Welsh provision and must –

(a) explain to the prospective adopter the procedure in relation to, and the legal implications of, adopting a child from the State of origin from which the prospective adopter wishes to adopt in accordance with the Convention; and
(b) provide him with written information about the matters referred to in sub-paragraph (a).

(2) Paragraph (1) does not apply if the adoption agency is satisfied that the requirements set out in that paragraph have been carried out in respect of the prospective adopter by another agency.

15 Procedure in respect of carrying out an assessment

(1) Regulation 22 of the Agencies Regulations (requirement to consider application for an assessment of suitability) or corresponding Welsh provision shall apply as if the reference to an application in those Regulations or corresponding Welsh provision was to an application made in accordance with regulation 13.

(2) Where the adoption agency is satisfied that the requirements in –

(a) regulation 14; and

(b) regulations 23 (police checks) and 24 (preparation for adoption) of the Agencies Regulations or corresponding Welsh provision,

have been meet, regulations 25 (prospective adopter's report) and 26 (adoption panel) of the Agencies Regulations or corresponding Welsh provisions shall apply.

(3) The adoption agency must place on the prospective adopter's case record any information obtained as a consequence of this Chapter.

(4) The adoption agency must include in the prospective adopter's report –

(a) the State of origin from which the prospective adopter wishes to adopt a child;
(b) confirmation that the prospective adopter is eligible to adopt a child under the law of that State;
(c) any additional information obtained as a consequence of the requirements of that State; and
(d) the agency's assessment of the prospective adopter's suitability to adopt a child who is habitually resident in that State.

(5) The references to information in regulations 25(5) and 26(2) of the Agencies Regulations or corresponding Welsh provisions shall include information obtained by the adoption agency or adoption panel as a consequence of this regulation.

16 Adoption agency decision and notification

The adoption agency must make a decision about whether the prospective adopter is suitable to adopt a child in accordance with regulation 27 of the Agencies Regulations and regulations made under section 45 of the Act, or corresponding Welsh provisions.

17 Review and termination of approval

The adoption agency must review the approval of each prospective adopter in accordance with regulation 29 of the Agencies Regulations or corresponding Welsh provision unless the agency has received written notification from the relevant Central Authority that the agreement under Article 17(c) of the Convention has been made.

18 Procedure following decision as to suitability to adopt

(1) Where an adoption agency has made a decision that the prospective adopter is suitable to adopt a child in accordance with regulation 16, it must send to the relevant Central Authority –

(a) written confirmation of the decision and any recommendation the agency may make in relation to the number of children the prospective adopter may be suitable to adopt, their age range, sex, likely needs and background;
(b) the enhanced criminal record certificate obtained under regulation 23 of the Agencies Regulations or corresponding Welsh provision;

(c)   all the documents and information which were passed to the adoption panel in accordance with regulation 25(9) of the Agencies Regulations or corresponding Welsh provision;

(d)   the record of the proceedings of the adoption panel, its recommendation and the reasons for its recommendation; and

(e)   any other information relating to the case as the relevant Central Authority or the CA of the State of origin may require.

(2) If the relevant Central Authority is satisfied that the adoption agency has complied with the duties and procedures imposed by the Agencies Regulations or corresponding Welsh provision, and that all the relevant information has been supplied by that agency, the Authority must send to the CA of the State of origin –

(a)   the prospective adopter's report prepared in accordance with regulation 25 of the Agencies Regulations or corresponding Welsh provision;

(b)   (*revoked*)

(c)   a copy of the adoption agency's decision and the adoption panel's recommendation;

(d)   any other information that the CA of the State of origin may require;

(da)   if the prospective adopter applied to the appropriate Minister for a review under section 12 of the Adoption and Children Act 2002, the record of the proceedings of the panel, its recommendation and the reasons for its recommendation; and

(e)   a certificate in the form set out in Schedule 1 confirming that the –

    (i)   prospective adopter is eligible to adopt;

    (ii)   prospective adopter has been assessed in accordance with this Chapter;

    (iii)   prospective adopter has been approved as suitable to adopt a child; and

    (iv)   child will be authorised to enter and reside permanently in the United Kingdom if entry clearance, and leave to enter or remain as may be necessary, is granted and not revoked or curtailed and a Convention adoption order or Convention adoption is made.

(3) The relevant Central Authority must notify the adoption agency and the prospective adopter in writing that the certificate and the documents referred to in paragraph (2) have been sent to the CA of the State of origin.

Amendment: SI 2005/3842.

19 Procedure following receipt of the Article 16 Information from the CA of the State of origin

(1) Where the relevant Central Authority receives from the CA of the State of origin, the Article 16 Information relating to the child whom the CA of the State of origin considers should be placed for adoption with the prospective adopter, the relevant Central Authority must send that Information to the adoption agency.

(2) The adoption agency must consider the Article 16 Information and –

  (a)   send that Information to the prospective adopter;
  (b)   meet with him to discuss –
         (i)   that Information;
         (ii)   the proposed placement;
         (iii) the availability of adoption support services; and
  (c)   if appropriate, offer a counselling service and further information as required.

(3) Where –

  (a)   the procedure in paragraph (2) has been followed; and
  (b)   the prospective adopter has confirmed in writing to the adoption agency that he wishes to proceed to adopt the child,

the agency must notify the relevant Central Authority in writing that the requirements specified in sub-paragraphs (a) and (b) have been satisfied and at the same time it must confirm that it is content for the adoption to proceed.

(4) Where the relevant Central Authority has received notification from the adoption agency under paragraph (3), the relevant Central Authority shall –

  (a)   notify the CA of the State of origin that –
         (i)   the prospective adopter wishes to proceed to adopt the child;
         (ii)   it is prepared to agree with the CA of the State of origin that the adoption may proceed; and
  (b)   confirm to the CA of the State of origin that –
         (i)   in the case where the requirements specified in section 1(5A) of the British Nationality Act 1981 are met that the child will be authorised to enter and reside permanently in the United Kingdom; or
         (ii)   in any other case, if entry clearance and leave to enter and remain, as may be necessary, is granted and not revoked or curtailed and a Convention adoption order or a Convention adoption is made, the child will be authorised to enter and reside permanently in the United Kingdom.

(5) The relevant Central Authority must inform the adoption agency and the prospective adopter when the agreement under Article 17(c) of the Convention has been made.

(6) For the purposes of this regulation and regulation 20 'the Article 16 Information' means –

  (a)   the report referred to in Article 16(1) of the Convention including information about the child's identity, adoptability, background, social environment, family history, medical history including that of the child's family and any special needs of the child;
  (b)   proof of confirmation that the consents of the persons, institutions and authorities whose consents are necessary for adoption have been obtained in accordance with Article 4 of the Convention; and

(c) the reasons for the CA of the State of origin's determination on the placement.

Amendment: SI 2009/2563.

20 Procedure where proposed adoption is not to proceed

(1) If, at any stage before the agreement under Article 17(c) of the Convention is made, the CA of the State of origin notifies the relevant Central Authority that it has decided the proposed placement should not proceed –

(a) the relevant Central Authority must inform the adoption agency of the CA of the State of origin's decision;
(b) the agency must then inform the prospective adopter and return the Article 16 Information to the relevant Central Authority; and
(c) the relevant Central Authority must then return those documents to the CA of the State of origin.

(2) Where at any stage before the adoption agency receives notification of the agreement under Article 17(c) of the Convention the approval of the prospective adopter is reviewed under regulation 29 of the Agencies Regulations or corresponding Welsh provision, and as a consequence, the agency determines that the prospective adopter is no longer suitable to adopt a child –

(a) the agency must inform the relevant Central Authority and return the documents referred to in regulation 19(1);
(b) the relevant Central Authority must notify the CA of the State of origin and return those documents.

(3) If, at any stage before any Convention adoption is made and before the child's entry into the United Kingdom, the prospective adopter notifies the adoption agency that he does not wish to proceed with the adoption of the child –

(a) that agency must inform the relevant Central Authority and return the documents to that Authority; and
(b) the relevant Central Authority must notify the CA of the State of origin of the prospective adopter's decision and return the documents to the CA of the State of origin.

Amendment: SI 2009/2563.

21 Applicable requirements in respect of prospective adopter entering the United Kingdom with a child

Following any agreement under Article 17(c) of the Convention, the prospective adopter must –

(a) notify the adoption agency of his expected date of entry into the United Kingdom with the child;
(b) confirm to the adoption agency when the child is placed with him by the competent authority in the State of origin; and

(c)   accompany the child on entering the United Kingdom unless, in the case of a couple, the adoption agency and the CA of the State of origin have agreed that it is necessary for only one of them to do so.

22 Applicable requirements in respect of an adoption agency before the child enters the United Kingdom

Where the adoption agency is informed by the relevant Central Authority that the agreement under Article 17(c) of the Convention has been made and the adoption may proceed, before the child enters the United Kingdom that agency must –

(a)   send the prospective adopter's general practitioner written notification of the proposed placement and send with that notification a written report of the child's health history and current state of health, so far as it is known; and

(b)   send the local authority (if that authority is not the adoption agency) and the Primary Care Trust or Local Health Board (Wales), in whose area the prospective adopter has his home, written notification of the proposed arrival of the child into England or Wales and, where the child is of compulsory school age, include in the notification to the local authority information about the child's educational history and whether the child has been or is likely to be assessed for special educational needs under the Education Act 1996

(c)   (*revoked*)

Amendment: SI 2010/1172.

23 Applicable provisions following the child's entry into the United Kingdom where no Convention adoption is made

Regulations 24 to 27 apply where –

(a)   following the agreement between the relevant Central Authority and the CA of the State of origin under Article 17(c) of the Convention that the adoption may proceed, no Convention adoption is made, or applied for, in the State of origin; and

(b)   the child is placed with the prospective adopter in the State of origin who then returns to England or Wales with that child.

24 Applicable requirements in respect of prospective adopter following child's entry into the United Kingdom

(1) A prospective adopter must within the period of 14 days beginning with the date on which the child enters the United Kingdom give notice to the relevant local authority –

(a)   of the child's arrival in the United Kingdom; and

(b)   of his intention –

    (i)   to apply for an adoption order in accordance with section 44(2) of the Act; or

    (ii)   not to give the child a home.

(2) In a case where a prospective adopter has given notice in accordance with paragraph (1) and he subsequently moves his home into the area of another local authority, he must within 14 days of that move confirm to that authority in writing the child's entry into the United Kingdom and that notice of his intention –

(a) to apply for an adoption order in accordance with section 44(2) of the Act has been given to another local authority; or

(b) not to give the child a home,

has been given.

25 Functions imposed on the local authority following the child's entry into the United Kingdom

(1) Where notice is given to a local authority in accordance with regulation 24, the functions imposed on the local authority by virtue of regulation 5 shall apply subject to the modifications in paragraph (2).

(2) Paragraph (1) of regulation 5 shall apply as if –

(a) in sub-paragraph (a) –
  (i) in head (i) for the words 'relevant foreign authority' there is substituted 'CA of the State of origin and competent foreign authority';
  (ii) in head (v) there is substituted 'the relevant Central Authority'; and
(b) sub-paragraphs (b) to (d) were omitted.

26 Prospective adopter unable to proceed with adoption

(1) Where the prospective adopter gives notice to the relevant local authority that he does not wish to proceed with the adoption and no longer wishes to give the child a home, he must return the child to that authority not later than the end of the period of seven days beginning with the date on which notice was given.

(2) Where a relevant local authority have received a notice in accordance with paragraph (1), that authority must give notice to the relevant Central Authority of the decision of the prospective adopter not to proceed with the adoption.

Amendment: SI 2005/3482.

27 Withdrawal of child from prospective adopter

(1) Where the relevant local authority are of the opinion that the continued placement of the child is not in the child's best interests –

(a) that authority must give notice to the prospective adopter of their opinion and request the return of the child to them; and
(b) subject to paragraph (3), the prospective adopter must, not later than the end of the period of seven days beginning with the date on which notice was given, return the child to that authority.

(2) Where the relevant local authority has given notice under paragraph (1), that authority must at the same time notify the relevant Central Authority that they have requested the return of the child.

(3) Where notice is given under paragraph (1) but –

(a) an application for a Convention adoption order was made prior to the giving of that notice; and

(b) the application has not been disposed of,

the prospective adopter is not required by virtue of paragraph (1) to return the child unless the court so orders.

(4) This regulation does not affect the exercise by any local authority or other person of any power conferred by any enactment or the exercise of any power of arrest.

28 Breakdown of placement

(1) This regulation applies where –

(a) notification is given by the prospective adopter under regulation 26 (unable to proceed with adoption);

(b) the child is withdrawn from the prospective adopter under regulation 27 (withdrawal of child from prospective adopter);

(c) an application for a Convention adoption order is refused;

(d) a Convention adoption which is subject to a probationary period cannot be made; or

(e) a Convention adoption order or a Convention adoption is annulled pursuant to section 89(1) of the Act.

(2) Where the relevant local authority are satisfied that it would be in the child's best interests to be placed for adoption with another prospective adopter habitually resident in the United Kingdom they must take the necessary measures to identify a suitable adoptive parent for that child.

(3) Where the relevant local authority have identified and approved another prospective adopter who is eligible, and has been assessed as suitable, to adopt in accordance with these Regulations –

(a) that authority must notify the relevant Central Authority in writing that –

(i)   another prospective adopter has been identified; and

(ii) the provisions in regulations 14, 15 and 16 have been complied with; and

(b) the requirements specified in regulations 18 and 19 have been complied with.

(4) Where the relevant Central Authority has been notified in accordance with paragraph (3)(a) –

(a) it shall inform the CA of the State of origin of the proposed placement; and

(b) it shall agree the placement with the CA of the State of origin in accordance with the provisions in this Chapter.

(5) Subject to paragraph (2), where the relevant local authority is not satisfied it would be in the child's best interests to be placed for adoption with another prospective adopter in England or Wales, it must liaise with the relevant Central Authority to arrange for the return of the child to his State of origin.

(6) Before coming to any decision under this regulation, the relevant local authority must have regard to the wishes and feelings of the child, having regard to his age and understanding, and where appropriate, obtain his consent in relation to measures to be taken under this regulation.

29 Convention adoptions subject to a probationary period

(1) This regulation applies where –

(a) the child has been placed with the prospective adopters by the competent authority in the State of origin and a Convention adoption has been applied for by the prospective adopters in the State of origin but the child's placement with the prospective adopter is subject to a probationary period before the Convention adoption is made; and
(b) the prospective adopter returns to England or Wales with the child before that probationary period is completed and the Convention adoption is made in the State of origin.

(2) The relevant local authority must, if requested by the competent authority of the State of origin, submit a report about the placement to that authority and such a report must be prepared within such timescales and contain such information as the competent authority may reasonably require.

30 Report of local authority investigation

The report of the investigation which a local authority must submit to the court in accordance with section 44(5) of the Act must include –

(a) confirmation that the Certificate of eligibility and approval has been sent to the CA of the State of origin in accordance with regulation 18;
(b) the date on which the agreement under Article 17(c) of the Convention was made; and
(c) details of the reports of the visits and reviews made in accordance with regulation 5 as modified by regulation 25.

31 Convention adoption order

An adoption order shall not be made as a Convention adoption order unless –

(a) in the case of –
    (i) an application by a couple, both members of the couple have been habitually resident in any part of the British Islands for a period of not less than one year ending with the date of the application; or

        (ii)   an application by one person, the applicant has been habitually resident in any part of the British Islands for a period of not less than one year ending with the date of the application;

   (b)   the child to be adopted was, on the date on which the agreement under Article 17(c) of the Convention was made, habitually resident in a Convention country outside the British Islands; and

   (c)   in a case where one member of a couple (in the case of an application by a couple) or the applicant (in the case of an application by one person) is not a British citizen, the Home Office has confirmed that the child is authorised to enter and reside permanently in the United Kingdom.

32 Requirements following a Convention adoption order or Convention adoption

(1) Where the relevant Central Authority receives a copy of a Convention adoption order made by a court in England or Wales that Authority must issue a certificate in the form set out in Schedule 2 certifying that the adoption has been made in accordance with the Convention.

(2) A copy of the certificate issued under paragraph (1) must be sent to the –

   (a)   CA of the State of origin;
   (b)   adoptive parent; and
   (c)   adoption agency and, if different, the relevant local authority.

(3) Where a Convention adoption is made and the relevant Central Authority receives a certificate under Article 23 of the Convention in respect of that Convention adoption, the relevant Central Authority must send a copy of that certificate to the –

   (a)   adoptive parent; and
   (b)   adoption agency and, if different, the relevant local authority.

33 Refusal of a court in England or Wales to make a Convention adoption order

Where an application for a Convention adoption order is refused by the court or is withdrawn, the prospective adopter must return the child to the relevant local authority within the period determined by the court.

34 Annulment of a Convention adoption order or a Convention adoption

Where a Convention adoption order or a Convention adoption is annulled under section 89(1) of the Act and the relevant Central Authority receives a copy of the order from the court, it must forward a copy of that order to the CA of the State of origin. Chapter 2

Chapter 2
Requirements, Procedure, Recognition and Effect of Adoptions in England and
Wales where the United Kingdom is the State of Origin

35 Application of Chapter 2

The provisions in this Chapter shall apply where a couple or a person
habitually resident in a Convention country outside the British Islands, wishes
to adopt a child who is habitually resident in the British Islands in accordance
with the Convention.

36 Counselling and information for the child

(1) Where an adoption agency is considering whether a child is suitable for an
adoption in accordance with the Convention, it must provide a counselling
service for and information to that child in accordance with regulation 13 of
the Agencies Regulations or corresponding Welsh provision and it must –

   (a) explain to the child in an appropriate manner the procedure in relation
       to, and the legal implications of, adoption under the Convention for
       that child by a prospective adopter habitually resident in the receiving
       State; and
   (b) provide him with written information about the matters referred to in
       sub-paragraph (a).

(2) Paragraph (1) does not apply if the adoption agency is satisfied that the
requirements set out in that paragraph have been carried out in respect of the
prospective adopter by another agency.

37 Counselling and information for the parent or guardian of the child etc

(1) An adoption agency must provide a counselling service and information in
accordance with regulation 14 of the Agencies Regulations or corresponding
Welsh provision for the parent or guardian of the child and, where
regulation 14(4) of the Agencies Regulations or corresponding Welsh provision
applies, for the father.

(2) The adoption agency must also –

   (a) explain to the parent or guardian, and, where regulation 14(4) of the
       Agencies Regulations or corresponding Welsh provision applies, the
       father the procedure in relation to, and the legal implications of,
       adoption under the Convention by a prospective adopter in a receiving
       State; and
   (b) provide him with written information about the matters referred to in
       sub-paragraph (a).

(3) Paragraphs (1) and (2) do not apply if the adoption agency is satisfied that
the requirements set out in that paragraph have been carried out in respect of
the prospective adopter by another agency.

38 Requirements in respect of the child's permanence report and information for the adoption panel

(1) The child's permanence report which the adoption agency is required to prepare in accordance with regulation 17 of the Agencies Regulations or corresponding Welsh provision must include –

(a)   a summary of the possibilities for placement of the child within the United Kingdom; and

(b)   an assessment of whether an adoption by a person in a particular receiving State is in the child's best interests.

(2) In a case falling within regulation 17(2C) of the Agencies Regulations or the corresponding Welsh provision, the adoption agency must send –

(a)   if received, the Article 15 Report; and

(b)   their observations on that Report,

together with the reports and information referred to in regulation 17(2D) of the Agencies Regulations or corresponding Welsh provision to the adoption panel.

(3) In a case falling within regulation 17(2) of the Agencies Regulations or the corresponding Welsh provision, the adoption agency must consider –

(a)   if received, the Article 15 Report; and

(b)   their observations on that Report together with the reports and information referred to in regulation 17(2D) of the Agencies Regulations or the corresponding Welsh provision

in deciding whether the child should be placed for adoption in accordance with the Convention.

Amendments: SI 2012/1410

39 Recommendation of adoption panel

Where an adoption panel make a recommendation in accordance with regulation 18(1) of the Agencies Regulations or corresponding Welsh provision it must consider and take into account the Article 15 Report, if available, and the observations thereon together with the information passed to it as a consequence of regulation 38.

40 Adoption agency decision and notification

Where the adoption agency decides in accordance with regulation 19 of the Agencies Regulations or corresponding Welsh provision that the child should be placed for an adoption in accordance with the Convention it must notify the relevant Central Authority of –

(a)   the name, sex and age of the child;

(b)   the reasons why they consider that the child may be suitable for such an adoption;

(c)   whether a prospective adopter has been identified and, if so, provide any relevant information; and

(d)   any other information that Authority may require.

41 Convention list

(1) The relevant Central Authority is to maintain a Convention list of children who are notified to that Authority under regulation 40 and shall make the contents of that list available for consultation by other Authorities within the British Islands.

(2) Where an adoption agency –

(a)   places for adoption a child whose details have been notified to the relevant Central Authority under regulation 40; or

(b)   determines that an adoption in accordance with the Convention is no longer in the best interests of the child,

it must notify the relevant Central Authority accordingly and that Authority must remove the details relating to that child from the Convention list.

42 Receipt of the Article 15 Report from the CA of the receiving State

(1) This regulation applies where –

(a)   the relevant Central Authority receives a report from the CA of the receiving State which has been prepared for the purposes of Article 15 of the Convention ('the Article 15 Report');

(b)   the Article 15 Report relates to a prospective adopter who is habitually resident in that receiving State; and

(c)   the prospective adopter named in the Article 15 Report wishes to adopt a child who is habitually resident in the British Islands.

(2) Subject to paragraph (3), if the relevant Central Authority is satisfied the prospective adopter meets the following requirements –

(a)   the age requirements as specified in section 50 of the Act in the case of adoption by a couple, or section 51 of the Act in the case of adoption by one person; and

(b)   in the case of a couple, both are, or in the case of adoption by one person, that person is habitually resident in a Convention country outside the British Islands,

that Authority must consult the Convention list and may, if the Authority considers it appropriate, consult any Convention list maintained by another Central Authority within the British Islands.

(3) Where a prospective adopter has already been identified in relation to a proposed adoption of a particular child and the relevant Central Authority is satisfied that prospective adopter meets the requirements referred to in paragraph (2)(a) and (b), that Authority –

(a)   need not consult the Convention list; and

(b)   must send the Article 15 Report to the local authority which referred the child's details to the Authority.

(4) The relevant Central Authority may pass a copy of the Article 15 Report to any other Central Authority within the British Islands for the purposes of enabling that Authority to consult its Convention list.

(5) Where the relevant Central Authority identifies a child on the Convention list who may be suitable for adoption by the prospective adopter, that Authority must send the Article 15 Report to the local authority which referred the child's details to that Authority.

43 Proposed placement and referral to adoption panel

(1) Where the adoption agency is considering whether a proposed placement should proceed in accordance with the procedure provided for in regulation 31 of the Agencies Regulations or corresponding Welsh provision it must take into account the Article 15 Report.

(2) Where the adoption agency refers the proposal to place the child with the particular prospective adopter to the adoption panel in accordance with regulation 31 of the Agencies Regulations or corresponding Welsh provision, it must also send the Article 15 Report to the panel.

44 Consideration by adoption panel

The adoption panel must take into account when considering what recommendation to make in accordance with regulation 32(1) of the Agencies Regulations or corresponding Welsh provision the Article 15 Report and any other information passed to it as a consequence of the provisions in this Chapter.

45 Adoption agency's decision in relation to the proposed placement

(1) Regulation 33 of the Agencies Regulations or corresponding Welsh provision shall apply as if paragraph (3) of that regulation or corresponding Welsh provision was omitted.

(2) As soon as possible after the agency makes its decision, it must notify the relevant Central Authority of its decision.

(3) If the proposed placement is not to proceed –

(a)   the adoption agency must return the Article 15 Report and any other documents or information sent to it by the relevant Central Authority to that Authority; and

(b)   the relevant Central Authority must then send that Report, any such documents or such information to the CA of the receiving State.

46 Preparation of the Article 16 Information

(1) If the adoption agency decides that the proposed placement should proceed, it must prepare a report for the purposes of Article 16(1) of the Convention which must include –

(a) the information about the child which is specified in Schedule 1 to the Agencies Regulations or corresponding Welsh provision; and

(b) the reasons for their decision.

(2) The adoption agency must send the following to the relevant Central Authority –

(a) the report referred to in paragraph (1);

(b) details of any placement order or other orders, if any, made by the courts; and

(c) confirmation that the parent or guardian consents to the proposed adoption.

(3) The relevant Central Authority must then send the documents referred to in paragraph (2) to the CA of the receiving State.

47 Requirements to be met before the child is placed for adoption with prospective adopter

(1) The relevant Central Authority may notify the CA of the receiving State that it is prepared to agree that the adoption may proceed provided that CA has confirmed that –

(a) the prospective adopter has agreed to adopt the child and has received such counselling as may be necessary;

(b) the prospective adopter has confirmed that he will accompany the child to the receiving State, unless in the case of a couple, the adoption agency and the CA of the receiving State have agreed that it is only necessary for one of them to do so;

(c) it is content for the adoption to proceed;

(d) in the case where a Convention adoption is to be effected, it has explained to the prospective adopter the need to make an application under section 84(1) of the Act; and

(e) the child is or will be authorised to enter and reside permanently in the Convention country if a Convention adoption is effected or a Convention adoption order is made.

(2) The relevant Central Authority may not make an agreement under Article 17(c) of the Convention with the CA of the receiving State unless –

(a) confirmation has been received in respect of the matters referred to in paragraph (1); and

(b) the adoption agency has confirmed to the relevant Central Authority that –

(i) it has met the prospective adopter and explained the requirement to make an application for an order under section 84 of the Act before the child can be removed from the United Kingdom;

(ii)   the prospective adopter has visited the child; and

(iii)   the prospective adopter is content for the adoption to proceed.

(3) An adoption agency may not place a child for adoption unless the agreement under Article 17(c) of the Convention has been made and the relevant Central Authority must advise that agency when that agreement has been made.

(4) In this regulation, the reference to 'prospective adopter' means in the case of a couple, both of them.

48 Requirements in respect of giving parental responsibility prior to a proposed Convention adoption

In the case of a proposed Convention adoption, the prescribed requirements for the purposes of section 84(3) of the Act (requirements to be satisfied prior to making an order) are –

(a)   the competent authorities of the receiving State have –
    (i)   prepared a report for the purposes of Article 15 of the Convention;
    (ii)   determined and confirmed in writing that the prospective adoptive parent is eligible and suitable to adopt;
    (iii) ensured and confirmed in writing that the prospective adoptive parent has been counselled as may be necessary; and
    (iv)   determined and confirmed in writing that the child is or will be authorised to enter and reside permanently in that State;

(b)   the report required for the purposes of Article 16(1) of the Convention has been prepared by the adoption agency;

(c)   the adoption agency confirms in writing that it has complied with the requirements imposed upon it under Part 3 of the Agencies Regulations or corresponding Welsh provision and this Chapter;

(d)   the adoption agency has obtained and made available to the court –
    (i)   the reports and information referred to in regulation 17(2D) of the Agencies Regulations or corresponding Welsh provision;
    (ii)   the recommendation made by the adoption panel in accordance with regulations 18, where applicable, and 33 of the Agencies Regulations or corresponding Welsh provisions; and
    (iii) the adoption placement report prepared in accordance with regulation 31(2) of the Agencies Regulations or corresponding Welsh provision;

(e)   the adoption agency includes in their report submitted to the court in accordance with section 43(a) or 44(5) of the Act as modified respectively by regulation 11, details of any reviews and visits carried out as consequence of Part 6 of the Agencies Regulations or corresponding Welsh provision; and

(f)   the prospective adopter has confirmed in writing that he will accompany the child on taking the child out of the United Kingdom to travel to the receiving State or in the case of a couple the agency and competent foreign authority have confirmed that it is necessary for only one of them to do so.

Amendments: SI 2012/1410.

49 Local authority report

In the case of a proposed application for a Convention adoption order, the report which a local authority must submit to the court in accordance with section 43(a) or 44(5) of the Act must include a copy of the –

(a)   Article 15 Report;
(b)   report prepared for the purposes of Article 16(1); and
(c)   written confirmation of the agreement under Article 17(c) of the Convention.

50 Convention adoption order

An adoption order shall not be made as a Convention adoption order unless –

(a)   in the case of –
    (i)   an application by a couple, both members of the couple have been habitually resident in a Convention country outside the British Islands for a period of not less than one year ending with the date of the application; or
(aa) an application by one person, the applicant has been habitually resident in a Convention country outside the British Islands for a period of not less than one year ending with the date of the application;
(b)   the child to be adopted was, on the date on which the agreement under Article 17(c) of the Convention was made, habitually resident in any part of the British Islands; and
(c)   the competent authority has confirmed that the child is authorised to enter and remain permanently in the Convention country in which the applicant is habitually resident.

51 Requirements following a Convention adoption order or Convention adoption

(1) Where the relevant Central Authority receives a copy of a Convention adoption order made by a court in England or Wales, that Authority must issue a certificate in the form set out in Schedule 2 certifying that the adoption has been made in accordance with the Convention.

(2) A copy of the certificate must be sent to the –

(a)   CA of the receiving State; and
(b)   the relevant local authority.

(3) Where a Convention adoption is made and the Central Authority receives a certificate under Article 23 in respect of that Convention adoption, the relevant Central Authority must send a copy of that certificate to the relevant local authority.

Chapter 3
Miscellaneous Provisions

52 Application, with or without modifications, of the Act

(1) Subject to the modifications provided for in this Chapter, the provisions of the Act shall apply to adoptions within the scope of the Convention so far as the nature of the provision permits and unless the contrary intention is shown.

53 Change of name and removal from the United Kingdom

In a case falling within Chapter 1 of this Part, section 28(2) of the Act shall apply as if –

(a)   at the end of paragraph (a), 'or' was omitted;
(b)   at the end of paragraph (b) there were inserted 'or (c) a child is placed by a competent foreign authority for the purposes of an adoption under the Convention,'; and
(c)   at the end of subsection (2) there were inserted 'or the competent foreign authority consents to a change of surname.'.

54 Removal of children

(1) In a case falling within Chapter 1 of this Part, sections 36 to 40 of the Act shall not apply.

(2) In a case falling within Chapter 2 of this Part –

(a)   section 36 of the Act shall apply, as if –
  (i)   for the words 'an adoption order' in paragraphs (a) and (c) in subsection (1) there were substituted 'a Convention adoption order'; and
  (ii)   subsection (2) was omitted; and
(b)   section 39 of the Act shall apply as if subsection (3)(a) was omitted.

55 Modifications of the Act in respect of orders under section 84 where child is to be adopted under the Convention

The modifications set out in regulation 11 shall apply in the case where a couple or person habitually resident in a Convention country outside the British Islands intend to adopt a child who is habitually resident in England or Wales in accordance with the Convention.

56 Child to live with adopters before application for a Convention adoption order

Section 42 of the Act shall apply as if –

(a)   subsections (1)(b) and (3) to (6) were omitted; and
(b)   in subsection (2) from the word 'If' to the end of paragraph (b) there were substituted 'In the case of an adoption under the Convention,'.

57 Notice of intention to adopt

Section 44 of the Act shall apply as if subsection (3) was omitted.

58 Application for Convention adoption order

Section 49 of the Act shall apply as if –

(a) in subsection (1), the words from 'but only' to the end were omitted;
(b) subsections (2) and (3) were omitted.

59 Offences

Any person who contravenes or fails to comply with –

(a) regulation 24 (requirements in respect of prospective adopter following child's entry into the United Kingdom);
(b) regulation 26(1) (return of child to relevant local authority where prospective adopter does not wish to proceed);
(c) regulation 27(1)(b) (return of child to relevant local authority on request of local authority or by order of court); or
(d) regulation 33 (refusal of a court in England or Wales to make a Convention adoption order)

is guilty of an offence and liable on summary conviction to imprisonment for a term not exceeding three months, or a fine not exceeding level 5 on the standard scale, or both.

Amendment: SI 2005/3842.

Schedule 1
Certificate of Eligibility and Approval

Regulation 18

To the Central Authority of the State of origin

Re ....[name of applicant]

In accordance with Article 5 of the Convention, I hereby certify on behalf of the Central Authority for [England] [Wales] that ....[name of applicant] has been counselled, is eligible to adopt and has been assessed and approved as suitable to adopt a child from ....[State of origin] by ....[public authority or accredited body for the purposes of the Convention].

The attached report has been prepared in accordance with Article 15 of the Convention for presentation to the competent authority in ....[State of origin].

This certificate of eligibility and approval and the report under Article 15 of the Convention are provided on the condition that a Convention adoption or Convention adoption order will not be made until the agreement under Article 17(c) of the Convention has been made.

I confirm on behalf of the Central Authority that if following the agreement under Article 17(c) of the Convention that –

[in the case, where the requirements specified in section 1(5A) of the British Nationality Act 1981 are met that the child ....[name] will be authorised to enter and reside permanently in the United Kingdom]; or

[in any other case, if entry clearance and leave to enter and remain, as may be necessary, is granted and not revoked, or curtailed and a Convention adoption order or Convention adoption is made, the child ....[name] will be authorised to enter and reside permanently in the United Kingdom.]

Name

[On behalf of the Secretary of State, the Central Authority for England]

Date

[the National Assembly for Wales, the Central Authority for Wales]

Schedule 2
Certificate That the Convention Adoption Order has Been Made in Accordance With the Convention

Regulations 32 and 51

1 The Central Authority as the competent authority for [England] [Wales] being the country in which the Convention adoption order was made hereby certifies, in accordance with Article 23(1) of the Convention, that the child:

(a) name ....[name on birth certificate, also known as/now known as ....]
sex: ....
date and place of birth: ....
habitual residence at the time of the adoption: ....
State of origin: ....
(b) was adopted on: ....
by order made by: ....court in [England] [Wales]
(c) by the following person(s):
(i) family name and first name(s): ....
sex: ....
date and place of birth: ....
Habitual residence at the time adoption order was made: ....
(ii) family name and first name(s): ....
sex: ....
date and place of birth: ....
habitual residence at the time adoption order made: ....

2 The competent authority for [England] [Wales] in pursuance of Article 23(1) of the Convention hereby certifies that the adoption was made in accordance with the Convention and that the agreement under Article 17(c) was given by:

    (a)   name and address of the Central Authority in State of origin: ....

date of the agreement: ....

    (b)   name and address of the Central Authority of receiving State: ....

date of the agreement: ....

Signed

Date

Appendix 3

ADOPTION AGENCIES REGULATIONS 2005

SI 2005/389

PART I
GENERAL

1 Citation, commencement and application

(1) These Regulations may be cited as the Adoption Agencies Regulations 2005 and shall come into force on 30th December 2005.

(2) These Regulations apply to England only.

2 Interpretation

(1) In these Regulations –

'the Act' means the Adoption and Children Act 2002;

'the 1989 Act' means the Children Act 1989;

'adoption panel' means a panel established in accordance with regulation 3;

'adoption placement plan' has the meaning given in regulation 35(2);

'adoption placement report' means the report prepared by the adoption agency in accordance with regulation 31(2)(d);

'adoption support services' has the meaning given in section 2(6)(a) of the Act and in any regulations made under section 2(6)(b) of the Act;

'adoptive family' has the meaning given in regulation 31(2)(a);

'CAFCASS' means the Children and Family Court Advisory and Support Service;

'care order' has the meaning given in section 105(1) of the 1989 Act;

'child's case record' has the meaning given in regulation 12;

'child's health report' means the report obtained in accordance with regulation 15(2)(b);

'child's permanence report' means the report prepared by the adoption agency in accordance with regulation 17(1);

'independent member' in relation to an adoption panel has the meaning given in regulation 3(3)(e);

'independent review panel' means a panel constituted under section 12 of the Act;

'joint adoption panel' means an adoption panel established in accordance with regulation 3(5);

'medical adviser' means the person appointed as the medical adviser by the adoption agency in accordance with regulation 9(1);

'proposed placement' has the meaning given in regulation 31(1);

'prospective adopter's case record' has the meaning given in regulation 22(1);

'prospective adopter's report' means the report prepared by the adoption agency in accordance with regulation 25(5);

'prospective adopter's review report' means the report prepared by the adoption agency in accordance with regulation 29(4)(a);

'qualifying determination' has the meaning given in regulation 27(4)(a);

'registration authority' means Her Majesty's Chief Inspector of Education, Children's Services and Skills;

'relevant foreign authority' means a person, outside the British Islands performing functions in the country in which the child is, or in which the prospective adopter is, habitually resident which correspond to the functions of an adoption agency or to the functions of the Secretary of State in respect of adoptions with a foreign element;

'relevant post-qualifying experience' means post-qualifying experience in child care social work including direct experience in adoption work;

'section 83 case' means a case where a person who is habitually resident in the British Islands intends to bring, or to cause another to bring, a child into the United Kingdom in circumstances where section 83 of the Act (restriction on bringing children into the United Kingdom) applies;

'social worker' means a person who is registered as a social worker in a register maintained by the General Social Care Council or the Care Council for Wales under section 56 of the Care Standards Act 2000 or in a corresponding register maintained under the law of Scotland or Northern Ireland;

'vice chair' has the meaning given in regulation 3(4) or, as the case may be, (5)(c);

'working day' means any day other than a Saturday, Sunday, Christmas Day, Good Friday or a day which is a bank holiday within the meaning of the Banking and Financial Dealings Act 1971.

Amendments: SI 2007/603; SI 2012/1410.

PART 2
ADOPTION AGENCY—ARRANGEMENTS FOR ADOPTION WORK

3 The central list

(1) Subject to regulation 5, an adoption agency must maintain a list of persons who are considered by it to be suitable to be members of an adoption panel ('the central list'), including –

(a) one or more social workers who have at least three years' relevant post-qualifying experience, and

(b) the medical adviser to the adoption agency (or at least one if more than one medical adviser is appointed).

(2) A person who is included in the central list may at any time ask to be removed from the central list by giving one month's notice in writing.

(3) Where the adoption agency is of the opinion that a person included in the central list is unsuitable or unable to remain in the list the agency may remove that person's name from the list by giving them one month's notice in writing with reasons.

Amendments: Regulations 3–8 substituted for original regs 3–10; SI 2011/589, regs 1, 2.

4 Constituting an adoption panel

(1) The adoption agency must constitute one or more adoption panels, as necessary, to perform the functions of an adoption panel under these Regulations and must appoint the panel members from the persons in the central list including –

- (a) a person to chair the panel, being an independent person, who has the skills and experience necessary for chairing an adoption panel, and
- (b) one or two persons who may act as chair if the person appointed to chair the panel is absent or that office is vacant ('the vice chairs').

(2) The adoption agency must ensure that an adoption panel has sufficient members, and that individual members have between them the experience and expertise necessary to effectively discharge the functions of the panel.

(3) Any two or more local authorities may jointly constitute an adoption panel ('a joint adoption panel') in which case the appointment of members must be by agreement between the authorities.

(4) A local authority may pay to any member of an adoption panel constituted by it such fee as it may determine, being a fee of a reasonable amount.

(5) Any adoption panel member may resign at any time by giving one month's notice in writing to the adoption agency which appointed them.

(6) Where an adoption agency is of the opinion that any member of the adoption panel appointed by it is unsuitable or unable to continue as a panel member, it may terminate that member's appointment at any time by giving the member notice in writing with reasons.

(7) A person ('P') is not an independent person for the purposes of this regulation and regulation 6 if –

- (a) in the case of a registered adoption society, P is a trustee or employee of that society, or
- (b) in the case of a local authority, P –
  - (i) is an elected member of that authority, or
  - (ii) is employed by that authority for the purposes of the adoption service or for the purposes of any of that local authority's functions relating to the protection or placement of children, or
- (c) P is the adoptive parent of a child who was –
  - (i) placed for adoption with P by the adoption agency ('agency A'), or

    (ii)   placed for adoption with P by another adoption agency where P had been approved as suitable to be an adoptive parent by agency A,

unless at least 12 months has elapsed since the adoption order was made in respect of the child.

Amendments: Regulations 3–8 substituted for original regs 3–10: SI 2011/589, regs 1, 2.

5 Adoption agencies operating only for certain purposes

Where an adoption agency operates only for the purpose of putting persons into contact with other adoption agencies and for the purpose of putting such agencies into contact with each other or for either of such purposes, regulations 3, 4, 8 and, to the extent that it requires consultation with persons in the central list, regulation 7 shall not apply to such an agency.

Amendments: Regulations 3–8 substituted for original regs 3–10; SI 2011/589, regs 1, 2.

6 Meetings of adoption panel

(1) No business may be conducted by an adoption panel unless at least the following meet as the panel –

    (a)   either the person appointed to chair the panel or one of the vice chairs,
    (b)   one person falling within regulation 3(1)(a),
    (c)   three, or in the case of an adoption panel established under regulation 4(3) four, other members and where the chair is not present and the vice chair is not an independent person, at least one other panel member must be an independent person.

(2) An adoption panel must make a written record of its proceedings, its recommendations and the reasons for its recommendations.

Amendments: Regulations 3–8 substituted for original regs 3–10; SI 2011/589, regs 1, 2.

7 Adoption agency arrangements for adoption work

An adoption agency must, in consultation with such persons in the central list as the agency considers appropriate and, to the extent specified in regulation 8(4) with the agency's medical adviser, prepare and implement written policy and procedural instructions governing the exercise of the functions of the agency and an adoption panel in relation to adoption and such instructions shall be kept under review and, where appropriate, revised by the agency.

Amendments: Regulations 3–8 substituted for original regs 3–10; SI 2011/589, regs 1, 2.

8 Requirement to appoint an agency adviser and a medical adviser

(1) The adoption agency must appoint a senior member of staff, or where local authorities agree to constitute joint adoption panels as necessary appoint a senior member of staff of one of them, (referred to in this regulation as the 'agency adviser') –

(a)   to assist the agency with the maintenance of the central list and the constitution of adoption panels,

(b)   to be responsible for the induction and training of persons in the central list,

(c)   to be responsible for liaison between the agency and an adoption panel, monitoring the performance of persons in the central list and members of the adoption panel and the administration of adoption panels, and

(d)   to give such advice to an adoption panel as the panel may request in relation to any case or generally.

(2) The agency adviser must be a social worker and have at least five years' relevant post-qualification experience and, in the opinion of the adoption agency, relevant management experience.

(3) The adoption agency must appoint at least one registered medical practitioner to be the agency's medical adviser.

(4) The medical adviser shall be consulted in relation to the arrangements for access to, and disclosure of, health information which is required or permitted by virtue of these Regulations.

Amendments: Regulations 3–8 substituted for original regs 3–10; SI 2011/589, regs 1, 2.

PART 3
DUTIES OF ADOPTION AGENCY WHERE THE AGENCY IS CONSIDERING ADOPTION FOR A CHILD

11 Application of regulations 12 to 17

Regulations 12 to 17 apply where the adoption agency is considering adoption for a child.

Amendments: SI 2005/3482.

12 Requirement to open the child's case record

(1) The adoption agency must set up a case record ('the child's case record') in respect of the child and place on it –

(a)   the information and reports obtained by the agency by virtue of this Part;

(b)   the child's permanence report;

(c)   where applicable the written record of the proceedings of the adoption panel under regulation 18, its recommendation and the reasons for its recommendation and any advice given by the panel to the agency;

(d)   the record of the agency's decision and any notification of that decision under regulation 19;

(e)   any consent to placement for adoption under section 19 of the Act (placing children with parental consent);

(f)   any consent to the making of a future adoption order under section 20 of the Act (advance consent to adoption);

(g) any form or notice withdrawing consent under section 19 or 20 of the Act or notice under section 20(4)(a) or (b) of the Act;

(h) a copy of any placement order in respect of the child; and

(i) any other documents or information obtained by the agency which it considers should be included in that case record.

(2) Where an adoption agency places on the child's case record a notice under section 20(4)(a) or (b) of the Act, the agency must send a copy of that notice to a court which has given the agency notice of the issue of an application for an adoption order.

Amendments: SI 2012/1410.

13 Requirement to provide counselling and information for, and ascertain wishes and feelings of, the child

(1) The adoption agency must, so far as is reasonably practicable –

(a) provide a counselling service for the child;

(b) explain to the child in an appropriate manner the procedure in relation to, and the legal implications of, adoption for the child and provide him with appropriate written information about these matters; and

(c) ascertain the child's wishes and feelings regarding –
   (i) the possibility of placement for adoption with a new family and his adoption;
   (ii) his religious and cultural upbringing; and
   (iii) contact with his parent or guardian or other relative or with any other person the agency considers relevant.

(2) Paragraph (1) does not apply if the adoption agency is satisfied that the requirements of that paragraph have been carried out in respect of the child by another adoption agency.

14 Requirement to provide counselling and information for, and ascertain wishes and feelings of, the parent or guardian of the child and others

(1) The adoption agency must, so far as is reasonably practicable –

(a) provide a counselling service for the parent or guardian of the child;

(b) explain to him –
   (i) the procedure in relation to both placement for adoption and adoption;
   (ii) the legal implications of –
   (aa) giving consent to placement for adoption under section 19 of the Act;
   (bb) giving consent to the making of a future adoption order under section 20 of the Act; and
   (cc) a placement order; and
   (iii) the legal implications of adoption,

and provide him with written information about these matters; and

(c)   ascertain the wishes and feelings of the parent or guardian of the child and, of any other person the agency considers relevant, regarding –

(i)   the child;

(ii)   the placement of the child for adoption and his adoption, including any wishes and feelings about the child's religious and cultural upbringing; and

(iii)   contact with the child if the child is authorised to be placed for adoption or the child is adopted.

(2) Paragraph (1) does not apply if the agency is satisfied that the requirements of that paragraph have been carried out in respect of the parent or guardian and any other person the agency considers relevant by another adoption agency.

(3) This paragraph applies where the father of the child does not have parental responsibility for the child and the father's identity is known to the adoption agency.

(4) Where paragraph (3) applies and the adoption agency is satisfied it is appropriate to do so, the agency must –

(a)   carry out in respect of the father the requirements of paragraph (1)(a), (b)(i) and (iii) and (c) as if they applied to him unless the agency is satisfied that the requirements have been carried out in respect of the father by another agency; and

(b)   ascertain so far as possible whether the father –

(i)   wishes to acquire parental responsibility for the child under section 4 of the 1989 Act (acquisition of parental responsibility by father, or paragraph 4ZA of the 1989 Act (acquisition of parental responsibility by second female parent)); or

(ii)   intends to apply for a residence order or contact order with respect to the child under section 8 of the 1989 Act (residence, contact and other orders with respect to children) or, where the child is subject to a care order, an order under section 34 of the 1989 Act (parental contact etc with children in care).

Amendments: SI 2009/1892.

15 Requirement to obtain information about the child

(1) The adoption agency must obtain, so far as is reasonably practicable, the information about the child which is specified in Part 1 of Schedule 1.

(2) Subject to paragraph (4), the adoption agency must –

(a)   make arrangements for the child to be examined by a registered medical practitioner; and

(b)   obtain from that practitioner a written report ('the child's health report') on the state of the child's health which shall include any treatment which the child is receiving, any need for health care and the matters specified in Part 2 of Schedule 1, unless the agency has received advice from the medical adviser that such an examination and report is unnecessary.

(3) Subject to paragraph (4), the adoption agency must make arrangements –

(a)   for such other medical and psychiatric examinations of, and other tests on, the child to be carried out as are recommended by the agency's medical adviser; and

(b)   for written reports of such examinations and tests to be obtained.

(4) Paragraphs (2) and (3) do not apply if the child is of sufficient understanding to make an informed decision and refuses to submit to the examinations or other tests.

16 Requirement to obtain information about the child's family

(1) The adoption agency must obtain, so far as is reasonably practicable, the information about the child's family which is specified in Part 3 of Schedule 1.

(2) The adoption agency must obtain, so far as is reasonably practicable, the information about the health of each of the child's natural parents and his brothers and sisters (of the full blood or half-blood) which is specified in Part 4 of Schedule 1.

17 Requirement to prepare child's permanence report

(1) The adoption agency must prepare a written report ('the child's permanence report') which shall include –

(a)   the information about the child and his family as specified in Parts 1 and 3 of Schedule 1;

(b)   a summary, written by the agency's medical adviser, of the state of the child's health, his health history and any need for health care which might arise in the future;

(c)   the wishes and feelings of the child regarding the matters set out in regulation 13(1)(c);

(d)   the wishes and feelings of the child's parent or guardian, and where regulation 14(4)(a) applies, his father, and any other person the agency considers relevant, regarding the matters set out in regulation 14(1)(c);

(e)   the views of the agency about the child's need for contact with his parent or guardian or other relative or with any other person the agency considers relevant and the arrangements the agency proposes to make for allowing any person contact with the child;

(f)   an assessment of the child's emotional and behavioural development and any related needs;

(g)   an assessment of the parenting capacity of the child's parent or guardian and, where regulation 14(4)(a) applies, his father;

(h)   a chronology of the decisions and actions taken by the agency with respect to the child;

(i)   an analysis of the options for the future care of the child which have been considered by the agency and why placement for adoption is considered the preferred option; and

(j)   any other information which the agency considers relevant.

(2) In a case where –

(a)   the adoption agency is a local authority and is considering whether the child ought to be placed for adoption, and

(b)   either paragraph (2A) or paragraph (2B) applies,

the adoption agency may not refer the case to the adoption panel.

(2A) This paragraph applies where –

(a)   the child is placed for adoption by the adoption agency or is being provided with accommodation by them,

(b)   no adoption agency is authorised to place the child for adoption, and

(c)   the child has no parent or guardian, or the agency consider that the conditions in section 31(2) of the 1989 Act are met in relation to the child.

(2B) This paragraph applies where –

(a)   an application has been made, and has not been disposed of, on which a care order might be made in respect of the child, or

(b)   the child is subject to a care order and the adoption agency are not authorised to place the child for adoption.

(2C) In a case not falling within paragraph (2), the adoption agency must send the information and reports referred to in paragraph (2D) to the adoption panel.

(2D) For the purposes of paragraph (2C) and regulation 19(1A) the information and reports are –

(i)   the child's permanence report,

(ii)   the child's health report and any other reports referred to in regulation 15, and

(iii)   the information relating to the health of each of the child's natural parents,

except that, in a case falling within paragraph (2C), the adoption agency may only send to the adoption panel the documents referred to in subparagraphs (ii) and (iii) if the agency's medical adviser advises it to do so.

(3) The adoption agency must obtain, so far as is reasonably practicable, any other relevant information which may be requested by the adoption panel and send that information to the panel.

Amendments: SI 2005/3482; SI 2012/1410.

18 Function of the adoption panel in relation to a child referred by the adoption agency

(1) The adoption panel must consider the case of every child referred to it by the adoption agency and make a recommendation to the agency as to whether the child should be placed for adoption.

(2) In considering what recommendation to make the adoption panel must have regard to the duties imposed on the adoption agency under section 1(2), (4), (5) and (6) of the Act (considerations applying to the exercise of powers in relation to the adoption of a child) and –

(a) must consider and take into account the reports and any other information passed to it in accordance with regulation 17;

(b) may request the agency to obtain any other relevant information which the panel considers necessary; and

(c) must obtain legal advice in relation to the case.

(3) Where the adoption panel makes a recommendation to the adoption agency that the child should be placed for adoption, it must consider and may at the same time give advice to the agency about –

(a) the arrangements which the agency proposes to make for allowing any person contact with the child; and

(b) where the agency is a local authority, whether an application should be made by the authority for a placement order in respect of the child.

19 Adoption agency decision and notification

(1) In any case falling within regulation 17(2C) the adoption agency must take into account the recommendation of the adoption panel in coming to a decision about whether the child should be placed for adoption.

(1A) In any case falling within regulation 17(2) the adoption agency must take into account the information and reports referred to in regulation 17(2D), and any other relevant information, in coming to a decision about whether the child ought to be placed for adoption.

(2) No member of the adoption panel or person on the central list shall take part in any decision made by the adoption agency under paragraph (1).

(3) The adoption agency must, if their whereabouts are known to the agency, notify in writing the parent or guardian and, where regulation 14(3) applies and the agency considers it is appropriate, the father of the child of its decision.

Amendments: SI 2012/1410.

20 Request to appoint an officer of the Service or a Welsh family proceedings officer

Where the parent or guardian of the child resides in England and Wales and[1] is prepared to consent to the placement of the child for adoption under section 19 of the Act and, as the case may be, to consent to the making of a future adoption order under section 20 of the Act, the adoption agency must request the CAFCASS to appoint an officer of the Service or the National Assembly for Wales to appoint a Welsh family proceedings officer for the purposes of the signification by that officer of the consent to placement or to adoption by that parent or guardian and send with that request the information specified in Schedule 2.

Amendments: SI 2005/3482.

20A (1) Where the parent or guardian resides outside England and Wales and is prepared to consent to the placement of the child for adoption under section 19 of the Act and, as the case may be, to consent to the making of a future adoption order under section 20 of the Act, the adoption agency must arrange for the appointment of an authorised person to witness the execution of the form of consent to placement or to adoption by that parent or guardian and send to that person the information specified in Schedule 2.

(2) 'Authorised person' for the purposes of this regulation means in relation to a form of consent executed—

(a) in Scotland, a Justice of the Peace or a Sheriff;

(b) in Northern Ireland, a Justice of the Peace;

(c) outside the United Kingdom, any person for the time being authorised by law in the place where the document is executed to administer an oath for any judicial or other legal purpose; a British Consular officer; a notary public; or, if the person executing the document is serving in any of the regular armed forces of the Crown, an officer holding a commission in any of those forces.

Amendments: SI 2005/3482.

PART 4
DUTIES OF ADOPTION AGENCY IN RESPECT OF A PROSPECTIVE ADOPTER

21 Requirement to provide counselling and information

(1) Where an adoption agency is considering a person's suitability to adopt a child, the agency must –

(a) provide a counselling service for the prospective adopter;

(b) in a section 83 case, explain to the prospective adopter the procedure in relation to, and the legal implications of, adopting a child from the country from which the prospective adopter wishes to adopt;

(c) in any other case, explain to him the procedure in relation to, and the legal implications of, placement for adoption and adoption; and

(d) provide him with written information about the matters referred to in sub-paragraph (b) or, as the case may be, (c).

(2) Paragraph (1) does not apply if the adoption agency is satisfied that the requirements set out in that paragraph have been carried out in respect of the prospective adopter by another adoption agency.

22 Requirement to consider application for an assessment of suitability to adopt a child

(1) Where the adoption agency, following the procedures referred to in regulation 21, receives an application in writing in the form provided by the agency from a prospective adopter for an assessment of his suitability to adopt

a child, the agency must set up a case record in respect of that prospective adopter ('the prospective adopter's case record') and consider his suitability to adopt a child.

(2) The adoption agency may ask the prospective adopter to provide any further information in writing the agency may reasonably require.

(3) The adoption agency must place on the prospective adopter's case record –

(a) the application by the prospective adopter for an assessment of his suitability to adopt a child referred to in paragraph (1);

(b) the information and reports obtained by the agency by virtue of this Part;

(c) the prospective adopter's report and his observations on that report;

(d) the written record of the proceedings of the adoption panel under regulation 26 (and, where applicable, regulation 27(6)), its recommendation and the reasons for its recommendation and any advice given by the panel to the agency;

(e) the record of the agency's decision under regulation 27(3), (5) or, as the case may be, (9);

(f) where the prospective adopter applied to the Secretary of State for a review by an independent review panel the recommendation of that review panel;

(g) where applicable, the prospective adopter's review report and his observations on that report; and

(h) any other documents or information obtained by the agency which it considers should be included in that case record.

23 Requirement to carry out police checks

(1) In respect of the prospective adopter and any other member of the prospective adopter's household who is aged 18 or over, an adoption agency must obtain an enhanced criminal record certificate issued under section 113B of the Police Act 1997 which includes suitability information relating to children (within the meaning of section 113BA(2) of that Act).

(2) An adoption agency may not consider a person suitable to adopt a child if he or any member of his household aged 18 or over –

(a) has been convicted of a specified offence committed at the age of 18 or over; or

(b) has been cautioned by a constable in respect of any such offence which, at the time the caution was given, he admitted.

(3) In paragraph (2), 'specified offence' means –

(a) an offence against a child;

(b) an offence specified in Part 1 of Schedule 3;

(c) an offence contrary to section 170 of the Customs and Excise Management Act 1979 in relation to goods prohibited to be imported under section 42 of the Customs Consolidation Act 1876 (prohibitions and restrictions relating to pornography) where the prohibited goods included indecent photographs of children under the age of 16;

(d) any other offence involving bodily injury to a child, other than an offence of common assault or battery,

and the expression 'offence against a child' has the meaning given to it by section 26(1) of the Criminal Justice and Court Services Act 2000 except that it does not include an offence contrary to section 9 of the Sexual Offences Act 2003 (sexual activity with a child) in a case where the offender was under the age of 20 and the child was aged 13 or over at the time the offence was committed.

(4) An adoption agency may not consider a person suitable to adopt a child if he or any member of his household aged 18 or over –

(a) has been convicted of an offence specified in paragraph 1 of Part 2 of Schedule 3 committed at the age of 18 or over or has been cautioned by a constable in respect of any such offence which, at the time the caution was given, was admitted; or

(b) falls within paragraph 2 or 3 of Part 2 of Schedule 3,

notwithstanding that the statutory offences specified in Part 2 of Schedule 3 have been repealed.

(5) Where an adoption agency becomes aware that a prospective adopter or a member of his household falls within paragraph (2) or (4), the agency must notify the prospective adopter as soon as possible that he cannot be considered suitable to adopt a child.

Amendments: SI 2009/1895.

24 Requirement to provide preparation for adoption

(1) Where an adoption agency is considering a person's suitability to adopt a child, the agency must make arrangements for the prospective adopter to receive such preparation for adoption as the agency considers appropriate.

(2) In paragraph (1) 'preparation for adoption' includes the provision of information to the prospective adopter about –

(a) the age range, sex, likely needs and background of children who may be placed for adoption by the adoption agency;

(b) the significance of adoption for a child and his family;

(c) contact between a child and his parent or guardian or other relatives where a child is authorised to be placed for adoption or is adopted;

(d) the skills which are necessary for an adoptive parent;

(e) the adoption agency's procedures in relation to the assessment of a prospective adopter and the placement of a child for adoption; and

(f) the procedure in relation to placement for adoption and adoption.

(3) Paragraph (1) does not apply if the adoption agency is satisfied that the requirements set out in that paragraph have been carried out in respect of the prospective adopter by another adoption agency.

25 Prospective adopter's report

(1) This regulation applies where the adoption agency, consider the prospective adopter may be suitable to adopt a child.

(2) The adoption agency must obtain the information about the prospective adopter which is specified in Part 1 of Schedule 4.

(3) The adoption agency must obtain –

  (a)   a written report from a registered medical practitioner about the health of the prospective adopter following a full examination which must include matters specified in Part 2 of Schedule 4 unless the agency has received advice from its medical adviser that such an examination and report is unnecessary; and

  (b)   a written report of each of the interviews with the persons nominated by the prospective adopter to provide personal references for him.

(4) The adoption agency must ascertain whether the local authority in whose area the prospective adopter has his home have any information about the prospective adopter which may be relevant to the assessment and if so obtain from that authority a written report setting out that information.

(5) The adoption agency must prepare a written report ('the prospective adopter's report') which shall include –

  (a)   the information about the prospective adopter and his family which is specified in Part 1 of Schedule 4;

  (b)   a summary, written by the agency's medical adviser, of the state of health of the prospective adopter;

  (c)   any relevant information the agency obtains under paragraph (4);

  (d)   any observations of the agency on the matters referred to in regulations 21, 23 and 24;

  (e)   the agency's assessment of the prospective adopter's suitability to adopt a child; and

  (f)   any other information which the agency considers to be relevant.

(6) In a section 83 case, the prospective adopter's report shall also include –

  (a)   the name of the country from which the prospective adopter wishes to adopt ('country of origin');

  (b)   confirmation that the prospective adopter meets the eligibility requirements to adopt from the country of origin;

  (c)   additional information obtained as a consequence of the requirements of the country of origin; and

  (d)   the agency's assessment of the prospective adopter's suitability to adopt a child who is habitually resident outside the British Islands.

(7) Where the adoption agency receives information under paragraph (2), (3) or (4) or other information in relation to the assessment of the prospective adopter and is of the opinion that a prospective adopter is unlikely to be considered suitable to adopt a child, it may make the prospective adopter's

report under paragraph (5) notwithstanding that the agency may not have obtained all the information about the prospective adopter which may be required by this regulation.

(7A) The report shall not be completed until the adoption agency has carried out police checks in accordance with regulation 23 and made arrangements for the prospective adopter to receive preparation for adoption in accordance with regulation 24.

(8) The adoption agency must notify the prospective adopter that his application is to be referred to the adoption panel and give him a copy of the prospective adopter's report, inviting him to send any observations in writing to the agency within 10 working days, beginning with the date on which the notification is sent.

(9) At the end of the period of 10 working days referred to in paragraph (8) (or earlier if any observations made by the prospective adopter are received before that period has expired) the adoption agency must send –

(a) the prospective adopter's report and the prospective adopter's observations;
(b) the written reports referred to in paragraphs (3) and (4);but in the case of reports obtained in accordance with paragraph (3) (a), only if the agency's medical adviser advises it to do so; and
(c) any other relevant information obtained by the agency,

to the adoption panel.

(10) The adoption agency must obtain, so far as is reasonably practicable, any other relevant information which may be required by the adoption panel and send that information to the panel.

Amendments: SI 2005/3482.

26 Function of the adoption panel

(1) Subject to paragraphs (2) and (2A), the adoption panel must consider the case of the prospective adopter referred to it by the adoption agency and make a recommendation to the agency as to whether the prospective adopter is suitable to adopt a child.

(2) In considering what recommendation to make the adoption panel –

(a) must consider and take into account all the information and reports passed to it in accordance with regulation 25;
(b) may request the adoption agency to obtain any other relevant information which the panel considers necessary; and
(c) may obtain legal advice as it considers necessary in relation to the case.

(2A) In relation to the case of a prospective adopter in respect of whom a report has been prepared in accordance with regulation 25(7), the adoption panel must either—

    (a)   request the adoption agency to prepare a further prospective adopter's report, covering all the matters set out in regulation 25(5); or

    (b)   recommend that the prospective adopter is not suitable to adopt a child.

(3) Where the adoption panel makes a recommendation to the adoption agency that the prospective adopter is suitable to adopt a child, the panel may consider and give advice to the agency about the number of children the prospective adopter may be suitable to adopt, their age range, sex, likely needs and background.

(4) Before making any recommendation, the adoption panel must invite the prospective adopters to attend a meeting of the panel.

Amendments: SI 2005/3482.

27 Adoption agency decision and notification

(1) The adoption agency must make a decision about whether the prospective adopter is suitable to adopt a child.

(2) No member of the adoption panel shall take part in any decision made by the adoption agency under paragraph (1).

(3) Where the adoption agency decides to approve the prospective adopter as suitable to adopt a child, it must notify him in writing of its decision.

(4) Where the adoption agency considers that the prospective adopter is not suitable to adopt a child, it must –

    (a)   notify the prospective adopter in writing that it proposes not to approve him as suitable to adopt a child ('qualifying determination');

    (b)   send with that notification its reasons together with a copy of the recommendation of the adoption panel if that recommendation is different;

    (c)   advise the prospective adopter that within 40 working days beginning with the date on which the notification was sent he may –

        (i)   submit any representations he wishes to make to the agency; or

        (ii) apply to the Secretary of State for a review by an independent review panel of the qualifying determination.

(5) If, within the period of 40 working days referred to in paragraph (4), the prospective adopter has not made any representations or applied to the Secretary of State for a review by an independent review panel, the adoption agency shall proceed to make its decision and shall notify the prospective adopter in writing of its decision together with the reasons for that decision.

(6) If, within the period of 40 working days referred to in paragraph (4), the adoption agency receives further representations from the prospective adopter, it may refer the case together with all the relevant information to the adoption panel for further consideration.

(7) The adoption panel must consider any case referred to it under paragraph (6) and make a fresh recommendation to the adoption agency as to whether the prospective adopter is suitable to adopt a child.

(8) The adoption agency must make a decision on the case but –

(a) if the case has been referred to the adoption panel under paragraph (6), the agency must make the decision only after taking into account the recommendations of the adoption panel made under both paragraph (7) and regulation 26; or

(b) if the prospective adopter has applied to the Secretary of State for a review by an independent review panel of the qualifying determination, the agency must make the decision only after taking into account the recommendation of the independent review panel and the recommendation of the adoption panel made under regulation 26.

(9) As soon as possible after making its decision under paragraph (8), the adoption agency must notify the prospective adopter in writing of its decision stating its reasons for that decision if they do not consider the prospective adopter suitable to adopt a child, and of the adoption panel's recommendation under paragraph (7), if this is different from the agency's decision.

(10) In a case where an independent review panel has made a recommendation, the adoption agency shall send to the Secretary of State a copy of the notification referred to in paragraph (9).

28 Information to be sent to the independent review panel

(1) If the adoption agency receives notification from the Secretary of State that a prospective adopter has applied for a review by an independent review panel of the qualifying determination, the agency must, within 10 working days of receipt of that notification, send to the Secretary of State the information specified in paragraph (2).

(2) The following information is specified for the purposes of paragraph (1) –

(a) all of the documents and information which were passed to the adoption panel in accordance with regulation 25;

(b) any relevant information in relation to the prospective adopter which was obtained by the agency after the date on which the documents and information referred to in sub-paragraph (a) were passed to the adoption panel; and

(c) the documents referred to in regulation 27(4)(a) and (b).

29 Review and termination of approval

(1) The adoption agency must review the approval of each prospective adopter in accordance with this regulation, unless –

(a) in a section 83 case, the prospective adopter has visited the child in the country in which the child is habitually resident and has confirmed in writing that he wishes to proceed with the adoption; and

(b)   in any other case, a child is placed for adoption with the prospective adopter or the agency is considering placing a child with the prospective adopter in accordance with regulations 31 to 33.

(2) A review must take place whenever the adoption agency considers it necessary but otherwise not more than one year after approval and thereafter at intervals of not more than a year.

(3) When undertaking such a review the adoption agency must –

(a)   make such enquiries and obtain such information as it considers necessary in order to review whether the prospective adopter continues to be suitable to adopt a child; and

(b)   seek and take into account the views of the prospective adopter.

(4) If at the conclusion of the review, the adoption agency considers that the prospective adopter may no longer be suitable to adopt a child, it must –

(a)   prepare a written report ('the prospective adopter's review report') which shall include the agency's reasons;

(b)   notify the prospective adopter that his case is to be referred to the adoption panel; and

(c)   give him a copy of the report inviting him to send any observations to the agency within 10 working days beginning with the date on which that report is given to him.

(5) At the end of the period of 10 working days referred to in paragraph (4)(c) (or earlier if the prospective adopter's comments are received before that period has expired), the adoption agency must send the prospective adopter's review report together with the prospective adopter's observations to the adoption panel.

(6) The adoption agency must obtain, so far as is reasonably practicable, any other relevant information which may be required by the adoption panel and send that information to the panel.

(7) The adoption panel must consider the prospective adopter's review report, the prospective adopter's observations and any other information passed to it by the adoption agency and make a recommendation to the agency as to whether the prospective adopter continues to be suitable to adopt a child.

(8) The adoption agency must make a decision as to whether the prospective adopter continues to be suitable to adopt a child and regulation 27(2) to (10) shall apply in relation to that decision by the agency.

Amendments: SI 2005/3482.

30 Duties of the adoption agency in a section 83 case

Where the adoption agency decides in a section 83 case to approve a prospective adopter as suitable to adopt a child, the agency must send to the Secretary of State –

(a) written confirmation of the decision and any recommendation the agency may make in relation to the number of children the prospective adopter may be suitable to adopt, their age range, sex, likely needs and background;

(b) all the documents and information which were passed to the adoption panel in accordance with regulation 25;

(c) the record of the proceedings of the adoption panel, its recommendation and the reasons for its recommendation;

(d) if the prospective adopter applied to the Secretary of State for a review by an independent review panel of a qualifying determination, the record of the proceedings of that panel, its recommendation and the reasons for its recommendation; and

(e) any other information relating to the case which the Secretary of State or the relevant foreign authority may require.

PART 5
DUTIES OF ADOPTION AGENCY IN RESPECT OF PROPOSED PLACEMENT OF CHILD WITH PROSPECTIVE ADOPTER

31 Proposed placement

(1) Where an adoption agency is considering placing a child for adoption with a particular prospective adopter ('the proposed placement') the agency must –

(a) provide the prospective adopter with a copy of the child's permanence report and any other information the agency considers relevant;

(b) meet with the prospective adopter to discuss the proposed placement;

(c) ascertain the views of the prospective adopter about –
  (i) the proposed placement; and
  (ii) the arrangements the agency proposes to make for allowing any person contact with the child; and

(d) provide a counselling service for, and any further information to, the prospective adopter as may be required.

(2) Where the adoption agency considers that the proposed placement should proceed, the agency must –

(a) where the agency is a local authority, carry out an assessment of the needs of the child and the prospective adopter and any children of the prospective adopter ('the adoptive family') for adoption support services in accordance with regulations made under section 4(6) of the Act;

(b) where the agency is a registered adoption society, notify the prospective adopter that he may request the local authority in whose area he has his home ('the relevant authority') to carry out an assessment of his needs for adoption support services under section 4(1) of the Act and pass to the relevant authority, at their request, a copy of the child's permanence report and a copy of the prospective adopter's report;

(c)   consider the arrangements for allowing any person contact with the child; and

(d)   prepare a written report ('the adoption placement report') which shall include –

    (i)   the agency's reasons for proposing the placement;

    (ii)   the information obtained by the agency by virtue of paragraph (1);

    (iii)   where the agency is a local authority, their proposals for the provision of adoption support services for the adoptive family;

    (iv)   the arrangements the agency proposes to make for allowing any person contact with the child; and

    (v)   any other relevant information.

(3) Where the adoption agency remains of the view that the proposed placement should proceed, it must notify the prospective adopter that the proposed placement is to be referred to the adoption panel and give him a copy of the adoption placement report, inviting him to send any observations in writing to the agency within 10 working days, beginning with the date on which the notification is sent.

(4) At the end of the period of 10 working days referred to in paragraph (3) (or earlier if observations are received before the 10 working days has expired) the adoption agency must send –

(a)   the adoption placement report;

(b)   the child's permanence report; and

(c)   the prospective adopter's report and his observations,

to the adoption panel.

(5) The adoption agency must obtain so far as is reasonably practicable any other relevant information which may be requested by the adoption panel in connection with the proposed placement and send that information to the panel.

(6) This paragraph applies where an adoption agency ('agency A') intends to refer a proposed placement to the adoption panel and another agency ('agency B') made the decision (in accordance with these Regulations) that –

(a)   the child should be placed for adoption; or

(b)   the prospective adopter is suitable to be an adoptive parent.

(7) Where paragraph (6) applies agency A may only refer the proposed placement to the adoption panel if it has consulted agency B about the proposed placement.

(8) Agency A must –

(a)   where paragraph (6)(a) applies, open a child's case record; or

(b)   where paragraph (6)(b) applies, open a prospective adopter's case record,

and place on the appropriate record, the information and documents received from agency B.

Amendments: SI 2005/3482.

32 Function of the adoption panel in relation to proposed placement

(1) The adoption panel must consider the proposed placement referred to it by the adoption agency and make a recommendation to the agency as to whether the child should be placed for adoption with that particular prospective adopter.

(2) In considering what recommendation to make the adoption panel shall have regard to the duties imposed on the adoption agency under section 1(2), (4) and (5) of the Act (considerations applying to the exercise of powers in relation to the adoption of a child) and –

(a) must consider and take into account all information and the reports passed to it in accordance with regulation 31;
(b) may request the agency to obtain any other relevant information which the panel considers necessary; and
(c) may obtain legal advice as it considers necessary in relation to the case.

(3) The adoption panel must consider –

(a) in a case where the adoption agency is a local authority, the authority's proposals for the provision of adoption support services for the adoptive family;
(b) the arrangements the adoption agency proposes to make for allowing any person contact with the child; and
(c) whether the parental responsibility of any parent or guardian or the prospective adopter should be restricted and if so the extent of any such restriction.

(4) Where the adoption panel makes a recommendation to the adoption agency that the child should be placed for adoption with the particular prospective adopter, the panel may at the same time give advice to the agency about any of the matters set out in paragraph (3).

(5) An adoption panel may only make the recommendation referred to in paragraph (1) if –

(a) that recommendation is to be made at the same meeting of the adoption panel at which a recommendation has been made that the child should be placed for adoption; or
(b) the adoption agency, or another adoption agency, has already made a decision in accordance with regulation 19 that the child should be placed for adoption,

and in either case that recommendation is to be made at the same meeting of the panel at which a recommendation has been made that the prospective adopter is suitable to adopt a child or the adoption agency, or another adoption agency, has made a decision in accordance with regulation 27 that the prospective adopter is suitable to adopt a child.

33 Adoption agency decision in relation to proposed placement

(1) The adoption agency must take into account the recommendation of the adoption panel in coming to a decision about whether the child should be placed for adoption with the particular prospective adopter.

(2) No member of the adoption panel shall take part in any decision made by the adoption agency under paragraph (1).

(3) As soon as possible after making its decision the adoption agency must notify in writing –

    (a)   the prospective adopter of its decision; and

    (b)   if their whereabouts are known to the agency, the parent or guardian and, where regulation 14(3) applies and the agency considers it is appropriate, the father of the child, of the fact that the child is to be placed for adoption.

(4) If the adoption agency decides that the proposed placement should proceed, the agency must, in an appropriate manner and having regard to the child's age and understanding, explain its decision to the child.

(5) The adoption agency must place on the child's case record –

    (a)   the prospective adopter's report;

    (b)   the adoption placement report and the prospective adopter's observations on that report;

    (c)   the written record of the proceedings of the adoption panel under regulation 32, its recommendation, the reasons for its recommendation and any advice given by the panel to the agency; and

    (d)   the record and notification of the agency's decision under this regulation.

34 Function of the adoption agency in a section 83 case

(1) This paragraph applies where in a section 83 case the adoption agency receives from the relevant foreign authority information about a child to be adopted by a prospective adopter.

(2) Where paragraph (1) applies, the adoption agency must –

    (a)   send a copy of the information referred to in paragraph (1) to the prospective adopter unless it is aware that the prospective adopter has received a copy;

    (b)   consider that information and meet with the prospective adopter to discuss the information; and

    (c)   if appropriate, provide a counselling service for, and any further information to, the prospective adopter as may be required.

PART 6
PLACEMENT AND REVIEWS

35 Requirements imposed on the adoption agency before the child may be placed for adoption

(1) This paragraph applies where the adoption agency –

   (a) has decided in accordance with regulation 33 to place a child for adoption with a particular prospective adopter; and
   (b) has met with the prospective adopter to consider the arrangements it proposes to make for the placement of the child with him.

(2) Where paragraph (1) applies, the adoption agency must, as soon as possible, send the prospective adopter a placement plan in respect of the child which covers the matters specified in Schedule 5 ('the adoption placement plan').

(3) Where the prospective adopter notifies the adoption agency that he wishes to proceed with the placement and the agency is authorised to place the child for adoption or, subject to paragraph (4), the child is less than 6 weeks old, the agency may place the child for adoption with the prospective adopter.

(4) Unless there is a placement order in respect of the child, the adoption agency may not place for adoption a child who is less than six weeks old unless the parent or guardian of the child has agreed in writing with the agency that the child may be placed for adoption.

(5) Where the child already has his home with the prospective adopter, the adoption agency must notify the prospective adopter in writing of the date on which the child is placed for adoption with him by that agency.

(6) The adoption agency must before the child is placed for adoption with the prospective adopter –

   (a) send to the prospective adopter's general practitioner written notification of the proposed placement and send with that notification a written report of the child's health history and current state of health; and
   (b) send to the local authority (if that authority is not the adoption agency) and Primary Care Trust or Local Health Board (Wales), in whose area the prospective adopter has his home, written notification of the proposed placement and, where the child is of compulsory school age, include in the notification to the local authority information about the child's educational history and whether the child has been or is likely to be assessed for special educational needs under the Education Act 1996
   (c) *(revoked)*

(7) The adoption agency must notify the prospective adopter in writing of any change to the adoption placement plan.

(8) The adoption agency must place on the child's case record –

(a) in the case of a child who is less than 6 weeks old and in respect of whom there is no placement order, a copy of the agreement referred to in paragraph (4); and

(b) a copy of the adoption placement plan and any changes to that plan.

Amendments: SI 2010/1172.

36 Reviews

(1) Where an adoption agency is authorised to place a child for adoption but the child is not for the time being placed for adoption the agency must carry out a review of the child's case –

(a) not more than 3 months after the date on which the agency first has authority to place; and

(b) thereafter not more than 6 months after the date of the previous review ('6 months review'),

until the child is placed for adoption.

(2) Paragraphs (3) and (4) apply where a child is placed for adoption.

(3) The adoption agency must carry out a review of the child's case –

(a) not more than 4 weeks after the date on which the child is placed for adoption ('the first review');

(b) not more than 3 months after the first review; and

(c) thereafter not more than 6 months after the date of the previous review,

unless the child is returned to the agency by the prospective adopter or an adoption order is made.

(4) The adoption agency must –

(a) ensure that the child and the prospective adopter are visited within one week of the placement and thereafter at least once a week until the first review and thereafter at such frequency as the agency decides at each review;

(b) ensure that written reports are made of such visits; and

(c) provide such advice and assistance to the prospective adopter as the agency considers necessary.

(5) When carrying out a review the adoption agency must consider each of the matters set out in paragraph (6) and must, so far as is reasonably practicable, ascertain the views of –

(a) the child, having regard to his age and understanding;

(b) if the child is placed for adoption, the prospective adopter; and

(c) any other person the agency considers relevant,

in relation to such of the matters set out in paragraph (6) as the agency considers appropriate.

(6) The matters referred to in paragraph (5) are –

(a)   whether the adoption agency remains satisfied that the child should be placed for adoption;

(b)   the child's needs, welfare and development, and whether any changes need to be made to meet his needs or assist his development;

(c)   the existing arrangements for contact, and whether they should continue or be altered;

(d)   the arrangements in relation to the exercise of parental responsibility for the child, and whether they should continue or be altered;

(e)   where the child is placed for adoption the arrangements for the provision of adoption support services for the adoptive family and whether there should be any re-assessment of the need for those services;

(f)   in consultation with the appropriate agencies, the arrangements for assessing and meeting the child's health care and educational needs;

(g)   subject to paragraphs (1) and (3), the frequency of the reviews.

(7) Where the child is subject to a placement order and has not been placed for adoption at the time of the first 6 months review, the local authority must at that review –

(a)   establish why the child has not been placed for adoption and consider what further steps the authority should take in relation to the placement of the child for adoption; and

(b)   consider whether it remains satisfied that the child should be placed for adoption.

(8) The adoption agency must, so far as is reasonably practicable, notify –

(a)   the child, where the agency considers he is of sufficient age and understanding;

(b)   the prospective adopter; and

(c)   any other person whom the agency considers relevant,

of any decision taken by the agency in consequence of that review.

(9) The adoption agency must ensure that –

(a)   the information obtained in the course of a review or visit in respect of a child's case including the views expressed by the child;

(b)   the details of the proceedings of any meeting arranged by the agency to consider any aspect of the review of the case; and

(c)   details of any decision made in the course of or as a result of the review,

are recorded in writing and placed on the child's case record.

(10) Where the child is returned to the adoption agency in accordance with section 35(1) or (2) of the Act, the agency must conduct a review of the child's case no earlier than 28 days, or later than 42 days, after the date on which the child is returned to the agency and when carrying out that review the agency must consider the matters set out in paragraph (6)(a), (b), (c) and (f).

Amendments: SI 2005/3482.

37 Independent reviewing officers

(1) An adoption agency which is –

    (a)   a local authority; or

    (b)   a registered adoption society which is a voluntary organisation who provide accommodation for a child,

must appoint a person ('the independent reviewing officer') in respect of the case of each child authorised to be placed for adoption by the agency to carry out the functions mentioned in section 26(2A) of the 1989 Act.

(2) The independent reviewing officer must be registered as a social worker in a register maintained by the General Social Care Council or by the Care Council for Wales under section 56 of the Care Standards Act 2000 or in a corresponding register maintained under the law of Scotland or Northern Ireland.

(3) The independent reviewing officer must, in the opinion of the adoption agency, have sufficient relevant social work experience to undertake the functions referred to in paragraph (1) in relation to the case.

(4) A person who is an employee of the adoption agency may not be appointed as an independent reviewing officer in a case if he is involved in the management of the case or is under the direct management of –

    (a)   a person involved in the management of the case;

    (b)   a person with management responsibilities in relation to a person mentioned in sub-paragraph (a); or

    (c)   a person with control over the resources allocated to the case.

(5) The independent reviewing officer must –

    (a)   as far as is reasonably practicable attend any meeting held in connection with the review of the child's case; and

    (b)   chair any such meeting that he attends.

(6) The independent reviewing officer must, as far as is reasonably practicable, take steps to ensure that the review is conducted in accordance with regulation 36 and in particular to ensure –

    (a)   that the child's views are understood and taken into account;

    (b)   that the persons responsible for implementing any decision taken in consequence of the review are identified; and

    (c)   that any failure to review the case in accordance with regulation 36 or to take proper steps to make the arrangements agreed at the review is brought to the attention of persons at an appropriate level of seniority within the adoption agency.

(7) If the child whose case is reviewed wishes to take proceedings on his own account, for example, to apply to the court for revocation of a placement order, it is the function of the independent reviewing officer –

    (a)   to assist the child to obtain legal advice; or

(b) to establish whether an appropriate adult is able and willing to provide such assistance or bring the proceedings on the child's behalf.

(8) The adoption agency must inform the independent reviewing officer of –

(a) any significant failure to make the arrangements agreed at a review; and

(b) any significant change in the child's circumstances after a review.

38 Withdrawal of consent

(1) This paragraph applies where consent given under section 19 or 20 of the Act in respect of a child is withdrawn in accordance with section 52(8) of the Act.

(2) Where paragraph (1) applies and the adoption agency is a local authority, on receipt of the form or notice given in accordance with section 52(8) of the Act the authority must immediately review their decision to place the child for adoption and where, in accordance with section 22(1) to (3) of the Act, the authority decide to apply for a placement order in respect of the child, they must notify as soon as possible –

(a) the parent or guardian of the child;

(b) where regulation 14(3) applies and the agency considers it is appropriate, the child's father; and

(c) if the child is placed for adoption, the prospective adopter with whom the child is placed.

(3) Where paragraph (1) applies and the adoption agency is a registered adoption society, the agency must immediately consider whether it is appropriate to inform the local authority in whose area the child is living.

PART 7
CASE RECORDS

39 Storage of case records

The adoption agency must ensure that the child's case record and the prospective adopter's case record and the contents of those case records are at all times kept in secure conditions and in particular that all appropriate measures are taken to prevent the theft, unauthorised disclosure, loss or destruction of, or damage to, the case record or its contents.

40 Preservation of case records

An adoption agency must keep the child's case record and the prospective adopter's case record for such period as it considers appropriate.

41 Confidentiality of case records

Subject to regulation 42, the contents of the child's case record and the prospective adopter's case record shall be treated by the adoption agency as confidential.

42 Access to case records and disclosure of information

(1) Subject to paragraph (3), an adoption agency shall provide such access to its case records and disclose such information in its possession, as may be required –

- (a) to those holding an inquiry under sections 3 and 4 of the Children Act 2004 (inquiries held by the Children's Commissioner) or under the Inquiries Act 2005 for the purposes of such an inquiry;
- (b) to the Secretary of State;
- (c) to the registration authority;
- (d) subject to the provisions of sections 29(7) and 32(3) of the Local Government Act 1974 (investigations and disclosure), to the Commission for Local Administration in England, for the purposes of any investigation conducted in accordance with Part 3 of that Act;
- (e) to any person appointed by the agency for the purposes of the consideration by the agency of any representations (including complaints);
- (f) by and to the extent specified in these Regulations;
- (g) to an officer of the Service or a Welsh family proceedings officer for the purposes of the discharge of his duties under the Act; and
- (h) to a court having power to make an order under the Act or the 1989 Act.

(2) Subject to paragraph (3), an adoption agency may provide such access to its case records and disclose such information in its possession, as it thinks fit for the purposes of carrying out its functions as an adoption agency.

(3) A written record shall be kept by an adoption agency of any access provided or disclosure made by virtue of this regulation.

Amendments: SI 2005/3482.

43 Transfer of case records

(1) An adoption agency may transfer a copy of a child's case record or prospective adopter's case record (or part of that record) to another adoption agency when itconsiders this to be in the interests of the child or prospective adopter to whom the record relates, and a written record shall be kept of any such transfer.

(2) Subject to paragraph (3), a registered adoption society which intends to cease to act or exist as such shall forthwith either transfer its case records to another adoption agency having first obtained the registration authority's approval for such transfer, or transfer its case records –

- (a) to the local authority in whose area the society's principal office is situated; or
- (b) in the case of a society which amalgamates with another registered adoption society to form a new registered adoption society, to the new body.

(3) An adoption agency to which case records are transferred by virtue of paragraph (2)(a) or (b) shall notify the registration authority in writing of such transfer.

44 Application of regulations 40 to 42

Nothing in this Part applies to the information which an adoption agency must keep in relation to an adopted person by virtue of regulations made under section 56 of the Act.

PART 8
MISCELLANEOUS

45 Modification of 1989 Act in relation to adoption

(1) This paragraph applies where –

(a) a local authority are authorised to place a child for adoption; or
(b) a child who has been placed for adoption by a local authority is less than 6 weeks old.

(2) Where paragraph (1) applies –

(a) section 22(4)(b) of the 1989 Act shall not apply;
(b) section 22(4)(c) of the 1989 Act shall apply as if for that sub-paragraph there were inserted '(c) any prospective adopter with whom the local authority has placed the child for adoption;';
(c) section 22(5)(b) of the 1989 Act shall apply as if for the words '(4)(b) to (d)' there were inserted '(4)(c) and (d)'; and
(d) paragraphs 15 and 21 of Schedule 2 to the 1989 Act shall not apply.

(3) This paragraph applies where a registered adoption society is authorised to place a child for adoption or a child who has been placed for adoption by a registered adoption society is less than 6 weeks old.

(4) Where paragraph (3) applies –

(a) section 61 of the 1989 Act is to have effect in relation to the child whether or not he is accommodated by or on behalf of the society;
(b) section 61(2)(b) of the 1989 Act shall not apply; and
(c) section 61(2)(c) of the 1989 Act shall apply as if for that sub-paragraph there were inserted '(c) any prospective adopter with whom the registered adoption society has placed the child for adoption;'.

Amendments: SI 2005/3482.

46 Contact

(1) This paragraph applies where an adoption agency decides that a child should be placed for adoption.

(2) Where paragraph (1) applies and subject to paragraph (3), the adoption agency must consider what arrangements it should make for allowing any

person contact with the child once the agency is authorised to place the child for adoption ('the contact arrangements').

(3) The adoption agency must –

(a)   take into account the wishes and feelings of the parent or guardian of the child and, where regulation 14(3) applies and the agency considers it is appropriate, the father of the child;

(b)   take into account any advice given by the adoption panel in accordance with regulation 18(3); and

(c)   have regard to the considerations set out in section 1(2) and (4) of the Act,

in coming to a decision in relation to the contact arrangements.

(4) The adoption agency must notify –

(a)   the child, if the agency considers he is of sufficient age and understanding;

(b)   if their whereabouts are known to the agency, the parent or guardian, and, where regulation 14(3) applies and the agency considers it is appropriate, the father of the child;

(c)   any person in whose favour there was a provision for contact under the 1989 Act which ceased to have effect by virtue of section 26(1) of the Act; and

(d)   any other person the agency considers relevant,

of the contact arrangements.

(5) Where an adoption agency decides that a child should be placed for adoption with a particular prospective adopter, the agency must review the contact arrangements in light of the views of the prospective adopter and any advice given by the adoption panel in accordance with regulation 32(3).

(6) If the adoption agency proposes to make any change to the contact arrangements which affects any person mentioned in paragraph (4), it must seek the views of that person and take those views into account in deciding what arrangements it should make for allowing any person contact with the child while he is placed for adoption with the prospective adopter.

(7) The adoption agency must –

(a)   set out the contact arrangements in the placement plan; and

(b)   keep the contact arrangements under review.

47 Contact: supplementary

(1) Where an adoption agency has decided under section 27(2) of the Act to refuse to allow the contact that would otherwise be required by virtue of an order under section 26 of the Act, the agency must, as soon as the decision is made, inform the persons specified in paragraph (3) and notify them of the decision, the date of the decision, the reasons for the decision and the duration of the period.

(2) The terms of an order under section 26 of the Act may be departed from by agreement between the adoption agency and any person for whose contact with the child the order provides subject to the following conditions –

(a) where the child is of sufficient age and understanding, subject to his agreement;

(b) where the child is placed for adoption, subject to consultation before the agreement is reached, with the prospective adopter with whom the child is placed for adoption; and

(c) written confirmation by the agency to the persons specified in paragraph (3) of the terms of that agreement.

(3) The following persons are specified for the purposes of paragraphs (1) and (2) –

(a) the child, if the adoption agency considers he is of sufficient age and understanding;

(b) the person in whose favour the order under section 26 was made; and

(c) if the child is placed for adoption, the prospective adopter.

Schedule 1
Information

PART 1
INFORMATION ABOUT THE CHILD

Regulation 15(1)

1 Name, sex, date and place of birth and address including the local authority area.

2 A photograph and physical description.

3 Nationality.

4 Racial origin and cultural and linguistic background.

5 Religious persuasion (including details of baptism, confirmation or equivalent ceremonies).

6 Whether the child is looked after or is provided with accommodation under section 59(1) of the 1989 Act.

7 Details of any order made by a court with respect to the child under the 1989 Act including the name of the court, the order made and the date on which the order was made.

8 Whether the child has any rights to, or interest in, property or any claim to damages under the Fatal Accidents Act 1976 or otherwise which he stands to retain or lose if he is adopted.

9 A chronology of the child's care since birth.

10 A description of the child's personality, his social development and his emotional and behavioural development.

11 Whether the child has any difficulties with activities such as feeding, washing and dressing himself.

12 The educational history of the child including –

    (a)   the names, addresses and types of nurseries or schools attended with dates;

    (b)   a summary of his progress and attainments;

    (c)   whether he is subject to a statement of special educational needs under the Education Act 1996;

    (d)   any special needs he has in relation to learning; and

    (e)   where he is looked after, details of his personal education plan prepared by the local authority.

13 Information about –

    (a)   the child's relationship with –

        (i)   his parent or guardian;

        (ii)   any brothers or sisters or other relatives he may have; and

        (iii)   any other person the agency considers relevant;

    (b)   the likelihood of any such relationship continuing and the value to the child of its doing so; and

    (c)   the ability and willingness of the child's parent or guardian or any other person the agency considers relevant, to provide the child with a secure environment in which he can develop, and otherwise to meet his needs.

14 The current arrangements for and the type of contact between the child's parent or guardian or other person with parental responsibility for him, his father, and any relative, friend or other person.

15 A description of the child's interests, likes and dislikes.

16 Any other relevant information which might assist the adoption panel and the adoption agency.

17 In this Part 'parent' includes the child's father whether or not he has parental responsibility for the child.

PART 2
MATTERS TO BE INCLUDED IN THE CHILD'S HEALTH REPORT

Regulation 15(2)

1 Name, date of birth, sex, weight and height.

2 A neo-natal report on the child, including –

(a)   details of his birth and any complications;

(b)   the results of a physical examination and screening tests;

(c)   details of any treatment given;

(d)   details of any problem in management and feeding;

(e)   any other relevant information which may assist the adoption panel and the adoption agency; and

(f)   the name and address of any registered medical practitioner who may be able to provide further information about any of the above matters.

3 A full health history of the child, including –

(a)   details of any serious illness, disability, accident, hospital admission or attendance at an out-patient department, and in each case any treatment given;

(b)   details and dates of immunisations;

(c)   a physical and developmental assessment according to age, including an assessment of vision and hearing and of neurological, speech and language development and any evidence of emotional disorder;

(d)   for a child over five years of age, the school health history (if available);

(e)   how his physical and mental health and medical history have affected his physical, intellectual, emotional, social or behavioural development; and

(f)   any other relevant information which may assist the adoption panel and the adoption agency.

PART 3
INFORMATION ABOUT THE CHILD'S FAMILY AND OTHERS

Regulation 16(1)

Information about each parent of the child

1 Name, sex, date and place of birth and address including the local authority area.

2 A photograph, if available, and physical description.

3 Nationality.

4 Racial origin and cultural and linguistic background.

5 Religious persuasion.

6 A description of their personality and interests.

Information about the child's brothers and sisters

7 Name, sex, and date and place of birth.

8 A photograph, if available, and physical description.

9 Nationality.

10 Address, if appropriate.

11 If the brother or sister is under the age of 18 –

    (a)   where and with whom he or she is living;

    (b)   whether he or she is looked after or is provided with accommodation under section 59(1) of the 1989 Act;

    (c)   details of any court order made with respect to him or her under the 1989 Act, including the name of the court, the order made, and the date on which the order was made; and

    (d)   whether he or she is also being considered for adoption.

Information about the child's other relatives and any other person the agency considers relevant

12 Name, sex and date and place of birth.

13 Nationality.

14 Address, if appropriate.

Family history and relationships

15 Whether the child's parents were married to each other at the time of the child's birth (or have subsequently married) and if so, the date and place of marriage and whether they are divorced or separated.

16 Where the child's parents are not married, whether the father has parental responsibility for the child and if so how it was acquired.

17 If the identity or whereabouts of the child's father are not known, the information about him that has been ascertained and from whom, and the steps that have been taken to establish paternity.

18 Where the child's parents have been previously married or formed a civil partnership, the date of the marriage or, as the case may be, the date and place of registration of the civil partnership.

19 So far as is possible, a family tree with details of the child's grandparents, parents and aunts and uncles with their age (or ages at death).

20 Where it is reasonably practicable, a chronology of each of the child's parents from birth.

21 The observations of the child's parents about their own experiences of being parented and how this has influenced them.

22 The past and present relationship of the child's parents.

23 Details of the wider family and their role and importance to –

(a) the child's parents; and
(b) any brothers or sisters of the child.

Other information about each parent of the child

24 Information about their home and the neighbourhood in which they live.

25 Details of their educational history.

26 Details of their employment history.

27 Information about the parenting capacity of the child's parents, particularly their ability and willingness to parent the child.

28 Any other relevant information which might assist the adoption panel and the adoption agency.

29 In this Part 'parent' includes the father of the child whether or not he has parental responsibility for the child.

PART 4
INFORMATION RELATING TO THE HEALTH OF THE CHILD'S NATURAL PARENTS AND BROTHERS AND SISTERS

Regulation 16(2)

1 Name, date of birth, sex, weight and height of each natural parent.

2 A health history of each of the child's natural parents, including details of any serious physical or mental illness, any hereditary disease or disorder, drug or alcohol misuse, disability, accident or hospital admission and in each case any treatment given where the agency consider such information to be relevant.

3 A health history of the child's brothers and sisters (of the full blood or half-blood), and the other children of each parent with details of any serious physical or mental illness and any hereditary disease or disorder.

4 A summary of the mother's obstetric history, including any problems in the ante-natal, labour and post-natal periods, with the results of any tests carried out during or immediately after the pregnancy.

5 Details of any present illness, including treatment and prognosis.

6 Any other relevant information which the adoption agency considers may assist the adoption panel and the agency.

Schedule 2
Information and Documents to be Provided to the Cafcass or the National Assembly for Wales

Regulation 20

1 A certified copy of the child's birth certificate.

2 Name and address of the child's parent or guardian.

3 A chronology of the actions and decisions taken by the adoption agency with respect to the child.

4 Confirmation by the adoption agency that it has counselled, and explained to the parent or guardian the legal implications of both consent to placement under section 19 of the Act and, as the case may be, to the making of a future adoption order under section 20 of the Act and provided the parent or guardian with written information about this together with a copy of the written information provided to him.

5 Such information about the parent or guardian or other information as the adoption agency considers the officer of the Service or the Welsh family proceedings officer may need to know.

Schedule 3

PART 1
OFFENCES SPECIFIED FOR THE PURPOSES OF REGULATION 23(3)(B)

Regulation 23(3)

Offences in England and Wales

1 Any of the following offences against an adult –

   (a)   an offence of rape under section 1 of the Sexual Offences Act 2003;
   (b)   an offence of assault by penetration under section 2 of that Act;
   (c)   an offence of causing a person to engage in sexual activity without consent under section 4 of that Act, if the activity fell within subsection (4) of that section;
   (d)   an offence of sexual activity with a person with a mental disorder impeding choice under section 30 of that Act, if the touching fell within subsection (3) of that section;
   (e)   an offence of causing or inciting a person with mental disorder impeding choice to engage in sexual activity under section 31of that Act, if the activity caused or incited fell within subsection (3) of that section;

(f) an offence of inducement, threat or deception to procure sexual activity with a person with a mental disorder under section 34 of that Act, if the touching involved fell within subsection (2) of that section; and

(g) an offence of causing a person with a mental disorder to engage in or agree to engage in sexual activity by inducement, threat or deception under section 35 of that Act, if the activity fell within subsection (2) of that section.

Offences in Scotland

2 An offence of rape.

3 An offence specified in Schedule 1 to the Criminal Procedure (Scotland) Act 1995 except, in a case where the offender was under the age of 20 at the time the offence was committed, an offence contrary to section 5 of the Criminal Law (Consolidation) (Scotland) Act 1995 (intercourse with a girl under 16), an offence of shameless indecency between men or an offence of sodomy.

4 An offence of plagium (theft of a child below the age of puberty).

5 Section 52 or 52A of the Civil Government (Scotland) Act 1982 (indecent photographs of children).

6 An offence under section 3 of the Sexual Offences (Amendment) Act 2000 (abuse of trust).

Offences in Northern Ireland

7 An offence of rape.

8 An offence specified in Schedule 1 to the Children and Young Person Act (Northern Ireland) 1968, except offences of common assault or battery or in the case where the offender was under the age of 20 at the time the offence was committed, an offence contrary to section 5 or 11 of the Criminal Law Amendment Act 1885 (unlawful carnal knowledge of a girl under 17 and gross indecency between males).

9 An offence under Article 3 of the Protection of Children (Northern Ireland) Order 1978 (indecent photographs).

10 An offence under Article 9 of the Criminal Justice (Northern Ireland) Order 1980 (inciting girl under 16 to have incestuous sexual intercourse).

11 An offence contrary to Article 15 of the Criminal Justice (Evidence, Etc) (Northern Ireland) Order 1988 (possession of indecent photographs of children).

PART 2
REPEALED STATUTORY OFFENCES

Regulation 23(4)

1 (1) An offence under any of the following sections of the Sexual Offences Act 1956 –

- (a) section 1 (rape);
- (b) section 5 (intercourse with a girl under 13);
- (c) subject to paragraph 4, section 6 (intercourse with a girl under 16);
- (d) section 19 or 20 (abduction of girl under 18 or 16);
- (e) section 25 or 26 of that Act (permitting girl under 13, or between 13 and 16, to use premises for intercourse); and
- (f) section 28 (causing or encouraging prostitution of, intercourse with or indecent assault on, girl under 16).

(2) An offence under section 1 of the Indecency with Children Act 1960 (indecent conduct towards young child).

(3) An offence under section 54 of the Criminal Law Act 1977 (inciting girl under sixteen to incest).

(4) An offence under section 3 of the Sexual Offences (Amendment) Act 2000 (abuse of trust).

2 A person falls within this paragraph if he has been convicted of any of the following offences against a child committed at the age of 18 or over or has been cautioned by a constable in respect of any such offence which, at the time the caution was given, he admitted –

- (a) an offence under section 2 or 3 of the Sexual Offences Act 1956 Act (procurement of woman by threats or false pretences);
- (b) an offence under section 4 of that Act (administering drugs to obtain or facilitate intercourse);
- (c) an offence under section 14 or 15 of that Act (indecent assault);
- (d) an offence under section 16 of that Act (assault with intent to commit buggery);
- (e) an offence under section 17 of that Act (abduction of woman by force or for the sake of her property); and
- (f) an offence under section 24 of that Act (detention of woman in brothel or other premises).

3 A person falls within this paragraph if he has been convicted of any of the following offences committed at the age of 18 or over or has been cautioned by a constable in respect of any such offence which, at the time the caution was given, he admitted –

- (a) an offence under section 7 of the Sexual Offences Act 1956 (intercourse with defective) by having sexual intercourse with a child;
- (b) an offence under section 9 of that Act (procurement of defective) by procuring a child to have sexual intercourse;

(c)   an offence under section 10 of that Act (incest by a man) by having sexual intercourse with a child;

(d)   an offence under section 11 of that Act (incest by a woman) by allowing a child to have sexual intercourse with her;

(e)   subject to paragraph 4, an offence under section 12 of that Act by committing buggery with a child under the age of 16;

(f)   subject to paragraph 4, an offence under section 13 of that Act by committing an act of gross indecency with a child;

(g)   an offence under section 21 of that Act (abduction of defective from parent or guardian) by taking a child out of the possession of her parent or guardian;

(h)   an offence under section 22 of that Act (causing prostitution of women) in relation to a child;

(i)   an offence under section 23 of that Act (procuration of girl under 21) by procuring a child to have sexual intercourse with a third person;

(j)   an offence under section 27 of that Act (permitting defective to use premise for intercourse) by inducing or suffering a child to resort to or be on premises for the purpose of having sexual intercourse;

(k)   an offence under section 29 of that Act (causing or encouraging prostitution of defective) by causing or encouraging the prostitution of a child;

(l)   an offence under section 30 of that Act (man living on earnings of prostitution) in a case where the prostitute is a child;

(m)   an offence under section 31 of that Act (woman exercising control over prostitute) in a case where the prostitute is a child;

(n)   an offence under section 128 of the Mental Health Act 1959 (sexual intercourse with patients) by having sexual intercourse with a child;

(o)   an offence under section 4 of the Sexual Offences Act 1967 (procuring others to commit homosexual acts) by –

   (i)   procuring a child to commit an act of buggery with any person; or

   (ii)   procuring any person to commit an act of buggery with a child;

(p)   an offence under section 5 of that Act (living on earnings of male prostitution) by living wholly or in part on the earnings of prostitution of a child; and

(q)   an offence under section 9(1)(a) of the Theft Act 1968 (burglary), by entering a building or part of a building with intent to rape a child.

4 Paragraphs 1(c) and 3(e) and (f) do not include offences in a case where the offender was under the age of 20 at the time the offence was committed.

Schedule 4

PART 1
INFORMATION ABOUT THE PROSPECTIVE ADOPTER

Regulation 25(2)

Information about the prospective adopter

1 Name, sex, date and place of birth and address including the local authority area.

2 A photograph and physical description.

3 Whether the prospective adopter is domiciled or habitually resident in a part of the British Islands and if habitually resident for how long he has been habitually resident.

4 Racial origin and cultural and linguistic background.

5 Religious persuasion.

6 Relationship (if any) to the child.

7 A description of his personality and interests.

8 If the prospective adopter is married or has formed a civil partnership and is applying alone for an assessment of his suitability to adopt, the reasons for this.

9 Details of any previous family court proceedings in which the prospective adopter has been involved.

10 Names and addresses of three referees who will give personal references on the prospective adopter, not more than one of whom may be a relative.

11 Name and address of the prospective adopter's registered medical practitioner.

12 If the prospective adopter –

    (a)   is married, the date and place of marriage;
    (b)   has formed a civil partnership, the date and place of registration of that partnership; or
    (c)   has a partner, details of that relationship.

Amendments: SI 2005/3482.

13 Details of any previous marriage, civil partnership or relationship.

14 A family tree with details of the prospective adopter, his siblings and any children of the prospective adopter, with their ages (or ages at death).

15 A chronology of the prospective adopter from birth.

16 The observations of the prospective adopter about his own experience of being parented and how this has influenced him.

17 Details of any experience the prospective adopter has had of caring for children (including as a parent, step-parent, foster parent, child minder or prospective adopter) and an assessment of his ability in this respect.

18 Any other information which indicates how the prospective adopter and anybody else living in his household is likely to relate to a child placed for adoption with the prospective adopter.

Wider family

19 A description of the wider family of the prospective adopter and their role and importance to the prospective adopter and their likely role and importance to a child placed for adoption with the prospective adopter.

Information about the home etc of the prospective adopter

20 Information about the prospective adopter's home and the neighbourhood in which he lives.

21 Details of other members of the prospective adopter's household (including any children of the prospective adopter whether or not resident in the household).

22 Information about the local community of the prospective adopter, including the degree of the family's integration with its peer groups, friendships and social networks.

Education and employment

23 Details of the prospective adopter's educational history and attainments and his views about how this has influenced him.

24 Details of his employment history and the observations of the prospective adopter about how this has influenced him.

25 The current employment of the prospective adopter and his views about achieving a balance between employment and child care.

Income

26 Details of the prospective adopter's income and expenditure.

Other information

27 Information about the prospective adopter's capacity to –

    (a)   provide for a child's needs, particularly emotional and behavioural development needs;

    (b)   share a child's history and associated emotional issues; and

    (c)   understand and support a child through possible feelings of loss and trauma.

28 The prospective adopter's –

    (a)   reasons for wishing to adopt a child;

    (b)   views and feelings about adoption and its significance;

    (c)   views about his parenting capacity;

    (d)   views about parental responsibility and what it means;

    (e)   views about a suitable home environment for a child;

    (f)   views about the importance and value of education;

    (g)   views and feelings about the importance of a child's religious and cultural upbringing; and

    (h)   views and feelings about contact.

29 The views of other members of the prospective adopter's household and wider family in relation to adoption.

30 Any other relevant information which might assist the adoption panel or the adoption agency.

PART 2
REPORT ON THE HEALTH OF THE PROSPECTIVE ADOPTER

Regulation 25(3)(a)

1 Name, date of birth, sex, weight and height.

2 A family health history of the parents, any brothers and sisters and the children of the prospective adopter, with details of any serious physical or mental illness and hereditary disease or disorder.

3 Infertility or reasons for deciding not to have children (if applicable).

4 Past health history, including details of any serious physical or mental illness, disability, accident, hospital admission or attendance at an out-patient department, and in each case any treatment given.

5 Obstetric history (if applicable).

6 Details of any present illness, including treatment and prognosis.

7 Details of any consumption of alcohol that may give cause for concern or whether the prospective adopter smokes or uses habit-forming drugs.

8 Any other relevant information which the adoption agency considers may assist the adoption panel and the adoption agency.

Schedule 5
Adoption Placement Plan

Regulation 35(2)

1 Whether the child is placed under a placement order or with the consent of the parent or guardian.

Amendments: SI 2005/3482.

2 The arrangements for preparing the child and the prospective adopter for the placement.

3 Date on which it is proposed to place the child for adoption with the prospective adopter.

4 The arrangements for review of the placement.

5 Whether parental responsibility of the prospective adopter for the child is to be restricted, and if so, the extent to which it is to be restricted.

6 Where the local authority has decided to provide adoption support services for the adoptive family, how these will be provided and by whom.

7 The arrangements which the adoption agency has made for allowing any person contact with the child, the form of contact, the arrangements for supporting contact and the name and contact details of the person responsible for facilitating the contact arrangements (if applicable).

8 The dates on which the child's life story book and later life letter are to be passed by the adoption agency to the prospective adopter.

9 Details of any other arrangements that need to be made.

10 Contact details of the child's social worker, the prospective adopter's social worker and out of hours contacts.

Appendix 4

CARE PLANNING, PLACEMENT AND CASE REVIEW (ENGLAND) REGULATIONS 2010

SI 2010/959

PART 1
GENERAL

1 Citation and commencement

(1) These Regulations may be cited as the Care Planning, Placement and Case Review (England) Regulations 2010 and come into force on 1st April 2011.

(2) These Regulations apply in relation to England only.

2 Interpretation

(1) In these Regulations –

'the 1989 Act' means the Children Act 1989;
'the Fostering Services Regulations' means the Fostering Services (England) Regulations 2011;
'appropriate person' means –
    (a)   P, where C is to live, or lives, with P;
    (b)   F, where C is to be placed, or is placed, with F;
    (c)   where C is to be placed, or is placed, in a children's home, the person who is registered under Part 2 of the Care Standards Act 2000 in respect of that home; or
    (d)   where C is to be placed, or is placed, in accordance with other arrangements under section 22C(6)(d), the person who will be responsible for C at the accommodation;

'area authority' means the local authority for the area in which C is placed, or is to be placed, where this is different from the responsible authority;
'C' means a child who is looked after by the responsible authority;
'care plan' means the plan for the future care of C prepared in accordance with Part 2;
'case record' has the meaning given in regulation 49;
'connected person' has the meaning given in regulation 24;
'director of children's services' means the officer of the responsible authority appointed for the purposes of section 18 of the Children Act 2004;

'F' means a person who is approved as a local authority foster parent and with whom it is proposed to place C or, as the case may be, with whom C is placed;

'fostering service provider' has the meaning given in regulation 2(1) of the Fostering Services Regulations;

'full assessment process' has the meaning given in regulation 24(2)(c);

'health plan' has the meaning given in regulation 5(b)(i);

'independent visitor' means the independent person appointed to be C's visitor under section 23ZB;

'IRO' means the independent reviewing officer appointed for C's case under section 25A(1);

'nominated officer' means a senior officer of the responsible authority nominated in writing by the director of children's services for the purposes of these Regulations;

'P' means –

(a)   a person who is C's parent;

(b)   a person who is not C's parent but who has parental responsibility for C; or

(c)   where C is in the care of the responsible authority and there was a residence order in force with respect to C immediately before the care order was made, a person in whose favour the residence order was made;

'pathway plan' has the meaning given in section 23E(1)(a);

'personal adviser' means the personal adviser arranged for C under paragraph 19C of Schedule 2 to the 1989 Act;

'personal education plan' has the meaning given in regulation 5(b)(ii);

'placement' means –

(i)   arrangements made by the responsible authority for C to live with P in accordance with section 22C(2), where C is in the care of the responsible authority, or

(ii)   arrangements made by the responsible authority to provide for C's accommodation and maintenance by any of the means specified in section 22C(6);

'placement plan' has the meaning given in regulation 9(1)(a);

'R' means the representative of the responsible authority who is appointed to visit C in accordance with arrangements made by them under section 23ZA;

'responsible authority' means the local authority that looks after C;

'special educational needs' and 'special educational provision' have the meanings given in section 312 of the Education Act 1996;

'temporary approval' has the meaning given in regulation 24(1); and

'working day' means any day other than –

(a)   a Saturday or a Sunday,

(b)   Christmas day or Good Friday, or

(c)   a bank holiday in England and Wales under the Banking and Financial Dealings Act 1971.

(2) In these Regulations any reference to any document or other record includes any such document or record that is kept or provided in a readily accessible form and includes copies of original documents and electronic methods of recording information.

(3) Save as otherwise appears –

(a) any reference in these Regulations to a numbered section is a reference to that section in the 1989 Act; and.

(b) any reference in these Regulations to a numbered regulation, Part or Schedule is a reference to that regulation, Part or Schedule in these Regulations.

Amendments: SI 2011/581.

3 These Regulations do not apply in relation to any child who is looked after by a local authority and who has been placed for adoption under the Adoption and Children Act 2002.

PART 2
ARRANGEMENTS FOR LOOKING AFTER A CHILD

4 Care planning

(1) Where C is not in the care of the responsible authority and a care plan for C has not already been prepared, the responsible authority must assess C's needs for services to achieve or maintain a reasonable standard of health or development, and prepare such a plan.

(2) Except in the case of a child to whom section 31A (care orders: care plans) applies, or where paragraph (6) applies, the care plan must be prepared before C is first placed by the responsible authority or, if it is not practicable to do so, within ten working days of the start of the first placement.

(3) When assessing C's needs under paragraph (1), the responsible authority must consider whether C's placement meets the requirements of Part 3 of the 1989 Act.

(4) Unless paragraph (5) applies, the care plan should, so far as is reasonably practicable, be agreed by the responsible authority with –

(a) any parent of C's and any person who is not C's parent but who has parental responsibility for C, or.

(b) if there is no such person, the person who was caring for C immediately before the responsible authority arranged a placement for C.

(5) Where C is aged 16 or over and agrees to be provided with accommodation under section 20, the care plan should be agreed with C by the responsible authority.

(6) Where C was first placed by the responsible authority before 1st April 2011, the care plan must be prepared as soon as reasonably practicable.

5 Preparation and content of the care plan

The care plan must include a record of the following information –

(a)   the long term plan for C's upbringing ('the plan for permanence'),

(b)   the arrangements made by the responsible authority to meet C's needs in relation to –

    (i)   health, including the information set out in paragraph 1 of Schedule 1 ('the health plan'),

    (ii)   education and training, including, so far as reasonably practicable, the information set out in paragraph 2 of Schedule 1 ('the personal education plan'),

    (iii)   emotional and behavioural development,

    (iv)   identity, with particular regard to C's religious persuasion, racial origin and cultural and linguistic background,

    (v)   family and social relationships and in particular the information set out in paragraph 3 of Schedule 1,

    (vi)   social presentation, and

    (vii)   self-care skills,

(c)   except in a case where C is in the care of the responsible authority but is not provided with accommodation by them by any of the means specified in section 22C, the placement plan,

(d)   the name of the IRO, and.

(e)   details of the wishes and feelings of the persons listed in section 22(4) about the arrangements referred to in sub-paragraph (b) and the placement plan that have been ascertained and considered in accordance with section 22(4) and (5) and the wishes and feelings of those persons in relation to any change, or proposed change, to the care plan.

6 (1) The responsible authority must keep C's care plan under review in accordance with Part 6 and, if they are of the opinion some change is required, they must revise the care plan or prepare a new care plan accordingly.

(2) Save as otherwise provided in these Regulations, the responsible authority must not make any significant change to the care plan unless the proposed change has first been considered at a review of C's case.

(3) Subject to paragraph (4), the responsible authority must give a copy of the care plan –

(a)   to C, unless it would not be appropriate to do so having regard to C's age and understanding,

(b)   to P,

(c)   to the IRO,

(d)   where C is to be placed, or is placed, with F, to the fostering service provider that approved F in accordance with the Fostering Services Regulations,

(e)   where C is to be placed, or is placed, in a children's home, to the person who is registered under Part 2 of the Care Standards Act 2000 in respect of that home, and

(f)   where C is to be placed, or is placed, in accordance with other arrangements under section 22C(6)(d), to the person who will be responsible for C at the accommodation.

(4) The responsible authority may decide not to give a copy of the care plan, or a full copy of the care plan, to P if to do so would put C at risk of significant harm.

Amendments: SI 2011/581.

7 Health care

(1) Before C is first placed by them or, if that is not reasonably practicable, before the first review of C's case, the responsible authority must make arrangements for a registered medical practitioner to –

(a)   carry out an assessment of C's state of health, and
(b)   provide a written report of the assessment, addressing the matters specified in paragraph 1 of Schedule 1,

as soon as reasonably practicable.

(2) Paragraph (1) does not apply if, within a period of three months immediately preceding the placement, an assessment of C's state of health has been carried out and the responsible authority has obtained a written report that meets the requirements of that paragraph.

(3) The responsible authority must make arrangements for a registered medical practitioner or a registered nurse or registered midwife acting under the supervision of a registered medical practitioner to review C's state of health and provide a written report of each review, addressing the matters specified in paragraph 1 of Schedule 1 –

(a)   at least once in every period of six months before C's fifth birthday, and
(b)   at least once in every period of 12 months after C's fifth birthday.

(4) Paragraphs (1) and (3) do not apply if C refuses consent to the assessment, being of sufficient age and understanding to do so.

(5) The responsible authority must take all reasonable steps to ensure that C is provided with appropriate health care services, in accordance with the health plan, including –

(a)   medical and dental care and treatment, and
(b)   advice and guidance on health, personal care and health promotion issues.

8 Contact with a child in care

(1) This regulation applies if C is in the care of the responsible authority and they have decided under section 34(6) (refusal of contact as a matter of

urgency) to refuse to allow contact that would otherwise be required by virtue of section 34(1) or an order under section 34 (parental contact etc with children in care).

(2) The responsible authority must immediately give written notification to the following persons of the information specified in paragraph (3) ('the specified information') –

    (a)   C, unless it would not be appropriate to do so having regard to C's age and understanding,

    (b)   P,

    (c)   where, immediately before the care order was made, a person had care of C by virtue of an order made in exercise of the High Court's inherent jurisdiction with respect to children, that person,

    (d)   any other person whose wishes and feelings the responsible authority consider to be relevant, and.

    (e)   the IRO.

(3) The specified information is –

    (a)   the responsible authority's decision,

    (b)   the date of the decision,

    (c)   the reasons for the decision,

    (d)   the duration of the decision (if applicable), and

    (e)   remedies available in case of dissatisfaction.

(4) The responsible authority may depart from the terms of any order made under section 34 by agreement with the person in relation to whom the order is made, provided that –

    (a)   C, being of sufficient age and understanding, also agrees, and

    (b)   written notification of the specified information is given within five working days to the persons listed in paragraph (2).

(5) Where the responsible authority has decided to vary or suspend any arrangements made (otherwise than under an order under section 34) with a view to affording any person contact with C, the responsible authority must immediately give written notification containing the specified information to the persons listed in paragraph (2).

(6) The responsible authority must record any decision made under this regulation in C's care plan.

PART 3
PLACEMENTS – GENERAL PROVISIONS

9 Placement plan

(1) Subject to paragraphs (2) and (4), before making arrangements in accordance with section 22C for C's placement, the responsible authority must –

    (a)   prepare a plan for the placement ('the placement plan') which –

      (i)   sets out how the placement will contribute to meeting C's needs, and

      (ii)   includes all the matters specified in Schedule 2 as are applicable, having regard to the type of the placement, and.

  (b)   ensure that –

      (i)   C's wishes and feelings have been ascertained and given due consideration, and

      (ii)   the IRO has been informed.

(2) If it is not reasonably practicable to prepare the placement plan before making the placement, the placement plan must be prepared within five working days of the start of the placement.

(3) The placement plan must be agreed with, and signed by, the appropriate person.

(4) Where the arrangements for C's placement were made before 1st April 2011, the responsible authority must prepare the placement plan as soon as reasonably practicable.

10 Avoidance of disruption in education

(1) Subject to paragraphs (2) and (3), if C is a registered pupil at a school in the fourth key stage, a decision to make any change to C's placement that would have the effect of disrupting the arrangements made for C's education must not be put into effect until it has been approved by a nominated officer.

(2) Before approving a decision under paragraph (1), the nominated officer must be satisfied that –

  (a)   the requirements of regulation 9(1)(b)(i) have been complied with,

  (b)   the educational provision made for C at the placement will promote C's educational achievement and is consistent with C's personal education plan,

  (c)   the designated teacher at the school has been consulted, and

  (d)   the IRO has been consulted.

(3) Paragraph (1) does not apply in any case where –

  (a)   the responsible authority terminates C's placement in accordance with regulation 14(3), or.

  (b)   it is necessary for any other reason to change C's placement in an emergency,

and in such a case the responsible authority must make appropriate arrangements to promote C's educational achievement as soon as reasonably practicable.

(4) In any case not falling within paragraph (1), but where the responsible authority propose making any change to C's placement that would have the effect of disrupting the arrangements made for C's education or training, the

responsible authority must ensure that other arrangements are made for C's education or training that meet C's needs and are consistent with C's personal education plan.

(5) In this regulation –

    (a)   'registered pupil' has the meaning given in section 20(7) of the Children and Young Persons Act 2008, and.

    (b)   'school' has the meaning given in section 4 of the Education Act 1996.

Placement out of area

11 Placement decision

(1) Subject to paragraphs (3) and (4), a decision to place C outside the area of the responsible authority (including a placement outside England) must not be put into effect until it has been approved by a nominated officer.

(2) Before approving a decision under paragraph (1), the nominated officer must be satisfied that –

    (a)   the requirements of regulation 9(1)(b)(i) have been complied with,

    (b)   the placement is the most appropriate placement available for C and consistent with C's care plan,

    (c)   C's relatives have been consulted, where appropriate,

    (d)   the area authority have been notified, and

    (e)   the IRO has been consulted.

(3) In the case of a placement made in an emergency, paragraph (2) does not apply and before approving a decision under paragraph (1) the nominated officer must –

    (a)   be satisfied that regulation 9(1)(b)(i) and the requirements of sub-paragraph (2)(b) have been complied with, and.

    (b)   take steps to ensure that regulation 9(1)(b)(ii) and the requirements set out in sub-paragraphs (2)(c) and (d) are complied with by the responsible authority within five working days of approval of the decision under paragraph (1).

(4) Paragraphs (1) and (2) do not apply to a decision to place C outside the area of the responsible authority with –

    (a)   F who is a connected person, or

    (b)   F who is approved as a local authority foster parent by the responsible authority.

12 Placements outside England and Wales

(1) This regulation applies if –

    (a)   C is in the care of the responsible authority, and

(b) the responsible authority make arrangements to place C outside England and Wales in accordance with the provisions of paragraph 19 of Schedule 2 to the 1989 Act (placement of a child in care outside England and Wales).

(2) The responsible authority must take steps to ensure that, so far as is reasonably practicable, requirements corresponding with the requirements which would have applied under these Regulations had C been placed in England, are complied with.

(3) The responsible authority must include in the care plan details of the arrangements made by the responsible authority to supervise C's placement.

13 Notification of placement

(1) Subject to paragraph (3), the responsible authority must give written notification to the persons listed in paragraph (2) of the arrangements for C's placement before the placement is made or, if the placement is made in an emergency, within five working days of the start of the placement, unless it is not reasonably practicable to do so.

(2) The persons referred to in paragraph (1) are –

(a) C, unless it would not be appropriate to do so having regard to C's age and understanding,

(b) P,

(c) if C is in the care of the responsible authority, any person who is allowed contact with C under section 34(1) and any person who has contact with C by virtue of an order under section 34,

(d) if C is looked after but is not in the care of the responsible authority, any person who has contact with C pursuant to an order made under section 8 (residence, contact and other orders with respect to children),

(e) any person who was caring for C immediately before the arrangements were made,

(f) the Primary Care Trust (or in the case of a child living or to be placed in Wales, the local health board) for the area in which C is living and, if different, for the area in which C is to be placed,

(g) C's registered medical practitioner and, where applicable, the registered medical practitioner with whom C is to be registered during the placement,

(h) any educational institution attended by, or person providing education or training for, C, and

(i) the IRO.

(3) The responsible authority may decide not to give notification to any of the persons listed in sub-paragraphs (b) to (e) if to do so would put C at risk of significant harm.

14 Termination of placement by the responsible authority

(1) Subject to paragraphs (3) and (5), the responsible authority may only terminate C's placement following a review of C's case in accordance with Part 6.

(2) Subject to paragraphs (3) and (4), before terminating C's placement, the responsible authority must –

    (a)   make other arrangements for C's accommodation, in accordance with section 22C,

    (b)   inform the IRO,

    (c)   so far as is reasonably practicable, give written notification of their intention to terminate the placement to –

        (i)   all the persons to whom notification of the placement was given under regulation 13,

        (ii)   the person with whom C is placed,

        (iii)   where C is placed in the area of another local authority, that authority.

(3) Where there is an immediate risk of significant harm to C, or to protect others from serious injury, the responsible authority must terminate C's placement, and in those circumstances –

    (a)   paragraph (1) does not apply, and

    (b)   they must comply with paragraph (2)(a) and (b) as soon as reasonably practicable.

(4) If it is not reasonably practicable to notify any person in accordance with paragraph (2)(c), then the responsible authority must give written notification to that person, within ten working days of the date on which the placement is terminated, of the fact that the placement has been terminated.

(5) This regulation does not apply where C's placement is terminated under regulation 19(c), regulation 23(2) or regulation 25(6), nor where section 22D (review of child's case before making alternative arrangements for accommodation) applies.

PART 4
PROVISION FOR DIFFERENT TYPES OF PLACEMENT

Chapter 1
Placement of a child in care with P

15 Application

(1) This Chapter applies if C is in the care of the responsible authority and they, acting in accordance with section 22C(2), propose to place C with P.

(2) Nothing in this Chapter requires the responsible authority to remove C from P's care if C is living with P before a placement decision is made about C.

16 Effect of contact order

The responsible authority must not place C with P if to do so would be incompatible with any order made by the court under section 34.

17 Assessment of P's suitability to care for a child

Before deciding to place C with P, the responsible authority must –

(a) assess the suitability of P to care for C, including the suitability of –
  (i)   the proposed accommodation, and
  (ii) all other persons aged 18 and over who are members of the household in which it is proposed that C will live,
(b) take into account all the matters set out in Schedule 3 in making their assessment,
(c) consider whether, in all the circumstances and taking into account the services to be provided by the responsible authority, the placement will safeguard and promote C's welfare and meet C's needs set out in the care plan, and
(d) review C's case in accordance with Part 6.

18 Decision to place a child with P

(1) The decision to place C with P must not be put into effect until it has been approved by a nominated officer, and the responsible authority have prepared a placement plan for C.

(2) Before approving a decision under paragraph (1), the nominated officer must be satisfied that –

(a) the requirements of regulation 9(1)(b)(i) have been complied with,
(b) the requirements of regulation 17 have been complied with,
(c) the placement will safeguard and promote C's welfare, and
(d) the IRO has been consulted.

19 Circumstances in which a child may be placed with P before assessment completed

Where the nominated officer considers it to be necessary and consistent with C's welfare, the responsible authority may place C with P before their assessment under regulation 17 ('the assessment') is completed provided that they –

(a) arrange for P to be interviewed in order to obtain as much of the information specified in Schedule 3 about P and the other persons living in P's household who are aged 18 and over as can be readily ascertained at that interview,
(b) ensure that the assessment and the review of C's case are completed in accordance with regulation 17 within ten working days of C being placed with P, and

(c)   ensure that a decision in accordance with regulation 18 is made and approved within ten working days after the assessment is completed, and –

    (i)   if the decision is to confirm the placement, review the placement plan and, if appropriate amend it, and

    (ii)   if the decision is not to confirm the placement, terminate the placement.

20 Support for P

Where C is placed, or is to be placed, with P, the responsible authority must provide such services and support to P as appear to them to be necessary to safeguard and promote C's welfare and must record details of such services and support in C's care plan.

Chapter 2
Placement with local authority foster parents

21 Interpretation

(1) In this Chapter 'registered person' has the same meaning as in the Fostering Services Regulations.

(2) Where C is placed jointly with two persons each of whom is approved as a local authority foster parent, any reference in these Regulations to a local authority foster parent is to be interpreted as referring equally to both such persons and any requirement to be satisfied by or relating to a particular local authority foster parent must be satisfied by, or treated as relating to, both of them.

Amendments: SI 2011/581.

22 Conditions to be complied with before placing a child with a local authority foster parent

(1) This regulation applies where the responsible authority propose to place C with F.

(2) The responsible authority may only place C with F if –

(a)   F is approved by –

    (i)   the responsible authority, or

    (ii)   provided that the conditions specified in paragraph (3) are also satisfied, another fostering service provider,

(b)   the terms of F's approval are consistent with the proposed placement, and

(c)   F has entered into a foster care agreement either with the responsible authority or with another fostering service provider in accordance with regulation 27(5)(b) of the Fostering Services Regulations.

(3) The conditions referred to in paragraph (2)(a)(ii) are that –

(a)   the fostering service provider by whom F is approved consents to the proposed placement, and

(b)   where any other local authority currently have a child placed with F, that local authority consents to the proposed placement.

Amendments: SI 2011/581.

23 Emergency placement with a local authority foster parent

(1) Where it is necessary to place C in an emergency, the responsible authority may place C with any local authority foster parent who has been approved in accordance with the Fostering Services Regulations, even if the terms of that approval are not consistent with the placement, provided that the placement is for no longer than six working days.

(2) When the period of six working days referred to in paragraph (1) expires, the responsible authority must terminate the placement unless the terms of that person's approval have been amended to be consistent with the placement.

Amendments: SI 2011/581.

24 Temporary approval of relative, friend or other person connected with C

(1) Where the responsible authority is satisfied that –

(a)   the most appropriate placement for C is with a connected person, notwithstanding that the connected person is not approved as a local authority foster parent, and

(b)   it is necessary for C to be placed with the connected person before the connected person's suitability to be a local authority foster parent has been assessed in accordance with the Fostering Services Regulations,

they may approve that person as a local authority foster parent for a temporary period not exceeding 16 weeks ('temporary approval') provided that they first comply with the requirements of paragraph (2).

(2) Before making a placement under paragraph (1), the responsible authority must –

(a)   assess the suitability of the connected person to care for C, including the suitability of –
  (i)   the proposed accommodation, and
  (ii)   all other persons aged 18 and over who are members of the household in which it is proposed that C will live,

taking into account all the matters set out in Schedule 4,

(b)   consider whether, in all the circumstances and taking into account the services to be provided by the responsible authority, the proposed arrangements will safeguard and promote C's welfare and meet C's needs set out in the care plan, and

(c)   make immediate arrangements for the suitability of the connected person to be a local authority foster parent to be assessed in accordance with the Fostering Services Regulations ('the full assessment process') before the temporary approval expires.

(3) In this regulation 'connected person' means a relative, friend or other person connected with C.

Amendments: SI 2011/581.

25 Expiry of temporary approval

(1) Subject to paragraph (4), the responsible authority may extend the temporary approval of a connected person if –

(a)   it is likely to expire before the full assessment process is completed, or
(b)   the connected person, having undergone the full assessment process, is not approved and seeks a review of the decision in accordance with Regulations made under paragraph 12F(1)(b) of Schedule 2 to the 1989 Act.

(2) In a case falling within paragraph (1)(a), the responsible authority may extend the temporary approval once for a further period of up to eight weeks.

(3) In a case falling within paragraph (1)(b), the responsible authority may extend the temporary approval until the outcome of the review is known.

(4) Before deciding whether to extend the temporary approval in the circumstances set out in paragraph (1), the responsible authority must first –

(a)   consider whether placement with the connected person is still the most appropriate placement available,
(b)   seek the views of the fostering panel established by the fostering service provider in accordance with the Fostering Services Regulations, and
(c)   inform the IRO.

(5) A decision to extend temporary approval must be approved by a nominated officer.

(6) If the period of temporary approval and of any extension to that period expires and the connected person has not been approved as a local authority foster parent in accordance with the Fostering Services Regulations, the responsible authority must terminate the placement after first making other arrangements for C's accommodation.

Amendments: SI 2011/581.

26 Independent fostering agencies – discharge of responsible authority functions

(1) A responsible authority may make arrangements in accordance with this regulation for the duties imposed on it as responsible authority by regulation 14(3) and regulation 22 to be discharged on their behalf by a registered person.

(2) No arrangements may be made under this regulation unless the responsible authority has entered into a written agreement with the registered person which includes the information set out in paragraph 1 of Schedule 5, and where the

responsible authority proposes to make an arrangement under this regulation in relation to a particular child, the written agreement must also include the matters set out in paragraph 2 of Schedule 5.

(3) The responsible authority must report to the Chief Inspector of Education, Children's Services and Skills any concerns they may have about the services provided by a registered person.

Chapter 3
Other arrangements

27 General duties of the responsible authority when placing a child in other arrangements

Before placing C in accommodation in an unregulated setting under section 22C(6)(d), the responsible authority must –

   (a)   be satisfied that the accommodation is suitable for C, having regard to the matters set out in Schedule 6,

   (b)   unless it is not reasonably practicable, arrange for C to visit the accommodation, and

   (c)   inform the IRO.

PART 5
VISITS BY THE RESPONSIBLE AUTHORITY'S REPRESENTATIVE ETC

28 Frequency of visits

(1) As part of their arrangements for supervising C's welfare, the responsible authority must ensure that their representative ('R') visits C in accordance with this regulation, wherever C is living.

(2) Subject to paragraphs (3) to (6), the responsible authority must ensure that R visits C –

   (a)   within one week of the start of any placement,

   (b)   at intervals of not more than six weeks for the first year of any placement, and

   (c)   thereafter –

      (i)   where the placement is intended to last until C is aged 18, at intervals of not more than three months,

      (ii)   and in any other case, at intervals of not more than six weeks.

(3) Where regulation 19 applies, the responsible authority must ensure that R visits C –

   (a)   at least once a week until the first review carried out in accordance with Part 6, and

   (b)   thereafter at intervals of not more than six weeks.

(4) Where regulation 24 applies, or where an interim care order has been made in relation to C under section 38 (interim orders) and C is living with P, the responsible authority must ensure that R visits C –

    (a)   at least once a week until the first review carried out in accordance with Part 6, and

    (b)   thereafter at intervals of not more than four weeks.

(5) Where a care order has been made in relation to C under section 31 (care and supervision orders) and C is living with P, the responsible authority must ensure that R visits C –

    (a)   within one week of the making of the care order, and

    (b)   thereafter at intervals of not more than six weeks.

(6) Where C is in the care of the responsible authority but another person is responsible for the arrangements under which C is living for the time being ('C's living arrangements'), the responsible authority must ensure that R visits C –

    (a)   within one week of the start of C's living arrangements and within one week of any change to C's living arrangements,

    (b)   at intervals of not more that six weeks for the first year thereafter, and

    (c)   at intervals of not more than three months in any subsequent year.

(7) In addition to visits in accordance with paragraphs (2) to (6), the responsible authority must ensure that R visits C –

    (a)   whenever reasonably requested to do so by –

        (i)   C,

        (ii)   where paragraphs (2), (3) or (4) apply, the appropriate person, or

        (iii)   where paragraph (5) applies, the person responsible for C's living arrangements,

    (b)   within one week of first receiving notification under section 30A of the Care Standards Act 2000 (notification of matters relating to persons carrying on or managing certain establishments or agencies), where the children's home in which C is placed for the time being is referred to in that notification.

29 Conduct of visits

On each visit, R must speak to C in private unless –

    (a)   C, being of sufficient age and understanding to do so, refuses,

    (b)   R considers it inappropriate to do so, having regard to C's age and understanding, or

    (c)   R is unable to do so.

30 Consequences of visits

Where, as the result of a visit carried out in accordance with this Part, R's assessment is that C's welfare is not adequately safeguarded and promoted by the placement, the responsible authority must review C's case in accordance with Part 6.

31 Advice, support and assistance for the child

When making arrangements in accordance with section 23ZA(2)(b) for advice, support and assistance to be available to C between R's visits, the responsible authority must ensure that –

(a) the arrangements –
   (i) are appropriate having regard to C's age and understanding, and
   (ii) give due consideration to C's religious persuasion, racial origin, cultural and linguistic background and to any disability C may have, and
(b) so far as is reasonably practicable having regard to C's age and understanding, C knows how to seek appropriate advice, support and assistance from them.

PART 6
REVIEWS OF THE CHILD'S CASE

32 General duty of the responsible authority to review the child's case

(1) The responsible authority must review C's case in accordance with this Part.

(2) The responsible authority must not make any significant change to C's care plan unless the proposed change has first been considered at a review of C's case, unless this is not reasonably practicable.

(3) Nothing in this Part prevents any review of C's case being carried out at the same time as any other review assessment or consideration of C's case under any other provision.

33 Timing of reviews

(1) The responsible authority must first review C's case within 20 working days of the date on which C becomes looked after.

(2) The second review must be carried out not more than three months after the first, and subsequent reviews must be carried out at intervals of not more than six months.

(3) The responsible authority must carry out a review before the time specified in paragraph (1) or (2) if –

(a) the IRO so requests,
(b) regulation 30 applies,
(c) C is provided with accommodation under section 21(2)(b) or (c) and a review would not otherwise occur before C ceases to be so provided with accommodation,
(d) C is in the care of the responsible authority and is detained in a secure training centre or a young offenders institution, and a review would not otherwise occur before C ceases to be so detained, or
(e) C is looked after but is not in the care of the responsible authority and

(i)   the responsible authority propose to cease to provide accommodation for C, and

(ii)   accommodation will not subsequently be provided for C by C's parents (or one of them) or any person who is not C's parent but who has parental responsibility for C.

Conduct of reviews

34 Local authority's policy on reviews

(1) The responsible authority must prepare and implement a written policy regarding the manner in which they will review cases in accordance with this Part.

(2) The responsible authority must provide a copy of their policy to –

(a)   C, unless it would not be appropriate to do so having regard to C's age and understanding,

(b)   C's parents, or any person who is not C's parent but who has parental responsibility for C, and

(c)   any other person whose views the responsible authority consider to be relevant.

35 Considerations to which the responsible authority must have regard

The considerations to which the responsible authority must have regard in reviewing each case are set out in Schedule 7.

36 The role of the IRO

(1) The IRO must –

(a)   so far as reasonably practicable, attend any meeting held as part of the review ('the review meeting') and, if attending the review meeting, chair it,

(b)   speak to C in private about the matters to be considered at the review unless C, being of sufficient understanding to do so, refuses or the IRO considers it inappropriate having regard to C's age and understanding,

(c)   ensure that, so far as reasonably practicable, the wishes and feelings of C's parents, or any person who is not C's parent but who has parental responsibility for C, have been ascertained and taken into account, and

(d)   ensure that the review is conducted in accordance with this Part and in particular –

    (i)   that the persons responsible for implementing any decision taken in consequence of the review are identified, and

    (ii)   that any failure to review the case in accordance with this Part or to take proper steps to implement decisions taken in consequence of the review are brought to the attention of an officer at an appropriate level of seniority within the responsible authority.

(2) The IRO may, if not satisfied that sufficient information has been provided by the responsible authority to enable proper consideration of any of the

matters in Schedule 7, adjourn the review meeting once for not more than 20 working days, and no proposal considered in the course of the review may be implemented until the review has been completed.

37 Arrangements for implementing decisions arising out of reviews

The responsible authority must –

(a) make arrangements to implement decisions made in the course, or as a result, of the review, and

(b) inform the IRO of any significant failure to make such arrangements, or any significant change of circumstances occurring after the review that affects those arrangements.

38 Records of reviews

The responsible authority must ensure that a written record of the review is prepared, and that the information obtained in the course of the review, details of proceedings at the review meeting, and any decisions made in the course, or as a result, of the review are included in C's case record.

PART 7
ARRANGEMENTS MADE BY THE RESPONSIBLE AUTHORITY FOR CEASING TO LOOK AFTER A CHILD

39 Arrangements for ceasing to look after a child who is not an eligible child

In any case where –

(a) C is not in the care of the responsible authority and is not an eligible child, and

(b) C's circumstances have changed such that the responsible authority are likely to cease to provide C with accommodation.

the care plan must include details of the advice, assistance and support that the responsible authority intend to provide for C when C ceases to be looked after by them.

Eligible children

40 Meaning of eligible child

(1) For the purposes of paragraph 19B(2)(b) of Schedule 2 to the 1989 Act (meaning of eligible child), the prescribed period is 13 weeks and the prescribed age is 14.

(2) For the purposes of paragraph 19B(3)(b) of that Schedule, if C is a child to whom regulation 48 applies, C is not an eligible child despite falling within paragraph 19B(2) of that Schedule.

41 General duties

If C is an eligible child, the responsible authority must –

(a)   assess C's needs in accordance with regulation 42, and
(b)   prepare C's pathway plan, in accordance with regulation 43.

42 Assessment of needs

(1) The responsible authority must complete the assessment of C's needs in accordance with paragraph 19B(4) of Schedule 2 to the 1989 Act not more than three months after the date on which C reaches the age of 16 or becomes an eligible child after that age.

(2) In carrying out their assessment of C's likely needs when C ceases to be looked after, the responsible authority must take account of the following considerations –

(a)   C's state of health (including physical, emotional and mental health) and development,
(b)   C's continuing need for education, training or employment,
(c)   the support that will be available to C from C's parents and other connected persons,
(d)   C's actual and anticipated financial resources and capacity to manage personal finances independently,
(e)   the extent to which C possesses the practical and other skills necessary for independent living,
(f)   C's need for continuing care, support and accommodation,
(g)   the wishes and feelings of –
   (i)   C,
   (ii)   any parent of C's and any person who is not C's parent but who has parental responsibility for C,
   (iii) the appropriate person,
(h)   the views of –
   (i)   any person or educational institution that provides C with education or training and, if C has a statement of special educational needs, the local authority who maintain the statement (if different),
   (ii)   the IRO,
   (iii) any person providing health (whether physical, emotional or mental health) or dental care or treatment to C,
   (iv)   the personal adviser appointed for C, and
   (v)   any other person whose views the responsible authority, or C, consider may be relevant.

43 The pathway plan

(1) The pathway plan must be prepared as soon as possible after the assessment of C's needs and must include, in particular –

(a)   C's care plan, and
(b)   the information referred to in Schedule 8.

(2) The pathway plan must, in relation to each of the matters referred to in paragraphs 2 to 10 of Schedule 8, set out –

(a) the manner in which the responsible authority propose to meet C's needs, and

(b) the date by which, and by whom, any action required to implement any aspect of the plan will be carried out.

44 Functions of the personal adviser

The personal adviser's functions in relation to C are to –

(a) provide advice (including practical advice) and support,

(b) participate in reviews of C's case carried out under Part 6,

(c) liaise with the responsible authority in the implementation of the pathway plan,

(d) co-ordinate the provision of services and take reasonable steps to ensure C makes use of such services,

(e) remain informed about C's progress and wellbeing, and

(f) maintain a written record of their contacts with C.

PART 8
INDEPENDENT REVIEWING OFFICERS AND INDEPENDENT VISITORS

45 Additional functions of independent reviewing officers

(1) The IRO must ensure that, having regard to C's age and understanding, C has been informed by the responsible authority of the steps C may take under the 1989 Act and in particular, where appropriate, of –

(a) C's rights to apply, with leave, for a section 8 order (residence, contact and other orders with respect to children) and, where C is in the care of the responsible authority, to apply for the discharge of the care order, and

(b) the availability of the procedure established by them under section 26(3) for considering any representations (including complaints) C may wish to make about the discharge by the responsible authority of their functions, including the availability of assistance to make such representations under section 26A (advocacy services).

(2) If C wishes to take legal proceedings under the 1989 Act, the IRO must –

(a) establish whether an appropriate adult is able and willing to assist C to obtain legal advice or bring proceedings on C's behalf, and

(b) if there is no such person, assist C to obtain such advice.

(3) In the following circumstances the IRO must consider whether it would be appropriate to refer C's case to an officer of the Children and Family Court Advisory and Support Service –

(a) in the opinion of the IRO, the responsible authority have failed in any significant respect to –

(i) prepare C's care plan in accordance with these Regulations,

(ii) review C's case in accordance with these Regulations, or effectively implement any decision taken in consequence of a review,

or are otherwise in breach of their duties to C in any material respect, and

(b) having drawn the failure or breach to the attention of persons at an appropriate level of seniority within the responsible authority, it has not been addressed to the satisfaction of the IRO within a reasonable period of time.

(4) When consulted by the responsible authority about any matter concerning C, or when informed of any matter relating to C in accordance with these Regulations, the IRO must –

(a) ensure that the responsible authority have ascertained and, subject to C's age and understanding, given due consideration to, C's wishes and feelings concerning the matter in question, and

(b) consider whether to request a review of C's case.

46 Qualifications and experience of independent reviewing officers

(1) The IRO must be registered as a social worker in a register maintained by the General Social Care Council or by the Care Council for Wales under section 56 of the Care Standards Act 2000, or in a corresponding register maintained under the law of Scotland or Northern Ireland.

(2) The IRO must have sufficient relevant social work experience with children and families to perform the functions of an independent reviewing officer set out in section 25B(1) and under these Regulations in an independent manner and having regard to C's best interests.

(3) The responsible authority must not appoint any of the following as the IRO –

(a) a person involved in preparing C's care plan or the management of C's case,

(b) R,

(c) C's personal adviser,

(d) a person with management responsibilities in relation to a person mentioned in sub-paragraphs (a) to (c), or

(e) a person with control over the resources allocated to the case.

47 Independent visitors

A person appointed by the responsible authority as an independent visitor under section 23ZB(1) is to be regarded as independent of that authority where the person appointed is not connected with the responsible authority by virtue of being –

(a) a member of the responsible authority or any of their committees or sub-committees, whether elected or co-opted,

(b) an officer of the responsible authority employed in relation to the exercise of the functions referred to in section 18(2) of the Children Act 2004, or

(c) a spouse, civil partner or other person (whether of different sex or the same sex) living in the same household as the partner of a person falling within sub-paragraph (a) or (b).

PART 9
MISCELLANEOUS

48 Application of these Regulations with modifications to short breaks

(1) In the circumstances set out in paragraph (2) these Regulations apply with the modifications set out in paragraph (3).

(2) The circumstances are that –

(a) C is not in the care of the responsible authority,

(b) the responsible authority have arranged to place C in a series of short-term placements with the same person or in the same accommodation ('short breaks'), and

(c) the arrangement is such that –

   (i)   no single placement is intended to last for longer than 17 days,

   (ii) at the end of each such placement, C returns to the care of C's parent or a person who is not C's parent but who has parental responsibility for C, and

   (iii) the short breaks do not exceed 75 days in total in any period of 12 months.

(3) The modifications are that –

(a) regulations 5 and 9 do not apply, but instead the care plan must set out the arrangements made to meet C's needs with particular regard to –

   (i)   C's health and emotional and behavioural development, in particular in relation to any disability C may have,

   (ii) promoting contact between C and C's parents and any other person who is not C's parent but who has parental responsibility for C, during any period when C is placed,

   (iii) C's leisure interests, and

   (iv) promoting C's educational achievement,

   and must include the name and address of C's registered medical practitioner, and the information set out in paragraph 3 of Schedule 2, where appropriate,

(b) regulations 7, 13 and 49(2)(b) do not apply,

(c) regulation 28(2) does not apply, but instead the responsible authority must ensure that R visits C on days when C is in fact placed, at regular intervals to be agreed with the IRO and C's parents (or any person who is not C's parent but who has parental responsibility for C) and recorded in the care plan before the start of the first placement, and in any event –

(i) the first visit must take place within three months of the start of the first placement, or as soon as practicable thereafter, and

(ii) subsequent visits must take place at intervals of not more than six months, for as long as the short breaks continue,

(d) regulation 33 does not apply, but instead –

(i) the responsible authority must first review C's case within three months of the start of the first placement, and

(ii) the second and subsequent reviews must be carried out at intervals of not more than six months.

Records

49 Establishment of records

(1) The responsible authority must establish and maintain a written case record for C ('C's case record'), if one is not already in existence.

(2) The case record must include –

(a) C's care plan, including any changes made to the care plan and any subsequent plans,

(b) reports obtained under regulation 7,

(c) any other document created or considered as part of any assessment of C's needs, or of any review of C's case,

(d) any court order relating to C,

(e) details of any arrangements that have been made by the responsible authority with any other local authority or with an independent fostering agency under regulation 26 and Schedule 5, or with a provider of social work services, under which any of the responsible authority's functions in relation to C are discharged by that local authority or independent fostering agency or provider of social work services.

50 Retention and confidentiality of records

(1) The responsible authority must retain C's case record either –

(a) until the seventy-fifth anniversary of C's birth, or

(b) if C dies before attaining the age of 18, for fifteen years beginning with the date of C's death.

(2) The responsible authority must secure the safe keeping of C's case record and take any necessary steps to ensure that information contained in it is treated as confidential subject only to –

(a) any provision of, or made under or by virtue of, a statute under which access to such a record or information may be obtained or given,

(b) any court order under which access to such a record or information may be obtained or given.

51 Revocations

The Regulations set out in Schedule 9 are revoked.

Schedule 1
Care plans

Regulation 5

1 Information to be included in the health plan

(1) C's state of health including C's physical, emotional and mental health.

(2) C's health history including, so far as practicable, C's family's health history.

(3) The effect of C's health and health history on C's development.

(4) Existing arrangements for C's medical and dental care including –

(a) routine checks of C's general state of health, including dental health,
(b) treatment for, and monitoring of, identified health (including physical, emotional and mental health) or dental care needs,
(c) preventive measures such as vaccination and immunisation,
(d) screening for defects of vision or hearing, and
(e) advice and guidance on promoting health and effective personal care.

(5) Any planned changes to existing arrangements.

(6) The role of the appropriate person, and of any other person who cares for C, in promoting C's health.

2 Information to be included in the personal education plan

(1) C's educational and training history, including information about educational institutions attended and C's attendance and conduct record, C's academic and other achievements, and C's special educational needs, if any.

(2) Existing arrangements for C's education and training, including details of any special educational provision and any other provision made to meet C's particular educational or training needs, and to promote C's educational achievement.

(3) Any planned changes to existing arrangements for C's education or training and, where any changes to the arrangements are necessary, provision made to minimise disruption to that education or training.

(4) C's leisure interests.

(5) The role of the appropriate person, and of any other person who cares for C, in promoting C's educational achievements and leisure interests.

3 Family and social relationships

(1) If C has a sibling for whom the responsible authority or another authority are providing accommodation, and the children have not been placed together, the arrangements made to promote contact between them, so far as is consistent with C's welfare.

(2) If C is looked after by, but is not in the care of, the responsible authority, details of any order relating to C made under section 8.

(3) If C is in the care of the responsible authority, details of any order relating to C made under section 34 (parental contact etc with children in care).

(4) Any other arrangements made to promote and maintain contact in accordance with paragraph 15 of Schedule 2 of the 1989 Act, so far as is reasonably practicable and consistent with C's welfare, between C and –

    (a)   any parent of C's and any person who is not C's parent but who has parental responsibility for C, and

    (b)   any other connected person.

(5) Where section 23ZB(1) applies, the arrangements made to appoint an independent visitor for C or, if section 23ZB(6) applies (appointment of independent visitor not made where child objects), that fact.

Schedule 2
Matters to be dealt with in the placement plan

Regulation 9

1 Information to be included in C's placement plan

(1) How on a day to day basis C will be cared for and C's welfare will be safeguarded and promoted by the appropriate person.

(2) Any arrangements made for contact between C and any parent of C's and any person who is not C's parent but who has parental responsibility for C, and between C and any other connected person including, if appropriate –

    (a)   the reasons why contact with any such person would not be reasonably practicable or would not be consistent with C's welfare,

    (b)   if C is not in the care of the responsible authority, details of any order made under section 8,

    (c)   if C is in the care of the responsible authority, details of any order relating to C made under section 34,

    (d)   the arrangements for notifying any changes in the arrangements for contact.

(3) The arrangements made for C's health (including physical, emotional and mental health) and dental care including –

    (a)   the name and address of C's registered medical and dental practitioners and, where applicable, any registered medical or dental practitioner with whom C is to be registered following the placement,

    (b)   any arrangements for the giving or withholding of consent to medical or dental examination or treatment for C.

(4) The arrangements made for C's education and training including –

    (a)   the name and address of any school at which C is a registered pupil,

    (b)   the name of the designated teacher at the school (if applicable),

    (c)   the name and address of any other educational institution that C attends, or of any other person who provides C with education or training,

    (d)   where C has a statement of special educational needs, details of the local authority that maintains the statement.

(5) The arrangements made for R to visit C in accordance with Part 5, the frequency of visits and the arrangements made for advice, support and assistance to be available to C between visits in accordance with regulation 31.

(6) If an independent visitor is appointed, the arrangements made for them to visit C.

(7) The circumstances in which the placement may be terminated and C removed from the appropriate person's care in accordance with regulation 14.

(8) The name and contact details of –

    (a)   the IRO,
    (b)   C's independent visitor (if one is appointed),
    (c)   R, and
    (d)   if C is an eligible child, the personal adviser appointed for C.

2 Additional information to be included where C is placed with P

(1) Details of support and services to be provided to P during the placement.

(2) The obligation on P to notify the responsible authority of any relevant change in circumstances, including any intention to change address, any changes in the household in which C lives, and of any serious incident involving C.

(3) The obligation on P to ensure that any information relating to C or C's family or any other person given in confidence to P in connection with the placement is kept confidential, and that such information is not disclosed to any person without the consent of the responsible authority.

(4) The circumstances in which it is necessary to obtain the prior approval of the responsible authority for C to live in a household other than P's household.

(5) The arrangements for requesting a change to the placement plan.

(6) The circumstances in which the placement will be terminated in accordance with regulation 19(c)(ii).

3 Additional information to be included where C is placed with F, in a children's home or in other arrangements

(1) The type of accommodation to be provided, the address and, where C is placed under section 22C(6)(d), the name of the person who will be responsible for C at that accommodation on behalf of the responsible authority (if any).

(2) C's personal history, religious persuasion, cultural and linguistic background, and racial origin.

(3) Where C is not in the care of the responsible authority –

(a)   the respective responsibilities of the responsible authority and C's parents, or any person who is not C's parent but who has parental responsibility for C,

(b)   any delegation of responsibility to the responsible authority for C's day to day care there has been by C's parents, or any person who is not C's parent but who has parental responsibility for C,

(c)   the expected duration of the arrangements and the steps which should be taken to bring the arrangements to an end, including arrangements for C to return to live with C's parents, or any person who is not C's parent but who has parental responsibility for C, and

(d)   where C is aged 16 or over and agrees to being provided with accommodation under section 20, that fact.

(4) Any circumstances in which F must obtain the prior approval of either the responsible authority or P before making decisions in relation to C or C's care.

(5) The responsible authority's arrangements for the financial support of C during the placement.

(6) Where C is placed with F, the obligation on F to comply with the terms of the foster care agreement made under regulation 27(5)(b) of the Fostering Services Regulations.

Amendments: SI 2011/581.

Schedule 3
**Matters to be taken into account when assessing the suitability of P
to care for C**

Regulation 17

1 In respect of P –

(a)   P's capacity to care for children and in particular in relation to C to –

(i)   provide for C's physical needs and appropriate medical and dental care,

(ii)   protect C adequately from harm or danger, including from any person who presents a risk of harm to C,

(iii) ensure that the home environment is safe for C,

(iv)   ensure that C's emotional needs are met and C is provided with a positive sense of self, including any particular needs arising from C's religious persuasion, racial origin and cultural and linguistic background, and any disability C may have,

(v)   promote C's learning and intellectual development through encouragement, cognitive stimulation and the promotion of educational success and social opportunities,

(vi)   enable C to regulate C's emotions and behaviour, including by modelling appropriate behaviour and interactions with others, and

(vii) provide a stable family environment to enable C to develop and maintain secure attachments to P and other persons who provide care for C,

(b) P's state of health including P's physical, emotional and mental health and medical history including any current or past issues of domestic violence, substance misuse or mental health problems,

(c) P's family relationships and the composition of P's household, including particulars of –

(i) the identity of all other members of the household, including their age and the nature of their relationship with P and with each other, including any sexual relationship,

(ii) any relationship with any person who is a parent of C,

(iii) other adults not being members of the household who are likely to have regular contact with C, and

(iv) any current or previous domestic violence between members of the household, including P,

(d) P's family history, including –

(i) particulars of P's childhood and upbringing including the strengths and difficulties of P's parents or other persons who cared for P,

(ii) P's relationships with P's parents and siblings, and their relationships with each other,

(iii) P's educational achievement and any specific learning difficulty or disability,

(iv) a chronology of significant life events, and

(v) particulars of other relatives and their relationships with C and P,

(e) particulars of any criminal offences of which P has been convicted or in respect of which P has been cautioned,

(f) P's past and present employment and other sources of income, and

(g) the nature of the neighbourhood in which P's home is situated and resources available in the community to support C and P.

2 In respect of members of P's household aged 18 and over, so far as is practicable, all the particulars specified in paragraph 1 except sub-paragraphs (d), (f) and (g).

Schedule 4
Matters to be taken into account when assessing the suitability of a connected person to care for C

Regulation 24

1 In respect of the connected person –

(a) the nature and quality of any existing relationship with C,

(b) their capacity to care for children and in particular in relation to C to –

(i) provide for C's physical needs and appropriate medical and dental care,

      (ii)   protect C adequately from harm or danger including from any person who presents a risk of harm to C,

      (iii) ensure that the accommodation and home environment is suitable with regard to the age and developmental stage of C,

      (iv) promote C's learning and development, and

      (v)   provide a stable family environment which will promote secure attachments for C, including promoting positive contact with P and other connected persons, unless to do this is not consistent with the duty to safeguard and promote C's welfare,

  (c)   their state of health including their physical, emotional and mental health and medical history including any current or past issues of domestic violence, substance misuse or mental health problems,

  (d)   their family relationships and the composition of their household, including particulars of –

      (i)   the identity of all other members of the household, including their age and the nature of their relationship with the connected person and with each other, including any sexual relationship,

      (ii) any relationship with any person who is a parent of C,

      (iii) any relationship between C and other members of the household,

      (iv) other adults not being members of the household who are likely to have regular contact with C, and

      (v)   any current or previous domestic violence between members of the household, including the connected person,

  (e)   their family history, including –

      (i)   particulars of their childhood and upbringing including the strengths and difficulties of their parents or other persons who cared for them,

      (ii) their relationships with their parents and siblings, and their relationships with each other,

      (iii) their educational achievement and any specific learning difficulty or disability,

      (iv) a chronology of significant life events, and

      (v)   particulars of other relatives and their relationships with C and the connected person,

  (f)   particulars of any criminal offences of which they have been convicted or in respect of which they have been cautioned,

  (g)   their past and present employment and other sources of income, and

  (h)   the nature of the neighbourhood in which their home is situated and resources available in the community to support C and the connected person.

Schedule 5
Agreement with an independent fostering agency relating to the discharge of the responsible authority's functions

Regulation 26

1 The agreement must contain the following information –

(1) the services to be provided to the responsible authority by the registered person,

(2) the arrangements for the selection by the responsible authority of F from those approved by the registered person,

(3) a requirement for the registered person to submit reports to the responsible authority on any placements as may be required by the responsible authority, and

(4) the arrangements for the termination of the agreement.

2 Where the agreement relates to a particular child, it must also contain the following information –

(1) F's details,

(2) details of any services that C is to receive and whether the services are to be provided by the responsible authority or by the registered person,

(3) the terms (including as to payment) of the proposed placement agreement,

(4) the arrangements for record keeping about C and for the return of records at the end of the placement,

(5) a requirement for the registered person to notify the responsible authority immediately in the event of any concerns about the placement, and

(6) whether, and on what basis, other children may be placed with F.

Schedule 6
Matters to be considered before placing C in accommodation in an unregulated setting under section 22(6)(d)

Regulation 27

1 In respect of the accommodation, the –

    (a)   facilities and services provided,
    (b)   state of repair,
    (c)   safety,
    (d)   location,
    (e)   support,
    (f)   tenancy status, and
    (g)   the financial commitments involved for C and their affordability.

2 In respect of C, C's –

    (a)   views about the accommodation,
    (b)   understanding of their rights and responsibilities in relation to the accommodation, and
    (c)   understanding of funding arrangements.

Schedule 7
Considerations to which the responsible authority must have regard when reviewing C's case

Regulation 35

1 The effect of any change in C's circumstances since the last review, in particular of any change made by the responsible authority to C's care plan, whether decisions taken at the last review have been successfully implemented, and if not, the reasons for that.

2 Whether the responsible authority should seek any change in C's legal status.

3 Whether there is a plan for permanence for C.

4 The arrangements for contact and whether there is any need for changes to the arrangements in order to promote contact between C and P, or between C and other connected persons.

5 Whether C's placement continues to be the most appropriate available, and whether any change to the placement plan or any other aspects of the arrangements made to provide C with accommodation is, or is likely to become, necessary or desirable before the next review of C's case.

6 C's educational needs, progress and development and whether any change to the arrangements for C's education or training is, or is likely to become, necessary or desirable to meet C's particular needs and to promote C's educational achievement before the next review of C's case, having regard to the advice of any person who provides C with education or training, in particular the designated teacher of any school at which C is a registered pupil.

7 C's leisure interests.

8 The report of the most recent assessment of C's state of health obtained in accordance with regulation 8 and whether any change to the arrangements for C's health care is, or is likely to become, necessary or desirable before the next review of C's case, having regard to the advice of any health care professional received since the date of that report, in particular C's registered medical practitioner.

9 Whether C's needs related to C's identity are being met and whether any particular change is required, having regard to C's religious persuasion, racial origin and cultural background.

10 Whether the arrangements made in accordance with regulation 31 continue to be appropriate and understood by C.

11 Whether any arrangements need to be made for the time when C will no longer be looked after by the responsible authority.

12 C's wishes and feelings, and the views of the IRO, about any aspect of the case and in particular about any changes the responsible authority has made since the last review or proposes to make to the C's care plan.

13 Where regulation 28(3) applies, the frequency of R's visits.

Amendments: SI 2011/581.

Schedule 8
Matters to be dealt with in the pathway plan

Regulation 43

1 The name of C's personal adviser.

2 The nature and level of contact and personal support to be provided to C, and by whom.

3 Details of the accommodation C is to occupy when C ceases to be looked after.

4 The plan for C's continuing education or training when C ceases to be looked after.

5 How the responsible authority will assist C in obtaining employment or other purposeful activity or occupation.

6 The support to be provided to enable C to develop and sustain appropriate family and social relationships.

7 A programme to develop the practical and other skills C needs to live independently.

8 The financial support to be provided to enable C to meet accommodation and maintenance costs.

9 C's health care needs, including any physical, emotional or mental health needs and how they are to be met when C ceases to be looked after.

10 The responsible authority's contingency plans for action to be taken in the event that the pathway plan ceases to be effective for any reason.

Schedule 9
Revocations

Regulation 51

The Regulations set out in the table are revoked –

Regulations Revoked	Series number
Contact with Children Regulations 1991	SI 1991/891
Definition of Independent Visitors (Children) Regulations 1991	SI 1991/892
Placement of Children with Parents etc Regulations 1991	SI 1991/898

Appendix 5

ADOPTION (INTERCOUNTRY ASPECTS) ACT 1999

Implementation of Convention

1 Regulations giving effect to Convention

(1) Subject to the provisions of this Act, regulations made by the Secretary of State may make provision for giving effect to the Convention on Protection of Children and Co-operation in respect of Intercountry Adoption, concluded at the Hague on 29th May 1993 ('the Convention').

(2) The text of the Convention (so far as material) is set out in Schedule 1 to this Act.

(3) Regulations under this section may –

    (a)   apply, with or without modifications, any provision of the enactments relating to adoption;

    (b)   provide that any person who contravenes or fails to comply with any provision of the regulations is to be guilty of an offence and liable on summary conviction to imprisonment for a term not exceeding three months, or a fine not exceeding level 5 on the standard scale, or both;

    (c)   make different provision for different purposes or areas; and

    (d)   make such incidental, supplementary, consequential or transitional provision as appears to the Secretary of State to be expedient.

(4) Regulations under this section shall be made by statutory instrument which shall be subject to annulment in pursuance of a resolution of either House of Parliament.

(5) Subject to subsection (6), any power to make subordinate legislation under or for the purposes of the enactments relating to adoption includes power to do so with a view to giving effect to the provisions of the Convention.

(6) Subsection (5) does not apply in relation to any power which is exercisable by the National Assembly for Wales.

(7) References in this section to enactments include references to Acts of the Scottish Parliament.

Amendments: Adoption and Children (Scotland) Act 2007, s 120(1), Sch 2, para 10; SI 2011/1740.

2 Central Authorities and accredited bodies

(1) The functions under the Convention of the Central Authority are to be discharged –

(a)   separately in relation to England and Scotland by the Secretary of State; and

(b)   in relation to Wales by the National Assembly for Wales.

(2)   A communication may be sent to the Central Authority in relation to any part of Great Britain by sending it (for forwarding if necessary) to the Central Authority in relation to England.

(2A)   A registered adoption society is an accredited body for the purposes of the Convention if, in accordance with the conditions of the registration, the society may provide facilities in respect of Convention adoptions and adoptions effected by Convention adoption orders.

(3)   An approved adoption society is an accredited body for the purposes of the Convention if the approval extends to the provision of facilities in respect of Convention adoptions and adoptions effected by Convention adoption orders.

(4)   The functions under Article 9(a) to (c) of the Convention are to be discharged by local authorities and accredited bodies on behalf of the Central Authority.

(5)   In this section, 'registered adoption society' has the same meaning as in section 2 of the Adoption and Children Act 2002 (basic definitions); and expressions used in this section in its application to England and Wales which are also used in that Act have the same meanings as in that Act.

(6)   In this section, 'approved adoption society' has the same meaning as in section 65(1) (interpretation) of the Adoption (Scotland) Act 1978 ('the 1978 Act'); and expressions used in this section in its application to Scotland which are also used in that Act have the same meanings as in that Act.

Amendments: Care Standards Act 2000, s 116, Sch 4, para 27(a); Adoption and Children Act 2002, s 139(1), Sch 3, paras 96, 97, 98, 99.

****

18   Short title, interpretation, commencement and extent

(1)   This Act may be cited as the Adoption (Intercountry Aspects) Act 1999.

(2)   (*repealed*)

'the 1976 Act' means the Adoption Act 1976;

'the 1978 Act' means the Adoption (Scotland) Act 1978;

'the Convention' means the Convention on Protection of Children and Co-operation in respect of Intercountry Adoption, concluded at the Hague on 29th May 1993.

(3)   This Act, except this section, shall come into force on such day as the Secretary of State may by order made by statutory instrument appoint and different days may be appointed for different purposes.

(4)   Subject to subsection (5), this Act extends to Great Britain only.

(5)   Any amendment of an enactment which extends to any other part of the British Islands or any colony also extends to that part or colony.

Amendments: Adoption and Children (Scotland) Act 2007, s 120(2), Sch 3; SI 2011/1740.

Schedule 1
Convention on Protection of Children and Co-operation in respect of Intercountry Adoption

Section 1

The States signatory to the present Convention.

Recognizing that the child, for the full and harmonious development of his or her personality, should grow up in a family environment, in an atmosphere of happiness, love and understanding,

Recalling that each State should take, as a matter of priority, appropriate measures to enable the child to remain in the care of his or her family of origin,

Recognizing that intercountry adoption may offer the advantage of a permanent family to a child for whom a suitable family cannot be found in his or her State of origin,

Convinced of the necessity to take measures to ensure that intercountry adoptions are made in the best interests of the child and with respect for his or her fundamental rights, and to prevent the abduction, the sale of, or traffic in children,

Desiring to establish common provisions to this effect, taking into account the principles set forth in international instruments, in particular the United Nations Convention on the Rights of the Child, of 20 November 1989, and the United Nations Declaration on Social and Legal Principles relating to the Protection and Welfare of Children, with Special Reference to Foster Placement and Adoption Nationally and Internationally (General Assembly Resolution 41/85, of 3 December 1986),

Have agreed upon the following provisions –

CHAPTER I
SCOPE OF THE CONVENTION

Article 1

The objects of the present Convention are–

(a)   to establish safeguards to ensure that intercountry adoptions take place in the best interests of the child and with respect for his or her fundamental rights as recognised in international law;

(b)   to establish a system of co-operation amongst Contracting States to ensure that those safeguards are respected and thereby prevent the abduction, the sale of, or traffic in children;

(c)   to secure the recognition in Contracting States of adoptions made in accordance with the Convention.

Article 2

1 The Convention shall apply where a child habitually resident in one Contracting State ('the State of origin') has been, is being, or is to be moved to another Contracting State ('the receiving State') either after his or her adoption in the State of origin by spouses or a person habitually resident in the receiving State, or for the purposes of such an adoption in the receiving State or in the State of origin.

2 The Convention covers only adoptions which create a permanent parent-child relationship.

Article 3

The Convention ceases to apply if the agreements mentioned in Article 17, sub-paragraph (c), have not been given before the child attains the age of eighteen years.

CHAPTER II
REQUIREMENTS FOR INTERCOUNTRY ADOPTIONS

Article 4

An adoption within the scope of the Convention shall take place only if the competent authorities of the State of origin –

   (a)   have established that the child is adoptable;

   (b)   have determined, after possibilities for placement of the child within the State of origin have been given due consideration, that an intercountry adoption is in the child's best interests;

   (c)   have ensured that –

      (i)   the persons, institutions and authorities whose consent is necessary for adoption, have been counselled as may be necessary and duly informed of the effects of their consent, in particular whether or not an adoption will result in the termination of the legal relationship between the child and his or her family of origin,

      (ii)   such persons, institutions and authorities have given their consent freely, in the required legal form, and expressed or evidenced in writing,

      (iii)   the consents have not been induced by payment or compensation of any kind and have not been withdrawn, and

      (iv)   the consent of the mother, where required, has been given only after the birth of the child; and

   (d)   have ensured, having regard to the age and degree of maturity of the child, that –

      (i)   he or she has been counselled and duly informed of the effects of the adoption and of his or her consent to the adoption, where such consent is required,

      (ii)   consideration has been given to the child's wishes and opinions,

    (iii)   the child's consent to the adoption, where such consent is required, has been given freely, in the required legal form, and expressed or evidenced in writing, and

such consent has not been induced by payment or compensation of any kind.

Article 5

An adoption within the scope of the Convention shall take place only if the competent authorities of the receiving State –

    (a)   have determined that the prospective adoptive parents are eligible and suited to adopt;

    (b)   have ensured that the prospective adoptive parents have been counselled as may be necessary; and

    (c)   have determined that the child is or will be authorised to enter and reside permanently in that State.

CHAPTER III
CENTRAL AUTHORITIES AND ACCREDITED BODIES

Article 6

1 A Contracting State shall designate a Central Authority to discharge the duties which are imposed by the Convention upon such authorities.

2 Federal States, States with more than one system of law or States having autonomous territorial units shall be free to appoint more than one Central Authority and to specify the territorial or personal extent of their functions. Where a State has appointed more than one Central Authority, it shall designate the Central Authority to which any communication may be addressed for transmission to the appropriate Central Authority within that State.

Article 7

1 Central Authorities shall co-operate with each other and promote co-operation amongst the competent authorities in their States to protect children and to achieve the other objects of the Convention.

2 They shall take directly all appropriate measures to –

    (a)   provide information as to the laws of their States concerning adoption and other general information, such as statistics and standard forms;

    (b)   keep one another informed about the operation of the Convention and, as far as possible, eliminate any obstacles to its application.

Article 8

Central Authorities shall take, directly or through public authorities, all appropriate measures to prevent improper financial or other gain in connection with an adoption and to deter all practices contrary to the objects of the Convention.

Article 9

Central Authorities shall take, directly or through public authorities or other bodies duly accredited in their State, all appropriate measures, in particular to –

(a)   collect, preserve and exchange information about the situation of the child and the prospective adoptive parents, so far as is necessary to complete the adoption;

(b)   facilitate, follow and expedite proceedings with a view to obtaining the adoption;

(c)   promote the development of adoption counselling and post-adoption services in their States;

(d)   provide each other with general evaluation reports about experience with intercountry adoption;

(e)   reply, in so far as is permitted by the law of their State, to justified requests from other Central Authorities or public authorities for information about a particular adoption situation.

Article 10

Accreditation shall only be granted to and maintained by bodies demonstrating their competence to carry out properly the tasks with which they may be entrusted.

Article 11

An accredited body shall –

(a)   pursue only non-profit objectives according to such conditions and within such limits as may be established by the competent authorities of the State of accreditation;

(b)   be directed and staffed by persons qualified by their ethical standards and by training or experience to work in the field of intercountry adoption; and

(c)   be subject to supervision by competent authorities of that State as to its composition, operation and financial situation.

Article 12

A body accredited in one Contracting State may act in another Contracting State only if the competent authorities of both States have authorised it to do so.

Article 13

The designation of the Central Authorities and, where appropriate, the extent of their functions, as well as the names and addresses of the accredited bodies shall be communicated by each Contracting State to the Permanent Bureau of the Hague Conference on Private International Law.

CHAPTER IV
PROCEDURAL REQUIREMENTS IN INTERCOUNTRY ADOPTION

Article 14

Persons habitually resident in a Contracting State, who wish to adopt a child habitually resident in another Contracting State, shall apply to the Central Authority in the State of their habitual residence.

Article 15

1 If the Central Authority of the receiving State is satisfied that the applicants are eligible and suited to adopt, it shall prepare a report including information about their identity, eligibility and suitability to adopt, background, family and medical history, social environment, reasons for adoption, ability to undertake an intercountry adoption, as well as the characteristics of the children for whom they would be qualified to care.

2 It shall transmit the report to the Central Authority of the State of origin.

Article 16

1 If the Central Authority of the State of origin is satisfied that the child is adoptable, it shall –

   (a) prepare a report including information about his or her identity, adoptability, background, social environment, family history, medical history including that of the child's family, and any special needs of the child;
   (b) give due consideration to the child's upbringing and to his or her ethnic, religious and cultural background;
   (c) ensure that consents have been obtained in accordance with Article 4; and
   (d) determine, on the basis in particular of the reports relating to the child and the prospective adoptive parents, whether the envisaged placement is in the best interests of the child.

2 It shall transmit to the Central Authority of the receiving State its report on the child, proof that the necessary consents have been obtained and the reasons for its determination on the placement, taking care not to reveal the identity of the mother and the father if, in the State of origin, these identities may not be disclosed.

Article 17

Any decision in the State of origin that a child should be entrusted to prospective adoptive parents may only be made if–

   (a) the Central Authority of that State has ensured that the prospective adoptive parents agree;

   (b)   the Central Authority of the receiving State has approved such decision, where such approval is required by the law of that State or by the Central Authority of the State of origin;

   (c)   the Central Authorities of both States have agreed that the adoption may proceed; and

   (d)   it has been determined, in accordance with Article 5, that the prospective adoptive parents are eligible and suited to adopt and that the child is or will be authorised to enter and reside permanently in the receiving State.

Article 18

The Central Authorities of both States shall take all necessary steps to obtain permission for the child to leave the State of origin and to enter and reside permanently in the receiving State.

Article 19

1 The transfer of the child to the receiving State may only be carried out if the requirements of Article 17 have been satisfied.

2 The Central Authorities of both States shall ensure that this transfer takes place in secure and appropriate circumstances and, if possible, in the company of the adoptive or prospective adoptive parents.

3 If the transfer of the child does not take place, the reports referred to in Articles 15 and 16 are to be sent back to the authorities who forwarded them.

Article 20

The Central Authorities shall keep each other informed about the adoption process and the measures taken to complete it, as well as about the progress of the placement if a probationary period is required.

Article 21

1 Where the adoption is to take place after the transfer of the child to the receiving State and it appears to the Central Authority of that State that the continued placement of the child with the prospective adoptive parents is not in the child's best interests, such Central Authority shall take the measures necessary to protect the child, in particular –

   (a)   to cause the child to be withdrawn from the prospective adoptive parents and to arrange temporary care;

   (b)   in consultation with the Central Authority of the State of origin, to arrange without delay a new placement of the child with a view to adoption or, if this is not appropriate, to arrange alternative long-term care; an adoption shall not take place until the Central Authority of the State of origin has been duly informed concerning the new prospective adoptive parents;

(c) as a last resort, to arrange the return of the child, if his or her interests so require.

2 Having regard in particular to the age and degree of maturity of the child, he or she shall be consulted and, where appropriate, his or her consent obtained in relation to measures to be taken under this Article.

Article 22

1 The functions of a Central Authority under this Chapter may be performed by public authorities or by bodies accredited under Chapter III, to the extent permitted by the law of its State.

2 Any Contracting State may declare to the depositary of the Convention that the functions of the Central Authority under Articles 15 to 21 may be performed in that State, to the extent permitted by the law and subject to the supervision of the competent authorities of that State, also by bodies or persons who –

(a) meet the requirements of integrity, professional competence, experience and accountability of that State; and

(b) are qualified by their ethical standards and by training or experience to work in the field of intercountry adoption.

3 A Contracting State which makes the declaration provided for in paragraph 2 shall keep the Permanent Bureau of the Hague Conference on Private International Law informed of the names and addresses of these bodies and persons.

4 Any Contracting State may declare to the depositary of the Convention that adoptions of children habitually resident in its territory may only take place if the functions of the Central Authorities are performed in accordance with paragraph 1.

5 Notwithstanding any declaration made under paragraph 2, the reports provided for in Articles 15 and 16 shall, in every case, be prepared under the responsibility of the Central Authority or other authorities or bodies in accordance with paragraph 1.

CHAPTER V
RECOGNITION AND EFFECTS OF THE ADOPTION

Article 23

1 An adoption certified by the competent authority of the State of the adoption as having been made in accordance with the Convention shall be recognised by operation of law in the other Contracting States. The certificate shall specify when and by whom the agreements under Article 17, sub-paragraph c, were given.

2 Each Contracting State shall, at the time of signature, ratification, acceptance, approval or accession, notify the depositary of the Convention of the identity and the functions of the authority or the authorities which, in that State, are competent to make the certification. It shall also notify the depositary of any modification in the designation of these authorities.

Article 24

The recognition of an adoption may be refused in a contracting State only if the adoption is manifestly contrary to its public policy, taking into account the best interests of the child.

Article 25

Any Contracting State may declare to the depositary of the convention that it will not be bound under this Convention to recognise adoptions made in accordance with an agreement concluded by application of Article 39, paragraph 2.

Article 26

1 The recognition of an adoption includes recognition of

    (a)   the legal parent-child relationship between the child and his or her adoptive parents;

    (b)   parental responsibility of the adoptive parents for the child;

    (c)   the termination of a pre-existing legal relationship between the child and his or her mother and father, if the adoption has this effect in the Contracting State where it was made.

2 In the case of an adoption having the effect of terminating a pre-existing legal parent-child relationship, the child shall enjoy in the receiving State, and in any other Contracting State where the adoption is recognised, rights equivalent to those resulting from adoptions having this effect in each such State.

3 The preceding paragraphs shall not prejudice the application of any provision more favourable for the child, in force in the Contracting State which recognises the adoption.

Article 27

1 Where an adoption granted in the State of origin does not have the effect of terminating a pre-existing legal parent-child relationship, it may, in the receiving State which recognises the adoption under the Convention, be converted into an adoption having such an effect–

    (a)   if the law of the receiving State so permits; and

    (b)   if the consents referred to in Article 4, sub-paragraphs c and d, have been or are given for the purpose of such an adoption.

2 Article 23 applies to the decision converting the adoption.

CHAPTER VI
GENERAL PROVISIONS

Article 28

The Convention does not affect any law of a State of origin which requires that the adoption of a child habitually resident within that State take place in that State or which prohibits the child's placement in, or transfer to, the receiving State prior to adoption.

Article 29

There shall be no contact between the prospective adoptive parents and the child's parents or any other person who has care of the child until the requirements of Article 4, sub-paragraphs a to c, and Article 5, sub-paragraph a, have been met, unless the adoption takes place within a family or unless the contact is in compliance with the conditions established by the competent authority of the State of origin.

Article 30

1 The competent authorities of a Contracting State shall ensure that information held by them concerning the child's origin, in particular information concerning the identity of his or her parents, as well as the medical history, is preserved.

2 They shall ensure that the child or his or her representative has access to such information, under appropriate guidance, in so far as is permitted by the law of that State.

Article 31

Without prejudice to Article 30, personal data gathered or transmitted under the Convention, especially data referred to in Articles 15 and 16, shall be used only for the purposes for which they were gathered or transmitted.

Article 32

1 No one shall derive improper financial or other gain from an activity related to an intercountry adoption.

2 Only costs and expenses, including reasonable professional fees of persons involved in the adoption, may be charged or paid.

3 The directors, administrators and employees of bodies involved in an adoption shall not receive remuneration which is unreasonably high in relation to services rendered.

Article 33

A competent authority which finds that any provision of the Convention has not been respected or that there is a serious risk that it may not be respected, shall immediately inform the Central Authority of its State. This Central Authority shall be responsible for ensuring that appropriate measures are taken.

Article 34

If the competent authority of the State of destination of a document so requests, a translation certified as being in conformity with the original must be furnished. Unless otherwise provided, the costs of such translation are to be borne by the prospective adoptive parents.

Article 35

The competent authorities of the contracting States shall act expeditiously in the process of adoption.

Article 36

In relation to a State which has two or more systems of law with regard to adoption applicable in different territorial units –

   (a)   any reference to habitual residence in that State shall be construed as referring to habitual residence in a territorial unit of that State;
   (b)   any reference to the law of that State shall be construed as referring to the law in force in the relevant territorial unit;
   (c)   any reference to the competent authorities or to the public authorities of that State shall be construed as referring to those authorised to act in the relevant territorial unit;
   (d)   any reference to the accredited bodies of that State shall be construed as referring to bodies accredited in the relevant territorial unit.

Article 37

In relation to a State which with regard to adoption has two or more systems of law applicable to different categories of persons, any reference to the law of that State shall be construed as referring to the legal system specified by the law of that State.

Article 38

A State within which different territorial units have their own rules of law in respect of adoption shall not be bound to apply the Convention where a State with a unified system of law would not be bound to do so.

Article 39

1 The convention does not affect any international instrument to which Contracting States are Parties and which contains provisions on matters governed by the Convention, unless a contrary declaration is made by the States parties to such instrument.

2 Any Contracting State may enter into agreements with one or more other Contracting States, with a view to improving the application of the Convention in their mutual relations. These agreements may derogate only from the provisions of Articles 14 to 16 and 18 to 21. The States which have concluded such an agreement shall transmit a copy to the depositary of the Convention.

Article 40

No reservation to the Convention shall be permitted.

Article 41

The Convention shall apply in every case where an application pursuant to Article 14 has been received after the Convention has entered into force in the receiving State and the State of origin.

Article 42

The Secretary General of the Hague Conference on Private International Law shall at regular intervals convene a Special Commission in order to review the practical operation of the Convention.

****

Appendix 6

CHILDREN AND ADOPTION ACT 2006

****

PART II
ADOPTIONS WITH A FOREIGN ELEMENT

9 Declaration of special restrictions on adoptions from abroad

(1) This section applies if the Secretary of State has reason to believe that, because of practices taking place in a country or territory outside the British Islands (the 'other country') in connection with the adoption of children, it would be contrary to public policy to further the bringing of children into the United Kingdom in the cases mentioned in subsection (2).

(2) The cases are that a British resident –

(a) wishes to bring, or cause another to bring, a child who is not a British resident into the United Kingdom for the purpose of adoption by the British resident, and, in connection with the proposed adoption, there have been, or would have to be, proceedings in the other country or dealings with authorities or agencies there, or

(b) wishes to bring, or cause another to bring, into the United Kingdom a child adopted by the British resident under an adoption effected, within the period of twelve months ending with the date of the bringing in, under the law of the other country.

(3) It is immaterial whether the other country is a Convention country or not.

(4) The Secretary of State may by order declare, in relation to any such country or territory, that special restrictions are to apply for the time being in relation to the bringing in of children in the cases mentioned in subsection (2).

(5) Before making an order containing such a declaration the Secretary of State must consult –

(a) the National Assembly for Wales, and

(b) the Department of Health, Social Services and Public Safety in Northern Ireland.

(6) A country or territory in relation to which such a declaration has effect for the time being is referred to below in this section as a 'restricted country'.

(7) The Secretary of State must publish reasons for making the declaration in relation to each restricted country.

(8) The Secretary of State must publish a list of restricted countries ('the restricted list') and keep the list up to date.

(9) The restricted list and the reasons are to be published in whatever way the Secretary of State thinks appropriate for bringing them to the attention of adoption agencies and members of the public.

(10) In this section –

- (a) 'British resident' means a person habitually resident in the British Islands, and the reference to adoption by a British resident includes adoption by a British resident and another person,
- (b) 'the Convention' means the Convention on Protection of Children and Co-operation in respect of Intercountry Adoption, concluded at The Hague on 29th May 1993,
- (c) 'Convention country' means a country or territory in which the Convention is in force.

10 Review

(1) The Secretary of State must keep under review, in relation to each restricted country, whether it should continue to be a restricted country.

(2) If the Secretary of State determines, in relation to a restricted country, that there is no longer reason to believe what is mentioned in subsection (1) of section 9, he must by order revoke the order containing the declaration made in relation to it under subsection (4) of that section.

(3) Before making a determination under subsection (2), the Secretary of State must consult –

- (a) the National Assembly for Wales, and
- (b) the Department of Health, Social Services and Public Safety in Northern Ireland.

(4) In this section, 'restricted country' has the same meaning as in section 9.

11 The special restrictions

(1) The special restrictions mentioned in section 9(4) are that, except as mentioned in subsection (2) of this section, the appropriate authority is not to take any step which he or it might otherwise have taken in connection with furthering the bringing of a child into the United Kingdom in the cases mentioned in section 9(2) (whether or not that step is provided for by or by virtue of any enactment).

(2) But nothing in subsection (1) prevents the appropriate authority from taking those steps if, in any particular case, the prospective adopters satisfy –

- (a) the appropriate authority, or
- (b) in relation to Northern Ireland, in a case which is not a Convention case, the Secretary of State,

that the appropriate authority should take those steps despite the special restrictions.

(3) The Secretary of State may make regulations providing for –

(a) the procedure to be followed by the appropriate authority (or, if subsection (2)(b) applies, the Secretary of State) in determining whether or not he or it is satisfied as mentioned in subsection (2),

(b) matters which the appropriate authority (or the Secretary of State) is to take into account when making such a determination (whether or not he or it also takes other matters into account).

(4) In this section –

'the appropriate authority' means, in a Convention case, the Central Authority in relation to England, to Wales or to Northern Ireland (as the case may be), and in any other case –

(a) in relation to England and Wales, the Secretary of State,

(b) in relation to Northern Ireland, the Secretary of State (for the purposes of steps which he takes) or the Department of Health, Social Services and Public Safety in Northern Ireland (for the purposes of steps which it takes),

'Central Authority' is to be construed in accordance with section 2 of the Adoption (Intercountry Aspects) Act 1999 (c 18) ('the 1999 Act') or, in relation to Northern Ireland, section 2 of the Adoption (Intercountry Aspects) Act (Northern Ireland) 2001 (c 11 (NI)) ('the 2001 Act'),

'Convention case' means a case where –

(a) the child is intended to be adopted under an adoption order which, by virtue of regulations under section 1 of the 1999 Act or section 1 of the 2001 Act (as appropriate), is made as a Convention adoption order, or

(b) the child is intended to be adopted under an adoption effected under the law of a Convention country outside the British Islands and certified in pursuance of Article 23(1) of the Convention,

and 'the Convention' and 'Convention country' have the meanings given by section 9(10).

12 Imposition of extra conditions in certain cases

(1) The Secretary of State may make regulations providing –

(a) for him to specify in the restricted list, in relation to any restricted country, a step which is not otherwise provided for by or by virtue of any enactment but which, by virtue of the arrangements between the United Kingdom and that country, the appropriate authority normally takes in connection with the bringing in of a child where that country is concerned, and

(b) that, if such a step has been so specified in relation to a restricted country, one or more conditions specified in the regulations are to be met in respect of a child brought into the United Kingdom in either of the cases mentioned in section 9(2) (reading the reference there to the 'other country' as being to the restricted country in question).

(2) Those conditions are in addition to any provided for by virtue of –

    (a)   section 83 of the Adoption and Children Act 2002 (c 38) (restriction on bringing children in), or

    (b)   Article 58ZA of the Adoption (Northern Ireland) Order 1987 (SI 1987/2203 (NI 22)) (restriction on bringing children in),

or under or by virtue of any other enactment.

(3) A person who brings, or causes another to bring, a child into the United Kingdom is guilty of an offence if any condition required to be met by virtue of subsection (1)(b) is not met.

(4) Subsection (3) does not apply if the step specified in the restricted list in relation to any country had already been taken before the publication of the restricted list.

(5) A person guilty of an offence under subsection (3) is liable –

    (a)   on summary conviction, to imprisonment for a term not exceeding 12 months (in England and Wales) or 6 months (in Northern Ireland), or a fine not exceeding the statutory maximum, or both,

    (b)   on conviction on indictment, to imprisonment for a term not exceeding 12 months, or a fine, or both.

(6) In relation to an offence committed before the commencement of section 154(1) of the Criminal Justice Act 2003 (c 44) (general limit on magistrates' court's power to impose imprisonment), the reference in subsection (5)(a) to 12 months is to be read as a reference to 6 months.

This subsection does not extend to Northern Ireland.

(7) In this section –

    (a)   'the appropriate authority' has the meaning given by section 11(4),

    (b)   'restricted country' and 'restricted list' have the same meanings as in section 9.

13 Power to charge

After section 91 of the Adoption and Children Act 2002 (c 38) insert –

"91A Power to charge

(1) This section applies to adoptions to which –

    (a)   section 83 applies, or

    (b)   regulations made under section 1 of the Adoption (Intercountry Aspects) Act 1999 apply.

(2) The Secretary of State may charge a fee to adopters for services provided or to be provided by him in relation to adoptions to which this section applies.

(3) The Assembly may charge a fee to adopters for services provided or to be provided by it as the Central Authority in relation to adoptions to which this section applies by virtue of subsection (1)(b).

(4) The Secretary of State and the Assembly may determine the level of fee as he or it sees fit, and may in particular –

(a)   charge a flat fee or charge different fees in different cases or descriptions of case, and

(b)   in any case or description of case, waive a fee.

(5) But the Secretary of State and the Assembly must each secure that, taking one financial year with another, the income from fees under this section does not exceed the total cost to him or, as the case may be, to it of providing the services in relation to which the fees are imposed.

(6) In this section –

references to adoptions and adopters include prospective adoptions and prospective adopters,

'Central Authority' is to be construed in accordance with section 2 of the Adoption (Intercountry Aspects) Act 1999,

'financial year' means a period of twelve months ending with 31st March."

****

Appendix 7

FAMILY LAW ACT 1986

****

PART III
DECLARATIONS OF STATUS

55 Declarations as to marital status

(1) Subject to the following provisions of this section, any person may apply to the High Court or a county court for one or more of the following declarations in relation to a marriage specified in the application, that is to say –

(a) a declaration that the marriage was at its inception a valid marriage;

(b) a declaration that the marriage subsisted on a date specified in the application;

(c) a declaration that the marriage did not subsist on a date so specified;

(d) a declaration that the validity of a divorce, annulment or legal separation obtained in any country outside England and Wales in respect of the marriage is entitled to recognition in England and Wales;

(e) a declaration that the validity of a divorce, annulment or legal separation so obtained in respect of the marriage is not entitled to recognition in England and Wales.

(2) A court shall have jurisdiction to entertain an application under subsection (1) above if, and only if, either of the parties to the marriage to which the application relates –

(a) is domiciled in England and Wales on the date of the application, or

(b) has been habitually resident in England and Wales throughout the period of one year ending with that date, or

(c) died before that date and either –

    (i) was at death domiciled in England and Wales, or

    (ii) had been habitually resident in England and Wales throughout the period of one year ending with the date of death.

(3) Where an application under subsection (1) above is made to a court by any person other than a party to the marriage to which the application relates, the court shall refuse to hear the application if it considers that the applicant does not have a sufficient interest in the determination of that application.

Amendments: Child Support, Pensions and Social Security Act 2000, s 83(5), Sch 8, paras 3, 4(a).

55A Declarations of parentage

(1) Subject to the following provisions of this section, any person may apply to the High Court, a county court or a magistrates' court for a declaration as to whether or not a person named in the application is or was the parent of another person so named.

(2) A court shall have jurisdiction to entertain an application under subsection (1) above if, and only if, either of the persons named in it for the purposes of that subsection –

(a)   is domiciled in England and Wales on the date of the application, or
(b)   has been habitually resident in England and Wales throughout the period of one year ending with that date, or
(c)   died before that date and either –
    (i)   was at death domiciled in England and Wales, or
    (ii) had been habitually resident in England and Wales throughout the period of one year ending with the date of death.

(3) Except in a case falling within subsection (4) below, the court shall refuse to hear an application under subsection (1) above unless it considers that the applicant has a sufficient personal interest in the determination of the application (but this is subject to section 27 of the Child Support Act 1991).

(4) The excepted cases are where the declaration sought is as to whether or not –

(a)   the applicant is the parent of a named person;
(b)   a named person is the parent of the applicant; or
(c)   a named person is the other parent of a named child of the applicant.

(5) Where an application under subsection (1) above is made and one of the persons named in it for the purposes of that subsection is a child, the court may refuse to hear the application if it considers that the determination of the application would not be in the best interests of the child.

(6) Where a court refuses to hear an application under subsection (1) above it may order that the applicant may not apply again for the same declaration without leave of the court.

(7) Where a declaration is made by a court on an application under subsection (1) above, the prescribed officer of the court shall notify the Registrar General, in such a manner and within such period as may be prescribed, of the making of that declaration.

Amendments: Child Support, Pensions and Social Security Act 2000, s 83(1), (2).

56 Declarations of parentage, legitimacy or legitimation

(1) Any person may apply to the High Court or a county court for a declaration –

(a)   (*repealed*)
(b)   that he is the legitimate child of his parents.

(2) Any person may apply to the High Court or a county court for one (or for one or, in the alternative, the other) of the following declarations, that is to say –

(a) a declaration that he has become a legitimated person;
(b) a declaration that he has not become a legitimated person.

(3) A court shall have jurisdiction to entertain an application under this section if, the applicant –

(a) is domiciled in England and Wales on the date of the application; or
(b) has been habitually resident in England and Wales throughout the period of one year ending with that date.

(4) Where a declaration is made by a court on an application under subsection (1) above, the prescribed officer of the court shall notify the Registrar General, in such a manner and within such period as may be prescribed, of the making of that declaration.

(5) In this section "legitimated person" means a person legitimated or recognised as legitimated –

(a) under section 2, 2A or 3 of the Legitimacy Act 1976;
(b) under section 1 or 8 of the Legitimacy Act 1926; or
(c) by a legitimation (whether or not by virtue of the subsequent marriage of his parents) recognised by the law of England and Wales and effected under the law of another country.

Amendments: Family Law Reform Act 1987, s 22; Child Support, Pensions and Social Security Act 2000, s 83(5), Sch 8, paras 3, 5(a); Human Fertilisation and Embryology Act 2008, s 56, Sch 6, Pt 1, para 23.

57 Declarations as to adoptions effected overseas

(1) Any person whose status as an adopted child of any person depends on whether he has been adopted by that person by either –

(a) a Convention adoption, or an overseas adoption, within the meaning of the Adoption and Children Act 2002, or
(b) an adoption recognised by the law of England and Wales and effected under the law of any country outside the British Islands,

may apply to the High Court or a county court for one (or for one or, in the alternative, the other) of the declarations mentioned in subsection (2) below.

(2) The said declarations are –

(a) a declaration that the applicant is for the purposes of section 39 of the Adoption Act 1976 or section 67 of the Adoption and Children Act 2002 the adopted child of that person;
(b) a declaration that the applicant is not for the purposes of that section the adopted child of that person.

(3) A court shall have jurisdiction to entertain an application under subsection (1) above if, and only if, the applicant –

(a)   is domiciled in England and Wales on the date of the application, or

(b)   has been habitually resident in England and Wales throughout the period of one year ending with that date.

(4) (*spent*)

Amendments: Adoption and Children Act 2002, s 139(1), Sch 3, paras 46, 49(a); Child Support, Pensions and Social Security Act 2000, s 83(5), Sch 8, paras 3, 6; Adoption and Children Act 2002, s 139(1), Sch 3, paras 46, 49(b).

58 General provisions as to the making and effect of declarations

(1) Where on an application to a court for a declaration under this Part the truth of the proposition to be declared is proved to the satisfaction of the court, the court shall make that declaration unless to do so would manifestly be contrary to public policy.

(2) Any declaration made under this Part shall be binding on Her Majesty and all other persons.

(3) A court, on the dismissal of an application for a declaration under this Part, shall not have power to make any declaration for which an application has not been made.

(4) No declaration which may be applied for under this Part may be made otherwise than under this Part by any court.

(5) No declaration may be made by any court, whether under this Part or otherwise –

(a)   that a marriage was at its inception void;

(b)   (*repealed*)

(6) Nothing in this section shall affect the powers of any court to grant a decree of nullity of marriage.

Amendments: Child Support, Pensions and Social Security Act 2000, s 83(5), Sch 8, paras 3, 7(a).

59 Provisions relating to the Attorney-General

(1) On an application to a court for a declaration under this Part the court may at any stage of the proceedings, of its own motion or on the application of any party to the proceedings, direct that all necessary papers in the matter be sent to the Attorney-General.

(2) The Attorney-General, whether or not he is sent papers in relation to an application to a court for a declaration under this Part, may –

(a)   intervene in the proceedings on that application in such manner as he thinks necessary or expedient, and

(b)   argue before the court any question in relation to the application which the court considers it necessary to have fully argued.

(3) Where any costs are incurred by the Attorney-General in connection with any application to a court for a declaration under this Part, the court may make such order as it considers just as to the payment of those costs by parties to the proceedings.

Amendments: Child Support, Pensions and Social Security Act 2000, s 83(5), Sch 8, paras 3, 8(a).

60 Supplementary provisions as to declarations

(1) Any declaration made under this Part, and any application for such a declaration, shall be in the form prescribed by rules of court.

(2) Rules of court may make provision –

(a) as to the information required to be given by any applicant for a declaration under this Part;

(b) as to the persons who are to be parties to proceedings on an application under this Part;

(c) requiring notice of an application under this Part to be served on the Attorney-General and on persons who may be affected by any declaration applied for.

(3) No proceedings under this Part shall affect any final judgment or decree already pronounced or made by any court of competent jurisdiction.

(4) The court hearing an application under this Part may direct that the whole or any part of the proceedings shall be heard in camera, and an application for a direction under this subsection shall be heard in camera unless the court otherwise directs.

(5) An appeal shall lie to a county court against –

(a) the making by a magistrates' court of a declaration under section 55A above,

(b) any refusal by a magistrates' court to make such a declaration, or

(c) any order under subsection (6) of that section made on such a refusal.

Amendments: Family Law Reform Act 1987, s 33(1), Sch 2, para 96; Child Support, Pensions and Social Security Act 2000, s 83(1), (4); SI 2009/871.

61 Abolition of right to petition for jactitation of marriage

No person shall after the commencement of this Part be entitled to petition the High Court or a county court for jactitation of marriage.

62 Repeal of Greek Marriages Act 1884

(1) *(repealed)*

(2) Any marriage in respect of which a declaration that it was a valid marriage could before the commencement of this Part have been made under the Greek Marriages Act 1884 is hereby declared to have been a valid marriage; but nothing in this subsection shall affect any status or right which would not have been affected by a declaration under that Act.

Amendments: Sub-s (1): repeals the Greek Marriages Act 1884.

63 (*repealed*)

Amendments: Repealed by the Child Support, Pensions and Social Security Act 2000, s 85, Sch 9, Pt IX.

Appendix 8

ADOPTION (DESIGNATION OF OVERSEAS ADOPTIONS) ORDER 1973

SI 1973/19

1 This Order may be cited as the Adoption (Designation of Overseas Adoptions) Order 1973 and shall come into operation on 1 February 1973.

2 The Interpretation Act 1889 shall apply to the interpretation of this Order as it applies to the interpretation of an Act of Parliament.

3 (1) An adoption of an infant is hereby specified as an overseas adoption if it is an adoption effected in a place in relation to which this Article applies and under the law in force in that place.

(2) Subject to paragraph (2A) of this Article, as respects any adoption effected before the date on which this Order comes into operation, this Article applies in relation to any place which, at that date, forms part of a country or territory described in Part I or II of the Schedule to this Order and as respects any adoption effected on or after that date, this Article applies in relation to any place which, at the time the adoption is effected, forms part of a country or territory which at that time is a country or territory described in Part I or II of the Schedule to this Order.

(2A) This Article also applies, as respects any adoption effected on or after 5th April 1993, in relation to any place which, at the time the adoption is effected, forms part of the People's Republic of China.

(3) In this Article the expression –

'infant' means a person who at the time when the application for adoption was made had not attained the age of 18 years and had not been married;
'law' does not include customary or common law.

Amendments: SI 1993/690.

4 (1) Evidence that an overseas adoption has been effected may be given by the production of a document purporting to be –

(a) a certified copy of an entry made, in accordance with the law of the country or territory concerned, in a public register relating to the recording of adoptions and showing that the adoption has been effected; or

(b)   a certificate that the adoption has been effected, signed or purporting to be signed by a person authorised by the law of the country or territory concerned to sign such a certificate, or a certified copy of such certificate.

(2) Where a document produced by virtue of paragraph (1) of this Article is not in English, the Registrar General or the Registrar General of Births, Deaths and Marriages for Scotland, as the case may be, may require the production of an English translation of the document before satisfying himself of the matters specified in section 8 of the Adoption Act 1968.

(3) Nothing in this Article shall be construed as precluding proof, in accordance with the Evidence (Foreign, Dominion and Colonial Documents) Act 1933, or the Oaths and Evidence (Overseas Authorities and Countries) Act 1963, or otherwise, that an overseas adoption has been effected.

Schedule

PART I
COMMONWEALTH COUNTRIES AND UNITED KINGDOM BRITISH OVERSEAS TERRITORIES

Australia	Malaysia
Bahamas	Malta
Barbados	Mauritius
Bermuda	Montserrat
Botswana	New Zealand
British Honduras	Nigeria
British Virgin Islands	Pitcairn
Canada	St. Christopher, Nevis and Anguilla
Cayman Islands	St. Vincent
The Republic of Cyprus	Seychelles
Dominica	Singapore
Fiji	Southern Rhodesia
Ghana	Sri Lanka
Gibraltar	Swaziland
Guyana	Tanzania
Hong Kong	Tonga
Jamaica	Trinidad and Tobago
Kenya	Uganda
Lesotho	Zambia
Malawi	

Amendment: British Overseas Territories Act 2002, s 2(3).

PART II
OTHER COUNTRIES AND TERRITORIES

Austria

Belgium

Denmark (including Greenland and the Faroes)

Finland

France (including Réunion, Martinique, Guadeloupe and French Guyana)

The Federal Republic of Germany and Land Berlin (West Berlin)

Greece

Iceland

The Republic of Ireland

Israel

Italy

Luxembourg

The Netherlands (including Surinam and the Antilles)

Norway

Portugal (including the Azores and Madeira)

South Africa and South West Africa

Spain (including the Balearics and the Canary Islands)

Sweden

Switzerland

Turkey

The United States of America

Yugoslavia

Appendix 9

ADOPTIONS WITH A FOREIGN ELEMENT (SPECIAL RESTRICTIONS ON ADOPTIONS FROM ABROAD) REGULATIONS 2008

SI 2008/1807

1 Citation and commencement

These Regulations may be cited as the Adoptions with a Foreign Element (Special Restrictions on Adoptions from Abroad) Regulations 2008 and come into force on 1st August 2008.

2 Interpretation

(1) In these Regulations –

'the Act' means the Children and Adoption Act 2006;
'the relevant authority' means the appropriate authority or, in relation to Northern Ireland, in a case which is not a Convention case, the Secretary of State;
'a request' means a request made in writing by prospective adopters that the appropriate authority should take any step as mentioned in section 11(1) of the Act despite an order having been made under section 9(4) of the Act in relation to the State of origin; and
'the State of origin' means the country or territory from which the prospective adopters wish to bring a child into the United Kingdom.

(2) For the purposes of these Regulations, the relevant authority is "satisfied that the case is exceptional" if that authority is satisfied that the appropriate authority should take any step as mentioned in section 11(1) of the Act despite an order having been made under section 9(4) of the Act in relation to the State of origin.

3 Receipt of a request

(1) On receipt of a request, the relevant authority must, subject to regulation 5 –

(a) acknowledge receipt of the request in writing as soon as is practicable,
(b) make such enquiries of the prospective adopters as appear to the relevant authority necessary to clarify –
   (i) the reasons why they consider that the relevant authority should be satisfied that the case is exceptional, or

    (ii)   any other information that the prospective adopters have submitted,

(c)   make such further enquiries as the relevant authority considers appropriate, and

(d)   ask the prospective adopters whether there exists any further information that they have not submitted but that they consider relevant to the request.

(2) The relevant authority may defer making a determination in accordance with regulation 4 until –

(a)   the prospective adopters confirm that there is no further information that they consider relevant to the request, or

(b)   where the prospective adopters indicate that there is further information that they have not submitted but that they consider relevant to the request, that information has been received.

4 Determining whether an exception to the special restrictions should be made

(1) The relevant authority must consider all the information the authority holds that is relevant to the request and take the matters referred to in regulation 6 into account in determining whether the authority is satisfied that the case is exceptional.

(2) The relevant authority must notify the prospective adopters in writing as to whether the authority is satisfied that the case is exceptional, giving reasons, where the authority is not so satisfied, why the authority is not so satisfied.

(3) If, in relation to Northern Ireland, in a case which is not a Convention case, the Secretary of State is satisfied that the case is exceptional, the Secretary of State must also notify the Department of Health, Social Services and Public Safety in Northern Ireland.

5 Further requests

(1) This regulation applies where the relevant authority has made a determination in accordance with regulation 4 and the prospective adopters submit a further request.

(2) The relevant authority need not consider that further request if the authority is of the view that –

(a)   the further request does not contain any new information, or

(b)   the new information is not such that, had that information been available to the relevant authority at the time that the authority made the determination, the information might have led to the relevant authority being satisfied that the case is exceptional.

6 Matters to be taken into account

(1) For the purposes of paragraph (1) of regulation 4, the matters that the relevant authority is to take into account, whether or not the authority also takes other matters into account, are as follow.

(2) Where the prospective adopters wish to adopt a particular child, the matters are –

    (a)   the circumstances leading to the child becoming available for adoption, including whether any competent authority in the State of origin has made a decision in relation to the adoption or availability for adoption of the child,

    (b)   the relationship that the child has with the prospective adopters, including how and when that relationship was formed,

    (c)   the child's particular needs and the capacity of the prospective adopters to meet those needs, and

    (d)   the reasons why the State of origin was placed on the restricted list.

(3) In any other case, the matter is the reasons why the State of origin was placed on the restricted list.

(4) In this regulation, a "competent authority" means a court or a person who performs functions which correspond to the functions of an adoption agency or to the functions of the Secretary of State in respect of intercountry adoption, and "adoption agency" has the meaning given in section 2 of the Adoption and Children Act 2002.

7 Imposition of extra conditions

(1) The Secretary of State may specify in the restricted list, in relation to any restricted country, a step which is not otherwise provided for by or by virtue of any enactment but which, by virtue of the arrangements between the United Kingdom and that country, the appropriate authority normally takes in connection with the bringing in of a child where that country is concerned.

(2) If a step has been specified under paragraph (1) in relation to a restricted country, the condition which is to be met for the purposes of section 12(1)(b) of the Act is that the relevant authority has notified the prospective adopters in writing that the adoption may proceed.

(3) A notification for the purpose of paragraph (2) must state that it is given for the purpose of that paragraph.

Appendix 10

FAMILY PROCEDURE RULES 2010

SI 2010/2955

****

PART 8
PROCEDURE FOR MISCELLANEOUS APPLICATIONS

Chapter 1
Procedure

8.1 Procedure

Subject to rules 8.13 and 8.24, applications to which this Part applies must be made in accordance with the Part 19 procedure.

****

Chapter 5
Declarations

8.18 Scope of this Chapter

The rules in this Chapter apply to applications made in accordance with –

(a) section 55 of the 1986 Act (declarations as to marital status) and section 58 of the 2004 Act (declarations as to civil partnership status);

(b) section 55A of the 1986 Act (declarations of parentage);

(c) section 56(1)(b) and (2) of the 1986 Act (declarations of legitimacy or legitimation); and

(d) section 57 of the 1986 Act (declaration as to adoptions effected overseas).

8.19 Where to start proceedings

The application may be made in the High Court or a county court and applications under section 55A of the 1986 Act may also be made in a magistrates' court.

8.20 Who the parties are

(1) In relation to the proceedings set out in column 1 of the following table, column 2 sets out who the respondents to those proceedings will be.

Proceedings	Respondent
Applications for declarations as to marital or civil partnership status.	The other party to the marriage or civil partnership in question or, where the applicant is a third party, both parties to the marriage or civil partnership.
Applications for declarations of parentage.	(i) The person whose parentage is in issue; and (ii) any person who is or is alleged to be the parent of the person whose parentage is in issue, except where that person is the applicant.
Applications for declarations of legitimacy or legitimation.	The applicant's father and mother or the survivor of them.
Applications for declarations as to adoption effected overseas.	The person(s) whom the applicant is claiming are or are not the applicant's adoptive parents.

(2) The applicant must include in his application particulars of every person whose interest may be affected by the proceedings and his relationship to the applicant.

(3) The acknowledgment of service filed under rule 19.5 must give details of any other persons the respondent considers should be made a party to the application or be given notice of the application.

(4) Upon receipt of the acknowledgment of service, the court must give directions as to any other persons who should be made a respondent to the application or be given notice of the proceedings.

(5) A person given notice of proceedings under paragraph (4) may, within 21 days beginning with the date on which the notice was served, apply to be joined as a party.

(6) No directions may be given as to the future management of the case under rule 19.9 until the expiry of the notice period in paragraph (5).

Amendments: SI 2012/679.

8.21 The role of the Attorney General

(1) The applicant must, except in the case of an application for a declaration of parentage, send a copy of the application and all accompanying documents to the Attorney General at least one month before making the application.

(2) The Attorney General may, when deciding whether to intervene in the proceedings, inspect any document filed at court relating to any family proceedings mentioned in the declaration proceedings.

(3) If the court is notified that the Attorney General wishes to intervene in the proceedings, a court officer must send the Attorney General a copy of any subsequent documents filed at court.

(4) The court must, when giving directions under rule 8.20(4), consider whether to ask the Attorney General to argue any question relating to the proceedings.

(5) If the court makes a request to the Attorney General under paragraph (4) and the Attorney General agrees to that request, the Attorney General must serve a summary of the argument on all parties to the proceedings.

8.22 Declarations of parentage

(1) If the applicant or the person whose parentage or parenthood is in issue, is known by a name other than that which appears in that person's birth certificate, that other name must also be stated in any order and declaration of parentage.

(2) A court officer must send a copy of a declaration of parentage and the application to the Registrar General within 21 days beginning with the date on which the declaration was made.

****

Chapter 9

Application for Consent to Marriage of a Child or to Registration of Civil Partnership of a Child

8.41 Scope of this Chapter

The rules in this Chapter apply to an application under –

  (a)   section 3 of the Marriage Act 1949; or
  (b)   paragraph 3, 4 or 10 of Schedule 2 to the 2004 Act.

8.42 Child acting without a children's guardian

The child may bring an application without a children's guardian, unless the court directs otherwise.

8.43 Who the respondents are

Where an application follows a refusal to give consent to –

  (a)   the marriage of a child; or
  (b)   a child registering as the civil partner of another person,

every person who has refused consent will be a respondent to the application.

****

PART 14
PROCEDURE FOR APPLICATIONS IN ADOPTION, PLACEMENT AND RELATED PROCEEDINGS

14.1 Application of this Part and interpretation

(1) The rules in this Part apply to the following proceedings –

    (a)   adoption proceedings;
    (b)   placement proceedings; and
    (c)   proceedings for –

        (i)   the making of a contact order under section 26 of the 2002 Act;
        (ii) the variation or revocation of a contact order under section 27 of the 2002 Act;
        (iii) an order giving permission to change a child's surname or remove a child from the United Kingdom under section 28(2) and (3) of the 2002 Act;
        (iv) a section 84 order;
        (v) a section 88 direction;
        (vi) a section 89 order; or
        (vii) any other order that may be referred to in a practice direction.

(2) In this Part –

'Central Authority' means –

    (a)   in relation to England, the Secretary of State; and
    (b)   in relation to Wales, the Welsh Ministers;

'Convention adoption order' means an adoption order under the 2002 Act which, by virtue of regulations under section 1 of the Adoption (Intercountry Aspects) Act 1999 (regulations giving effect to the Convention on Protection of Children and Co-operation in Respect of Intercountry Adoption, concluded at the Hague on 29th May 1993), is made as a Convention adoption order;

'guardian' means –

    (a)   a guardian (other than the guardian of the estate of a child) appointed in accordance with section 5 of the 1989 Act; and
    (b)   a special guardian within the meaning of section 14A of the 1989 Act;

'provision for contact' means a contact order under section 8 or 34 of the 1989 Act or a contact order under section 26 of the 2002 Act;

'section 88 direction' means a direction given by the High Court under section 88 of the 2002 Act that section 67(3) of that Act (status conferred by adoption) does not apply or does not apply to any extent specified in the direction.

14.2 Application for a serial number

(1) This rule applies to any application in proceedings by a person who intends to adopt the child.

(2) If, before the proceedings have started, the applicant requests a court officer to assign a serial number to identify the applicant in connection with the proceedings in order for the applicant's identity to be kept confidential in those proceedings, a serial number will be so assigned.

(3) The court may at any time direct that a serial number identifying the applicant in the proceedings referred to in paragraph (2) must be removed.

(4) If a serial number has been assigned to a person under paragraph (2) –

(a) the court officer will ensure that any application form or application notice sent in accordance with these rules does not contain information which discloses, or is likely to disclose, the identity of that person to any other party to that application who is not already aware of that person's identity; and

(b) the proceedings on the application will be conducted with a view to securing that the applicant is not seen by or made known to any party who is not already aware of the applicant's identity except with the applicant's consent.

14.3 Who the parties are

(1) In relation to the proceedings set out in column 1 of the following table, column 2 sets out who the application may be made by and column 3 sets out who the respondents to those proceedings will be.

Proceedings for	*Applicants*	*Respondents*
An adoption order (section 46 of the 2002 Act).	The prospective adopters (sections 50 and 51 of the 2002 Act).	Each parent who has parental responsibility for the child unless that parent has given notice under section 20(4)(a) of the 2002 Act (statement of wish not to be informed of any application for an adoption order) which has effect; any guardian of the child unless that guardian has given notice under section 20(4)(a) of the 2002 Act (statement of wish not to be informed of any application for an adoption order) which has effect;

Proceedings for	Applicants	Respondents
		any person in whose favour there is provision for contact;
		any adoption agency having parental responsibility for the child under section 25 of the 2002 Act;
		any adoption agency which has taken part at any stage in the arrangements for adoption of the child;
		any local authority to whom notice under section 44 of the 2002 Act (notice of intention to adopt or apply for a section 84 order) has been given;
		any local authority or voluntary organisation which has parental responsibility for, is looking after or is caring for, the child; and
		the child where –
		– permission has been granted to a parent or guardian to oppose the making of the adoption order (section 47(3) or 47(5) of the 2002 Act);
		– the child opposes the making of an adoption order;
		– a children and family reporter recommends that it is in the best interests of the child to be a party to the proceedings and that recommendation is accepted by the court;

Proceedings for	Applicants	Respondents
		– the child is already an adopted child;
		– any party to the proceedings or the child is opposed to the arrangements for allowing any person contact with the child, or a person not being allowed contact with the child after the making of the adoption order;
		– the application is for a Convention adoption order or a section 84 order;
		– the child has been brought into the United Kingdom in the circumstances where section 83(1) of the 2002 Act applies (restriction on bringing children in);
		– the application is for an adoption order other than a Convention adoption order and the prospective adopters intend the child to live in a country or territory outside the British Islands after the making of the adoption order; or
		– the prospective adopters are relatives of the child.
A section 84 order.	The prospective adopters asking for parental responsibility prior to adoption abroad.	As for an adoption order.

Proceedings for	Applicants	Respondents
A placement order (section 21 of the 2002 Act).	A local authority (section 22 of the 2002 Act).	Each parent who has parental responsibility for the child: any guardian of the child; any person in whose favour an order under the 1989 Act is in force in relation to the child; any adoption agency or voluntary organisation which has parental responsibility for, is looking after, or is caring for, the child; the child; and the parties or any persons who are or have been parties to proceedings for a care order in respect of the child where those proceedings have led to the application for the placement order.
An order varying a placement order (section 23 of the 2002 Act).	The joint application of the local authority authorised by the placement order to place the child for adoption and the local authority which is to be substituted for that authority (section 23 of the 2002 Act).	The parties to the proceedings leading to the placement order which it is sought to have varied except the child who was the subject of those proceedings; and any person in whose favour there is provision for contact.
An order revoking a placement order (section 24 of the 2002 Act).	The child; the local authority authorised to place the child for adoption; or	The parties to the proceedings leading to the placement order which it is sought to have revoked; and

Proceedings for	Applicants	Respondents
	where the child is not placed for adoption by the authority, any other person who has the permission of the court to apply (section 24 of the 2002 Act).	any person in whose favour there is provision for contact.
A contact order (section 26 of the 2002 Act).	The child; the adoption agency; any parent, guardian or relative; any person in whose favour there was provision for contact under the 1989 Act which ceased to have effect on an adoption agency being authorised to place a child for adoption, or placing a child for adoption who is less than six weeks old (section 26(1) of the 2002 Act); a person in whose favour there was a residence order in force immediately before the adoption agency was authorised to place the child for adoption or placed the child for adoption at a time when the child was less than six weeks old;	The adoption agency authorised to place the child for adoption or which has placed the child for adoption; the person with whom the child lives or is to live; each parent with parental responsibility for the child; any guardian of the child; and the child where – – the adoption agency authorised to place the child for adoption or which has placed the child for adoption or a parent with parental responsibility for the child opposes the making of the contact order under section 26 of the 2002 Act; – the child opposes the making of the contact order under section 26 of the 2002 Act; – existing provision for contact is to be revoked;

Proceedings for	*Applicants*	*Respondents*
	a person who by virtue of an order made in the exercise of the High Court's inherent jurisdiction with respect to children had care of the child immediately before that time; or any person who has the permission of the court to make the application (section 26 of the 2002 Act).	– relatives of the child do not agree to the arrangements for allowing any person contact with the child, or a person not being allowed contact with the child; or – the child is suffering or is at risk of suffering harm within the meaning of the 1989 Act.
An order varying or revoking a contact order (section 27 of the 2002 Act).	The child; the adoption agency; or any person named in the contact order (section 27(1) of the 2002 Act).	The parties to the proceedings leading to the contact order which it is sought to have varied or revoked; and any person named in the contact order.
An order permitting the child's name to be changed or the removal of the child from the United Kingdom (section 28(2) and (3) of the 2002 Act).	Any person including the adoption agency or the local authority authorised to place, or which has placed, the child for adoption (section 28(2) of the 2002 Act).	The parties to proceedings leading to any placement order; the adoption agency authorised to place the child for adoption or which has placed the child for adoption; any prospective adopters with whom the child is living; each parent with parental responsibility for the child; and any guardian of the child.

Proceedings for	Applicants	Respondents
A section 88 direction.	The adopted child; the adopters; any parent; or any other person.	The adopters; the parents; the adoption agency; the local authority to whom notice under section 44 of the 2002 Act (notice of intention to apply for a section 84 order) has been given; and the Attorney-General.
A section 89 order.	The adopters; the adopted person; any parent; the relevant Central Authority; the adoption agency; the local authority to whom notice under section 44 of the 2002 Act (notice of intention to adopt or apply for a section 84 order) has been given; the Secretary of State for the Home Department; or any other person.	The adopters; the parents; the adoption agency; and the local authority to whom notice under section 44 of the 2002 Act (notice of intention to adopt or apply for a section 84 order) has been given.

(2) The court may at any time direct that a child, who is not already a respondent to proceedings, be made a respondent to proceedings where –

    (a)   the child –
        (i)   wishes to make an application; or
        (ii)   has evidence to give to the court or a legal submission to make which has not been given or made by any other party; or
    (b)   there are other special circumstances.

(3) The court may at any time direct that –

    (a)   any other person or body be made a respondent to proceedings; or

(b)   a party be removed.

(4) If the court makes a direction for the addition or removal of a party, it may give consequential directions about –

(a)   serving a copy of the application form on any new respondent;
(b)   serving relevant documents on the new party; and
(c)   the management of the proceedings.

14.4 Notice of proceedings to person with foreign parental responsibility

(1) This rule applies where a child is subject to proceedings to which this Part applies and –

(a)   a parent of the child holds or is believed to hold parental responsibility for the child under the law of another State which subsists in accordance with Article 16 of the 1996 Hague Convention following the child becoming habitually resident in a territorial unit of the United Kingdom; and
(b)   that parent is not otherwise required to be joined as a respondent under rule 14.3.

(2) The applicant shall give notice of the proceedings to any parent to whom the applicant believes paragraph (1) applies in any case in which a person who was a parent with parental responsibility under the 1989 Act would be a respondent to the proceedings in accordance with rule 14.3.

(3) The applicant and every respondent to the proceedings shall provide such details as they possess as to the identity and whereabouts of any parent they believe to hold parental responsibility for the child in accordance with paragraph (1) to the court officer, upon making, or responding to the application as appropriate.

(4) Where the existence of such a parent only becomes apparent to a party at a later date during the proceedings, that party must notify the court officer of those details at the earliest opportunity.

(5) Where a parent to whom paragraph (1) applies receives notice of proceedings, that parent may apply to the court to be joined as a party using the Part 18 procedure.

14.5 Who is to serve

(1) The general rules about service in Part 6 are subject to this rule.

(2) In proceedings to which this Part applies, a document which has been issued or prepared by a court officer will be served by the court officer except where –

(a)   a practice direction provides otherwise; or
(b)   the court directs otherwise.

(3) Where a court officer is to serve a document, it is for the court to decide which of the methods of service specified in rule 6.23 is to be used

14.6 What the court or a court officer will do when the application has been issued

(1) As soon as practicable after the application has been issued in proceedings –

(a) the court will –

    (i) if section 48(1) of the 2002 Act (restrictions on making adoption orders) applies, consider whether it is proper to hear the application;

    (ii) subject to paragraph (4), set a date for the first directions hearing;

    (iii) appoint a children's guardian in accordance with rule 16.3(1);

    (iv) appoint a reporting officer in accordance with rule 16.30;

    (v) consider whether a report relating to the welfare of the child is required, and if so, request such a report in accordance with rule 16.33;

    (vi) set a date for the hearing of the application; and

    (vii) do anything else that may be set out in a practice direction; and

(b) a court officer will –

    (i) subject to receiving confirmation in accordance with paragraph (2)(b)(ii), give notice of any directions hearing set by the court to the parties and to any children's guardian, reporting officer or children and family reporter;

    (ii) serve a copy of the application form (but, subject to sub-paragraphs (iii) and (iv), not the documents attached to it) on the persons referred to in Practice Direction 14A;

    (iii) send a copy of the certified copy of the entry in the register of live-births or Adopted Children Register and any health report attached to an application for an adoption order to –

        (aa) any children's guardian, reporting officer or children and family reporter; and

        (bb) the local authority to whom notice under section 44 of the 2002 Act (notice of intention to adopt or apply for a section 84 order) has been given;

    (iv) if notice under rule 14.9(2) has been given (request to dispense with consent of parent or guardian), in accordance with that rule inform the parent or guardian of the request and send a copy of the statement of facts to –

        (aa) the parent or guardian;

        (bb) any children's guardian, reporting officer or children and family reporter;

        (cc) any local authority to whom notice under section 44 of the 2002 Act (notice of intention to adopt or apply for a section 84 order) has been given; and

        (dd) any adoption agency which has placed the child for adoption; and

    (v) do anything else that may be set out in a practice direction.

(2) In addition to the matters referred to in paragraph (1), as soon as practicable after an application for an adoption order or a section 84 order has been issued the court or the court officer will –

    (a)   where the child is not placed for adoption by an adoption agency –
        (i)   ask either the Service or the Assembly to file any relevant form of consent to an adoption order or a section 84 order; and
        (ii)   ask the local authority to prepare a report on the suitability of the prospective adopters if one has not already been prepared; and
    (b)   where the child is placed for adoption by an adoption agency, ask the adoption agency to –
        (i)   file any relevant form of consent to –
            (aa) the child being placed for adoption;
            (bb) an adoption order;
            (cc) a future adoption order under section 20 of the 2002 Act; or
            (dd) a section 84 order;
        (ii)   confirm whether a statement has been made under section 20(4)(a) of the 2002 Act (statement of wish not to be informed of any application for an adoption order) and if so, to file that statement;
        (iii)   file any statement made under section 20(4)(b) of the 2002 Act (withdrawal of wish not to be informed of any application for an adoption order) as soon as it is received by the adoption agency; and
        (iv)   prepare a report on the suitability of the prospective adopters if one has not already been prepared.

(3) In addition to the matters referred to in paragraph (1), as soon as practicable after an application for a placement order has been issued –

    (a)   the court will consider whether a report giving the local authority's reasons for placing the child for adoption is required, and if so, will direct the local authority to prepare such a report; and
    (b)   the court or the court officer will ask either the Service or the Assembly to file any form of consent to the child being placed for adoption.

(4) Where it considers it appropriate the court may, instead of setting a date for a first directions hearing, give the directions provided for by rule 14.8.

14.7 Date for first directions hearing

Unless the court directs otherwise, the first directions hearing must be within 4 weeks beginning with the date on which the application is issued.

14.8 The first directions hearing

(1) At the first directions hearing in the proceedings the court will –

    (a)   fix a timetable for the filing of –

(i)   any report relating to the suitability of the applicants to adopt a child;

(ii)   any report from the local authority;

(iii)   any report from a children's guardian, reporting officer or children and family reporter;

(iv)   if a statement of facts has been filed, any amended statement of facts;

(v)   any other evidence, and

(vi)   give directions relating to the reports and other evidence;

(b)   consider whether the child or any other person should be a party to the proceedings and, if so, give directions in accordance with rule 14.3(2) or (3) joining that child or person as a party;

(c)   give directions relating to the appointment of a litigation friend for any protected party or child who is a party to, but not the subject of, proceedings unless a litigation friend has already been appointed;

(d)   consider whether the case needs to be transferred to another court and, if so, give directions to transfer the proceedings to another court in accordance with any order made by the Lord Chancellor under Part 1 of Schedule 11 to the 1989 Act;

(e)   give directions about –

(i)   tracing parents or any other person the court considers to be relevant to the proceedings;

(ii)   service of documents;

(iii)   subject to paragraph (2), disclosure as soon as possible of information and evidence to the parties; and

(iv)   the final hearing.

(By rule 3.3 the court may also direct that the case be adjourned if it considers that alternative dispute resolution is appropriate.)

(2) Rule 14.13(2) applies to any direction given under paragraph (1)(e)(iii) as it applies to a direction given under rule 14.13(1).

(3) In addition to the matters referred to in paragraph (1), the court will give any of the directions listed in Practice Direction 14B in proceedings for –

(a)   a Convention adoption order;

(b)   a section 84 order;

(c)   a section 88 direction;

(d)   a section 89 order; or

(e)   an adoption order where section 83(1) of the 2002 Act applies (restriction on bringing children in).

(4) The parties or their legal representatives must attend the first directions hearing unless the court directs otherwise.

(5) Directions may also be given at any stage in the proceedings –

(a)   of the court's own initiative; or

(b)   on the application of a party or any children's guardian or, where the direction concerns a report by a reporting officer or children and family reporter, the reporting officer or children and family reporter.

(6) For the purposes of giving directions or for such purposes as the court directs –

    (a)   the court may set a date for a further directions hearing or other hearing; and

    (b)   the court officer will give notice of any date so fixed to the parties and to any children's guardian, reporting officer or children and family reporter.

(7) After the first directions hearing the court will monitor compliance by the parties with the court's timetable and directions.

14.9 Requesting the court to dispense with the consent of any parent or guardian

(1) This rule applies where the applicant wants to ask the court to dispense with the consent of any parent or guardian of a child to –

    (a)   the child being placed for adoption;

    (b)   the making of an adoption order except a Convention adoption order; or

    (c)   the making of a section 84 order.

(2) The applicant requesting the court to dispense with the consent must –

    (a)   give notice of the request in the application form or at any later stage by filing a written request setting out the reasons for the request; and

    (b)   file a statement of facts setting out a summary of the history of the case and any other facts to satisfy the court that –

        (i)   the parent or guardian cannot be found or is incapable of giving consent; or

        (ii)   the welfare of the child requires the consent to be dispensed with.

(3) If a serial number has been assigned to the applicant under rule 14.2, the statement of facts supplied under paragraph (2)(b) must be framed so that it does not disclose the identity of the applicant.

(4) On receipt of the notice of the request –

    (a)   a court officer will –

        (i)   inform the parent or guardian of the request unless the parent or guardian cannot be found; and

        (ii)   send a copy of the statement of facts filed in accordance with paragraph (2)(b) to –

            (aa)   the parent or guardian unless the parent or guardian cannot be found;

            (bb)   any children's guardian, reporting officer or children and family reporter;

            (cc)   any local authority to whom notice under section 44 of the 2002 Act (notice of intention to adopt or apply for a section 84 order) has been given; and

            (dd)   any adoption agency which has placed the child for adoption; and

(b)   if the applicant considers that the parent or guardian is incapable of giving consent, the court will consider whether to –

  (i)   appoint a litigation friend for the parent or guardian under rule 15.6(1); or

  (ii)   give directions for an application to be made under rule 15.6(3)

  (iii) unless a litigation friend is already appointed for that parent or guardian.

14.10 Consent

(1) Consent of any parent or guardian of a child –

(a)   under section 19 of the 2002 Act, to the child being placed for adoption; and

(b)   under section 20 of the 2002 Act, to the making of a future adoption order,

must be given in the form referred to in Practice Direction 5A or a form to the like effect.

(2) Subject to paragraph (3), consent –

(a)   to the making of an adoption order; or

(b)   to the making of a section 84 order,

may be given in the form referred to in Practice Direction 5A or a form to the like effect or otherwise as the court directs.

(3) Any consent to a Convention adoption order must be in a form which complies with the internal law relating to adoption of the Convention country of which the child is habitually resident.

(4) Any form of consent executed in Scotland must be witnessed by a Justice of the Peace or a Sheriff.

(5) Any form of consent executed in Northern Ireland must be witnessed by a Justice of the Peace.

(6) Any form of consent executed outside the United Kingdom must be witnessed by –

(a)   any person for the time being authorised by law in the place where the document is executed to administer an oath for any judicial or other legal purpose;

(b)   a British Consular officer;

(c)   a notary public; or

(d)   if the person executing the document is serving in any of the regular armed forces of the Crown, an officer holding a commission in any of those forces.

14.11 Reports by the adoption agency or local authority

(1) The adoption agency or local authority must file the report on the suitability of the applicant to adopt a child within the timetable fixed by the court.

(2) A local authority that is directed to prepare a report on the placement of the child for adoption must file that report within the timetable fixed by the court.

(3) The reports must cover the matters specified in Practice Direction 14C.

(4) The court may at any stage request a further report or ask the adoption agency or local authority to assist the court in any other manner.

(5) A court officer will send a copy of any report referred to in this rule to any children's guardian, reporting officer or children and family reporter.

(6) A report to the court under this rule is confidential.

14.12 Health reports

(1) Reports by a registered medical practitioner ('health reports') made not more than 3 months earlier on the health of the child and of each applicant must be attached to an application for an adoption order or a section 84 order except where –

(a) the child was placed for adoption with the applicant by an adoption agency;
(b) the applicant or one of the applicants is a parent of the child; or
(c) the applicant is the partner of a parent of the child.

(2) Health reports must contain the matters set out in Practice Direction 14D.

(3) A health report is confidential.

14.13 Confidential reports to the court and disclosure to the parties

(1) The court will consider whether to give a direction that a confidential report be disclosed to each party to the proceedings.

(2) Before giving such a direction the court will consider whether any information should be deleted including information which –

(a) discloses, or is likely to disclose, the identity of a person who has been assigned a serial number under rule 14.2(2); or
(b) discloses the particulars referred to in rule 29.1(1) where a party has given notice under rule 29.1(2) (disclosure of personal details).

(3) The court may direct that the report will not be disclosed to a party.

14.14 Communication of information relating to proceedings

For the purposes of the law relating to contempt of court, information (whether or not it is recorded in any form) relating to proceedings held in private may be communicated –

(a)   where the court gives permission;

(b)   unless the court directs otherwise, in accordance with Practice Direction 14E; or

(c)   where the communication is to –

    (i)   a party;

    (ii)   the legal representative of a party;

    (iii)   a professional legal adviser;

    (iv)   an officer of the service or a Welsh family proceedings officer;

    (v)   a welfare officer;

    (vi)   the Legal Services Commission;

    (vii)   an expert whose instruction by a party has been authorised by the court for the purposes of the proceedings; or

    (viii)   a professional acting in furtherance of the protection of children.

14.15 Notice of final hearing

A court officer will give notice to the parties, any children's guardian, reporting officer or children and family reporter and to any other person to whom a practice direction may require such notice to be given –

(a)   of the date and place where the application will be heard; and

(b)   of the fact that, unless the person wishes or the court requires, the person need not attend.

14.16 The final hearing

(1) Any person who has been given notice in accordance with rule 14.15 may attend the final hearing and, subject to paragraph (2), be heard on the question of whether an order should be made.

(2) A person whose application for the permission of the court to oppose the making of an adoption order under section 47(3) or (5) of the 2002 Act has been refused is not entitled to be heard on the question of whether an order should be made.

(3) Any member or employee of a party which is a local authority, adoption agency or other body may address the court at the final hearing if authorised to do so.

(4) The court may direct that any person must attend a final hearing.

(5) Paragraphs (6) and (7) apply to –

(a)   an adoption order;

(b)   a section 84 order; or

(c)   a section 89 order.

(6) Subject to paragraphs (7) and (8), the court cannot make an order unless the applicant and the child personally attend the final hearing.

(7) The court may direct that the applicant or the child need not attend the final hearing.

(8) In a case of adoption by a couple under section 50 of the 2002 Act, the court may make an adoption order after personal attendance of one only of the applicants if there are special circumstances.

(9) The court cannot make a placement order unless a legal representative of the applicant attends the final hearing.

14.17 Proof of identity of the child

(1) Unless the contrary is shown, the child referred to in the application will be deemed to be the child referred to in the form of consent –

  (a)   to the child being placed for adoption;
  (b)   to the making of an adoption order; or
  (c)   to the making of a section 84 order,

where the conditions in paragraph (2) apply.

(2) The conditions are –

  (a)   the application identifies the child by reference to a full certified copy of an entry in the registers of live-births;
  (b)   the form of consent identifies the child by reference to a full certified copy of an entry in the registers of live-births attached to the form; and
  (c)   the copy of the entry in the registers of live-births referred to in sub-paragraph (a) is the same or relates to the same entry in the registers of live-births as the copy of the entry in the registers of live-births attached to the form of consent.

(3) Where the child is already an adopted child paragraph (2) will have effect as if for the references to the registers of live-births there were substituted references to the Adopted Children Register.

(4) Subject to paragraph (7), where the precise date of the child's birth is not proved to the satisfaction of the court, the court will determine the probable date of birth.

(5) The probable date of the child's birth may be specified in the placement order, adoption order or section 84 order as the date of the child's birth.

(6) Subject to paragraph (7), where the child's place of birth cannot be proved to the satisfaction of the court –

  (a)   the child may be treated as having been born in the registration district of the court where it is probable that the child may have been born in –
    (i)   the United Kingdom;
    (ii)   the Channel Islands; or
    (iii) the Isle of Man; or
  (b)   in any other case, the particulars of the country of birth may be omitted from the placement order, adoption order or section 84 order.

(7) A placement order identifying the probable date and place of birth of the child will be sufficient proof of the date and place of birth of the child in adoption proceedings and proceedings for a section 84 order.

14.18 Disclosing information to an adopted adult

(1) The adopted person has the right, on request, to receive from the court which made the adoption order a copy of the following –

(a)   the application form for an adoption order (but not the documents attached to that form);

(b)   the adoption order and any other orders relating to the adoption proceedings;

(c)   orders allowing any person contact with the child after the adoption order was made; and

(d)   any other document or order referred to in Practice Direction 14F.

(2) The court will remove any protected information from any copy of a document or order referred to in paragraph (1) before the copies are given to the adopted person.

(3) This rule does not apply to an adopted person under the age of 18 years.

(4) In this rule 'protected information' means information which would be protected information under section 57(3) of the 2002 Act if the adoption agency gave the information and not the court.

14.19 Translation of documents

(1) Where a translation of any document is required for the purposes of proceedings for a Convention adoption order the translation must –

(a)   unless the court directs otherwise, be provided by the applicant; and

(b)   be signed by the translator to certify that the translation is accurate.

(2) This rule does not apply where the document is to be served in accordance with the Service Regulation.

14.20 Application for recovery orders

(1) An application for any of the orders referred to in section 41(2) of the 2002 Act (recovery orders) may –

(a)   in the High Court or a county court, be made without notice in which case the applicant must file the application –

　　(i)   where the application is made by telephone, the next business day after the making of the application; or

　　(ii)   in any other case, at the time when the application is made; and

(b)   in a magistrates' court, be made, with the permission of the court, without notice in which case the applicant must file the application at the time when the application is made or as directed by the court.

(2) Where the court refuses to make an order on an application without notice it may direct that the application is made on notice in which case the application will proceed in accordance with rules 14.1 to 14.17.

(3) The respondents to an application under this rule are –

(a) in a case where –
    (i) placement proceedings;
    (ii) adoption proceedings; or
    (iii) proceedings for a section 84 order,
    are pending, all parties to those proceedings;
(b) any adoption agency authorised to place the child for adoption or which has placed the child for adoption;
(c) any local authority to whom notice under section 44 of the 2002 Act (notice of intention to adopt or apply for a section 84 order) has been given;
(d) any person having parental responsibility for the child;
(e) any person in whose favour there is provision for contact;
(f) any person who was caring for the child immediately prior to the making of the application; and
(g) any person whom the applicant alleges to have effected, or to have been or to be responsible for, the taking or keeping of the child.

14.21 Inherent jurisdiction and fathers without parental responsibility

Where no proceedings have started an adoption agency or local authority may ask the High Court for directions on the need to give a father without parental responsibility notice of the intention to place a child for adoption.

14.22 Timing of applications for section 89 order

An application for a section 89 order must be made within 2 years beginning with the date on which –

(a) the Convention adoption or Convention adoption order; or
(b) the overseas adoption or determination under section 91 of the 2002 Act,

to which it relates was made.

14.23 Custody of documents

All documents relating to proceedings under the 2002 Act must, while they are in the custody of the court, be kept in a place of special security.

14.24 Documents held by the court not to be inspected or copied without the court's permission

Subject to the provisions of these rules, any practice direction or any direction given by the court –

(a) no document or order held by the court in proceedings under the 2002 Act will be open to inspection by any person; and

(b)   no copy of any such document or order, or of an extract from any such document or order, will be taken by or given to any person.

14.25 Orders

(1) An order takes effect from the date when it is made, or such later date as the court may specify.

(2) In proceedings in Wales a party may request that an order be drawn up in Welsh as well as English.

14.26 Copies of orders

(1) Within 7 days beginning with the date on which the final order was made in proceedings, or such shorter time as the court may direct, a court officer will send –

(a)   a copy of the order to the applicant;
(b)   a copy, which is sealed, authenticated with the stamp of the court or certified as a true copy, of –
    (i)   an adoption order;
    (ii)   a section 89 order; or
    (iii) an order quashing or revoking an adoption order or allowing an appeal against an adoption order,
    to the Registrar General;
(c)   a copy of a Convention adoption order to the relevant Central Authority;
(d)   a copy of a section 89 order relating to a Convention adoption order or a Convention adoption to the –
    (i)   relevant Central Authority;
    (ii)   adopters;
    (iii) adoption agency; and
    (iv)   local authority;
(e)   unless the court directs otherwise, a copy of a contact order under section 26 of the 2002 Act or a variation or revocation of a contact order under section 27 of the 2002 Act to the –
    (i)   person with whom the child is living;
    (ii)   adoption agency; and
    (iii) local authority; and
(f)   a notice of the making or refusal of –
    (i)   the final order; or
    (ii)   an order quashing or revoking an adoption order or allowing an appeal against an order in proceedings,
    to every respondent and, with the permission of the court, any other person.

(2) The court officer will also send notice of the making of an adoption order or a section 84 order to –

(a)   any court in Great Britain which appears to the court officer to have made any such order as is referred to in section 46(2) of the 2002 Act (order relating to parental responsibility for, and maintenance of, the child); and

(b)   the principal registry, if it appears to the court officer that a parental responsibility agreement has been recorded at the principal registry.

(3) A copy of any final order may be sent to any other person with the permission of the court.

(4) The court officer will send a copy of any order made during the course of the proceedings to the following persons or bodies, unless the court directs otherwise –

(a)   all the parties to those proceedings;
(b)   any children and family reporter appointed in those proceedings;
(c)   any adoption agency or local authority which has prepared a report on the suitability of an applicant to adopt a child;
(d)   any local authority which has prepared a report on placement for adoption.

(5) If an order has been drawn up in Welsh as well as English in accordance with rule 14.25(2) any reference in this rule to sending an order is to be taken as a reference to sending both the Welsh and English orders.

14.27 Amendment and revocation of orders

(1) Subject to paragraph (2), an application under –

(a)   section 55 of the 2002 Act (revocation of adoptions on legitimation); or
(b)   paragraph 4 of Schedule 1 to the 2002 Act (amendment of adoption order and revocation of direction),

may be made without serving a copy of the application notice.

(2) The court may direct that an application notice be served on such persons as it thinks fit.

(3) Where the court makes an order granting the application, a court officer will send the Registrar General a notice –

(a)   specifying the amendments; or
(b)   informing the Registrar General of the revocation,

giving sufficient particulars of the order to enable the Registrar General to identify the case.

14.28 Keeping registers in the family proceedings court

(1) A magistrates' court officer will keep a register in which there will be entered a minute or memorandum of every adjudication of the court in proceedings to which this Part applies.

(2) The register may be stored in electronic form on the court computer system and entries in the register will include, where relevant, the following particulars –

(a) the name and address of the applicant;
(b) the name of the child including, in adoption proceedings, the name of the child prior to, and after, adoption;
(c) the age and sex of the child;
(d) the nature of the application; and
(e) the minute of adjudication.

(3) The part of the register relating to adoption proceedings will be kept separately to any other part of the register and will –

(a) not contain particulars of any other proceedings; and
(b) be kept by the court in a place of special security.

****

PART 19
ALTERNATIVE PROCEDURE FOR APPLICATIONS

19.1 Types of application for which Part 19 procedure may be followed

(1) The Part 19 procedure is the procedure set out in this Part.

(2) An applicant may use the Part 19 procedure where the Part 18 procedure does not apply and –

(a) there is no form prescribed by a rule or referred to in Practice Direction 5A in which to make the application;
(b) the applicant seeks the court's decision on a question which is unlikely to involve a substantial dispute of fact; or
(c) paragraph (5) applies.

(3) The court may at any stage direct that the application is to continue as if the applicant had not used the Part 19 procedure and, if it does so, the court may give any directions it considers appropriate.

(4) Paragraph (2) does not apply if a practice direction provides that the Part 19 procedure may not be used in relation to the type of application in question.

(5) A rule or practice direction may, in relation to a specified type of proceedings –

(a) require or permit the use of the Part 19 procedure; and
(b) disapply or modify any of the rules set out in this Part as they apply to those proceedings.

19.2 Applications for which the Part 19 procedure must be followed

(1) The Part 19 procedure must be used in an application made in accordance with –

(a) section 60(3) of the 2002 Act (order to prevent disclosure of information to an adopted person);

(b) section 79(4) of the 2002 Act (order for Registrar General to give any information referred to in section 79(3) of the 2002 Act); and

(c) rule 14.21 (directions of High Court regarding fathers without parental responsibility).

(2) The respondent to an application made in accordance with paragraph (1)(b) is the Registrar General.

19.3 Contents of the application

Where the applicant uses the Part 19 procedure, the application must state –

(a) that this Part applies;

(b) either –

    (i) the question which the applicant wants the court to decide; or

    (ii) the order which the applicant is seeking and the legal basis of the application for that order;

(c) if the application is being made under an enactment, what that enactment is;

(d) if the applicant is applying in a representative capacity, what that capacity is; and

(e) if the respondent appears or is to appear in a representative capacity, what that capacity is.

(Part 17 requires a statement of case to be verified by a statement of truth.)

19.4 Issue of application without naming respondents

(1) A practice direction may set out circumstances in which an application may be issued under this Part without naming a respondent.

(2) The practice direction may set out those cases in which an application for permission must be made by application notice before the application is issued.

(3) The application for permission –

(a) need not be served on any other person; and

(b) must be accompanied by a copy of the application which the applicant proposes to issue.

(4) Where the court gives permission, it will give directions about the future management of the application.

19.5 Acknowledgment of service

(1) Subject to paragraph (2), each respondent must –

(a) file an acknowledgment of service within 14 days beginning with the date on which the application is served; and

(b) serve the acknowledgment of service on the applicant and any other party.

(2) If the application is to be served out of the jurisdiction, the respondent must file and serve an acknowledgment of service within the period set out in Practice Direction 6B.

(3) The acknowledgment of service must –

(a)   state whether the respondent contests the application;
(b)   state, if the respondent seeks a different order from that set out in the application, what that order is; and
(c)   be signed by the respondent or the respondent's legal representative.

19.6 Consequence of not filing an acknowledgment of service

(1) This rule applies where –

(a)   the respondent has failed to file an acknowledgment of service; and
(b)   the time period for doing so has expired.

(2) The respondent may attend the hearing of the application but may not take part in the hearing unless the court gives permission.

19.7 Filing and serving written evidence

(1) The applicant must, when filing the application, file the written evidence on which the applicant intends to rely.

(2) The applicant's evidence must be served on the respondent with the application.

(3) A respondent who wishes to rely on written evidence must file it when filing the acknowledgment of service.

(4) A respondent who files written evidence must also, at the same time, serve a copy of that evidence on the other parties.

(5) Within 14 days beginning with the date on which a respondent's evidence was served on the applicant, the applicant may file further written evidence in reply.

(6) An applicant who files further written evidence must also, within the same time limit, serve a copy of that evidence on the other parties.

19.8 Evidence – general

(1) No written evidence may be relied on at the hearing of the application unless –

(a)   it has been served in accordance with rule 19.7; or
(b)   the court gives permission.

(2) The court may require or permit a party to give oral evidence at the hearing.

(3) The court may give directions requiring the attendance for cross-examination of a witness who has given written evidence.

(Rule 22.1 contains a general power for the court to control evidence.)

19.9 Procedure where respondent objects to use of the Part 19 procedure

(1) A respondent who contends that the Part 19 procedure should not be used because –

(a) there is a substantial dispute of fact; and

(b) the use of the Part 19 procedure is not required or permitted by a rule or practice direction,

must state the reasons for that contention when filing the acknowledgment of service.

(2) When the court receives the acknowledgment of service and any written evidence, it will give directions as to the future management of the case.

(Rule 19.7 requires a respondent who wishes to rely on written evidence to file it when filing the acknowledgment of service.)

(Rule 19.1(3) allows the court to make an order that the application continue as if the applicant had not used the Part 19 procedure.)

****

Appendix 11

RESTRICTION ON THE PREPARATION OF ADOPTION REPORTS REGULATIONS 2005

SI 2005/1711

1 Citation and commencement

These Regulations may be cited as the Restriction on the Preparation of Adoption Reports Regulations 2005 and shall come into force on 30th December 2005.

2 Interpretation

In these Regulations –

'the Act' means the Adoption and Children Act 2002;

'the 2000 Act' means the Care Standards Act 2000;

'the Adoption Agencies Regulations' means the Adoption Agencies Regulations 2005;

'the Adoptions with a Foreign Element Regulations' means the Adoptions with a Foreign Element Regulations 2005;

'corresponding Welsh provision', in relation to the Adoption Agencies Regulations or to a regulation of the Adoption Agencies Regulations, means the provision of regulations made by the Assembly under section 9 of the Act which corresponds to, as the case may be, the Adoption Agencies Regulations or to that regulation of the Adoption Agencies Regulations;

'Council' means either the English Council or the Welsh Council and 'the English Council' and 'the Welsh Council' have the same meaning as in section 54 of the 2000 Act;

'pre-adoption report' means a report prepared otherwise than in accordance with the Adoption Agencies Regulations or corresponding Welsh provision at the request of a relevant foreign authority following the placement for adoption of a child from the country in which that authority performs its functions and prior to that child's adoption and includes a report prepared in accordance with regulation 29(2) of the Adoptions with a Foreign Element Regulations;

'post-adoption report' means a report prepared otherwise than in accordance with the Adoption Agencies Regulations or corresponding Welsh provision at the request of a relevant foreign authority following the adoption of a child from the country in which that authority performs its functions;

'relevant foreign authority' has the meaning given in regulation 2 of the Adoptions with a Foreign Element Regulations; and

'social worker' means a person who is registered in –

    (a)   the register for social workers maintained in accordance with section 56 of the 2000 Act;

    (b)   the register maintained by the Scottish Social Services Council under section 44 of the Regulation of Care (Scotland) Act 2001; or

    (c)   the register maintained by the Northern Ireland Social Care Council under section 3 of the Health and Personal Social Services Act (Northern Ireland) 2001.

3 A person within a prescribed description

(1) A person is within a prescribed description for the purposes of section 94(1) of the Act if –

    (a)   he is a social worker who is employed by a local authority or registered adoption society and who satisfies at least one of the conditions set out in paragraph (2)(a) or (b);

    (b)   he is a person who –

        (i)   is participating in a course approved by a Council under section 63 of the 2000 Act for persons wishing to become social workers;

        (ii)   is employed by, or placed with, a local authority or registered adoption society as part of that course; and

        (iii)   satisfies the condition set out in paragraph (2)(b); or

    (c)   he is acting on behalf of a local authority or a registered adoption society and is a social worker who satisfies the conditions in paragraph (2)(a) and (b).

(2) The conditions referred to in paragraph (1) are that the person –

    (a)   has at least three years' post-qualifying experience in child care social work, including direct experience of adoption work;

    (b)   is supervised by a social worker who –

        (i)   is employed by the local authority or registered adoption society in question; and

        (ii)   has at least three years' post-qualifying experience in child care social work, including direct experience of adoption work.

4 The prescribed circumstances

The circumstances prescribed for the purposes of section 94(1) of the Act are –

    (a)   preparing a report about whether a child should be placed for adoption, in accordance with regulation 17(1) of the Adoption Agencies Regulations or corresponding Welsh provision;

    (b)   preparing a report about the suitability of a prospective adopter to adopt a child, in accordance with regulation 25(5) of the Adoption Agencies Regulations or corresponding Welsh provision;

(c)   preparing a report about whether a child should be placed for adoption with a particular prospective adopter, in accordance with regulation 31(2)(d) of the Adoption Agencies Regulations or corresponding Welsh provision;

(d)   preparing a report of a visit in accordance with regulation 36(4)(b) of the Adoption Agencies Regulations or corresponding Welsh provision;

(e)   preparing a report of a visit or review in accordance with regulation 5(1)(h)(ii) of the Adoptions with a Foreign Element Regulations;

(f)   preparing a report of a review of a child's case in accordance with regulation 5(3) of the Adoptions with a Foreign Element Regulations;

(g)   preparing a pre-adoption report;

(h)   preparing a post-adoption report;

(i)   preparing a report in accordance with section 43 (reports in agency cases) or section 44(5) (reports in non-agency cases) of the Act; and

(j)   preparing a report in the case of an application under section 84(1) (parental responsibility prior to adoption abroad) of the Act.

Appendix 12

BRITISH NATIONALITY ACT 1981

PART I
BRITISH CITIZENSHIP

Acquisition after commencement

1 Acquisition by birth or adoption

(1) A person born in the United Kingdom after commencement, or in a qualifying territory on or after the appointed day, shall be a British citizen if at the time of the birth his father or mother is –

    (a)   a British citizen; or
    (b)   settled in the United Kingdom or that territory.

(1A) A person born in the United Kingdom or a qualifying territory on or after the relevant day shall be a British citizen if at the time of the birth his father or mother is a member of the armed forces.

(2) A new-born infant who, after commencement, is found abandoned in the United Kingdom, or on or after the appointed day is found abandoned in a qualifying territory, shall, unless the contrary is shown, be deemed for the purposes of subsection (1) –

    (a)   to have been born in the United Kingdom after commencement or in that territory on or after the appointed day; and
    (b)   to have been born to a parent who at the time of the birth was a British citizen or settled in the United Kingdom or that territory.

(3) A person born in the United Kingdom after commencement who is not a British citizen by virtue of subsection (1), (1A) or (2) shall be entitled to be registered as a British citizen if, while he is a minor –

    (a)   his father or mother becomes a British citizen or becomes settled in the United Kingdom; and
    (b)   an application is made for his registration as a British citizen.

(3A) A person born in the United Kingdom on or after the relevant day who is not a British citizen by virtue of subsection (1), (1A) or (2) shall be entitled to be registered as a British citizen if, while he is a minor –

    (a)   his father or mother becomes a member of the armed forces; and
    (b)   an application is made for his registration as a British citizen

(4) A person born in the United Kingdom after commencement who is not a British citizen by virtue of subsection (1), (1A) or (2) shall be entitled, on an application for his registration as a British citizen made at any time after he has attained the age of ten years, to be registered as such a citizen if, as regards

each of the first ten years of that person's life, the number of days on which he was absent from the United Kingdom in that year does not exceed 90.

(5) Where –

    (a)   any court in the United Kingdom or, on or after the appointed day, any court in a qualifying territory makes an order authorising the adoption of a minor who is not a British citizen; or

    (b)   a minor who is not a British citizen is adopted under a Convention adoption, effected under the law of a country or territory outside the United Kingdom,

that minor shall, if the requirements of subsection (5A) are met, be a British citizen as from the date on which the order is made or the Convention adoption is effected, as the case may be.

(5A) Those requirements are that on the date on which the order is made or the Convention adoption is effected (as the case may be) –

    (a)   the adopter or, in the case of a joint adoption, one of the adopters is a British citizen; and

    (b)   in a case within subsection (5)(b), the adopter or, in the case of a joint adoption, both of the adopters are habitually resident in the United Kingdom or in a designated territory.

(6) Where an order or a Convention adoption in consequence of which any person became a British citizen by virtue of subsection (5) ceases to have effect, whether on annulment or otherwise, the cesser shall not affect the status of that person as a British citizen.

(7) If in the special circumstances of any particular case the Secretary of State thinks fit, he may for the purposes of subsection (4) treat the person to whom the application relates as fulfilling the requirement specified in that subsection although, as regards any one or more of the first ten years of that person's life, the number of days on which he was absent from the United Kingdom in that year or each of the years in question exceeds 90.

(8) In this section and elsewhere in this Act 'settled' has the meaning given by section 50.

(9) The relevant day for the purposes of subsection (1A) or (3A) is the day appointed for the commencement of section 42 of the Borders, Citizenship and Immigration Act 2009 (which inserted those subsections).

Amendments: British Overseas Territories Act 2002, s 5, Sch 1, para 1(1), (2)(a); Borders, Citizenship and Immigration Act 2009, s 42(1), (2); Adoption (Intercountry Aspects) Act 1999, s 7(1); Adoption and Children Act 2002, ss 137(3), (4)(c), 139(3), Sch 5.

****

3 Acquisition by registration: minors

(1) If while a person is a minor an application is made for his registration as a British citizen, the Secretary of State may, if he thinks fit, cause him to be registered as such a citizen.

****

50 Interpretation

(1) In this Act, unless the context otherwise requires –

'the 1948 Act' means the British Nationality Act 1948;

'alien' means a person who is neither a Commonwealth citizen nor a British protected person nor a citizen of the Republic of Ireland;

'appointed day' means the day appointed by the Secretary of State under section 8 of the British Overseas Territories Act 2002 for the commencement of Schedule 1 to that Act;

'association' means an unincorporated body of persons;

'British National (Overseas)' means a person who is a British National (Overseas) under the Hong Kong (British Nationality) Order 1986, and 'status of a British National (Overseas)' shall be construed accordingly;

'British Overseas citizen' includes a person who is a British Overseas citizen under the Hong Kong (British Nationality) Order 1986;

'British overseas territory' means a territory mentioned in Schedule 6;

'British protected person' means a person who is a member of any class of person declared to be British protected persons by an Order in Council for the time being in force under section 38 or is a British protected person by virtue of the Solomon Islands Act 1978;

'commencement', without more, means the commencement of this Act;

'Commonwealth citizen' means a person who has the status of a Commonwealth citizen under this Act;

'company' means a body corporate;

'Convention adoption' means an adoption effected under the law of a country or territory in which the Convention is in force, and certified in pursuance of Article 23(1) of the Convention;

'Crown service' means the service of the Crown, whether within Her Majesty's dominions or elsewhere;

'Crown service under the government of the United Kingdom' means Crown service under Her Majesty's government in the United Kingdom or under Her Majesty's government in Northern Ireland or under the Scottish Administration or under the Welsh Assembly Government;

'designated territory' means a qualifying territory, or the Sovereign Base Areas of Akrotiri and Dhekelia, which is designated by Her Majesty by Order in Council under subsection (14);

'enactment' includes an enactment comprised in Northern Ireland legislation;

'foreign country' means a country other than the United Kingdom, a British overseas territory, a country mentioned in Schedule 3 and the Republic of Ireland;

'the former nationality Acts' means –

    (a)   the British Nationality Acts 1948 to 1965;

    (b)   the British Nationality and Status of Aliens Acts 1914 to 1943; and

    (c)   any Act repealed by the said Acts of 1914 to 1943 or by the Naturalization Act 1870;

'Governor', in relation to a British overseas territory, includes the officer for the time being administering the government of that territory;

'High Commissioner' includes an acting High Commissioner;

'immigration laws' –

    (a)   in relation to the United Kingdom, means the Immigration Act 1971 and any law for purposes similar to that Act which is for the time being or has at any time been in force in any part of the United Kingdom;

    (b)   in relation to a British overseas territory, means any law for purposes similar to the Immigration Act 1971 which is for the time being or has at any time been in force in that territory;

'the Islands' means the Channel Islands and the Isle of Man;

'minor' means a person who has not attained the age of eighteen years;

'prescribed' means prescribed by regulations made under section 41;

'qualifying territory' means a British overseas territory other than the Sovereign Base Areas of Akrotiri and Dhekelia;

'settled' shall be construed in accordance with subsections (2) to (4);

'ship' includes a hovercraft;

'statutory provision' means any enactment or any provision contained in –

    (a)   subordinate legislation (as defined in section 21(1) of the Interpretation Act 1978); or

    (b)   any instrument of a legislative character made under any Northern Ireland legislation;

'the United Kingdom' means Great Britain, Northern Ireland and the Islands, taken together;

'United Kingdom consulate' means the office of a consular officer of Her Majesty's government in the United Kingdom where a register of the births is kept or, where there is no such office, such office as may be prescribed.

****

Amendments: British Overseas Territories Act 2002, s 5, Sch 1, para 5(1), (2); Adoption and Children Act 2002, s 137(3), (6)(a); SI 1999/1042, art 3, Sch 1, para 10.

Appendix 13

HOUSING ACT 1985

****

325 The room standard

(1) The room standard is contravened when the number of persons sleeping in a dwelling and the number of rooms available as sleeping accommodation is such that two persons of opposite sexes who are not living together as husband and wife must sleep in the same room.

(2) For this purpose –

    (a)   children under the age of ten shall be left out of account, and

    (b)   a room is available as sleeping accommodation if it is of a type normally used in the locality either as a bedroom or as a living room.

326 The space standard

(1) The space standard is contravened when the number of persons sleeping in a dwelling is in excess of the permitted number, having regard to the number and floor area of the rooms of the dwelling available as sleeping accommodation.

(2) For this purpose –

    (a)   no account shall be taken of a child under the age of one and a child aged one or over but under ten shall be reckoned as one-half of a unit, and

    (b)   a room is available as sleeping accommodation if it is of a type normally used in the locality either as a living room or as a bedroom.

(3) The permitted number of persons in relation to a dwelling is whichever is the less of –

    (a)   the number specified in Table I in relation to the number of rooms in the dwelling available as sleeping accommodation, and

    (b)   the aggregate for all such rooms in the dwelling of the numbers specified in column 2 of Table II in relation to each room of the floor area specified in column 1.

No account shall be taken for the purposes of either Table of a room having a floor area of less than 50 square feet.

TABLE 1

Number of rooms	Number of persons
1	2
2	3
3	5
4	7 $\frac{1}{2}$
5 or more	2 for each room

TABLE 2

Floor area of room	Number of persons
110 sq ft or more	2
90 sq ft or more but less than 110 sq ft	1 $\frac{1}{2}$
70 sq ft or more but less than 90 sq ft	1
50 sq ft or more but less than 70 sq ft	1/2

****

Appendix 14

IMMIGRATION ACT 1971

****

3C Continuation of leave pending variation decision

(1) This section applies if –

    (a)   a person who has limited leave to enter or remain in the United Kingdom applies to the Secretary of State for variation of the leave,

    (b)   the application for variation is made before the leave expires, and

    (c)   the leave expires without the application for variation having been decided.

(2) The leave is extended by virtue of this section during any period when –

    (a)   the application for variation is neither decided nor withdrawn,

    (b)   an appeal under section 82(1) of the Nationality, Asylum and Immigration Act 2002 could be brought, while the appellant is in the United Kingdom against the decision on the application for variation (ignoring any possibility of an appeal out of time with permission), or

    (c)   an appeal under that section against that decision, brought while the appellant is in the United Kingdom, is pending (within the meaning of section 104 of that Act).

(3) Leave extended by virtue of this section shall lapse if the applicant leaves the United Kingdom.

(4) A person may not make an application for variation of his leave to enter or remain in the United Kingdom while that leave is extended by virtue of this section.

(5) But subsection (4) does not prevent the variation of the application mentioned in subsection (1)(a).

(6) The Secretary of State may make regulations determining when an application is decided for the purposes of this section; and the regulations –

    (a)   may make provision by reference to receipt of a notice,

    (b)   may provide for a notice to be treated as having been received in specified circumstances,

    (c)   may make different provision for different purposes or circumstances,

    (d)   shall be made by statutory instrument, and

    (e)   shall be subject to annulment in pursuance of a resolution of either House of Parliament.

Amendments: Nationality, Immigration and Asylum Act 2002, s 118.

****

33 Interpretation

(1) For purposes of this Act, except in so far as the context otherwise requires –

'aircraft' includes hovercraft, 'airport' includes hoverport and 'port' includes airport;

'captain' means master (of a ship) or commander (of an aircraft);

'certificate of entitlement' means a certificate under section 10 of the Nationality, Immigration and Asylum Act 2002 that a person has the right of abode in the United Kingdom;

'Convention adoption' has the same meaning as in the Adoption Act 1976 and the the Adoption and Children (Scotland) Act 2007 or in the Adoption and Children Act 2002;

'crew', in relation to a ship or aircraft, means all persons actually employed in the working or service of the ship or aircraft, including the captain, and 'member of the crew' shall be construed accordingly;

'entrant' means a person entering or seeking to enter the United Kingdom and 'illegal entrant' means a person –

    (a)   unlawfully entering or seeking to enter in breach of a deportation order or of the immigration laws, or

    (b)   entering or seeking to enter by means which include deception by another person,

and includes also a person who has entered as mentioned in paragraph (a) or (b) above;

'entry clearance' means a visa, entry certificate or other document which, in accordance with the immigration rules, is to be taken as evidence or the requisite evidence of a person's eligibility, though not a British citizen, for entry into the United Kingdom (but does not include a work permit);

'immigration laws' means this Act and any law for purposes similar to this Act which is for the time being or has (before or after the passing of this Act) been in force in any part of the United Kingdom and Islands;

'immigration rules' means the rules for the time being laid down as mentioned in section 3(2) above;

'the Islands' means the Channel Islands and the Isle of Man, and 'the United Kingdom and Islands' means the United Kingdom and the Islands taken together;

'legally adopted' means adopted in pursuance of an order made by any court in the United Kingdom and Islands, under a Convention adoption or by any adoption specified as an overseas adoption by order of the Secretary of State under section 87 of the Adoption and Children Act 2002 or by regulations made by the Scottish Ministers under section 67(1) of the Adoption and Children (Scotland) Act 2007;

'limited leave' and 'indefinite leave' mean respectively leave under this Act to enter or remain in the United Kingdom which is, and one which is not, limited as to duration;

'settled' shall be construed in accordance with subsection (2A) below;

'ship' includes every description of vessel used in navigation;

'United Kingdom passport' means a current passport issued by the Government of the United Kingdom, or by the Lieutenant-Governor of any of the Islands or by the Government of any territory which is for the time being a British overseas territory within the meaning of the British Nationality Act 1981;

'work permit' means a permit indicating, in accordance with the immigration rules, that a person named in it is eligible, though not a British citizen, for entry into the United Kingdom for the purpose of taking employment.

(1A) A reference to being an owner of a vehicle, ship or aircraft includes a reference to being any of a number of persons who jointly own it.

(2) It is hereby declared that, except as otherwise provided in this Act, a person is not to be treated for the purposes of any provision of this Act as ordinarily resident in the United Kingdom or in any of the Islands at a time when he is there in breach of the immigration laws.

(2A) Subject to section 8(5) above, references to a person being settled in the United Kingdom are references to his being ordinarily resident there without being subject under the immigration laws to any restriction on the period for which he may remain.

(3) The ports of entry for purposes of this Act, and the ports of exit for purposes of any Order in Council under section 3(7) above, shall be such ports as may from time to time be designated for the purpose by order of the Secretary of State made by statutory instrument.

(4) For the purposes of this Act, the question of whether an appeal is pending shall be determined in accordance with section 104 of the Nationality, Immigration and Asylum Act 2002 (pending appeals).

(5) This Act shall not be taken to supersede or impair any power exercisable by Her Majesty in relation to aliens by virtue of Her prerogative.

Amendments: Nationality, Immigration and Asylum Act 2002, s 10(5)(b); Adoption (Intercountry Aspects) Act 1999, s 15(1), Sch 2, para 2(a); Adoption and Children Act 2002, s 139(1), Sch 3, para 15(a).

****

Appendix 15

NATIONALITY, IMMIGRATION AND ASYLUM ACT 2002

****

78 No removal while appeal pending

(1) While a person's appeal under section 82(1) is pending he may not be –

(a) removed from the United Kingdom in accordance with a provision of the Immigration Acts, or

(b) required to leave the United Kingdom in accordance with a provision of the Immigration Acts.

(2) In this section "pending" has the meaning given by section 104.

(3) Nothing in this section shall prevent any of the following while an appeal is pending –

(a) the giving of a direction for the appellant's removal from the United Kingdom,

(b) the making of a deportation order in respect of the appellant (subject to section 79), or

(c) the taking of any other interim or preparatory action.

(4) This section applies only to an appeal brought while the appellant is in the United Kingdom in accordance with section 92.

****

82 Right of appeal: general

(1) Where an immigration decision is made in respect of a person he may appeal to the Tribunal.

(2) In this Part "immigration decision" means –

(a) refusal of leave to enter the United Kingdom,

(b) refusal of entry clearance,

(c) refusal of a certificate of entitlement under section 10 of this Act,

(d) refusal to vary a person's leave to enter or remain in the United Kingdom if the result of the refusal is that the person has no leave to enter or remain,

(e) variation of a person's leave to enter or remain in the United Kingdom if when the variation takes effect the person has no leave to enter or remain,

(f) revocation under section 76 of this Act of indefinite leave to enter or remain in the United Kingdom,

(g)   a decision that a person is to be removed from the United Kingdom by way of directions under section 10(1)(a), (b), (ba) or (c) of the Immigration and Asylum Act 1999 (c 33) (removal of person unlawfully in United Kingdom),

(h)   a decision that an illegal entrant is to be removed from the United Kingdom by way of directions under paragraphs 8 to 10 of Schedule 2 to the Immigration Act 1971 (c 77) (control of entry: removal),

(ha)   a decision that a person is to be removed from the United Kingdom by way of directions under section 47 of the Immigration, Asylum and Nationality Act 2006 (removal: persons with statutorily extended leave),

(i)   a decision that a person is to be removed from the United Kingdom by way of directions given by virtue of paragraph 10A of that Schedule (family),

(ia)   a decision that a person is to be removed from the United Kingdom by way of directions under paragraph 12(2) of Schedule 2 to the Immigration Act 1971 (c 77) (seamen and aircrews),

(ib)   a decision to make an order under section 2A of that Act (deprivation of right of abode),

(j)   a decision to make a deportation order under section 5(1) of that Act, and

(k)   refusal to revoke a deportation order under section 5(2) of that Act.

(3) *(repealed)*

(3A) Subsection (2)(j) does not apply to a decision to make a deportation order which states that it is made in accordance with section 32(5) of the UK Borders Act 2007; but –

(a)   a decision that section 32(5) applies is an immigration decision for the purposes of this Part, and

(b)   a reference in this Part to an appeal against an automatic deportation order is a reference to an appeal against a decision of the Secretary of State that section 32(5) applies.

(4) The right of appeal under subsection (1) is subject to the exceptions and limitations specified in this Part.

Amendments: Asylum and Immigration (Treatment of Claimants, etc) Act 2004, s 26(2); Immigration, Asylum and Nationality Act 2006, s 2.

****

84 Grounds of appeal

(1) An appeal under section 82(1) against an immigration decision must be brought on one or more of the following grounds –

(a)   that the decision is not in accordance with immigration rules;

(b)   that the decision is unlawful by virtue of Article 20A of the Race Relations (Northern Ireland) Order 1997 (discrimination by public authorities);

(c)   that the decision is unlawful under section 6 of the Human Rights Act 1998 (c 42) (public authority not to act contrary to Human Rights Convention) as being incompatible with the appellant's Convention rights;

(d)   that the appellant is an EEA national or a member of the family of an EEA national and the decision breaches the appellant's rights under the EU Treaties in respect of entry to or residence in the United Kingdom;

(e)   that the decision is otherwise not in accordance with the law;

(f)   that the person taking the decision should have exercised differently a discretion conferred by immigration rules;

(g)   that removal of the appellant from the United Kingdom in consequence of the immigration decision would breach the United Kingdom's obligations under the Refugee Convention or would be unlawful under section 6 of the Human Rights Act 1998 as being incompatible with the appellant's Convention rights.

(2) In subsection (1)(d) "EEA national" means a national of a State which is a contracting party to the Agreement on the European Economic Area signed at Oporto on 2nd May 1992 (as it has effect from time to time).

(3) An appeal under section 83 must be brought on the grounds that removal of the appellant from the United Kingdom would breach the United Kingdom's obligations under the Refugee Convention.

(4) An appeal under section 83A must be brought on the grounds that removal of the appellant from the United Kingdom would breach the United Kingdom's obligations under the Refugee Convention.

Amendments: SI 2001/1060.

****

Exceptions and limitations

88 Ineligibility

(1) This section applies to an immigration decision of a kind referred to in section 82(2)(a), (b), (d) or (e).

(2) A person may not appeal under section 82(1) against an immigration decision which is taken on the grounds that he or a person of whom he is a dependant –

(a)   does not satisfy a requirement as to age, nationality or citizenship specified in immigration rules,

(b)   does not have an immigration document of a particular kind (or any immigration document),

(ba)   has failed to supply a medical report or a medical certificate in accordance with a requirement of immigration rules,

(c)   is seeking to be in the United Kingdom for a period greater than that permitted in his case by immigration rules, or

(d)   is seeking to enter or remain in the United Kingdom for a purpose other than one for which entry or remaining is permitted in accordance with immigration rules.

(3) In subsection (2)(b) "immigration document" means –

(a)   entry clearance,
(b)   a passport,
(c)   a work permit or other immigration employment document within the meaning of section 122, and
(d)   a document which relates to a national of a country other than the United Kingdom and which is designed to serve the same purpose as a passport.

(4) Subsection (2) does not prevent the bringing of an appeal on any or all of the grounds referred to in section 84(1)(b), (c) and (g).

Amendments: Immigration, Asylum and Nationality Act 2006, s 5.

****

89 Refusal of leave to enter

(1) A person may not appeal under section 82(1) against refusal of leave to enter the United Kingdom unless –

(a)   on his arrival in the United Kingdom he had entry clearance, and
(b)   the purpose of entry specified in the entry clearance is the same as that specified in his application for leave to enter.

(2) Subsection (1) does not prevent the bringing of an appeal on any or all of the grounds referred to in section 84(1)(b), (c) and (g).

Amendments: Immigration, Asylum and Nationality Act 2006, s 6.

****

92 Appeal from within United Kingdom: general

(1) A person may not appeal under section 82(1) while he is in the United Kingdom unless his appeal is of a kind to which this section applies.

(2) This section applies to an appeal against an immigration decision of a kind specified in section 82(2)(c), (d), (e), (f), (ha) and (j).

(3) This section also applies to an appeal against refusal of leave to enter the United Kingdom if –

(a)   at the time of the refusal the appellant is in the United Kingdom, and
(b)   on his arrival in the United Kingdom the appellant had entry clearance.

(3A) But this section does not apply by virtue of subsection (3) if subsection (3B) or (3C) applies to the refusal of leave to enter.

(3B) This subsection applies to a refusal of leave to enter which is a deemed refusal under paragraph 2A(9) of Schedule 2 to the Immigration Act 1971 (c 77) resulting from cancellation of leave to enter by an immigration officer –

(a) under paragraph 2A(8) of that Schedule, and
(b) on the grounds specified in paragraph 2A(2A) of that Schedule.

(3C) This subsection applies to a refusal of leave to enter which specifies that the grounds for refusal are that the leave is sought for a purpose other than that specified in the entry clearance.

(3D) This section also applies to an appeal against refusal of leave to enter the United Kingdom if at the time of the refusal the appellant –

(a) is in the United Kingdom,
(b) has a work permit, and
(c) is any of the following (within the meaning of the British Nationality Act 1981 (c 61)) –
    (i)   a British overseas territories citizen,
    (ii) a British Overseas citizen,
    (iii) a British National (Overseas),
    (iv) a British protected person, or
    (v)   a British subject.

(4) This section also applies to an appeal against an immigration decision if the appellant –

(a) has made an asylum claim, or a human rights claim, while in the United Kingdom, or
(b) is an EEA national or a member of the family of an EEA national and makes a claim to the Secretary of State that the decision breaches the appellant's rights under the EU Treaties in respect of entry to or residence in the United Kingdom.

Amendments: Immigration, Asylum and Nationality Act 2006, s 47(7); Asylum and Immigration (Treatment of Claimants, etc) Act 2004, s 28.

****

104 Pending appeal

(1) An appeal under section 82(1) is pending during the period –

(a) beginning when it is instituted, and
(b) ending when it is finally determined, withdrawn or abandoned (or when it lapses under section 99).

(2) An appeal under section 82(1) is not finally determined for the purpose of subsection (1)(b) while –

(a) an application for permission to appeal under section 11 or 13 of the Tribunals, Courts and Enforcement Act 2007 could be made or is awaiting determination,

(b)   permission to appeal under either of those sections has been granted and the appeal is awaiting determination, or

(c)   an appeal has been remitted under section 12 or 14 of that Act and is awaiting determination.

(3) (*repealed*)

(4) An appeal under section 82(1) brought by a person while he is in the United Kingdom shall be treated as abandoned if the appellant leaves the United Kingdom.

(4A) An appeal under section 82(1) brought by a person while he is in the United Kingdom shall be treated as abandoned if the appellant is granted leave to enter or remain in the United Kingdom (subject to subsections (4B) and (4C)).

(4B) Subsection (4A) shall not apply to an appeal in so far as it is brought on the ground relating to the Refugee Convention specified in section 84(1)(g) where the appellant –

(a)   is granted leave to enter or remain in the United Kingdom for a period exceeding 12 months, and

(b)   gives notice, in accordance with Tribunal Procedure Rules, that he wishes to pursue the appeal in so far as it is brought on that ground.

(4C) Subsection (4A) shall not apply to an appeal in so far as it is brought on the ground specified in section 84(1)(b) where the appellant gives notice, in accordance with Tribunal Procedure Rules, that he wishes to pursue the appeal in so far as it is brought on that ground.

(5) An appeal under section 82(2)(a), (c), (d), (e) or (f) shall be treated as finally determined if a deportation order is made against the appellant.

Amendments: Asylum and Immigration (Treatment of Claimants, etc) Act 2004, ss 26(7), 47, Sch 2, Pt 1, paras 16, 20(b), Sch 4; Immigration, Asylum and Nationality Act 2006, s 9; SI 2010/21.

****

Appendix 16

IMMIGRATION (EUROPEAN ECONOMIC AREA) REGULATIONS 2006

SI 2006/1003

****

7 Family member

(1) Subject to paragraph (2), for the purposes of these Regulations the following persons shall be treated as the family members of another person –

    (a)   his spouse or his civil partner;

    (b)   direct descendants of his, his spouse or his civil partner who are –

        (i)   under 21; or

        (ii)   dependants of his, his spouse or his civil partner;

    (c)   dependent direct relatives in his ascending line or that of his spouse or his civil partner;

    (d)   a person who is to be treated as the family member of that other person under paragraph (3).

****

PART 2
EEA RIGHTS

11 Right of admission to the United Kingdom

(1) An EEA national must be admitted to the United Kingdom if he produces on arrival a valid national identity card or passport issued by an EEA State.

(2) A person who is not an EEA national must be admitted to the United Kingdom if he is a family member of an EEA national, a family member who has retained the right of residence, a person who meets the criteria in paragraph (5) or a person with a permanent right of residence under regulation 15 and produces on arrival –

    (a)   a valid passport; and

    (b)   an EEA family permit, a residence card, a derivative residence card or a permanent residence card.

(3) An immigration officer may not place a stamp in the passport of a person admitted to the United Kingdom under this regulation who is not an EEA national if the person produces a residence card, a derivative residence card or permanent residence card.

(4) Before an immigration officer refuses admission to the United Kingdom to a person under this regulation because the person does not produce on arrival a document mentioned in paragraph (1) or (2), the immigration officer must give the person every reasonable opportunity to obtain the document or have it brought to him within a reasonable period of time or to prove by other means that he is –

(a)   an EEA national;
(b)   a family member of an EEA national with a right to accompany that national or join him in the United Kingdom;
(ba) a person who meets the criteria in paragraph (5); or
(c)   a family member who has retained the right of residence or a person with a permanent right of residence under regulation 15.

(5) A person ('P') meets the criteria in this paragraph where –

(a)   P previously resided in the United Kingdom pursuant to regulation 15A(3) and would be entitled to reside in the United Kingdom pursuant to that regulation were P in the country;
(b)   P is accompanying an EEA national to, or joining an EEA national in, the United Kingdom and P would be entitled to reside in the United Kingdom pursuant to regulation 15A(2) were P and the EEA national both in the United Kingdom;
(c)   P is accompanying a person ('the relevant person') to, or joining the relevant person in, the United Kingdom and –
      (i)   the relevant person is residing, or has resided, in the United Kingdom pursuant to regulation 15A(3); and
      (ii)   P would be entitled to reside in the United Kingdom pursuant to regulation 15A(4) were P and the relevant person both in the United Kingdom.
(d)   P is accompanying a person who meets the criteria in (b) or (c) ('the relevant person') to the United Kingdom and –
      (i)   P and the relevant person are both –
             (aa) seeking admission to the United Kingdom in reliance on this paragraph for the first time; or
             (bb) returning to the United Kingdom having previously resided there pursuant to the same provisions of regulation 15A in reliance on which they now base their claim to admission; and
      (ii)   P would be entitled to reside in the United Kingdom pursuant to regulation 15A(5) were P and the relevant person there.

(6) Paragraph (7) applies where –

(a)   a person ('P') seeks admission to the United Kingdom in reliance on paragraph (5)(b) or (c); and
(b)   if P were in the United Kingdom, P would have a derived right of residence by virtue of regulation 15A(7)(b)(ii).

(7) Where this paragraph applies a person ('P') will only be regarded as meeting the criteria in paragraph (5)(b) or (c) where P –

(a)   is accompanying the person with whom P would on admission to the United Kingdom jointly share care responsibility for the purpose of regulation 15A(7)(b)(ii); or

(b)   has previously resided in the United Kingdom pursuant to regulation 15A(2) or (4) as a joint primary carer and seeks admission to the United Kingdom in order to reside there again on the same basis.

(8) But this regulation is subject to regulations 19(1) and (2).

Amendments: SI 2012/1547.

12 Issue of EEA family permit

(1) An entry clearance officer must issue an EEA family permit to a person who applies for one if the person is a family member of an EEA national and –

(a)   the EEA national –
    (i)   is residing in the UK in accordance with these Regulations; or
    (ii)   will be travelling to the United Kingdom within six months of the date of the application and will be an EEA national residing in the United Kingdom in accordance with these Regulations on arrival in the United Kingdom; and

(b)   the family member will be accompanying the EEA national to the United Kingdom or joining the EEA national there.

(1A) An entry clearance officer must issue an EEA family permit to a person who applies and provides proof that, at the time at which he first intends to use the EEA family permit, he –

(a)   would be entitled to be admitted to the United Kingdom by virtue of regulation 11(5); and

(b)   will (save in the case of a person who would be entitled to be admitted to the United Kingdom by virtue of regulation 11(5)(a)) be accompanying to, or joining in, the United Kingdom any person from whom his right to be admitted to the United Kingdom under regulation 11(5) will be derived.

(1B) An entry clearance officer must issue an EEA family permit to a family member who has retained the right of residence.

(2) An entry clearance officer may issue an EEA family permit to an extended family member of an EEA national who applies for one if –

(a)   the relevant EEA national satisfies the condition in paragraph (1)(a);

(b)   the extended family member wishes to accompany the relevant EEA national to the United Kingdom or to join him there; and

(c)   in all the circumstances, it appears to the entry clearance officer appropriate to issue the EEA family permit.

(3) Where an entry clearance officer receives an application under paragraph (2) he shall undertake an extensive examination of the personal circumstances

of the applicant and if he refuses the application shall give reasons justifying the refusal unless this is contrary to the interests of national security.

(4) An EEA family permit issued under this regulation shall be issued free of charge and as soon as possible.

(5) But an EEA family permit shall not be issued under this regulation if the applicant or the EEA national concerned is not entitled to be admitted to the United Kingdom as a result of regulation 19(1A) or falls to be excluded in accordance with regulation 19(1B).

(6) An EEA family permit will not be issued under this regulation to a person ('A') who is the spouse, civil partner or durable partner of a person ('B') where a spouse, civil partner or durable partner of A or B holds a valid EEA family permit.

Amendments: SI 2011/1247; SI 2012/1547.

****

15 Permanent right of residence

(1) The following persons shall acquire the right to reside in the United Kingdom permanently –

- (a) an EEA national who has resided in the United Kingdom in accordance with these Regulations for a continuous period of five years;
- (b) a family member of an EEA national who is not himself an EEA national but who has resided in the United Kingdom with the EEA national in accordance with these Regulations for a continuous period of five years;
- (c) a worker or self-employed person who has ceased activity;
- (d) the family member of a worker or self-employed person who has ceased activity;
- (e) a person who was the family member of a worker or self-employed person where –
  - (i) the worker or self-employed person has died;
  - (ii) the family member resided with him immediately before his death; and
  - (iii) the worker or self-employed person had resided continuously in the United Kingdom for at least the two years immediately before his death or the death was the result of an accident at work or an occupational disease;
- (f) a person who –
  - (i) has resided in the United Kingdom in accordance with these Regulations for a continuous period of five years; and
  - (ii) was, at the end of that period, a family member who has retained the right of residence.

(1A) Residence in the United Kingdom as a result of a derivative right of residence does not constitute residence for the purpose of this regulation.

(2) The right of permanent residence under this regulation shall be lost only through absence from the United Kingdom for a period exceeding two consecutive years.

(3) A person who satisfies the criteria in this regulation will not be entitled to a permanent right to reside in the United Kingdom where the Secretary of State has made a decision under regulation 19(3)(b), 20(1) or 20A(1)

Amendments: SI 2012/1547.

****

PART 6
APPEALS UNDER THESE REGULATIONS

25 Interpretation of Part 6

(1) In this Part—

'Asylum claim' has the meaning given in section 113(1) of the 2002 Act;
'Commission' has the same meaning as in the Special Immigration Appeals Commission Act 1997;
'Human rights claim' has the meaning given in section 113(1) of the 2002 Act.

(2) For the purposes of this Part, and subject to paragraphs (3) and (4), an appeal is to be treated as pending during the period when notice of appeal is given and ending when the appeal is finally determined, withdrawn or abandoned.

(3) An appeal is not to be treated as finally determined while a further appeal may be brought; and, if such a further appeal is brought, the original appeal is not to be treated as finally determined until the further appeal is determined, withdrawn or abandoned.

(4) A pending appeal is not to be treated as abandoned solely because the appellant leaves the United Kingdom.

Amendments: SI 2010/21; SI 2012/1547.

26 Appeal rights

(1) Subject to the following paragraphs of this regulation, a person may appeal under these Regulations against an EEA decision.

(2) If a person claims to be an EEA national, he may not appeal under these Regulations unless he produces a valid national identity card or passport issued by an EEA State.

(3) If a person claims to be a family member who has retained the right of residence or the family member or relative of an EEA national he may not appeal under these Regulations unless he produces –

(a) a valid national identity card issued by an EEA State or a passport; and

(b)   either –
    (i)   an EEA family permit;
    (ii)   proof that he is the family member or relative of an EEA national; or
    (iii) in the case of a person claiming to be a family member who has retained the right of residence, proof that he was a family member of the relevant person.

(3A) If a person claims to be a person with a derivative right of residence he may not appeal under these Regulations unless he produces a valid national identity card issued by an EEA State or a passport, and either –

(a)   an EEA family permit; or
(b)   proof that –
    (i)   where the person claims to have a derivative right of residence under regulation 15A(2), he is a direct relative or guardian of an EEA national who is under the age of 18;
    (ii)   where the person claims to have a derivative right of residence under regulation 15A(3), he is the child of an EEA national;
    (iii) where the person claims to have a derivative right of residence under regulation 15A(4), he is a direct relative or guardian of the child of an EEA national;
    (iv)   where the person claims to have a derivative right of residence under regulation 15A(5), he is under the age of 18 and is a dependant of a person satisfying the criteria in (i) or (iii).

(4) A person may not bring an appeal under these Regulations on a ground certified under paragraph (5) or rely on such a ground in an appeal brought under these Regulations.

(5) The Secretary of State or an immigration officer may certify a ground for the purposes of paragraph (4) if it has been considered in a previous appeal brought under these Regulations or under section 82(1) of the 2002 Act.

(6) Except where an appeal lies to the Commission, an appeal under these Regulations lies to the First-tier Tribunal.

(7) The provisions of or made under the 2002 Act referred to in Schedule 1 shall have effect for the purposes of an appeal under these Regulations to the First-tier Tribunal in accordance with that Schedule.

Amendments: SI 2012/1547; SI 2010/21.

27 Out of country appeals

(1) Subject to paragraphs (2) and (3), a person may not appeal under regulation 26 whilst he is in the United Kingdom against an EEA decision—

(a)   to refuse to admit him to the United Kingdom;
(aa)   to make an exclusion order against him;
(b)   to refuse to revoke a deportation or exclusion order made against him;
(c)   to refuse to issue him with an EEA family permit;

(ca) to revoke, or to refuse to issue or renew any document under these Regulations where that decision is taken at a time when the relevant person is outside the United Kingdom; or

(d) to remove him from the United Kingdom after he has entered the United Kingdom in breach of a deportation or exclusion order.

(2) Paragraphs (1)(a) and (aa) do not apply where the person is in the United Kingdom and –

(a) the person held a valid EEA family permit, registration certificate, residence card, derivative residence card, document certifying permanent residence or permanent residence card on his arrival in the United Kingdom or can otherwise prove that he is resident in the United Kingdom;

(b) the person is deemed not to have been admitted to the United Kingdom under regulation 22(3) but at the date on which notice of the decision to refuse to admit him is given he has been in the United Kingdom for at least 3 months; or

(c) has made an asylum or human rights claim (or both), unless the Secretary of State has certified that the claim or claims is or are clearly unfounded.

(3) Paragraph (1)(d) does not apply where the person has made an asylum or human rights claim (or both), unless the Secretary of State has certified that the claim or claims is or are clearly unfounded.

Amendments: SI 2009/1117; SI 2010/21; SI 2012/1547.

****

29 Effect of appeals to the First-tier Tribunal or Upper Tribunal

(1) This Regulation applies to appeals under these Regulations made to the First-tier Tribunal or Upper Tribunal.

(2) If a person in the United Kingdom appeals against an EEA decision to refuse to admit him to the United Kingdom, any directions for his removal from the United Kingdom previously given by virtue of the refusal cease to have effect, except in so far as they have already been carried out, and no directions may be so given while the appeal is pending.

(3) If a person in the United Kingdom appeals against an EEA decision to remove him from the United Kingdom, any directions given under section 10 of the 1999 Act or Schedule 3 to the 1971 Act for his removal from the United Kingdom are to have no effect, except in so far as they have already been carried out, while the appeal is pending.

(4) But the provisions of Part I of Schedule 2, or as the case may be, Schedule 3 to the 1971 Act with respect to detention and persons liable to detention apply to a person appealing against a refusal to admit him or a decision to remove him as if there were in force directions for his removal from

the United Kingdom, except that he may not be detained on board a ship or aircraft so as to compel him to leave the United Kingdom while the appeal is pending.

(5) In calculating the period of two months limited by paragraph 8(2) of Schedule 2 to the 1971 Act for –

(a)   the giving of directions under that paragraph for the removal of a person from the United Kingdom; and

(b)   the giving of a notice of intention to give such directions,

any period during which there is pending an appeal by him under is to be disregarded.

(6) If a person in the United Kingdom appeals against an EEA decision to remove him from the United Kingdom, a deportation order is not to be made against him under section 5 of the 1971 Act while the appeal is pending.

(7) Paragraph 29 of Schedule 2 to the 1971 Act (grant of bail pending appeal) applies to a person who has an appeal pending under these Regulations as it applies to a person who has an appeal pending under section 82(1) of the 2002 Act.

Amendments: SI 2010/21.

Schedule 1
Appeals to the First-tier Tribunal

Regulation 26(7)

1 The following provisions of, or made under, the 2002 Act have effect in relation to an appeal under these Regulations to the First-tier Tribunal as if it were an appeal against an immigration decision under section 82(1) of that Act:

section 84(1), except paragraphs (a) and (f);
sections 85 to 87;
section 105 and any regulations made under that section; and
section 106 and any rules made under that section.

2 Tribunal Procedure Rules have effect in relation to appeals under these Regulations.

Amendments: SI 2010/21.

****

Appendix 17

IMMIGRATION RULES

****

6 In these Rules the following interpretations apply:

****

'adoption' unless the contrary intention appears, includes a de facto adoption in accordance with the requirements of paragraph 309A of these Rules, and 'adopted' and 'adoptive parent' should be construed accordingly.

****

'public funds' means

    (a)   housing under Part VI or VII of the Housing Act 1996 and under Part II of the Housing Act 1985, Part I or II of the Housing (Scotland) Act 1987, Part II of the Housing (Northern Ireland) Order 1981 or Part II of the Housing (Northern Ireland) Order 1988;

    (b)   attendance allowance, severe disablement allowance, carer's allowance and disability living allowance under Part III of the Social Security Contribution and Benefits Act 1992; income support, council tax benefit and housing benefit under Part VII of that Act; a social fund payment under Part VIII of that Act; child benefit under Part IX of that Act; income based jobseeker's allowance under the Jobseekers Act 1995, income related allowance under Part 1 of the Welfare Reform Act 2007 (employment and support allowance) state pension credit under the State Pension Credit Act 2002; or child tax credit and working tax credit under Part 1 of the Tax Credits Act 2002.

    (c)   attendance allowance, severe disablement allowance, carer's allowance and disability living allowance under Part III of the Social Security Contribution and Benefits (Northern Ireland) Act 1992; income support, council tax benefit and, housing benefit under Part VII of that Act; a social fund payment under Part VIII of that Act; child benefit under Part IX of that Act; income based jobseeker's allowance under the Jobseekers (Northern Ireland) Order 1995 or income related allowance under Part 1 of the Welfare Reform Act (Northern Ireland) 2007.

'settled in the United Kingdom' means that the person concerned:

    (a)   is free from any restriction on the period for which he may remain save that a person entitled to an exemption under Section 8 of the Immigration Act 1971 (otherwise than as a member of the home forces) is not to be regarded as settled in the United Kingdom except in so far as Section 8(5A) so provides; and

(b)   is either:
   (i)   ordinarily resident in the United Kingdom without having entered or remained in breach of the immigration laws; or
   (ii)   despite having entered or remained in breach of the immigration laws, has subsequently entered lawfully or has been granted leave to remain and is ordinarily resident.

'a parent' includes

(a)   the stepfather of a child whose father is dead and the reference to stepfather includes a relationship arising through civil partnership;

(b)   the stepmother of a child whose mother is dead and the reference to stepmother includes a relationship arising through civil partnership and;

(c)   the father as well as the mother of an illegitimate child where he is proved to be the father;

(d)   an adoptive parent, where a child was adopted in accordance with a decision taken by the competent administrative authority or court in a country whose adoption orders are recognised by the United Kingdom or where a child is the subject of a de facto adoption in accordance with the requirements of paragraph 309A of these Rules (except that an adopted child or a child who is the subject of a de facto adoption may not make an application for leave to enter or remain in order to accompany, join or remain with an adoptive parent under paragraphs 297–303);

(e)   in the case of a child born in the United Kingdom who is not a British citizen, a person to whom there has been a genuine transfer of parental responsibility on the ground of the original parent(s)' inability to care for the child.

****

'present and settled' means that the person concerned is settled in the United Kingdom, and, at the time that an application under these Rules is made, is physically present here or is coming here with or to join the applicant and intends to make the United Kingdom their home with the applicant if their application is successful.

For the purposes of Appendix FM a member of HM Forces serving overseas, or a permanent member of HM Diplomatic Service, or a comparable UK-based staff member of the British Council on a tour of duty abroad, or a staff member of the Department for International Development or the Home Office, who is a British Citizen or settled in the UK, is to be regarded as present and settled in the UK.

****

'adequate' and 'adequately' in relation to a maintenance and accommodation requirement shall mean that, after income tax, national insurance contributions and housing costs have been deducted, there must be available to the family the level of income that would be available to them if the family was in receipt of income support.

'occupy exclusively' in relation to accommodation shall mean that part of the accommodation must be for the exclusive use of the family.

'must not be leading an independent life' means that the applicant does not have a partner as defined in Appendix FM; is living with their parents (except where they are at boarding school, college or university as part of their full-time education); is not employed full-time (unless aged 18 years or over); is wholly or mainly dependent upon their parents for financial support (unless aged 18 years or over); and is wholly or mainly dependent upon their parents for emotional support.

****

6A For the purpose of these Rules, a person (P) is not to be regarded as having (or potentially having) recourse to public funds merely because P is (or will be) reliant in whole or in part on public funds provided to P's sponsor unless, as a result of P's presence in the United Kingdom, the sponsor is (or would be) entitled to increased or additional public funds (save where such entitlement to increased or additional public funds is by virtue of P and the sponsor's joint entitlement to benefits under the regulations referred to in paragraph 6B).

6B Subject to paragraph 6C, a person (P) shall not be regarded as having recourse to public funds if P is entitled to benefits specified under section 115 of the Immigration and Asylum Act 1999 by virtue of regulations made under sub-sections (3) and (4) of that section or section 42 of the Tax Credits Act 2002.

6C A person (P) making an application from outside the United Kingdom will be regarded as having recourse to public funds where P relies upon the future entitlement to any public funds that would be payable to P or to P's sponsor as a result of P's presence in the United Kingdom, (including those benefits to which P or the sponsor would be entitled as a result of P's presence in the United Kingdom under the regulations referred to in to paragraph 6B).

'For the purposes of an application as a fiancé(e) or proposed civil partner under Appendix FM, an EEA national who holds a registration certificate or a document certifying permanent residence issued under the 2006 EEA Regulations (including an EEA national who holds a residence permit issued under the Immigration (European Economic Area) Regulations 2000 which is treated as if it were such a certificate or document by virtue of Schedule 4 to the 2006 EEA Regulations) is to be regarded as present and settled in the United Kingdom.'

****

PART 1
GENERAL PROVISIONS REGARDING LEAVE TO ENTER OR
REMAIN IN THE UNITED KINGDOM

****

27 An application for entry clearance is to be decided in the light of the circumstances existing at the time of the decision, except that an applicant will not be refused an entry clearance where entry is sought in one of the categories contained in paragraphs 296–316 or paragraph EC-C of Appendix FM solely on account of his attaining the age of 18 years between receipt of his application and the date of the decision on it.

****

Transitional provisions and interaction between Part 8, Appendix FM and Appendix FM-SE

PART 8
FAMILY MEMBERS

Transitional provisions and interaction between Part 8 and Appendix FM

A277 From 9 July 2012 Appendix FM will apply to all applications to which Part 8 of these rules applied on or before 8 July 2012 except where the provisions of Part 8 are preserved and continue to apply, as set out in paragraph A280.

A277A Where the Secretary of State is considering an application for indefinite leave to remain to which Part 8 of these rules continues to apply (excluding an application from a family member of a Relevant Points Based System Migrant), and where the applicant:

(a)   does not meet the requirements of Part 8 for indefinite leave to remain, and

(b)   continues to meet the requirements for limited leave to remain on which the applicant's last grant of limited leave to remain under Part 8 was based,

further limited leave to remain under Part 8 may be granted of such a period and subject to such conditions as the Secretary of State deems appropriate.

A277B Where the Secretary of State is considering an application for indefinite leave to remain to which Part 8 of these rules continues to apply (excluding an application from a family member of a Relevant Points Based System Migrant) and where the application does not meet the requirements of Part 8 for indefinite leave to remain or limited leave to remain:

(a)   the application will also be considered under paragraphs R-LTRP.1.1. (a), (b) and (d), R-LTRPT.1.1.(a), (b) and (d) and EX.1. of Appendix FM (family life) and paragraphs 276ADE to 276DH (private life) of these rules;

(b) if the applicant meets the requirements for leave under those paragraphs of Appendix FM or paragraphs 276ADE to 276DH (except the requirement for a valid application under that route), the applicant will be granted leave under those provisions; and

(c) if the applicant is granted leave under those provisions, the period of the applicant's continuous leave under Part 8 at the date of application will be counted towards the period of continuous leave which must be completed before the applicant can apply for indefinite leave to remain under those provisions.

A277C Subject to paragraphs A277 to A280 and paragraph GEN.1.9. of Appendix FM of these rules, where the Secretary of State is considering any application to which the provisions of Appendix FM (family life) and paragraphs 276ADE to 276DH (private life) of these rules do not already apply, she will also do so in line with those provisions.

A278 The requirements to be met under Part 8 after 9 July 2012 may be modified or supplemented by the requirements in Appendix FM and Appendix FM-SE.

A279 The requirements of sections 'S-EC: Suitability – entry clearance' and 'S-LTR: Suitability – leave to remain' of Appendix FM shall apply to all applications made under Part 8 and paragraphs 276A–276D; and paragraphs 398–399A shall apply to all immigration decisions made further to applications under Part 8 and paragraphs 276A–276D where a decision is made on or after 9 July 2012, irrespective of the date the application was made.

A280 The following provisions of Part 8 and Appendix FM apply in the manner and circumstances specified:

(a) The following paragraphs apply in respect of all applications made under Part 8, irrespective of the date of application or decision:

Paragraph number
277–280
289AA
295AA
296

(b) The following paragraphs of Part 8 continue to apply to all applications made on or after 9 July 2012. The paragraphs apply in their current form unless an additional requirement by reference to Appendix FM is specified:

Paragraph number	Additional requirement
295J	None
297–300	None
304–309	None
309A–316F	Where the applicant: • falls under paragraph 314(i)(a); or • falls under paragraph 316A(i)(d) or (e); and • is applying on or after 9 July 2012 the application must also meet the requirements of paragraphs E-ECC 2.1–2.3 (entry clearance applications) or E-LTRC 2.1–2.3 (leave to remain applications) of Appendix FM.

Paragraph number	Additional requirement
	Where the applicant: • falls under paragraph 314(i)(d); • is applying on or after 9 July 2012; and • has two parents or prospective parents and one of the applicant's parents or prospective parents does not have right of abode, indefinite leave to enter or remain, is not present and settled in the UK or being admitted for settlement on the same occasion as the applicant is seeking admission the application must also meet the requirements of paragraphs E-ECC 2.1–2.3 (entry clearance applications) or E-LTRC 2.1–2.3 (leave to remain applications) of Appendix FM.
319X	None

(c) The following provisions of Part 8 continue to apply on or after 9 July 2012, and are not subject to any additional requirement listed in (b) above:
  (i) to persons who have made an application before 9 July 2012 under Part 8 which was not decided as at 9 July 2012; and
  (ii) to applications made by persons who have been granted entry clearance or limited leave to enter or remain under Part 8 before 9 July 2012 and this leave to enter or limited leave to remain is extant:

281–289
289A–289C
290–295
295A–295O
297–316F
317–319

319L–319U
319V–319Y

(d) The following provisions of Part 8 continue to apply to applications made on or after 9 July 2012, and are not subject to any additional requirement listed in (b) above, by persons who have made an application for entry clearance, leave to enter or remain as the fiancé(e), proposed civil partner, spouse, civil partner, unmarried partner, same sex partner, or child or other dependant relative of a British citizen or settled person who is a full-time member of HM Forces:

281–289
289A–289C
290–295
295A–295O
297–316F
317–319

(e) The following provisions of Part 8 shall continue to apply to applications made on or after 9 July 2012, and are not subject to any additional requirement listed in (b) above, by a spouse, civil partner, unmarried partner or same sex partner who was admitted to the UK before 9 July 2012 further to paragraph 282(c) or 295B(c) of these Rules who has not yet applied for indefinite leave to remain:

284–286
287(a)(i)(c)
287(a)(ii)–(vii)
287(b)
288–289
289A–289C
295D–295F
295G(i)(c)
295G(ii)–(vii)

295H–295I

(f)   Paragraphs 301–303F continue to apply to applications made under this route on or after 9 July 2012, and are not subject to any additional requirement listed in (b) above, by a child of a person to whom those paragraphs relate who has been granted limited leave to enter or remain or an extension of stay following an application made before 9 July 2012,

(g)   For the avoidance of doubt, notwithstanding the introduction of Appendix FM, paragraphs 319AA–319J of Part 8 continue to apply, and are not subject to any additional requirement listed in paragraph (b) above, to applications for entry clearance or leave to enter or remain as the spouse, civil partner, unmarried partner, same sex partner, or child of a Relevant Points Based System Migrant.

Requirements for indefinite leave to enter the United Kingdom as the child of a parent, parents or a relative present and settled or being admitted for settlement in the United Kingdom

A281 In Part 8 "specified" means specified in Appendix FM-SE, unless otherwise stated, and "English language test provider approved by the Secretary of State" means a provider specified in Appendix O.

****

Children

297 The requirements to be met by a person seeking indefinite leave to enter the United Kingdom as the child of a parent, parents or a relative present and settled or being admitted for settlement in the United Kingdom are that he:

(i)   is seeking leave to enter to accompany or join a parent, parents or a relative in one of the following circumstances:

    (a)   both parents are present and settled in the United Kingdom; or

    (b)   both parents are being admitted on the same occasion for settlement; or

    (c)   one parent is present and settled in the United Kingdom and the other is being admitted on the same occasion for settlement; or

    (d)   one parent is present and settled in the United Kingdom or being admitted on the same occasion for settlement and the other parent is dead; or

    (e)   one parent is present and settled in the United Kingdom or being admitted on the same occasion for settlement and has had sole responsibility for the child's upbringing; or

    (f)   one parent or a relative is present and settled in the United Kingdom or being admitted on the same occasion for settlement and there are serious and compelling family or other considerations which make exclusion of the child undesirable and suitable arrangements have been made for the child's care; and

(ii)   is under the age of 18; and

(iii) is not leading an independent life, is unmarried and is not a civil partner, and has not formed an independent family unit; and

(iv)   can, and will, be accommodated adequately by the parent, parents or relative the child is seeking to join without recourse to public funds in accommodation which the parent, parents or relative the child is seeking to join, own or occupy exclusively; and

(v)   can, and will, be maintained adequately by the parent, parents, or relative the child is seeking to join, without recourse to public funds; and

(vi)   holds a valid United Kingdom entry clearance for entry in this capacity; and

(vii) does not have one or more unspent convictions within the meaning of the Rehabilitation of Offenders Act 1974.

****

Adopted children

309A For the purposes of adoption under paragraphs 310–316C a de facto adoption shall be regarded as having taken place if:

(a)   at the time immediately preceding the making of the application for entry clearance under these Rules the adoptive parent or parents have been living abroad (in applications involving two parents both must have lived abroad together) for at least a period of time equal to the first period mentioned in sub-paragraph (b)(i) and must have cared for the child for at least a period of time equal to the second period material in that sub-paragraph; and

(b)   during their time abroad, the adoptive parent or parents have:

   (i)   lived together for a minimum period of 18 months, of which the 12 months immediately preceding the application for entry clearance must have been spent living together with the child; and

   (ii)   have assumed the role of the child's parents, since the beginning of the 18 month period, so that there has been a genuine transfer of parental responsibility.

309B Inter-country adoptions which are not a de facto adoption under paragraph 309A are subject to the Adoption and Children Act 2002 and the Adoptions with a Foreign Element Regulations 2005. As such all prospective adopters must be assessed as suitable to adopt by a competent authority in the UK, and obtain a Certificate of Eligibility from the Department for Education, before travelling abroad to identify a child for adoption. This Certificate of Eligibility must be provided with all entry clearance adoption applications under paragraphs 310–316F.

Requirements for indefinite leave to enter the United Kingdom as the adopted child of a parent or parents present and settled or being admitted for settlement in the United Kingdom

310 The requirements to be met in the case of a child seeking indefinite leave to enter the United Kingdom as the adopted child of a parent or parents present and settled or being admitted for settlement in the United Kingdom are that he:

(i) is seeking leave to enter to accompany or join an adoptive parent or parents in one of the following circumstances;

    (a) both parents are present and settled in the United Kingdom; or

    (b) both parents are being admitted on the same occasion for settlement; or

    (c) one parent is present and settled in the United Kingdom and the other is being admitted on the same occasion for settlement; or

    (d) one parent is present and settled in the United Kingdom or being admitted on the same occasion for settlement and the other parent is dead; or

    (e) one parent is present and settled in the United Kingdom or being admitted on the same occasion for settlement and has had sole responsibility for the child's upbringing; or

    (f) one parent is present and settled in the United Kingdom or being admitted on the same occasion for settlement and there are serious and compelling family or other considerations which make exclusion of the child undesirable and suitable arrangements have been made for the child's care; or

    (g) in the case of a de facto adoption one parent has a right of abode in the United Kingdom or indefinite leave to enter or remain in the United Kingdom and is seeking admission to the United Kingdom on the same occasion for the purposes of settlement; and

(ii) is under the age of 18; and

(iii) is not leading an independent life, is unmarried and is not a civil partner, and has not formed an independent family unit; and

(iv) can, and will, be accommodated and maintained adequately without recourse to public funds in accommodation which the adoptive parent or parents own or occupy exclusively; and

(v) (*deleted*)

(vi) (a) was adopted in accordance with a decision taken by the competent administrative authority or court in his country of origin or the country in which he is resident, being a country whose adoption orders are recognised by the United Kingdom; or

    (b) is the subject of a de facto adoption; and

(vii) was adopted at a time when:

    (a) both adoptive parents were resident together abroad; or

    (b) either or both adoptive parents were settled in the United Kingdom; and

(viii) has the same rights and obligations as any other child of the adoptive parent's or parents' family; and

(ix) was adopted due to the inability of the original parent(s) or current carer(s) to care for him and there has been a genuine transfer of parental responsibility to the adoptive parents; and

(x)   has lost or broken his ties with his family of origin; and

(xi) was adopted, but the adoption is not one of convenience arranged to facilitate his admission to or remaining in the United Kingdom; and

(xii) holds a valid United Kingdom entry clearance for entry in this capacity; and

(xiii) does not have one or more unspent convictions within the meaning of the Rehabilitation of Offenders Act 1974.

Requirements for indefinite leave to remain in the United Kingdom as the adopted child of a parent or parents present and settled in the United Kingdom

311 The requirements to be met in the case of a child seeking indefinite leave to remain in the United Kingdom as the adopted child of a parent or parents present and settled in the United Kingdom are that he:

(i)   is seeking to remain with an adoptive parent or parents in one of the following circumstances:
  (a) both parents are present and settled in the United Kingdom; or
  (b) one parent is present and settled in the United Kingdom and the other parent is dead; or
  (c) one parent is present and settled in the United Kingdom and has had sole responsibility for the child's upbringing; or
  (d) one parent is present and settled in the United Kingdom and there are serious and compelling family or other considerations which make exclusion of the child undesirable and suitable arrangements have been made for the child's care; or
  (e) in the case of a de facto adoption one parent has a right of abode in the United Kingdom or indefinite leave to enter or remain in the United Kingdom and is seeking admission to the United Kingdom on the same occasion for the purpose of settlement; and

(ii) has limited leave to enter or remain in the United Kingdom, and
  (a) is under the age of 18; or
  (b) was given leave to enter or remain with a view to settlement under paragraph 315 or paragraph 316B; and

(iii) is not leading an independent life, is unmarried and is not a civil partner, and has not formed an independent family unit; and

(iv) can, and will, be accommodated and maintained adequately without recourse to public funds in accommodation which the adoptive parent or parents own or occupy exclusively; and

(v)   (*deleted*)

(vi) (a) was adopted in accordance with a decision taken by the competent administrative authority or court in his country of origin or the country in which he is resident, being a country whose adoption orders are recognised by the United Kingdom; or

(b)   is the subject of a de facto adoption; and

(vii)   was adopted at a time when:

(a)   both adoptive parents were resident together abroad; or

(b)   either or both adoptive parents were settled in the United Kingdom; and

(viii)   has the same rights and obligations as any other child of the adoptive parent's or parents' family; and

(ix)   was adopted due to the inability of the original parent(s) or current carer(s) to care for him and there has been a genuine transfer of parental responsibility to the adoptive parents; and

(x)   has lost or broken his ties with his family of origin; and

(xi)   was adopted, but the adoption is not one of convenience arranged to facilitate his admission to or remaining in the United Kingdom; and

(xii)   does not have one or more unspent convictions within the meaning of the Rehabilitation of Offenders Act 1974.

Indefinite leave to enter or remain in the United Kingdom as the adopted child of a parent or parents present and settled or being admitted for settlement in the United Kingdom

312 Indefinite leave to enter the United Kingdom as the adopted child of a parent or parents present and settled or being admitted for settlement in the United Kingdom may be granted provided a valid United Kingdom entry clearance for entry in this capacity is produced to the Immigration Officer on arrival. Indefinite leave to remain in the United Kingdom as the adopted child of a parent or parents present and settled in the United Kingdom may be granted provided the Secretary of State is satisfied that each of the requirements of paragraph 311 is met.

Refusal of indefinite leave to enter or remain in the United Kingdom as the adopted child of a parent or parents present and settled or being admitted for settlement in the United Kingdom

313 Indefinite leave to enter the United Kingdom as the adopted child of a parent or parents present and settled or being admitted for settlement in the United Kingdom is to be refused if a valid United Kingdom entry clearance for entry in this capacity is not produced to the Immigration Officer on arrival. Indefinite leave to remain in the United Kingdom as the adopted child of a parent or parents present and settled in the United Kingdom is to be refused if the Secretary of State is not satisfied that each of the requirements of paragraph 311 is met.

Requirements for limited leave to enter or remain in the United Kingdom with a view to settlement as the adopted child of a parent or parents given limited leave to enter or remain in the United Kingdom with a view to settlement

314 The requirements to be met in the case of a child seeking limited leave to enter or remain in the United Kingdom with a view to settlement as the

adopted child of a parent or parents given limited leave to enter or remain in the United Kingdom with a view to settlement are that he:

    (i)   is seeking leave to enter to accompany or join or remain with a parent or parents in one of the following circumstances:

        (a)   one parent is present and settled in the United Kingdom or being admitted on the same occasion for settlement and the other parent is being or has been given limited leave to enter or remain in the United Kingdom with a view to settlement; or

        (b)   one parent is being or has been given limited leave to enter or remain in the United Kingdom with a view to settlement and has had sole responsibility for the child's upbringing; or

        (c)   one parent is being or has been given limited leave to enter or remain in the United Kingdom with a view to settlement and there are serious and compelling family or other considerations which make exclusion of the child undesirable and suitable arrangements have been made for the child's care; or

        (d)   in the case of a de facto adoption one parent has a right of abode in the United Kingdom or indefinite leave to enter or remain in the United Kingdom and is seeking admission to the United Kingdom on the same occasion for the purpose of settlement; and

    (ii)   is under the age of 18; and

    (iii) is not leading an independent life, is unmarried and is not a civil partner, and has not formed an independent family unit; and

    (iv) can, and will, be accommodated and maintained adequately without recourse to public funds in accommodation which the adoptive parent or parents own or occupy exclusively; and

    (v)   (a) was adopted in accordance with a decision taken by the competent administrative authority or court in his country of origin or the country in which he is resident, being a country whose adoption orders are recognised by the United Kingdom; or

        (b)   is the subject of a de facto adoption; and

    (vi) was adopted at a time when:

        (a)   both adoptive parents were resident together abroad; or

        (b)   either or both adoptive parents were settled in the United Kingdom; and

    (vii) has the same rights and obligations as any other child of the adoptive parent's or parents' family; and

    (viii) was adopted due to the inability of the original parent(s) or current carer(s) to care for him and there has been a genuine transfer of parental responsibility to the adoptive parents; and

    (ix) has lost or broken his ties with his family of origin; and

    (x)   was adopted, but the adoption is not one of convenience arranged to facilitate his admission to the United Kingdom; and

    (xi) (where an application is made for limited leave to remain with a view to settlement) has limited leave to enter or remain in the United Kingdom; and

(xii) if seeking leave to enter, holds a valid United Kingdom entry clearance for entry in this capacity.

Limited leave to enter or remain in the United Kingdom with a view to settlement as the adopted child of a parent or parents given limited leave to enter or remain in the United Kingdom with a view to settlement

315 A person seeking limited leave to enter the United Kingdom with a view to settlement as the adopted child of a parent or parents given limited leave to enter or remain in the United Kingdom with a view to settlement may be admitted for a period not exceeding 12 months provided he is able, on arrival, to produce to the Immigration Officer a valid United Kingdom entry clearance for entry in this capacity. A person seeking limited leave to remain in the United Kingdom with a view to settlement as the adopted child of a parent or parents given limited leave to enter or remain in the United Kingdom with a view to settlement may be granted limited leave for a period not exceeding 12 months provided the Secretary of State is satisfied that each of the requirements of paragraph 314 (i)–(xi) is met.

Refusal of limited leave to enter or remain in the United Kingdom with a view to settlement as the adopted child of a parent or parents given limited leave to enter or remain in the United Kingdom with a view to settlement

316 Limited leave to enter the United Kingdom with a view to settlement as the adopted child of a parent or parents given limited leave to enter or remain in the United Kingdom with a view to settlement is to be refused if a valid United Kingdom entry clearance for entry in this capacity is not produced to the Immigration Officer on arrival. Limited leave to remain in the United Kingdom with a view to settlement as the adopted child of a parent or parents given limited leave to enter or remain in the United Kingdom with a view to settlement is to be refused if the Secretary of State is not satisfied that each of the requirements of paragraph 314 (i)–(xi) is met.

Requirements for limited leave to enter the United Kingdom with a view to settlement as a child for adoption

316A The requirements to be satisfied in the case of a child seeking limited leave to enter the United Kingdom for the purpose of being adopted (which, for the avoidance of doubt, does not include a de facto adoption) in the United Kingdom are that he:

(i)   is seeking limited leave to enter to accompany or join a person or persons who wish to adopt him in the United Kingdom (the 'prospective parent(s)'), in one of the following circumstances:
  (a) both prospective parents are present and settled in the United Kingdom; or
  (b) both prospective parents are being admitted for settlement on the same occasion that the child is seeking admission; or

(c)   one prospective parent is present and settled in the United Kingdom and the other is being admitted for settlement on the same occasion that the child is seeking admission; or

(d)   one prospective parent is present and settled in the United Kingdom and the other is being given limited leave to enter or remain in the United Kingdom with a view to settlement on the same occasion that the child is seeking admission, or has previously been given such leave; or

(e)   one prospective parent is being admitted for settlement on the same occasion that the other is being granted limited leave to enter with a view to settlement, which is also on the same occasion that the child is seeking admission; or

(f)   one prospective parent is present and settled in the United Kingdom or is being admitted for settlement on the same occasion that the child is seeking admission, and has had sole responsibility for the child's upbringing; or

(g)   one prospective parent is present and settled in the United Kingdom or is being admitted for settlement on the same occasion that the child is seeking admission, and there are serious and compelling family or other considerations which would make the child's exclusion undesirable, and suitable arrangements have been made for the child's care; and

(ii)   is under the age of 18; and

(iii) is not leading an independent life, is unmarried and is not a civil partner, and has not formed an independent family unit; and

(iv)   can, and will, be maintained and accommodated adequately without recourse to public funds in accommodation which the prospective parent or parents own or occupy exclusively; and

(v)   will have the same rights and obligations as any other child of the marriage or civil partnership; and

(vi)   is being adopted due to the inability of the original parent(s) or current carer(s) (or those looking after him immediately prior to him being physically transferred to his prospective parent or parents) to care for him, and there has been a genuine transfer of parental responsibility to the prospective parent or parents; and

(vii) has lost or broken or intends to lose or break his ties with his family of origin; and

(viii) will be adopted in the United Kingdom by his prospective parent or parents in accordance with the law relating to adoption in the United Kingdom, but the proposed adoption is not one of convenience arranged to facilitate his admission to the United Kingdom.

Limited leave to enter the United Kingdom with a view to settlement as a child for adoption

316B A person seeking limited leave to enter the United Kingdom with a view to settlement as a child for adoption may be admitted for a period not exceeding 24 months provided he is able, on arrival, to produce to the Immigration Officer a valid United Kingdom entry clearance for entry in this capacity.

Refusal of limited leave to enter the United Kingdom with a view to settlement as a child for adoption

316C Limited leave to enter the United Kingdom with a view to settlement as a child for adoption is to be refused if a valid United Kingdom entry clearance for entry in this capacity is not produced to the Immigration Officer on arrival.

Requirements for limited leave to enter the United Kingdom with a view to settlement as a child for adoption under the Hague Convention

316D The requirements to be satisfied in the case of a child seeking limited leave to enter the United Kingdom for the purpose of being adopted in the United Kingdom under the Hague Convention are that he:

(i)   is seeking limited leave to enter to accompany one or two people each of whom are habitually resident in the United Kingdom and who wish to adopt him under the Hague Convention ('the prospective parents');
(ii)   is the subject of an agreement made under Article 17(c) of the Hague Convention; and
(iii)   has been entrusted to the prospective parents by the competent administrative authority of the country from which he is coming to the United Kingdom for adoption under the Hague Convention; and
(iv)   is under the age of 18; and
(v)   can, and will, be maintained and accommodated adequately without recourse to public funds in accommodation which the prospective parent or parents own or occupy exclusively; and
(vi)   holds a valid United Kingdom entry clearance for entry in this capacity.

Limited leave to enter the United Kingdom with a view to settlement as a child for adoption under the Hague Convention

316E A person seeking limited leave to enter the United Kingdom with a view to settlement as a child for adoption under the Hague Convention may be admitted for a period not exceeding 24 months provided he is able, on arrival, to produce to the Immigration Officer a valid United Kingdom entry clearance for entry in this capacity.

Refusal of limited leave to enter the United Kingdom with a view to settlement as a child for adoption under the Hague Convention

316F Limited leave to enter the United Kingdom with a view to settlement as a child for adoption under the Hague Convention is to be refused if a valid United Kingdom entry clearance for entry in this capacity is not produced to the Immigration Officer on arrival.

****

FAMILY LIFE AS A CHILD OF A PARENT WITH LIMITED LEAVE AS A PARTNER OR PARENT

****

Financial requirement

E-ECC.2.1 The applicant must provide specified evidence, from the sources listed in paragraph E-ECC.2.2, of –

(a) a specified gross annual income of at least –
  (i) £18,600;
  (ii) an additional £3,800 for the first child; and
  (iii) an additional £2,400 for each additional child; alone or in combination with
(b) specified savings of
  (i) £16,000; and
  (ii) additional savings of an amount equivalent to 2.5 times the amount which is the difference between the gross annual income from the sources listed in paragraph E-ECC.2.2(a)–(f) and the total amount required under paragraph E-ECC.2.1(a); or
(c) the requirements in paragraph E-ECC.2.3 being met.

In this paragraph 'child' means the applicant and any other dependent child of the applicant's parent who is –

(a) under the age of 18 years, or who was under the age of 18 years when they were first granted entry under this route;
(b) in the UK;
(c) not a British Citizen or settled in the UK; and
(d) not an EEA national with a right to remain in the UK under the Immigration (EEA) Regulations 2006.

E-ECC.2.2 When determining whether the financial requirement in paragraph EECC.2.1 is met only the following sources may be taken into account –

(a) income of the applicant's parent's partner from specified employment or self-employment; which, in respect of an applicant's parent's partner returning to the UK with the applicant, can include specified employment or self-employment overseas and in the UK;
(b) income of the applicant's parent from specified employment or self-employment if they are in the UK unless they are working illegally;
(c) specified pension income of the applicant's parent and that parent's partner;
(d) any specified maternity allowance or bereavement benefit received by the applicant's parent and that parent's partner in the UK;
(e) other specified income of the applicant's parent and that parent's partner;
(f) income from the sources at (b), (d) or (e) of a dependent child of the applicant's parent under paragraph E-ECC.2.1 who is aged 18 years or over; and

(g) *specified savings of the applicant's parent, that parent's partner and a dependent child of the applicant's parent under paragraph E-ECC.2.1 who is aged 18 years or over.*

E-ECC.2.3 The requirements to be met under this paragraph are –

(a) *the applicant's parent's partner must be receiving one or more of the following –*
   (i) *disability living allowance;*
   (ii) *severe disablement allowance;*
   (iii) *industrial injury disablement benefit;*
   (iv) *attendance allowance; or*
   (v) *carer's allowance; and*

(b) *the applicant must provide evidence that their parent's partner is able to maintain and accommodate themselves, the applicant's parent, the applicant and any dependants adequately in the UK without recourse to public funds.*

****

Financial requirements

E-LTRC.2.1 The applicant must provide specified evidence, from the sources listed in paragraph E-LTRC.2.2, of –

(a) *a specified gross annual income of at least –*
   (i) *£18,600;*
   (ii) *an additional £3,800 for the first child; and*
   (iii) *an additional £2,400 for each additional child; alone or in combination with*

(b) *specified savings of –*
   (i) *£16,000; and*
   (ii) *additional savings of an amount equivalent to 2.5 times (or if the parent is applying for indefinite leave to remain 1 times) the amount which is the difference between the gross annual income from the sources listed in paragraph E-LTRC.2.2(a)–(f) and the total amount required under paragraph E-LTRC.2.1(a); or*

(c) *the requirements in paragraph E-LTRC.2.3 being met.*

In this paragraph 'child' means the applicant and any other dependent child of the applicant's parent who is –
   (i) *under the age of 18 years, or who was under the age of 18 years when they were first granted entry under this route;*
   (ii) *in the UK;*
   (iii) *not a British Citizen or settled in the UK; and*
   (iv) *not an EEA national with a right to remain in the UK under the Immigration (EEA) Regulations 2006.*

E-LTRC.2.2 When determining whether the financial requirement in paragraph E-LTRC.2.1 is met only the following sources may be taken into account –

(a) income of the applicant's parent's partner from specified employment or self-employment;

(b) income of the applicant's parent from specified employment or self-employment;

(c) specified pension income of the applicant's parent and that parent's partner;

(d) any specified maternity allowance or bereavement benefit received by the applicant's parent and that parent's partner;

(e) other specified income of the applicant's parent and that parent's partner in the UK;

(f) income from the sources at (b), (d) or (e) of a dependent child of the applicant's parent under paragraph E-LTRC.2.1 who is aged 18 years or over; and

(g) specified savings of the applicant's parent, that parent's partner and a dependent child of the applicant's parent under paragraph E-ECC.2.1 who is aged 18 years or over.

E-LTRC.2.3 The requirements to be met under this paragraph are –

(a) the applicant's parent's partner must be receiving one or more of the following –

    (i)   disability living allowance;

    (ii)   severe disablement allowance;

    (iii) industrial injury disablement benefit;

    (iv)   attendance allowance; or

    (v)   carer's allowance; and

(b) the applicant must provide evidence that their parent's partner is able to maintain and accommodate themselves, the applicant's parent, the applicant and any dependants adequately in the UK without recourse to public funds.

E-LTRC.2.4 The applicant must provide evidence that there will be adequate accommodation in the UK, without recourse to public funds, for the family, including other family members who are not included in the application but who live in the same household, which the family own or occupy exclusively; accommodation will not be regarded as adequate if –

(a) it is, or will be, overcrowded; or

(b) it contravenes public health regulations.

****

Appendix 18

FORMS

Application for a
Convention adoption order
Section 46 Adoption and
Children Act 2002

Name of court	
Case no./Serial no.	
Date received by the court	
Date issued	

Notes to applicants

- This form should only be used if you wish to apply for a Convention adoption order.
- You shall need to complete Form A61 (Application for parental responsibility prior to adoption abroad) if you intend to adopt a child who is habitually resident in the United Kingdom (or who is a Commonwealth citizen) in a place outside of the British Islands (and provided you do not already have an order to remove the child under the Adoption (Scotland) Act 1978 or the Adoption (Northern Ireland) Order 1987), even if you will be applying for a Convention adoption order in a place outside the British Islands.
- Before filling in this form, please read the guidance notes on completing the form.
- Please complete every Part. If you are not sure of the answer to any question, or you do not think that it applies to you, please say so.
- If there is not enough room on the form for your reply, you may continue on a separate sheet. Please put the child's full name, the number of the Part and the paragraph reference at the head of the continuation sheet.
- Please use black ink when filling in the form.

I/We the undersigned _____

(and _____)

wish to adopt _____ ◄ See Note 1

and give the following details in support of my/our application

I/We want my/our identity to be kept confidential and
wish to apply for a serial number   ☐ Yes   ☐ No   ◄ See Note 2

Part 1 About you

First applicant

a) Title

☐ Mr   ☐ Mrs   ☐ Miss

☐ Ms   ☐ Other _____

b) My name is

First name(s) in full

Last name

Second applicant

a) Title

☐ Mr   ☐ Mrs   ☐ Miss

☐ Ms   ☐ Other _____

b) My name is   ◄ See Note 3

First name(s) in full

Last name

c) My address is (including postcode)   c) My address is (including postcode)

d) My telephone number is   d) My telephone number is

e) My date of birth is   e) My date of birth is

f) My nationality is   f) My nationality is

Habitual Residence   ◀ See Note 4

Please indicate whether the United Kingdom is the receiving State or State of origin by ticking the relevant box and the statement that applies to you (or both of you):

☐ The United Kingdom is the receiving State and [I (in the case of an application by one person)][both of us] have been habitually resident in a part of the British Islands for a period of not less than one year ending with the date of the application.

☐ The United Kingdom is the State of origin and [I am (in the case of an application by one person)][both of us are] habitually resident in a Convention country outside the British Islands on the date of the application.

Note: If the United Kingdom is the receiving State and you are (or if you are applying as a couple, either of you is) not a British citizen, please complete the following statement. Otherwise delete the following statement:

The First Applicant/the Second Applicant is not a British citizen, but the Home Office has confirmed that the child is authorised to enter and reside permanently in the United Kingdom. Evidence of the authorisation from the Home Office is attached.

g) My occupation is   g) My occupation is   ◀ See Note 5

h) I am   h) I am
   ☐ Male   ☐ Female   ☐ Male   ☐ Female

i) My relationship to the child is   i) My relationship to the child is   ◀ See Note 6

j) My/Our solicitor in these proceedings is

Name of solicitor	
Name of firm	
Address (including postcode)	

Telephone no.		Fax no.	
DX no.			
E-mail address			

Status

If you are applying to adopt as a couple, please go straight to **Part 2 About the Child.** Paragraphs (k) to (p) do not apply to you

If you are applying to adopt alone, please tick the box at (k) to (p) below that applies to your circumstances. **If you tick (k), (l) or (p), please give the additional information asked for.**

k) ☐ I am the partner of the child's

   ☐ Father   ☐ Mother

If you have ticked box (k), please go straight to Part 2 About the Child. Paragraphs (l) to (p) do not apply to you.

◄ See Note 7

l) ☐ I am the partner (not the spouse or civil partner) of a person who is not the child's parent and I am applying to adopt alone because:

If you have ticked box (l), please go straight to Part 2 About the Child. Paragraphs (m) to (p) do not apply to you.

◄ See Note 8

(please give reasons below, continuing on a separate sheet if necessary)

m) ☐ I am not married/I do not have a civil partner

◄ See Note 9

or

n) ☐ I am divorced/my civil partnership has been dissolved

◄ See Note 9

or

o) ☐ I am a widow/a widower/a surviving civil partner

◄ See Note 9

or

p) ☐ I am married/I have a civil partner, and I can satisfy the court that:

◄ See Note 10

   ☐ my husband/wife/civil partner cannot be found

      or

   ☐ I have separated from my husband/wife/civil partner, we are living apart and the separation is likely to be permanent

      or

   ☐ my husband/wife/civil partner is not capable of making an application due to ill-health

Part 2 About the child

a) The child is a

☐Boy   ☐Girl

b) The child was born on

```
[ ][ ][ ][ ][ ][ ]
```

and is the person to whom the attached certified copy of the child's orginial birth certificate, or other evidence attached regarding the child's identity relates.

or To the best of my/our knowledge the child was born on or about   ◀ See Note 11

```
[ ][ ][ ][ ][ ][ ][ ]
```

in (give place and country of birth)

c) The child's nationality is

d) I/we confirm that the child is not and has never been married or a civil partner   ◀ See Note 12

☐Yes   ☐No

e) The child has had his/her home with me/us continuously since

```
[ ][ ][ ][ ][ ][ ][ ]
```

Habitual Residence

Please indicate whether the United Kingdom is the receiving State or the State of origin by ticking the relevant box and the statement that applies to the child:

☐ The United Kingdom is the receiving State and the child to be adopted was, on the date on which the Article 17(c) agreement was made, habitually resident in a Convention country outside the British Islands.

☐ The United Kingdom is the State of origin and the child to be adopted was, on the date on which the agreement under Article 17(c) was made, habitually resident in a part of the British Islands.

f) The child was placed with me/us for adoption by an adoption agency

☐Yes (If you ticked this box, please complete paragraphs (g) and (h) and then go straight to paragraph (j). Paragraph (i) does not apply to you.)

☐No (If you ticked this box, please go straight to paragraph (i). Paragraphs (g) and (h) do not apply to you.)

g) The child was placed with me/us for adoption on

```
[ ][ ][ ][ ][ ][ ][ ]
```
by

Name of adoption agency	
Address (including post code)	
Name of your contact in the agency	
Telephone no.	

h) ☐   No other adoption agency has been involved in placing the child

   or

   ☐   The following adoption agency has also been involved in placing the child

Name of adoption agency	
Address (including post code)	
Name of your contact in the agency	
Telephone no.	

i)   I/we have notified in writing my/our local authority of my/our intention to apply for an adoption order (give details)   ◀ See Note 13

Name of local authority	
Address (including post code)	
Date notified	
Name of your contact in the local authority	
Telephone no.	

Care

j) ☐   No local authority or voluntary organisation has parental responsibility for the child

   or

   ☐   The following local authority/voluntary organisation has parental responsibility for the child:

Name of local authority or voluntary organisation	
Address (including post code)	
Name of your contact in the authority/organisation	
Telephone no.	

Maintenance

k) ☐ No maintenance order/agreement or award of child support maintenance under the
      Child Support Act 1991 has been made in respect of the child

   or

   ☐ The following maintenance order/agreement/award of child support maintenance   ◀ See Note 14
      has been made

Person liable to pay maintenance	
Address (including post code)	

Court and date of order	
Date of maintenance agreement/child support maintenance award	

About other orders or proceedings that affect the child

l) ☐ To the best of my/our knowledge, no proceedings relating to the child (other than
      any maintenance order given above) have been completed or commenced in any
      court, whether in the United Kingdom or elsewhere

   or

   ☐ The following proceedings relating to the child have been completed/commenced   ◀ See Note 15
      (in addition to any maintenance order given above)

Type of order made (or applied for)	Date of order (or date of next hearing)	Name of court (and country if not in the UK)	Case number (or serial number)

Cases concerning a related child

m)☐ To the best of my knowledge, no proceedings relating to a full, half or step brother or
      sister of the child have been completed or commenced in any court, whether in the
      United Kingdom or elsewhere

   or

   ☐ The following proceedings relating to a full, half or step brother or sister of the child
      have been completed/commenced (please give details below and, if you were a
      party to any proceedings that have been completed, attach a copy of the final order)

Relationship to child (eg. sister, half-brother)	Type of order made (or applied for)	Date of order (or date of next hearing)	Name of court (and country if not in the UK)	Case number (or serial number)

Part 3 About the child's parents or guardian

The child's mother | **The child's father**

See Note 16

a) The name of the child's mother is

First name(s) in full

Last name

b) Her address is (if deceased, please write 'Deceased' in the address box)

c) Her nationality is

d) The name of the child's father is

First name(s) in full

Last name

e) His address is (if deceased, please write 'Deceased' in the address box)

f) His nationality is

g) Does he have parental responsibility for the child?

See Note 17

☐ Yes   ☐ No

If No, does he intend to apply for an order under section 4(1)(c) of the Children Act 1989 (a parental responsibility order) or a residence or contact order in respect of the child?

☐ Yes   ☐ No

The child's guardian

h) The name of the child's guardian is

First name(s) in full

Last name

i) His/Her address is

See Note 18

Parent/guardian consent to adoption

See Note 19

The child's parent(s)/guardians has/have consented to a Convention adoption order being made.

Part 4 General

Child's name on adoption

◀ See Note 20

If the adoption order is made, I/We want the
child to be known as

First name(s) in full

Last name

Declarations

I/We have not received or given payment or reward in respect of the proposed adoption
(except as follows:) (give details below)

To the best of my/our knowledge, only the person(s) or organisation(s) named in Part 2 of
this application have taken part in the arrangements for the child's adoption.

Part 5 Statement of truth

Proceedings for contempt of court may be brought against a person who makes or causes
to be made, a false statement in a document verified by a statement of truth.

I believe that the facts stated in this
application are true.

I believe that the facts stated in this
application are true.

Signature of first applicant

Signature of second applicant

Print full name

Print full name

Signed

Signed

Date

Date

If you attend the court for a hearing

1. Do you/either of you have a disability for which you require special assistance or special facilities?   ◄ See Note 21

    ☐ Yes   ☐ No

If Yes, please say what your needs are below
(the court staff will get in touch with you about your requirements)

2. Do you/either of you want to use the services of an interpreter?

    ☐ Yes   ☐ No

If Yes, please specify which language
(court staff will get in touch with you about your requirements)

3. Are there any dates on which you know you will not be able to attend the court, or any particular dates that would especially suit you? If so, please give details below

Unavailable dates	Preferred dates

(Please note that, although the court will try to fit in with your preferences, it may not be always be possible to do so)

What to do now

Once you have completed and signed this form, you should take or send the form and three copies to the court, together with the court fee* and the following documents:

- where the UK is the State of origin, a certified copy of the full entry in the Register of Live Births that relates to the child or, where the child has been adopted, a certified copy of the entry in the Adopted Children Register;

- where the UK is the receiving State, a certified copy of the child's original birth certificate, any abandonment certificate/declaration, or where the child has been adopted, a certified copy of the entry in the register of adoptions as recognised in the State of origin or a certified copy of the adoption certificate;

- if you were a party to the proceedings, a copy of any final order relating to the child that has effect and, if possible, a copy of any maintenance agreement or maintenance award relating to the child;

- if you were a party to the proceedings, a copy of any final order relating to a full, half or step brother or sister of the child that has effect;

- where a parent of the child has died, a certified copy of the entry in the Register of Deaths;

- if you are submitting evidence of marriage or civil partnership, a certified copy of the entry in the Register of Marriages or the Register of Civil Partnerships;

- where your husband, wife or civil partner has died, a certified copy of the entry in the Register of Deaths;

- a copy of any decree absolute of divorce or decree of nullity of your marriage;

- in relation to a civil partnership, a copy of any dissolution order or nullity order of your civil partnership;

- any documentary evidence supporting the reasons why you are applying to adopt the child without your husband, wife or civil partner, such as a decree of judicial separation;

- where the UK is the receiving State and the applicant (or in the case of a couple, either or both of the applicants) is not a British citizen, the child's passport containing confirmation the Home Office authorisation for the child to enter and reside permanently in the United Kingdom;

- if your name as entered on the application form is different from the name shown on any evidence of marriage or civil partnership you are sending with your application, any documentary evidence to explain the difference.

*If you are not sure about the court fee payable for your application, or think that you may be exempt from paying all or part of the fee, you should contact the court for information.

Click here to print form

Click here to reset form	Click here to print form

Name of court	

Application for an adoption order (excluding a Convention adoption order) where the child is habitually resident outside the British Islands and is brought into the United Kingdom for the purposes of adoption

Case no./Serial no.	
Date received by the court	
Date issued	

Section 46 Adoption and Children Act 2002

Notes to applicants
This form can be used where:

- a child who is habitually resident outside the British Islands is brought into the United Kingdom for the purpose of adoption by a British resident; or

- a child adopted by a British resident under the law of any country or territory outside the British Islands is brought into the United Kingdom and the British resident wants to apply for an adoption order, and the application is not for a Convention adoption order.

However, you will need to complete Form A61 (Application for parental responsibility prior to adoption abroad) if you intend to adopt a child who is habitually resident in the United Kingdom (or who is a Commonwealth citizen) in a place outside of the British Islands (and provided you do not already have an order to remove the child under the Adoption and Children (Scotland) Act 2007 and the Adoption (Scotland) Act 1978 or the Adoption (Northern Ireland) Order 1987).

Before filling in this form, please read the guidance notes on completing the form.

Please complete every Part. If you are not sure of the answer to any question, or you do not think that it applies to you, please say so.

If there is not enough room on the form for your reply, you may continue on a separate sheet. Please put the child's full name, the number of the Part and the paragraph reference at the head of the continuation sheet.

Please use black ink when filling in the form.

I/We the undersigned _____

(and _____)

wish to adopt _____ ◄ See Note 1

and give the following details in support of my/our application

---

I/We want my/our identity to be kept confidential and
wish to apply for a serial number   ☐ Yes   ☐ No   ◄ See Note 2

Part 1 About you

First applicant

a) Title

☐ Mr   ☐ Mrs   ☐ Miss

☐ Ms   ☐ Other _____

b) My name is

First name(s) in full

Last name

c) My address is (including postcode)

d) My telephone number is

e) My date of birth is

f) My nationality is

g) My occupation is

h) I am

☐ Male   ☐ Female

i) My relationship to the child is

Second applicant

a) Title

☐ Mr   ☐ Mrs   ☐ Miss

☐ Ms   ☐ Other _____

b) My name is   ◄ See Note 3

First name(s) in full

Last name

c) My address is (including postcode)

d) My telephone number is

e) My date of birth is

f) My nationality is

g) My occupation is   ◄ See Note 4

h) I am

☐ Male   ☐ Female

i) My relationship to the child is   ◄ See Note 5

j) My/Our solicitor in these proceedings is

Name of solicitor	
Name of firm	
Address (including postcode)	

Telephone no.		Fax no.	
DX no.			
E-mail address			

Domicile and habitual residence

◀ See Note 6

k) ☐ I am/We are/One of us, namely _____

is domiciled in a part of the British Islands.

or

☐ I have/We have both been habitually resident in a part of the British Islands for a period of at least one year, ending with the date of this application.

Status

If you are applying to adopt as a couple, please go straight to **Part 2 About the Child.** Paragraphs (l) to (r) do not apply to you

If you are applying to adopt alone, please tick the box at (l) to (r) below that applies to your circumstances. **If you tick (l), (m), (q) or (r), please give the additional information asked for.**

l) ☐ I am the partner of the child's

    ☐ Father   ☐ Mother
    or other parent

If you have ticked box (l), please go straight to Part 2 About the Child. Paragraphs (m) to (r) do not apply to you.

◀ See Note 7

m) ☐ I am the partner (not the spouse or civil partner) of a person who is not the child's parent and I am applying to adopt alone because:

If you have ticked box (m), please go straight to Part 2 About the Child. Paragraphs (n) to (r) do not apply to you.

◀ See Note 8

(please give reasons below, continuing on a separate sheet if necessary)

n) ☐ I am not married/I do not have a civil partner   ◀ See Note 9

   or

o) ☐ I am divorced/my civil partnership has been dissolved   ◀ See Note 9

   or

p) ☐ I am a widow/a widower/a surviving civil partner   ◀ See Note 9

   or

q) ☐ I am married/I have a civil partner, and I can satisfy the court that: ◀ See Note 10

   ☐ my husband/wife/civil partner cannot be found

   or

   ☐ I have separated from my husband/wife/civil partner, we are living apart and the separation is likely to be permanent

   or

   ☐ my husband/wife/civil partner is physically incapable of making an application or lacks capacity (within the meaning of the Mental Capacity Act 2005) to do so.

   or

r) ☐ I am applying alone for an adoption order in respect of my own child and I can   ◀ See Note 11
   satisfy the court that

   ☐ the other natural parent has died

   or

   ☐ the other natural parent cannot be found

   or

   ☐ by virtue of section 28 of the Human Fertilisation and Embryology Act 1990, (disregarding subsections (5A) to (5I) of that section) and sections 34 to 47 of the Human Fertilisation and Embryology Act 2008 (disregarding sections 39, 40 and 46 of that Act) there is no other parent.

   or

   ☐ the other natural parent's exclusion from this application is justified
   (please give reasons below)

   [ ]

Part 2 About the child

a) The child is a

   ☐ Boy   ☐ Girl

b) The child was born on   **or**   To the best of my/our knowledge the child   ◀ See Note 12
                                                          was born on or about

   [| | | | | |]   [| | | | | |]

   and is the person to whom the attached   in (give place and country of birth)
   certified copy of the entry in the Register
   of Live Births/Register of Adopted   [ ]
   Children relates

c) The child's nationality is

   [ ]

Note: Please complete the following statements. Otherwise delete the following statements: ◀ See Note 13

☐ The Child is habitually resident in a country outside the British Islands

☐ The Child is not a British citizen, however, the Department for Children, Schools and Families has certified to the foreign authority that the child is authorised to enter and will be authorised to reside permanently in the United Kingdom if an adoption order is made.

☐ I attach a copy of the relevant notification letter from the Department for Children, Schools and Families.

d) I/we confirm that the child is not and has never been married or a civil partner ◀ See Note 14

  ☐ Yes   ☐ No

e) The child has had his/her home with me/us continuously since ◀ See Note 15

  ☐☐☐☐☐☐☐☐

f) I/we have notified in writing my/our local authority of my/our intention to apply for an ◀ See Note 16
   adoption order (give details below)

Name of local authority	
Address (including post code)	
Date notified	
Name of your contact in the local authority	
Telephone no.	

Care

g) ☐ No local authority or voluntary organisation has parental responsibility for the child

or

☐ The following local authority/voluntary organisation has parental responsibility for the child:

Name of local authority or voluntary organisation	
Address (including post code)	
Name of your contact in the authority/organisation	
Telephone no.	

Maintenance

h) ☐ No maintenance order/agreement or award of child support maintenance by the ◄ See Note 17
Child Support Agency has been made in respect of the child

or

☐ The following maintenance order/agreement/award of child support maintenance
has been made

Person liable to pay maintenance	
Address (including post code)	

Court and date of order	
Date of maintenance agreement/child support maintenance award	

About other orders or proceedings that affect the child

i) ☐ To the best of my/our knowledge, no proceedings relating to the child (other than ◄ See Note 18
any maintenance order as given above) have been completed or commenced in any
court, whether in the United Kingdom or elsewhere

or

☐ The following proceedings relating to the child have been completed/commenced
(in addition to any maintenance order given above)

Type of order made (or applied for)	Date of order (or date of next hearing)	Name of court (and country, if not in the UK)	Case number (or serial number)

Cases concerning a related child

j) ☐ To the best of my knowledge, no proceedings relating to a full, half or step brother or
sister of the child have been completed or commenced in any court, whether in the
United Kingdom or elsewhere.

or

☐ The following proceedings relating to a full, half or step brother or sister of the child
have been completed/commenced (please give details below and, if you were a
party to any proceedings that have been completed, attach a copy of the final order)

Relationship to child (eg. sister, half-brother)	Type of order made (or applied for)	Date of order (or date of next hearing)	Name of court (and country, if not in the UK)	Case number (or serial number)

Part 3 About the child's parents or guardian

The child's mother

a) The name of the child's mother

First name(s) in full

Last name

b) Her address is (if deceased, please write 'Deceased' in the address box)

c) Her nationality is

The child's father or other parent   See Note 19

d) What is their relationship to the child?

☐ Father   ☐ Other parent

The name of the child's father or other parent

First name(s) in full

Last name

e) Address is (if deceased, please write 'Deceased' in the address box)

f) Nationality is

The child's guardian   See Note 20

g) The name of the child's guardian is

First name(s) in full

Last name

h) His/Her address is

Parent/guardian consent to adoption

See Note 21
See Note 22

i) ☐   The child's parent(s)/guardian(s) has/have consented to the making of an adoption order

or

☐   The following parent(s)/guardian(s) of the child has/have not consented to the making of an adoption order (give name(s) below)

```



```

and I/we ask the court to dispense with his/her/their consent on the following grounds: (please tick the grounds that apply)

☐ he/she/they cannot be found

☐ he/she/they lack capacity (within the meaning of the Mental Capacity Act 2005) to give consent

☐ the welfare of the child requires it.

You must attach a brief statement of facts (and two copies of the statement) setting out a summary of the history of the case and any other facts to satisfy the court that the grounds for your request apply.

IMPORTANT: The court will send a copy of your statement of facts to each parent or guardian of the child. If you intend to ask the court to keep your identity confidential, you should make sure that the statement of facts does not include any information that could identify you, where you live, or where the child goes to school or nursery.

Part 4 General

Child's name on adoption

◀ See Note 23

If the adoption order is made, I/We want the child to be known as

First name(s) in full

Last name

Health reports

◀ See Note 24

Separate reports on my/our health and the health of the child made by a registered medical practitioner on (give date(s))

are attached to this application.

Declarations

I/We have not received or given payment or reward in respect of the proposed adoption (except as follows:) (give details below)

To the best of my/our knowledge, only the person(s) or organisation(s) named in Part 2 of this application have taken part in the arrangements for the child's adoption.

Part 5 Statement of truth

Proceedings for contempt of court may be brought against a person who makes or causes to be made, a false statement in a document verified by a statement of truth.

I believe that the facts stated in this application are true.

I believe that the facts stated in this application are true.

Signature of first applicant

Signature of second applicant

Print full name

Print full name

Signed

Signed

Date

Date

If you attend the court for a hearing

1. Do you/either of you have a disability for which you require special assistance or special facilities?　　◀ See Note 25

　　☐ Yes　　　☐ No

　　If Yes, please say what your needs are below
　　(the court staff will get in touch with you about your requirements)

　　┌───┐
　　│   │
　　│   │
　　│   │
　　│   │
　　│   │
　　└───┘

2. Do you/either of you want to use the services of an interpreter?

　　☐ Yes　　　☐ No

　　If Yes, please specify which language
　　(court staff will get in touch with you about your requirements)

　　┌──────────────────────────┐
　　│   │
　　└──────────────────────────┘

3. Are there any dates on which you know you will not be able to attend the court, or any particular dates that would especially suit you? If so, please give details below

Unavailable dates	Preferred dates

(Please note that, although the court will try to fit in with your preferences, it may not be always be possible to do so)

What to do now

Once you have completed and signed this form, you should take or send the form **and three copies** to the court, together with the court fee* and the following documents:

- a certified copy of the child's original birth certificate, any abandonment certificate, or where the child has been adopted, a certified copy of the entry in the register of adoptions as recognised in the State of origin or a certified copy of the adoption certificate;

- if you are asking the court to dispense with the consent of any parent or guardian to the adoption, a brief statement of facts relied on in support of the request, **and two copies** of the statement;

- if you were a party to the proceedings, a copy of any final order relating to the child that has effect and, if possible, a copy of any maintenance agreement or maintenance award relating to the child;

- if you were a party to the proceedings, a copy of any final order relating to a full, half or step brother or sister of the child that has effect;

- reports by a registered medical practitioner on the health of the child and the applicant(s) covering the matters specified in the Practice Direction 'Reports by a registered medical practitioner ("health reports")', **and two copies** of the reports.
  Note: you do not have to supply health reports if:

  - the child was placed with you for adoption by an adoption agency, or

  - he/she is your child, or the child of the other applicant, or

  - you are applying alone as the partner (including the husband, wife or civil partner) of the child's mother or father or other parent;

- where a parent of the child has died, a certified copy of the entry in the Register of Deaths;

- if you are submitting evidence of marriage or civil partnership, a certified copy of the entry in the Register of Marriages or the Register of Civil Partnerships;

- where your husband, wife or civil partner has died, a certified copy of the entry in the Register of Deaths;

- a copy of any decree absolute of divorce or decree of nullity of your marriage;

- in relation to a civil partnership, a copy of any dissolution order or nullity order of your civil partnership;

- any documentary evidence supporting the reasons why you are applying to adopt the child without your husband, wife or civil partner, such as a decree of judicial separation;

- the notification letter from the Department for Children, Schools and Families that they have issued a "certificate of eligibility" to the foreign authority and that the child is authorised to enter and remain and will be authorised to reside permanently in the United Kingdom if an adoption order is made;

- if your name as entered on the application form is different from the name shown on any evidence of marriage or civil partnership you are sending with your application, any documentary evidence to explain the difference.

Attach two photocopies of each of the following:
- Photo page of the child's passport
- Page showing date of enry stamp by Immigration on child's passport

Attach two photocopies of each of the following:
- Photo page of passport of each of the applicants
- any Visa, if applicable
- any page showing date of enry stamp by Immigration on passport, if applicable

*If you are not sure about the court fee payable for your application, or think that you may be exempt from paying all or part of the fee, you should contact the court for information.

| Click here to print form |

Click here to reset form	Click here to print form

C65

Application

For declaration as to adoption effected overseas under section 57 of the Family Law Act 1986

To be completed by the court
Name of court
Date issued
Case number

You must file with the application a certified copy of the adoption order made overseas and one of the following documents:

a. a certified copy of the entry in the register of adoptions as recognised in the State in which the adoption was effected;

b. a certified copy of the adoption certificate; or

c. a certified copy of the birth certificate made after the adoption referred to in the application

If any of the documents to be provided are not in English, you must include English translations certified by a notary public or authenticated by a statement of truth.

If you are filling in the application by hand, please **use black ink** and write in **BLOCK CAPITAL LETTERS**.

1. About you (**the applicant** - a person whose status as an adopted child depends upon an adoption effected overseas)

Your first name	
Middle name(s)	
Surname	
Previous surnames (if any)	
Date of birth	/ / Gender ☐ Male ☐ Female
Place of birth (town/county/country)	

If you do not wish your address to be made known to the respondent, leave the address details blank and complete Confidential contact details form C8.

Address	
	Postcode
Home telephone number	
Mobile telephone number	

C65 Application For declaration as to adoption effected overseas under section 57 of the Family Law Act 1986 (04.11)   © Crown copyright 2011

Have you lived at this address for more than 5 years?

☐ Yes ☐ No

If No, please provide details of all previous addresses you have lived at during the last 5 years.

Your solicitor's details

Do you have a solicitor acting for you?

☐ Yes ☐ No

If Yes, please give the following details

Your solicitor's name

Name of firm

Address

Postcode ☐☐☐☐ ☐☐☐☐☐

Telephone number

Fax number

DX number

Email

Solicitor's Reference

2

Applicant 2 (if applicable) ——————————

Your first name

Middle name(s)

Surname

Previous surnames (if any)

Date of birth ⬚⬚ / ⬚⬚ / ⬚⬚⬚⬚   Gender ☐ Male   ☐ Female

Place of birth (town/county/country)

If you do not wish your address to be made known to the respondent, leave the address details blank and complete Confidential contact details form C8.

Address

Postcode ⬚⬚⬚⬚ ⬚⬚⬚

Home telephone number

Mobile telephone number

If you have a solicitor acting for you and your solicitor is different from the first applicant please provide details of these on a separate sheet.

What is your relationship to Applicant 1?

3

2. About the adoption order

Date of adoption order ☐☐ / ☐☐ / ☐☐☐☐

Place of adoption order

Court or Tribunal which made adoption order

Address of court or Tribunal (if known)

Postcode ☐☐☐☐ ☐☐☐

Telephone number

Court Reference (if known)

3. Why are you making this application?

Please give brief details about why you are making this application. You should include details of the facts you allege justify making this application and the declaration you are seeking.

Do not give a full statement, please provide a summary.
You may be asked to provide a full statement later.

4

4. Your connection with England and Wales

1) Please state whether you:

a) are domiciled in England and Wales on the date of the application, or

☐ Yes   ☐ No

b) have been habitually resident in England and Wales throughout the period of one year ending with that date

☐ Yes   ☐ No

2) If the court's jurisdiction to hear the application is based on habitual residence please state the addresses where you have lived and the length of residence at each place during the period of one year ending with the date of the application.

5. The respondents

The respondents to the application will be:-
1. the people you claim are your adoptive parents, or
2. the people you claim are **not** your adoptive parents.

If there are more than 2 respondents please continue on a separate sheet.

Respondent 1 _____

Respondent's first name	
Middle name(s)	
Surname	
Previous surnames (if known)	

Date of birth [ ] [ ] / [ ] [ ] / [ ] [ ] [ ] [ ]   Gender [ ] Male [ ] Female

Place of birth
(town/county/country, if known)

Address

Postcode [ ] [ ] [ ] [ ] [ ] [ ] [ ]

Telephone number

Mobile telephone number

Have they lived at this address
for more than 5 years?   [ ] Yes   [ ] No   [ ] Don't know

If No, please provide all previous addresses for the
last 5 years below, if known.

6

Respondent 2 _____

Respondent's first name	
Middle name(s)	
Surname	
Previous surnames (if known)	

Date of birth [ ] / [ ] / [ ]   Gender ☐ Male ☐ Female

Place of birth
(town/county/country, if known)

Address

Postcode [ ] [ ]

Telephone number

Mobile telephone number

Have they lived at this address
for more than 5 years?   ☐ Yes   ☐ No   ☐ Don't know

If No, please provide all previous addresses for the
last 5 years below, if known.

6. Statement of truth

*[I believe] [the applicant believes] that the facts stated in this application are true

*I am duly authorised by the applicant to sign this statement
*Delete as appropriate

Print full name

Address for service

Name of applicant solicitor's firm

Signed   Dated

*(Applicant) (Applicant's solicitor)

Position or office held
(if signing on behalf of firm or company)

Proceedings for contempt of court may be brought against a person who makes or causes to be made a false statement in a document verified by a statement of truth.

8

7. Attending the court

Section N of the the booklet **'CB1 - Making an application - Children and the Family Courts'** provides information about attending court.

If you require an interpreter, you must tell the court now so that one can be arranged.

Do you or any of the parties need an interpreter at court?

☐ Yes   ☐ No

If Yes, please specify the language and dialect:

If attending the court, do you or any of the parties involved have a disability for which you require special assistance or special facilities?

☐ Yes   ☐ No

If Yes, please say what the needs are

Please say whether the court needs to make any special arrangements for you to attend court (e.g. providing you with a separate waiting room from the respondent or other security provisions).

Court staff may get in touch with you about the requirements

continued over the page ➪

What to do now

You must file with the application a certified copy of the adoption order made overseas and one of the following documents:

a. a certified copy of the entry in the register of adoptions as recognised in the State in which the adoption was effected;

b. a certified copy of the adoption certificate; or

c. a certified copy of the birth certificate made after the adoption referred to in the application

If any of the documents to be provided are not in English, you must include English translations certified by a notary public or authenticated by a statement of truth.

☐ Check you have **signed** Section 6 of this form.

☐ You must provide a **copy** of this application and attached documents for each of the respondents.

☐ Details of the additional respondents if there are more than 2 in Section 5.

☐ Check you have attached the correct fee. The leaflet 'EX50 Civil and Family Court Fees' provides information about court fees you will have to pay.

Now take or send your application with the correct fee and correct number of copies to the court.

Court fees

You may be exempt from paying all or part of the fee. The combined booklet and application form 'EX160A Court Fees - Do you have to pay them' gives more information. You can get a copy from the court or download a copy from our website at www.hmcourts-service.gov.uk

11

Guidance Notes for applicant on completing this form

- Please read all of these guidance notes before you begin completing the application. The notes follow the order in which information is required on the application.
- Court staff can help you fill in the application and give information about procedure once it has been issued, but they cannot give legal advice. If you need legal advice, for example, about the likely success of your application or the evidence you need to support it, you should contact a solicitor or a Citizens Advice Bureau.
- If you are filling in the application by hand, please use black ink and write in block capitals.
- You must file any written evidence to support your application either in or with the application. Your written evidence must be verified by a statement of truth.
- Copy the completed application, the respondent's notes for guidance and your written evidence so that you have a copy for yourself, one copy for the court and one copy for each respondent. Send or take the applications and evidence to the court office with the appropriate fee. The court will tell you how much this is.

Applicant and Respondent details

As the person making the application, you are called the 'applicant'; any other party is called a 'respondent'. Applicants who are under 18 years old (unless otherwise permitted by the court) and persons who lack capacity within the meaning of the Mental Capacity Act 2005 must have a litigation friend to make the application and conduct court proceedings on their behalf. Court staff will tell you more about what you need to do if this applies to you.

You must provide the following information about yourself and each respondent (if known):

- all known forenames and surname;
- whether Mr, Mrs, Miss, Ms or Other (e.g. Dr);and
- residential address (including postcode and telephone number).

Where ant person listed in the application form is:

- under 18, write ("a child, by 'Mr Joe Bloggs' his/her litigation friend")
- a person who lacks capacity within the meaning of the Mental Capacity Act 2005, write (", by Mr Joe Bloggs, his/her litigation friend")
- appearing in a representative capacity, you must say what that capacity is, eg. "Mr Joe Bloggs as the representative of Mrs Sharon Bloggs"

Your solicitor's name and address

If you are represented by solicitor in these proceedings, enter in this box your solicitor's full name and address, and other contact details as requested.

Details of application

Under this heading you must set out either:

- the question(s) you wish the court to decide; or
- the order you are seeking and the legal basis for your application; and
- if your application is being made under a specific rule or practice direction, you must state which.

Depending on the Declaration you are applying for you must set out specific information.

Statement of truth

This must be signed by you, by your solicitor or your litigation friend, as appropriate.

INDEX

References are to paragraph numbers.